A Chanticleer Press Edition

A Chanticleer Press Edition

ATLANTIC & GULF COASTS

By William H. Amos and Stephen H. Amos

Birds
John Bull, Field Associate, The American Museum of Natural History; and John Farrand, Jr., Editor, *American Birds,* National Audubon Society

Fishes, Whales, and Dolphins
Herbert T. Boschung, Jr., Professor of Zoology, University of Alabama; and David K. Caldwell and Melba C. Caldwell, Research Scientists, University of Florida

Insects and Spiders
Lorus Milne and Margery Milne, Lecturers, University of New Hampshire

Mammals
John O. Whitaker, Jr., Professor of Life Sciences, Indiana State University

Reptiles and Amphibians
John L. Behler, Curator of Herpetology, New York Zoological Society; and F. Wayne King, Director, Florida State Museum

Seashells
Harald A. Rehder, Zoologist Emeritus, Smithsonian Institution

Seashore Creatures
Norman A. Meinkoth, Professor Emeritus of Zoology, Swarthmore College

Alfred A. Knopf, New York

This is a Borzoi Book.
Published by Alfred A. Knopf, Inc.

Copyright © 1985, 1997 by Chanticleer Press, Inc. All rights
reserved under International and Pan-American Copyright
Conventions. Published in the United States by Alfred A.
Knopf, Inc., New York, and simultaneously in Canada by
Random House of Canada Limited, Toronto. Distributed by
Random House, Inc., New York.

Prepared and produced by Chanticleer Press, Inc., New York.

Printed and bound by Toppan Printing Co., Ltd., Tokyo, Japan.
Typeset in Garamond by Dix Type, Inc., Syracuse, New York.

Published March 1985
Sixth Printing, March 1997

Library of Congress Cataloging-in-Publication Data
Amos, William, 1921–
The National Audubon Society nature guides. Atlantic and
Gulf coasts.
Includes index.
1. Natural history–Atlantic Coast (U.S.)–Handbooks,
manuals, etc. 2. Natural history–Gulf Coast (U.S.)–
Handbooks, manuals, etc. 3. Coastal ecology–Atlantic Coast
(U.S.)–Handbooks, manuals, etc. 4. Coastal ecology–Gulf
Coast (U.S.)–Handbooks, manuals, etc. 5. Zoology–Atlantic
Coast (U.S.)–Handbooks, manuals, etc. 6. Zoology–Gulf
Coast (U.S.)–Handbooks, manuals, etc. 7. Botany–Atlantic
Coast (U.S.)–Handbooks, manuals, etc. 8. Botany–Gulf
Coast (U.S.)–Handbooks, manuals, etc. 9. Coastal flora–
Atlantic Coast (U.S.)–Identification. 10. Coastal flora–Gulf
Coast (U.S.)–Identification. 11. Animals–Identification.
I. Amos, Stephen, 1955–   II. National Audubon Society.
III. Title.   IV. Title: Atlantic and Gulf coasts.
QH104.5.A84A47   1985   574.5'2638'0974   84-48676
ISBN 0-394-73109-3 (pbk.)

Cover photograph: At sunset, gulls gather for the night along
Herring Cove Beach in Cape Cod National Seashore,
Massachusetts.

For Catherine and Carol, our wives, who have understood our
preoccupation and supported our efforts.

CONTENTS

NATIONAL AUDUBON SOCIETY

The mission of the NATIONAL AUDUBON SOCIETY *is to conserve and restore natural ecosystems, focusing on birds and other wildlife, for the benefit of humanity and the earth's biological diversity.*

With more than 560,000 members and an extensive chapter network, our staff of scientists, educators, lobbyists, lawyers, and policy analysts works to save threatened ecosystems and restore the natural balance of life on our planet. Through our sanctuary system we manage 150,000 acres of critical habitat. *Audubon* magazine, sent to all members, carries outstanding articles and color photography on wildlife, nature, and the environment. We also publish *Field Notes,* a journal reporting bird sightings, and *Audubon Adventures,* a bimonthly children's newsletter reaching 600,000 students.

NATIONAL AUDUBON SOCIETY produces television documentaries and sponsors books, electronic programs, and nature travel to exotic places.

For membership information:

NATIONAL AUDUBON SOCIETY
700 Broadway
New York, NY 10003-9562
(212) 979-3000

THE AUTHORS

William H. Amos

After thirty-seven years of research and teaching, William Amos has recently retired to his farm in Vermont. Mr. Amos grew up in the Philippines and Japan, where he first began his studies of the marine environment at the Misaki Marine Biological Laboratory. Since then, he has been affiliated with numerous institutions, including the Mount Desert Biological Laboratory in Maine, Rutgers University Department of Biophotography, St. Andrew's School in Delaware, the University of Delaware Marine Laboratories, the Systematics-Ecology Program at the Marine Biological Laboratory in Woods Hole, Massachusetts, the Department of Zoology of the University of Hawaii, and the Fairbanks Museum of Science. In his retirement, Mr. Amos has accepted a three-year appointment as visiting scientist in the Department of Natural Sciences at Lyndon State College near his home.

Mr. Amos holds degrees from Rutgers University and the University of Delaware, and has been a member of several scientific expeditions, including the Smithsonian-Bredin Caribbean Expedition to the Lesser Antilles, the Westward Expedition in the Hawaiian Archipelago, and the St. Andrew's Expedition to the Galápagos Islands. He is the author of numerous books, among them *Wildlife of the Islands, Wildlife of the Rivers, Life of the Pond, Life of the Seashore,* and *The Infinite River,* and has written many articles and professional papers.

Stephen H. Amos

Senior aviculturist at the National Aquarium in Baltimore, Stephen Amos is in charge of the Aquarium's large South American rain forest exhibit as well as the exhibit on North Atlantic seabirds. He received his B.S. degree in psychobiology from Hiram College in Ohio, and later served as the senior keeper of birds at the Baltimore Zoo before taking on his present position. He is a professional fellow with the American Association of Zoos, Parks, and Aquariums.

Mr. Amos has traveled extensively to pursue his interest in ornithology and vertebrate ecology. He has studied waterfowl in England, wildlife in the Amazon and Andes, and was one of the coleaders as well as ornithologist and ethologist for the 1984 St. Andrew's Expedition to the Galápagos Islands. Most recently, he has completed a trip to the Amazon of Peru, bringing back tropical reptiles and amphibians for the National Aquarium. He is currently doing research on the Atlantic Puffin and the Gray-necked Wood Rail.

HOW TO USE THIS GUIDE

This guide is designed for use both at home and in the field. Its clear arrangement in four parts—habitat essays, color plates, species descriptions, and appendices—puts information at your fingertips that would otherwise only be accessible through a small library of field guides.

The habitat essays enable you to discover the many kinds of habitats on the Atlantic and Gulf coasts, the relationships among the plants and animals found there, and highlights not to be missed. The color plates feature coastal scenes and over 600 photographs of different plant and animal species. The species descriptions cover the most important information about a plant or animal, including a description, the range, specific habitat, and comments. Finally, the appendices include a bibliography, a glossary, and a comprehensive index.

Using This Guide at Home

Before planning an outing, you will want to know what you can expect to see.

1. Begin by leafing through the color plates for a preview of the Atlantic and Gulf coasts.

2. Read the habitat section. For quick reference, at the end of each chapter you will find a list of some of the most common animals found in that habitat.

3. Look at the color plates of some of the animals and plants so that you will be able to recognize them later in the field. The table called How to Use the Color Plates provides a visual table of contents to the color section, explains the arrangement of the plates, and tells the caption information provided. The habitats where you are likely to encounter the species are listed in blue type so that you can easily refer to the correct habitat chapter. The page number for the full species description is also included in the caption.

4. Turn to the species descriptions to learn more about the plants and animals that interest you. A range map or drawing appears in the margin for birds, reptiles, amphibians, and many of the mammals. Poisonous fishes, seashore creatures, reptiles, and dangerous whales are indicated by the danger symbol ⊗ next to the species name.

5. Consult the appendices for definitions of technical terms and suggestions for further reading.

Using This Guide in the Field

When you are out in the field, you will want to find information quickly and easily.

1. Turn to the color plates to locate the plant or animal you have seen. At a glance the captions will help you narrow down the possibilities. First, verify the general habitat by checking the blue type information to the left of the color plate. Next, look for additional information in blue type—for example, the specific habitat of fishes and seashore creatures or an insect's food. To find out whether a bird, mammal, reptile, amphibian, or plant is in your area, check the range map or range description next to the color plate.

2. Now turn to the species description to confirm your identification and to learn more about the species.

First frontispiece: Herring gulls scavenge for food washed up by the tide on the coast of Nova Scotia.

Second frontispiece: A pair of Horseshoe Crabs mating at high tide in late spring along the shore of Delaware Bay.

Third frontispiece: A commensal cleaning shrimp makes its home among a Collared Sand Anemone's tentacles in coral reefs off the Florida Keys.

Fourth frontispiece: Two Atlantic Decorator Crabs from subtropical waters near the Florida Keys carry different species of sponges on their backs as protective camouflage.

Fifth frontispiece: Northern Rock Barnacles sweep planktonic food with their feathery appendages from shallow water along the shore of Pratt's Island, Maine.

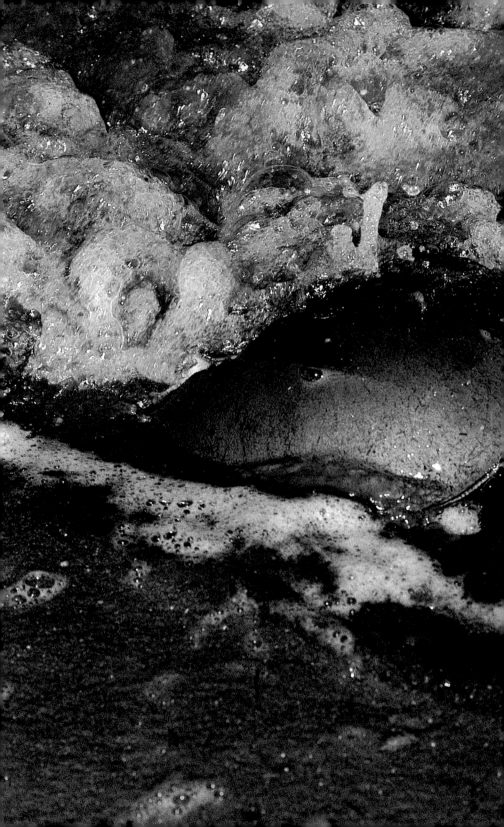

PREFACE

Thomas Henry Huxley, Charles Darwin's friend and champion, once wrote, "To a person uninstructed in natural history, a country or seaside stroll is a walk through a gallery filled with wonderful works of art, nine-tenths of which have their faces turned to the wall." We pass through this extraordinary world of ours often unseeing and little understanding the natural phenomena that surround us. We are terrestrial creatures—albeit ones with a distant aquatic past—so our attention is drawn mostly to those plants and animals that live on land with us. Another and larger world exists on this planet: the world of water, principally that lying in ocean basins. But this is a world we do not see clearly and enter only briefly and with difficulty. A preponderance of life exists in the oceans and includes creatures that date back largely unchanged to the earliest beginnnings of life on Earth. Only those marine scientists and students specially equipped to do so are able to penetrate the interface separating "our" world from that of the dolphin, jellyfish, and octopus.

Almost without exception during a visit to the seashore, we engage in an idle activity—beach-combing. That is, it is idle until something remarkable catches our eye and we stop to look and wonder. We observe organisms that are as different from terrestrial creatures as would be life from another planet. Nowhere on land do we find animals shooting along by jet propulsion, ejecting poison darts at the end of long threads, using a hydraulic system instead of muscles for movement, or employing the surrounding medium as the major constituent of their bodies. Marine organisms are not only ancient, they are well-tested and some of the most successful forms of life on Earth, even though they seem strange to our eyes.

A stroll along a seashore, then, can be rewarding and illuminating if—to use Huxley's metaphor—we begin turning some of the wonderful works of art to the light. Every walk along every shore yields information and surprises, and it is the purpose of this book to encourage you to seek further sources of information.

Here we take you on a journey of many thousands of miles, selecting only a very few—about 600—of the different plants and animals associated with the marine world. Most live in water, at least part of the time, while others are found along the maritime fringe of a continent. Different regions of the seashore from Labrador to Texas are considered in broadly descriptive chapters. The chapters cannot describe every aspect of a given section of coast, but serve to highlight its geological formation and the complex ecology of some of its biotic communities. The organisms and their associations have been chosen for their likelihood of being seen by the seashore visitor; some, to be sure, do not present themselves in obvious fashion, but need to be sought out.

Getting Started

No matter which kind of shoreline you visit, certain items will enhance the pleasure of finding new and interesting forms of life. This book should serve to answer many questions when a specimen or phenomenon arouses your curiosity. A notebook, preferably one that will withstand the dampness of salt mist, records your questions and observations for later study. Binoculars are useful for those who follow shorebirds, watch dolphins arcing out of the water half a mile away, or wish to study an inaccessible rock face across a wave-battered cove. Another, far simpler optical accessory is a must: a small magnifier that will enlarge specimens about ten times. Popular models of these fold into their own metal cases and are very inexpensive, considering the uses to which they can be put. Another useful item would be a small clear plastic vial or container. This is not for removing specimens to your home or picnic location on the beach, but to provide a temporary aquarium in which you can observe the activity of marine animals within their natural medium of sea water. In air, these animals simply do not behave normally; they may collapse and most certainly will soon die. Select a plastic container that is perfectly clear, such as a wide medicine vial obtained at a drugstore. Small organisms from tide pools can be placed in this miniature aquarium and studied with the magnifier, revealing their extraordinary shapes, colors, appendages, and behavior. After being examined, however, they should be returned to the place they were taken from. An added cautionary note is not to pluck off marine organisms from the rocks or wharf pilings, for almost all will be unable to fasten themselves again. Removing them effectively kills them, although not always at once.

If the wave surge is not great, the water is clear, and you are not a swimmer or have no mask and snorkel, a glass-bottomed bucket is a wonderful window to the subsurface world. Such items are not found in stores, but are easily constructed. A plastic bucket—even a small child's one for portability—is easy to alter: cut a square out of the bottom and place a somewhat larger square of window glass inside, cemented by household silicone sealer. In use, you can eliminate skylight reflections on the glass by draping a towel over both your head and the bucket. Once you have such a viewing aid, you will never visit a shore without it.

For a real treat, visit a seashore at night with a good flashlight. Ghost crabs on beaches are confused by directional light at night and can be approached closely; if the shallows along the shoreline are quiet—as they may be with a nighttime land breeze—fishes and crabs can be seen close to shore. Many creatures that are impossible to see in daytime, either because of reflection or their reluctance to leave protective burrows or hiding places, are immediately obvious at night. The human visitor to a tide pool after dark is likely to lose track of time and make a late night of it!

Almost everyone visiting a seashore brings a camera along. Even the simplest kind is capable of recording some of the attractions and activities found there, especially if you are after scenic photographs. If your camera has controls, your photographs may be planned a bit more. For example, a slow shutter speed blurs waves, often giving the feeling of motion and power. On the other hand, a fast shutter speed may freeze the exact moment of a wave breaking or spray shooting high into the air. If you attempt to photograph life within a tide pool, be sure to use a polarizing filter, and rotate it until reflections are eliminated.

The shore is one place where your camera should be protected at all times if you are not using it. Keep your lens in a sealed case whenever it is not actually being used. Many photographers like to use "zip-lock" plastic bags in which their cameras, lenses, and film are placed while at the shore. Such a bag can actually be drawn up over a camera while it is hanging around your neck, then dropped briefly while a photograph is being taken. An inexpensive all-rubber syringe, obtainable at a drugstore, provides a narrow blast of air to dislodge sand grains from lens or camera body. Your breath is too moist to do the job safely.

Some Cautionary Notes

It is not safe to be too adventuresome at night. Swimming after dark is never advisable, and brisk walking along wet rocks that are nearly black, their contours obscured and not revealed by flashlights, can be very hazardous. Even in daytime, look closely at the rock surface and test it before stepping with your full weight. A rock can shift unexpectedly. Furthermore, in intertidal regions, certain zones, especially the black zone, where primitive blue-green algae grow, is so slippery it is almost impossible to keep your footing.

Beaches generally present few hazards day or night, provided you remain above the wave action. But if sandbars lie offshore, and there is a good longshore current, inspect the inshore waters for a powerful, discolored rip current flooding out to sea, for this is a movement of water against which no swimmer can contend.

The one summertime hazard a beach offers is familiar to all: sunburn. The power of the sun is obvious to anyone lying on a towel or attempting to walk across the searing sands of a dune. But close to the water's edge, where you seem to be cooled by ocean breezes, an hour spent examining life in a tide pool or at the water line can produce a serious burn. Use the proper lotions or cover yourself sensibly, and the day at the seashore will be remembered with pleasure, not with pain.

Salt marshes are not especially dangerous, but their muds are very slippery and clinging, and the biting insect population often is intensely active, so the right kinds of boots, protective clothing, and insect repellent are necessary.

A mangrove swamp is best entered by boat in daylight. Trying to walk through or across one is extremely difficult under any conditions. The mud under the prop roots is thick, slippery, and often not firm; the prop roots themselves create such a tangle that it is like threading your way through a dense jungle gym. Furthermore, mangrove swamps sometimes harbor the venomous Cottonmouth, although it prefers fresher waters farther inland.

Fascination for a coral reef can exact a toll from the careless visitor. Coral rubble makes for unsure footing along the shore or reef crest. Snorkeling in shallows gives you a good view of the reef architecture, and an idea where wave surge is strong. Try not to enter powerful currents that can throw you against sharp, rough coral heads. There are creatures to be avoided in the reef as well: bristly Fire Worms, Fire Coral, the Long-spined Urchin, or a defensive octopus or moray in its lair (they are neither of them actually aggressive, nor do they appreciate intruders). Some of the more dangerous sharks may penetrate reef waters, although most sharks found there are inoffensive.

Some Reminders

Seashores are fragile places, although they seem permanent and almost unchanging to our short-term perspective. The sea is constantly at work altering them, while different kinds of organisms are at work building totally new shorelines. A study of geological history shows us that shores have never been stable, but have changed with each epoch as sea levels rise or fall and temperatures alter with climatological developments. Through hundreds of millions of years these natural events have produced fluctuations that, in the long run, display a dynamic equilibrium. Today, for the first time in the history of the world, a new force is at work that permanently alters shorelines and may poison them almost beyond recovery— man. Our salt marshes are ditched or obliterated, mangroves are restricted, beaches allowed to wash away due to construction practices, or artificially built up where natural forces will not permit them to remain. A concrete and steel condominium is no match for the sea in the long run; it opposes the waves and tides, while a barrier dune gives way when necessary, then reforms again. Enormous oil spills wash over shorelines, eliminating almost every form of intertidal life, and toxic effluent from coastal industries and power plants either wipe the biological slate clean or encourage severely unbalanced populations of organisms.

On a far lesser scale, we as visitors to seashores leave our mark —often it is a deleterious one. Beach buggies destroy fragile plants that stabilize sand dunes, and the sand begins to shift, blown by the wind. Closer to the water line, the same vehicles compress sand, killing the hidden animals that otherwise exist securely within burrows.

A picnic at the shore, as anywhere else, should not leave behind the trash of a pleasant event. Photographs abound of sea birds, crabs, and seals caught in the snares of plastic containers, perishing in their inability to feed or swim or fly. The creatures we find at the shore are fascinating beyond compare, but they are specialists living under conditions we cannot duplicate in a collecting container or aquarium. Even in the best of the world's great public aquariums, longevity for most marine animals is less than their counterparts in the sea, while seaweeds find it almost impossible to survive even briefly. As visitors to the regions where the ocean washes the land, we should study and marvel at the extraordinary forms of life that exist there—but we should not interrupt their

habitats or their lives, or remove them from the only place
where they are adapted to survive after long ages of evolution.
All of us need to learn more about the sea and its importance
to the world ecosystem. Beginning with the seashore is not a
poor idea—it is a pursuit that has been engaged in by
naturalists and scientists the world over for many years. Three
thousand years ago Aristotle studied and described coastal
marine life in the Mediterranean with such accuracy and
enthusiasm that much of what he wrote is still valuable today.

An Invitation

One of the greatest pleasures of walking the shore is the effect
it has upon you. Even in the company of friends, there is a
sense of solitude—not loneliness, but a splendid isolation that
separates you from the noisy, busy world you left behind.
While you walk or rest just beyond the reach of the waves, the
ocean's rhythm soothes a taut body and cares ebb away. Your
mind is washed as clean as the sand. As surely as the tide
rises, your footprints will be erased, leaving nothing of your
passage behind.

It matters little when you choose to be at the shore. The heat
of noon on a midsummer day is familiar enough, but other
hours and other seasons can have an even more powerful effect.
A black moonless night or a fog-wrapped day in early fall are
times when other senses become alive. Ears sharpen in the
darkness when vision is subdued and we listen to the rustling
of sand, the murmur of small waves, the cry of a bird on the
dark water. In the quiet of an early morning, tendrils of fog
roll in and envelop us until we are surrounded by a vaporous
blanket—our world of perception is reduced to a luminous
hemisphere, where seaweed-draped rocks loom from nothing
and flat, steel-gray water fades into the mist.

Do not avoid the shore in times of weather that invites you to
remain indoors. Cold, gust-driven northeasters, with sleeting
rain and low, gray, scudding clouds, create a shore in
monochrome. Silt-laden waves turn dark with debris, cresting
with foam and flinging spume into the air. Sand grains lifted
from the beach and driven at high velocity sting exposed skin.
As you lean into the gale, calling upon invigorating reserves of
strength, the experience seals itself within your experience and
remains for a lifetime. In later years and far away, your walk
on a storm-swept shore returns in reverie with sounds of
booming surf, pressure of the wet gale, and a sea-fragrance
whose aroma is known nowhere else.

Beaches, high rocky bluffs, coral reef shores—all have a
powerful effect upon our psyche. Beyond this there is an
awakening to the wonder of life in the sea that began and
grew and flourished eons before creatures of our design
ventured into freshwater rivers and emerged upon the land.
Studying and appreciating the remarkable plants and creatures
of the sea, even during a brief visit to the shore, will be as
memorable an experience as you are likely to have in this life.

INTRODUCTION

The sea draws us to its shore, whether we know it or not. We are terrestrial creatures by origin and habit, yet spellbound by the mist of sea air and the lulling rhythm of waves upon a beach. It is not impossible to imagine our distant ancestors, men who were hardly men by contemporary standards, standing for the first time upon a beach or rocky headland wondering what was before them—and what was beyond. To this day we do the same.

No oceanographer has answers to all the puzzles of waves and currents; no marine biologist can tell precisely what organisms exist beneath the surface at a given spot, or why some creatures are found on one intertidal rock face and not on another. The sea is a frontier in knowledge as well as in geography, and one that the novice and casual visitor can explore along with the seasoned scientist. Let the sea pull you to its edge; enjoy its effect, and learn a bit about the enormous, complex world of life it harbors in its shallow and intertidal waters.

The seashore is the earth's greatest meeting place. Creatures and plants from the two entirely different worlds of land and sea mingle there, many of them unable to live anywhere else. Ecologists everywhere are interested in ecotones—zones where one habitat impinges upon another. Although most ecotones are much smaller regions, by far the largest example is that of land meeting sea—where the sea washes the land's edge. Most ecotones have certain features in common: They tend to have a greater concentration of life than either of the two adjacent habitats—a condition scientists call the edge effect. Ecotones permit members of each different place to intrude upon one another, yet they possess their own inhabitants in great profusion. Physical factors play a basic role in establishing an ecotone's range, but it is the biological factors that give an ecotone its character and determine the community of life present in it. This book attempts to explain a little of both, perhaps sufficiently to encourage you to pursue the subject further.

Coastal seas and the great ocean masses have a profound influence upon world climate and also serve as a modifier of local weather patterns; we must take what we get, and accept their effects. We are aware that huge cyclonic storms, called hurricanes and typhoons, begin at sea. But it may be less well known that it is the equable temperature of the oceans that stabilizes the temperature of our entire planet. Water temperature, unlike that of the air, changes very, very slowly. On land, rocks and soil are quickly heated by the sun and cooled at night—but not the ocean. Thus by day, air warmed over the land rises, and breezes flow in from the sea. At night the flow reverses itself: The land cools quickly, and the comparative warmth of the ocean causes air to rise, drawing breezes seaward.

Evaporation of water occurs mostly from oceans. Lakes, rivers, and forests contribute comparatively little. It is this water, transported through the atmosphere, that eventually falls upon continents. There it does its work, often far inland, sculpturing the surface and creating great rivers that flow to the sea. Finally, these rivers become estuaries; fresh water and salt water mix; and the cycle is complete.

No matter how terrestrial an organism may be, the sea persists in it—and in all life. Life originated in the sea, and much of it evolved to its present form in the sea. When our air-breathing fish and amphibian ancestors left the freshwater swamps—to which they had migrated from the sea long before—they took with them their watery nature. Every cell of our bodies is in effect an aquatic living unit, with water and various salts in varying dilutions playing essential roles in our continuing existence. It is often remarked that the chemical composition of our body fluids is not entirely dissimilar to that of the ocean. Who can say what echoes are felt within our being when we find ourselves drawn back to the sea?

For each of us, a visit to the seashore has a special and often private meaning. We may go in company with others or seek, in a long and solitary walk along a deserted shore, a renewal within ourselves. We may watch children stand awash in wavelets, or we may cling for support upon a cliff top as huge storm waves batter the rocks below. We marvel at the agility of seabirds gliding on rising currents or skimming the wave tops. And we pursue a popular pastime: beachcombing— finding shells and seaweed and fragments of marine creatures, or the oddities of jetsam from ships and ports far away. A visit to a shore brings pleasure and solace and, if we will permit it, enlightenment.

The Origins of Shorelines

There is great variation among shorelines, for they are created by different forces. Some are fairly ancient (although still young in geological terms); others are the products of sand brought by currents or a new lava flow. There are three kinds of shorelines along the Atlantic: piedmont, which is part of the ancient continent; coastal alluvium, which consists of sediments carried down by rivers and washed in from the sea; and the edges of old mountains. It is clear that rocky bluffs plunging into the ocean are the edge of an extremely old land mass, while a sandy barrier island consisting of little more than a wide beach may not even appear on early navigational charts.

In geological time, a shoreline is an ephemeral margin, which, over centuries and millennia, migrates back and forth according to climatological and geological events. During glacial epochs, when enormous quantities of water are locked up in polar ice caps, the sea level is lower and more land is exposed. In interglacial periods, the ice masses at the poles melt, liberating water into the oceans and flooding coastal plains and even penetrating far inland over low-lying continents. The life of seashores—plant or animal; burrowing, attached, or motile—must migrate with the continental waterline. Only now are scientists able to uncover and study the fossil remnants left behind.

Certain types of shoreline along our eastern coasts have been altered by organisms; salt marshes and mangrove swamps are both notable examples. As pioneers in shallow, protected water, marsh grasses and mangrove trees trap sediment and increase their hold by spreading widely until vast areas are under their domination. The two kinds of vegetation do not compete with each other, for salt marshes are more northerly; toward the south, they diminish and vanish altogether along the central Florida coast, where conditions are right for the tropical mangrove forests.

Coral shores have been created entirely by living organisms. For the most part they are submerged, while salt marshes and mangrove swamps are distinctly intertidal and clearly visible to a visitor. All three create habitats and unique opportunities for colonization by a wide variety of life forms, many of which can be found nowhere else. Shorelines that are biological in origin are said to be formed by organogenesis. Not only are they often extensive, but they are also some of the most nutritionally important of all marine environments.

Types of Shorelines

Seashores consist of rock, sand, or finer sedimentary particles that form mud. Each type has a specific origin made possible by physical and sometimes biological processes.

A rocky shore might be called the most primitive type of coast because it has been altered the least. Even so, except for moraine and lava rocks recently extruded from volcanoes far from our Atlantic and Gulf coasts, all rocky shores have been heavily weathered, and many of them north of Long Island have been affected by glaciation. Although a rocky bluff may appear to be impervious even to the power of storm waves, it gradually gives way to the relentless force of the sea. Over thousands of years, waves sculpture terraces, caverns, ledges, arches, and a wide range of other intriguing architectural configurations. As shapes of a rocky shore change, so do the opportunities for intertidal life to attach and survive. Each shoreline of this sort must be examined anew, for no two are identical, although basic principles of zonation always apply. As time passes and waves do their work, fractures occur and boulders fall from granite bluffs. Rubble collects at the foot of cliffs, where it is pounded, rolled about, smoothed, and reduced in size, eventually taking shape as ovoid cobbles. If the process continues long enough, the result is sand— although where rocky shores predominate, waves and tidal currents are so strong and the shoreline topography so abrupt that sandy beaches have little chance to develop or persist. Nevertheless, beaches are formed, although they do not conform to the usual image of a sandy shore. In northeastern Massachusetts, for example, some beaches are composed of large, rounded granite rocks. While larger rocks were dropped by glaciers, relatively smaller ones, too heavy for a person to lift or move, are kept there by the action of tides and waves. The particles from which many northern sandy beaches are made generally have an ancient origin, derived from the fragmentation of granite as it was scoured in swollen glacial streams and rivers. These sand grains are the crystals that once gave the rock its coarse texture: clear, polished quartz, light-colored feldspar, red garnet, and dark iron magnetite. Because each kind of grain has a density or weight different from that of the others, some are transported over longer distances by waves and water than are others. This sorting action results in concentrations of certain grains—and therefore of certain colors. Washouts through a barrier dune can illustrate this principle: Intensely dark bands may indicate the presence of magnetite, either deposited at the time of erosion or laid bare as lighter sand was carried away.

The sand of southern beaches is composed of very different materials—mostly calcite, or calcium carbonate, that has its origin in life processes. This comparatively soft substance results from the breaking down of worn, discarded mollusk shells, sea-urchin spines and bodies, pulverized coral, and the limey deposits inside certain algae. A strong magnifying glass reveals that the sand of Florida's beaches is a treasure trove of biological fragments—sometimes even of whole animal structures, if they are small enough. If not moved by waves or wind for long periods of time, calcite beaches may become consolidated into rocklike masses of calcium carbonate, creating a kind of rocky shore where none had existed before. Many major beaches along the Atlantic and Gulf shores consist of such enormous volumes of sand that they create major—if geologically temporary—coastal features. Capes and barrier islands are examples of new land created by currents and wave action, providing extensive habitats where formerly there had been nothing but ocean.

Rivers and Currents

It is a mistake to believe that our seashores are purely the products of marine phenomena. Rivers running across the land, transporting sediment and dissolved substances, are powerful influences upon a coastline. Estuaries, salt marshes, bays, and deltas with their bayous are some of the features that can develop as a result of the activity of rivers, past and present. Each of these is a distinct type of marine environment, inhabited by its own association of plants and animals. Sediment carried by a river may total millions of tons a year—land literally lost to the sea or rearranged along the seacoast, creating new conditions for coastal marine life. A great river such as the Mississippi transports such enormous quantities of suspended materials that it makes the Gulf of Mexico opaque and discolored far beyond the many outlets of its delta. Eventually this fine sediment must descend to the Gulf floor, however, building it up and providing a soft substrate suitable for burrowing creatures.

Along the Atlantic Coast, over long periods of time, sediment has built a wide continental shelf. This stretches out a long way from the coast before plunging steeply to the oceanic abyss, creating a shallow sea that slopes gently away from the shoreline. Many creatures found just below the low-tide mark also live far out in the shallow waters over the shelf.

Waves invariably approach a beach at an angle, known as the angle of incidence. Water rushes up the beach and is bounced off, receding at an equivalent—but opposite—angle (the angle of reflection). Where the receding water meets the incoming wave, a current is created that flows parallel to the beach not far offshore, often behind an outlying sandbar. This current, called a longshore current, is capable of eroding a trough just beyond the low tide level, a deeper place sought by small inshore fishes, crabs, and other creatures. It also creates a surprise for a person who wades out in shin-deep water, then suddenly finds himself in water nearly waist-high. Much larger currents and ocean phenomena have relatively little effect upon a beach. Major currents, such as the Gulf Stream, flow past a continent many miles out to sea. Where such a current comes close to land, it washes away the continental shelf to a narrow band but never actually flows along the shoreline. Therefore, they take small part in creating a longshore current or causing other major effects unless in concert with other kinds of waves generated closer to shore.

Tides

To those who dwell by the sea, tides are a planetary clock by which to live. But the occasional visitor may be somewhat baffled by them. The person who understands that the timing of the tides advances approximately fifty minutes each day must often still consult tide tables to learn exactly when the tides are high or low, or just how high or low they will be. The oceans, composed of fluid water held in their basins, are free to be moved by external forces. The earth's gravity holds the water in place, but there are two other bodies in our solar system—the moon and the sun—with sufficient gravitational attraction to affect our seas. The position of these bodies and that of the earth are maintained by the countering and balanced effects of centrifugal force and gravitational pull.

It is the moon's gravity acting upon the earth that determines the major tidal effect. Because the earth rotates on its axis, the gravitational influence of the moon is felt at different times of day at different places on the earth. The part of the earth that is closest to the moon at any given moment will feel the moon's gravitational pull most strongly. (There is, understandably, a certain lag time—the time it takes the fluid mass to respond.) In the oceans, this pull is experienced as high tide.

On the opposite side of the earth, farthest from the moon, there is an interesting corollary effect that also results in a high tide. Here, the moon's gravity exerts less influence on the water than it does on the solid earth that intervenes. Thus the earth is pulled more forcefully toward the moon than the waters are; the effect is that the waters on the side of the earth opposite the moon bulge *away* from the earth—and the result is a high tide. Low tides occur exactly halfway between the two high tides.

It takes about twenty-four hours for the earth to complete one rotation, and there are usually two high tides and two low tides each day. (There are certain places where this rule does not hold true.) But because of the rate at which the moon orbits the earth, the timing of the tides advances by fifty minutes each day. Thus, if high tide occurs in Boston Harbor at noon on Tuesday, it will occur at 12:50 PM on Wednesday, 1:40 PM on Thursday, and 2:30 PM on Friday.

If the moon were the only force working upon the oceans, then each day's tides would rise and fall to the same levels. It is apparent, though, that within a two-week period, tides gradually reach their maximum extent and then grow less again. These differences are the result of the sun's influence. When the sun, moon, and earth are in a straight line, the effect of gravity from both sun and moon is combined (at the time of full moon and new moon); and exceptionally high and low tides—known as spring tides—are produced. When the sun and moon are at right angles to each other, their gravitational pulls are at odds and the tidal rise and fall are diminished, creating neap tides. The amount of water by which a surface is covered at high tide differs from day to day as the position of the moon relative to the sun changes over a two-week cycle.

For the shore-watcher and naturalist, spring tides are the most rewarding, for it is then that intertidal plants and animals are most fully exposed. If you have a choice, time your arrival at a shoreline with a low spring tide and you will see more marine life aired in the intertidal zone than at any other time. At any given time, there is a high-tide line and a low-tide level; these change slightly with each succeeding tide. During a tidal rise and fall, it is possible to arbitrarily divide the vertical distance between the high-tide and low-tide marks into halves (the halfway point being mid-tide), quarters, or any fractions you wish. This is useful because, as you will see in other chapters, intertidal plants and animals have their preferred zones in which to live; indeed, many are found only at certain intertidal levels and never anywhere else. The reason for this is that each marine organism has its own degree of tolerance for exposure to air—some more, others less.

Tides can be modified by shoreline features. The most extreme example would be a long bay that narrows toward its head, entering a river and creating an estuary. It should be obvious that if a tidal surge enters a bay and is increasingly compressed as it flows upstream, it should rise higher. This is precisely what it does. For example, in the Delaware River system, the tide about ninety miles upstream (at Philadelphia) is exactly twice as high as it is at the bay mouth, at Capes May and Henlopen. The Bay of Fundy, a deep narrow bay in Nova Scotia, has high spring tides of more than fifty feet that expose wide areas of tidal flats when the tide falls to its lowest level. Tides along the Atlantic Coast are regular, with each being very similar to the next, although more northerly tides are greater than those to the south. In the Gulf of Mexico, however, a day's tides are irregular or fluctuating, with one high tide being a little lower than the high tides preceding it and following it. In a similar fashion, one low tide is lower than the following ones. This might seem to present difficulties both to intertidal organisms and to people venturing along the seashore, but the truth is that Gulf tides generally rise and fall only one or two feet. Part of the reason for these alternating tides is that the Gulf of Mexico is sufficiently large to feel the effects of moon and sun by itself, for it is a small sea almost enclosed by Cuba and the Yucatán peninsula. (In theory, even a bathtub can have tides.) Water from the far larger Atlantic Ocean surges through the channels, thoroughly confusing the picture. Obviously, water that enters the Gulf must eventually leave. But the Gulf is wide, so near Florida it feels the effects of the Atlantic quite differently than it does far across the water along the Texas coast. The tidal picture in the Gulf is extremely complex, and visitors are fortunate that the overall rise and fall is so small, sparing them almost hopeless confusion.

Tides profoundly affect different kinds of shorelines. Rocky shores seem to suffer the least, yet that is only a geological myopia—we simply do not live long enough to see them worn away by the endless waves that thunder against them, first at high tide, then at low. On the other hand, we easily see the effects of tidal action upon a sandy coastline. A storm blowing onshore at the time of a high tide is devastating, destroying barrier dunes, shorefront property, and perhaps removing many miles of beach sand. Tides write their signatures on beaches more clearly than upon any other shoreline, leaving lines of jetsam, called wrack, at their highest limit.

Salt wetlands are properly called tidal marshes. Their flatness and extent are the combined product of rooted vegetation and regular tides that keep them level, flushing their muddy nutrients back and forth between bay and salt marsh.

While the physical structure of shorelines responds to the forces of tides, it is the rhythm of the tides that most deeply affects life along a shoreline. This rhythm is echoed within the biology and behavior of many coastal creatures—bodily processes change, colors fade or increase, and activity at one tidal level may be very different from that a few hours before or after. Remember this when you look for fiddler crabs in salt marshes, watch shorebirds probing the wet sand of a beach, or notice sea anemones among seaweeds along a rocky shore. Some animals migrate with the tides, following them just above or below the waterline. Other animals are attached to rocks or live in permanent burrows and must adjust to the changes that occur when water floods over them or drops below their level. One of the most interesting aspects of a seaside visit is to understand how a particular intertidal creature survives in its changeable world. Is it quiet when the tide covers it? Does it emerge or become active only when it is submerged under water? How do you explain the presence of two different kinds of barnacles stretched in separate horizontal bands upon a rocky shore? It doesn't take long to realize that the barnacle species that lives higher up is immersed for shorter periods of time and can tolerate greater exposure to air than the barnacles in the lower zone can. This zonation is repeated among every kind of plant and animal found within the intertidal region. Each is a specialist in its adaptations to submergence or exposure. And superimposed upon this, of course, is the effect of waves and currents, or tidal waters in action.

Tides follow precisely the same patterns throughout the year, month after month. While they are regular and predictable, another environmental factor—temperature—changes markedly over a year's time. A midwinter low tide with freezing air temperatures poses a very different challenge than the same sort of tide on a day in July. For this reason, there are clear differences, coinciding with seasonal changes, between the populations of certain plants and animals.

Since seasons affect coastal organisms, it is logical that many of them synchronize their spawning habits with favorable conditions. As is true on land, the oceans have a surge in the production of spores, eggs, and larvae in the spring. Growth is accentuated during the summer months and slows in the fall. Winter for some may be a quieter time, even an occasion for closing down most activities in a way that, on land, we call hibernation.

Winters also bring far greater forces to bear within the water itself—the heavy waves of winter are larger and more powerful than those of summer. Not only do they affect beaches—washing them down to narrow strips or even removing them almost entirely—they also create hazardous conditions for inshore animals and plants. The patterns of larval distribution that many invertebrate animals depend upon are altered by winter current changes, so this is not a favorable time for their release.

In the warm months, tidal currents can be filled with countless larval forms produced by worms, mollusks, and crustaceans, to name a few. Oyster, mussel, and clam larvae—small, top-shaped creatures with fine little hairs (cilia)—drift as clouds of plankton in enclosed bays. Predators following the swarms of plankton, such as Leidy's Comb Jelly, reproduce prolifically to take advantage of the tidal circulation; these creatures sometimes fill inshore waters so abundantly that they blunt the waves and make the surface appear almost semisolid with their gelatinous bodies.

The endless adaptations of coastal plants and animals to tidal variations did not occur overnight. Life originated along the shores of ancient oceans over three and one half billion years ago, when tides were just as much in effect as they are today. The earliest forms of life existing in intertidal zones had to cope with exposure and submergence in their own primitive fashion. As eons passed, populations along the shoreline proliferated in number and kind—the seashore has always been a popular place to live. Portions of the ocean—the open sea and especially the abyssal, or deep sea—were populated much later than the seashore. Some of the early adjustments to a tidal situation were so successful that they have hardly changed since.

The hydrozoans—animal phylum containing the jellyfish

(medusae) and hydroids—developed a system of alternating generations that is eminently suited to their way of life. One generation consists of an asexual, branching hydroid colony that grows from its solid place of attachment. It does so quickly and abundantly until whole surfaces are covered. Later, it produces tiny sexual medusae that break free and pulsate their way out into currents to be swept away to new opportunities for colonization. The mortality rate is high, but the method is sure. It is possible to find clear impressions of both stages in ancient rocks that are now exposed. So closely do these fossils resemble modern forms that we can almost visualize the shoreline and the conditions under which they lived long before there was any life on land.

Patterns of Succession

Whenever a new surface appears along a shoreline—a recent rockfall from a cliff, or a structure of our own devising like a jetty—colonization by attaching life forms commences at once. The very first arrivals, bacteria, are invisible to all but specialists. Within hours a bacterial film establishes itself across the surface. These are not harmful bacteria but representatives of free-living forms that exist everywhere in the world, the oceans included.

Once they arrive and settle into an extensive population, the scene is set for more and different organisms to follow. Just which they will be is not predictable, although one-celled protozoans are very likely to attach within the first day. Some of these build small tubes that are cemented to the rock; from within these tubes, the animals extend palm-shaped extensions, fringed with cilia, to create miniature vortices, or "whirlpools," that bring in food. By the end of the same day, the planktonic larvae of hydroids usually arrive, settling down and growing the first tentacled polyp of what eventually will be a colony of hundreds or thousands.

From now on, new arrivals follow the pioneers in rapid order; often the kinds and proportions of creatures that will eventually form the attached community—known as the climax population—are determined in the early stages of succession. Algal spores settle and grow into brown or red seaweeds; ciliated mussel larvae attach, and tiny active barnacle larvae explore the rock surface in a meticulous fashion, searching for precisely the right place to cement themselves for life. In the lower intertidal region, it is quite possible that any one of these three may establish itself so completely that the others always remain secondary in abundance. A kind of sweepstakes occurs in the immediate colonization of a newly exposed rock surface in coastal waters, and the scramble for attachment is especially energetic in the lower regions of the intertidal zone.

The Zonation of Shores

Taken all together—regardless of the form of the seashore or its many specific characteristics—every shoreline has certain definable zones. The region where the sea meets the land is known as the littoral zone, although in this book we will often use the more familiar term "intertidal" in an equivalent sense. Maritime influence can be felt well above the littoral region, principally in the form of splash, spray, and salt mist zones. Collectively, these regions above the intertidal may be called the supralittoral zone. A splash zone offers real opportunities —albeit rather difficult ones—for certain organisms that do not require periodic complete seawater immersion during high tide, making do, instead, with seawater afforded by the splash of waves. It is only during high tide that waves throw seawater up to where these creatures live, yet this splash is an absolutely vital condition. On coasts lacking regular and dependable waves that splash above the normal waterline, such life cannot exist. The Little Gray Barnacle is one species that is able to live a little above the high-tide mark by relying upon wave splash to bring food and carry away its larvae. Along a windswept coast, salt spray from the wave tops is carried inland, creating saline conditions farther than would occur on a quiet shore. Small pools high up on a rock face may be replenished by this spray rather than by tides, often growing more and more saline as water evaporates, while salt water continues to arrive. Salt mist usually discourages terrestrial plants from growing on the crest, whether of rock or sand, although a few forms do tolerate salty conditions. Some perennial shrubs and trees growing not far inland show scars on their windward sides caused by salt damage.

Along some coasts, there are areas where sand and soil allow penetration by seawater that is not flushed out by fresh water flowing from the land. In such spots, the water table becomes saline for a considerable distance inland. This condition makes it impossible for most plants to grow, since they lack the necessary adaptations to their root systems or the physiological means of adjusting to salt water. Only in salt marshes, with their highly specialized seed plants, do heavy stands of vegetation flourish.

The littoral, or intertidal, region is covered by water at least part of the time during the cycle of spring and neap tides. Because it may be quite wide—made up of gently sloped beaches or salt marshes, for example—the intertidal can be divided into subzones: upper intertidal, midtidal, and lower intertidal. It is here that the true shoreline flora and fauna exist, the organisms that play such an important role in our seashore visits and that comprise the bulk of the descriptions in this book.

Organisms in the upper intertidal spend relatively less time covered by salt water and are exposed to air much of the time, while creatures in the lower intertidal are immersed far longer than they are exposed. Life forms in the midtidal are submerged and exposed alternately, for about equal lengths of time. These varying conditions clearly have an impact upon shoreline life, with the result that distinct bands or zones of plants and animals are recognizable along every shore.

Any visitor to a seashore realizes that the open ocean does not begin immediately below the low-tide line. The sublittoral zone is a definable habitat that stretches out for varying distances into shallow water. It is populated by its own forms of life, only some of which continue to be found far out in much deeper water. The Atlantic and Gulf coasts are bordered by a wide continental shelf that gradually deepens until reaching the continental slope, at which point the contours plunge deeply to the oceanic abyssal plain far below. What distinguishes the sublittoral zone from regions farther out is the continental influence—the flow of fresh water from rivers, sediments washed off the land, and the action of tides, waves, and currents upon the shoreline. All combine to affect the quality, salinity, transparency, and amount of nutrients of inshore waters. Creatures living in this area depend upon its characteristic features, most of which eventually diminish or vanish with increased distance from the land. The seashore's effects, then, continue well beyond where we walk and observe intertidal life.

Individuals of a single species of plant or animal in an intertidal region may compete with one another for space or food. On the other hand, separate species have ways of life, or ecological niches, that are usually so distinct that one particular species will seldom affect another. For this reason, we see long, horizontal bands composed of almost a pure population of one kind of organism stretching for miles along a shore. The entire phenomenon owes its existence mostly to one environmental factor—the tides.

Thus, the rise and fall of tides determines exactly which plants and animals are able to take hold and survive at specific levels. For example, larvae of one species of barnacle take hold at the upper level of the intertidal zone, a region inhospitable to another barnacle species, which must attach lower down, where the animals can spend more time underwater during tidal exchange. Seaweeds are even more clearly zoned, with perhaps a half-dozen species growing in horizontal bands across a rock face. Some of these are discussed in the chapter on rocky shores.

Temperature also influences the way zones become established along a shoreline. Tides rising and falling upon an open oceanfront will be colder than those that have crossed many miles of a shallow, warm, protected bay. This means that intertidal life in such a bay—in addition to having to tolerate exposure or submergence—may find itself favored or discouraged by a range of temperatures not normally encountered along much of the seashore.

Direct exposure to sunlight, with its bright intensity and accompanying heat, is a related factor that to a degree determines the presence of intertidal plants and animals. Seaweeds, although rather simple plants, nevertheless must photosynthesize organic nutrients; they can hardly grow far back in a deep, shadowy crevice. But such a place, washed regularly by tides and constantly wet because of reduced evaporation, may be a fine place for delicate, soft-bodied animals like hydroids, sea anemones, sponges, and bryozoans, or moss animals.

These are but some of the environmental features that

determine the presence, absence, or local abundance of seashore organisms. A visitor walking the shore should consider every possible influence that may help explain the appearance of shoreline populations and communities. The complexities and variations are not only endless—they are endlessly fascinating.

Waves

Tides become apparent to us only with the passing of hours. But the one feature every visitor watches with awe is the approach of waves traveling in from the sea. Their rhythm lulls us or excites us and, at times, justifiably frightens us. They march in, rank upon rank, yet we soon discern differences among them. Swimmers and surfers wait to take advantage of certain waves having characteristics out of the ordinary. A wave is a manifestation of energy passing through a fluid medium, yet its dynamics are so complex that they challenge scientist and engineer alike. Waves also establish a wide variety of conditions with which seashore plants and animals must contend—and these organisms do so with extraordinary and almost infinite adaptations.

How does a wave begin? Nature provides only two origins: the wind, or a geological disturbance such as an earthquake, volcanic eruption, or collapse of a cliff into the sea. Since the latter kind of wave is infrequent anywhere, the only cause we need to consider is pressure from the wind. When we stand on an Atlantic beach watching waves roll in, we have little means of knowing just where they began. A series of waves may have got its start 2000 miles away, as a calm portion of the ocean gradually felt the effects of an approaching storm. The storm did not cross the Atlantic, but the energy it imparted to the water did.

A gentle breeze that we can hardly feel slips across the water's surface without disturbing it, even though a bit of friction exists between the two media. When the wind picks up, it begins to tug at the elastic film on the water, and small ripples appear, soon growing into wavelets. If the wind blows faster than the waves move, aerial eddies begin to develop on the lee (protected) side of a wave, lowering the pressure there. But on the windward side of a wave, the pressure increases, pushing against this fluid obstacle, moving it a little more rapidly. The more a wave is pressed by a faster wind, the larger it becomes.

A large wave is not only high—it also takes up more space than a small wave. Wavelength is defined as the distance between the crest of one wave and the crest of the next; large waves are farther apart than small ones. An ocean swell in the Atlantic may have a wavelength of more than 2300 feet, while the wavelength of a storm wave in the same area may be less than 480 feet. Fair-weather waves are much shorter and correspondingly smaller in height, usually no more than a yard tall. The velocity of a wave in open water is impressive, with speeds of twenty-two feet a second for a wave 330 feet long. The speed of even larger waves is accordingly greater.

While the velocity of an ocean wave may be rapid, the water itself does not flow along at all. It simply moves in a small, narrow, circular course—forward, up, back, and down, in a roller effect. A log floating on the surface can be watched to follow this circular motion; if it continues to move forward at all, it is because it is carried by currents or it is blown by the wind. Waves do not push it along. The roller motion of small waves is shallow, but great storm waves may have an effect far beneath the surface, disturbing bottom sediments nearly 1000 feet down. If it is difficult to visualize this internal motion of water, think of a field of grain being blown by the wind. Waves are clearly apparent across the wide expanse, but surely the stalks of grain are not going anywhere—they bend forward, down, then back and up. The head of a grain stalk is equivalent to a "particle" of water. A wave, therefore, is an oscillation, not a form of transport; it is a surface phenomenon, and the effect diminishes quickly with increased depth.

At sea, it is possible to see many wave forms at the same place and time. There are great swells widely separated from one another; waves are superimposed upon the swells, and racing up and down the waves may be little wavelets. Furthermore, not all these wave forms may flow in the same direction. Waves of similar magnitude may approach one another from different angles, but they do not collide—they merely pass through one another, undiminished. But eventually all swells and waves reach a shoreline, and there dramatic changes take place.

As long as the roller motion of waves does not feel the bottom, waves tend to proceed in even, rounded, watery hills— although a very strong wind may force them to crest and break into foam. When waves enter shallow water, however, the lower portion of the roller strikes the bottom and is slowed, but the upper part of the wave travels as rapidly as before. It grows steeper and ultimately unstable, tipping forward and spilling water down its front in what is known as a breaker. Furthermore, because of this slowing, waves crowd in upon one another, shortening the wavelength they maintained in open water. The area of a seashore where the waves begin to break is called the surf zone; it may begin far out over a sandbar or almost directly upon the shore—it all depends upon how close to shore the water becomes shallow. At this point, and for the first time in the existence of the wave, water is actually moved, and it may move with great force. This tremendous pressure of a heavy fluid in rapid motion is sufficient to move boulders, beaches, ships, and shorefront hotels. It is also a force with which every seashore creature must contend. That they are able to do so with such success speaks volumes for their evolutionary adaptations.

If you are flying over an ocean toward a shoreline, you will not be surprised to find waves approaching the coast obliquely from the sea. Winds blow from different directions, and a coastline always has irregular contours. Yet when waves reach actual shore, they seem to turn to rush directly toward it, crashing upon beaches or cliffs in near-parallel array. Once again the slowing effect of a shallow bottom is at work: When one end of a wave touches the shore, its speed is reduced, while the part of the wave still out in open water continues rapidly. The slowdown steadily works its way along the wave until the entire front approaches the shore almost face-on. This means the shore and its associated plants and animals must bear the full brunt of a wave's power.

As long as you are flying over a shoreline, it would be a mistake not to note the effect that a solid mass has upon waves. Where a coast has headlands and bays, waves are refracted in predictable patterns: They converge upon headlands and spread outward into bays. When waves approach a point of land or a breakwater, the ones that strike it are diffracted into semicircular patterns that bend around the obstacle, eventually interacting with the other waves that have missed the land and continued straight on. The pattern you see of circular waves passing through an array of parallel waves is known as a diffraction pattern and can be demonstrated in bathtubs or swimming pools. In a coastal ocean, a diffraction pattern is confused and choppy, difficult for small swimming and drifting organisms to pass through. Complex wave patterns, such as the ones caused by refraction and diffraction, also have their effects upon shoreline organisms, especially those that attach to solid surfaces and have varying degrees of tolerance for the force of waves striking them. A headland may be populated only by plants and animals that can adhere securely to rocks, while a bay offers a haven for more delicate forms unable to withstand heavy wave pressures.

The effects of waves breaking upon beaches and rocky shores are described further in the corresponding chapters. There too you will find information on some of the plants and animals that exist under such apparently difficult conditions. It needs to be remembered, however, that these situations are precisely what such organisms require because of their specialties and adaptations. In other words, a seacoast may seem a stressful and seemingly chaotic place from our terrestrial perspective, but for countless simple plants and a host of small, fragile, highly specialized creatures, it is the norm—it is home and the only possible place to live.

No organism on a seashore is there by accident. Each is the product of hundreds of millions of years of evolutionary adaptation, an exquisite example of genetic alteration that results in a precise fit with a particular habitat. A limpet, a barnacle, a rockweed, a mole crab, a mangrove—to human eyes these have attained a capacity to survive where other living things may not. It is the purpose of this book to take us —as land-dwelling outsiders—into the nearby marine world of the seashore, a world far larger and less well known than the terrestrial one we inhabit. The seashore, as an ecotone in which land and sea meet, is a unique and special world deserving understanding and appreciation.

ROCKY SHORES

Of all the shorelines of the world, it may be that none holds the appeal of a rugged, sculptured rocky coast with cliffs, islets, and crashing waves. Every step along a headland reveals a new vista, a surprise, a pulse of excitement. In quiet weather, ocean swells rise and fall across vertical rock faces, but when waves build, their smashing assault sends jets of mist and clouds of spray high into the air, accompanied by a thunderous roar. It seems as though the headlands of such a coast tear the waves apart, but in the long run, it is the waves that bring about the greatest change in a rocky shoreline, for they are a major force in altering its contours.

Along the Atlantic Coast, rocky shores predominate north of Cape Cod. South of this huge spit of land, outcroppings of rock occur through Rhode Island, but diminish until no natural rocky shorelines exist at all in the Middle Atlantic States and farther south. However, man's hand has provided opportunities—by creating breakwaters and rock jetties—both for the visitor and for the marine plants and animals seeking places of attachment. On a rocky jetty in Maryland, for example, it is possible to find a sea anemone that otherwise would be restricted to New England waters. The coral rocks and rubble of Florida's coast support very different forms of life but display the basic principles that apply to rocky shores everywhere.

Over the ages, waves, wind, weathering, and sea-level changes along the famed and scenic Maine coast have created rugged beauty typical of rocky shores from Labrador to Massachusetts. Cliffs, bays, and headlands have become caves, arches, ledges, and even great fjords. Sections of cliff face have collapsed into massive rubble where rocks are ground by wave action into gravel and sand; this sand is carried by currents to adjacent coves and deposited as small beaches. It is this irregularity that fascinates and surprises visitors, for no two views are ever the same.

Once the grandeur of the topography has been accepted, new features are recognized. Even from a distance, a rocky shoreline is seen to have distinct horizontal bands of different subdued colors, almost as though brushed by a giant painter. The lower greenish-brown lines are correctly assumed to be seaweeds of various kinds, but what of the white and black bands above? Only close inspection will prove them also to be evidence of living organisms, some of them very small: barnacles, dark algae, and lichens.

Walking the rocks raises more questions. Crevices extending down from the crest allow terrestrial plants to invade the granite shoreline well beyond their source in pine and moss woodlands. And crevices penetrating the rocks from the sea permit marine plants and animals to live higher above tide levels than an exposed surface allows. Depressions in a rock ledge hold water in one of the most fascinating of all shoreline features—a tide pool, which is a natural aquarium of unrivaled richness and beauty.

Visiting the same spot day after day reveals even more differences as high- and low-tide levels change over a two-week interval. Seasons have their effect upon the life that is present, and storms wreak sudden changes of great magnitude. The moods of a rocky shore are varied and ephemeral. On a misty morning, the sun shines weakly through dense sea mist, and the scene is subdued in quiet pastel tones. A few hours later, with the air cleared and a brilliant blue sky above, the bright contrasts of color, shape, and shadow of a rocky shore are almost more than the eye can encompass.

Approaching a rocky shore from the wooded interior, the first animal life a visitor sees might be gulls, wheeling over a school of offshore fishes, crying their familiar *kyow-kyow-kyow*. If the tide is low, smaller creatures are visible. Your visit should be timed to coincide with low tide (especially spring tides rather than neap tides), for it is then that the intertidal regions are most exposed. Some of the life is inactive while the water level is down, for barnacles, limpets, and periwinkles must remain closed against the drying effects of sun and air.

Northern Sea Roach
Ligia oceanica
180

Lower down, Northern Sea Roaches scurry across a rock face to the security of a clump of rockweed, and sea stars move slowly through a film of moisture to a water-filled crevice.

A glimpse into a tide pool reveals marine life in full action, undeterred by the fallen water level. Hermit crabs sift through bottom sediment, whelks cruise about in search of molluskan prey, barnacles strain water for its planktonic contents, sea anemones stretch out their tentacles, and tiny shrimp and fishes dart through the clear, still water. At still lower levels, you may wish to inspect the rockweeds and other seaweeds, strange plants to the eyes of those used to landlocked trees, shrubs, and grasses. Lifting a tangled mat of knotted wrack (*Ascophyllum* spp.) may reveal clusters of brightly colored Dog Whelks—flattened amphipod crustaceans that scamper away —or lithe and elusive worms.

Common Eastern Dog Whelk
Nassarius vibex
55

If the rocky shore faces a bay with small waves and little surf, a plunge into the cold, clear water with a face mask (and wet suit if you have one!) will open an entirely new world unlike that of the exposed intertidal zone above. Actually, it may be even more interesting to examine, after the tide has risen, the same intertidal zone you formerly walked over, for everything changes. The rockweeds and wrack that formerly hung damp and limp downward across the rock face now stand almost erect, buoyed by bladders within their fronds, swaying rhythmically in the slow surge of the ocean swell. Crabs, active and very much in evidence, emerge from their low-tide hiding places. Sea urchins, with spines and tube feet waving slowly about, creep from spot to spot; limpets browse away from their home territories; and hosts of barnacles, now open, busily sweep the water with feeding appendages, looking for planktonic food. Your underwater visit to Maine's waters will be of short duration, most likely, for the frigid water takes your breath away, but even a brief glimpse of what lies just beneath the surface will be remembered for a lifetime.

Range
Rocky shores of the type described here are scarce south of

Cape Cod, but from the north shore of the Cape to Labrador
they are virtually unbroken. Below the Cape, beaches and salt
marshes become common and finally are the only kind of
natural shoreline habitats. The only other natural hard
seashore within the scope of this book is very different: It is
composed of coral blocks and rubble in southern Florida.
On the other hand, artificial rocky habitats in the form of
breakwaters and jetties occur the entire length of the Atlantic
and Gulf coasts. The flora and fauna of these sporadically
placed rock structures show a distinct north-south gradient,
with cold-water forms appearing down into the Middle
Atlantic States and a few even as far as Cape Hatteras, North
Carolina. Certain warm-water tropical forms from Florida are
found north to Hatteras and sometimes well beyond, as far as
New Jersey if the season and currents are favorable.
The Gulf Coast, while possessing some coral shores and lava
rock islets, consists essentially of sand and mud. Deep beneath
these deposits, however, the complex Gulf Coast geology is
hidden and unavailable today to marine flora and fauna.

Features

The rocky northern shoreline of New England and Canada is
varied and complicated. Its form depends largely upon the
type of rock exposed, the range of the tides washing it, and
whether it is open to heavy wave action and oceanic currents.
Two rock faces only 100 yards apart can be very different
habitats supporting divergent communities.
Rocks exposed along the Maine coast are primarily
metamorphic and granitic rock. Heated igneous rock in the
form of basalt flowed into the cracks, hardened, and formed
straight walls, or dikes. Subsequent geological events,
weathering, wave action, and glaciation shaped these rocks
into rough and irregular forms. Walking along the shore today
shows us these dikes in some areas, but in other places, they
have eroded and vanished, leaving large, deep slots that run
straight through massive granite formations. Waves surge
through such places with great force, creating a turbulent
habitat for fish and well-anchored marine plants and animals.
Prior to about 380 million years ago, what is today New
England lay under an ancient, shallow sea called the Proto-
Atlantic. At about that time, North America-Greenland
collided with Africa and Europe, eliminating a large part of
this ocean and forming a supercontinent. A line of mountains
rose along the line of contact between these two land masses,
heating and compressing marine sediments and volcanic
material, which became metamorphic rock. Later on, granite
entered folds in this altered rock, and then the entire
formation gradually rose until it emerged above sea level. It is
this granite that today forms much of the rocky New England
coast. This shoreline now faces the comparatively young
Atlantic Ocean, which began to open about sixty million years
ago, although a very narrow sea remained in the vicinity of
Labrador and Greenland until only a little more than ten
million years ago. For a long period, then, the Atlantic Coast

of North America was in close proximity to that of Europe; this near continuity explains the striking similarity between many of their intertidal and coastal forms of life, nearly all of which have swimming or planktonic stages, allowing dispersal.

Over the ages, the rocky bulwark against the sea was slowly shaped by forces of wind, temperature, and, above all, water. Promontories were cut back, caves and ledges were shaped, and everywhere gradually collapsing cliffs allowed boulders to separate and fall into the surge below, where they were slowly and inexorably ground into cobbles and finally to sand.

The great irregularity of a rocky shore offers a wide variety of habitats, some directly exposed to the onslaught of powerful waves, others so sheltered that water movement is scarcely felt. All, however, know the effects of tides, although plants and animals living in a deep, rooted crevice are likely to remain moist during low tide and suffer little from evaporation. Those on open rock faces must contend with heat, drying, and (in winter) scouring by ice. No wonder that a visit to a rocky promontory reveals clear differences in the assemblages of organisms within just a few yards of one another. Life on a rocky shore is impossible to understand unless the nature of the precise habitat is first considered.

North of Cape Cod, tidal rise and fall is very great; indeed, in the Bay of Fundy, which separates New Brunswick from Nova Scotia, it has the greatest range of anywhere in the world— more than twenty feet at the mouth and fifty-three feet at the head in Minas Basin. For much of New England, a rise and fall of between six and eight feet is common. Wide tidal excursions such as these provide a mixing of waters, upwelling, and temperature fluctuations; these are aspects with which all intertidal animals must contend. Because of the northerly latitude, intertidal portions of rocky coasts in this part of North America are subject to extremely low temperatures, often below freezing in winter. Even in midsummer, should there be a sudden upwelling along the coast, creatures in shallow water may have to tolerate temperature changes of almost 70° F within an hour, causing severe physiological stress. An animal that is exposed to warm air and sunlight and then immersed in such frigid waters must have remarkable adaptations shared by few other animals in the world. In short, a rocky coast seems to be a difficult and even hazardous place to live, yet the organisms present are beautifully and successfully adapted to flourish there.

Ecology

Like the other shorelines included in this book, rocky shores are affected by tides; it is these periodic risings and fallings that give such character to northern coasts. For one thing, because tides above Cape Cod tend to be greater than those along the Middle Atlantic, Florida, and Gulf coasts, the intertidal regions are both steeper and wider. There are more faces to the shore than on sandy beaches, salt marshes, or mangrove swamps. The angle of wave attack—therefore its power—is of enormous significance to a plant or animal living attached to a rock face. Crevices become vitally important to those more delicate organisms that cannot withstand the great force of waves driving in from the ocean.

The levels or zones of a rocky shore may be defined in two ways: by the extent of tidal incursion and by the graded composition of living things present. The levels affected by tides are named as they are elsewhere. The supralittoral region is above high-water level but may be affected by wave splash or sea mist. The littoral zone is the area between high and low water; it can be subdivided in itself depending upon how long it is exposed or submerged as tides rise and fall. The subtidal region extends downward and out to sea from just below the low spring tide level. The physical nature of being covered or uncovered by seawater sets the stage for plant and animal communities on a rocky shore, yet so many other factors enter into the picture that this simplified zonation in no way predicts what will be found at a particular level.

It is the living organisms present in a particular place that best define the zones of a rocky shore, for each species has its own degree of tolerance for wave action, exposure to air (or to seawater, if the organisms are of terrestrial origin), temperature variations, desiccation, feeding possibilities, reproductive opportunities, security against predators, and much more. Two sides of a waterfront boulder may exhibit distinctly different assemblages of life.

If you approach a rocky coast from the top of a hill, passing from a coniferous woodland where it grows upon a granite dome, you will find little life out in the open. Sometimes a few grasses, weeds, insects, and spiders penetrate down the slope in a crack filled with organic matter. But soon they too vanish, giving way to a zone almost devoid of life—but not quite, for hardy lichens, often the attractive orange and yellow Xanthoria, dot the granite crest. Rock Tripe (*Umbilicaria* spp.), another lichen, sometimes grows in thin, nearly black scales upon the steeper portions of the higher rocks. Although these two species of lichens tolerate salt mist, they actually are the last of the terrestrial forms of life to invade a rocky shore. Another lichen that lives farther down the slope, Verrucaria, consists of a black, asphaltlike crust commonly seen on these shores. It is so tolerant of a salty maritime influence, it almost seems to be a life form in transition between two vastly different ecosystems. Lichens are not single organisms but result from an intimate association between algae, which are photosynthetic, and fungi, which provide the supporting matrix. They are capable of surviving some of the most extreme environmental conditions the world has to offer— such as along a rocky shore, with searing temperatures in summer, ice-scour and sub-zero conditions in winter, a heavy concentration of salt (left as seawater evaporates), and occasional copious freshwater runoff. Verrucaria is seldom covered by waves (except by huge, storm-generated ones), but spray and salt-laden mist are constant along a northern rocky coast.

Zones of Life

Below the area where lichens grow, rocks are generally bare unless invaded briefly by insects, spiders, mites, or other land animals hunting for food. Verrucaria lichens, if extensive, may sufficiently darken the rocks to create black splotches, but the most common black zone, the first of the horizontal zones of marine life, is caused by a thick growth of blue-green algae (*Calothrix* spp.) and almost microscopic lichens of another kind. In fair weather, these organisms are so small and dry that they appear simply as a dark, discolored streak that runs parallel to the water level and always a short distance above the highest tide mark. The region may be wet by spray, and, because the blue-green algae are encased in gelatinous sheaths, the area is extremely slippery and treacherous to walk upon. The slimy covering ensures that the microscopic cells will remain moist even during periods of hot and dry weather. These hardy plants are able to withstand not only heat and severe cold but also temporary immersion in the fresh water that runs off the rocks above after a heavy rain. This blue-green alga is not attractive to most shoreline grazers but provides an important food source for the Rough Periwinkle, which ascends into this zone to browse.

Rough Periwinkle
Littorina saxatilis

Proceeding seaward, the next horizontal association of organisms is the upper littoral zone. This zone is not heavily populated, but those plants and animals living there are well adapted to survival under conditions that are often difficult and adverse. A slender tubular green alga, Enteromorpha, grows at the highest reaches of this zone. It can sometimes be found in an upper-level tide pool, where temperature and salinity fluctuations make it almost impossible for other algae and animals to live. Two kinds of red alga grow just a bit lower: a fine filamentous species, Thread Alga (*Bangia* spp.), and wide, ruffled sheets or ribbons of Laver (*Porphyra* spp.). Both of these simple plants are highly resistant to the multiple changes that occur high in the intertidal region.

This area is the favored habitat of the Rough Periwinkle, which breathes and breeds well removed from its marine origins. This snail takes in atmospheric oxygen through moist membranes that function almost like gills, and it retains its developing embryos within its shell until they emerge fully developed and capable of existing on the rock face. Their adaptations to the upper littoral or rocks are so well developed that they often ascend even higher when the tide rises, cementing themselves with mucus secretions to dry rock, remaining there without difficulty for several days or more before returning to the algal mats upon which they feed. If a Rough Periwinkle is dislodged and falls to lower levels, it follows a complex series of moves to regain its preferred location—for rocky shores are highly irregular, and their contours are unpredictable, so moving back up is not a simple procedure. Crawling straight upward, the snail is drawn toward light, but as soon as it comes to a crevice and of necessity crawls in, it reacts negatively to light, going deep inside until it comes to the back wall; then it begins crawling

up and out, drawn to light again. In this fashion, the slow
snail will eventually reach the upper intertidal zone again.
The region between the upper and lower intertidal zones
supports a large variety of organisms, all of them showing
remarkable adaptations to surviving in an area that twice a day
is underwater and twice exposed to the air. These organisms
too are zoned according to the degree to which they can
withstand exposure.

The Barnacle Zone

Without question, barnacles are the outstanding examples of
a highly specialized intertidal animal. The barnacles found
highest on the shore are the Little Gray Barnacles, which .
extend in scattered numbers even into the splash zone, where
their feeding opportunities are restricted to short periods every
twelve hours. Below them, the Northern Rock Barnacle often
forms a thickly packed carpet that excludes all other forms of
life. The bleached calcareous shells of these animals give this
horizontal community the name white zone. From a distance,
it appears that the rocks at low tide have been painted with
whitewash in a band stretching as far as the eye can see. When
they are closely packed together, individual Northern Rock
Barnacles cannot grow in diameter but must extend upward in
a columnar fashion. This is fine as long as no mishap occurs,
but if a few are knocked off, the neighboring barnacles are
easily undercut, and soon whole sections peel away, baring the
rock for colonization by new generations.

Barnacles are crustaceans and go through a series of larval
stages not unlike those of their more familiar crustacean
relatives, such as crabs, shrimps and lobsters—although the
stages of barnacle development are not as complex. When the
last larval stage has been reached—and the barnacle is a small,
oval, swimming creature—it begins seeking a place of
attachment, but it does so in a most particular manner,
examining a surface with great care and selecting precisely the
right spot. This is not always easy to do, for space is at a
premium in the mid-intertidal zone. Nevertheless, a barnacle
larva looks for a roughened place with good exposure and
settles into a minute, preferably oval, depression.

As a barnacle population begins to grow across a rock surface,
competition is keen, although it is so slow it is almost
invisible to human eyes. When two barnacles grow large
enough in diameter to touch each other, each one tries to
undercut its neighbor, thereby forcing it up and eventually off
the rock, to be washed away by waves and die.

An adult barnacle looks nothing like any other crustacean, for
its form is vastly altered to suit its surroundings. The outer
shell is cone-shaped and composed of six fitted and
overlapping calcareous plates. At the top of the cone, the
aperture is closed at low tide by four additional movable
plates. When the water level rises, the "door" plates open; the
animal extends six feathery, branched legs into the water and
sweeps rhythmically for planktonic food. If you can catch a
glimpse of a barnacle-covered rock face underwater, it will

Little Gray Barnacle
Chthamalus fragilis
238

Northern Rock Barnacle
Balanus balanoides
240

appear as an animated carpet of frenzied activity, as thousands of delicate appendages reach out and then retract in their search for diatoms and other minute organisms to feed upon. The size of individual barnacles is graded somewhat according to height of attachment. Those higher in the intertidal zone tend to be smaller than those lower down; they are submerged for a shorter time when the tide rises, so they acquire a little less food and grow proportionately less in size.

The conical shape of a barnacle is admirably suited to withstand even the most powerful waves. Furthermore, the cement with which a barnacle's base is attached to the rock is one of the most powerful known. Long after a barnacle dies, the brown, oval, ribbed base remains.

A conical shape—broad base, sloping sides, and a narrow apex—is so successful a form in the face of powerful waves that other creatures have adopted it as well. The Atlantic Plate Limpet, a snail with its shell formed as an oval cone, is admirably suited both by shape and behavior to life in the wave surge. During low tide, it clamps down onto a "home" spot to which its shell margin is precisely fitted. This neat fit is due in part to the manner in which the shell has grown, but these spots, or limpet scars, on rocks are also the result of centuries and countless generations of limpets adhering to precisely the same place, day after day, securely protected both from drying out and from being dislodged by waves. The very rock itself, then, is worn by their presence. When the tide rises, each limpet leaves its particular spot and ranges out about a yard away, browsing upon algae. Limpets are such efficient herbivores that an area free of significant algal growth usually exists around each one, perhaps requiring the snail to venture even farther afield.

Limpets are snails, although their shells are not spiraled. Like most snails, a limpet scrapes its food off the surface by means of a toothed rasp known as a radula. The rasping effect is so energetic that the rock itself is worn away over time. Some tide pools are slowly deepened by such activity.

Living lower in the mid-tidal region than barnacles, limpets are neighbors to an increased variety of life forms. One of the highly conspicuous residents of this region is the Common Periwinkle, one of the most adaptable and successful of all intertidal creatures. It does not ascend into the range of the Rough Periwinkle nor venture down into the lower intertidal province of the Smooth Periwinkle. It travels only as high as neap tides and as low as spring tides allow. When the tide falls, a Common Periwinkle retreats into its shell and secretes mucus; this hardens, cementing the shell to the drying rock. This way, the Periwinkle remains securely protected against desiccation until the tide rises again in a few hours.

Still another snail, the colorful Atlantic Dogwinkle, is found intertidally among seaweeds; a number of these creatures often cluster together in the wetness when the tide is low. The color of this snail's shell is determined by its diet, for it is a predator and feeds upon other shelled creatures, including the Blue Mussels and various barnacles. Its eggs, in vase-shaped

Atlantic Plate Limpet
Notoacmaea testudinalis
83

Common Periwinkle
Littorina littorea
57

Northern Yellow
Periwinkle
Littorina obtusata
68

Atlantic Dogwinkle
Nucella lapillus
51

Blue Mussel
Mytilus edulis
117

Common Northern
Whelk
Buccinum undatum
48

Acadian Hermit Crab
Pagurus acadianus
157

Chevron Amphiporus
Amphiporus angulatus
309

Clam Worm
Nereis virens
305

Spiral Rockweed
Fucus spiralis

clusters, are found under seaweed and in rocky crevices. The Common Northern Whelk is a larger snail; it lives close to the low-tide mark and below, where it scavenges upon dead and dying marine animals. Often its heavy shell is splotched and decorated by encrusting red coralline algae, such as *Lithothamnium* spp., which lend it a pinkish hue. After one of these snails dies, its empty shell is almost immediately occupied by a large hermit crab.

A hermit crab, such as the Acadian Hermit Crab, is not a true crab but actually a crustacean. The animal has a long, soft, coiled abdomen that requires protection—this comes in the surprising form of an empty snail shell, which the hermit crab appropriates. Hooklike structures on the hermit crab's tail appendages make it possible not only to hold on to a shell once the animal is inside but also to resist being drawn out in such a determined fashion that its body will be pulled in two before the animal can be extracted. A shell is the animal's home, into which it can withdraw while blocking off the opening with its large flattened claws, which are usually shaped to fit almost precisely. Of course, like any crustacean, a hermit crab must grow; eventually it outgrows its shell and is forced to seek a new one of appropriate size.

The Blue Mussel is far and away the most common bivalve mollusk of the lower intertidal zone; there, it can grow in enormous colonies in places that otherwise might support seaweed. Mussels are so closely packed together that they form a tight blanket of dark elliptical shells; each is tied to the rock by strong filaments, called byssi, that are secreted by a gland at the base of the mussel's small, slender, muscular foot. If the threads are broken or the mussel needs to change its location, new threads can be produced; so, unlike a barnacle, the mussel —although primarily fixed in place—is able to move a bit when conditions require. It is a plankton feeder, straining diatoms and other minute organisms from seawater that flows across the broad expanse of its twin gills, which are covered by hairlike, beating cilia. Beneath a mussel mat, where sediment accumulates, a host of smaller animals find refuge and feeding opportunities: The red, ribbonlike worm Chevron Amphiporus; the predaceous Clam Worm and other segmented worms; and minute crustaceans—such as copepods and amphipods—abound, often in the company of nearly microscopic mites, which have a terrestrial origin.

Seaweeds
On rocky shores, one can see that barnacles and mussels make a strong visual impression, even from far away; nonetheless, the largest and most extensive zones are those of seaweeds, notably rockweeds and certain other algae. These seaweeds are very clearly zoned, with certain species living at one level replaced by other species at adjacent levels. For example, Spiral Rockweed, with its short, heavy, brownish fronds that end in inflated swellings, lives in the highest intertidal reaches of North America. From a distance, the Spiral Rockweed band is seen to be narrow. Below Spiral Rockweed, Knotted

Knotted Rockweed
Ascophyllum nodosum
472

Bladder Rockweed
Fucus vesiculosus
473

Irish Moss
Chondrus crispus
477

Sea Lettuce
Ulva lactuca
474

Club Hydroid
Clava leptostyla
249

Sinistral Spiral Tube
Worm
Spirorbis borealis
294

Rockweed occurs; growing on rocks that do not directly face ocean waves, it sometimes covers vast areas. With moderate exposure to the sea, there may be a zone occupied by Bladder Rockweed, a smaller, tougher brown alga that is sturdy enough to withstand even powerful storm waves. At low tide, such plants are not especially attractive or interesting to the visitor, for they hang down wet and limp across rock faces in great tangled masses of ill-defined plant material. Separated out, each one becomes more specific and identifiable, but it is only when they are submerged during high tide that their true nature and special adaptations become apparent. The small gas-filled floats that so many shoreline seaweeds have in their fronds buoy up the flexible and pliant plants until they stand erect, straining toward the surface. But the underwater view is unlike that of a terrestrial forest, for everything is in motion: The thickets of large algae sway rhythmically in the surge of the waves, constantly changing position yet always remaining securely anchored to the rocks by firm disks or tendrils known as holdfasts. For the most part, the plants are untangled, for their surfaces are smooth and even slippery, a condition that also inhibits the attachment of sessile plants and animals— known as fouling organisms—that normally seek every available surface. Below the rockweed zone, Irish Moss, Sea Lettuce, and the encrusting red algae of the genus *Hildenbrandia* appear. They are soon followed by various kelp living just below the low-tide mark.

Owing to the physical and chemical nature of most seaweeds, not many marine animals eat them, although in the intertidal zone limpets and periwinkles browse upon their fronds. Certain small and finely branched red seaweeds, such as *Polysiphonia* spp., grow on the surface of the much larger brown Knotted Rockweed, but evenly spaced and not in sufficient numbers to affect them. Two rather obvious creatures that attach to rockweeds include colonies of Club Hydroids and scattered individual Sinistral Spiral Tube Worms, hidden in their coiled, white, limey tubes. From swaying fronds of rockweed, both these small creatures feed upon minute plankton.

The associations between seaweeds and intertidal animals are almost beyond accounting. Sediment accumulates around the bases, or holdfasts, of these large algae; in this rich, organic material, an enormous number of organisms find shelter and food. Ribbon worms, or nemerteans, wind their soft bodies through the tangled plant structures in writhing knots; tiny segmented worms construct tubes, while larger worms seek prey that may have found refuge there. And small crustaceans of many kinds may be found.

Not all marine algae are large seaweeds, however. Besides planktonic diatoms, which float in a rich blanket in offshore waters, every moist surface along the shore is coated with multitudes of microscopic algae beyond reckoning. These miniature pastures make excellent grazing—not only for the snails already mentioned but also for other creatures, including their molluskan relatives, the chitons. A chiton is a

Coralline Alga
Corallina officinalis
478, 479

Hairy Bryozoan
Electra pilosa
288

Forbes' Common Sea Star
Asterias forbesi
189

Green Sea Urchin
Strongylocentrotus droebachiensis
197

Orange-footed Sea Cucumber
Cucumaria frondosa
297

primitive animal with an ancient ancestry. Unlike other mollusks, it has not one or two shells but eight overlapping ones. It creeps slowly along on a broad, muscular foot that adheres to rock so securely that powerful waves cannot dislodge the animal. Like the periwinkles, a chiton rasps off algal coatings from the rocks with a filelike radula.

Irish Moss is a purplish-red alga that grows in dense carpets in the lower intertidal zone down to levels below the lowest tides. It is an edible seaweed, once used in Ireland for flavoring and jellies. It provides a heavy cover upon the lower rocks, where its stubby, tightly packed fronds offer a haven for all kinds of small mobile creatures that cannot tolerate the heavy surge of waves. If you examine it very closely, you will see dozens of worms and crustaceans moving about within the security of this miniature forest. Another even more curious red alga lives in the same region, Coralline Alga.

Its narrow, cylindrical fronds are strengthened by deposits of lime, making its clusters tough and firm, almost to the point of seeming brittle. Invariably, this plant is populated by large numbers of small organisms.

The lower intertidal and shallow subtidal regions are inhabited by a host of animals, some unfamiliar and others large and well known to the shore visitor. Flat colonies of the Hairy Bryozoan encrust themselves upon Irish Moss. This is the region where young sea stars, such as Forbes' Common Sea Star, tend to get their start in adult life, after completing planktonic stages. At low tide, much of this area may be carpeted by hundreds of Green Sea Urchins, their long greenish spines making them look like animated horse chestnuts. Sea stars and sea urchins are echinoderms; another member of this group, the Orange-footed Sea Cucumber, lives close by, just a little farther down.

From a human's viewpoint, each of these echinoderms represents a curious approach to life. These creatures are radially symmetrical: that is, their bodies are arranged on a circular plan and contain one of the most remarkable organ systems known. It is the water vascular system, a complex network of tubes and valves, that permits the animals to move by hydraulic pressure. Long, slender tube feet, each ending in a suction cup, extend from the undersides of sea stars and from the bottoms and sides of sea urchins and sea cucumbers. In the case of the sea urchin, tube feet allow the animal to move across rock faces and through tide pools as it scrapes off algal coatings with the most remarkable jaw apparatus in the animal kingdom: five triangular teeth arranged in a circle, activated by many muscles and "bony" working parts. This mouth even has an exotic name: Aristotle's lantern.

A sea star's tube feet not only make it possible for the creature to walk slowly over the bottom and rock faces when the tide is up, but also to clamp down upon the shells of its favorite food —mussels and other bivalve mollusks. A sea star folds its body over the mussel, then sets up a constant pressure against the muscles of the mollusk that hold its shell closed. Muscle strength is no match for hydraulic pressure, so eventually the mussel or clam tires, and its shell begins to gape open. At this point, the sea star extrudes the lower portion of its centrally located stomach through its mouth; it wraps its stomach around the visceral mass of the mollusk, and digests it! Later, the stomach with its meal is withdrawn back into the sea star's body. The large sea cucumber of northern shores has no such dramatic method of feeding, but simply extends a large brush of feathery arms outward around its mouth, sifting plankton. The lowest level of the intertidal zone is uncovered only twice each month, during the period of spring tides. It is here that the plants and animals least tolerant of exposure to air dwell. Echinoderms are generally limited to this zone, although some survive at higher places if they are surrounded by wet seaweeds or are submerged in water in a tide pool. The lowest part of the littoral zone is easily recognized by its plants, the largest and most obvious being kelp. On northern Atlantic coasts, kelp are the dominant plants of the sublittoral fringe. They are large—often enormous—brown algae, some species of which consist of solitary, straplike fronds stretching several yards in length. Others have about a dozen smaller straps radiating out from a common stem. Kelp holdfasts are gnarled, stoutly built structures. Because of their size, these holdfasts offer protection and surfaces for attachment to a wide variety of other organisms.

It is in this zone that populations of the Blue Mussel begin to diminish, to be replaced by the much larger Northern Horse Mussel, which may reach lengths of more than seven inches. Its dark outer shells are often eroded, displaying the white, iridescent layers beneath. Small amphipod crustaceans work their way among the attaching threads of the mussels and through the holdfasts of seaweeds. The Red-eyed Amphipod is an especially common species and proves to be an attractive, sprightly little creature when viewed closely. It feeds primarily upon diatoms attached to nearby surfaces, but often rests within a sheltered nook, peering outward with its scarlet compound eyes. Other species of amphipods live in the same region. Some of them are not as flattened from side to side as the Red-eyed Amphipod but nearly cylindrical and tube-dwelling—like the Mottled Tube-Maker, a small shrimp that constructs its shelter out of mud particles and organic debris. The Red-eyed Amphipod's external skeleton is translucent and uniformly colored, while a few of the other amphipods are brightly and dramatically marked, often with bright-red splotches. Although most of these small crustaceans are wary and quite well protected, they are nevertheless choice food items for predatory animals, such as fishes.

The realm of sea squirts, or tunicates, commences below the lowest tide levels. Some are solitary, others colonial, yet all individuals are built upon a basic plan: They are filter feeders equipped with siphons to bring in water and exhale it (hence the name sea squirt). The water, once in their bodies, is strained of its plankton contents through a basketlike structure. Their rather simple and inelegant appearance may belie it, but tunicates are in fact cousins of ours, belonging to

Northern Horse Mussel
Modiolus modiolus
116, 132

Red-eyed Amphipod
Ampithoe rubricata
168

Mottled Tube-Maker
Jassa falcata
176

Northern Sea Pork
Aplidium constellatum
236

Golden Star Tunicate
Botryllus schlosseri
290

Stalked Tunicate
Boltenia ovifera
248

Jonah Crab
Cancer borealis
139

Green Crab
Carcinus maenas
145

Northern Lobster
Homarus americanus
162

the same phylum, Chordata. Among the colonial tunicates, the Northern Sea Pork and the Golden Star Tunicate are common along rocky shores, where they attach to rocks and seaweed holdfasts. The Stalked Tunicate, a creature standing more than a foot high on a tough, slender stalk, has an oval, reddish body that almost resembles a peach. The stalk is not always easy to distinguish, for it is usually covered with a thick coat of encrusting algae, moss animals (bryozoans), and hydroids; but the round body, with its siphons pointed to one side, emerges clear and rosy from the confused mass. Underwater, a rocky shore possesses as many crevices, caverns, and irregularities as are found above the high-tide level. There is a difference, however, because space is at a premium, and every square millimeter of submerged rock is populated by an enormous variety of living organisms, many of them microscopic. A Jonah Crab, one of the familiar crustaceans of northern rocky coastlines and a relatively quiet, stocky, and powerful animal, may be wedged in a horizontal crevice. The handsomely marked Green Crab, a likely neighbor, is of lighter build and comes equipped with sharp claws; this crab tends to be more active as it hunts for prey.

Beyond Low Tide

Not far beneath the low-tide level, the largest of all North Atlantic crustaceans can be found, lurking deep in a crevice by day or exploring the rocky bottom at night. The Northern Lobster is an impressive and formidable creature when it reaches adulthood. It has been known to reach a length of almost three feet and weigh as much as forty-five pounds! Probably because of heavy fishing pressure, the largest specimens are found far away from shore, in deep water along the edge of the continental shelf. The Northern Lobster is an indiscriminate feeder, consuming living, dead, and decaying plant and animal matter. Its two powerful claws differ from each other: One is a heavy crusher for cracking open shells, and the other acts as shears, cutting food.

All crustaceans molt periodically, a process that is obvious in the larger species. The jointed exoskeleton of a crab, shrimp, or lobster is composed of a compound known as chitin, and is fortified with calcium salts that make the covering hard and almost inflexible. The animal must grow, however; at intervals, a new tender and flexible exoskeleton forms beneath the outer one; the old covering splits and the animal crawls out. For a while it is vulnerable, until the calcium salts stored in its body can migrate to the new covering and strengthen it. Molting occurs at frequent intervals among larval and juvenile crustaceans, but becomes a rare event in very old specimens. During the process of molting, a crustacean has an opportunity to regenerate lost appendages. For example, should a crab lose a leg to a predator, a tiny new leg begins to form under the old exoskeleton. At the time of molting, this small leg reappears in a nonfunctional form. With each succeeding molt, the leg grows larger, until at last it is indistinguishable from the others.

The realm of crabs and lobsters—the sublittoral zone—is truly the edge of the sea, for it continues out into the open ocean in ever-increasing depths. The widely varied marine animals living there have no tolerance for exposure to air and hence are not found in the intertidal zone. They depend upon the complex but stable chemistry of seawater, a sufficiency of oxygen, a fairly constant temperature, and light filtering down from the surface. Bottom-dwellers require certain types of substrates upon which to attach, or to burrow in.

The sublittoral zone, with its abundance of attached and crawling life, is an attraction to fishes. Indeed, some spend much of their lives there. Where sand and sediment collect to form a flat floor between boulders, the Winter Flounder may settle, lying quietly until a crab or worm passes by. Instantly, the fish erupts from beneath the thin layer of sand that had obscured its body, snatches its victim, and settles down again, all but hidden. A Winter Flounder, like all other flatfishes, starts off life looking like any other very young fish. As it grows and matures, however, one eye migrates across the head; the fins change location somewhat, one side loses pigmentation while the other is darkly colored and, finally, the whole animal assumes a permanent horizontal orientation.

Winter Flounder
Pseudopleuronectes americanus
357

The Puffer is another inshore dweller that feeds upon worms, mollusks, sea urchins, barnacles, and mobile crustaceans that abound along a rocky shore. Normally a Puffer is quite slender, but if threatened or irritated, it inflates its body with water (or air if the fish is removed from the sea) until it becomes almost globular. An attacking fish generally either is intimidated or loses interest in this sudden change in its intended victim's appearance and leaves the scene. Soon the Puffer deflates and resumes its normal activity.

Northern Puffer
Sphoeroides maculatus
354

Several hundred meters and more out to sea, many of the shoreline creatures from the highest edge of the sublittoral zone are still present and flourishing. But other animals there are seldom if ever found near shore. Snorkeling in northern waters, although uncomfortable, offers some extraordinary sights. The world's largest jellyfish, the Lion's Mane, is common off Maine coasts. Most are about the size of dinner plates or a bit larger, but they have been measured to be almost eight feet in diameter, with tentacles trailing a hundred feet beyond their reddish, umbrella-shaped bodies.

Lion's Mane
Cyanea capillata
219

Some of the most curious jellyfish in any ocean are not free-swimming but become attached to kelp and other near-shore seaweeds. One species, the Trumpet Stalked Jellyfish, sometimes also called the Clown, is a beautiful red or orange creature that lives inverted, its bell-shaped body opening upward and fringed with knobby tentacles emerging from eight arms. When irritated, it contracts into a tight ball upon its stalk, but only after a slight delay, for its nervous system, like that of any jellyfish, is not sophisticated.

Trumpet Stalked Jellyfish
Haliclystus salpinx
247

Details of zonation upon rocky shores differ from coast to coast, continent to continent, ocean to ocean. Yet every ocean rises and falls in tides, no matter how great or small, so overall patterns are familiar everywhere. Wherever you examine a rocky coast, the same principles apply, and endless hours of fascination await you.

Cliff-dwelling Birds

Where high rock cliffs plunge hundreds of feet to the dark sea below, birds of a special nature cluster in enormous numbers on the narrow, shelflike ledges that interrupt the sheer walls. These North Atlantic seabirds are members of the auk family, and expert fishermen all. A visit to such a rookery—for this is where they lay their eggs and brood their young—is a more precarious venture for a human than for the eggs or fledglings that are balanced or cling to the shallow ledges. Such a visit is also a bewildering experience, for adult birds circle and cry overhead and in front of one's face, wheeling and swooping by the hundreds and thousands.

Each mated pair of adult birds has its own brooding spot—it can hardly be called a nest in the usual sense. Returning from the sea with their catch of fish, the birds recognize their spot without difficulty, just as they recognize their own young among the hundreds of noisy nestlings on the cliff. Birds of these regions include the Razorbill, Black Guillemot, Common Murre, Dovekie, and Atlantic Puffin. All are wonderfully adapted to their northern rocky seacoast habitat.

Razorbill
Alca torda
522

Black Guillemot
Cepphus grylle

Common Murre
Uria aalge
520

Dovekie
Alle alle
523

Atlantic Puffin
Fratercula arctica
521

The Puffin, with its brightly colored, clownlike face in breeding plumage, is known even to those who have never seen one. It swims and dives skillfully, feeding on mollusks and crustaceans, but mostly it pursues shoals of small fish near the surface. Because the edges of its bill have sharp serrations, a Puffin can hold as many as three dozen fish crosswise; it can carry them back to it's chick awaiting deep within its earthen burrow above the rocky ledge. As the chick grows, both parents remain busy at their fishing and feeding tasks for about six weeks. By then, the young bird has become overfed and overweight; it is abandoned by its parents to develop into adult form, while relying upon the food stored in its body. Only after growing its flight feathers is the young Puffin able to leave its rocky home.

The Common Murre, like other members of its family, uses its wings underwater to "fly" with grace and skill in pursuit of its marine prey. All of these birds still maneuver well in the air, but until not long ago there was another family member that had lost the power of flight. Although totally unrelated to the penguins, the Great Auk was the Northern Hemisphere's counterpart of the penguin below the equator. A large bird thirty inches long and weighing eleven pounds, it was an excellent swimmer and diver, but unable to avoid the predations of humans who sought it for food. In addition, volcanic eruptions destroyed some of the bird's breeding grounds. The Great Auk's numbers fell steadily, until in 1844 the last pair were caught and killed by humans.

Great Auk
Pinguinus impennis

Northern Gannet
Sula bassanus
517

The Northern Gannet lives on the same cliffs amidst the auks, but it is a creature of a very different sort. In the air it is a large and graceful bird, flapping and gliding until it spots a shoal of fish. A Gannet's dive is extraordinarily accurate and thrilling to watch: The bird tilts downward, with its wings still partly outstretched, then folds them tightly the instant before hitting the water. Taking into account the size of the bird, the height from which it dives, and its velocity at the moment of impact, there is remarkably little splash—just a narrow column of water that rises and falls. The force of the strike is considerable, but the bird is protected from injury by an unusual system of shock-absorbing air sacs in the breast, a strengthened skeleton, and closed nostrils. When one bird dives, other Gannets immediately follow suit; soon hundreds upon hundreds of bright white spears can be seen plummeting to penetrate the surface like aerial torpedoes, the water everywhere erupting in small geysers. After only a few seconds —during which time, on successful dives, a fish or two is swallowed—each bird bobs to the surface, buoyed by air trapped within its feathers. Then with strong wing beats, the Gannets take off and gain altitude.

A Gannet's fishing success is undoubtedly high, for a school of fish is driven into a frenzy by the sudden intrusion of the large birds. Once they lose their close-knit school structure, fish become vulnerable and easier to select.

Tide Pools

One feature of a rocky shore offers more opportunities for observing marine life than any other on any coastline—a tide pool. Tide pools are precisely what their name suggests: They are products of the tides or, in the highest pools, of waves and splash. These latter pools are of some interest to the biologist but are impoverished in their populations and not very attractive to the seashore visitor. After all, they are not flushed regularly, grow hot in the summer sun, and have little oxygen dissolved in their water; what is more, they may be very salty because of evaporation, or composed almost purely of fresh water because of rain. It is the lower pools, well within the intertidal region, that are most worthy of study.

Most rocky shores will have a variety of good tide pools, so you can select one to suit your needs and interests. A large and fairly deep pool will maintain its temperature between tidal flushings and will probably have the greatest variety of life. A smaller, shallower pool may be easier to study, however, with many creatures close to the surface and directly in front of your eyes if you lie prone and look into the clear, still water. The plants and animals attached there are permanent residents, and the snails and small crustaceans might as well be. Fishes and medium-sized crustaceans, such as Opossum Shrimps (*Mysis* spp.) are usually only temporarily trapped in the pool, and leave with the next tide. By and large the interactions within a well-populated tide pool make it a true miniature ecosystem. Close examination will reveal erect branching objects; they seem to be delicate plants but are actually animals, probably hydroids or bryozoans.

Bryozoans are filter feeders with finely ciliated tentacles; these tentacles create minute currents to draw in microscopic plankton. Hydroids superficially resemble the erect and bushy

Opossum Shrimp
Mysis spp.
173

Feathered Hydroid
Pennaria tiarella
259

**Bushy Wine-glass
Hydroid**
Obelia spp.
260

Tubularian Hydroid
Tubularia crocea
256

Frilled Anemone
Metridium senile
246

bryozoans but in effect are far more primitive, being related to jellyfish and sea anemones. Two common hydroids likely to be found in tide pools are the Feathered Hydroid and Bushy Wine-glass Hydroids. Both are exceedingly delicate in appearance, and their true nature is revealed only through magnification. Under a powerful hand lens, it may be seen that each "bud" is actually a very small polyp bearing tentacles. In the case of the Feathered Hydroid, each polyp can retreat into a transparent wine-glass-shaped cup. Both species of hydroids form true colonies in which every individual is linked to every other by slender strands of tissue that run through the "stems." If luck is with the observer, the tide pool may contain yet another hydroid, the much larger Tubularian Hydroid, sometimes called Sea Strawberries, principally because of their color rather than their shape.

The reproduction of Bushy Wine-glass Hydroids is well known to generations of biology students, but is nonetheless remarkable. The colony consists of two kinds of polyps: one for feeding and one for reproduction. The reproductive sort grow small disks internally; these, when they finally emerge through a pore, become tiny medusae. They swim off as members of the plankton and, if they survive, later reproduce sexually. The product is a microscopic ciliated creature that swims to any available surface and attaches, then grows into a new colony. This alternating of generations allows the species to grow prolifically as a colony and also to distribute itself widely in the medusa form, which furthermore injects the genetic advantages of sexual reproduction with all its evolutionary potential. On the other hand, asexual reproduction has advantages in producing large numbers of individuals in a colony in a short period of time, but each individual in effect is a clone of the others—they do not in the least vary genetically from one another. Without the exchange of genetic traits during sexual reproduction, evolutionary change would be so slow as to be almost nonexistent.

A tide pool may contain giant members of the Cnidarian phylum—the same group to which the Hydrozoans belong. These large Cnidarians are sea anemones and, as their name implies, may very well be flowerlike in superficial appearance, although certainly not in structure or behavior. A sea anemone is built rather like a huge and much more complex hydroid polyp, but is muscular, thick-walled, and behaves very differently. Many species of sea anemone populate rocky coastal waters, and a likely candidate for close examination in a tide pool is one of the largest species, the Frilled Anemone. Its thick, stalked body is often a dark reddish-brown, while the abundance of tentacles surrounding its mouth at the top of the body is much paler—yellow or flesh-colored. A sea anemone seems fixed to one place for life, yet this is not the case, for it can glide very slowly along on its disk-shaped base. If a Frilled Anemone is well covered in a tide pool, the chances are it will extend its body upward and display its many hundreds of tentacles in an attempt to capture passing plankton or larger invertebrates. A sea anemone that is partly exposed on the wall of a pool will contract into a tough, muscular sphere, protecting itself against drying and possible attack by a probing shorebird. If you find a sea anemone that is open and expanded, poke it gently with your finger (it will not hurt you) to watch it contract in defense.

Close examination of the bottom and the life present in a tide pool invariably produces surprises. An erect hydroid colony may be the temporary perch for a Linear Skeleton Shrimp. Although it is an amphipod crustacean related to those described earlier, it in no way resembles them. It is highly elongated, with grasping legs at the rear of its body and large sicklelike claws toward the front. Above its head are two pairs of long antennae; if it is a female, there may be a brood pouch filled with developing young in the middle of its body. What makes these little shrimps so appealing is their behavior, which consists of a continual waving and bowing, and feinting motions with their claws. In their own small world, of course, they are formidable predators, and their motions are simply a means of coming into contact with potential prey.

Linear Skeleton Shrimp
Caprella linearis
172

Down at the bottom of the tide pool among the algae, you may spot what appears to be a dense cluster of short seaweeds, but within moments a shape can be clearly seen to be moving along in a determined fashion. At first it is difficult to make out, then it resolves itself and becomes a remarkable mollusk —a nudibranch, the Bushy-backed Sea Slug. This elegant creature, with its spotted body and branched bushy projections along its back, feeds almost exclusively upon hydroids such as the Wine-glass Hydroids. Not only does it acquire nourishment from them, but it does something that is so extraordinary no accurate explanation exists for how it is accomplished. In eating a hydroid polyp, the nudibranch— which actually is a shell-less snail—swallows the poisonous stinging capsules of its victim intact; in other words, the capsules are not discharged, although in almost every other instance they are shot out at once in defense. These capsules then migrate through the nudibranch's body, taking up positions in the branched projections along its back, orienting themselves with "triggers" pointing outward, ready to discharge if touched. The nudibranch snail, then, steals another creature's armament for its own means of defense!

Bushy-backed Sea Slug
Dendronotus frondosus
208

Fish are occasionally trapped in tide pools. One species, the Grubby, or Little Sculpin, survives very well in its small isolated world. Its color varies with the bottom, so it is hard to make out, but once it darts through the still water to snatch an amphipod or worm, its presence is unmistakable. It is a spiny, armored-looking little fish, very much at home along rockbound coasts.

Grubby Sculpin
Myoxocephalus aeneus

No one can predict what a tide pool will contain and what activity will occur. Every pool is an isolated and complete ecosystem, dependent only upon the exchange of water as the tides rise. Not every kind of plant or animal can survive there, but those that do are admirably suited to living in the ocean's equivalent to an island—that is, a small body of water isolated and surrounded by terrestrial rocks.

ROCKY SHORES: ANIMALS

BEACHES AND DUNES

A beach is never the same from day to day. A return visit is not a predictable experience: conditions and contours may seem similar, but a closer look reveals that subtle changes are always taking place. A beach is always becoming something new—either wider or narrower, steeper or flatter, washed clean or littered with jetsam. Storms along a beach sometimes reveal unexpected items hidden for years, or even centuries, by the sand. A shipwreck or a whale skeleton may suddenly appear, or a whole forest of cedar stumps, where once there had been land. Beaches attract multitudes of visitors for a variety of reasons, not the least of which is the thought of finding something cast ashore, or looking for a change in the rhythm of the surf.

Beaches appear clean, pure and simple, yet both sand and the forces of wind and water that move it constantly about are extraordinarily complex. On a visit to the beach, we tend to hasten over the sand toward the water, where, if the surf is high, the force of crashing waves may be felt under bare feet as vibrations in the wet sand. Waves approach the shore rank upon rank, rising higher as the water becomes shallower. Finally, the circular rolling energy within causes a wave to tower high and break forward in foam and spray, water rushing up the sloping beach in white-edged sheets that ultimately halt and partly sink into the sand before slipping back to the sea. On windy days, spume and mist are whipped off the tops of breaking waves and stream landward, misting the beach and dunes behind.

If you stand in the ebb and flow of spent waves, letting the thin film of water wash over toes and heels, you will sink slowly into the loose and disturbed sand as water flows out from under your feet. This is dramatic proof of the unstable nature of the beach as a shifting marine habitat.

The place you are standing in is called the intertidal zone—regardless of the stage of the tide. Behind you, where jetsam has been deposited by an earlier high tide in the wrack zone, the backshore commences, ascending slightly upward to the first sand ridge, which is known as the barrier dune. Behind this are other dunes and sand flats, largely invisible from where you stand at the water's edge.

After repeated trips to a beach, familiarity may give rise to increased curiosity. One sees details that at first were obscure. The composition of sand is found to differ from one spot to another: the more vigorous the wave action and water movement, the greater the distance fine grains are carried, leaving heavier and larger ones exposed in wide patches. Composition of the particles determines color as well as size—thus some areas may shine with quartz and feldspar, while others are dark with magnetite; some are white, some brown, some gray or black. In Florida, beaches gleam white with fine particles derived from pulverized coral, shells, and algae.

If you stand on the barrier dune, you may notice that the waterline is scalloped in a regular fashion; the cause of this is wave attack, which is discussed fully in the Features section of this chapter. You may also notice that a piece of driftwood tossed beyond the surf moves slowly parallel to the beach, perhaps for long distances, before being caught by the waves and thrown back to land. This phenomenon, you surmise, must be due to a current of some kind—explained later as a longshore current.

Beaches attract multitudes of wildlife, for shore birds of every description arrive there to feed and to nest. At certain latitudes, seals or large sea turtles come to shore, and terrestrial animals may stray from their usual inland ranges to forage on the beach. Shallow-water fishes, crabs, and other marine creatures live just below the low-tide mark, while specialized forms of life exist in and among the moist grains of sand, or dig into wet sand to feed in the swash of waves.

The row of dunes behind a beach may reach far inland or end abruptly, depending upon certain topographical features. At times, dunes are thought of as wastelands or recreational areas for dune buggies, although in reality these fragile places are important and fascinating habitats in themselves. Their vegetation is sparse and their summer temperatures searing, yet their ever-shifting contours reveal intricacies and specialties of life found nowhere else. The fine sand of which dune habitats are composed shows the passage of every inhabitant, from the dimpled footprints of insects to the sinuous tracing of a snake. Grasses scribe circles, and marks of rolling pine cones baffle the human tracker. The eradication of a dune by the action of waves or wind can expose its structure. The interested observer can see how countless layers of sand were deposited over many decades. One storm, however, may remove millions of tons of sand from beach and dunes, as though the work of years was nothing.

Although most beachgoers think that summer is the only season, spring and autumn are often more rewarding and pleasant months for visiting. And providing one is well-protected against the wind and cold, winter walks along a beach are some of the most memorable visits of all. To see a raft of Surf Scoters tucked into the cold gray water beyond the waves, to listen to the dry rattling of dune grasses in the wind, or to inspect the wrack zone for treasures few others are likely to see—all are experiences not soon forgotten.

Surf Scoter
Melanitta perspicillata
549

Range
A large portion of the Atlantic and Gulf coasts are bordered by sandy beaches that are exposed to powerful ocean waves. The only exceptions are rocky edges on the original ancient continent that form cliffs, sheltered waters where silt and fine sediment accumulate, such as salt marshes and mangrove swamps, and coral shores. In Labrador, some beaches are composed not of sand but of rounded cobbles rising steeply from the sea.

Features
Beaches are the most restless and responsive of shorelines. Sand is constantly on the move, shifting under the influences of winds and tides, waves and currents. Beaches grow and diminish and are again replenished. Their long cycles of

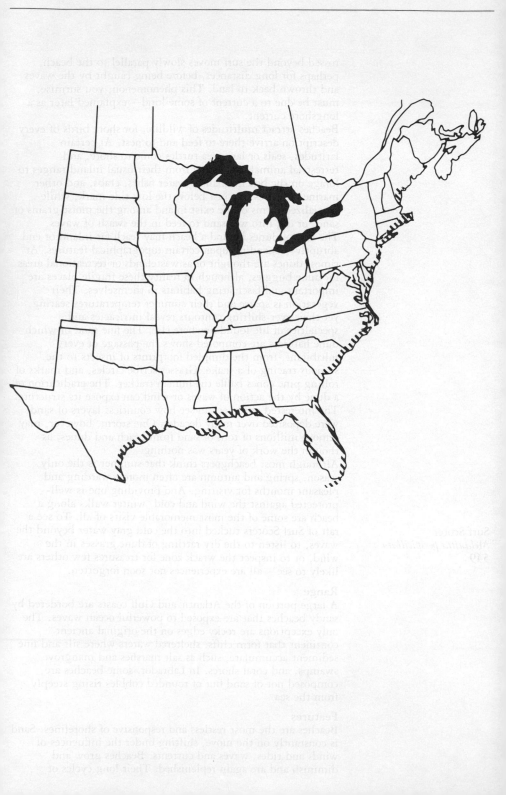

change are measured by the seasons, their short ones by storms. Their composition varies from heavy cobbles in Labrador, through the thousand miles of light-colored granitic sands of quartz and feldspar along the Atlantic Coast, to the hard, fine-grained calcite beaches of Florida.

Where does beach sand come from? Along much of the Atlantic and Gulf coasts, the particles were created long ago by great glacial rivers and carried to the sea, there to be eventually distributed in largely the same patterns we know today. In addition, some sand is eroded and pulverized along nearby coasts, some is carried shoreward from the sea floor, and a little is blown to the coast from inland where topsoil has been lost. In southern Florida, the calcite beaches are predominantly organic in origin, composed of fragments derived from the disintegration of old coral, broken shells and sea urchin spines, and deposits within coralline algae.

Sand varies greatly in its size and composition. The beaches composed of feldspar and quartz usually contain a coarse sand, light-colored but never really white. The calcareous sands of tropical Florida, however, are often blindingly white from the irregularly shaped limey fragments of which they are made. The different composition of these two kinds of beaches makes for differences in the physical nature of the shore as well as the success—or lack of it—of the organisms that live there. Calcareous sand is difficult for burrowing animals to live in because of the wide range of sizes of sharp-edged particles. On the other hand, the granitic sand found in mid-Atlantic and northern beaches is usually well sorted, and the rounded particles offer an inviting substrate for burrowers. Subtropical calcite beaches tend to be wide, but the breadth of others varies with the seasons and at certain times may be quite steep. Cobble beaches are the steepest of all, approaching a twenty-degree grade, while the steepness of shingle and gravel beaches averages about twelve degrees. The slope of granite sand beaches is often less than this, and calcareous beaches have a barely perceptible incline.

It is possible to judge the size of beach-sand particles simply by pinching the sand and rubbing it between two fingers. Comparing samples allows one to identify sand as coarse, fine, or silty; the finest sand is made up of silts and clays.

Beaches are never quiet, because of the forces working upon them; as a result, sand particles are constantly being resorted. Fine sands pack together closely, enhancing the movement of water across the surface. When you stand on wet fine sand, your feet hardly sink in; in fact, it may be possible to run vehicles close to the water along such beaches, although the practice is destructive. Coarse-sand beaches, on the other hand, pack loosely, and feet sink and disappear almost at once; water percolates quickly downward, with little flow across the crumbly surface. Because particle size affects the amount of water retained within beach sand, the coarse-grained beaches have a water table that is almost precisely that of the sea, and responds—at least for a short distance inland—to the tides. Thus the water content may be high or low, depending on the

tides. Fine-sand beaches are not as porous. Water is slow to
sink in, but is retained at a rate of about twenty percent.
Therefore, water movement beneath the surface, either
vertically or horizontally, is less pronounced.

What exactly is a beach? Some say a beach extends only as
far as the highest waves can carry sand; others—especially
summer visitors—consider a beach to include everything from
the water line to the barrier dune. The upper portion beyond
the reach of waves is called the berm, or backshore, while the
intertidal region is known as the foreshore.

The movement of the water and wave line up and down the
foreshore slope provides ample evidence that tides are at work.
In summer, when the slope of beaches is relatively flat and
wide, the movement of the water line with each rise and fall of
the tides is extensive. But in winter, after heavy storm waves
have eroded the foreshore and berm, the slope is increased and
the beach is subsequently much narrower; at this time of year,
waves crash almost against the barrier dune, which may lose
some of its face. Unusually powerful winter waves can break
through the barrier dune in a washout, flooding sand flats
behind it to a depth uncomfortable for dune inhabitants—
animal or human—as well as for vegetation.

In northern areas, narrow beaches lie in thin layers over rock
between high headlands; here, winter waves can be responsible
for temporarily obliterating them, carrying all their sand to
the sea and exposing the underlying rock and cobbles. Only
with the return of milder seasons is the sand returned and
deposited in its former location. Such a condition is
characteristic of a geologically youthful shoreline.

Seasons have other effects upon beach and sand. The small
waves of summer, adding sand to the shore, fail to maintain
underwater sandbars just offshore, using them as a major
source of sand for the beach. But in the turbulence of winter,
sandbars are built back up again.

Beaches can be very hot in the midsummer sun;·however, it is
cooler just an inch or two beneath the surface, where
temperatures fall rapidly to a point almost equal to that of the
nearby seawater. Organisms that burrow in wet or dry sand are
favored in summer with increased beach width; moreover, they
find an opportunity to select depth of sand that corresponds to
the temperature of their preference.

It has already been mentioned that the slope of a beach is
related to particle size, with the coarsest beaches being the
steepest. Particle size and incline are also related to wave
height, for the greater the waves, the more pronounced their
ability to transport heavy materials. Fine sand can be moved
by gentle waves and currents; it takes more energy to carry
coarse sand, and great power is required to shift cobbles.

Waves and Currents

Water action near the sea's edge—a never-ending source of
fascination—reveals much about the dynamics of waves,
currents, and sand movement. When a wave breaks just
offshore, sheets of water race up the sandy slope, slowing and

eventually stopping as momentum is lost. This effect is known as the swash; it is followed by the backwash, a less copious flow back to the sea. Examined closely, both swash and backwash can be seen to transport sand. The swash pushes a thin line of suspended particles ahead of its curving front. After the water begins to recede, these particles are left as a fine, ridged arc, a clear record of the extent of that particular wave. The next wave may erase it, or none may extend that far again, at least for this one tidal cycle's excursion. The backwash moves sand in a different manner—as the water tends to flow downslope in a delicate tracery of minute channels, sometimes etching a dendritic pattern reminiscent of aerial views of a great river system.

Even on hard beaches some water sinks into the sand, displacing air as it does so. The air may rise in lines of bubbles or form sand blisters; the next sheet of water flowing overhead sinks into the holes and smoothes them into tiny funnels. Visitors sometimes believe they have found the workings of subsurface creatures, but these are only the effects of water, air, and sand interacting.

The best time to examine a beach is early in the morning, when traces of the previous day's activities of humans and perhaps their machines have been erased. Part of the fascination of beach walking is that of finding a clean slate each day, at least where water and wind have done their night's work. Delicate marks and engravings are evidence of precise events. There are the swash and backwash marks, little holes, funnels, blisters, and domes. There are also ripples— parallel ridges and depressions in the sand—which are one of the most enchanting and familiar of all beach records. Ripples may be of any size, but generally they are only inches apart from one another. The exact mechanics of ripple formation are not always visible; they are related to particle size, the velocity of water passing over sand, and the amount of sand suspended within the water. As water moves over sand, small irregularities in the surface cause it to tumble in a kind of long, invisible cylindrical roller; each roller of water lifts a few of the coarser sand particles, which are then moved shoreward and deposited there. The backwash currents, being weaker, transport finer sand seaward, so a continual sorting action is carried on. Exaggerated examples of this are found in the long bands of very coarse particles distributed along the beach, quite distant in composition from the rest of the sand. But ripples, being regular and consisting mostly of grains of the same size, remain mysteries to the average beach walker. The sorting action may affect the lives of burrowing creatures, for each has its preference for the kind of sand in which to live. Waves also sort out the jetsam in the wrack zone: animal fragments, bits of flotsam from ships, timbers, shells, seaweed, bottles, and much more. Finally, ripples are not restricted to present-day beaches but are also found in the deep sea, in streambeds and riverbeds, and frozen in fossil seabeds, often with the tracks and traces of long-extinct creatures— worms, trilobites and dinosaurs—passing across them.

When water moves sand, the movement is not a simple matter of shifting particles up and down the face of the beach. Sand is also transported laterally by currents. Waves seldom approach a beach straight on, but come in at angles. There is almost always a longshore current just beyond the water's edge, sometimes carving out a long trough parallel to the beach. Any object drifting on or in the water tends to move along the beachfront just beyond the waves for long distances before being caught by the waves and thrown back to shore. Much-feared undertows are actually seldom a serious threat and can be overcome. But swimmers can be carried parallel to the beach by a longshore current and, if not careful, may be quickly thrust out to sea in a dangerous current known as a riptide. A riptide is simply the result of too great an accumulation of water traveling along a beach face, trapped there by an outlying sandbar. Sooner or later, usually at regular intervals, the excess water must escape and surge outward toward the ocean. It is almost impossible to fight against such a powerful seaward current, although keeping one's head makes it possible to return safely to a beach. A riptide is a relatively narrow current, so a swimmer has only to cease his struggles to swim back to shore, and direct himself instead at right angles to the current and swim parallel to the beach. Soon he will regain calmer water and can use the force of waves to help carry him safely to shore. From the air, riptides are seen as not only turbulent but also dark and cloudy areas with suspended sediment being carried forcibly away from the beach.

In addition to longshore currents, which are primarily the result of wave action, winds and tides may also have an effect on shorelines—especially when storms or tides come flooding into bay waters along a confining shore. They carry enough sand so that when a longshore current reaches a point where the shoreline abruptly ends and a bay begins, the sand that it carries arrives in quiet water and is deposited in a long spit. Although a spit will at first lie underwater, it accumulates over time and eventually becomes a new feature of the beach. Over a long enough period, such a spit may grow into a cape that slowly begins to curve in upon itself; the tip of Cape Cod is a huge example of this, but under the right conditions, smaller ones are found along almost all sandy shores.

Longshore currents are biologically valuable because they transport food to fixed or sessile organisms, and because they are the means by which larval forms are distributed. These and other currents close to land have certain overall effects: outside the surf zone (beyond where the waves break), the net effect is an onshore movement, whereas on the bottom within the surf zone, these currents have a net offshore direction. Shoreline animals depend upon such patterns, and often their life stages are adapted to making use of the free but often hazardous transportation that currents offer.

Oxygen is distributed only in the surface layers of a wet beach, so it is only here that most microscopic life can exist between wet sand grains. Under any beach there is a dark, stagnant layer, usually odorous, deficient in oxygen but rich in iron oxides. It may be a foot or two down in exposed and active beaches but only a few inches beneath the surface in quiet areas. It is, of course, a lifeless zone. If exposed, it is quickly altered by air and water. Bacteria adapted for life in oxygenless places are found far down; they are in part responsible for the dark subsurface layer.

One of the curious and still not thoroughly understood features of a sandy beach is the formation of the scalloped edges on the shoreline where it meets the water. These cusps, as they are called, seem to form only where waves attack the beach head-on and meet with some irregularity when they reach the shore. This irregularity deflects the impact of the wave. One eroded spot begets another, until from high above, a beach will show miles of a gently toothed margin. The spacing of cusps is related to the height of the waves, yet there is still no satisfying explanation of why, once begun, they continue to form spontaneously.

Much of the Atlantic and Gulf coasts is characterized by barrier islands. These islands get their start as large sandbars that lie offshore parallel to the coast. They reach their fullest development where the tidal rise and fall is not great, as their wide extent along the Texas coast testifies. A bar, whether it rises above the surface as a barrier island or remains beneath it, alters the shoreline environment, acting as a bulwark against waves and trapping sediment. If a barrier island rises, then the space behind becomes a quiet lagoon, a nursery for all kinds of marine life that flourishes in warm, shallow placid water. Lesser bars are temporary but for a while provide miniature counterparts of the lagoon in shallow beach tide pools, which are catchalls for small fish, crustaceans, and mollusks. If these creatures survive the rising temperature of the tide pool and excessive feeding by shorebirds, they may be lucky enough to be flushed out by the next tide and returned to sea.

Beaches, sandbars, and barrier islands are ephemeral, geologically speaking. They are the most changeable of shorelines and differ from day to day, season to season, year to year. A comparison of dated maps reveals that over a person's lifetime—and certainly over a few centuries—capes, sand islands, inlets, and beaches are dramatically altered. The forces at work include storms, seasons, tides, longshore currents, river flow, rising sea levels, and subsiding coastlines. If one could look down upon a sandy coast from a high altitude and compress hundreds of years into a few moments—as time-lapse photography is able to do—then sand formations would be seen to writhe, to extend and retract, appear and disappear, almost as wraiths of smoke or clouds in the sky. The tiny, unconsolidated particles that compose a sandy beach are at the mercy of wind and water currents and are stabilized only temporarily when conditions are relatively quiet or when held together by binding mud or the roots of plants.

Dune Formation

Where low-lying land extends back from a sandy beach,

conditions are right for the growth of coastal sand dunes. From the air, such dunes can resemble great white waves frozen in motion. Occasionally they rise to considerable heights and slowly progress inland, swallowing forests and even human settlements.

Sand dunes have specific origins, but these are difficult to identify. Often a dune begins with a small irregularity—perhaps a bit of driftwood or a cluster of beach grass—on a flat sandy area beyond the berm. Flotsam left by high storm tides or a few timbers from a ship's broken hull will suffice. Any obstruction interrupts the landward flow of winds from the sea, causing their freight of sand grains to be dropped in the lee of the object (that is, the side protected from the wind). Soon a long, elevated, pointed spit of sand streams from behind the obstruction in a wind shadow; this in turn becomes an even larger and more inviting barrier to the sand-laden sea wind. As a ridge builds at right angles to the beach, more plants begin to take hold in the protection it offers.

American Beach Grass
Ammophila breviligulata
465

American Beach Grass, which has extensive root systems, anchors the sand, and soon various little streamlined wind-shadow elevations begin to be joined laterally, until a different kind of ridge develops parallel to the beach. The second kind of ridge continues to build higher as the wind flow is affected and slowed; this is the beginning of what is known as a secondary dune.

Beach Grass, now anchored in the secondary dune, grows seaward and creates new interruptions in the wind flow over the beach. Before long, another dune rises just above the berm; this becomes the primary dune. A hollow develops between the two enlarging dunes, and it remains perhaps for many years, a sparsely vegetated sand flat, at times flooded and denuded, when storm waves break through the primary dune. Gradually, vegetation grows higher and more dense, until it becomes a thoroughly stabilized region, a hollow in which the sand darkens with collected organic material, setting the stage for still newer kinds of plants.

In extensive regions of sand dunes, primary and secondary dunes are only the first of many that extend inland. Despite colonizing vegetation, no dunes are permanent; the whole area is subject to extensive and sometimes violent change by wind and water breaking through the first protecting sand ridges. At any one time, a series of dunes is gradually subsiding inland, as the innermost ones are stabilized by vegetation. Where the depressions between dunes are lower than the water table, small temporary ponds or freshwater marshes appear. Often, these are very healthy from a biological point of view because they are new and uncontaminated. The aquatic forms of life they harbor, both plant and animal, exist in great variety, providing they have been able to reach open water by flight or by being carried by wind. The interactions in such water-filled depressions are extremely complex.

A dune system behind a beach serves a number of important functions. First, it is a barrier, although not a thoroughly impenetrable one, to high storm tides and powerful winds. O very windy days, the tops of high dunes "smoke," as long trails of sand are whipped up from their crests. Sand dunes also serve as reservoirs of sand for the rebuilding of destroyed beaches—not just by heavy machinery but also by winds that originate inland and blow to the sea, carrying sand shoreward. Beaches without a dune system behind them may erode more quickly and more completely.

The searing summer temperatures of sand dunes may create an environment hostile to life forms: Plants and animals show special adaptations to survival in such places. At the surface, temperatures can soar above 120° F, but the air just above and the subsurface sand both quickly fall to more tolerable levels. Hollows between dunes may serve as giant reflectors, creating an uncomfortable intensity of heat and light.

The slow progression of dunes inland reveals certain physical characteristics that are universal. Sea winds follow a long, fairly gentle slope up the crest of a dune. Once there, however, with air currents now confused and velocity lost, the wind drops the load of sand it has carried or pushed up-slope; the sand tumbles down the lee side to create what is known as the slipface. This steep side of a dune lies at the angle of repose (about thirty-two degrees from the vertical)—an angle beyond which all particles, regardless of their size or configuration, slip upon one another and tumble down, coming to rest at the bottom. Attempting to climb such a slipface is arduous work, for it seems that with every step one slides back half the distance. This very problem is invoked by an extraordinary inhabitant of the dunes, the larva of the Antlion, which is described in the following section.

When it rains on dunes, the sand is pitted by the force of the drops, but water immediately disappears beneath the surface, sinking down to wherever the water table lies. At some point, sand grains temporarily begin to hold water in a thin film surrounding each particle; the force that holds the water is known as capillarity. Because sand is so porous, only about twenty percent of the weight of moist sand consists of water. Plants have difficulty extending their roots down to this essential fluid, whether it is in the form of capillary moisture or the water table itself.

Dunes are seaside worlds that must be seen to be appreciated, for it is then that their wonders are revealed. Most visitors are attracted only to the beach and shore itself, yet only a short distance away are dunelands waiting to be explored, the features that make them so special ready to be understood.

Ecology

While seemingly barren, a beach is actually an enormously complex ecosystem, although all but the shorebirds and an occasional seal or sea turtle are hidden from view. Much of a beach's life is so small that it at first escapes notice. Success, for most creatures associated with a beach, is determined by how well they burrow in the shifting, unstable sand. Burrowing is essential below the tidemark, in the intertidal region, and on the berm. Because each of these regions poses special problems for organisms, they are considered distinctly different habitats, yet all are part of the beach system.

First there is the sublittoral zone, which lies beneath the water even at low tide. Just out from the low-water line may be a longshore trough, and beyond that, a sand flat or sandbar. Both are covered by seawater; they are well-aerated, and their temperatures tend to be moderated by that of the ocean beyond. While life may come and go—depending upon waves, currents, and food availability—the animals most characteristic of the sublittoral zone are bottom-dwellers, many of them burrowing beneath the substrate.

The intertidal, or littoral, zone is a dynamic region of great change, covered and uncovered by water and battered and altered by the force of waves. Its temperature varies markedly with exposure and submergence, with light and drying, and these fluctuations are dangerous to many organisms that attempt to live there.

The upper beach, or berm (also—logically—called the supralittoral zone) is never wet except by storm waves. Yet salt water is available to animals that burrow well beneath the surface, and salt spray blown in by sea winds deposits a crusty mineral coating upon the surface sand. Temperatures fluctuate wildly in the summer here, and in winter the berm may be colder than the other two zones.

With surface sand particles constantly being moved about, an animal's need to remain secure and established is answered only by burrowing to lower levels. Every sand-dweller has its own unique means of finding safety beneath the surface, but there are problems down below as well. If the animal lives in water, the supply of dissolved oxygen it needs for respiration may be severely reduced just an inch or so under the sand. This is especially true for those living in water. Animals existing in flooded burrows covered by seawater are able to feed and to ventilate their retreats effectively if they create water currents in and out of the tubes in which they live. On the other hand, an animal of the supralittoral zone may have enough oxygen in its burrow but little food, so it must emerge into a potentially dangerous world to scavenge or hunt.

Because of the danger from predators and the drying effects of the sun, most creatures of the supralittoral zone come out only at night or during twilight hours, remaining safely cool and hidden in the daytime.

Some sand-dwellers are blind; others have reduced eyes or eyes that protrude on long stalks to rise above the sand. Streamlined or thin bodies are characteristic of most burrowers, as are special digging and anchoring devices.

A great many organisms living in sand feed on organic detritus trapped between sand grains, often passing large quantities of sand through their intestinal tracts after digesting nutritious organic material. Other creatures filter particles of suspended food from water passing overhead, either trapping it with appendages extended into the moving water or drawing it into their burrows on currents of water. There is a great deal of scavenging among both the water and the land creatures, for the very nature of waves is to bring in large quantities of dead and decaying plants and animals. In the whole supralittoral zone there are but few predators, although those that are present have some remarkable adaptations for detecting and capturing their victims. Some of the smallest of beach inhabitants show the greatest specializations, although they are by and large invisible to the human eye. Tiny animals and certain microscopic motile plants live in the water between sand grains and compose a vast flora and fauna. The plantlike organisms are mostly what are known as dinoflagellates—yellowish-green photosynthetic beings that swim by means of two whiplike extensions (flagella) of their one-celled bodies. Dinoflagellates can be examined closely only with a miscroscope; nonetheless, their accumulated numbers sometimes color wet sand. The colors may abruptly fade as the creatures swim downward between the saturated sand grains when surface conditions become less favorable for them. Interstitial animals—as creatures living between sand grains are called—are without exception long and thin, allowing them easy and rapid passage through the wet sand. They include slender roundworms, or nematodes, as well as small crustaceans. The latter have long bodies and greatly reduced legs and antennae but are otherwise similar to their copepod cousins that swim freely in the sea. One-celled animals and a host of other minute creatures in wet sand make up one of the most fascinating and little understood of all coastal communities.

Above the Waves

Of all three zones, the supralittoral is the most sparsely populated. The dry sands of the upper beach shift a great deal from wind and storm waves and, unlike the dunes, are not anchored even tenuously by grasses. There are but few animals characteristic of this zone, and the species vary according to where a beach is situated—in the mid-Atlantic region, Florida, or the Gulf Coast. The most obvious animal—because of its size, the large open burrows it makes, and the radiating tracks it leaves from the previous night's forays—is the Ghost Crab. Rarely seen in the daytime, Ghost Crabs are easily spotted at dusk; they can be seen even more clearly at night in a flashlight's beam, which confuses their sense of direction enough so they won't run off.

The Ghost Crab is, at first glance, a perfectly ordinary crab in its external appearance, although as an adult it leads a terrestrial existence. (Ghost Crabs return to the sea only to release eggs, which must pass through the conventional planktonic stages common to all crabs.) When a Ghost Crab metamorphoses into its adult form, however, it emerges upon the beach, scurries to dry sand above the wrack line in the supralittoral zone, and immediately digs a little burrow. It goes through progressive molts over a period of time until it is quite large, having severed all dependency upon the ocean except the occasional need to dash down to the water to wet its reduced gills. The Ghost Crab obtains oxygen by circulating

Ghost Crab
Ocypode quadrata
44

air across the moist gill membranes, and thus is an almost completely terrestrial creature. Were it not for the need to deposit fertile eggs in the water, Ghost Crabs could move inland almost any distance. As it is, large specimens may be found several hundred yards from the high-tide mark. They move so incredibly rapidly, and their light color blends so perfectly with the background, that the name Ghost Crab is very appropriate.

A male Ghost Crab has another adaptation that is shared by a few of its marine cousins: It is capable of making recognizable sounds by rubbing a bumpy, ridged area on its claws against its body. The grating, or stridulating, sounds it makes are true examples of animal communication.

Another and much smaller crustacean, the Beach Flea, remains closer to the wrack line. There it feeds, living in sand that is dry at the surface and only slightly moist beneath. Like the Ghost Crab, beach fleas (*Talorchestia* spp.) make burrows in the lower, moister, levels where gills and body are prevented from drying out during hot daylight hours. The small creatures are highly active on the surface in twilight and evening hours, often to the annoyance of humans stretched out upon the sand, for Beach Fleas can nip the skin in an irritating fashion. On some beaches, as evening approaches, great numbers of the small crustaceans can be seen hopping about, changing their feeding places while seeking bits of decaying seaweed and other organic material.

The wrack zone itself harbors a large and unpredictable animal population, as well as remnants of all kinds of marine life. Land Hermit Crabs forage in the litter of Florida beaches, along with many other animals from the land and the air above. On mid-Atlantic beaches, Earwigs, Soft-winged Flower Beetles, and various kinds of ants can be found. Predators like the Hemispherical Savage Beetles, rove beetles, and large wolf spiders (*Geolycosa* spp.) hunt the scavenger insects. Flies and midges alight on wrack; some lay eggs in the flesh of decaying marine animals, from which consuming maggots quickly develop. Among scavenging birds, Boat-tailed Grackles and Fish Crows, Herring Gulls, Ring-billed Gulls, and Black Vultures may arrive to pick over organic remains. The Bald Eagle was once a frequent visitor to the Atlantic wrack zone. The wrack itself is a useful indicator of what lives just offshore, for remains of almost every kind of marine life can be found there. Not only are there bits of seaweed from nearby locations, but some of the rockweeds (*Fucus* spp.), which have floats in their fronds, may drift to beaches from great distances. In Florida and the Gulf, sargassum weed (*Sargassum* spp.) is often stranded upon the shore, one species of which comes from the Sargasso Sea in the mid-Atlantic and is carried by the Gulf Stream. Shells of every description are cast ashore: hard clams, soft clams, razor clams, scallops, ark shells, angel wings, conchs, mussels, periwinkles, whelks, and moon snails are just a few. Some shells are extraordinarily beautiful and, if recently dead, retain their colors; the cowries and Common Purple Sea Snails of Florida waters are often lovely.

Land Hermit Crab
Coenobita clypeatus
156

Earwig
Labidura riparia

Black-headed Soft-winged
Flower
Collops nigriceps
488

Boat-tailed Grackle
Quiscalus major
607

Fish Crow
Corvus ossifragus
608

Herring Gull
Larus argentatus
503

Ring-billed Gull
Larus delawarensis
502

Black Vulture
Coragyps atratus

Bald Eagle
Haliaeetus leucocephalus
606

Common Purple Sea Snail
Janthina janthina
69

Occasionally a shell tells a story: a cleanly drilled hole in a tellin clam (*Tellina* spp.) is proof of the work of a predatory snail; the galleries in the shell of an Eastern Oyster have been eroded by a Boring Sponge. Shells may be encrusted with dead colonies and tubes of many other creatures, such as hydroids, bryozoans, and tube worms. Bits of crab and shrimp shells provide additional information about nearby marine life, as do mermaid's purses, the dark egg cases of skates.

Wrack is an accurate indicator of life in the nearby sea, and jetsam will vary from one region to another. For example, in Maine waters—where beaches are few but rocky shores abound—the sand usually includes the broken tests (shells) of sea urchins, fragments of rock crabs, and shells of barnacles, periwinkles, and mussels. From New Jersey to Virginia, parts of swimming crabs, whelks, clams, and moon snails are common. In Florida, Purple Sea Snails and the collapsed floats of Portuguese Men-of-War can be found at certain seasons.

Between the Tides

Below the wrack line the intertidal zone begins. In this constantly changing region, sand-dwellers must have special adaptations. A highly specialized amphipod crustacean, the Sand Amphipod, leaves no trace of its presence beneath the wet sand, so it is found only after much stirring and sifting. This animal is about half an inch long and is stoutly built, with large protective plates along the sides of its body. Its feeding appendages are specialized for drawing in and filtering water from between sand grains; it keeps trapped food particles in a food basin beneath its mouth.

One of the most enchanting creatures lives a little lower down: the Atlantic Mole Crab, which is about the size and shape of the end joint of a human thumb. A beach visitor can walk for miles and see none, then suddenly come across droves of the small active creatures when they burst up into the swash of a wave from their hidden positions in the sand. They scurry to a new location in the thin sheet of water, then quickly burrow down again, back toward the sea. After the next wave floods over them and begins to slip back downslope as backwash, each Mole Crab unfurls a special pair of long, feathery antennae, which filter plankton and food particles from the rushing water. Other antennae and eyes on long stalks keep these crabs in touch with the above-sand world, so they know precisely when to extend and when to retract their feeding appendages. A Mole Crab is an extraordinarily efficient digger; its compact, oval body comes complete with sculling, excavating, and anchoring appendages at the rear. As the tidal level slowly rises or falls, favorable feeding conditions gradually change and are detected by the small animal. Triggered apparently by a signal (of which we are unaware), hordes of Mole Crabs erupt from their feeding positions and rush up or down the beach slope to locations where feeding opportunities are once again at their optimum.

A totally different creature, a mollusk known as the Coquina, lives in much the same way. It too may be locally abundant

Lug Worm
Arenicola cristata
317

Sanderling
Calidris alba
586

Least Sandpiper
Calidris minutilla
588

Semipalmated Sandpiper
Calidris pusilla

Piping Plover
Charadrius melodus
581

Semipalmated Plover
Charadrius semipalmatus
582

Black-bellied Plover
Pluvialis squatarola
584

Wilson's Plover
Charadrius wilsonia

Ruddy Turnstone
Arenaria interpres
583

Willet
Catoptrophorus semipalmatus
590

American Oystercatcher
Haematopus palliatus
576

Red Knot
Calidris canutus

Atlantic Jackknife Clam
Ensis directus
120

and absent elsewhere; sometimes Coquinas are common one year and rare the next. These pretty little clams live just beneath the wet sand surface of the intertidal zone, each extending its two siphons into the water above. As the tide begins to rise, the Coquina senses altered wave patterns through vibrations in the sand and, with an incoming wave, quickly emerges from the sand; from there, it is carried to a new location higher on the beach, leaping and flashing in the sunlight before burrowing in again. When the tide falls, the pattern is the reverse. The result is that the greatest density of their populations is always a little higher than mid-tide level on the flood (rising) tide, and a little lower than mid-tide level on the ebb tide.

Every Coquina's shell is colored differently from all others. This variability, some experts suggest, is a defense against predation by shorebirds. The idea is that because all Coquinas are different, birds cannot recognize the clams on the basis of shell color, and a moment's hesitation might well mean survival for some of the small clams.

Members of another family of clams, the tellins, live closer to the low-tide mark and feed in the same fashion as Coquinas, but do not change position readily. This is also the habitat of the large, stout Lug Worm, which builds its U-shaped burrows in gently sloping shores. Lugworms are dark red-brown, about a foot long, and about the diameter of a man's finger. Each lives its entire life (except for a planktonic larval stage) tucked away in a parchment-lined tube, drawing water in and sending it out again after food and oxygen have been removed. Such well-protected worms as these have few successful natural enemies.

Nonetheless, Coquinas, Mole Crabs, tellins, and worms living in the intertidal zone do have some enemies, almost all of them shorebirds. Depending upon the season and the type of beach, many birds find almost their entire sustenance in the sandy and muddy shorelines. Sanderlings, Least and Semipalmated sandpipers, Piping, Semipalmated, Black-bellied and Wilson's plovers, Ruddy Turnstones, Willets, American Oystercatchers, and Red Knots all feed actively near the water's edge of the Atlantic and Gulf coasts. Yet few of them compete directly with one another, for each has its own ecological niche, which includes its preferred foods, as well as the time, place, and condition of the hunting ground.

A host of marine creatures feed and reproduce just beyond the intertidal zone in sandy bottoms that extend seaward from the beach. The Atlantic Jackknife Clam comes close enough to the intertidal zone to sometimes be a part of it. This highly elongated bivalve is one of the fastest diggers in the marine world extending its long, muscular, pointed foot downward, anchoring itself, then contracting the foot's length so rapidly that the streamlined shell is pulled down through the sand, instantly disappearing from sight. It is difficult for predatory birds or other creatures to capture full-grown Atlantic Jackknife Clams, although young ones are often picked up by skates, dogfish, and other bottom-feeding fishes.

Blue Crab
Callinectes sapidus
147

Lady Crab
Ovalipes ocellatus
135

Sand Shrimp
Crangon septemspinosa
177

Long-clawed Hermit
Crab
Pagurus longicarpus
158

Eelgrass
Zostera marina
467

Common Tern
Sterna hirundo
511

Great Black-backed Gull
Larus marinus
504

Peregrine Falcon
Falco peregrinus
603

It is hard to make a distinction between the zone immediately beyond the low-tide mark and the shallow sea stretching beyond. Nonetheless, one distinguishing feature is the usually greater concentrations of certain kinds of animals in the area immediately following the low-tide mark. Organic nutrients tend to collect near shore, either driven by waves and currents or washed from land, creating opportunities for filter feeders, deposit feeders, and scavengers working their way across the bottom.

The Blue Crab and the Lady Crab consume great quantities of organic detritus drifting along the bottom. Among the rich accumulation of nutrients, smaller crustaceans—such as the Sand Shrimp and Long-clawed Hermit Crabs—forage as well. If beds of Eelgrass occur close to shore, an entire ecosystem is supported on their long blades and within their swaying growth. But Eelgrass is more characteristic of bay mouths and estuaries and is discussed in that section rather than here.

Birds of the Beach
Along northern beaches, Common Terns are among the most familiar and attractive birds, especially when they hover and dive cleanly into the water after small fish and shrimp. Should a human visitor intrude upon their dune nesting sites, the commotion is fearful, with dozens or hundreds of adult birds circling overhead, calling loudly, and diving to strike with their sharp bills at the vulnerable human head.

Herring Gulls are found on every shoreline, but the impressive Great Black-backed Gull is less common. As the largest of North American gulls, it is a fierce predator of smaller birds, waterfowl, fish, clams, and the eggs and nestlings.

Once, an even more remarkable predator frequented Atlantic beaches—the Peregrine Falcon. This beautiful and spectacular bird, capable of diving at 180 miles an hour, would snatch shorebirds on the wing or on the beach before they had a chance to take off. Although severely reduced in numbers by pesticides in contaminated food, the Peregrine is now protected, and its numbers are beginning to increase slightly. Perhaps someday this extraordinary bird will once again be frequently seen soaring over beaches in search of prey.

With the exception of the excitable gulls and terns, shorebirds are not an especially noisy lot. But one birdcall familiar along the coast is the *per-will-willet* of the Willet, one of the most vocal of all birds near beaches and marshes. The Willet may be difficult to see on the ground among dunes and grass, but as soon as it flies, its striking black-and-white wing pattern identifies it.

Feeding opportunities vary considerably along a sandy shore. Long-legged, long-billed shorebirds that probe into the wet sand along the water's edge have already been mentioned, but there are other sources of food as well. The American Oystercatcher, also an inhabitant of rocky shores, explores beaches and mud flats for mussels and other bivalves, quickly inserting its strong, bladelike bill between the mollusk's paired shells before they can snap shut. Crows may seem unlikely denizens of a beach, but the Fish Crow is a genuine shore-dweller and an omnivorous feeder. It takes its name from its preferred food of weakened and dead fish cast ashore by waves into the wrack zone. In more southerly beaches, this bird flies to nearby heron and seabird rookeries, where it feeds upon unprotected eggs and young chicks.

Black Skimmer
Rynchops niger
516

The Black Skimmer is one of the most skillful and specialized shorebirds. While it feeds throughout the day, it is in the early evening, when water just offshore may lie quietly, that the Skimmer's beautifully controlled flight and almost surgical means of feeding can be best seen and appreciated. One or two individuals fly just above the water's surface, long powerful wings beating steadily, with lower mandible of the red-and-black bill just cleaving the water in search of surface minnows, leaving V-shaped ripples widening behind the bird.

Loggerhead Turtle
Caretta caretta
434

Once, beaches at least as far north as New Jersey saw the great Loggerhead Turtles struggle ashore to excavate nests, where clutches of more than a hundred eggs were laid. With present numbers severely reduced, nesting sites are much fewer and widely separated. With continuing development of beaches, it is unlikely that these giant reptiles will ever again be so abundant.

Ecology of Sand Dunes

Although coastal sand dunes are not actually a part of the true marine environment, they are so closely associated with the seashore in a visitor's mind that their plant and animal inhabitants are objects of unusual interest. Almost all the dunes within the scope of this book are composed of quartz and feldspar sand, which originated long ago from pulverized granite in rivers far inland.

The "soil" of sand dunes is an inhospitable medium for most plants; only those that are tolerant of abrasive sand movement, extremely high temperatures, few nutrients, little water, and possible salt spray from the sea are capable of surviving. American Beach Grass, or marram grass, is a prime example of successful adaptation. It is able to tolerate shifting sands by producing both vertical and horizontal rhizomes, or rootstocks. A seedling taking root on a flat sand surface soon sends out a horizontal rhizome that, after a short distance, produces a new leafy shoot above the sand. Sand accumulating around the slight windbreak afforded by the original clump of leaves now moves on to embrace the second cluster of blades, and a small dune is on its way. Rhizomes keep extending outward as still more sand builds. If the new dune grows too high, vertical rootstocks keep close enough to the surface to allow shoots to reach the sun and air. A reciprocal condition between American Beach Grass and sand is established: sand produces the right conditions for this specialized plant, and the plant in turn attracts more sand. There are other plants, such as Beach Heather and Sea Oats, that initiate and help build primary dunes along the Atlantic and Gulf coasts, but American Beach Grass is the most common. Once Beach Grass is established, new conditions are created for other kinds of

Beach Heather
Hudsonia tomentosa
455

Sea Oats
Uniola paniculata
462

Maritime Locust
Timeropteris maritima

Eastern Sand Wasp
Bembix americana spinolae
482

Bee Fly
Anthrax analis
485

Red Velvet-ant
Dasymutilla magnifica
486

life to appear. The Maritime Locust, while resting briefly on the sand in the hot summer sun, rises high on its legs to elevate its body away from the searing heat before flying away. Dune insects and spiders share certain common adaptations to cope with their habitat. Many are extremely hirsute with dense "fur" composed of hairlike extensions of their exoskeletons. This coating traps a thin layer of air that serves as insulation. On a few insects, the coating is silvery, creating a highly reflective surface that, at certain angles, glistens in the sun. Some insects spend much of their time on dune plants above the hot sand; others burrow down to cooler levels an inch or so beneath the surface.

One small insect provides a fascinating display of behavioral adaptation to its hot, sandy world. It is the Eastern Sand Wasp, a light yellow-and-black-banded wasp with pale blue eyes and a silvery reflective forehead over its tiny brain. It descends to the sand surface—usually on the steeper side of a dune—and digs briefly like a terrier. The surface heat is too much for it, however, so it rises, hovers in the cooler air above its burrow, then returns to its digging task. This process continues until the burrow is sufficiently far beneath the surface for the wasp to remain cool. Every once in a while it can be seen backing to the entrance and thrusting out a load of sand. Its front legs, curved and equipped with stout hairs that form a comblike structure, are specially adapted to efficient digging.

Sand Wasps provision their burrows with paralyzed flies; one victim is the Bee Fly, which is common on dunes. The Sand Wasp lays a single egg upon its paralyzed victim. When the larva emerges from its egg, it is assured of a fresh food supply. The adults memorize the location of each burrow by nearby landmarks, such as stalks of American Beach Grass in particular patterns, a bit of driftwood, or other features. If the landmarks are changed, the wasp fails to find its burrow again. It is critically important for the insect to know where the burrow is, for the female plugs its entrance after laying an egg, and later must return repeatedly to bring more food to the developing larva.

The Red Velvet-ant is another unique insect found in coastal sand dunes. It is actually a wasp (the large female is wingless). Its dense velvety "hair" offers protection against the sun during brief forays across a dune at midday. The brilliant scarlet-and-black markings warn away would-be predators, for its sting is potent and painful.

Robberflies, Bee Flies, tiger beetles (*Cicindelidae* spp.), and antlion larvae are all found in coastal dune areas. Most specialized is the antlion young, quite unlike the graceful, weak-flying adult. The larva is a grotesque little creature, heavy of body, with long, sicklelike jaws. Its legs are directed backward so it can walk only to the rear . . . and then in circles! This activity allows it to excavate a conical pit, throwing sand outward from the top of its broad, flat head. The pit grows deeper and larger in diameter until finally it is a well-constructed conical trap, with the antlion larva lying hidden in the bottom, only the tips of its jaws showing slightly. The sandy sides of the pit form a slipface lying at about thirty-two degrees (the angle of repose for sand grains). Any insect unlucky enough to tumble into the pit cannot get out, for the steep walls are so unstable that every step upward results in sand slipping down, carrying the victim toward the center of the cone. The larva helps matters by flipping sand overhead so that it cascades down upon the struggling prey. Once at the bottom, the victim is pierced by the larva's long, hollow jaws; a tissue-dissolving enzyme is injected, and its struggles are over.

Beautiful Tiger Beetle
Cicindela formosa
489

Sand-dwelling tiger beetles, such as the Beautiful Tiger Beetle, are fierce enough as adults, flying or scurrying about with huge jaws poised at the ready, but their larvae reveal equally extraordinary predatory adaptations. A tiger beetle larva constructs and occupies a vertical burrow in the sand; its long body has gripping bumps on its back to provide a secure grasp within the burrow. The larva's head is flat and armored and, like the antlion's, is also equipped with sicklelike jaws. When an insect comes running along close to the burrow entrance, the larva pops out and grabs it, then retreats down into its burrow. While its body is naked, its head, like the bodies of adult dune insects, has a coating of white reflective hairs and an iridescent sheen beneath.

Dune Wolf Spider
Geolycosa pikei
492

Even Dune Wolf Spiders of dunes are densely covered with light-colored hairs, although they spend their days deep within web-lined burrows, emerging only at night to forage for prey. If a Dune Wolf Spider happens to be caught in the open in daylight, it blends with the sand in perfect mimicry; but if disturbed, it raises contrasting dark-bottomed legs in a threat posture that is often enough to discourage predators.

Woodhouse's (Fowler's)
Toad
Bufo woodhousei fowleri
437

Eastern Hognose Snake
Heterodon platyrhinos
444

Meadow Vole
Microtus pennsylvanicus

Eastern Cottontail
Sylvilagus floridanus

Common Grackle
Quiscalus quiscula

Other larger animals live in the dunes or visit them frequently. Light-colored Woodhouse's (Fowler's) Toads emerge at dusk from their retreats beneath small bushes or logs in search of insects. Eastern Fence Lizards scurry along the sand among scrub trees fringing the last dunes, and Eastern Hognose Snakes leave evidence of their nocturnal forays in the form of sinuous trails across smooth sand surfaces. The Meadow Vole constructs nests and complex runways beneath logs or timbers carried inland on high storm tides years earlier. The Eastern Cottontail deposits fecal evidence of its presence throughout the dunes, although the rabbit is generally seen only in twilight hours.

Hawks circle overhead, Common Grackles call in the swaying shrubbery, and smaller birds briefly hop across the hot sand before flying to cooler levels, leaving a maze of tracks behind. Where the dunes finally stabilize, as pines and other substantial trees take hold, the transition to a terrestrial habitat is abrupt, with common inland plants and animals finding little opportunity or tolerance for invading the sandy seaward stretches of their accustomed region. But the coastal belt of sand dunes, terrestrial though they may be, are nevertheless a product of the sea; therefore, they comprise a real maritime habitat.

BEACHES AND DUNES: ANIMALS

Ivory Barnacle 242
Keyhole Urchin 202
Keyhole Urchin Spoon
Worm 316
Lady Crab 135
Land Hermit Crab 156
Large-eyed Feather
Duster 250
Leidy's Comb Jelly 228
Lesser Sponge Crab 152
Limulus Leech 310
Lion's Mane 219
Long-clawed Hermit
Crab 158
Long-horn Skeleton
Shrimp 169
Long-spined Sea
Biscuit 206
Milky Nemertean 312
Moon Jellyfish 223
Mottled Tube Maker 176
Opossum Shrimps 173
Orange Sea Grape 234
Pink Shrimp 166
Plumed Worm 296
Portuguese Man-of-
war 218
Red Beard Sponge 275
Red-gilled
Nudibranch 209
Red-lined Cleaning
Shrimp 169
Red Opossum Shrimp 163
Sand Fiddler 142
Sargassum Crab 136
Sea Gooseberry 225
Sea Nettle 220
Sea Whip 267
Six-hole Urchin 203
Slate-pencil Urchin 194
Snail Fur 254
Sponge Crab 151
Spotted Sea Hare 207
Stinker Sponge 282
Stone Crab 134
Striped Anemone 244
Thorny Sea Star 190
Upside-down Jellyfish 221
Variegated Urchin 205
Vase Sponge 278
West Indies Spiny
Lobster 161
Wharf Crab 146
Zebra Flatworm 216

Zig-zag Wine-glass
Hydroid 261

Insects and Spiders
Bearded Robber Fly 481
Beautiful Tiger Beetle 489
Bee Fly 485
Cow Killer 486
Deer Fly 483
Dune Wolf Spider 492
Eastern Sand Wasp 482
Field Cricket 491
Seaside Grasshopper 490

Fishes
Atlantic Cod 389
Atlantic Croaker 384
Atlantic Mackerel 399
Atlantic Needlefish 412
Black Drum 380
Blacktip Shark 417
Blue Shark 415
Bluefish 401
Bonefish 404
Bull Shark 419
Clearnose Skate 426
Cobia 408
Cunner 341
Eyed Flounder 358
Florida Pompano 347
Gizzard Shad 391
Goosefish 355
Gray Snapper 374
Haddock 388
Hogchoker 359
Inland Silverside 407
Jewfish 377
Lined Seahorse 432
Lumpfish 346
Naked Sole 360
Nassau Grouper 382
Northern Puffer 354
Ocean Pout 430
Ocean Surgeon 365
Oyster Toadfish 427
Pinfish 372
Porkfish 371
Red Snapper 375
Rock Hind 383
Sand Perch 379
Sand Tiger 421
Sandbar Shark 418
Sargassumfish 351
Scrawled Filefish 348

Sea Lamprey 411
Smalltooth Sawfish 422
Southern Stingray 425
Spiny Dogfish 414
Spotted Eagle Ray 424
Spotted Moray 431
Striped Anchovy 403
Striped Bass 373
Striped Blenny 428
Striped Burrfish 352
Striped Mullet 405
Tarpon 402
Tautog 338
White Flounder 357
White Shark 420
Windowpane 356

Birds
American
Oystercatcher 576
Arctic Tern 513
Black-bellied Plover 584
Black Scoter 550
Black Skimmer 516
Boat-tailed Grackle 607
Bonaparte's Gull 506
Common Tern 511
Double-crested
Cormorant 575
Dunlin 585
Fish Crow 608
Forster's Tern 512
Great Black-backed
Gull 504
Herring Gull 503
Horned Lark 612
Laughing Gull 505
Least Tern 514
Northern Gannet 517
Oldsquaw 552
Osprey 605
Peregrine Falcon 603
Piping Plover 581
Purple Sandpiper 587
Ring-billed Gull 502
Royal Tern 510
Sanderling 586
Sandwich Tern 508
Semipalmated Plover 582
Sooty Tern 515
Surf Scoter 549
Whimbrel 592
White Winged Scoter 551
Willet 590

ESTUARIES AND BAYS

Throughout geological time, the contours of a shoreline constantly change. The sea level rises and falls as polar ice caps melt—returning more water to the sea—or grow, locking up more water in their icy mass. Furthermore, continents are elevated or depressed by geological forces. Over thousands of years, then, the precise coastline fluctuates, migrating seaward or landward in response to these forces. Today the Atlantic Coast is about midway between its highest possible level and its lowest. Along much of its length there are old river valleys, now flooded or "drowned" by the sea. To the north, many such valleys are rockbound and deep. But south of Cape Cod, these river valleys become enlarged shallow basins, often very wide at the mouth, narrowing upstream into estuaries and inland rivers. The wide bays and their estuarine rivers are mixing places for fresh water from the land and salt water from the sea.

Throughout the history of the earth, estuaries, or tidal rivers, have been comparatively rare, existing only when sea level conditions are about as they are at present. The age in which we live favors the development and proliferation of estuarine creatures; for this reason, estuaries are not only extremely interesting places to study but also enormously important from the biological point of view.

During the evolutionary process, estuaries have been routes of invasion and migration by organisms, particularly those changing from marine forms to inland freshwater forms of life. For example, modern bony fishes evolved in fresh water after distant ancestors of a more primitive nature had entered continental waters at a much earlier time. Today's freshwater fishes are descended from species that simply remained there, evolving further; other fishes returned to the sea, becoming the bony fishes that populate the oceans from shoreline to deep sea. (This history does not apply to sharks; they are not bony fishes, but possess cartilaginous skeletons and, with very few exceptions, they have never left the ocean.)

A bay is a protected portion of the coastal sea. In a bay, tides rise and fall as they do outside on the open coast, but bays do not feel the full effect of the enormous swells and monstrous storm waves that are generated far out to sea. Storms do, however, have serious effects upon bays and their life, for in shallow water sizable choppy waves are quickly created by powerful winds. Shorelines become inundated and eroded, and bay water soon grows turbid with muds and sediments that are washed in. Most of the time, though, a bay is a quiet place for a marine organism to live.

Currents within a bay consist basically of three kinds: tidal, river flow, and those created by the rotation of the earth. The mouth and mid-portions of a bay tend to be nurseries for a great many marine animals, from fishes to planktonic invertebrates. In fact, some oceanic fishes are incapable of maintaining their kind without bays, where their young find both food and shelter. Walking the shore of a bay near its mouth reveals ample evidence of a multitude of marine organisms. Where rocks are present, they support almost the same populations as do rocky shores facing the sea; beaches toward the mouth of a bay contain the same communities of life found on an ocean beach. It is only when one goes farther up a bay and into the river estuary that significant differences become evident.

People visit and use bays heavily for sport, pleasure, commerce, and industry. Some bays support large commercial fisheries as well as sport fishing activities, although in too many instances our Atlantic and Gulf bays are polluted by industry, shipping, and the outpouring of garbage from nearby cities. Bays provide excellent boating in their protected waters, and their beaches—if clean—are safe and attractive swimming spots. A bay also offers immediate access to ocean shipping routes from protected waters. So bays attract many interests, not all of them compatible with one another.

Where a bay narrows and meets the mouth of a river estuary, its nature changes, for here it feels the effects of fresh water flowing from distant inland sources. While this change is gradual (and is described more fully later), without question the scene alters from the visitor's point of view. The tang of salt air diminishes, as does evidence of marine life. Sea stars might have been present at the bay mouth, but not here. Farther up the river, surprising mixtures of marine and freshwater life are found: There may be some barnacles and crabs, but on the surface there could also be a few aquatic insects. The shorelines are often muddy and fringed with marsh, which, in the lower reaches, is true salt marsh but is more likely to be a cattail or reedgrass marsh upriver.

Your first attraction to a bay may be the opportunity for bird-watching, since a great many shorebirds, and especially waterfowl, find a sheltered bay an attractive place for nesting, feeding, and resting during migration. In fact, for many northern birds, an Atlantic coastal bay is the final winter destination, a moderate place indeed compared with their Arctic summer grounds. It may be thought that our own visits to seashores and bays should be only summertime events, but a wealth of opportunities are missed if that is the only time chosen. In fall and spring, and even on the darkest, coldest days of winter, a bay is an excellent spot for birding. Take, for example, the waterfowl that might be seen during seasons

Brant
Branta bernicla
555

other than summer. The Brant is a small, dark goose, not much larger than the bigger ducks. It breeds high in the Arctic and goes south to winter along the Atlantic Coast in protected waters. Rafts of a few dozen or more Brant tucked low in the water are a common sight in bays in late fall and throughout the winter.

White-winged Scoter
Melanitta fusca
551

Another dark bird that summers and breeds in the far North, the White-winged Scoter, is identified as it flies in long lines low over the water, its white wing patches conspicuously flashing with every beat. Winter on the bay does not call for much flying, however, so many birds are spotted on the

Greater Scaup
Aythya marila
543

surface. The Greater Scaup, a black, brown, and gray bird, drifts together in huge rafts numbering many hundreds. Keen eyes and binoculars scanning the dark water may pick out

Bufflehead
Bucephala albeola
542

Canvasback
Aythya valisineria
530

Oldsquaw
Clangula hyemalis
552

Snow Goose
Chen caerulescens
553, 556

Tundra Swan
Cygnus columbianus
557

Canada Goose
Branta canadensis
554

little Buffleheads, the males unmistakable with their broad white patches across the sides and rear of their heads. The larger Canvasbacks also congregate in large winter flocks, their white bodies and reddish heads distinguishing them from others on the water. Oldsquaws, like the others, are birds from the North that winter in protected bays, the cold-weather plumage of males mostly white, with long, dark tail feathers. Oldsquaws dive to depths of one hundred feet or more, using their wings to power their descent, something very few other waterfowl are capable of.

The thrill of discovering birds on winter bays comes when brilliant flocks of Snow Geese are found riding on the gray water, their high-pitched yelps coming clearly across to where you stand. But even these lovely birds fade when the great, magnificent Tundra Swans sweep overhead with haunting fluting calls, descending with enormous wings held bowed and still, until their outstretched feet furrow the water. Once these birds are on the surface, with wings folded and heads held high, their size dwarfs everything else. They settle into bays before the winter evening commences, having fed inland in corn fields, and they remain on the water until the sun is well up the following day. Hundreds group together, each individual keeping its distance from its neighbors, quieting down while nearby Canada Geese talk much of the night. In the morning the swans begin to look restless as, calling actively, small groups of one or two dozen at a time begin taking off; they are followed shortly by others, until the sky is etched with their lines and Vs. A winter day spent watching such birds on the bay will not soon be forgotten.

A good way of approaching a study or developing an appreciation of a bay and estuarine complex is to map out a shoreline route beginning at the bay's mouth, where the marine influence is at its maximum; visit selected spots at intervals of several miles along the bay shore, progressing up into the estuary until, in every respect, it is a typical river. With this itinerary, you should be able to find much of what will be described in this chapter under Features and Ecology. In learning about a bay and its one or several estuarine tributaries, you may develop the almost passionate attraction so many people feel for these remarkable bodies of water, each unique and not duplicated anywhere else. All one need do is listen to advocates of the virtues of the Bay of Fundy, Narragansett Bay, Delaware Bay, the Chesapeake Bay, Pamlico Sound, Florida Bay, Tampa Bay, Mobile Bay, and Atchafalaya Bay—to name just a few. And one should not overlook the proponents of river life, for many rivers empty into the ocean with little or no widening that can be called a bay. A river is a grand and majestic highway to the sea and has figured in all of human history, as well as in evolution, since time began.

Range
The entire Atlantic and Gulf coasts are watersheds of extensive proportions, punctuated every few miles by rivers flowing

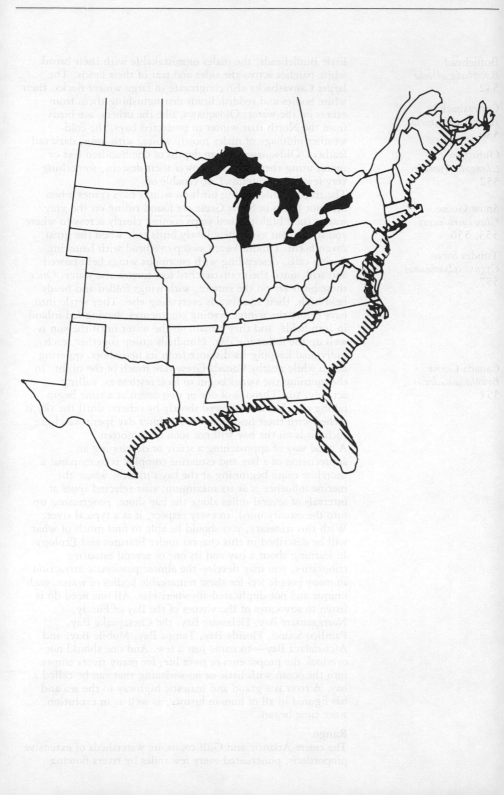

toward the sea. Some are great rivers, carrying an enormous volume of water and suspended sediments down their courses, while others are modest by comparison yet no less complex in their gradation of life. From Labrador to Mexico estuaries abound, and bays, large or small, indent the shoreline. Those farther north tend to be deep, cold, often narrow, with rockbound walls for a shoreline. In the Middle Atlantic States, the wide, shallow rivers empty into huge bays. In North Carolina and parts of Florida, Alabama, and Texas, rivers open into lagoonlike bays behind barrier islands. Because the geology, hydrology, and biology of each are unlike any other, no further geographic subdivisions should be made.

Features
Along the Atlantic Coast, tides flood and ebb in bays on a regular twelve-hour basis. At a bay's mouth, the rise and fall is the same as it is outside on the open shoreline. But farther up a bay, and particularly within the confines of a river estuary, incoming tides become delayed and compressed, and the rise in water level may be considerably greater than at the mouth. All this time, of course, the river's flow continues, but it is impeded when the tide enters and accelerated when the tide recedes. The net movement of water is always downstream toward the ocean, but it progresses in a halting, somewhat interrupted fashion over a daily cycle.

Currents on the surface of an ocean obey certain forces generated by the rotation of the planet. Because seawater that enters a bay is deflected to the right (clockwise), one side of a bay remains saltier than the other, at least along the bottom. This condition is augmented by fresh river water flowing into the bay from the opposite direction; this water is also deflected to the right, and thus ends up concentrating on the opposite side of a bay. This means, then, that a line drawn straight across an Atlantic Coast bay will find greater salinities and, therefore, a bit more true marine life, on one side than on the other. Remember that the concentrations, no matter what they are or where they are within a bay, are constantly being pushed in and pulled out by the tides.

There is a further complication: Fresh water is lighter in weight, or less dense, than salt water. River water coming down an estuary and entering a bay tends to float over the heavier salt water, with little mixing for perhaps many miles. It is possible, therefore, for organisms with a marine origin to penetrate a bay and estuary farther along the bottom than at the surface. It also means, of course, that certain freshwater animals that swim in or float near the surface of a river may be found farther downstream than might be expected.

It is apparent that an estuarine system is a remarkably complex environment for any form of life, and it is not surprising to find a number of organisms that are so suited, or highly adapted—structurally, physiologically, and behaviorally—to estuarine life that they are found nowhere else. The question arises, therefore, what precisely is an estuary? Part of the sea? Or part of the system of inland waters? The answer is that it is both, yet a distinct entity and habitat in itself. It is the recognition of this fact that makes an estuary both challenging and fascinating to learn about.

Estuaries along the Atlantic and Gulf coasts are of two basic kinds: those that are dominated by the ocean because the contribution of rivers is relatively small, and those with river inflow so large that its influence is felt far out to sea—as is the case with the Mississippi. Major examples of the first kind are found in the Delaware and Chesapeake bays, but there are many others along the Atlantic Coast.

Because bays and estuaries are sheltered waters, their regions of high and medium salinity create exactly the right conditions for the development of salt marshes (the subject of another chapter in this book). All that need be said now is that salt marshes are some of the most important wetlands in the world in terms of their biology and the production of organic materials that nourish the coastal oceans far beyond a bay or estuarine system.

It would be good if all we needed to know about estuaries and bays were natural geological, hydrological, and biological phenomena. Unfortunately, there is no such thing, anywhere in the world, as a completely unpolluted river. The rivers that come within the scope of this book are all, to one degree or another, affected by human presence and development along their shores and in their waters. To study the ecology of any of our rivers and bays, we must be aware of how they have been altered and how the life they contain has been touched by the presence of factors that never before existed in these marine ecosystems. Major pollution is obvious to all, but it is the small, insidious, almost undetectable events that baffle us and mysteriously affect estuarine and bay life. Just a degree or two of temperature rise—the result of BTUs given off by a cooling facility—may profoundly affect the ability of certain larval forms to develop or even survive. Even in great dilution, chemicals that never before existed in marine waters may affect normal development or put an end to it altogether. Those bays that are still comparatively healthy are natural treasures and must be recognized and protected before being altered further by our thoughtlessness or ignorance.

Ecology

Bays and estuaries are extremely complex; they have many features, and conditions change almost minute to minute. For these reasons, ecologists have been obliged to construct arbitrary zones based upon varying degrees of salinity. The Venice System (so called because of a symposium held in that city many years ago) divides an estuarine system into a large number of regions based upon ranges of salinity. All we need do here, however, is term the river portion of the estuary "brackish," and the region where the estuary widens into a bay "brackish-marine." The major portion of the bay, if there is one, is simply referred to as being "marine." It must be remembered that within each of these large areas there are many factors affecting the makeup of the water: a horizontal gradation of salinity at any given moment; probably a vertical stratification of salinity, with fresher water overlying saltier water; and river flow, with a countering tidal ebb and flow. If all these factors can be kept in mind, then the stage is set for looking at an estuary and a bay with appreciation.

When estuarine flora and fauna are compared with communities either in fresh water or in the ocean, it is generally true that there are fewer species present. But in all likelihood, those creatures that are present may be there in enormous populations. A small crustacean, the estuarine copepod (*Acartia* spp.), is rare both in the upper estuary and the ocean, but in a bay and lower estuary, it may be so abundant as to clog plankton nets. Apparently it is admirably suited to life in the changing world of the estuary, and nowhere else.

Those marine animals that live in estuaries often reveal a form of dwarfism that is the result of lowered salinity in the upper bay and estuary. The Clam Worm inhabits many Atlantic Coast bays but reaches adulthood in a significantly smaller form than its ocean-shore cousins. When marine creatures live well up into an estuary, they may lose the ability to reproduce successfully, so their populations are replaced by larvae from more fertile populations farther downstream.

All estuarine organisms have means of tolerating the great changes that occur with every tidal cycle and every season. The two problems they must solve are how to maintain their position in what may be powerful tidal and river currents, and how to adjust to the changes in salinity. When the tide floods, the salt "front" advances up into the bay and estuary, but when it ebbs, the flow of fresh water from the river causes the front to recede. Conditions vary with the season—in spring, the runoff of fresh water is heavy from snows melting far inland, but in late summer and fall, river flow is lessened, allowing salt water to penetrate farther in its daily tidal cycles. How does an animal contend with such events?

If it is a bivalve mollusk, such as the Blue Mussel, it simply closes up when conditions are unfavorable. If it is a burrowing worm or an amphipod crustacean, it digs deeper and waits it out, since salts remain in the substrate for long periods of time, even when fresh water flows overhead. If the animal can swim well, it follows the concentration of salts of its preference; if it is planktonic and swims only feebly, like the estuarine copepod, it must depend upon staying in a mass of water that suits its needs as the tides oscillate. Finally, and most remarkably of all, an animal may adapt in a physiological sense, changing its body chemistry to meet varying conditions. The Blue Crab, one of the best known of all estuarine species, is found from the salt water of the open sea all the way up into water with only the slightest tinge of salt. It possesses an extraordinary degree of physiological adaptation. Of course, the Blue Crab does not breed far up into the estuary but does best in the mid- and lower regions. When an organism must adjust to the salt content of the surrounding water, it has three different basic means for doing

Clam Worm
Nereis virens
305

Blue Mussel
Mytilus edulis
117

Blue Crab
Callinectes sapidus
147

so: It can excrete the salt as fast as it comes in (and a great many estuarine organisms employ this method); it can increase its internal pressure to equal that outside, chiefly by constricting its body, or contracting (a common means among certain worms); or it must possess an impermeable surface covering—but only insects, reptiles, birds, and mammals have such a provision. (A clam or mussel with its shell closed is only temporarily watertight.) Animals lacking these abilities are absent from estuaries.

No two estuaries are identical. For example, those in widely separated latitudes have different capacities for allowing invasion by animals. An estuary in a warm climate is more readily entered, because the warmer water makes it easier to adjust to lessened salinities. But estuaries in colder latitudes allow fewer cold-adapted species to invade the region. Where an estuary has a small tidal range (i.e. extent of tidal flow) and a relatively stable gradient from fresh to salt water, there is a greater penetration of the region both by freshwater animals and by those from the sea. A great tidal range and rapidly changing salt content present severe difficulties to organisms. And in any estuary, in the zone of transition where brackish water is about half fresh and half salt, the total number of species and their populations are decreased from the greater numbers upriver or down in the saltwater bay.

A true estuarine species, therefore, is one that can become established within a fluctuating environment according to its limits for tolerating such changes. That, of course, is the case under all normal conditions, but when storms occur inland, with heavy rainfall, the flooding fresh water floating down over the heavier salt water in the lower estuary and bay wreaks havoc with most animals and plants living there. Oyster mortality, for example, may be severe. In a bay, the lethal effects of fresh water on saltwater organisms can result in wholesale killing as far down the bay as the flood of fresh water reaches and to the depth of the freshwater level.

Oftentimes, closely related animals live in different regions of an estuary but do not overlap in their home ranges. A small crustacean, the Locust Amphipod, lives from the bay's mouth to the upper bay, while a very similar form, the Flea Amphipod, thrives at the head of the estuary. In similar fashion, the Virgin Nerite, a dramatically marked snail, is found near the mouth of southern bays, while the Olive Nerite prefers the middle reaches and the heads of the same bays. Such ranges and limitations have wide-reaching effects upon the ecology of a bay and an estuary. The most famous of all estuarine creatures, the Eastern Oyster, an animal very tolerant of wide fluctuations of salinity, reaps benefits from the manner in which its predators react to a decreased salt content within a bay. It has two major predators that can seriously decimate oyster populations in some regions: Forbes' Common Sea Star and the Atlantic Oyster Drill. Oysters at the bay's mouth have a very difficult time of it; there, both predators busily attack beds of the bivalves. But Sea Stars cannot tolerate much dilution of seawater, so they disappear shortly inside the bay's

Locust Amphipod
Gammarus locusta

Flea Amphipod
Gammarus pulex

Virgin Nerite
Neritina virginea
67

Olive Nerite
Neritina reclivata

Eastern Oyster
Crassostrea virginica
111

Forbes' Common Sea Star
Asterias forbesi
189

Atlantic Oyster Drill
Urosalpinx cinerea
41

mouth, leaving only the Oyster Drill as a major threat. This snail can survive diluted seawater up to a point, yet where the mix is about one-third salt water and two-thirds fresh, it too disappears. The oyster survives in even lesser dilutions, but it never reaches its full size or productivity. Nevertheless, it can live free of predators, although admittedly not under very favorable conditions.

Underwater in a bay, visibility is restricted by the enormous quantities of sediment carried down by the river, making the upper bay turbid and the bay's mouth at least rather cloudy. A bay bottom is never regular, but includes sandbars, oyster beds, and the rubble of old oyster communities. Often, vast expanses of bay bottom are covered a foot or more in depth with old shells, not just of oysters but of jackknife clams, razor clams, other bivalves and various snails, the latter usually occupied by small hermit crabs. It is here that the slow, spindly-legged Common Spider Crab carefully picks over the debris, scavenging for organic material. These crabs are dull-colored and somewhat camouflaged by the growth of algal filaments and silt upon their backs. Several species of smaller crabs, such as the Flat Mud Crabs, live and feed in the same locality; their stout and powerful claws are capable of crushing the shells of young clams and other bivalves.

A shell-strewn bottom is a perfect habitat for the Flat-clawed Hermit Crab—not a true crab at all but a highly specialized crustacean adapted to living in old snail shells—which scavenges busily among the debris. Usually it is not the sole occupant of its borrowed shell, for inside the cavity may be the Zebra Flatworm and the Fifteen-scaled Worm. Both these commensals not only find security within but also take advantage of the current of water created by the Hermit Crab's own efforts to secure oxygen. They also find nourishment in scraps and finer organic matter derived from the Hermit Crab's rather messy eating habits.

If you could look across the rubble-covered bottom, large rock-sized mounds might be seen rising above the mass of old shells. At first they could be taken for clumps of coral, although the animals extending outward from the surface are very different. These creatures have tentacles that are complex affairs, feathered and ciliated to create feeding and respiratory currents; furthermore, the tentacles may be reddish or orange, bluish and purple, mottled black, or light yellow and white. These are segmented worms, Atlantic Tube Worms; they excrete a limey compound, from which the tubes are made, and they live in a colony of calcareous tubes they have gradually extended upward and outward. Originally, one or more of the worm larvae settled upon a hard surface, grew, and established the beginnings of the colony. Once it is well developed, the colony becomes a haven for a host of other creatures, including the Polydora Mud Worm, which finds sediment collected between the limey tubes to its liking. Empty worm tubes may be occupied by tube-dwelling amphipods, which face toward the opening with outstretched antennae to sample what passes by. The surface of the mass of

Common Spider Crab
Libinia emarginata
138

Flat Mud Crab
Eurypanopeus depressus
133

Flat-clawed Hermit Crab
Pagurus pollicaris
155

Zebra Flatworm
Stylochus zebra
216

Fifteen-scaled Worm
Harmothoe imbricata

Atlantic Tube Worm
Hydroides uncinata

Polydora Mud Worm
Polydora ligni
307

Plumed Worm
Diopatra cuprea
296

Ice Cream Cone Worm
Pectinaria gouldii
301

**Soft-shell Clam or
Steamer Clam**
Mya arenaria
99

Common White Synapta
Leptosynapta inhaerens
315

Hairy Sea Cucumber
Sclerodactyla briareus
298

**Atlantic Purple Sea
Urchin**
Arbacia punctulata
196

Common Mantis Shrimp
Squilla empusa
167

worm tubes is often covered by the miniature cobblestonelike effect created by the various bryozoan colonies. Not all worms construct tubes of this kind. The Plumed Worm constructs a long, parchmentlike tube that extends far beneath the bottom sediments, but its upper end projects four or five inches into the water above. This portion of the tube is strengthened and camouflaged by a large collection of adhering shell fragments, bits of algae, and other debris cemented to the membranous shelter by the worm. The worm, when feeding, extends the anterior (front) portion of its body out from the tube's mouth, sweeping around in circular fashion, its bright-red, hemoglobin-filled gills and iridescent body gleaming in the pale light.

One of the most unusual tube builders in the estuarine world is the Ice Cream Cone Worm. It lives head downward in the sand and mud bottom amidst the rubble, the open tip to its long conical tube projecting just above the floor of the bay. Two things make this worm remarkable: First, it has two sets of comblike golden bristles that glisten exactly like pure metal, even though they are composed of a protein substance; these bristles are used for digging in the bottom. The other characteristic is the construction of the tube, which is made of carefully selected sand grains all of the same size, arranged so that their flat surfaces face both the interior of the cone and the exterior. So precisely is the cone constructed that it appears to have been manufactured—as of course it was, but by a worm!

The bay bottom harbors creatures other than worms. The most familiar is the popular Soft-shell Clam, also known as the Steamer Clam. Clams of this kind are deep burrowers, able to retract their elongated siphons at once but never getting them completely within the shell, which is too small to enclose the entire body of the clam. Two other burrowers are both sea cucumbers, but of very different kinds. The smaller of the two is the delicate-looking Common White Synapta, which is colorless, transparent, and so fragile it breaks almost at once when handled (if not too severely injured it can later regenerate lost portions). Since it seldom comes out in the open to crawl about, it is well protected most of the time. The other is the Hairy Sea Cucumber, which also stays mostly buried, its body almost entirely covered by tube feet, with only its bushy tentacles extended into the water.

The Atlantic Purple Sea Urchin is common on the rock and shell bottom, where it feeds primarily upon algal coatings that line the hard surfaces. In contrast with the reddish spines and body are the bright-yellow suction cups at the end of its long tube feet; these wave about, seeking new places of attachment, while the animal makes its slow way across the floor of the bay. It is relatively immune from predation, even from the Common Mantis Shrimp, whose diet does not include sea urchins. The Mantis Shrimp is one of the fiercest predators in the entire bay-estuary region; this powerfully built shrimplike animal has large, folding, knifelike claws, each equipped with a half-dozen extremely sharp spines. The body is also spiny, and its muscular abdomen makes this animal particularly difficult to hold. It lies buried just beneath the bottom, with only its elongated eyes, shaped somewhat like rounded croquet mallets, projecting above the surface. The jackknife claws are held at the ready, and when any creature passes by, the claws slash out and snare the victim. It is a powerful swimmer and often changes its location, but it is a solitary creature that defends its territory against intrusion by others of its kind. There is no such thing as two Mantis Shrimps lying side by side: Placed together, there will soon be but one.

The Oyster Community

Where the main current from the river flows, a deeper channel develops, but elsewhere a bay may be shallow enough for sufficient diffused light to penetrate and permit the growth of algae on the bottom. It is in the wider, shallower areas of a bay that oysters flourish best, and the community of life that they support is one of enormous complexity.

Although bays and estuaries are the favored habitats of the Eastern Oyster, life there is still not easy for this specialized bivalve mollusk. Any bottom—whether firm mud or rock and shell rubble—capable of supporting massive and heavy clusters of oysters is suitable for the establishment and growth of an oyster bed. Soft bottoms, into which oysters sink and suffocate, are devoid of oyster communities. In a river-fed estuary and its wide bay, there clearly are regions where oysters cannot be found; at the same time, there are other areas in which their populations become enormous and attractive to commensals, parasites, predators, and commercial fishermen. One of the factors favoring oysters is a vigorous water exchange, which delivers oxygen and nutrients and flushes away wastes and suffocating sediment. Although oysters can tolerate somewhat reduced salinity, if bay water grows too fresh, they grow inactive, sicken, and die. Sudden floods of the kind mentioned above can destroy whole oyster banks in shallow water. Temperature is also a factor in their survival, and high temperatures especially are unwelcome and dangerous. Finally, there must be sufficient food suspended in the water to nourish these filter feeders, food that consists primarily of microscopic planktonic algae.

If an oyster community is to continue for generation after generation, currents must play a favorable role in the distribution of their tiny planktonic larvae and allow them to arrive—after circulating about for a while—in the most hospitable regions for settlement. The most favorable areas are old established oyster beds that have existed for centuries. When small young oysters (called spat) attempt to make a new settlement, it is often a hazardous affair, with many failing to attach properly or to escape a multitude of hungry predators. In the lower estuary and throughout the bay, one of the chief dangers to an oyster community is sediment carried down by the river, which, as it loses velocity in the widened areas, deposits silt and sand in thick, suffocating blankets upon the bottom. Geological deposits deep under a bay's bottom often consist of remnants of ancient fossil oyster beds, some of them so old that the shape and species of oyster are different from ours today.

Numerous estuarine animals, not all of them large or formidable in appearance, create difficulties for oysters. One such creature, the Polydora Mud Worm, collects mud to build its tube, but its populations are so great and its tube-building activities so strenuous that large quantities of sediment are soon trapped on top of the oyster shells where the worms prefer to live. At times, entire oyster populations have been killed by the activity of vast numbers of this one species of worm alone.

Protozoan and fungal diseases affect oysters, sometimes wiping them out almost completely from an entire large bay. This has happened in the Chesapeake Bay, but it is an affliction that has its peak years and declines again later. Some diseases affect the oyster's shell, others the internal organs. There are also parasites, such as roundworms and copepod crustaceans, although the latter are rare among Atlantic Coast oysters.

Boring Sponge
Cliona celata
292

Boring Sponges erode shells, even to the point of penetrating straight through and allowing other organisms to enter and destroy the oyster. Shells attacked by the Boring Sponge may be easily broken in two with your hands; their normally heavy shell structure can then be seen to resemble a labyrinth of interconnected chambers.

Planktonic larvae of commensal crabs enter the mantle cavities of oysters, and once inside they mature and develop into adults. Ostensibly, the crab is a harmless commensal, simply living within the oyster's mantle cavity; actually, it may have a damaging effect upon the mollusk's gills, perhaps impairing their functioning. Both algae and a wide variety of small animals attach permanently to the outside of oyster shells, although perhaps not remaining long enough to cause

Ghost Anemone
Diadumene leucolena
245

problems. At times, groups of the lovely Ghost Anemone stretch up from the back of an oyster, tentacles swaying gracefully in the tidal bay currents.

Common Sea Grape
Molgula manhattensis

The muddy-looking Common Sea Grape has a tunic, or body covering, layered with sediment and debris, making this sea squirt difficult to see. But beneath the covering is a delicate and wonderfully constructed filter-feeding apparatus that strains quantities of plankton from the bay water. Clusters of

Common Atlantic Slipper Shell
Crepidula fornicata
82

the Atlantic Slipper Shell, a curious kind of gregarious snail, cause no difficulty for American oysters as they grow, but the snail has been inadvertently transported abroad. There it attaches in similar fashion to foreign species of oysters and prevents their larvae from settling, causing whole communities to diminish and even disappear.

Thick-lipped Drill
Eupleura caudata
40

Two major predators of oysters in bays and estuaries have already been mentioned, and there are many more. Aside from the Atlantic Oyster Drill, other kinds of predatory snails include the Thick-lipped Drill, which is less abundant but still a menace to oysters. The Florida Rock Shell, which

Florida Rock Shell
Thais haemastoma floridana
42

extends from North Carolina around Florida and along the

Knobbed Whelk
Busycon carica
33

Channeled Whelk
Busycon canaliculatum
34

Atlantic Rock Crab
Cancer irroratus
140

Gulf Coast, feeds more extensively upon oysters than upon other mollusks. Very large whelks, the Knobbed Whelk and the Channeled Whelk, are also powerful predators. Among other large predators, there are sea stars, especially Forbes' Common Sea Star, which feed upon oysters. Blue Crabs—the greatest threat to bivalves among crustaceans—and the Atlantic Rock Crab devour young oysters, often in large quantities.

Creatures that feed upon oysters may not always do so when the bivalves are attached, growing, or mature. When oyster larvae are swarming in the bay, carried along as plankton on their way to favorable grounds for settling as spat, they are vulnerable to a host of swimming plankton feeders. One that seems unlikely to be a major threat because of its delicate, transparent body is Leidy's Comb Jelly, but its appearance belies its effect upon oyster larvae. When the latter are produced in enormous quantities, these comb jellies swarm in unbelievable numbers, each individual sweeping up hundreds and thousands of larvae. The result is a very significant predation that may threaten successful settlement. A comb jelly is not a true jellyfish, or medusa, but is included in a group by itself. Comb jellies are propelled not by rhythmic contractions (as in true jellyfish) but by the steady bearing of eight rows of ciliary plates, known as comb plates because each looks like the teeth of a comb. These rows of cilia beat in waves, so if the animal is looked at in surface waters with sunlight filtering down upon it, lovely flashes of colored light produced by prismatic refraction ripple along the transparent body. These animals are also visible at night; the beating of their bioluminescent comb plates is signaled by cool bluish flashes in the dark nighttime waters of the bay.

Leidy's Comb Jelly
Mnemiopsis leidyi
228

Black Drum
Pogonias cromis
380

Not all of an oyster's predators are invertebrates, for at least one fish, the Black Drum, crushes even full-grown oysters between bony, toothed plates in its pharynx. Of course, the oyster's greatest predator today is man, who harvests the animals in increasing numbers to satisfy an enormous demand. But it is apparent that we are not the only creatures who seek oysters for nourishment, and who is to say whether or not the animals mentioned above may not relish oysters too?

Singing Fish and Forests of Grass

It used to be said that the ocean is a silent world. We know today that this is nonsense: There are as many sounds in the ocean as there are on land. In fact, there may be more, for water is a better conductor of sound than air. A bay—a small part of the sea—has its own songsters and noisemakers. It is not unusual for a fisherman, sitting quietly in his small boat in mid-bay, to start in alarm at a growing wave of sound coming from beneath him, one that develops into a submarine roaring sound, slowly passing unseen in the water and fading away. A swimmer, submerged beneath the gentle waves near shore, may hear croaks, rasps, booms, grunts, and little chirping noises. In each instance, a human has entered the noisy world of marine sounds created by various inhabitants of a bay, mostly fishes. Some crabs stridulate, rasping a claw against a roughened body file; but the truly wonderful variety of songs and calls come from the jaws, throats, muscles, and air bladders of fishes. Underwater microphones have recorded these sounds, which are as characteristic of the animals making them as are the songs of birds.

The fisherman in his boat probably was interrupted by a large school of croakers passing underneath. An Atlantic Croaker emits its loud vocalization by means of a pair of sound-producing muscles and a resonating air bladder. This croak is loud enough to be heard over a considerable distance, and an entire school of hundreds of croakers passing by is almost deafening.

Atlantic Croaker
Micropogonias undulatus
384

The Oyster Toadfish not only looks a little like a toad—broad and squat with bulging eyes—but even sounds like one. Its call is a croaking grunt, uttered singly at intervals from where the lumpy fish rests on the bottom. Although it is not an active animal, it is a successful predator, consuming passing crabs and shrimps caught in its wide-toothed mouth. The Oyster Toadfish is not averse to eating decaying material and even garbage thrown from a boat. It is not a fish to be handled, for its spines and powerful jaws lined with sharp teeth make the Toadfish a formidable antagonist capable of inflicting a painful wound.

Oyster Toadfish
Opsanus tau
427

While Northern Searobins don't warble like their avian namesakes, they chirp and sing their own sprightly song. When Searobins are seen underwater, their behavior seems to reflect the sounds they make, for they perch high on well-developed pectoral and pelvic fins, and even walk along the bottom on them. The lower three rays of each pectoral fin are modified into long "feelers" that constantly probe the bottom. The entire head is well armored with bony plates, decorated and protected by sharp spines along the sides. Like the Toadfish, a Searobin is a bottom-dweller, but it swims more readily and moves across the substrate easily in search of food. The largest and individually the loudest of all bay fishes is the Black Drum, a heavily built animal that may reach more than four feet in length and weigh as much as 150 pounds. A bay is a favored feeding ground for this great creature, with a multitude of smaller fishes, crabs, and oyster grounds readily available as prey. Once the Black Drum has a victim in its mouth, no shell is too hard to crack. At the back of the mouth lies a thick, triangular, bony plate, studded with large, blunt teeth. It is with this apparatus that the huge fish crushes its prey—a process that is far from silent.

Northern Searobin
Prionotus carolinus
378

Bays harbor remarkable forms of life. In the plant world, one assumes marine and brackish-water plants must be algae, either seaweeds or simpler kinds. But a few seed plants of terrestrial origin took to the sea—or at least to shallow marine waters—long ago and successfully live there. Turtle Grass, of southern waters, Widgeon Grass, and Eelgrass are examples found along the Atlantic Coast. The story of Eelgrass communities is one of unusual complexity, for a whole miniature world, or ecosystem, is associated with this

Turtle Grass
Thalassia testudinum
468

Widgeon Grass
Ruppia maritima

Eelgrass
Zostera marina
467

ribbonlike plant. Where it grows on the bottom, shelter is afforded for many fishes, crustaceans, and other invertebrates, but the most fascinating details of the community are found on the blades of the grass.

Eelgrass is not actually a grass but a member of the pondweed family, so undoubtedly it descended from fresh water through estuaries into bays, where it evolved a tolerance for salt water. It grows in dense stands in shallow, protected water, excluding all other plants—normally, in the bay-estuarine world, algae of various kinds. The roots of Eelgrass, arising from a creeping rhizome, are more for anchorage than for absorption, since the entire plant is immersed in water that bathes it in nutrients.

Eelgrass is a true flowering plant, although the flowers are hardly recognizable as such, for they grow in sheaths along the blade, hidden from view. After flowering, however, the ovoid seeds develop within a cup and are easily visible before they drop off and are carried away by the current. Tidal currents are the life means for Eelgrass, and the long streaming single blades wave like banners in the flow, or if the current is strong in one direction, they whip out almost at right angles.

Close examination of a mature stand of Eelgrass reveals that each blade is zoned along its length according to both the age of that portion of the leaf and the life that grows upon it. Down near the rhizome from which it arises, the blade is light green and clean; out at the tip, half a yard away, the leaf is frayed from constant whipping in the current and may be blackened where cells have died. The real zonation, though, comes from the multitude of attaching life, both plant and animal. Organisms that attach to underwater surfaces of other organisms are known as fouling organisms (a nautical term, from the fouling of a ship's bottom); if they are plants, they are called epiphytes, while such animals are known as epizoa. It stands to reason that the oldest part of an Eelgrass blade has been exposed the longest, and therefore should have the most epibiota (life growing on it). Actually, the tip of a blade is so battered and worn that populations diminish there, but a little farther back, the zonation displays a sequence: pioneers, which attach first, succeeded by other species, until a climax population of plants and animals is established.

If a blade is divided into four quarters, the lowest and first is one upon which pioneers become established and is the route for migrants from the bay bottom as they ascend the leaf. The second quarter supports a greatly increased population, and the third becomes the richest and most varied. The fourth quarter may have enormous populations of certain organisms but usually displays less variety.

Among the first, and always the most abundant, organisms on an Eelgrass blade are the diatoms, tiny silica-shelled plants consisting of only one cell each. They may grow in clusters, chains, and other assortments. Accompanying them are small copepod crustaceans that vary precisely in accordance with the diatom population, for that is their primary food. Larger epiphytes in the form of green and red algae grow from the blade in the second and later quarters. Several species of amphipod shrimp comb these epiphytes for detritus and diatoms that have been trapped or that grow there. Some of these same amphipods use the detritus to build tubes along the blade into which they can retreat, protected from currents and predators. The amphipods show strictly defined modes of life: Some species are found only in certain temperatures or current velocities, while some are more prevalent higher on the blade than others. They tend to have staggered breeding cycles that do not interfere with one another.

Small snails browse over the diatoms and other algae; most of them are shelled, but a few are devoid of shells—nudibranchs. The larger epiphytes not only provide food for some of the grazers but also offer refuge and protection to nearly all the organisms present. Worms and crustaceans hide beneath the tiny plants, while almost all organisms present benefit from the shelter Eelgrass provides against strong current.

Careful studies of the Eelgrass community have shown even more complexities, some of which the visitor to a bay could see if a few blades of Eelgrass are collected and immediately placed in a shallow basin. The wealth of life supported by even a single blade is beyond imagination: hydroids, bryozoans, sea squirts, round worms, segmented worms, and much more.

On the bottom, beneath the swaying Eelgrass forest, other larger creatures feed or make their homes. A sudden spurt of muddy sand rising into the water may signal the abrupt departure of an Atlantic Bay Scallop, one of the most remarkable mollusks in the world. Unlike most bivalves that are restricted to life on the bottom, the Bay Scallop uses jet propulsion to blast itself off the bottom, often escaping predators, shooting away with considerable velocity and very little accuracy: It doesn't really matter where the scallop goes, as long as it is a safe distance away. The jet is created when the animal claps the two ribbed shells together very rapidly; it is this clapping muscle that we eat, not the entire animal, as we do with clams and oysters. Even more remarkable are the scallop's brilliant blue eyes—about forty of them arranged in two rows along the two edges of the shell-secreting mantle. Each eye is fixed in focus with a bright-blue iris, but the lens and the retina behind (in basic structure much like our own eyes) reflect light with starry brilliance.

Atlantic Bay Scallop
Argopecten irradians
85

The Living Past

Were you down amid the Eelgrass watching the scene, you might see a creature lumbering along out of the murk, thrusting aside the waving blades, like something out of the ancient past—which is exactly what it is. It is fitting to leave the subject of bays and estuaries with an animal that sums up the wonder and mystery of estuarine systems, a creature like no other in the world today, related to nothing else alive.

The Horseshoe Crab is no crab at all. If one looks for any kind of relationship, then spiders would have to be chosen, yet this ancient creature is not poisonous and shares relatively few characteristics with spiders. Its outer carapace is a smooth,

Horseshoe Crab
Limulus polyphemus
160

pleasing, rounded shape, almost perfectly streamlined in the face of the rushing currents or waves that it must pass through to spawn upon bay beaches. The long, pointed tail, which frightens some visitors, is harmless and serves as an engineering wonder: If the animal is turned upside down, the tail bends sharply at right angles to the body, tipping it up into an unstable position, and the whole creature then gently rolls over along the front margin of its rounded body until it is rightside up again! Toward the front of the massive body are a widely separated pair of compound eyes and a pair of tiny simple eyes on either side of a small spine in the front center. Except for some attached fouling organisms, such as colonial bryozoans or clusters of Common Slipper Shells, the outside of the animal is smooth and featureless.

Underneath the carapace, its anatomy is revealed. The huge helmet-shaped outer body, composed of tough and flexible material, is mostly a kind of thick shield, its inner spaces filled with digestive glands. There are five pairs of heavily built legs: The first pair, in the male, ends in claspers that hold the female while mating; the next three pairs have weak pincers that cannot hurt a person but are able to pick food off the bottom; the final pair of legs terminates in folding, flattened spines that serve as pushers to move the animal along the bottom. Five pairs of gills follow the legs, and in motion they fan slowly back and forth, often revealing between their leaves, as between pages in a book, small commensal flatworms known as the Limulus Leech. The worm is not a parasite but is restricted to life only on a Horseshoe Crab's gills, and nowhere else: It feeds upon organic matter that drifts by as the larger animal eats. If a Horsehoe Crab must swim, it can do so slowly but with surprising grace, using the fanning motion of its gills. This mode of locomotion is especially important when it is young and small.

Limulus Leech
Bdelloura candida
310

The Horseshoe Crab preys upon bottom-dwelling invertebrates such as worms and clams, which it extracts from the muddy sand with its pincered legs. It grinds the food between spiny pads on its "shoulders," which are located near its mouth. Except when it is young, the creature itself is not preyed upon by others, for it is well protected, and not much of it is edible anyway.

A visitor to a mid-Atlantic bay, such as Delaware Bay, has an opportunity to witness an archaic scene out of the very distant past, a time before the land was properly invaded and creatures were not only restricted to water but largely to the sea. It occurs only a few days each spring, at the time of the highest spring tides (not neap tides), and is best seen at night with the aid of flashlights.

The gentle waves of a bay shore seem to generate hordes of these massive creatures, two by two, the male riding upon the back of the female, securely clasped to the rear of her body. With each wave, they are pushed farther up the sand, and at the peak of the highest spring tide, they are at least where they need to be. After scooping out a depression in the sand, the female begins producing masses of eggs, which are fertilized by the male. Covered by sand, and with each succeeding tide—now past the peak height—a little lower than the last, the eggs are protected and undergo development. That is, they should be protected, but this is a time for multitudes of shorebirds to descend on the beaches and gorge themselves upon the eggs not far beneath the surface. But there are enough eggs for many to go through their complete development until the time the next high spring tide arrives, about two weeks later. By then, the small light-green eggs have shed their tough outer skin and have become transparent inflated spheres, each containing a tiny active animal that slowly rotates within its delicate membrane. The name by which these larvae are known says something about the ancient nature of the Horseshoe Crab and its relationship to a huge and varied group of animals now vanished from the earth: The little animals are called trilobite larvae. This is an apt description, for they look much like those ancient animals. With a curved carapace, segmented body, but lacking a spiny tail, they are almost perfect replicas. When the tide finally reaches them and washes them out of their nests, abrasion with sand particles ruptures the thin transparent membrane, and the larvae are set free and carried out in the waves. At this time, however, the shorebirds are joined by great numbers of bay fishes, whose biological clocks are timed to coincide with the emergence of the larval Horseshoe Crabs. Hundreds of thousands, even millions, of the larvae are eaten at once, but enough survive, as they have through the ages, to disappear into the protection of the bay bottom and grow to adulthood.

Are the adults entirely safe? From natural predators, generally yes, although when they emerge to spawn, some of the larger gulls are capable of flipping them over and devouring their lightly protected bodies. There is one being, however, that in a short period has accounted for the destruction of vast numbers of these extraordinary animals that have survived so long—man. During the past century and the early part of this one, the crabs were harvested as fast as they came ashore in the spring, cast up into great enclosures to die, and converted into fertilizer. They obtained a reprieve several decades ago as technology achieved better results through chemical manufacturing plants, but today there are signs the animals may once again be taken in even larger numbers for other purposes, such as being converted into animal feed. No major attempts are yet under way, but the threat exists.

Of all creatures considered in this book, the uniqueness of the Manatee notwithstanding, there is nothing so remarkable in the coastal seas as Limulus, the Horseshoe Crab. It conveys to us the sense of wonder; it must be appreciated, not converted to fertilizer or poultry food. Limulus has been a survivor for more than 300 million years, and seeing it come up by the thousands upon bay beaches early on a mist-shrouded morning takes us back, as no time machine ever could, to days before our kind or anything remotely resembling us walked the land.

ESTUARIES AND BAYS: ANIMALS

Seashells
Alternate Bittium 59
Apple Murex 37
Atlantic Ribbed
Mussel 115
Atlantic Oyster Drill 41
Carolina Marsh Clam 102
Channeled Whelk 34
Common Atlantic
Bubble 78
Costate Horn Shell 61
Eastern Mud Whelk 56
Eastern Oyster 111
False Angel Wing 95
File Yoldia 97
Florida Crown Conch 36,
124
Florida Lace Murex 38,
123
Great Piddock 98
Green Jackknife Clam 119
Northern Quahog 101
Thick-lipped Drill 40
True Tulip 44
Virgin Nerite 67

Seashore Creatures
Atlantic Long-fin
Squid 181
Atlantic Purple Sea
Urchin 196
Atlantic Rock Crab 140
Baltic Isopod 178
Banded Feather
Duster 253
Bay Barnacle 239
Big-eyed Beach Flea 179
Blue Crab 147
Boring Sponge 292
Brackish-water
Fiddler 143
Chevron Amphiporus 309
Clam Worm 305
Common Atlantic
Octopus 183
Common Mantis
Shrimp 167
Common Red
Bryozoan 286
Common Spider Crab 138
Common White
Synapta 315
Finger Sponge 270
Flat-browed Crab 148

Flat-browed Mud
Shrimp 175
Flat-clawed Hermit
Crab 155
Flat Mud Crab 133
Forbes' Common Sea
Star 189
Garland Hydroid 263
Ghost Crab 144
Golden Star Tunicate 290
Green Crab 145
Green Paddle Worm 306
Hairy Bryozoan 287
Hairy Sea Cucumber 298
Horseshoe Crab 160
Ice Cream Cone
Worm 301
Ivory Barnacle 242
Lady Crab 135
Large-eyed Feather
Duster 250
Leafy Paddle Worm 304
Leidy's Comb Jelly 228
Limulus Leech 310
Lion's Mane 219
Long-clawed Hermit
Crab 158
Long-horn Skeleton
Shrimp 171
Lug Worm 317
Milky Nemertean 312
Moon Jellyfish 223
Northern Lobster 162
Northern Rock
Barnacle 240
Opossum Shrimps 173
Orange Sea Grape 234
Ornate Worm 293
Plumed Worm 296
Red Beard Sponge 275
Red-eyed Amphipod 168
Red-gilled
Nudibranch 209
Red-lined Cleaning
Shrimp 169
Red Opossum Shrimp 163
Rubbery Bryozoan 276
Sand Fiddler 142
Sandy Shrimp 177
Sea Gooseberry 225
Sea Nettle 220
Single-horn Bryozoan 291
Six-hole Urchin 203
Snail Fur 254
Spiral-tufted Bryozoan 242

SALT MARSHES

Of the three chief kinds of shoreline—rocky coasts, sandy beaches, and salt marshes—only salt marshes are mistakenly deemed unworthy of a visit. They are avoided because of the mosquitoes they harbor and the rich organic odors that arise from their thick muds. The mud itself makes traversing the marshes extremely difficult, if not impossible. Salt-marsh topography is flat and seemingly monotonous, without features to attract or excite the casual visitor. Worse than merely being avoided, salt marshes are drained, sprayed, filled, and otherwise obliterated to make way for resorts, homesteads, and commercial development. What is wrong with this? It is largely unknown that salt marshes are among the most important, and certainly the most naturally productive, lands on earth. Except for cultivated sugar cane, there is no crop in the world that exceeds their production of organic nutrients—and salt marshes do this without any attention from us. What is the significance? Salt marshes nourish bays and coastal seas in a way that is absolutely essential to the continuation of large numbers of marine plants, shellfish, and other invertebrates, as well as fishes. The links in these chains may be complex and obscure to the nonscientist, but they are nonetheless real.

Salt marshes are delicate ecosystems that cannot exist just anywhere along a shoreline. It is impossible for them to develop along exposed seashores, for even moderate waves would destroy their fragile structure. Nor can they grow far up in rivers, since the plants that are the basis for their biological economy require a salinity nearly equal to that of the ocean. Where, then, do they occur? Only along the shores of bays or in lagoons behind barrier islands, and only on terrain that is flat enough to allow their development. If a slope rises steeply from the bay shore, it is no place for a salt marsh.

Salt marshes build in shallow, quiet water, where sediment is permitted to drop out of suspension in the water and carpet the bottom. As the substrate rises to the level of the water's surface, special grasses that are tolerant of salt water take hold and trap even more suspended particles, which become compacted as mud. Salt marshes are absolutely the products of tides, which flood their wide expanse twice a day, keeping them flat and level and drawing off the organic detritus that results from plant decay. Out in the bay and beyond, bacteria already at work in the marsh mud continue their breakdown of minute plant fragments. They free chemical compounds needed by marine plants, especially members of the plankton that float as a rich blanket across the inshore waters.

It is important for visitors to coastal regions to look at salt marshes with understanding and appreciation. To be sure, one does not have to enter them to learn. Almost any salt marsh may be examined from roadsides or nearby rises, preferably with binoculars to bring details in close. Marshes near national seashores and wildlife refuges often may be inspected from observation towers built for the purpose. Their supposedly featureless terrain begins to take on meaning: zones of plants are seen, and tidal flooding and drainage patterns become

Clapper Rail
Rallus longirostris
598

Purple Marsh Crab
Sesarma reticulatum

obvious. The dynamics of a marsh start to become apparent. It is then that the animal life is first noticed. Much of it is hidden for a while after you arrive, but soon birds, crabs, muskrats, turtles, and fishes begin to appear, until it is clear that this is indeed a heavily populated habitat.

For more adventuresome souls, a trip by canoe or small boat along the tidal creeks winding through a salt marsh can be rewarding. The quieter your passage, the more you will see, including one of the most secretive birds in North America, the almost invisible Clapper Rail. Fiddler crabs (*Uca* spp.) and Purple Marsh Crabs tend not to become alarmed by a boat as quickly as they are by an upright figure. Even if a salt marsh covers relatively little area, the meandering channels of its tidal-drainage creeks make an exploratory trip seem long, with unexpected rewards around every bend.

Only the hardiest should attempt to walk into salt marshes, for the sticky mud tires one quickly, and falls are common on the slippery surface. It is impossible to be quiet about your progress—especially in heavy rubber boots—so expect to see little in the way of animal life except for snails and the hordes of mosquitoes and flies that follow you closely. It is, however, the only way to inspect the plants that make up the marsh and see the smaller forms of life in the mud and on the plants.

For those who live near salt marshes and those who visit them frequently, these tidal wetlands take on an attractiveness that is difficult to convey to others. The heavy organic odors are welcome, not repulsive; the vast sweep of green in summer and sere brown in winter are scenes of beauty. The salt-marsh watcher sees nuances of change that others miss completely. If nothing else, this chapter should induce you to visit a salt marsh at least once to test your powers of observation, with the hope that, upon departure, you may appreciate these diminishing lands. If somehow you can help reduce the rate at which salt marshes are disappearing, you will have become an important link in preserving the vital chain of events that maintains the productivity of our coastal seas.

Range

Salt marshes are rare north of Cape Cod, although a few can be found wherever conditions are right. However, geology and topography do not favor salt-marsh formation in northern latitudes along the Atlantic Coast. Heavy glacial erosion sculptured deep river valleys, unlike the rivers of the South that never knew glacial action, and it is almost impossible for river-carried sediment to fill their fjordlike mouths. Furthermore, the hard rocks of northern coasts do not erode easily or grind down into fine sediments that settle as mud. Moving down to the south shore of the Cape and along the Rhode Island and Connecticut coasts, salt marshes begin to appear with increasing frequency. It is from the New Jersey coast south to northern Florida that salt marshes form an almost unbroken band in protected waters behind barrier islands and in bays and estuaries. These regions receive enormous quantities of sediment from large rivers. Some rivers

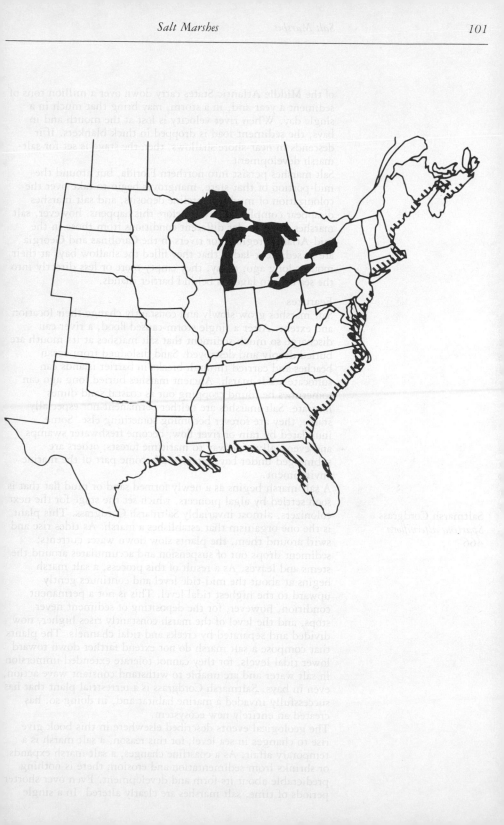

of the Middle Atlantic States carry down over a million tons of
sediment a year and, in a storm, may bring that much in a
single day. When river velocity is lost at the mouth and in
bays, the sediment load is dropped in thick blankets. If it
descends in near-shore shallows, then the stage is set for salt-
marsh development.

Salt marshes persist into northern Florida, but around the
mid-portion of that state, mangroves begin to take over the
colonization of muddy shoreline deposits, and salt marshes
disappear completely. Even before this happens, however, salt
marshes occur under different conditions from those in the
mid-Atlantic region, for rivers in the Carolinas and Georgia
are so sediment-laden that they filled the shallow bays at their
mouths long ago; today, they empty more or less directly into
the sea or into lagoons behind barrier islands.

Features

Salt marshes grow slowly and constantly change their location
and extent. After a single storm-caused flood, a river can
discharge so much sediment that salt marshes at its mouth are
buried deeply and destroyed. Sand dislodged from ocean
beaches and carried through breaks in barrier islands can
suffocate a salt marsh. Ancient marshes buried long ago can
sometimes be found cropping out as coastal sand dunes
migrate. Salt marshes are neither permanent nor especially
stable; they are forever becoming something else. Some,
inundated by rain or river flow, become freshwater swamps
and eventually give way to maritime forests; others are
submerged under bay waters and become part of the marine
environment.

Saltmarsh Cordgrass
Spartina alterniflora
466

A salt marsh begins as a newly formed sand or mud flat that is
soon settled by algal pioneers, which set the stage for the next
colonizers, almost invariably Saltmarsh Cordgrass. This plant
is the one organism that establishes a marsh: As tides rise and
swirl around them, the plants slow down water currents;
sediment drops out of suspension and accumulates around the
stems and leaves. As a result of this process, a salt marsh
begins at about the mid-tide level and continues gently
upward to the highest tidal level. This is not a permanent
condition, however, for the depositing of sediment never
stops, and the level of the marsh constantly rises higher, now
divided and separated by creeks and tidal channels. The plants
that compose a salt marsh do not extend farther down toward
lower tidal levels, for they cannot tolerate extended immersion
in salt water and are unable to withstand constant wave action,
even in bays. Saltmarsh Cordgrass is a terrestrial plant that has
successfully invaded a marine habitat and, in doing so, has
created an entirely new ecosystem.

The geological events described elsewhere in this book give
rise to changes in sea level; for this reason, a salt marsh is a
temporary affair. As a coastline changes, a salt marsh expands
or shrinks from sedimentation and erosion; there is nothing
predictable about its form and development. Even over shorter
periods of time, salt marshes are clearly altered. In a single

lifetime, coastal residents may see open water become an extensive marsh, or marshland become part of a bay. It does not take many years to notice changes that occur in the patterns of tidal creeks and channels; they twist and turn, some of them forming meanders so tightly curved that they rejoin themselves, cutting off a portion in what is called an oxbow. This now-stagnant body of water supports very different forms of life from those found in the creeks in which tidal currents surge back and forth. The creeks tend to build levees along the banks; these elevated stream banks encourage plant and animal life that is recognizably different from that of the flat marsh extending far beyond. These creeks are vitally important to maintaining a functioning salt marsh, for they allow seawater to enter and flood the inner reaches of a marsh and serve as drainage channels back to the bay.

If you are able to look over a salt marsh from a higher vantage point, you will see distinct round or oval patches of vegetation interrupting the monotony of cordgrass. These are salt pans; they are formed by slight irregularities of the surface mud, usually depressions in which salt water is retained as the tide falls. Salt pans are tide pools, but the substrate is not impervious, and the lack of shade allows the sun to beat upon them directly. Water therefore sinks down into the mud and drains away, and at the same time evaporation is enhanced. As the water leaves, salts are left behind in high concentrations. Crystalline salt may be apparent, and in addition, these pans are distinguished by the kinds of plants that can survive there, which are different from those in the rest of the marsh. Looking down on a salt pan reveals concentric rings of vegetation, with perhaps a shallow pool of very saline water remaining in the center.

Your survey of a salt marsh from a sideline elevation will take in the entire sweep of zones, from open water below the midtide level, the channels, and the vast expanse of marsh itself, to the bands of differing vegetation that grow as the slope inland begins to rise a little, allowing less and less inundation by the tides. Finally, there is the land itself, unaffected by seawater except during great ocean storms.

A salt marsh, then, is created through the interaction of living organisms and tidal forces, becoming a habitat unlike any other on earth. It is inevitable that highly specialized forms of life exist and interact there in complex fashion. It is a pity that so few of us know anything at all about these extraordinary places.

Ecology

Salt marshes do not yield their secrets easily. At first glance they seem to be uncomplicated, with only a few kinds of plants and not many visible animals. A few superficial glances during a brief stop along the margin of a marsh will not alter this opinion. But spend time inspecting one—even without entering the marsh proper—and the intricate ecosystem of a salt marsh begins to unfold.

Because salt marshes are literally the products of plant

colonization and growth, plants are not only the most apparent life forms but also the ones we need to understand first. Almost without exception, every animal found in a salt marsh is dependent, either directly or indirectly, upon the plants growing there.

Although many plant species can be found in a salt marsh, it is necessary for a newcomer to know only a few—the ones that establish the basic habitat. Each has its own zone, determined by its tolerance for existing conditions, mostly having to do with salinity and the degree of immersion in water.

The plant closest to water in the channels is Saltmarsh Cordgrass, a seven-foot-tall plant with stiff, narrow, pointed leaves. It lines the banks of tidal creeks, clearly distinguishing them from the grassland that stretches beyond. When the channels fill as the tide rises, the lower portions of Saltmarsh Cordgrass may be completely submerged, and at times of high spring tides, the entire plant may be underwater. Just behind the creekside growth of this tall, intensely green plant, another shorter variety of the same species occurs in a narrow parallel band. The growth of this second variety is probably the result of fewer available nitrogen compounds in the mud. Certainly there is very little oxygen in the wet soil, so the plants must adjust their respiration accordingly.

Saltmeadow Cordgrass
Spartina patens
464

The major part of the salt marsh, a vast expanse of grass, is occupied by Saltmeadow Cordgrass, which is also known as salt hay, for earlier in history it was harvested extensively. It also is covered by high tides and forms such a dense growth of stiff leaves that few other plants are able to establish themselves. Among the ones that can occasionally be found are brown seaweeds, which on rocky shores are known as rockweeds; here they find a firm enough substrate on the mud to attach to securely. Throughout the marsh, both *Spartina* species tend to grow more vigorously in lower regions closer to their sources of salt water. It is here that tidal flushing brings nutrients to the plants from the bay and washes away the accumulated organic detritus resulting from their decay.

Spike Grass
Distichlis spicata
461

Toward the back of the salt marsh, as the terrain begins to rise slightly, other plants make their appearance. Spike Grass, a plant that looks very much like Saltmeadow Cordgrass, grows under much the same conditions. Then, almost invariably, there is a conspicuous band of Blackgrass (*Juncus* spp.); two closely related species are common on Atlantic shores, one in northern marshes and the other in southern. Blackgrass is seldom covered by average high tides and is actually a very dark green. Beyond the Blackgrass belt, other grasses that tolerate salt in the soil form tussocks, after which vegetation typical of a higher terrain commences.

Sea Lavender
Limonium carolinianum
451

Glasswort
Salicornia virginica
470

Close examination reveals an unexpectedly large variety of highly specialized salt-marsh plants that are able to withstand saline conditions. Some are found along the margins, some are associated with salt pans, and a few are found in with the Saltmeadow Grass and Cordgrass. Sea Lavender, a plant that manages to squeeze among the Cordgrass, produces lovely delicate flowers. Glasswort catches the eye with its stubby,

Saltmarsh Bulrush
Scirpus robustus
460

fleshy, translucent stems, which, if tasted, prove to be extremely salty. In the fall, this plant turns an intensely brilliant red, providing bright spots of color through a marsh that is beginning to show shades of yellow and brown. The Saltmarsh Bulrush, a grass that grows almost six feet high in some places, provides seeds for birds, while its roots are eaten by muskrats and larger waterfowl.

Plant life in a salt marsh must contend with conditions never faced by terrestrial plants. The latter take in water by osmosis through tiny hairs covering the tips of their roots—a process that is possible because the concentration of water molecules is greater in soil-water than in the cells of the land plants themselves. For plants living in a salt marsh, the concentration of water molecules in seawater almost equals that of the plants' bodies, so there is no flow from a greater to a lesser concentration. The plants solve this otherwise impossible situation by collecting and keeping large quantities of salts in their roots, thereby creating an imbalance again, so water molecules begin flowing in. This water, which is "fresh" in that it contains few salts, is transported throughout the plant by mechanisms identical to those in terrestrial plants. On the other hand, the salts this water does contain, if not concentrated in the roots to allow an inflow, must be excreted. Cordgrass has salt glands in its leaves and stems, and often at low tide it is possible to see either droplets of water along the sides of the leaves—which taste very salty—or crystals of pure salt on the outside of leaves.

Salt-marsh plants have one additional problem not shared by their inland relatives. Ordinary soil is loose and permeated with oxygen-containing air, but the dense mud of a marsh allows no oxygen in. Such gases that may exist are those resulting from organic decomposition. What to do? Salt-marsh grasses and other plants have an unusually well-developed system of air tubes that conducts vital oxygen into even the deepest roots. A long evolutionary development solved these two problems, allowing terrestrial plants to invade the shallow sea and creating salt marshes.

There are other plants important to salt-marsh ecology, but they go unnoticed by most visitors, for they are individually microscopic, although collectively they may color the mud surface. These are photosynthetic algae that live directly upon the uppermost layer of marsh mud, where oxygen is plentiful. They consist of single cells, filaments, and extensive thin mats of beautiful, shelled diatoms, whose symmetry and perfection of form cannot be appreciated without a microscope. Sometimes tiny mobile plant-animals known as dinoflagellates are also present and add to the photosynthetic layer on the mud surface. All these small forms of life are active year-round, primarily during high tides in the summer and low tides in winter, when the mud and its minute inhabitants tend to be warmed by the weak sun. Despite their size, they are important in the productivity of a salt marsh.

Perhaps it is now possible to realize, purely from the standpoint of its vegetation, how intensely alive a salt marsh is. The density and enormous biological activity of grasses and algae result in the production of organic materials in excess of any other natural crop in the world. A salt marsh manufactures more than it or the herbivores living there can possibly consume. Over ninety percent goes unused in the marsh and is flushed off to be utilized in the bay and beyond. This is not to say a marsh is unoccupied by vegetarians, for many insects, a few kinds of crabs, some birds, and the ever-present Muskrat depend largely or exclusively upon plants growing there. Yet even those animals that eat salt-marsh grasses and other vegetation may not—in a biological sense—utilize all they consume; much passes through their digestive tracts only slightly altered, ready to be worked upon by bacteria in the mud or water. By far the largest amount of organic material, in the form of detritus, leaves the marsh to be converted by decomposers in the bay or eaten directly by animals, like the Northern Horse Mussel, that live in marsh-creek inlets.

Muskrat
Ondatra zibethicus

Northern Horse Mussel
Modiolus modiolus
116, 132

Animals of a Salt Marsh

The Muskrat may not be the first sign of animal life seen in a salt marsh, but very likely its houses are. In summer these large mounds, constructed from marsh grasses, may be partly hidden by the height of the surrounding plants, but in winter they stand out as conspicuous domes dotting the entire expanse of marsh. Furthermore, winter houses are enlarged by more cut grass that the Muskrat piles on top to serve as insulation above the several chambers within. The mounds are evenly spaced, indicating a form of territoriality, although the animals themselves share feeding and working grounds. In some seasons, a house may shelter several individuals, but in the warm-weather breeding season, there is usually just one Muskrat per house. Throughout the marsh, Muskrats build feeding platforms from the same kinds of vegetation; on these, or surrounding them, are numerous signs of the animals' presence, including cut leaves and partly eaten stems, and crab, clam, snail, and mussel shells. Generally, only one Muskrat uses a feeding platform at a time.

A Muskrat can be seen in daytime, although its periods of greatest activity begin as darkness falls. Look over a marsh and watch the water of the creeks; if you see the surface furrowed by a wet, dark brown head moving along smoothly and rapidly, leaving Vs behind it, you have spotted a Muskrat. It swims well by using its rear feet, which are equipped with a fringe of stiff bristles instead of webbing; it steers itself with a scaly tail. When a Muskrat dives, a fold of skin seals off its ear opening; this feature and the highly water-repellent nature of the fur are both adaptations to an aquatic life. If you are very quiet, the animal may be unaware of your presence and climb from the water onto a mud bank, leaving a distinctive trail of footprints with a center line scribed by its dragging tail. But when alarmed, a Muskrat quickly submerges and swims away invisibly in the turbid creek, remaining underwater, if it must, for more than fifteen minutes at a time.

Contrary to expectations, a salt marsh is an unusually good place to find birds. Some are seasonal, some secretive, and others are present and visible much of the time. Among the birds that remain largely hidden, the Clapper Rail makes its presence known with a series of penetrating calls, *kek-kek-kek-kek-kek*—a ventriloquist effect masking the bird's exact location. This bird is so closely associated with salt marshes that in some places it is called a marsh hen—for it is about the size and general shape of a chicken. As it stalks along the marsh surface hidden beneath the grass, the Clapper Rail seeks a wide variety of food, including seeds and buds, snails, young crabs, and insects. It is a good candidate for the salt marsh's most representative bird.

Examined from its margins, a salt marsh appears a still place with little discernible motion. But with luck you may spot a slender-bodied Northern Harrier—also known as the Marsh Hawk—as it flies with keen attention low over the marsh grasses. Its hunting flight is agile, without wasted motion, and exciting to the observer. Its excellent vision and unusually acute hearing—a sense few other birds of prey rely upon—allow a Harrier to detect small animals in the grass and to capture them by surprise before they are aware the bird has appeared overhead. In its deliberate inspection of the terrain, this raptor does not miss a square yard. When it sights prey, it stops in midair, seeming almost to back up as it takes aim; it hovers only a few yards overhead, then performs an instantaneous acrobatic dive, disappearing in the thick grass, where it devours its prey on the spot. At other times, it ascends with powerful wing beats while clutching the victim in its talons and proceeds straight over the marsh to a nest on the ground, hidden among the vegetation and close to water. Unlike other hawks, these birds remain in the air much of the time, usually low over the ground, circling, hovering, ascending, diving, always on the move. Following a Harrier through binoculars demands a great deal of attention but provides an extraordinary thrill.

If you proceed down a marshside road or glide silently along a tidal channel in a small boat, you may happen upon a strikingly marked bird standing motionless on the mud bank inspecting the water. The Black-crowned Night-Heron may be largely nocturnal in other places, but in salt marshes it is perfectly willing to be abroad in daylight, examining the turbid shallows for fishes, most likely minnows and killifish (*Fundulus* spp.). Salt marshes support other herons as well, such as the beautiful Snowy Egret, which can be found as far north as Maine, although it is usually associated with Florida's mangrove swamps.

Once your eyes are attuned to watching birds, you may identify the small long-billed Marsh Wren toward the rear of the marsh, clinging to rushes, sedges, and reeds swaying in the wind. This is a vocal little bird, the male's song consisting of rattling, gurgling liquid notes, ending in a rasping trill. The females construct functional nests, but not before the males have built a number of false nests; these are never used

Northern Harrier
Circus cyaneus
604

Black-crowned Night
Heron
Nycticorax nycticorax
572

Snowy Egret
Egretta thula
563

Marsh Wren
Cistothorus palustris
613

and are possibly intended to create a diversion for would-be predators.

In the fall, when the migration of waterfowl is under way, it would be a mistake not to visit a marsh—especially one that has some sort of elevated spot, such as a tower or hillside, next to it. Such a place provides an excellent vantage point for seeing the ducks, geese, and swans that arrive and remain for a while. Some of the large federal wildlife refuges in the Middle Atlantic States have proved to be such good winter havens for waterfowl that many birds are now resident all through the most difficult months of the year. The back margin of a salt marsh, among the sedges and rushes, is a transitional region that is alive with birds that nest and feed there during spring and summer. One of the most familiar of all native birds (although most Americans have never seen one) is the Bald Eagle; today it is once more returning to the banks of tidal creeks, where it collects dead and weakened fish. In increasing numbers, Bald Eagles are seen perched on bare branches of tall trees bordering salt marshes, looking out over the terrain in search of food.

Bald Eagle
Haliaeetus leucocephalus
606

The salt marshes are also home to a few kinds of reptiles. The Diamondback Terrapin is one animal invariably associated with these marshes. It is a rather pale creature, but it is handsomely marked with a gray head and neck flecked with dark spots. Its shell, or carapace, is sculptured with concentrically ringed plates and is colored a bit differently according to the variety of subspecies it belongs to, for the turtle ranges from Cape Cod all the way through the Gulf of Mexico to southeastern Texas. Diamondback Terrapins forage for invertebrate animal prey in tidal creeks, feeding on marine worms and mollusks. They, in turn, have been heavily hunted by man to serve as a base for soup, but today they enjoy an increased measure of protection.

Diamondback Terrapin
Malaclemys terrapin
435

Looked at closely, the cordgrass and muddy surface of the marsh are surprisingly well populated by insects, crustaceans, mollusks, and worms. Without question, it is ill advised to plan a summertime invasion of a salt marsh if you are unprotected against biting insects. Hordes of female Golden Saltmarsh Mosquitoes can turn a short walk into a nightmare; they make some areas absolutely impenetrable except with the most effective protective measures. The female American Horse Fly can bite severely and painfully; the insect injects an anticoagulant saliva with its bite, and often draws blood. It is possible to ward these creatures off with good repellents and proper clothing, and it is worth doing so, for the remainder of the small hidden life of a salt marsh includes some remarkable and fascinating creatures that must be examined closely to be understood.

Golden Saltmarsh Mosquito
Aedes solicitans
487

American Horse Fly
Tabanus americanus
484

Low tide in the network of marsh creeks reveals mud banks pockmarked with hundreds of holes; at this time, the scene is set for the emergence of hordes of fiddler crabs. The Mud Fiddler, a dark little crab with a bluish spot in the middle of its "forehead," crawls out of the burrows where it spent the high tide hours protected by mud plugs. It begins at once to

Mud Fiddler
Uca pugnax

sift through the rich organic mud, raising small chunks to its mouth with one claw at a time. Females, with two claws of equal size, seem to eat twice as effectively as males, which possess only one huge claw, which is useless for feeding. As a matter of fact, it is almost useless for defense as well, for the two fingers of the claw do not meet along their edges, as do those of most crabs, but only at the tips, and even then the force they exert is not great. This large claw has only one primary function: to be waved about in a courtship display, attracting females and presumably warning away other males. While this display is going on among many hundreds of crabs, the scene is somewhat absurd to the human observer; nonetheless, it has an important role in mate selection and in the transmission of genetic traits from the largest and most vigorous males.

The territory of the Mud Fiddler is encroached upon by two other species of fiddler crab; one of those is the Sand Fiddler, which is very similar in size and habit to those living exclusively in salt marshes. Both kinds are equipped with biological clocks that cause them to descend into their burrows at the approach of high tide; the little creatures plug their burrows securely with mud and wait out the hours until the water level falls again. In experiments, when they are removed to a laboratory setting, these crabs continue to go into and emerge from their burrows in perfect synchrony with the tides —which may be many miles away.

Sand Fiddler
Uca pugilator
142

The other fiddler crab is the Brackish-water Fiddler. In this species, which is larger, the males possess an imposing red-jointed claw, but it is no more effective an appendage than those of the other two species. In marshes, the Brackish-water Fiddler prefers the rear areas, where salinity levels are lower due to the inflow of fresh water from the land. This species tends not to herd together in such large groups as do the others, and its burrows are more likely to be found on the marsh flats rather than in creek banks.

Brackish-water Fiddler
Uca minax
143

The Purple Marsh Crab is quite different: stoutly built with two heavy claws. It is solitary and constructs larger burrows in the wide expanse of the marsh, often constructing a "porch" of mud that shields the burrow's entrance. The Marsh Crab does not obtain nourishment from the mud as fiddlers do but directly harvests both kinds of cordgrass. It simply crawls over to a plant, cuts it down with its powerful claws, and separates it into convenient lengths, which it manipulates lengthwise into its jaws. In this fashion, it quickly reduces marsh vegetation to fecal matter and detritus.

Though they may be land dwellers most of their lives, fiddler crabs and Marsh Crabs nevertheless are marine animals and must go through the typical crustacean life cycle. This entails liberating their eggs in water so that the emerging larvae are able to go through a series of planktonic stages. At certain times, the plankton surging back and forth in the salt-marsh tidal creeks is rich with crab larvae, each species identifiable by the shape and arrangement of long spines on its body.

The other crustaceans associated with salt marshes live in tidal

Blue Crab
Callinectes sapidus
147

Grass Shrimp
Palaemonetes pugio
143

Common Shore Shrimp
Palaemonetes vulgaris
174

Marsh Periwinkle
Littorina irrorata
58

Eastern Melampus
Melampus bidentatus
74

Eastern Mud Snail
Ilynassa obsoleta
56

Atlantic Ribbed Mussel
Geukensia demissa
115

streams and never emerge on land. The largest and most familiar is the Blue Crab, a formidable predator and scavenger. Marsh creeks are good places for this crab to shed its outer skeleton, something it must do periodically in the molting process that all crustaceans share. During this vulnerable time, Blue Crabs seek shelter and places to cling to, both of which are offered in tidal channels. Humans who seek these crabs for food find that marsh creeks yield far more of them, both soft-shell and hard-shell, than do nearby bay waters, where the animals are not so restricted in their movements.

The other crustacean is the Grass Shrimp, which is almost indistinguishable from the Common Shore Shrimp. It chews into smaller pieces bits of decaying marsh grass that float down the creek, only some of which it can eat. The uneaten grass fragments may be consumed directly by other animals or may decay further as they are washed into the bay; the principal decomposers of this material are bacteria from the intestinal tracts of Grass Shrimp, which continue to work upon detrital material in open water.

Mollusks play vital roles in salt-marsh ecology by consuming both decaying vegetation and living algae that coat the uppermost surface of the marsh. The Marsh Periwinkle is found abundantly along the high-tide mark on cordgrass and upon the algal mats farther back in the marsh. Normally, its shell is a soiled white, finely spotted with brown, but may become greenish from a thin coating of algae of the sort that form a thin blanket on the mud. The Eastern Melampus feeds in much the same way on the outer cells of marsh grasses and algal films covering both plant stems and surface mud. This common little snail often climbs up grass stems to escape high tide, for it breathes air with a single lung and cannot live underwater. At the same time, it is of marine ancestry; it deposits its eggs in gelatinous strings that must remain moist until the larvae hatch and are carried away as members of the plankton. Hatching is coordinated precisely with the lunar cycle during late spring and early summer, when the tiny larvae are at the mercy of tidal currents in the creeks for two weeks until they mature sufficiently to settle down upon the marsh again.

One other snail, the Eastern Mud Snail, is often found in immense numbers on exposed flats at low tide, well below the grass margin. Its dark brown, often battered-looking shell so blends with the sediment that a local population of snails appears as an almost infinite array of small clods of mud. Closer examination reveals long wandering trails in the wet mud, which are left as the snails travel along, extracting nourishment from the organic surface. The Eastern Mud Snail is somewhat omnivorous and may feed on dead marine animals and, rarely, even upon defenseless living invertebrates.

The one abundant bivalve present in salt marshes is the large Atlantic Ribbed Mussel. Because it has wide ranges of tolerance for temperature and salinity, it is admirably suited to survival here. Depressions and salt pans in marshes can develop excessively high salinities, and freshwater runoff from inland streams can markedly diminish the salt content of creeks, conditions that create difficulties for many other animals in the marsh. The Ribbed Mussel not only withstands both conditions unusually well but also is able to live and breathe high in the intertidal region of a marsh. It manages this by opening its shells slightly during low tide, allowing air to pass over its moist gills.

The surface mud of a salt marsh is the habitat for a number of worms from widely differing groups. The Clam Worm, common to several other shoreline habitats, takes advantage of favorable opportunities to hunt and breed in this marine grassland. The Red Lineus can often be found in northern salt marshes, entangled among the anchoring threads of Ribbed Mussels, while other kinds of these smooth nemertean worms live farther south. Though both Clam Worms and Red Lineus worms live in marsh mud, they function in their habitat in very different ways. The Clam Worm, which is segmented, feeds on organic detritus, while the nemertean Red Lineus is a predator, impaling its small victims on its eversible pharynx (which cannot possibly penetrate a human finger).

Clam Worm
Nereis virens
305

Red Lineus
Lineus ruber
311

Many of these salt-marsh creatures are unfamiliar to visitors or are small enough to go unnoticed even when a marsh's surface is examined closely. There are, of course, a great many more inhabitants of salt marshes, some of them extremely important to the marshes' ecology. One such is a little crustacean, the Salt Marsh Amphipod. Large populations of this small shrimplike animal consume great quantities of decaying cordgrass and marsh algae, but the small creature is itself prey to the abundant Killifish that swarm in the tidal creeks. Its role in the complex food web of a salt marsh is both as a consumer of nutrient material and as an item of food.

Salt Marsh Amphipod
Gammarus palustris

As you leave a salt marsh in the evening after dark, glowing eyes may reflect your light's beam, and you will find yourself looking at one of the most familiar faces in North America, the Raccoon. This opportunist, which ranges from far-inland mountainsides to coastal plains (and even large cities), long ago discovered the benefits of hunting in salt marshes where crabs, Ribbed Mussels, Clapper Rail eggs, the eggs and young of various waterfowl, and young Muskrats are plentiful. At the Raccoon's level of predation, there is little competition, and because it is not a specialist in dietary preferences, a vast amount of food is available to it.

Raccoon
Procyon lotor

Today, among much of the public, salt marshes are still considered wastelands to be altered or obliterated. If those who think in this vein could spend just a single day seeing some of the extraordinary plant and animal lives interact in a marsh, and learn how vital these wetlands are to the coastal oceans, then the full impact of their beauty and importance would ensure their preservation and management. Salt marshes are, without question, among the world's most extraordinary ecosystems, created entirely by living organisms and possessing a biological dynamism and level of productivity unmatched anywhere else.

SALT MARSHES: ANIMALS

Seashells

Atlantic Ribbed
Mussel 115
Eastern Melampus 74
Florida Crown Conch 36,
124
Great Piddock 98
Marsh Periwinkle 58

Seashore Creatures

Brackish-water
Fiddler 143
Red Lineus 311
Sand Fiddler 142

Insects and Spiders

American Horse Fly 484
Bearded Robber Fly 481
Beautiful Tiger Beetle 489
Bee Fly 485
Collops Beetle 488
Cow Killer 486
Deer Fly 483
Dune Wolf Spider 492
Eastern Sand Wasp 482

Fishes

Diamond Killifish 394
Gulf Killifish 393
Gulf Pipefish 410
Sailfin Molly 396
Sheepshead Minnow 395

Reptiles and Amphibians

American Alligator 439
Cottonmouth 442
Diamondback
Terrapin 435
Snapping Turtle 433
Southern Water Snake 443

Birds

American Avocet 577
American Bittern 567
American Black Duck 534
American Wigeon 535
Black-bellied Plover 584
Black-crowned Night
Heron 572
Black-necked Stilt 578
Boat-tailed Grackle 607
Brant 555
Canada Goose 554, 556
Caspian Tern 509

Clapper Rail 598
Fish Crow 608
Forster's Tern 512
Gadwall 533
Glossy Ibis 569
Great Blue Heron 565
Great Egret 562
Green-backed Heron 571
Hooded Merganser 540
Least Sandpiper 588
Least Tern 514
Lesser Yellowlegs 593
Little Blue Heron 564,
570
Long-billed
Dowitcher 595
Mallard 544
Marsh Wren 613
Mottled Duck 532
Northern Harrier 604
Northern Pintail 529
Northern Shoveler 545
Osprey 605
Red-winged
Blackbird 609
Reddish Egret 566
Redhead 531
Ring-necked Duck 546
Seaside Sparrow 617
Sharp-tailed Sparrow 615
Short-billed
Dowitcher 594
Snow Goose 553
Snowy Egret 563
Spotted Sandpiper 591
Stilt Sandpiper 589
Swamp Sparrow 614
Tree Swallow 610
Tricolored Heron 568
White Ibis 561
Willet 590
Wood Stork 560
Yellow-crowned Night
Heron 573
Yellow-rumped
Warbler 618

CORAL REEFS

A coral reef is overwhelming in its architecture, riot of submarine colors, and astonishing variety of life. No other shoreline in North America compares in these respects. Worldwide, coral reefs account for more than 68 million square miles—a suggestion of their considerable importance to the marine ecosystem. Yet corals are restricted to growth only in warm waters. Where temperatures fall below 64° F, reefs are absent, so in the continental United States they are found only in southern Florida and especially off the southeastern shores of the Keys.

The fringing reefs of Florida are barely apparent from the shore. Beach rubble contains bleached coral fragments, broken and often pulverized into sand. Sifting through the coarse sand, one finds bits of coral and chips of calcareous (limey, calcium-rich) material from coralline algae, shells of one-celled foraminiferans (large marine relatives of amoebae), sea-urchin spines, worn mollusk shells, and other remnants from the complex reef world hidden below the surface just offshore. While beaches tell a partial story, it is necessary either to go out in a glass-bottomed boat or to snorkel over the shallow reef to gain a full appreciation of the complexities of a reef community.

It is not always possible to see details in an inshore reef, no matter how shallow it is, because wind-driven waves stir up the sandy bottom between coral heads and in the lagoon, raising nearly opaque milky clouds that reduce visibility to disappointingly short distances. Days for observing must be chosen with care.

The snorkeling intruder need not cover great distances or even be experienced; simply drifting overhead, with an occasional dip down a few feet beneath the surface, presents a kaleidoscopic array of shapes and colors. In the shadows of an overhanging coral head an octopus or a moray lurks, neither as fearsome as its reputation suggests. Close inspection of a coral head reveals the delicate traceries of spiraled feather-duster worms, which disappear instantly when an exploratory finger approaches. The closer one gets to the reef, the more intense the colors: rich purple sponges, deep orange-red sea-squirt colonies, emerald star coral, neon-bright gobies, and everywhere the brilliance of reef fishes, each flashing its own colors in species recognition or in deceptive markings.

The snorkeler, freed from the restriction of gravity, becomes a part of this totally different world, lazily keeping up with jellyfish as they pump along, or entering schools of porkfish and grunts that part, as if by magic, to let the human intruder through, closing after him as though he had never passed. Strange sights materialize: Bright-eyed squid hover in formation just out of reach, waiting almost motionless until approached, then darting into the distance, their speed so astonishingly fast that the human eye is tricked and fails to follow them. In the distance, the graceful shape of a lemon shark or hammerhead sculls across the reef heads, intent only on weakened, isolated fish as a possible meal—not the large and unfamiliar human shape, which they tend to avoid.

The reef is not a silent place. At first one is conscious of the patter of wavelets overhead, or the liquid splashes of waves striking the forereef; then sounds occur that have no source other than the animals that make them. There are chirps, squeaks, whistles, grunts, croaks, and drumming booms—all against a backdrop of a million tiny firecracker pops of snapping shrimp communicating within their places of refuge in coral heads or the inner chambers of sponges.

Range
In the southern United States, good reefs extend out to the Dry Tortugas. Beyond Hawk Channel, just off Key Largo, White Bank extends over five miles to sea where the submarine slope begins and the Gulf Stream flows. More than twenty miles of this heavily populated marine community is protected as the John Pennekamp Coral Reef State Park. The reef itself extends both north and south of the Park, and similar fringing reefs are found along the southern Keys. Coral growth in lesser patches is found along much of the entire Florida coastline and into the Gulf of Mexico, but it is in the Keys that extensive fringing reefs are best developed. Of all the areas where coral communities exist in Florida waters, it is only within the State Park that marine life is protected. In other accessible regions, certain attractive and valuable animals, including the coral, may be seriously depleted.

Features
A fringing reef, which is the only major type of coral reef found in Florida's coastal waters, develops from a hard substrate upon which the free-swimming coral larvae can settle. It is composed of a wide variety of corals, hard and soft, although only a few species are dominant both in numbers and in the mass they produce. Shallow water makes it difficult for corals to grow well, but they increase dramatically as depths approach twenty feet. The water must be clear and clean, free of pollution. Chemical and thermal pollution from shoreline installations and oil from ships quickly kill the delicate polyps that are instrumental in maintaining the reef ecosystem.

The basic structure of a reef is made up of a limey compound, calcium carbonate, that is secreted by stony corals, coralline algae, and some tube-dwelling invertebrate worms and other creatures. Each coral polyp's anatomy resembles, in simplified form, that of its much larger cousins, the sea anemones. A coral is basically a tubular animal, mouth ringed by tentacles possessing stinging cells, securely tucked into a cup of stone-hard lime it has secreted. As the calcareous cups are deposited next to one another by neighboring polyps, the whole mass becomes fused into one colony. Depending upon the species of coral, the overall structure assumes whatever the creature's genetic code determines it to be: delicate and whiplike, treelike, mushroomlike, or boulderlike, to name a few shapes. Although every individual colony is unique in itself, the basic pattern of a species is sufficiently similar to make identifying it, even from a distance, an easy task. An Elkhorn Coral is readily distinguished from a Staghorn Coral, although both are

Elkhorn Coral
Acropora palmata
272

Staghorn Coral
Acropora cervicornis
273

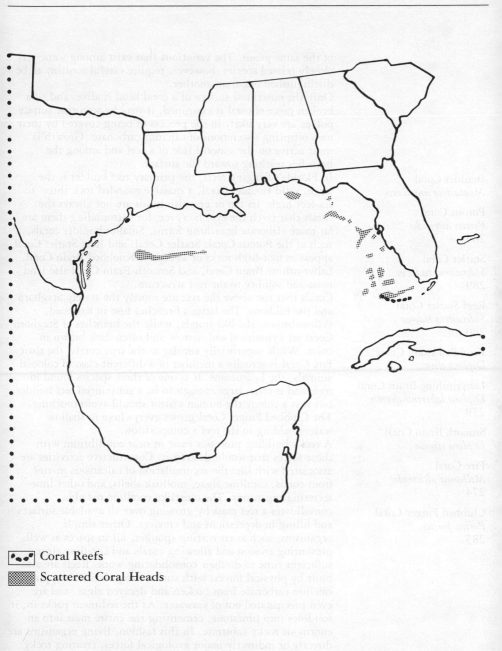

••• Coral Reefs

▨ Scattered Coral Heads

Boulder Coral
Montastrea annularis

Porous Coral
Porites astreoides
284

Starlet Coral
Siderastrea radians
289

Reef Starlet Coral
Siderastrea siderea
280

Knobbed Brain Coral
Diplora clivosa

Labyrinthine Brain Coral
Diplora labyrinthiformis
279

Smooth Brain Coral
Diplora stigosa

Fire Coral
Millepora alcicornis
274

Clubbed Finger Coral
Porites porites
283

of the same genus. The variations that exist among some very closely related species, however, require careful scrutiny to be distinguished one from another.

Only the outermost surface of a coral head is alive, and, if a broken piece of coral is examined, it may be seen that surface polyps are very likely in the process of being covered by their own offspring's secretions of calcium carbonate. Growth is most active on the seaward side of a reef and among the branches reaching toward the surface.

In Florida's fringing reefs, the primary reef builder is the large, solid Boulder Coral, a massive rounded rock three- to six-feet high. Its tan or greenish heads are not always the corals that catch the eye, however, for surrounding them are far more elaborate branching forms. Smaller boulder corals, such as the Porous Coral, Starlet Coral, and Reef Starlet Coral, appear as foot-high rocks or as crusts. Knobbed Brain Coral, Labyrinthine Brain Coral, and Smooth Brain Coral also lend mass and solidity to the reef structure.

Corals that rise above the rest are mostly the stately Staghorn and the Elkhorn. The latter's branches fuse in flattened, yellow-brown, slablike fronds, while the branches of Staghorn Coral are cylindrical and narrow and often dark brown in color. While superficially similar to the true corals, the toxic Fire Coral is actually a member of a different class of colonial animals, the hydrozoans. It is one of three species found in reefs and is often large enough to be a substantial reef builder, but it is a colony the human visitor should avoid touching. The Clubbed Finger Coral grows everywhere in shallow waters, adding to the reef's composition.

A reef's building processes exist in near equilibrium with those forces that would destroy it. Constructive activities are associated with life: the accumulation of calcareous matter from corals, coralline algae, mollusk shells, and other lime-secreting organisms. The crustlike coralline red alga consolidates a reef mass by growing over all available surfaces and filling in depressions and crevices. Other simple organisms, such as encrusting sponges, fill in spaces as well, preventing erosion and allowing corals and coralline algae sufficient time to do their consolidating work. Reefs are also built by physical forces, with surface irregularities trapping calcium carbonate from broken and decayed algae, and are even precipitated out of seawater. As the sediment packs in, it solidifies into limestone, cementing the entire mass into an enormous rocky substrate. In this fashion, living organisms are directly or indirectly major geological forces, creating rocky marine habitats where formerly there were none. Changes in sea level and rising ocean floors may thrust these formations into the air: the upper Florida Keys are just such ancient elevated reefs.

Destructive forces are at work as well, primarily through the action of a multitude of boring organisms that tunnel into and through a reef's structure. While certain kinds of algae are capable of dissolving calcareous coral rock, it is the invertebrate animals that by slow or seemingly minor

Rock-boring Urchin
Echinometra lucunter
195

Long-spined Urchin
Diadema antillarum
198

Boring Sponge
Cliona celata
292

Atlantic Palolo Worm
Eunice schemacephala

Giant Date Mussel
Lithophaga antillarum

Mahogany Date Mussel
Lithophaga bisulcata

Atlantic Gastrochaena
Gastrochaena hians

Blue Parrotfish
Scarus coeruleus
345

alterations of reef mass eventually cause major changes. The Rock-boring Urchin may take years to excavate a burrow in coral rock, but it does so inexorably. Long-spined Black Urchins also grind out hollows in coral.

The Boring Sponge not only attacks and excavates galleries within mollusk shells but also enters dead coral rocks and tunnels deep into the calcareous mass, so riddling the coral that it eventually collapses. Its tunnels open the way for other, even more vigorous, animals. Gnawing with powerful jaws, the Atlantic Palolo Worm burrows into coral, weakening it. Both the Giant Date Mussel and the Mahogany Date Mussel, after first attaching themselves by temporary byssus threads, enter coral by means of acidic secretions that dissolve the hard calcareous rock. They may allow themselves to be surrounded by growing coral but at the same time maintain an opening through which they can feed and breathe. The Atlantic Gastrochaena bores into coral by rotating its shell valves against the rock and also by chemical means that cause softening of the limestone.

Large colorful parrotfishes, such as the Blue Parrotfish, are common on coral reefs, where they are major destroyers of hard coral. Their teeth are fused into beaklike plates and are used to grind off flakes and chunks of coral to get at the algae present. They then either spit out the coral or allow the pulverized material to pass through their digestive tracts, after which it falls to the bottom as fine calcareous sand, where it may fill in chinks of the reef, helping to cement it together again. Coral heads clearly show the scrape marks from the powerful jaws of parrotfishes.

Storms, especially hurricanes that attack the Florida coast, are enormously destructive to reefs. At the very least, the force of large waves can kill coral polyps in the heavy surge. After a severe storm, great broken branches of the treelike corals litter the bottom, dramatic evidence of destruction, within hours, of what took many years to build. If coastal waters remain healthy and unpolluted by human activities, a slow rebuilding commences at once after a storm. Some epochs of geological time have been kinder to coral reef formation than others, but there seems never to have been a time when reefs weren't being constructed in tropical waters; this state of affairs should continue to hold true so long as we care for our shores.

Ecology

Unlike sandy beaches or rocky shores, which have clearly marked intertidal zones, a fringing reef has little obvious zonation. Nonetheless, broad zones, suitable to certain kinds of life and subject to different environmental influences, occur with increased distance from the shore and proximity of the reef to waves from the open ocean. The continental shoreline behind a reef supports few living corals among the great masses of coral rubble. This is largely a specialized and depopulated zone. Farther out from the shore, the water deepens to about twenty feet into a lagoon carpeted with calcareous sand, its breadth dependent upon prevailing currents and the reef formation beyond. As the bottom rises again, the reef proper commences, and coral reaches upward in a flattened array to less than a yard from the surface. The rear of the reef (the part closest to shore) is composed of broken and dead coral debris, but more life appears as one moves seaward across the reef. Finally, living coral branches interrupt the internal rolling motion of waves and create foaming breakers overhead. Here the variety of life again diminishes because of the precarious nature of existence in the wave surge, but as the seaward reef face descends into deeper water of the ocean, whole new associations of life appear.

The Lagoon

This is a quiet place to snorkel and usually contains an interesting variety of life if the visibility is good. Merman's Shaving Brush, a curious tufted alga supported by a stiff stalk, contrasts with different kinds of flat fan algae that also rise from the sandy bottom. Both Udotea Fan Algae and the abundant Disk Algae deposit calcium carbonate within their tissues; this is freed when they decay and serves both to help cement the reef together and to add sand to the shoreline.

Turtle Grass may grow in large underwater "meadows" in lagoons, providing a unique habitat in itself. Turtle Grass is something of a rarity in the oceans: It is a true seed-bearing plant with terrestrial origins and even produces tiny white flowers near the base of its stem. The dense growth of Turtle Grass traps sediment by slowing passing water, so it affords a quiet place for smaller plants and a host of animals. Many small algae and sessile creatures live attached to the broad blades of Turtle Grass, much as living organisms grow from the leaves of Eelgrass in the waters of estuaries farther north. Both the Green Sea Urchin and the Long-spined Black Urchin may carpet portions of the sandy lagoon bottom, but the Long-spined Black Urchins are to be avoided. Their needle-sharp spines, equipped with a mild toxin, cause temporarily painful wounds when they penetrate human flesh.

Queen Conchs and Tulip Shells were once common in Florida's lagoons, but the huge, beautiful Queen Conch has been so sought after it is almost gone from these waters. The predatory Tulip Shell is still found as it hunts for other snails on the sandy bottom. The large Tiger Lucine is a clam that lies buried beneath the bottom, one of many kinds of bivalve mollusks to live in the soft, loose substrate. Sea hares, such as the Spotted Sea Hare, a large, yellowish, fleshy mollusk with an internal shell, can be abundant in Turtle Grass beds, where its spotted coloration makes it extremely difficult to see. Its close relative, the Black Sea Hare, may emerge at night and swim gracefully with rippling undulations of its winglike mantle, making it appear in a flashlight's beam like a great, lazy marine bat.

Sandy lagoons are favored habitats for odd little crustaceans known as bashful crabs, or box crabs. The Yellow Box Crab and the Flame-streaked Box Crab pick through bottom sediment for food but, if bothered, either quickly bury

Upside-down Jellyfish
Cassiopeia xamachana
221

Porkfish
Anisotremus virginicus
371

Southern Stingray
Dasyatis americana
425

themselves in the sand or hold up broad, flat claws in front of their faces, creating a nearly impregnable armored casing. The quiet waters of a lagoon favor comb jellies, or ctenophores, which swim by means of eight rows of beating ciliary plates, as well as true jellyfish, which pulsate through the shallow water. An unusual creature is the Upside-down Jellyfish, a foot-wide disk that throbs through the water like any other jellyfish, but soon settles to the sandy bottom upside down. At times, whole lagoon floors may be carpeted with thousands of these creatures, their translucent bodies soaking up sunlight to activate yellowish microscopic algae held within their tissues. They gain nourishment from the photosynthetic activity of the algae, as well as from animal food caught in the water.

Schools of fish, such as Porkfish, may flash by on their way from one part of the reef to another, but the one animal to watch out for in lagoons is the Southern Stingray, which lies partly buried in the sand with only its eyes, spiracles (breathing holes), and whiplike tail exposed. A Stingray is capable of inflicting a severe wound in a person if the tail is lashed upward, driving the serrated spine deep into flesh. The spine bears poison that causes great pain, inflammation, and sometimes fainting and heart irregularities.

The Reef
No matter how calm a lagoon or how interesting its specialized inhabitants, it is the reef beyond, with its complex ecology, that holds the greatest fascination. As the lagoon floor slopes upward, coral heads, especially the boulder corals, become more numerous. At the rear of the reef many of these are dead, although they provide exposed surfaces to which algae and other forms of life attach. Deep crevices between coral boulders are places of refuge sought by crabs, small fishes, and nocturnal creatures. Healthy living corals appear increasingly as one enters the reef, with Staghorn and Elkhorn corals, Starlet and Brain corals, Fire Corals, and sea fans among the common species.

Passing seaward across the reef, one encounters the breaker zone. Here ocean waves are affected by the great arms and main branches of Elkhorn Coral, which mostly point toward the attacking waves. Staghorn Coral is rare or absent from this zone because its flattened branches do not easily withstand the force of moving water. Fire Coral is the only other erect form of life in this turbulent region of wave surge. Where the reef faces the deeper ocean, its front has open channels and ridges. The spurs are the result of coral growth, while in the open channels the movement of sand and coral rubble along the floor discourages living coral colonies from taking hold. Corals with photosynthetic algae held in their tissues are the originators of a reef's ecosystem, creating feeding grounds, places of attachment, and nurseries for every kind of marine organism. One square yard of reef supports not only tens of thousands of living corals but also a hundred or more distinct species, every one of which is a specialist in its manner of life.

Common Atlantic
Octopus
Octopus vulgaris
183

Long-armed Octopus
Octopus macropus
182

Flamingo Tongue
Cyphoma gibbosum
77, 128

Striped Tunicate
Styela plicata

Green Encrusting
Tunicate
Symplegma viride
237

Sheep's Wool Sponge
Hippiospongia lachne

Fire Sponge
Tedania ignis

Spiral-gilled Tube Worm
Spirobranchus giganteus
251

Magnificent Feather
Duster Worm
Sabellastarte magnifica

Star Tube Worm
Pomatostegus stellatus

Orange Fire Worm
Eurythoe complanata

Green Fire Worm
Hermodice carunculata
303

Furthermore, a reef seen during the day is entirely unlike the same place after dark, as one population quiets down or disappears and another assembly of organisms becomes active. Four different kinds of squirrelfish and two kinds of octopus, the Common Atlantic Octopus and the Long-armed Octopus, are but a few of the animals that emerge in the darkness. Once a reef has become established and begins to grow in size and complexity, the number of species increases almost beyond reckoning. Whether stony corals remain alive or as dead masses of limestone, the hard substrate that they create provides unlimited opportunities for other organisms to thrive in. Now the soft corals can take hold, their beautiful erect fronds and filaments waving in the currents. Some are slender tendrils, while others are delicately colored fans. Sea fans are preyed upon by the dramatically colored Flamingo Tongue, a small snail that extrudes a pinkish mantle, patterned with black-outlined orange squares and rectangles, to completely cover its polished shell. The snail is best found browsing on the polyps of broad sea fans at night, for during the day it clings to the base of the soft coral near the floor of the reef.

Reef Inhabitants
On the surface of the reef, sponges and sea squirts, or tunicates, live their quiet lives, sucking in water through siphons or tiny pores and extracting food and oxygen. Tunicates may be solitary, like the Striped Tunicate, or colonial, like the Green Encrusting Tunicate. Each individual has an incurrent and an excurrent siphon to allow a constant flow of water to pass through a meshed strainer in the globular body. Sponges, on the other hand, take in water through minute pores scattered over their entire surface, then allow it to pass out through a single, much larger pore; in tubelike sponges, this pore is at the top of the sponge, while a rounded sponge has similar large openings scattered over the surface. Some of the large sponges have a labyrinth of interior chambers where they harbor a multitude of small animals, including worms, crustaceans, and mollusks. These creatures are commensal—that is, they live in the sponge and share its food, but they seldom harm it. The sponge simply offers a secure communal dwelling place, safe from predators that cannot enter. Among the more colorful sponges are the purplish Stinker Sponge and the bright red, very toxic Fire Sponge, which attracts few other animals and should be avoided.

Although the surge of waves keeps soft corals, algae, and other delicate organisms moving in a constant rhythm, there is more purposeful activity among the coral heads. Spiral-gilled Tube Worms, Magnificent Feather Duster Worms, and Star Tube Worms extend their colorful, feathery antennae outward in radiating patterns, where they trap microscopic planktonic food passing by in the water. Orange Fire Worms and Green Fire Worms crawl across coral heads and rubble in search of other invertebrate prey in the form of coral polyps and colonial sea anemones, which they attack and kill with a protrusible pharynx. If disturbed, both fire worms extend clusters of sharp and toxic bristles that easily penetrate the skin of a person, breaking off and causing a severe irritation. Fire worms are rarely abroad in daylight but emerge from their coral hiding places in the evening to begin nightly forays for food.

Shrimps and crabs are also members of the reef community, but they are often difficult to see; many are small and protectively colored, and many hide securely. The most delicate of crabs, the Arrow Crab, perches high on coral heads, its slender body and head pointed upward while it moves slowly along on very long, extremely thin legs. It is attractively patterned with a striped body and spots of red and blue on its legs and claws, an assortment of markings and colors that makes such a slender animal very hard to observe. Another crab, the Sponge Crab, is even harder to recognize, for it camouflages itself with a sponge it has shaped to fit over its body, held securely in place by its hind legs. The sponge remains alive and may grow so large that the crab is completely hidden beneath the concave living helmet it occupies. Sponges are sometimes associated with other kinds of crustaceans. Snapping or pistol shrimps live inside chambers within a large sponge; there they feed upon organic matter brought in by the current, upon smaller animals also living in the sponge, and occasionally upon the sponge itself.

The Brown Pistol Shrimp, closely related to those found in sponges, lives in coral rubble and is therefore easier to find and examine. The snapping mechanism is found on a greatly enlarged claw of a pistol shrimp and is much like the hammer of a gun. The movable finger cocks upward at about ninety degrees and is then ready to be released. When it snaps down into the socket of the rest of the claw, the penetrating sound can be heard over great distances underwater. When hundreds or thousands of these shrimps carry on their explosive communications, the noise can be almost deafening. This background cacophony is punctuated by the grunts and groans of the blue-and-yellow-striped White Grunt, a reef fish that makes its characteristic noise by grinding pharyngeal teeth together. Each fish capable of producing sounds has its own distinctive calls: rasps, trills, squeaks, drumming sounds, and more. A Scrawled Filefish often stands head-down while searching for food on the bottom, at the same time keeping in touch with others of its kind by producing a grunting sound.

Cooperative Relationships

Some small shrimps have very important roles in reef ecology, for they set up "service stations," where they advertise their presence both by ritualized activity and by their brilliant colors. Fishes are attracted to such spots and remain there quietly while the shrimps remove parasites from their scales and fins, and even from inside their open mouths. The most dramatic of the cleaning shrimps is the two-inch-long Banded Coral Shrimp, which is pure white with bright red bands across its body and claws. It stands in one spot, often the opening to a crevice, and waves its antennae to catch the

Arrow Crab
Stenorhynchus seticornis
200

Sponge Crab
Dromia erythropus
151

Brown Pistol Shrimp
Alpheus armatus
170

White Grunt
Haemulon plumieri

Scrawled Filefish
Aluterus scriptus
348

Banded Coral Shrimp
Stenopus hispidus
164

Spotted Cleaning Shrimp
Periclimenes yucatanicus
165

Pink-tipped Anemone
Condylactis gigantea
268

Pederson's Cleaning
Shrimp
Periclimenes pedersoni

Ringed Anemone
Bartholomea annulata
269

Neon Goby
Elecatinus oceanops

Spanish Hogfish
Bodianus rufus
342

Queen Angelfish
Holacanthus ciliaris
363

Rock Beauty
Holacanthus tricolor

Queen Triggerfish
Balistes vetula

Agassiz's Sea Cucumber
Actinopyga agassizii

Spiny Brittle Star
Ophiocoma echinata

Reticulate Brittle Star
Ophionereis reticulata

attention of passing fish that approach, some assuming almost vertical headstands or tailstands as their own signals to the shrimp that they are ready for cleaning.

Not all cleaning shrimps associate with fishes, however. The Spotted Cleaning Shrimp, a beautiful transparent crustacean decorated with tannish, white-bordered spots, lives unharmed among the stinging tentacles of the Pink-tipped Anemone, the largest sea anemone of the reefs. Pederson's Cleaning Shrimp, a closely related species, chooses to live among the tentacles of the Ringed Anemone, without being stung, and may even share the same cleaning station as the Neon Goby described below.

Some "service stations" are worked by small fishes rather than crustaceans. Several species of wrasse, gobies, and, by means of their bright colors, the young of certain larger reef fishes actively solicit the attention of fishes in need of cleaning— quivering, darting, and swimming back and forth in one spot. The purple and yellow Spanish Hogfish is one such cleaning fish; another is the Neon Goby, with an electric-blue stripe down its side, which perches on coral heads waiting for passersby. It stays in place even in the surge of waves, using its pair of fused ventral fins as a suction cup; when a large grouper or other fish comes by, it stops and waits for the Neon Goby to remove irritating parasitic crustaceans from its scales and its cavernous mouth.

Reef fishes swim from one spot to another or occupy their home territories in a bewildering array of form, blazing colors, and varied behavior. The Queen Angelfish and the Rock Beauty feed upon algae, sea squirts, and sponges, their conspicuous colors actually allowing them to blend with the multicolored reef background. A Queen Triggerfish swims in stately fashion, waving its large dorsal and anal fins from side to side until a black Long-spined Urchin is in sight, then it attacks with its powerful bony jaws, jabbing at the urchin and grabbing at its spines or blowing sand away from underneath the animal until it is flipped upside down. The triggerfish then is able to tear open the vulnerable underside of the urchin and extract its internal organs.

Of the several kinds of sea cucumbers living in reefs and lagoons, Agassiz's Sea Cucumber is one of the most common. This dark, mottled animal with leathery skin lives in remarkable association with the small Pearlfish. The fish dwells in an enlarged portion of the hind gut, or cloaca, of the sea cucumber, just inside the anus. Sea cucumbers breathe through this opening, bringing water to internal gills known as a respiratory tree; for this reason, the fish is assured of oxygen. The little fish can leave at will, but always returns to the security of its large, tough-skinned host.

A sea cucumber is an echinoderm; though different in its elongated proportions, it is related to the radially symmetrical brittle stars, sea stars, sand dollars, sea biscuits, and sea urchins, all of which are found in association with a Florida reef. Among the brittle stars, the Spiny Brittle Star is the largest, and the Reticulate Brittle Star is one of the most common. Both live under old coral rocks and remain hidden from sight during the day. They are easily found by lifting a dead coral head, but when exposed, the sea stars immediately squirm away to find new security elsewhere. When grasped by one of their arms, they quickly sever it from the body. There is no harm in the long run, for a brittle star is able to regenerate its lost limbs. Even so, these animals should not be handled.

A Word of Caution

The reef is not without hazards to human visitors, but harm need not come to the cautious and forewarned snorkeler. For example, the Great Barracuda, which reaches a length of almost six feet, is an inquisitive and swift predator that may hover quietly near a human diver, watching and following but not attacking. There are no reported cases of a barracuda attacking a person simply for a meal, although a bright, shiny bit of metal might attract it as would a small, silvery fish. Belt buckles and silvery cameras could serve as lures.

Great Barracuda
Sphyraena barracuda

Sharks of different kinds cruise across the reef, perhaps in search of fish they can catch for food. Although a shark is never entirely predictable, the chance of one attacking a human in such surroundings is slight. If a shark exhibits agitated behavior and swims rapidly about in one area, it is time for human divers to leave the scene.

Only familiarity will tell divers which animals to avoid touching, for there are many that sting, burn, or otherwise irritate human skin. Avoid Long-spined Urchins, with their waving poisonous needles, and Fire Worms, which have sharp, glassy, toxic bristles. Fire Corals are painful if brushed against, and the two toxic sponges, the Fire Sponge and the Do-not-touch-me Sponge both cause severe blisters if handled.

Do-not-touch-me Sponge
Neofibularia nolitangere

The Portuguese Man-of-war appears on the surface as a purple-and-rose-colored float; its long tentacles, however, can stream out horizontally with the current, extending several yards from the base of this colony of stinging hydroid polyps.

Portuguese Man-of-war
Physalia physalis
218

Both Spotted Moray Eels and the two species of octopus in Florida's reefs inspire dread among some divers, yet they are not aggressive and prefer to remain tucked away in crevices during the daytime. Of course, if provoked by an intruding hand, the powerful moray, with its sharp teeth, and the octopus, with its shearing "parrot's beak" jaws, can deliver painful and even dangerous wounds.

Spotted Moray Eel
Gymnothorax moringa
431

The Alphabet Cone Shell, like cone shells everywhere, can stab grasping fingers with a poisonous barb at the tip of its proboscis (protruding mouthpart). Any cone shell should be handled with extreme caution, if at all.

Alphabet Cone Shell
Conus spurius
46

Care must also be taken with certain reef fishes. In addition to stringrays, scorpionfishes living in reefs even look dangerous, when they are recognized behind their camouflaging colors and sharp spines. The stings inflicted by their dorsal-fin spines are very painful but have no dangerous side effects.

The flesh of some reef fishes may be poisonous to eat, either predictably or only under certain conditions. Barracuda are known to cause ciguatera, a type of poisoning that can cause serious illness and sometimes death. Some barracuda are perfectly safe to eat; nonetheless, those that occupy the end of a food web that begins with certain microscopic algae may be dangerous. Apparently the difference occurs with the region in which these territorialistic fishes dwell. Members of the ubiquitous puffer, or blowfish, family can also be deadly and should not be eaten. Some species invariably cause fatalities, while some produce severe symptoms but not death. Oddly, some species are safe. Still, it is best to avoid eating all blowfishes or puffers, for there is no antidote, and no recovery is possible when one of the most poisonous ones is eaten.

Essential Relationships

The reef crest scene is awesome in its architecture and rich palette of color. But its most remarkable feature is the manner in which the myriad plants and animals interact, making the reef crest the most complex of marine habitats. The marine algae of coral reefs tend to be small and individually inconspicuous; yet their importance to reef ecology is enormous. A great many corals harbor one-celled algae within their tissues, often an indispensable arrangement for the two partners. There can be an exchange of nutrients in some cases; in others, the algae produce toxic substances that prevent other animals either from eating coral polyps or from attaching to the coral colony.

In other reef associations, the Tricolor Anemone is almost always found attached to the shell occupied by a hermit crab, or, more rarely, to the carapace of an ordinary crab. Both the hermit crab and the anemone "seek" the relationship: when they are near each other, they exhibit behavior that encourages attachment. The result of this relationship, of course, is one of mutual benefit. The predatory Long-armed Octopus finds large hermit crabs attractive prey but almost always avoids those with anemones attached. Moreover, a hermit crab is usually an untidy eater, and bits of food is shreds float off to be captured by the anemone's tentacles. The hermit crab provides mobility and new feeding opportunities for the anemone, which otherwise would be restricted to one place.

Above the surface of a reef there are few predictable forms of life to be seen. Of the many birds found along Florida's coast, perhaps the Brown Pelican is the most obvious, flying low over reef areas or skimming the surface in small groups. If fish are spotted in the lagoon or just beyond the breakers of the forereef, the bird plummets down in a specatacular dive, head outstretched and wings folded just as it hits the surface. Underwater, the fleshy pouch swells enormously to trap fish and carry them to the surface, extruding water as it does so. This great bird, a visitor from the airy world of the shore, thus reaps a full harvest from the richness provided by a coral reef.

Tricolor Anemone
Calliactis tricolor

Brown Pelican
Pelecanus occidentalis
519

CORAL REEFS: ANIMALS

Seashells
Atlantic Thorny
Oyster 109
Flamingo Tongue 77, 128
Florida Lace Murex 38, 123
Frons Oyster 110
Turkey Wing 86
West Indian Worm Shell 63

Seashore Creatures
Arrow Crab 200
Atlantic Long-fin Squid 181
Atlantic Purple Sea
Urchin 196
Banded Coral Shrimp 164
Blue Crab 147
Brown Pistol Shrimp 170
By-the-wind Sailor 217
Cannonball Jellyfish 222
Clubbed Finger Coral 283
Commensal Crab 149
Common Atlantic
Octopus 183
Common Lettuce Slug 214
Common Spider Crab 138
Coral Crab 141
Cushion Star 191
Dwarf Brittle Star 184
Elkhorn Coral 272
Encrusted Tunicate 277
Feathered Hydroid 259
Fire Coral 274
Florida Sea Cucumber 318
Forbes' Common Sea
Star 189
Ghost Crab 144
Green Encrusting
Tunicate 237
Keyhole Urchin 202
Labyrinthine Brain Coral 279
Land Hermit Crab 156
Large Star Coral 285
Lentil Sea Spider 199
Loggerhead Sponge 281
Long-armed Octopus 182
Long-spined Sea
Biscuit 206
Long-spined Urchin 198
Northern Sea Pork 236
Painted Tunicate 100
Pink Shrimp 166
Pink-tipped Anemone 268
Porous Coral 284
Portuguese Man-of- war 218

Red-lined Cleaning
Shrimp 169
Reef Starlet Coral 280
Ringed Anemone 269
Rock-boring Urchin 195
Sargassum Crab 136
Sea Fans 271
Sea Plumes 264
Sea Whip 267
Slate Pencil Urchin 194
Spiral-gilled Tube
Worm 251
Sponge Crab 151
Spotted Cleaning
Shrimp 165
Spotted Sea Hare 207
Staghorn Coral 273
Starlet Coral 289
Stinker Sponge 282
Thorny Sea Star 190
Upside-down Jellyfish 221
Variegated Urchin 205
West Indies Spiny
Lobster 161

Fishes
Banded Butterflyfish 369
Bigeye 339
Blue Parrotfish 345
Blue Tang 366
Bonefish 404
Cobia 408
Diamond Killifish 394
Foureye Butterflyfish 367
French Angelfish 362
Gray Angelfish 361
Gray Snapper 374
Jewfish 377
Longspine Squirrelfish 340
Nassau Grouper 382
Oyster Toadfish 427
Porkfish 371
Princess Parrotfish 343
Queen Angelfish 363
Queen Parrotfish 344
Reef Butterflyfish 368
Rock Hind 383
Sand Perch 379
Sergeant Major 370
Sharpnose Puffer 349
Snook 406
Spanish Hogfish 342
Spotted Moray 431
Yellowtail Damselfish 337

MANGROVE SHORES

Red Mangrove
Rhizophora mangle
447

Black Mangrove
Avicennia nitidia
446

Frons Oyster
Dendeostrea frons
110

In southern Florida, there is a unique shoreline that is neither land nor sea nor easily visited by humans. It consists of one of the largest mangrove swamp areas in the world, created by several kinds of trees known collectively as mangroves. A mangrove swamp is the tropical or subtropical equivalent of the temperate and northern salt marsh. Like cordgrass and other marsh plants, mangroves not only tolerate salt water, they also must have it to grow. They invade shallow tidal waters, eventually converting them to higher and drier land by stabilizing the muddy sediment and adding new soil. Where they grow from shallow sand banks off the Florida coast, they can be responsible for creating new islands that rise above sea level.

Mangroves, with their unusual habitat preference, have been known for more than 2000 years. In 325 B.C., Nearchus—one of Alexander the Great's officers—made a brief reference to mangroves in the Persian Gulf, but it was Theophratus who, twenty years later, described both Red Mangroves and Black Mangroves in that same area and in the Red Sea.

The first Western visitor to the New World mangroves was Christopher Columbus, who, in 1494, wrote about a strange tree that grew in the shallow sea. Years later Sir Walter Raleigh mistakenly reported that oysters were produced by trees. What he saw and failed to understand was that certain oysters, mostly the Frons Oyster, commonly live attached to mangrove prop roots and are exposed at low tide. Not only oysters but also sponges, sea squirts, hydroids, sea anemones, and a variety of crustaceans grow on the submerged roots. Close inspection of a mangrove forest reveals it to be filled with creatures of every description, small and large. It is probably this animal life that first attracts visitors to a mangrove swamp; nonetheless, these swamps are difficult places for human beings. The air is extremely humid and the heat oppressive; the vast expanse of mud is unpleasantly odorous and sometimes covered with slippery mats of algae. There are biting flies and mosquitoes as well as more interesting crabs, fish, shells, and worms.

Trying to pass through a mangrove swamp is very nearly impossible because of the dense tangle of unyielding stems and prop roots, which form impenetrable thickets. The mud from which they grow is thick, soft, clinging, and very slippery. Farther back in the swamp, the erect aerial roots that rise upward from the mud in clusters make walking very difficult. Indeed, about the only way to traverse a mangrove swamp, or penetrate it even slightly, is to enter an open channel and cruise along slowly in a small shallow boat, running quietly so as not to disturb the many creatures that live in the dense foliage.

In the sun-drenched upper canopy of mangroves, five or ten yards above the water, large gleaming birds perch or make their nests, sometimes in great congregations. Although the birds are not completely free from predators, mangroves are relatively safe places compared with low inland forests. Even close to the mangrove thicket one may see climbing crabs,

Raccoon
Procyon lotor

White Mangrove
Laguncularia racemosa
445

darting anole lizards, insects, and air-breathing snails. Other crabs run across the soft mud, while far back in the shadows a rail creeps along, a Raccoon peers out, or a snake moves slowly from one prop root to another.

Only in a few areas of the Everglades National Park are visitors able to get close to a mangrove swamp on foot, walking along elevated boardwalks. Such an opportunity should not be missed, for the mangrove complex is one of the most fascinating and ecologically important coastlines.

Range

Mangroves cannot survive where frosts are common. They extend northward along the Florida Atlantic Coast as far as the Cape Canaveral area, where they exist as isolated trees or, at most, a narrow fringe along estuaries. Red Mangroves are almost nonexistent here; the species that survive are Black Mangroves and White Mangroves.

The great mangrove swamps of southern Florida are among the most extensive in the world. They begin in Biscayne Bay but develop most abundantly along the southwestern portion of the peninsula. They flourish northward along the west coast past the Ten Thousand Islands in Gullivan Bay. The myriad mangrove islands of this region of the Gulf Coast probably grew from shallow sandbars, where the seedlings of pioneering Red Mangroves were able to take root. Some of the islands have merged, and more will do so, the inner ones eventually joining with the coastline to form new land. On a smaller scale, the same thing is happening in Whitewater Bay behind Cape Sable.

In southwestern Florida, the belt of mangrove vegetation ranges from a third of a mile wide to three and even four miles wide in some spots. As far as six miles inland, mangroves line river banks, growing upon thick peat soils that in turn lie on top of ancient coral reefs and beach ridges. The spearhead penetration of mangroves inland has taken over tropical marshes that once existed alongside open bodies of water.

On the west coast of Florida, almost precisely opposite Cape Canaveral (at 28° N. latitude), mangroves grow increasingly sparse around Tampa and the Crystal River. Here too they begin being replaced by salt marshes, the grasses of which are able to withstand the frosts that are lethal to their southern counterparts. Beyond the Crystal River, only Black Mangrove stands are able to survive.

Black Mangroves are also established in certain areas of the Louisiana coast west of the Mississippi River, but the only other place in the United States where Red Mangroves are found is Hawaii.

Features

The region in which mangroves grow in southern Florida reaches closer to the tropical zone than any other part of the continental United States, with mild and equable temperatures. Winter temperatures average above the mangrove's limit of 64° F, and damaging frosts are rare or lacking. Only one hundred miles north, however, the climatic

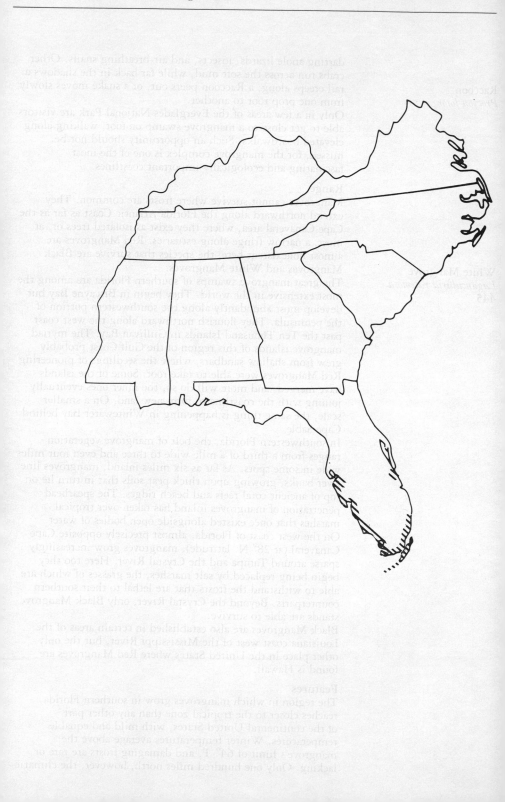

zone changes, and coastal mangroves disappear along with other tropical plants that are unable to flourish within an increased range of seasonal differences.

The substrate beneath most mangrove shores and islands is sand, although these forests may also grow on an old, raised, rock-hard coral bottom. In Florida the pioneer plant is the Red Mangrove, which becomes established upon limey sands of organic origin as well as on those composed largely of glassy silica (crushed quartz, feldspar, and other minerals). This pioneer will also readily colonize bare mud. Seedlings must take root in shallow areas, where the water seldom rises more than six inches over the young plants. Silting of the region around the first plants greatly accelerates the growth of new seedlings and the establishment of a permanent colony, but silt accumulation can occur only where currents and wave action are quiet.

As the mangroves produce leaves and prop roots, loose plant material and sediment are trapped within the thickening tangle, creating a muddy substrate. The prop root systems serve as effective barriers against erosion of the accumulated silt, allowing thick deposits to build up. The mangrove colonization, therefore, is dynamic; the silting process allows the colony to push farther out to sea; as it does so, the water becomes shallower, allowing everything composing the shoreline to advance seaward and creating changes in substrate and soil, in water depth and in salinity. In turn, these alterations bring about changes in vegetation as new species invade the region left by the advancing Red Mangrove. Inland, on the protected side of a mature stand of Red Mangroves, the Black Mangrove begins to appear in clusters. Still later and farther inland, the White Mangrove and other salt-tolerant plants take over as the Black Mangrove advances, following its Red Mangrove predecessor. Farthest inland of all, Buttonwood and a variety of hardwoods become the established climax forest of the region. Not only are mangrove swamps and forests zoned in this fashion, they alter the very nature of the coastal land by their own needs and invasive way of life—for as the mangroves move out to sea, they leave behind the proper environment for the establishment of the climax forest that follows.

For example, within the dense, suffocating mud on which they grow, all mangroves have problems obtaining oxygen for the essential life functions within their root systems. Immediately beneath the mud bottom, a Red Mangrove's roots spread widely; just a little farther down into the mud, oxygen is absent and only hydrogen sulfide, a foul-smelling gas produced by organic decay, is present. The tiny root hairs of the Red Mangrove are primary (that is, closest to the soil) absorptive cells emerging from root tips that grow only from the roots closest to the surface of the mud. Air is taken directly into roots through small pores, called lenticels, scattered over the exposed portion of prop roots.

In another adaptation, Black Mangroves lack the prop roots that are characteristic of Red Mangroves because they grow in

Buttonwood
Conocarpus erectus

Gumbo Limbo
Bursera simarouba

Sweetbay
Magnolia virginiana

Cabbage Palmetto
Sabal palmetto

Slash Pine
Pinus elliottii

Saw Palmetto
Serenoa repens

more densely consolidated mud that offers better support. Yet oxygen is still lacking, so Black Mangroves send up aerial "roots," or pneumatophores, that project into the air or into water when the tide is exceptionally high. In either case, they secure oxygen for subterranean root tissues and their vital respiratory processes. Black Mangrove stems and aerial roots are washed or covered only by the highest tides, for by the time the trees have produced so much growth, enough new muddy soil has accumulated to raise the land level. They stand exposed on the new land first created by the Red Mangroves.

As more organic material builds up around Black Mangroves, the soil level rises even higher. Other trees take hold and grow as the first two kinds of mangrove slowly advance seaward in successive generations: White Mangrove and Buttonwood; Gumbo Limbo; and plants of the hardwood hammocks, such as Sweet Bay, Cabbage Palmetto, and Saw Grass, begin to appear. Still farther back on even higher land, one finds Slash Pine and Saw Palmetto.

The building of new coastal lands and shorelines by living organisms has important geological consequences both for the land and for the shallow surrounding sea. Entirely new kinds of sediments are laid down, and chemical changes occur that affect subsequent life. Fossil evidence of both Red and Black mangroves and Buttonwoods from Gulf Coast deposits almost sixty million years old prove that this is nothing new. It is a well-established process that continues today.

Florida and its southern mangrove swamps have not always had the same boundaries, for deep beneath south Florida is an ancient rocky plain that has only occasionally been exposed. Florida as we know it today has been elevated to its present level for approximately twenty million years, but the sea level has not always been the same. During the several periods of glaciation and melting in the past million years, the seas have fallen and risen significantly, creating slow but continual changes for plants and animals living along the shoreline. The mangrove community, then, has constantly been faced with challenges and opportunities for survival and change.

At present, sea level rise is less than two centimeters (three-fourths of an inch) in a hundred years. Such a rate would seem to be of little consequence, but its effect on a very nearly flat shoreline translates into rather considerable horizontal differences. Mangroves work well under changing conditions, and their activity is a bit more than might be expected: not only do they add more land by advancing seaward, but they are doing so in the face of a rising sea level or a submerging coastline. The accretion of the soil they produce exceeds the rate of land subsidence. Also, as the sea level rises and floods inland through bays and estuaries, and as the soil becomes more saline, conditions are established for Red Mangroves to invade the region as well, thereby broadening their area of dominance. These are the reasons the mangrove swamp area of southwestern Florida is so enormous.

While tides have some effect upon the establishment and

nourishment of mangroves, they are also responsible for flushing out the loose surface mud and carrying nutrients away to the coastal seas. It is apparent that mangroves must be tolerant of small tidal differences: Along southeastern Florida, tides are regular and semidaily, while along southwestern Florida, they are semidaily but irregular, a condition that persists along part of the Gulf Coast. Tides for the region have minimal limiting effects upon the hardy mangroves.

Dense stands of mangroves have a profound effect upon waves that approach the shore. Whether these waves are of ordinary size and force, or powerful and driven by gale-force winds, mangroves hold fast and immediately quiet the waves that crash against their tangled thickets. Water levels may rise with onshore storm winds, but the force of the waves is eliminated by the tough, resilient stems and prop roots of these remarkable plants. The result is that a mangrove island or shoreline is a haven for animal life during storms, making it possible for many small creatures to emerge later to repopulate nearby devastated areas.

Mangroves may withstand storms and gales, but hurricanes are another matter. Florida is in the hurricane track and is periodically ravaged by these enormous and dangerous cyclonic storms. Major hurricanes are capable of destroying entire ecosystems, wiping out large tracts of mangrove swamp.

Fires are also significant ecological factors. Some are the result of natural phenomena, but too many have been set, accidentally or purposely, by people. After a period of decay and cleansing, succession patterns may recommence, with pioneering Red Mangroves paving the way for other species. Fires can release nutrients, but severe fires bring destruction so complete that recovery may be greatly delayed or even impossible if erosion alters the nature of the ecosystem.

The human impact upon mangrove shorelines has also been heavy and damaging. Because the swamps are recognized as not being fit for human habitation, too often they are considered wastelands to be altered or obliterated. Extensive regions have been completely destroyed by removing all the plants and filling with wet soil. In other places, the muddy lands have been ditched to drain, with water confined between concrete seawalls to provide channels for the passage of pleasure boats. Mangrove swamps, with all their varied wildlife, once stood where residential and amusement areas, served by dredged canals to allow yacht traffic, now lie. There is no question that housing is needed and that it is desirable to have waterfront property, but we fail to realize that mangrove shores are some of the most productive and stabilizing lands on earth and that they are a haven for a multitude of specialized and irreplaceable creatures.

Ecology

The Red Mangrove, advancing into the shallow sea, is the most evident plant to visitors passing just offshore. It is also highly unusual in its reproduction and means of survival. Mangroves tolerate salt water, but first they must rid themselves of the salt itself before using the water in their photosynthetic processes. Some species of mangrove do this by means of special salt-secreting glands; others prevent salt from entering their tissues at the cell membranes.

Both the Red Mangrove and the Black Mangrove grow in dense, decaying mud that denies them oxygen; for this reason, they must obtain the vital gas by special means. As already described, a Red Mangrove produces prop roots with pores, while the Black Mangrove sends up aerial roots, or pneumatophores. Both have vessels within these root systems that conduct air—with its component oxygen—deep into living root tissues.

The sediment that accumulates beneath mangroves, especially the Red Mangrove, is composed of decaying fragments of leaves, twigs, bark, and logs. Bits of vegetable matter are first worked over by larger creatures such as crabs and snails, after which this organic material is reduced to a smaller and simpler form by bacteria and yeasts. A prodigious amount of the detrital material is flushed out to sea by tides, as much as 7800 pounds per acre per year. In the ocean, this detritus nourishes offshore bottom grasses and planktonic organisms that, in turn, form the basis for complex food webs.

In the mangrove swamp, the detritus-laden mud is a direct food source for young shrimp, crabs, small fishes, worms, and filter-feeding clams. This mud is inhabited by, and consumed by, a wide variety of bacteria, single-celled protozoans, microscopic algae, and fungi. More than twenty species of small invertebrate animals depend directly upon this nutritious mud in Florida waters, as do six species of juvenile fishes. Mangrove swamp mud, therefore, is biologically and ecologically vital to the region, despite its thick consistency and heavy odor, neither of which is pleasant to humans.

Because of the decay and general lack of oxygen just below the surface, peat tends to form as the typical soil in the swamp. Peat releases acids into the water, and this slight acidity sometimes affects mollusks, such as oysters and snails, by thinning and weakening their calcareous shells; occasionally the shells may become so weak that they erode or break, with lethal results for the animals.

Reproduction of the Red Mangrove is unlike that of any other shoreline plant. The flowers are quite large and grow in clusters of twos or threes. The flower parts, both petals and reproductive organs, are arranged in fours or multiples of four. How Red Mangroves are pollinated is not clear; insects are not frequent visitors to the flowers, so wind may be the agent of pollen dispersal. Once pollination has occurred and the embryo begins to grow within the ovary, the resulting fruit does not detach from the flower stem. Instead, it germinates as a long, dartlike, bottom-heavy seedling, protruding as much as twelve inches through the two seed "leaves," or cotyledons. The developing seedling is retained by the parent plant as it grows to its full length, and nutrients and water are provided by the tree that bore it. Eventually the seedling becomes too heavy to remain attached and drops off. If it falls into the water, it immediately floats away in a horizontal position. The upper portion—consisting of embryo and seed leaves—is slightly elevated above the water level, where light and oxygen are available. The seedling can float and live in this condition for months before coming to rest, but as it grows, its center of gravity shifts, and the penlike root drops below the surface until the entire seedling floats upright. As soon as it comes to rest against a sandy or muddy shoreline, internal activity and growth commence: The juvenile root digs in, and, often within hours, small prop root buds begin their growth outward to stabilize the young plant.

If there is little or no water underneath when the seedling drops, it spears the soft mud and immediately begins to grow. Under these conditions, it may develop straight upward for a longer period than usual before sending out the characteristic prop roots. In such cases, the little mangrove has planted itself as effectively as any gardener could do. As noted earlier, the tiny absorptive root hairs needed to take in nutrients and water are restricted to those portions of the main root system just under the surface of the mud. The roots grow deeply purely to serve as anchors against storm winds and waves, not for absorption of nutrients. As the layers of oxygenless mud accumulate, the role of the prop roots with their many air pores, or lenticels, becomes increasingly important. Subsurface roots may actually turn and grow upward to bring root hairs closer to the surface of the bottom.

Mangrove Zonation

Red Mangroves live only in shallow water, and in southern Florida the rise and fall of tides requires exposed portions of prop roots to be submerged approximately forty percent of the time. As detritus accumulates around the prop roots, water depth diminishes or vanishes completely, leaving only mud, even at high tide. This chain of events creates conditions that are no longer suitable for the Red Mangrove, and the Black Mangrove takes over.

Although Black Mangroves grow in peaty muds left by the advancing Red Mangroves, they too have similar problems obtaining oxygen for their subterranean root tissues. They solve this dilemma by sending up large numbers of erect, foot-high aerial roots, or pneumatophores, that look like woody spikes surrounding the tree. Each pneumatophore has internal channels that allow the passage of oxygen downward for the respiration of living root cells.

As the accumulation of detritus and mud continues to elevate and extend the land seaward, the Black Mangrove is replaced by White Mangrove, Buttonwood, and other plants. These latest arrivals must still tolerate a degree of saltiness in the soil and occasional flooding by high storm tides. By the time these plants arrive, however, the soil surface is looser, and air can penetrate it, so the need for aerial roots—whether spikes or props—with lenticels, or pores, no longer exists. The plants in this last zone live much like those in any inland forest, not feeling the effects of salt or tidal submersion.

In south Florida's great mangrove swamps, trees seldom grow higher than about twenty feet, but up the Gulf Coast in the Ten Thousand Island region they become much larger. In the Shark River region, some mangroves reach a height of more than eighty feet, with a circumference of more than seven feet. It is not the size of the trees that makes mangrove swamps and forests so ecologically important, but their vast expanse. In Florida alone, they are estimated to cover more than 1000 square miles.

Although Florida is the only place in the continental United States where all three species of mangrove form a well-developed swamp area, Black Mangroves grow in dense thickets along the bayous of islands off the Louisiana coast west of the Mississippi delta. Here they are the pioneers, barely managing to survive when damaging frosts occur.

In mangrove swamp forests, there is an almost complete absence of the climbing, ropy vines that are so characteristic of inland tropical forests. There is also a scarcity of epiphytes, or air plants, in the branches of host trees; even parasites are rare on mangroves—none of these plants can tolerate salt water. The mangroves have a hard enough life as it is, because their saltwater environment creates a kind of physiological drought condition. To assure themselves of sufficient water, they store water in special tissues in their leaves.

Animal Life in Mangrove Swamps

Since a mangrove swamp is a broad, protected transitional zone between sea and land, it provides a specialized habitat for animals that is unlike any other. Just as the plants are broadly zoned according to the water level, as well as the gradually increasing height of newly accumulated land, animal life also differs from one zone to the next.

Offshore from the mangroves, the shallow sea bottom is of sand, marl (clay with limey deposits), or coral, or is overgrown with Turtle Grass. There, marine life consists of fishes, crustaceans, mollusks, and other creatures, and it is similar to that of any other warm, illuminated coastal region. But where the prop roots of Red Mangroves form tangled thickets, new conditions are established. It is possible for the careful visitor to walk or snorkel in the shallow water close to the tangle of roots and look beneath the surface. Long- and short-spined sea urchins are common, and crabs and an occasional spiny lobster may be seen. The tangle is a nursery for young fishes, but older individuals may also be seen among the hordes of juveniles. Mangrove Snappers and Schoolmasters, grunts (*Haemulon* spp.), Snook, and Tarpon may feed or hide there. The Sailfin Molly, Mosquitofish, and various killifishes (*Fundulus* spp.) are among its smaller fishes.

Close inspection of the underwater portion of prop roots reveals an astonishing assemblage of marine life, most of it animals that are permanently attached or that move slowly along the tough woody roots and stems. Colorful sponges and colonial sea squirts, or tunicates, are common. Sea squirts have a free-swimming larval stage that may well have played an

Turtle Grass
Thalassia testudinum
468

Schoolmaster
Lutjanus apodus

Snook
Centropomus undecimalus
406

Tarpon
Megalops atlanticus
402

Sailfin Molly
Poecilia latipinna
396

Mosquitofish
Gambusia affinis
392

Mangrove Tunicate
Ecteinascidia turbinata
235

Painted Tunicate
Clavelina picta
231

Flat Tree Oyster
Isognomon alatus
112

Florida Crown Conch
Melongena corona
36, 124

Rose Petal Tellin
Tellina lineata

Eastern Melampus
Melampus bidentatus
74

Coffee Melampus
Melampus coffeus
73

Bubble Melampus
Melampus bullaoides
75

Admirable Pedipes
Pedipes mirabilis

Beaded Pira
Pira monile

Hubbard's Top
Strobilops hubbardi stevensoni

Angulate Periwinkle
Littorina scabra angulifera

Blue Crab
Callinectes sapidus
147

important role in the evolution of all chordates and vertebrates by providing the basic plan upon which subsequent developments elaborated. The Mangrove Tunicate, a colorless, transparent creature with yellow or pink internal organs, lives in spiral clusters on submerged prop roots. The Painted Tunicate, so named because of the red and purple bands on its body and colorful internal organs, may live in colonies of more than a thousand individuals growing upon underwater mangrove roots. Both species are filter feeders, drawing in water and expelling it through a pair of siphons, and extracting planktonic food in the process.

Other creatures live in profusion on the roots: Delicate hydroids sway in the gentle currents; sea anemones spread their fleshy, stinging tentacles; barnacles rhythmically sweep the water for planktonic algae and microscopic animals. Often the most abundant and obvious attached creature is the ragged-looking Frons Oyster, which clings in large clusters to the prop roots by means of fingerlike extensions along the margin of its shell. Another kind of oyster, the very thin Flat Tree Oyster, grows in large and compact clumps in the same habitat. The larger Crown Conch may be found nearby preying upon the sedentary oysters.

The underwater scene becomes more complex when red and green algae grow from the roots, providing patches of new color and new grazing opportunities for herbivorous animals. Small mollusks are everywhere, but they are not always obvious at first glance. The beautifully delicate Rose Petal Tellin can be abundant, although completely hidden in burrows deep within the mud. Its presence is detected only by a scattering of dead shells lying on the surface.

The most common mollusks are snails, in seemingly endless variety. Eastern Melampus and Coffee Melampus snails are numerous, and although similar, they have different preferences in their food and places to live. The former are common on roots and the back reaches of a mangrove swamp, where they climb up into the air on vegetation at high tide. At low tide, when they browse on the mud, they are almost invisible, looking like small irregularities of the surface. The Coffee Melampus feeds among decaying mangrove leaves at low tide, where it deposits its eggs under rotting logs. A reclusive relative, another air breather with a small saclike lung, has a highly specialized habitat: It lives in burrows deep inside decaying mangrove logs that lie only at the high-tide mark. Still other members of the same family that live on mangrove roots and debris include the Bubble Melampus and the Admirable Pedipes. Two other snails, the Beaded Pira and Hubbard's Top, are both common to the Florida mangrove swamps, but it is the Angulate Periwinkle that is one of the most characteristic of all mangrove snails living on roots and branches above the high-tide mark.

With patient exploration, a mangrove swamp can soon be seen to crawl with crabs. Blue Crabs swim in shallow water, only clinging to submerged roots when they are in the vulnerable condition of shedding their exoskeleton (outer shell) in order

Fiddler
Uca pugilator
142

Mangrove Mud Crab
Eurytium limosum

Land Hermit Crab
Coenibita clypeata
136

Mangrove Tree Crab
Aratus pisonii

Green Anole
Anolis carolinensis
440

Mangrove Diamondback
Terrapin
*Malaclemys terrapin
rhizophorarum*
435

Mangrove Water Snake
*Neroidia fasciata
compressicauda*
443

Cottonmouth
Agkistrodon pisicivorus
442

Marsh Rabbit
Sylvilagus palustris paludicola

to grow larger. Other than that, they are aggressive and formidable creatures. Some of the more readily seen crabs are those that have forsaken life in the water except to release eggs. Nearly all crabs must spend time as planktonic larvae, but many spend their adult lives on land.

The Fiddler is probably the most abundant crab in the mangrove swamp. It scurries about the exposed mud surface at high tide, feeding upon organic detritus. The rich mud, consisting of fine organic particles, is the sole food of Fiddlers. They have special mouth parts that are able to separate the nutritious material from the silty mud, leaving the latter deposited across the surface as little "pills" or pellets. A male Fiddler has one greatly enlarged claw that is useless as a feeding appendage but is waved as a signal to other males encroaching upon his territory; it also serves as a rather ineffectual weapon and, to some degree, as a plug to the burrow. Both males and females burrow deeply into the soft mud, where they retreat when the tide rises, usually plugging the openings with pellets of mud.

The Mangrove Mud Crab, with its colorful orange and white claws, forages among mangrove debris, keeping its gills moist for respiration. The Land Hermit Crab has the ability to retreat inside its snail-shell shelter not only for protection but also to keep its own gills from drying out when it is out in the open for long periods. Another crab that lives high in the foliage, the Mangrove Tree Crab, releases its hold on a branch and drops straight down into the water when it is alarmed. More than one naturalist struggling to pass through the tangle of mangrove stems and roots has been startled by an active, frightened crab landing on his head or shoulders.

For many visitors, the most striking inhabitants of mangrove swamps are the vertebrates, chiefly the birds. There are reptiles present, however, including the familiar Green Anole Lizard, which is found throughout the southern states and is not restricted to mangrove areas. There are several other species of anole in southern Florida, some of which have taken up residence in mangrove swamps, but all except the Green Anole have been introduced to Florida from Caribbean islands. The Mangrove Diamondback Terrapin, a handsome and rather ornate aquatic turtle, wanders through the warm waters of a mangrove thicket in search of worms, snails, and small clams. The Mangrove Water Snake, while harmless to humans, is often frightening because it is irritable and may be confused with the Florida Cottonmouth, which tends to live further inland in freshwater conditions. The Mangrove Water Snake is a good swimmer and feeds primarily upon fishes and crustaceans in the shallow water.

The two mammals most often encountered in mangrove swamps are also found over large regions of North America, far removed from coasts and the specialized vegetation of coastal swamps. The Marsh Rabbit finds a favorable habitat among the mangroves and their associated vegetation away from open water. The vegetation cover is so thick that the animal's presence is usually indicated only by its distinctive tracks. The Marsh Rabbit can swim or float low in the water if pursued, becoming even more difficult to see. The other mammal of the mangrove swamp, the Raccoon, is one of the best known of all American animals. It is an opportunist wherever it lives, and those that inhabit southern Florida find mangrove swamps good places in which to hunt or scavenge for their varied diet.

Unlike mammals and reptiles, the birds of Florida's mangrove regions are strikingly obvious. There are only a few secretive ones, and birds catch the eye in every part of a mangrove forest. What is more, the noise of the mangrove bird community can be nearly deafening to humans close by, with croaks, squawks, and grunts constantly emerging from the thousands of birds nesting in the large rookeries.

Great Egret
Casmerodius albus
562

For example, the male and female Great Egret take turns at incubating duties at the nest; during the changing of the guard, there is a great deal of loud croaking that accompanies plumage displays. This species' nests are conspicuous affairs constructed of sticks and lined with Spanish Moss brought from inland trees. The nests are interspersed among those of several other heron species throughout the mangrove thickets. After the breeding season, Great Egrets disperse throughout the United States, especially to the South and both coasts, at times penetrating as far north as southern Canada.

Mangrove swamps seem made to order for heron rookeries.

Tricolored Heron
Egretta tricolor
568

The Tricolored Heron breeds in very large colonies, constructing nests of rushes or sticks in the lowest mangroves. It feeds chiefly on several species of killifish, which are abundant in the shallows of the mangrove areas. The beautiful Snowy Egret nests in equally large colonies, interspersed among those of the Tricolored and Little Blue heron. Snowy Egrets were brought to the verge of extinction earlier in the century because of their decorative courtship plumes, which were sought for millinery. After legislation was enacted barring the collection of birds for their feathers, their populations slowly recovered.

Snowy Egret
Egretta thula
563

Little Blue Heron
Egretta caerulea
564, 570

Green-backed Heron
Butorides striatus
571

Green Herons place their nests close to the water on the prop roots of Red Mangrove, sometimes no more than six inches above the water's surface. This spot is also the chosen nesting site of the Boat-tailed Grackle; the Green Heron, finding an old grackle nest, may build its own directly on top of the other.

Boat-tailed Grackle
Quiscalus major
607

White Ibis
Eudocimus albus
561

Other large birds also favor mangroves as nesting places. The White Ibis, a highly gregarious bird that constructs its nest of twigs and leaves low off the muddy ground, breeds in mangrove thickets, where its young are raised, but it feeds inland primarily upon freshwater crayfish. The Roseate Spoonbill is distinctive not only because of its attractive red, pink, and orange coloration but also because of its remarkable flattened, spoon-shaped bill. The bird swings the bill back and forth in long arcs through the water, where it sifts out shellfish, crustaceans, and fish fry. It chooses dense mangrove thickets for its sturdy nests, which are constructed of sticks and lined with strips of moss and bark.

Roseate Spoonbill
Ajaia ajaja
559

Mangrove Cuckoo
Coccyzus minor
611

Black-whiskered Vireo
Vireo altiloquus
615

Wood Stork
Mycteria americana
560

Double-crested Cormorant
Phalacrocorax auritus
575

Brown Pelican
Pelecanus occidentalis
519

Osprey
Pandion haliaetus
605

Some birds of the mangroves live only in this one habitat; the Mangrove Cuckoo, for example, is found almost exclusively in these thickets. Because of the plentiful food supply—consisting mainly of caterpillars, grasshoppers, mantids, and spiders—the Mangrove Cuckoo is able to raise two broods of young a year in its flat twig nest. The Black-whiskered Vireo is also found mainly in mangrove swamps along southern and southwestern Florida. It nests in the forks of branches and hunts primarily for spiders, which live in such large numbers in the thickets.

Other birds that may be more widely distributed nevertheless find mangrove forests excellent places in which to breed and raise their young, spend the winter, or feed. The large Wood Stork can be locally abundant in Florida mangroves, and, in places, its nests may almost touch one another. In the muddy shallows it stamps around, causing fish and invertebrates to come to the surface; as each creature does so, the stork strikes and kills it, leaving it lying there. When a good number have been assembled, the bird eats its catch all at once.

Mangrove swamps are host to the Double Crested Cormorant, a widely distributed coastal bird that finds the thickets excellent nesting sites. This preference is evidently shared by the Brown Pelican, which constructs bulky nests of green twigs in the low branches of mangroves. Even the great Osprey sometimes builds its huge nests high in the tops of the tallest mangroves.

In retrospect, what makes mangrove shores so important in an ecological sense and so rewarding to study is their transformation of one kind of coastline into an entirely different habitat that previously did not exist there. Before the first mangrove seedling takes root along a coral shore or a coarse beach or a muddy estuary, plant and animal life is of one sort. After the thick tangle of mangroves becomes established, a whole new ecosystem comes into existence.

The prop roots of Red Mangroves stand mostly submerged in shallow water, exposed only part of the time during extremely low tide. They offer, perhaps for the first time in the region, a firm and secure surface to a host of attaching marine organisms, both plant and animal. Some forms of life, such as oysters and algae, are cemented in place; others, such as snails and crabs, move about but seldom leave the prop roots. The emergent stems, branches, higher prop roots, and leaves of mangroves support a host of terrestrial and aerial animals: reptiles, insects, birds, and mammals. The upper levels of mangroves provide some of the most crowded and productive roosting and nesting sites for birds anywhere along the southern coastline.

Tracing the zones of a mangrove shore from open water to inland regions, the level of accumulated sediment and mud rises higher, until it is finally no longer washed even by the highest tides. A whole new continental margin has been established over many years—by the action of pioneering mangroves.

MANGROVE SHORES: ANIMALS

Seashells
Bubble Melampus 75
Coffee Melampus 73
Eastern Melampus 74
Flat Tree Oyster 112
Florida Crown Conch 36,
124
Frons Oyster 110
Virgin Nerite 67

Seashore Creatures
Blue Crab 147
Brackish Water
Fiddler 143
Mangrove Tunicate 235
Painted Tunicate 231
Variegated Urchin 205

Fishes
Gray Snapper 374
Killifish 393
Mosquitofish 392
Sailfin Molly 396
Snook 406
Tarpon 402

Reptiles and Amphibians
American Crocodile 438
Florida Cottonmouth 442
Green Anole 440
Southern Water Snake 443

Birds
American
Oystercatcher 576
Anhinga 574
Belted Kingfisher 602
Black-whiskered
Vireo 615
Boat-tailed Grackle 607
Brown Pelican 519
Double-crested
Cormorant 575
Great Egret 562
Green-backed Heron 571
Little Blue Heron 564,
570
Mangrove Cuckoo 611
Osprey 605
Purple Gallinule 600
Roseate Spoonbill 559
Snowy Egret 563
Tricolored Heron 568
White Ibis 561

Wood Stork 560
Yellow-crowned Night
Heron 573
Yellow-rumped
Warbler 618

Mammal
Manatee 331

GULF SHORES

For many centuries, the vast and varied Gulf of Mexico has been the focus of energetic study and exploration. Knowledge of the region has been accumulating since Christopher Columbus first sailed close by in 1492. Amerigo Vespucci, whose name is permanently associated with the New World, apparently was the first European to visit actual shoreline portions of the Gulf. A host of explorers who followed him, some well-known and some not, added information concerning this great body of water. Yet for many hundreds of years before the time of Columbus, parts of the Gulf were thoroughly familiar to native Americans living along its shores. In particular, the Aztecs developed detailed and accurate systems of navigation and maps, and they and other Indians of Central America sailed through the Gulf in vessels fully as large as any operated by the Spanish.

Today's visitors to the Gulf Coast do not find just a single characteristic pattern to the shoreline. It varies enormously with respect to its geology, topography, vegetation, and marine life. Coral shores, alluvium, limestone plateaus, sand dunes, tidal flats, salt-evaporation basins, beaches, mangrove ridges, lagoons, barrier islands, deltas and bayous, mud flats, and salt marshes are all part of the Gulf.

Some of the types of coastline here are considerably more ancient than others; some are dominated by the continent and others by the sea. Inshore waters are without exception shallow as a result of a wide shelf that extends out to the hundred-fathom mark, many miles offshore. Even at its center, the Gulf lacks the great depths of the Atlantic Ocean.

Because generalizations are impossible for this conglomeration of habitats, several of the more prominent and interesting types of shoreline and inshore associations of life are described below. It must be remembered, however, that the difference —measured by perhaps only a few miles—between a sandy beach ridge and a delta's muddy alluvial fan are so great that comparisons are very difficult to make.

Range

The Gulf of Mexico, a body of water covering approximately 615,000 square miles, is very nearly an inland sea. Its entrance is pinched together by Florida and the Yucatán Peninsula of Mexico, with Cuba lying in the middle directly between the two. Florida, Alabama, Mississippi, Louisiana, and Texas line the eastern, northern, and part of the western shores, while Mexico and the Yucatán comprise the remainder. Although the Florida mainland is a limestone plain, most of its shoreline from the southern tip and the Keys and the north along the west coast is of living origin. It includes patches of ancient and modern coral growth and broad expanses of mangrove swamps, including the multitude of mangrove islands in the Ten Thousand Island region of western Florida. All the rest of the Gulf Coast (the United States portion) is composed of alluvial sandy and muddy sediments derived long ago from ancient rivers and glaciers. Barrier islands border much of the Gulf, creating additional habitats.

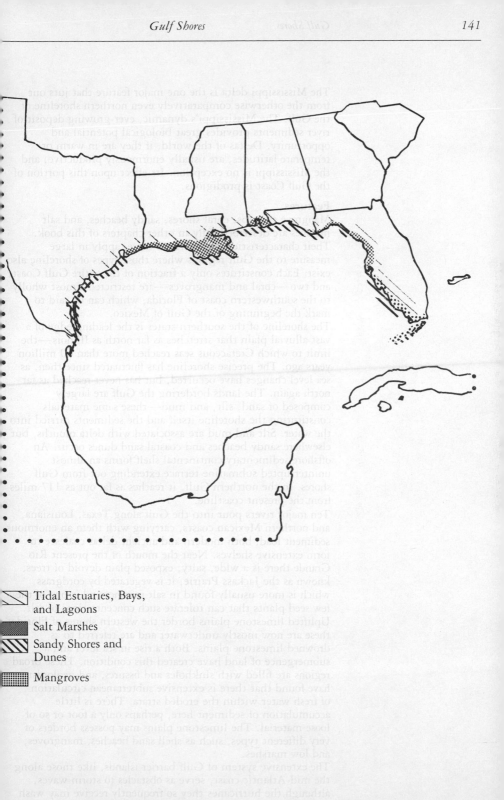

Tidal Estuaries, Bays, and Lagoons

Salt Marshes

Sandy Shores and Dunes

Mangroves

The Mississippi delta is the one major feature that juts out from the otherwise comparatively even northern shoreline of the Gulf. The Mississippi's dynamic, ever-growing deposit of river sediments provides great biological potential and opportunity. Deltas of the world, if they are in warm or temperate latitudes, are usually enormously productive, and the Mississippi is no exception. Its effect upon this portion of the Gulf Coast is prodigious.

Features

Mangrove swamps, coral shores, sandy beaches, and salt marshes are described fully in other chapters of this book. Their characteristics, as described there, apply in large measure to the Gulf regions where those types of shoreline also exist. Each constitutes only a fraction of the entire Gulf Coast, and two—coral and mangroves—are restricted almost wholly to the southwestern coast of Florida, which can be said to mark the beginning of the Gulf of Mexico.

The shoreline of the southern states is the leading edge of a vast alluvial plain that stretches as far north as Illinois—the limit to which Cretaceous seas reached more than 60 million years ago. The precise shoreline has fluctuated since then, as sea level changes have occurred, but has never reached as far north again. The lands bordering the Gulf are largely composed of sand, silt, and mud—these same materials constituting the shoreline itself and the sediments carried into the water. Silt and mud are associated with delta mouths, but elsewhere sandy beaches and coastal sand dunes occur. An offshore sedimentary continental shelf forms an almost uninterrupted submarine terrace extending out from Gulf shores. In the northern Gulf, it reaches as far out as 117 miles from the present coastline.

Ten major rivers pour into the Gulf along Texas, Louisiana, and northern Mexican coasts, carrying with them an enormous sediment load; both modern and ancient deltas coalesce to form extensive shelves. Near the mouth of the present Rio Grande there is a wide, salty, exposed plain devoid of trees; known as the Jackass Prairie, it is vegetated by cordgrass, which is more usually found in salt marshes and is one of the few seed plants that can tolerate such concentrations of salt.

Uplifted limestone plains border the western shores of Florida; these are now mostly underwater and are referred to as drowned limestone plains. Both a rise in sea level and a submergence of land have created this condition. These broad regions are filled with sinkholes and fissures, and geologists have found that there is extensive subterranean circulation of fresh water within the eroded strata. There is little accumulation of sediment here, perhaps only a foot or so of loose material. The limestone plains may possess borders of very different types, such as shell sand beaches, mangroves, and low marshes.

The extensive system of Gulf barrier islands, like those along the mid-Atlantic coast, serve as obstacles to storm waves, although the hurricanes they so frequently receive may wash over them with great destruction to vegetation, wildlife, and human developments. Barrier islands result from wave and current forces in the sea, but deltas are clearly the products of rivers. The Mississippi River, for example, delivers more than two million tons of sediment to its mouth each day; as river velocity is lost and the sediment drops to the bottom, it is this material that builds the delta both outward and to the sides. The finely dissected branching channels of the river throughout the delta create huge changes in shoreline conditions. River sediments drop out of suspension quickly in the Gulf of Mexico, for less than a hundred miles out from the Mississippi the water is as clear as anywhere in the world. That the river has not always emptied into the Gulf in the same spot is suggested by the discovery of an ancient, now-buried channel thirty miles from the present river mouth.

Climate, Tides, and Water Circulation

The Gulf is known for its hurricanes, four-fifths of which form far outside of the region and enter moving northwest through the Florida Straits and the Yucatán Channel. These enormous storms, which may range up to 500 miles in diameter, cause most of the damage by generating wind-driven tides and waves that crash into vulnerable inshore areas across breakwaters and seawalls.

Except for storm tides, tidal fluctuation in the Gulf of Mexico exhibits no impressive range, with a rise and fall in most places less than about one or two feet. Other than in regions with a gently sloped topography, the actual shoreline remains much the same from high to low tide, without the wide intertidal zones seen along the Atlantic Coast. On the other hand, the fluctuation in the timing of tides in the Gulf is highly complex, baffling the visitor and challenging the oceanographer. Tides throughout most of the Gulf are daily—that is, there is one high tide and one low tide every day (rather than two of each a day). In some parts of the Gulf Coast, especially southwestern Florida, there are two of each a day, but they do not resemble one another, one high tide being much higher than the following one, and one low tide much lower than the next before returning to the high level again. These are known as "mixed" tides because they occur in places where the twice-daily Atlantic tides come into conflict with Gulf tides. The effect of such tidal irregularities upon intertidal plants and animals is not fully known, although surely some effects are inevitable.

Still more complicating factors in the enclosed Gulf are winds, barometric pressure changes, and the flow of many large rivers. Each has an effect upon the rise and fall of tides; onshore winds are able to push water against the coast, and differing atmospheric pressures turn the Gulf into a huge barometer as water levels rise and fall. The contribution from rivers carrying runoff from inland sources changes with the seasons: Melting of snow and ice produce greater volumes, but during late-summer droughts smaller amounts are the rule. River flow alone can have a marked effect upon water level

along the coastal regions of this huge, almost enclosed sea.
The comfortable, predictable intertidal rhythm of the Atlantic
shore is missing from the Gulf of Mexico.
Every shoreline is bathed by ocean currents. But because the
Gulf is an almost circular basin with only two narrow
openings to the ocean beyond, the currents there are complex.
In general terms, water enters through the Yucatán Channel,
circulates around the shoreline in various patterns, then leaves
through the Florida Straits. Water flowing northward into the
Gulf from the Caribbean obviously brings warmth to the area,
which is further heated by the sun acting upon the broad
expanse. Surface temperatures range between 70° to 80° F, so
the marine life of Gulf shores is representative of near-tropical
plant and animal communities.

Ecology

The different soil and intertidal conditions along Gulf
shorelines give rise to a variety of vegetation almost beyond
accounting. Each shore habitat has its own community of
plants, many of them not found in adjacent areas. The diverse
coastal habitats to be seen in the Gulf include the following:
mud flats; shifting sandy beaches and stable sandy areas;
lagoons; channels; protected coves; bays; mangrove thickets;
tidal streams; shallows composed of sand, shell, and coral
rubble; reefs; and rocky shores. Drifting Gulfweed
(*Sargassum* spp.) may form large floating aggregates,
sometimes cast in huge windrows upon the shore. This seaweed
also drifts through the Sargasso Sea of the mid-Atlantic;
in fact, the two areas exchange some of these simple plants
when they are caught in major current flows. Almost every
other kind of red, green, and brown alga associated with
seaweeds of the world may be found in one spot or another
along the Gulf Coast, making generalization difficult.
Flowering plants growing in shallow shoreline waters can be
common where conditions are right. These highly specialized
plants of terrestrial origin form important feeding and
breeding habitats for a variety of marine creatures, many of

Manatee Grass
Syringodium filiforme

Turtle Grass
Thalassia testudinum
468

Widgeon Grass
Ruppia maritima

Horned Pondweed
Zannichellia palustris

Saltmarsh Cordgrass
Spartina alterniflora
466

which are small animals that find refuge there. Manatee Grass
and Turtle Grass are two of the five kinds of seed plants living
in the waters around the Florida Keys. Widgeon Grass and
Horned Pondweed are rarely found in salt water, but they
flourish in northern Gulf regions of reduced salinity. These
and the few other marine flowering plants of Gulf waters are
restricted to shallow, warm, clear water with bottoms
composed of sand, mud, or marl.
Salt-tolerant plant communities associated with mangrove and
Saltmarsh Cordgrass habitats grow only in certain areas,
although the salt marshes of the northern Gulf Coast are
extensive and are similar in most respects to those found along
Atlantic shores.
Even more than the plant ecology of the region, the
distribution of animals within the Gulf reveals both an
interesting historical background and relationships with
organisms in other localities. Changes in the geology of the

region have left their mark upon its biology as well. At one time, the Gulf was in direct contact with the Atlantic across the area now occupied by Florida. The Gulf Coast was simply an extension of the Atlantic shore, and many of the same animals were found widely distributed along the curving coastline. When the Florida peninsula rose and blocked access, creatures that did not find it possible to migrate through the Yucatán Channel or the Florida Straits were isolated. Minor evolutionary changes brought about slight differences in species. Nonetheless, many of the organisms along the northern Gulf Coast are almost identical to those of the mid-Atlantic coast, yet are not found along the shores of southwestern Florida or the Yucatán Peninsula. The animals in those areas are more closely related to, or the same as, tropical forms from the Caribbean. In a broad and general sense, the Gulf of Mexico has two rather different life provinces, each containing innumerable lesser habitats.

Within the 3600-mile shoreline of the United States' portion of the Gulf, there are several distinctly different kinds of biotic associations that may be seen or sampled by visitors: bottom communities, including large ones of oysters and sponges; breakwater and jetty communities; sandy beach associations; shrimp grounds; and coral communities.

Each habitat along the Gulf Coast has its own association of mollusks, with the gastropods (snails) and bivalves predominating. Only in a few instances do snails or clams from one habitat live plentifully in another, for most are specialists with highly developed adaptations. The molluskan association on a rocky outcrop or jetty is very different from that found in shallow sandy and muddy flats or near beaches. Those in lagoons or bays filled with brackish water of low salinity are not the same as those in similar bays or lagoons that are regularly flushed by seawater of high salinity. Furthermore, there are the deeper waters of the Gulf to which visitors have no access unless they are able to inspect the contents of a deep-sea dredge brought to the surface. Shell collecting along the northern Gulf states is not as rewarding as it is along the southwestern Florida coast or along the southern Texas shoreline, but a variety of interesting and specialized forms are possible to find in each of the Gulf habitats.

Bottom communities are not easily seen from the surface unless there is an exceptionally low tide. Large populations of clams are commonly found living in beds of muddy sand, in assemblages that are very similar to shrimp grounds.

Bottom Communities

By far the greatest, most complex, and most important bottom community is formed by oysters, ninety-five percent of which are the familiar edible Eastern Oyster. The Mangrove or Frons Oyster and the Crested or Horse Oyster may also be present. Along the Florida coast, the Sponge Oyster occurs, but none of these last three species is an important contributor to the building of an oyster reef.

Free-living segmented worms that are not parasitic find the

Eastern Oyster
Crassostrea virginica
11

Frons Oyster
Dendrostrea frons
10

Horse Oyster
Ostrea equestris

Sponge Oyster
Ostrea permollis

irregular surfaces of an oyster reef a perfect place to live in. About a dozen of the sixty species found in the Gulf are known to associate with oysters, not harming them in any way but benefiting from opportunities provided. Some burrow into sand or mud, usually lining their tubes with a thin, parchmentlike material. Others construct erect tubes made of calcium carbonate they secrete or sand grains selected from the bottom—that stick up into the water. The burrowers draw water into their tubes for breathing and eating, while those that live above the bottom have tentacles or featherlike fans with which they capture food.

The inshore bottom of the Gulf supports a surprising variety of marine animals. Among the many kinds of sea anemones present close to shore are the Pale Anemone, which ranges from whitish to brown, and the Warty Sea Anemone, whose dark body is covered with little bumps but whose tentacles may be bluish with reddish stripes on the back. Two other anemones do not subscribe to the usual habit of attaching to rocks, pilings, or other solid objects. A burrowing sea anemone is common in shallow Texan waters; its white columnar body lies beneath the substrate, but its tentacles are displayed from a green-and-orange rosette at the surface. An even odder sea anemone is the Balloon Anemone. It holds an air-filled float on its basal disk and hangs its mouth and tentacles downward; it is occasionally cast ashore, having traveled great distances across the Gulf.

Spiny-skinned animals, or echinoderms, are especially abundant in the Gulf, mostly in the area around the Florida Keys and Cuba. Sea urchins and sand dollars, sea stars, sea cucumbers, and sea lilies are all present, but the most abundant group is the brittle stars, with over twice as many species as any other echinoderm group in the Gulf. The Spiny Brittle Stars are likely to be found in the daytime under submerged objects. When their shelters are picked up, these agile creatures scuttle off to new hiding places.

Slate-pencil Urchins, with their heavy, thick spines, play host to many attaching organisms that find the surface of spines a good place to settle. The urchin's spines may be decorated with colorful coralline algae, encrusting sponges, or speckled crusts of bryozoans, sometimes called moss animals. Unlike brittle stars, the Slate-pencil Urchin is exposed and visible in daytime, although its many attaching colonizers help it to blend with the background.

Crustaceans, from minute members of the plankton to the large West Indies Spiny Lobster, abound in Gulf waters and along the shores. From the standpoint of human interests, by far the most important crustacean in this region is the White Shrimp, for it forms at least ninety-five percent of the commercial shrimp fishery-industry off the Louisiana and Mississippi coasts. This animal flourishes in areas where brackish inland waters are connected to shallow, high-salinity offshore seas with muddy bottoms. Several larval stages are passed at sea, where spawning occurs, but the young soon take up residence and grow rapidly in the low-salinity inland

Pale Anemone
Aiptasia pallida

Warty Sea Anemone
Bunodosoma cavernata

Spiny Brittle Star
Ophicoma echinatra

Slate-pencil Urchins
Eucidaris tribuloides
194

West Indies Spiny Lobster
Panulirus argas
161

White Shrimp
Penaeus setiferus

Muller's Sea Pansy
Renilla muelleri

Sea Whip
Leptogorgia virgulata
267

Tricolor Anemone
Calliactis tricolor

Giant Hermit Crab
Petrochirus diogenes
159

Calico Crab
Hepatus epheliticus

Flame-streaked Box Crab
Calappa flammea
153

Purse Crab
Persephona punctata

Lightning Whelk
Busycon contrarium
35

Apple Murex
Phyllonotus pomum
37

True Tulip
Fasciolaria tulipa
44, 125

Common Mantis Shrimp
Squilla empusa
167

waters. With gradually increasing size, they migrate slowly back to the sea, where they live their adult lives—and where many are harvested by shrimpers. Spawning takes place from late spring through summer; growth is most accelerated in the warm season, but it nearly stops as temperatures fall.

The shrimp ground community takes its name from this populous and important crustacean, but there are many other life forms that are characteristic of the community. The odd, flat-topped Muller's Sea Pansy looks a bit like a fleshy mushroom with polyps protruding from the top surface; it is a colonial animal related to corals and sea anemones. In places, it carpets the bottom in very large numbers. The Sea Whip, which lives in the same habitat, is a horned coral that may be red, yellow, or purple, and has long slender branches. The Tricolor Anemone, a colorful creature with hundreds of graceful tentacles, commonly lives attached to the shells occupied by the Giant Hermit Crab. Another anemone that burrows into the bottom, the Pointed Anemone, is occasionally washed out of its burrow by storms and cast upon the beach. Calico Crabs, Flame-streaked Box Crabs, and Purse Crabs stalk the bottom in search of food in the form of small organisms and detrital material. If they are quick, they may catch onuphid tube worms, which are common throughout the community. Characteristic snails of the shrimp grounds include the very large, predatory Lightning Whelk, whose shell spirals to the left—an unusual pattern in most snails. The Apple Murex and the True Tulip Snail prey upon other mollusks, the Murex preferring oysters and bivalves and the Tulip attacking large snails. The Common Mantis Shrimp is a solitary, burrowing, highly ferocious creature that makes short work of other crustaceans and invertebrates it captures with its sicklelike claws. It is also called a shrimp snapper by fishermen—who handle it with utmost caution, for it can inflict deep and painful wounds.

The northern Gulf Shore is a favorable zone for mollusks of all types, with more than 340 species known from the Texas coast alone. Off the Louisiana coast, however, the molluskan fauna, with only ninety-odd species present, appears impoverished compared with that of Texas and other more southerly shores on either side of the Gulf. There seem to be somewhat fewer species near the Mississippi delta, so one might infer that lowered salinities or increased sediment as well as temperature have a restricting effect.

Swimmers and Fliers

The fish fauna of the Gulf has several major components, two of which are not within the reach of most visitors. The deep-sea fishes of the Gulf are inaccessible and, from a geological point of view, fairly recent arrivals into this great basin. These fishes of the open Gulf swim freely into the Caribbean and the Atlantic; they are largely unseen unless they happen to be sought-after sports species. Shore fishes, however, include many familiar kinds.

Some shore species occur only in the Gulf but not in the West

Sheepshead
Archosargus probatocephalus
353

Red Drum
Scianenops ocellatus
385

Weakfish
Cynoscion regalis
386

Green Turtle
Chelonia mydas

Loggerhead Turtle
Caretta caretta
434

Hawksbill Turtle
Eretmochelys impricata

Leatherback Turtle
Dermochelys coriacea

West Indian Monk Seal
Monachus tropicalis

Indies. The distribution of other species allows them to pass through the Yucatán Channel and the Florida Straits, with the result that they may be found along the Central American coast as well as north along the Atlantic Coast. The Sheepshead, with its blunt-headed striped body, should be handled with care because of its broad, chisel-like incisor teeth and sharp spines. It is common along Gulf shores and along the Atlantic Coast but is completely absent from the Caribbean. The Red Drum has essentially the same distribution but migrates from inshore to offshore waters according to its life-cycle and the season. The silvery Weakfish, which prefers shallow inshore waters for feeding and brackish estuaries for breeding, is still another Gulf-shore fish that is also found along the Atlantic Coast but not in the Caribbean. None of the three, nor others with similar distribution patterns, are tropical fishes; experts assume that the warm Gulf Stream's path is a barrier to their dispersal into the Caribbean and the West Indies. This great ocean current is not an obstacle to a far larger number of shore fishes that now live in the Gulf but that originated in tropical West Indian waters. Therefore, the Gulf harbors a curious mix of temperate and tropical fishes living side by side, each having carved out its own ecological niche.

It is certain that the Gulf of Mexico was once a major habitat for four or five of the great sea turtles, but today these creatures range from being uncommon to almost absent, having been caught excessively by humans. The Green Turtle was once common along northern and western Gulf shores yet now is only seen frequently around the Florida Keys—and even there its numbers are greatly reduced. Shoreline nesting along the Gulf coast probably no longer exists. It is unlikely that this turtle will return without special efforts by biologists, for each Green Turtle returns with unerring accuracy to the precise beach where it was hatched.

Loggerhead Turtles, huge creatures that in former days may have reached 1000 pounds, are still found in the Gulf of Mexico, concentrated primarily toward the Florida coast. Some nesting occurs along the Gulf coasts where sandy beaches are either isolated or protected, but even the open water is hazardous for them since many are caught and drowned inadvertently in nets set by shrimp fishermen. The Hawksbill Turtle is rare anywhere in the Gulf except near the Florida Keys; fortunately it still lives in fair numbers throughout the Caribbean and can be seen off southern Florida and the Keys. The Leatherback Turtle, the largest of all sea turtles, may weigh as much as 1600 pounds. It nests occasionally along the western Florida shores but is rarely seen anywhere in the Gulf today. Because it prefers deep tropical waters, it may never have been populous in the Gulf except for nesting. Today, nesting sites everywhere are restricted, and this magnificent creature is seriously threatened with eventual extinction.

Man's excessive predation upon large and vulnerable animals is no less lamentable in the Gulf than anywhere else in the world. The West Indian Monk Seal, whose herds only 50 years

Manatee
Trichechus manatus
331

White Pelican
Pelecanus erythrorhynchos
518

Brown Pelican
Pelecanus occidentalis
519

Clapper Rail
Rallus longirostris
598

Marsh Wren
Cistothorus palustris
613

ago visited shorelines near Galveston, Texas, is now probably extinct. It was a mild-mannered animal, unsuspicious of humans who were not recognized as predators, so it was easy prey in shallows or on sandy beaches. The Manatee came under protection in Florida in 1948, barely escaping extinction. Once it was seen occasionally from New Orleans to Pensacola, and bones have been found in Louisiana and Texas. Perhaps Manatees were never numerous along the north coast of the Gulf because they are very sensitive to cold weather, and even in Florida they may succumb to its effects if caught in unfavorable locations. Normally these animals herd together in shallow water for warmth when low winter temperatures occur; otherwise, they disperse to feed in grassy shallows. The Manatee is larger than any other Gulf creature except the whale, reaching more than fifteen feet and weighing as much as 1922 pounds. It is purely herbivorous and feeds upon marine and brackish-water plants, collecting its food with extraordinarily mobile split lips as it grazes along the bottom, submerging for twelve to fifteen minutes at a time. A Manatee is unable to leave the water by itself; if one is taken out by humans, the weight of its internal organs may collapse its lungs and cause it to suffocate. While it is a slow and inoffensive creature, when alarmed or wounded it is capable of driving itself through the water with considerable power and speed in an attempt to escape.

A discussion of the birds of the Gulf Coast introduces certain complexities not affecting other creatures—simply put, some birds fly from far inland to the sea and back, passing over the shoreline entirely or resting there only briefly. Some, of course, nest there, and many feed at the water's edge or in its shallows. Certain birds are present only in the winter, finding the mild climate and warm water far preferable to the frozen northern latitudes, where they breed in spring and early summer and remain until the first chill of fall. But very few birds spend their entire lives along Gulf coasts.

The huge White Pelican is abundant not only from Texas to Florida but is probably also the most conspicuous of all. It nests in colonies on marshy islands, and its gleaming white feathers and great yellow bill make it impressive enough—but in flight, with black wing tips showing, this bird is truly magnificent. White Pelicans ride rising air currents, usually in long lines of individuals sailing along, then flapping in unison to gain more altitude and make way against a headwind. Unlike its relative the Brown Pelican, which is a common resident throughout the Gulf, the White Pelican does not dive for its food but, with beating wings, works cooperatively with others of its kind to drive fish into the shallows, then catches them in its massive, pouched bill.

There are resident populations of birds in the Gulf that, although their species are not restricted to the area, spend their lives along its shores. Salt marshes are the habitat of the Clapper Rail; the loud, harsh, clattering call of this secretive bird is often the only indication of its presence. Long-billed Marsh Wrens are also found here, calling in chorus from

Seaside Sparrow
Ammodramus maritima
617

Long-billed Curlew
Numenius americanus

Royal Tern
Sterna maxima
510

Caspian Tern
Sterna caspia
509

Gull-billed Tern
Sterna nilotica

Common Loon
Gavia immer
525

Horned Grebe
Podiceps auritus
524

Least Sandpiper
Calidris minutilla
588

Marbled Godwit
Limosa fedoa
597

Short-billed Dowitcher
Limnodromus griseus
594

Ruddy Turnstone
Arenaria interpres
583

Sora
Porzana carolina
599

brackish marshes; and Seaside Sparrows sing their buzzing song from nests woven in cordgrass above the high-tide level in salt marshes. The Long-billed Curlew, the largest North American shorebird, is migrant along the Gulf; it calls its name from marsh and beach as it searches for prey.

Three species of graceful terns inhabit Gulf shores as residents. The Royal Tern, conspicuous for the black bushy crest at the back of its head, is strictly limited to saltwater habitats, where it dives for small fish. The largest of North American terns, the Caspian Tern, is sometimes found associated with fresh water elsewhere on the continent; it uses its size to advantage by often robbing other seabirds of their fish catch. The Gull-billed Tern is unlike its relatives in its preference for food, for it hunts insects on the wing and only occasionally goes after fishes and crustaceans or other marine invertebrates. All three terns nest in sandy areas, either amidst beach or dune grasses or in scraped depressions in open sand. Tern colonies are noisy places when an intruder comes along, with birds of several species wheeling overhead, crying their rasping, grating calls and diving swiftly in near-attacks. In addition to the species mentioned above, there are about fifty more that breed, either widely or locally, along the Gulf Coast.

In winter the Gulf shores receive a multitude of additional bird species, at least seventy more, from the north. These birds nest in Canada or the northern United States, where the winter climate is intolerably severe; the warm, food-rich Gulf waters attract them. When they arrive, they represent almost every latitude and a wide variety of bird families. Even the Common Loon, so closely associated with cool northern lakes, is a Gulf resident in winter. The Horned Grebe, which nests all through northwestern Canada and southern Alaska, finds a haven in the Gulf when its summer waters freeze over. It appears suddenly, almost without warning, for it migrates only at night.

Shorebirds of a great many kinds arrive in the fall, seeking the beach or marsh habitat to which they are accustomed and adapted. They range from the smallest of North American shorebirds, the Least Sandpiper, to the largest of the godwits, the Marbled Godwit. Short-billed Dowitchers migrate to Gulf coastal areas in flocks numbering into the thousands; once on the beaches and flats, they probe deeply into the mud with rapid-fire thrusts seeking mollusks, marine worms, and crustaceans. These seasonal arrivals seek habitats as varied as the shoreline: Ruddy Turnstones explore rock rubble and sandy beaches, investigate under stones, shells, and seaweed for small crustaceans and other invertebrates. The Sora, on the other hand, immediately disappears into salt marshes, where it utters a sharp *keek* and emerges into view only when prompted by sudden loud noises, such as hand clapping.

Seasonal changes along the northern Gulf Coast may drive Manatees away in winter (if there are any left) and cause the great sea turtles to migrate farther south, but it is a birder's delight as these fascinating and specialized creatures arrive from all over North America to spend mild winter months.

GULF SHORES: ANIMALS

Seashells
Alphabet Cone 46
Angel Wing 96
Angulate Wentletrap 60
Atlantic Nut Clam 107
Atlantic Slipper Shell 82
Banded Tulip 43
Blood Ark 84
Brown Sargassum Snail 54
Carolina Marsh Clam 102
Common Atlantic Margin
Shell 72
Common Eastern Dog
Whelk 55
Common Jingle Shell 108
Common Nutmeg 49
Common Purple Snail 69
Costate Horn Shell 61
Disk Dosinia 104
Eastern Oyster 111
False Angel Wing 95
Florida Crown Conch 36
Florida Horse Conch 39, 122
Giant Atlantic Cockle 90,
130
Green Jackknife Clam 119
Lettered Olive 76, 127
Lightning Whelk 35
Marsh Periwinkle 58
Northern Quahog 101
Ponderous Ark 88
Saw-toothed Pen Shell 114
Scotch Bonnet 47
Shark Eye 71, 129
True Tulip 44, 125
Virgin Nerite 67

Seashore Creatures
Arrow Crab 200
Atlantic Long-fin
Shrimp 181
Atlantic Mole Crab 154
Atlantic Purple Sea
Urchin 196
Blue Crab 147
Boring Sponge 292
Bushy Wine-glass
Hydroids 260
By-the-wind Sailor 217
Cannonball Jellyfish 222
Clubbed Finger Coral 283
Commensal Crab 149
Common Atlantic
Octopus 183

Common Mantis
Shrimp 167
Common Spider Crab 138
Elkhorn Coral 272
Encrusted Tunicate 277
Feathered Hydroid 259
Flame-streaked Box
Crab 153
Flat-browed Crab 148
Flat-clawed Hermit
Crab 155
Flat Mud Crab 133
Forbes' Common Sea
Star 189
Ghost Crab 144
Giant Hermit Crab 159
Hairy Sea Cucumber 298
Horseshoe Crab 160
Labyrinthine Brain
Coral 279
Large Star Coral 285
Leafy Paddle Worm 304
Lentil Sea Spider 199
Lesser Sponge Crab 152
Limulus Leech 310
Lion's Mane 219
Long-spined Urchin 198
Long-clawed Hermit
Crab 158
Lug Worm 317
Mangrove Tunicate 235
Milky Nemertean 312
Moon Jellyfish 223
Northern Sea Pork 236
Pink Shrimp 166
Pink-tipped Anemone 268
Plumed Worm 296
Porous Coral 284
Portuguese Man-of-
war 218
Reef Starlet Coral 280
Ringed Anemone 269
Rock-boring Urchin 195
Sand Fiddler 142
Sargassum Crab 136
Sea Nettle 220
Single-horn Bryozoan 291
Slate Pencil Urchin 194
Snail Fur 254
Spiral-gilled Tube
Worm 251
Spotted Sea Hare 207
Stinker Sponge 282
Stone Crab 134

Striped Anemone 244
Tubularian Hydroid 256
Two-gilled Blood
Worm 308
Upside-down Jellyfish 221
Vase Sponge 278
West Indies Spiny
Lobster 161
Wharf Crab 146
Wine-glass Hydroids 262
Zebra Flatworm 216
Zig-zag Wine-glass
Hydroid 261

Fishes
Atlantic Croaker 384
Banded Butterflyfish 369
Black Drum 380
Blacktip Shark 417
Blue Tang 366
Bluefish 401
Bonnethead 416
Bull Shark 419
Clearnose Skate 426
Cobia 408
Eyed Flounder 358
Florida Pompano 347
Gizzard Shad 391
Gray Snapper 374
Gulf Killifish 393
Gulf Pipefish 410
Harvestfish 364
Hogchoker 359
Inland Silverside 407
Jewfish 377
Lined Seahorse 432
Nassau Grouper 382
Northern Puffer 354
Ocean Surgeon 365
Pinfish 372
Porkfish 371
Queen Angelfish 363
Queen Parrotfish 344
Red Snapper 375
Rock Hind 383
Sand Perch 379
Sandbar Shark 418
Sargassumfish 351
Sergeant Major 370
Scrawled Filefish 348
Sheepshead 353
Sheepshead Minnow 395
Smalltooth Sawfish 422
Snook 406

Southern Stingray 425
Spanish Hogfish 342
Spotted Eagle Ray 424
Spotted Moray 431
Striped Anchovy 403
Striped Bass 373
Striped Blenny 428
Striped Burrfish 352
Striped Mullet 405
Tarpon 402
Yellowtail Damselfish 337

Reptiles and Amphibians
American Alligator 439
Cottonmouth 442
Diamondback
Terrapin 435
Eastern Hognose
Snake 444
Green Anole 440
Gulf Coast Toad 436
Loggerhead 434
Snapping Turtle 433
Southern Water Snake 443

Birds
American Avocet 577
American Bittern 567
American Black Duck 534
American Coot 601
American
Oystercatcher 576
American White
Pelican 518
Anhinga 574
Bald Eagle 606
Black-bellied Plover 584
Black-crowned Night
Heron 572
Black-necked Stilt 578
Black Skimmer 516
Black-whiskered
Vireo 615
Blue-winged Teal 537
Boat-tailed Grackle 607
Bonaparte's Gull 506
Brown Pelican 519
Bufflehead 542
Canada Goose 554, 556
Canvasback 530
Caspian Tern 509
Clapper Rail 598
Common Loon 525
Common Tern 511

Double-crested
Cormorant 575
Forster's Tern 512
Fulvous Whistling
Duck 536
Great Blue Heron 565
Great Egret 562
Greater Scaup 543
Herring Gull 503
Horned Grebe 524
Laughing Gull 505
Least Sandpiper 588
Least Tern 514
Lesser Yellowlegs 593
Little Blue Heron 564,
570
Magnificent
Frigatebird 494
Mangrove Cuckoo 611
Marbled Godwit 597
Marsh Wren 613
Mottled Duck 532
Northern Shoveler 545
Osprey 605
Purple Gallinule 600
Red-breasted
Merganser 541
Red-winged
Blackbird 609
Reddish Egret 566
Redhead 531
Ring-billed Gull 502
Ring-necked Duck 546
Roseate Spoonbill 559
Roseate Tern 507
Royal Tern 510
Ruddy Turnstone 583
Sanderling 586
Seaside Sparrow 617
Semipalmated Plover 582
Sharp-tailed Sparrow 616
Short-billed Dowitcher 59
Snow Goose 553
Snowy Egret 563
Snowy Plover 580
Sora 599
Spotted Sandpiper 591
Stilt Sandpiper 589
Tricolored Heron 568
Willet 590
Wood Stork 560

Mammal
Manatee 361

PART II   COLOR PLATES

1 South Coast

Newfoundland

Rocky Shores

2 A cobble beach at Bonavista Bay

Windmill Bight, Newfoundland

Rocky Shores

3 Dunes

Gros Morne National Park, Newfoundland

Sandy Shores

4 Percé Rock   Gaspé Peninsula, Quebec

Rocky Shores

5 Stanhope Beach   Prince Edward Island

Sandy Shores

6 Bay at low tide   Digby Neck, Nova Scotia

Sandy Shores

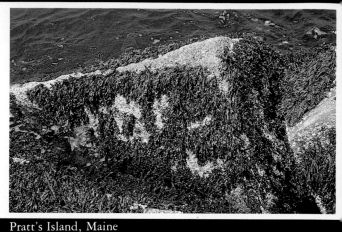

10 Tidepool with Irish Moss and rockweeds   Pratt's Island, Maine

Rocky Shores

11 Crest of rocky shore in fog   Pratt's Island, Maine

Rocky Shores

12 Rockweeds, black zone, and barnacles   Pratt's Island, Maine

Rocky Shores

13 Rising tide at Crow Neck

Cobscook Bay, Washington County, Maine

Bays and Estuaries

14 Dunes

Provincetown National Forest, Massachusetts

Sandy Shores

15 Marsh grasses

Provincetown, Massachusetts

Salt Marshes

16 Fringe of cordgrass Long Island Sound Marshlands Conservancy, Rye, New York
at high tide

Salt Marshes

17 Dunes with Beach Bethany Beach, Delaware
Plum in flower

Sandy Shores

18 Traveling dunes Cape Henlopen, Delaware
invading coastal forest

Sandy Shores

19 Bayside margin of salt marsh

Assawoman Bay, Delaware

Bays and Estuaries

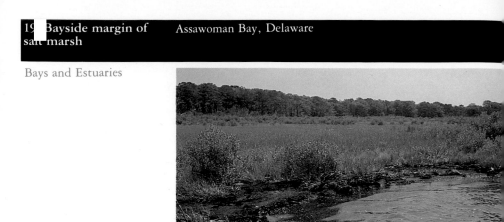

20 Salt marsh on barrier island

Assateague Island, Maryland

Salt Marshes

21 Barrier island with grasses and goldenrod

Assateague Island, Maryland

Sandy Shores

22 Saltmarsh Cordgrass and Seaside Lavender Lewes, Delaware

Salt Marshes

23 American Beach Grass on dunes Cape Hatteras National Seashore, North Carolina

Sandy Shores

24 Dunes at Jockey's Ridge Outer Banks, North Carolina

Sandy Shores

25 Beach with Saltwort   Laguna Atascosa National Wildlife Refuge, Texas

Gulf Shores

26 Dunes with Beach Morning Glory   Padre Island, Texas

Gulf Shores

27 Coastline   Aransas National Wildlife Refuge, Texas

Gulf Shores

28 Whooping Crane in salt marsh   Aransas National Wildlife Refuge, Texas

Gulf Shores

29 Red Mangroves on coral sand   Off Key Largo, Florida

Mangrove Shores

30 Red Mangroves in rocky shallows   Islamorada, Florida

Mangrove Shores

HOW TO USE THE COLOR PLATES

The color plates on the following pages include eight major groups of animals and plants: seashells, seashore creatures, mammals, fishes, reptiles and amphibians, plants, insects and spiders, and birds.

Table of Contents
For easy reference, a table of contents precedes the color plates. The table is divided into two sections. On the left, we list each major group of animals or plants. On the right, the major groups are usually subdivided into smaller groups, and each small group is illustrated by a symbol. For example, the large group of seashore creatures is divided into small groups made up of distinctive animals, such as crabs or barnacles. Similarly, the large group of fishes is divided into small groups, such as eel-like fishes or rays and skates.

Captions for the Color Plates
The black bar above each color plate contains the following information: the plate number, the common and scientific names of the animal or plant, its dimensions, and the page number of the full species description. To the left of each color plate, the habitats where you are likely to encounter the species are always indicated in blue type. Additionally, you will find either a fact helpful in field identification, such as the food that an insect eats (also in blue type), or a range map. The chart on the facing page lists the dimensions given and the blue-type information or map provided for each major group of animals or plants.

CAPTION INFORMATION

Dimensions	Blue Type/Art
Seashells	
Length, width, or height	Specific habitat
Seashore Creatures	
Length, width, or height	Phylum and class
Mammals	
Length of adult	Range map or range description
Fishes	
Maximum length of adult	Specific habitat
Reptiles and Amphibians	
Maximum length of adult	Range map
Plants	
Plant height or length or flower width	Range description
Insects and Spiders	
Length of adult, excluding antennae and appendages	Major food
Birds	
Length, usually of adult male, from tip of bill to tail	Range map showing breeding, winter, and/or permanent range

Fishes (*continued*)

Wrasses, Parrotfishes, Surgeonfishes, and Tripletail

Squirrelfish, Pompano, Striped Bass, Mackerels, and Bluefish

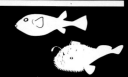

Lumpfish, Puffers, Sargassumfish, Burrfish, and Goosefish

Filefishes, Angelfishes, Harvestfish, and Butterflyfish

Flatfishes

Sea Basses and Blenny

Searobin, Drum, and Codfishes

Herrings, Tarpon, Anchovy, and Bonefish

Livebearers, Killifishes, and Needlefish

Mullet, Snook, and Silverside

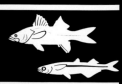

| 31 Queen Helmet | *Cassis madagascariensis* p. 371 | Height: 4–14″ |

Sandy Shores

Habitat
On sand

| 32 Pink Conch | *Strombus gigas* p. 371 | Height: 7–12″ |

Southern Sandy Shores

Habitat
In sand and rubble, usually among or near eelgrass

| 33 Knobbed Whelk | *Busycon carica* p. 372 | Height: 4–9″ |

Sandy Shores

Habitat
On sand

34 Channeled Whelk
Busycon canaliculatum   Height: 3½–7½"
p. 372

Sandy Shores; Bays and
Estuaries

Habitat
On sand or mud

35 Lightning Whelk
Busycon contrarium   Height: 2½–16"
p. 373

Sandy and Gulf shores

Habitat
In sand

36 Florida Crown Conch
Melongena corona   Height: 1–8"
p. 373

Sandy and Gulf shores;
Bays and Estuaries; Salt
Marshes

Habitat
On mud or muddy sand,
often among mangroves

37 Apple Murex

Phyllonotus pomum
p. 374

Height: 2–4¾"

Rocky and Sandy shores;
Bays and Estuaries

Habitat
Among rocks or on sand

38 Florida Lace Murex

*Chicoreus florifer
dilectus*
p. 374

Height: 1–3¼"

Sandy Shores; Bays and
Estuaries; Coral Reefs

Habitat
Among coral rubble or in
sandy or muddy areas

39 Florida Horse Conch

Pleuroploca gigantea
p. 374

Height: 4–19"

Sandy and Gulf shores

Habitat
On sand or muddy sand

40 Thick-lipped Drill	*Eupleura caudata* p. 375	Height: ½–1⅝″

Rocky Shores; Bays and
Estuaries

Habitat
On or near oyster beds

41 Atlantic Oyster Drill	*Urosalpinx cinerea* p. 375	Height: ½–1¾″

Rocky Shores; Bays and
Estuaries

Habitat
On or among rubble near
oyster beds

42 Florida Rock Shell	*Thais haemastoma* *floridana* p. 376	Height: 1½–4″

Rocky Shores

Habitat
On rocks and oyster reefs

43 Banded Tulip

Fasciolaria lilium
p. 377

Height: 2¼–4⅛"

Southern Sandy and Gulf shores

Habitat
On sand or muddy sand

44 True Tulip

Fasciolaria tulipa
p. 377

Height: 2½–9½"

Sandy and Gulf shores;
Bays and Estuaries

Habitat
On sand and mud

45 Junonia

Scaphella junonia
p. 378

Height: 2½–4"

Southern Sandy Shores

Habitat
In sand

46 Alphabet Cone
Conus spurius atlanticus
p. 378
Height: 1¾–3″

Southern Sandy and Gulf shores

Habitat
In sand

47 Scotch Bonnet
Phalium granulatum
p. 378
Height: 1–3⅝″

Southern Sandy and Gulf shores

Habitat
On sand

48 Common Northern Whelk
Buccinum undatum
p. 379
Height: 1⅜–5½″

Rocky and Northern Sandy shores

Habitat
On rocks, sand or gravel

49 Common Nutmeg

Cancellaria reticulata
p. 379

Height: 1–2¼"

Southern Sandy and Gulf
shores

Habitat
In sand among turtle
grasses

50 Common Dove Shell

Columbella mercatoria
p. 380

Height: ⅜–⅞"

Southern Sandy Shores

Habitat
On sand and stones among
turtle grasses

51 Atlantic Dogwinkle

Nucella lapillus
p. 380

Height: ⅞–2"

Rocky Shores

Habitat
On rocks, often among
seaweeds

52 New England Basket Whelk

Nassarius trivittatus
p. 381

Height: ½–⅞"

Southern Sandy Shores

Habitat
On sand and muddy sand

53 Greedy Dove Shell

Anachis avara
p. 381

Height: ⅜–¾"

Rocky and Sandy shores

Habitat
In eelgrass and on stones

54 Brown Sargassum Snail

Litiopa melanostoma
p. 382

Height: ⅛"

Gulf Shores and Offshore Waters

Habitat
On floating sargassum weeds or on dead shells in beach drift and dredge hauls

55 Common Eastern Dog Whelk

Nassarius vibex
p. 382

Height: ³⁄₈–³⁄₄″

Sandy and Gulf shores

Habitat
On sand

56 Eastern Mud Whelk

Ilynassa obsoleta
p. 383

Height: ⅝–1¼″

Bays and Estuaries

Habitat
On mud flats

57 Common Periwinkle

Littorina littorea
p. 383

Height: ⅝–1½″

Rocky Shores

Habitat
On rocks

58 Marsh Periwinkle

Littorina irrorata
p. 384

Height: ¾–1¼"

Salt Marshes and Gulf
Shores

Habitat
On and among vegetation

59 Alternate Bittium

Bittium alternatum
p. 384

Height: ⅛–⅜"

Bays and Estuaries

Habitat
On tidal flats

60 Angulate Wentletrap

Epitonium angulatum
p. 384

Height: ½–⅞"

Sandy and Gulf shores

Habitat
On sand or rubble

| 61 **Costate Horn Shell** | *Cerithidea costata*
p. 385 | Height: ⅜–⅝" |

Bays and Estuaries; Gulf
Shores

Habitat
On mud

| 62 **Common American
Auger** | *Terebra dislocata*
p. 385 | Height: 1¼–2⅜" |

Sandy Shores

Habitat
In sand

| 63 **West Indian Worm
Shell** | *Vermicularia spirata*
p. 386 | Length: 1–5" |

Southern Sandy Shores and
Coral Reefs

Habitat
Often growing in or with
sponges or other colonial
marine animals

Northern Sandy Shores

Habitat
On sand and rubble

Southern Sandy Shores

Habitat
In sand

Rocky Shores

Habitat
On rocks

67 Virgin Nerite

Neritina virginea
p. 387

Height: ¼–¾"

Bays and Estuaries;
Mangrove and Gulf shores

Habitat
On stones or mangrove
roots

68 Northern Yellow Periwinkle

Littorina obtusata
p. 388

Height: ⅜–¾"

Rocky Shores

Habitat
On rocks among seaweeds

69 Common Purple Snail

Janthina janthina
p. 388

Width: 1–1½"

Gulf Shores and Offshore
Waters

Habitat
Suspended upside down
from a frothy bubble raft

Sandy Shores

Habitat
In sand

Sandy and Gulf shores

Habitat
On sandy shores

Sandy and Gulf shores

Habitat
In sand and among grasses

73 Coffee Melampus

Melampus coffeus
p. 390

Height: ½–¾"

Mangrove Shores

Habitat
On mud in mangrove areas

74 Eastern Melampus

Melampus bidentatus
p. 390

Height: ⅜–¾"

Salt Marshes and Mangrove
Shores

Habitat
On edges of marshes or
mangrove swamps or on
seacoasts

75 Bubble Melampus

Detracia bullaoides
p. 391

Height: ⅜–½"

Mangrove Shores

Habitat
In mud in mangroves and
under debris

| **76 Lettered Olive** | *Oliva sayana* | Height: 1¾–2¾" |
| | p. 391 | |

Southern Sandy and Gulf shores

Habitat
In sand

| **77 Flamingo Tongue** | *Cyphoma gibbosum* | Length: ⅞–1¾" |
| | p. 392 | |

Coral Reefs

Habitat
On sea fans and sea whips

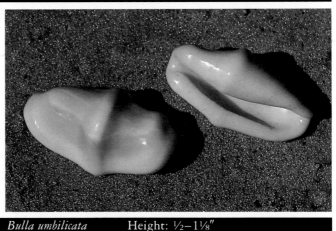

| **78 Common Atlantic Bubble** | *Bulla umbilicata* | Height: ½–1⅛" |
| | p. 392 | |

Southern Sandy Shores; Bays and Estuaries

Habitat
In mud and sand

Stenoplax floridana
p. 392

Length: ½–1⅞"

Southern Sandy Shores

Habitat
Under stones

Chaetopleura apiculata
p. 393

Length: ⅜–¾"

Rocky and Sandy shores

Habitat
On shells or stones

81 Red Northern Chiton

Tonicella rubra
p. 393

Length: ½–1"

Rocky Shores

Habitat
On and among rocks

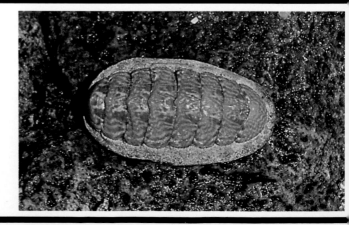

82 Atlantic Slipper Shell

Crepidula fornicata
p. 394

Length: ¾–2½"

Rocky and Gulf shores

Habitat
On rocks, other shells and horseshoe crabs

83 Atlantic Plate Limpet

Notoacmaea testudinalis
p. 394

Length: ⅞–1¾"

Rocky Shores

Habitat
Abundant on rocks

84 Cayenne Keyhole Limpet

Diodora cayenensis
p. 394

Length: ⅝–1¾"

Rocky Shores

Habitat
On and among rocks

Northern Sandy Shores

Habitat
On muddy sand in eelgrass

Coral Reefs

Habitat
Attached to coral rocks and
in crevices

Gulf Shores

Habitat
In sand and mud

88 Ponderous Ark

Noetia ponderosa
p. 396

Length: 1½–2¾"

Sandy and Gulf shores

Habitat
In sand

89 Atlantic Strawberry Cockle

Americardia media
p. 397

Height: ⅞–2"

Southern Sandy Shores

Habitat
In sand

90 Giant Atlantic Cockle

Dinocardium robustum
p. 397

Height: 2¼–5¼"

Sandy and Gulf shores

Habitat
In mud and sand

91 Yellow Cockle

Trachycardium muricatum
p. 398

Height: 1¼–2½"

Southern Sandy Shores

Habitat
In sand or mud

92 Dwarf Tiger Lucine

Codakia orbiculata
p. 398

Length: ½–1"

Southern Sandy Shores

Habitat
In sand and mud

93 Coquina Shell

Donax variabilis
p. 398

Length: ½–1"

Sandy Shores

Habitat
In sand on beaches

94 Sunray Venus

Macrocallista nimbosa   Length: 3–6"
p. 399

Southern Sandy Shores

Habitat
In sandy mud or sand

95 False Angel Wing

Petricola pholadiformis   Length: 1½–2¼"
p. 399

Bays and Estuaries; Gulf
Shores

Habitat
In heavy mud, clay or peat

96 Angel Wing

Cyrtopleura costata   Length: 4–8"
p. 400

Southern Sandy and Gulf
shores

Habitat
In deep, soft, sandy mud

97 File Yoldia

Yoldia limatula
p. 400

Length: 1–2½"

Bays and Estuaries

Habitat
In mud and muddy sand

98 Great Piddock

Zirfaea crispata
p. 401

Length: 1¼–3½"

Bays and Estuaries; Salt Marshes

Habitat
In salt marsh peat, or mud or clay

99 Soft-shell Clam

Mya arenaria
p. 401

Length: 1–5½"

Sandy Shores

Habitat
In sand and mud

100 Atlantic Surf Clam
Spisula solidissima
p. 401
Length: 1¾–7"

Sandy Shores

Habitat
Just beneath surface in
sand, mud or gravel

101 Northern Quahog
Merceneria mercenaria
p. 402
Length: 2¾–4¼"

Bays and Estuaries; Gulf
Shores

Habitat
In sand or mud

102 Carolina Marsh Clam
Polymesoda caroliniana
p. 402
Length: 1–2"

Bays and Estuaries; Gulf
Shores

Habitat
In mud

103 Ocean Quahog

Arctica islandica
p. 403

Length: 2–5"

Sandy Shores

Habitat
In sand

104 Disk Dosinia

Dosinia discus
p. 403

Length: 1¾–3"

Sandy and Gulf shores

Habitat
In sand and sandy mud in
protected beaches

105 Common Egg
Cockle

*Laevicardium
laevigatum*
p. 404

Height: 1¼–3"

Southern Sandy Shores

Habitat
In sand or mud

106 Northern Dwarf Tellin

Tellina agilis
p. 404

Length: ½–⅝"

Sandy Shores

Habitat
In sandy mud

107 Atlantic Nut Clam

Nucula proxima
p. 405

Length: ¼–⅜"

Sandy and Gulf shores

Habitat
In mud and sand

108 Common Jingle Shell

Anomia simplex
p. 405

Length: ¾–2¼"

Rocky and Sandy shores

Habitat
On rocks, shells, logs, boats, and piers

109 Atlantic Thorny Oyster

Spondylus americanus
p. 406

Length: 1½–5½"

Rocky Shores and Coral Reefs

Habitat
On rocks, coral reefs, submerged wrecks and sea walls

110 Frons Oyster

Dendrostrea frons
p. 406

Height: 1–2¾"

Coral Reefs

Habitat
On gorgonians, corals, cables, or wire nets

111 Eastern Oyster

Crassostrea virginica
p. 406

Length: 2–8"

Bays and Estuaries; Gulf Shores

Habitat
On hard or soft bottom

Mangrove Shores

Habitat
On mangroves, rocks or
concrete structures

Southern Sandy Shores

Habitat
In sandy mud

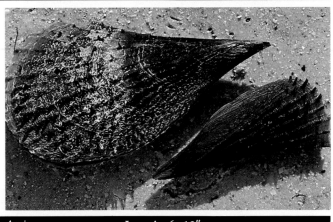

Southern Sandy and Gulf
shores

Habitat
In sandy mud

115 Atlantic Ribbed Mussel	*Geukensia demissa* p. 408	Length: 2–5"

Bays and Estuaries; Salt Marshes

Habitat
Buried in mud or peat or fastened to pilings at surface of mud

116 Northern Horse Mussel	*Modiolus modiolus* p. 409	Length: 2–9"

Rocky Shores

Habitat
Among gravel and rocks

117 Blue Mussel	*Mytilus edulis* p. 409	Length: 1¼–4"

Rocky Shores

Habitat
Attached to rocks and wooden structures

118 Atlantic Razor Clam *Siliqua costata* Length: 1½–2⅝″
p. 409

Sandy Shores

Habitat
In sand or mud

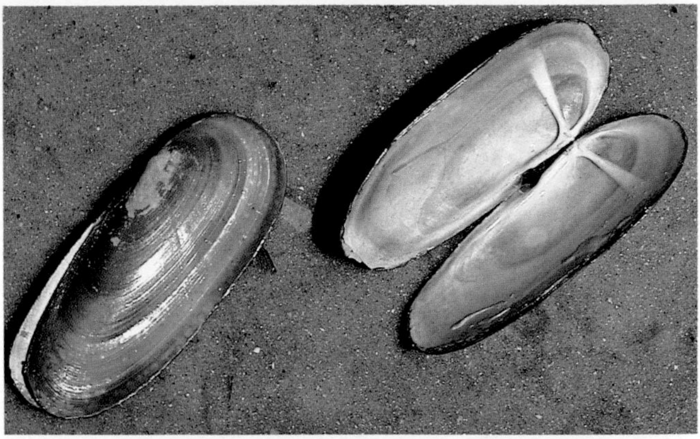

119 Green Jackknife Clam *Solen viridis* Length: 2–2⅝″
p. 410

Bays and Estuaries; Gulf Shores

Habitat
In sand

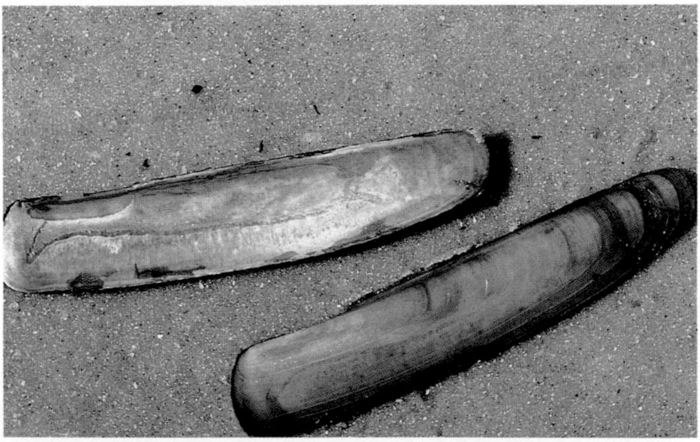

120 Atlantic Jackknife Clam *Ensis directus* Length: 3–8″
p. 410

Sandy Shores

Habitat
In sand

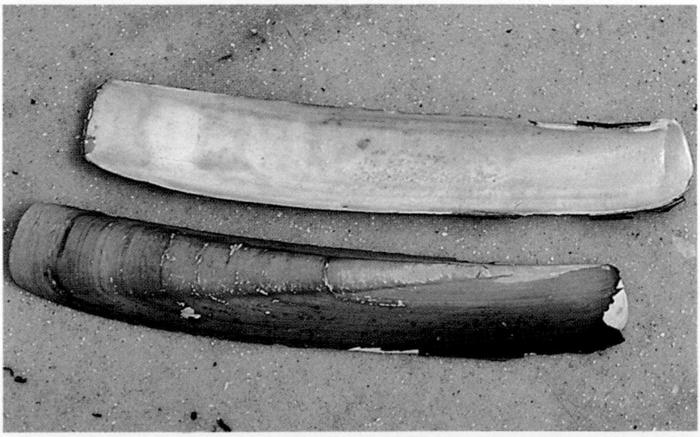

| 121 Pink Conch | *Strombus gigas* | Height: 7–12" |
| | *p. 371* | Juvenile |

Southern Sandy Shores

Habitat
In sand and rubble, usually
among or near eelgrass

| 122 Florida Horse Conch | *Pleuroploca gigantea* | Height: 4–19" |
| | *p. 374* | |

Sandy and Gulf shores

Habitat
On sand or muddy sand

123 Florida Lace Murex	*Chicoreus florifer*	Height: 1–3¼"
	dilectus	
	p. 374	

Sandy Shores; Bays and
Estuaries; Coral Reefs

Habitat
Among coral rubble or in
sandy or muddy areas

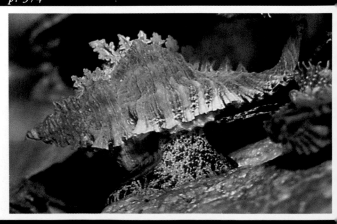

124 Florida Crown Conch

Melongena corona
p. 373

Height: 1–8"

Sandy and Gulf shores; Bays and Estuaries; Salt Marshes

Habitat
On mud or muddy sand, often among mangroves

125 True Tulip

Fasciolaria tulipa
p. 377

Height: 2½–9½"

Sandy and Gulf shores; Bays and Estuaries

Habitat
On sand and mud

126 Junonia

Scaphella junonia
p. 378

Height: 2½–4"

Southern Sandy Shores

Habitat
In sand

127 Lettered Olive   *Oliva sayana*   Height: 1¾–2¾"
                           p. 391

Southern Sandy and Gulf
shores

Habitat
In sand

128 Flamingo Tongue   *Cyphoma gibbosum*   Length: ⅞–1¾"
                           p. 392

Coral Reefs

Habitat
On sea fans and sea whips

129 Shark Eye   *Neverita duplicata* Height: ⅞–3"
                           p. 389

Sandy and Gulf shores

Habitat
On sandy shores

130 Giant Atlantic Cockle

Dinocardium robustum
p. 397

Height: 2¼–5¼"

Sandy and Gulf shores

Habitat
In mud and sand

131 Coquina Shell

Donax variabilis
p. 398

Length: ½–1"

Sandy Shores

Habitat
In sand on beaches

132 Northern Horse Mussel

Modiolus modiolus
p. 409

Length: 2–9"

Rocky Shores

Habitat
Among gravel and rocks

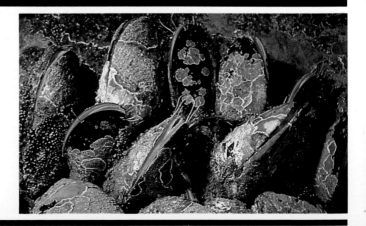

133 Flat Mud Crab

Eurypanopeus depressus Width: ¾"
p. 412

Bays and Estuaries; Gulf
Shores

Phylum Arthropoda, Class
Crustacea

134 Stone Crab

Menippe mercenaria Width: 4⅝"
p. 412

Sandy and Gulf shores;
Bays and Estuaries

Phylum Arthropoda, Class
Crustacea

135 Lady Crab

Ovalipes ocellatus Width: 3"
p. 412

Sandy Shores; Bays and
Estuaries

Phylum Arthropoda, Class
Crustacea

136 Sargassum Crab
Portunus sayi
p. 413
Width: 2⅛"

Sandy and Gulf shores;
Coral Reefs

Phylum Arthropoda, Class
Crustacea

137 Toad Crab
Hyas araneus
p. 414
Length: 3¾"

Rocky Shores

Phylum Arthropoda, Class
Crustacea

138 Common Spider Crab
Libinia emarginata
p. 414
Length: 4"

Rocky, Sandy, and Gulf
shores; Bays and Estuaries;
Coral Reefs

Phylum Arthropoda, Class
Crustacea

139 Jonah Crab   *Cancer borealis*   Width: 6¼"
p. 415

Rocky Shores

Phylum Arthropoda, Class
Crustacea

140 Atlantic Rock Crab   *Cancer irroratus*   Width: 5¼"
p. 415

Rocky and Sandy shores;
Bays and Estuaries

Phylum Arthropoda, Class
Crustacea

141 Coral Crab   *Carpilius corallinus*   Width: 6"
p. 415

Coral Reefs

Phylum Arthropoda, Class
Crustacea

Sandy and Gulf shores;
Bays and Estuaries; Salt
Marshes

Phylum Arthropoda, Class
Crustacea

Bays and Estuaries; Salt
Marshes

Phylum Arthropoda, Class
Crustacea

Sandy and Gulf shores;
Bays and Estuaries; Coral
Reefs

Phylum Arthropoda, Class
Crustacea

145 Green Crab
Carcinus maenas
p. 417
Width: 3⅛"

Rocky and Sandy shores; Bays and Estuaries

Phylum Arthropoda, Class Crustacea

146 Wharf Crab
Sesarma cinereum
p. 418
Width: ⅞"

Sandy and Gulf shores; Bays and Estuaries

Phylum Arthropoda, Class Crustacea

147 Blue Crab
Callinectes sapidus
p. 418
Width: 9¼"

Rocky, Sandy, and Gulf shores; Bays and Estuaries; Coral Reefs

Phylum Arthropoda, Class Crustacea

Sandy and Gulf shores;
Bays and Estuaries

Phylum Arthropoda, Class
Crustacea

Rocky, Sandy, and Gulf
shores; Bays and Estuaries;
Coral Reefs

Phylum Arthropoda, Class
Crustacea

Bays and Estuaries

Phylum Arthropoda, Class
Crustacea

| 151 Sponge Crab | *Dromia erythropus*
p. 420 | Width: 5″ |

Sandy Shores and Coral
Reefs

Phylum Arthropoda, Class
Crustacea

| 152 Lesser Sponge Crab | *Dromidia antillensis*
p. 420 | Length: 1⅜″ |

Sandy and Gulf shores

Phylum Arthropoda, Class
Crustacea

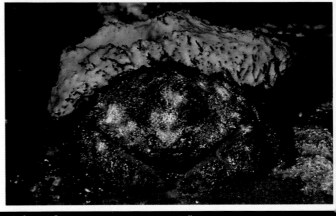

| 153 Flame-streaked Box
Crab | *Calappa flammea*
p. 420 | Width: 5½″ |

Sandy and Gulf shores

Phylum Arthropoda, Class
Crustacea

154 Atlantic Mole Crab
Emerita talpoida
p. 421
Length: 1"

Sandy and Gulf shores

Phylum Arthropoda, Class Crustacea

155 Flat-clawed Hermit Crab
Pagurus pollicaris
p. 421
Length: 1¼"

Sandy and Gulf shores; Bays and Estuaries

Phylum Arthropoda, Class Crustacea

156 Land Hermit Crab
Coenobita clypeatus
p. 422
Length: 1½"

Sandy Shores and Coral Reefs

Phylum Arthropoda, Class Crustacea

157 Acadian Hermit Crab

Pagurus acadianus
p. 422

Length: 1¼″

Rocky Shores

Phylum Arthropoda, Class Crustacea

158 Long-clawed Hermit Crab

Pagurus longicarpus
p. 422

Length: ½″

Rocky, Sandy, and Gulf shores; Bays and Estuaries

Phylum Arthropoda, Class Crustacea

159 Giant Hermit Crab

Petrochirus diogenes
p. 423

Length: 4¾″

Sandy and Gulf shores

Phylum Arthropoda, Class Crustacea

160 Horseshoe Crab

Limulus polyphemus
p. 423

Length: 24″

Rocky, Sandy, and Gulf shores; Bays and Estuaries

Phylum Arthropoda, Class Merostomata

161 West Indies Spiny Lobster

Panulirus argas
p. 424

Length: 24″

Sandy and Gulf shores; Coral Reefs

Phylum Arthropoda, Class Crustacea

162 Northern Lobster

Homarus americanus
p. 424

Length: 34″

Rocky Shores; Bays and Estuaries

Phylum Arthropoda, Class Crustacea

163 Red Opossum Shrimp   *Heteromysis formosa*   Length: ⅜"
p. 425

Rocky and Sandy shores;
Bays and Estuaries

Phylum Arthropoda, Class
Crustacea

164 Banded Coral Shrimp   *Stenopus hispidus*   Length: 2"
p. 425

Coral Reefs

Phylum Arthropoda, Class
Crustacea

165 Spotted Cleaning Shrimp   *Periclimenes yucatanicus*   Length: 1"
p. 426

Coral Reefs

Phylum Arthropoda, Class
Crustacea

166 Pink Shrimp *Penaeus duorarum* Length: 6½″ (males); 8⅜″ (females)
p. 426

Sandy and Gulf shores;
Coral Reefs

Phylum Arthropoda, Class
Crustacea

**167 Common Mantis
Shrimp** *Squilla empusa* Length: 10″
p. 427

Sandy and Gulf shores;
Bays and Estuaries

Phylum Arthropoda, Class
Crustacea

168 Red-eyed Amphipod *Ampithoe rubricata* Length: ¾″
p. 427

Rocky Shores; Bays and
Estuaries

Phylum Arthropoda, Class
Crustacea

**169 Red-lined Cleaning
Shrimp**   *Lysmata wurdemanni*   Length: 2¾"
          p. 427

Sandy Shores; Bays and
Estuaries; Coral Reefs

Phylum Arthropoda, Class
Crustacea

**170 Brown Pistol
Shrimp**   *Alpheus armatus*   Length: 1½"
          p. 428

Coral Reefs

Phylum Arthropoda, Class
Crustacea

**171 Long-horn Skeleton
Shrimp**   *Aeginella longicornis*   Length: 2⅛"
          p. 428

Rocky and Sandy shores;
Bays and Estuaries

Phylum Arthropoda, Class
Crustacea

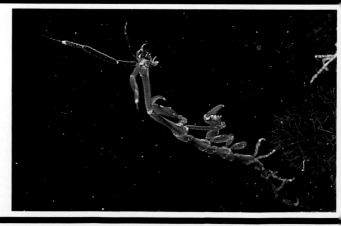

Rocky and Sandy shores;
Bays and Estuaries

Phylum Arthropoda, Class
Crustacea

Rocky and Sandy shores;
Bays and Estuaries

Phylum Arthropoda, Class
Crustacea

Sandy Shores

Phylum Arthropoda, Class
Crustacea

175 Flat-browed Mud Shrimp

Upogebia affinis
p. 430

Length: 2½″

Sandy Shores; Bays and Estuaries

Phylum Arthropoda, Class Crustacea

176 Mottled Tube-maker

Jassa falcata
p. 430

Length: ⅜″

Rocky and Sandy shores; Bays and Estuaries

Phylum Arthropoda, Class Crustacea

177 Sand Shrimp

Crangon septemspinosa
p. 430

Length: 2¾″

Rocky and Sandy shores; Bays and Estuaries

Phylum Arthropoda, Class Crustacea

178 Baltic Isopod
Idotea baltica
p. 431
Length: 1″

Rocky Shores; Bays and Estuaries

Phylum Arthropoda, Class Crustacea

179 Big-eyed Beach Flea
Talorchestia megalophthalma
p. 431
Length: 1″

Sandy Shores; Bays and Estuaries

Phylum Arthropoda, Class Crustacea

180 Northern Sea Roach
Ligia oceanica
p. 432
Length: 1″

Rocky Shores

Phylum Arthropoda, Class Crustacea

181 Atlantic Long-fin Squid   *Loligo pealei*   Length: 17"
                                   p. 432

Rocky, Sandy, and Gulf
shores; Bays and Estuaries;
Coral Reefs

Phylum Mollusca, Class
Cephalopoda

182 Long-armed Octopus   *Octopus macropus*   Length: 36"
                             p. 432

Coral Reefs

Phylum Mollusca, Class
Cephalopoda

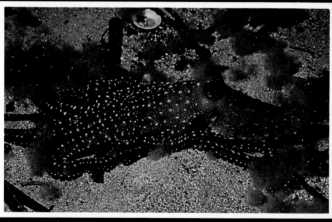

183 Common Atlantic Octopus   *Octopus vulgaris*   Length: 120"
                                  p. 433

Sandy and Gulf shores;
Bays and Estuaries; Coral
Reefs

Phylum Mollusca, Class
Cephalopoda

184 Dwarf Brittle Star   *Axiognathus*   Width: 2¼"
                              squamatus
                              p. 433

Rocky and Sandy shores;
Coral Reefs

Phylum Echinodermata,
Class Stelleroidea

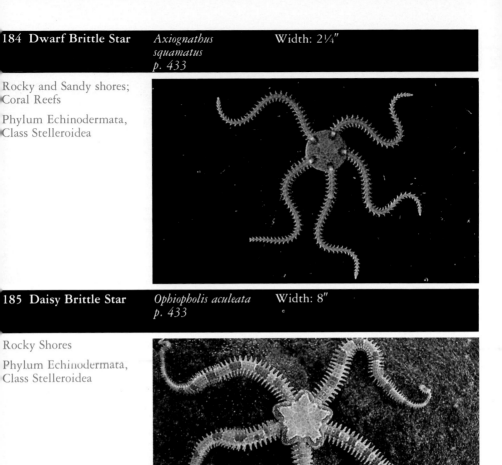

185 Daisy Brittle Star   *Ophiopholis aculeata*   Width: 8"
                              p. 433

Rocky Shores

Phylum Echinodermata,
Class Stelleroidea

186 Slender Sea Star   *Leptasterias tenera*   Width: 3"
                            p. 434

Rocky Shores

Phylum Echinodermata,
Class Stelleroidea

187 Blood Star *Henricia sanguinolenta* Width: 8"
p. 434

Rocky Shores

Phylum Echinodermata,
Class Stelleroidea

188 Northern Sea Star *Asterias vulgaris* Width: 16"
p. 435

Rocky Shores

Phylum Echinodermata,
Class Stelleroidea

**189 Forbes' Common
Sea Star** *Asterias forbesi* Width: 10¼"
p. 435

Rocky, Sandy, and Gulf
shores; Bay Mouths; Coral
Reefs

Phylum Echinodermata,
Class Stelleroidea

190 Thorny Sea Star
Echinaster sentus
p. 436
Width: 4½"

Rocky and Sandy shores;
Coral Reefs

Phylum Echinodermata,
Class Stelleroidea

191 Cushion Star
Oreaster reticulatus
p. 436
Width: 20"

Sandy Shores and Coral
Reefs

Phylum Echinodermata,
Class Stelleroidea

192 Smooth Sun Star
Solaster endeca
p. 436
Width: 16"

Rocky Shores

Phylum Echinodermata,
Class Stelleroidea

193 Spiny Sun Star   *Crossaster papposus*   Width: 14"
                           p. 437

Rocky Shores

Phylum Echinodermata,
Class Stelleroidea

194 Slate-pencil Urchin   *Eucidaris tribuloides*   Width: 2¼"
                                p. 437

Sandy and Gulf shores;
Coral Reefs

Phylum Echinodermata,
Class Echinoidea

195 Rock-boring Urchin   *Echinometra lucunter*   Width: 2"
                               p. 437

Coral Reefs and Gulf
Shores

Phylum Echinodermata,
Class Echinoidea

Rocky, Sandy, and Gulf shores; Bay Mouths; and Coral Reefs

Phylum Echinodermata, Class Echinoidea

Rocky Shores

Phylum Echinodermata, Class Echinoidea

Coral Reefs and Gulf Shores

Phylum Echinodermata, Class Echinoidea

199 Lentil Sea Spider
Anoplodactylus lentus Length: ¼"
p. 439

Rocky and Gulf shores;
Bays and Estuaries; Coral
Reefs

Phylum Arthropoda, Class
Pycnogonida

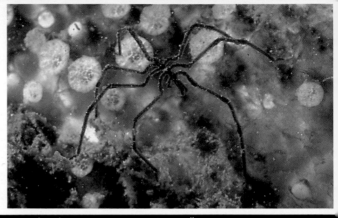

200 Arrow Crab
Stenorhynchus seticornis Length: 2¼"
p. 439

Sandy and Gulf shores;
Coral Reefs

Phylum Arthropoda, Class
Crustacea

201 Northern Basket Star
Gorgonocephalus arcticus Width: 32"
p. 440

Rocky Shores

Phylum Echinodermata,
Class Stelleroidea

202 Keyhole Urchin　　*Mellita*　　Width: 6"
　　　　　　　　　　　　　quinquiesperforata
　　　　　　　　　　　　　p. 440

Sandy Shores and Coral
Reefs

Phylum Echinodermata,
Class Echinoidea

203 Six-hole Urchin　　*Mellita sexiesperforata*　　Width: 4¼"
　　　　　　　　　　　　　p. 441

Sandy Shores and Bay
Mouths

Class Echinodermata, Class
Echinoidea

**204 Common Sand
Dollar**　　　　　　　*Echinarachnius parma*　　Width: 3⅛"
　　　　　　　　　　　p. 441

Rocky and Sandy shores

Phylum Echinodermata,
Class Echinoidea

205 Variegated Urchin
Lytechinus variegatus
p. 441
Width: 3"

Sandy and Mangrove shores; Coral Reefs

Phylum Echinodermata, Class Echinoidea

206 Long-spined Sea Biscuit
Plagiobrissus grandis
p. 442
Length: 10"

Sandy Shores and Coral Reefs

Phylum Echinodermata, Class Echinoidea

207 Spotted Sea Hare
Aplysia dactylomela
p. 442
Length: 5"

Sandy and Gulf shores; Coral Reefs

Phylum Mollusca, Class Gastropoda

208 Bushy-backed Sea Slug   *Dendronotus frondosus*   Length: 4⅝"
p. 442

Rocky Shores

Phylum Mollusca, Class Gastropoda

209 Red-gilled Nudibranch   *Coryphella rufibranchialis*   Length: 1¼"
p. 443

Rocky and Sandy shores; Bays and Estuaries

Phylum Mollusca, Class Gastropoda

210 Rough-mantled Doris   *Onchidoris bilamellata*   Length: 1"
p. 443

Rocky Shores

Phylum Mollusca, Class Gastropoda

211 White Atlantic Cadlina

Cadlina laevis
p. 443

Length: 1″

Rocky Shores

Phylum Mollusca, Class Gastropoda

212 Hairy Doris

Acanthodoris pilosa
p. 444

Length: 1¼″

Rocky Shores

Phylum Mollusca, Class Gastropoda

213 Atlantic Ancula

Ancula gibbosa
p. 444

Length: ½″

Rocky Shores

Phylum Mollusca, Class Gastropoda

| 214 Common Lettuce Slug | *Tridachia crispata*
p. 445 | Length: 1½" |

Sandy Shores and Coral
Reefs

Phylum Mollusca, Class
Gastropoda

| 215 Warty Sea Cat | *Dolabrifera dolabrifera*
p. 445 | Length: 6" |

Sandy Shores

Phylum Mollusca, Class
Gastropoda

| 216 Zebra Flatworm | *Stylochus zebra*
p. 445 | Length: 1½" |

Sandy and Gulf shores

Phylum Platyhelminthes,
Order Polycladida

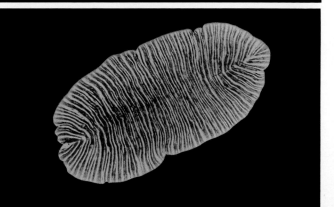

217 By-the-wind Sailor   *Velella velella*   Length: 4″
                                         p. 446

Sandy and Gulf shores;
Coral Reefs

Phylum Cnidaria, Class
Hydrozoa

218 Portuguese Man-of-war   *Physalia physalis*   Length: 12″   ⊗
                                         p. 446

Sandy and Gulf shores;
Coral Reefs

Phylum Cnidaria, Class
Hydrozoa

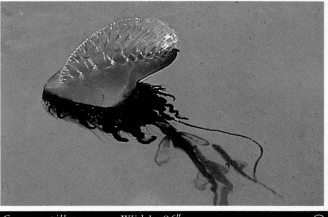

219 Lion's Mane   *Cyanea capillata*   Width: 96″   ⊗
                                         p. 446

Rocky, Sandy, and Gulf
shores; Bays and Estuaries

Phylum Cnidaria, Class
Scyphozoa

220 Sea Nettle   *Chrysaora*   Width: 10″   ⊗
quinquecirrha
p. 447

Sandy and Gulf shores;
Bays and Estuaries

Phylum Cnidaria, Class
Scyphozoa

221 Upside-down   *Cassiopeia xamachana*   Width: 12″   ⊗
Jellyfish   *p. 447*

Sandy and Gulf shores;
Coral Reefs

Phylum Cnidaria, Class
Scyphozoa

222 Cannonball Jellyfish   *Stomolophus meleagris*   Width: 7″
p. 448

Sandy and Gulf shores;
Coral Reefs

Phylum Cnidaria, Class
Scyphozoa

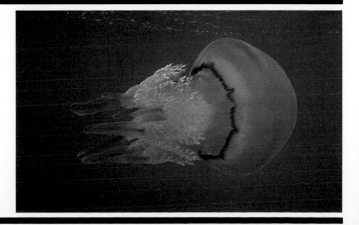

223 Moon Jellyfish *Aurelia aurita* Width: 16"
p. 448

Rocky, Sandy, and Gulf
shores; Bays and Estuaries

Phylum Cnidaria, Class
Scyphozoa

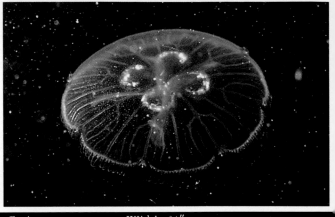

**224 Angled
Hydromedusa** *Gonionemus vertens* Width: ¾"
p. 448

Rocky Shores; Bays and
Estuaries

Phylum Cnidaria, Class
Hydrozoa

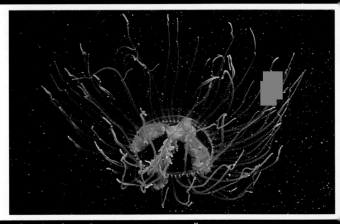

225 Sea Gooseberry *Pleurobrachia pileus* Height: 1⅛"
p. 449

Rocky and Sandy shores;
Bays and Estuaries

Phylum Ctenophora, Class
Tentaculata

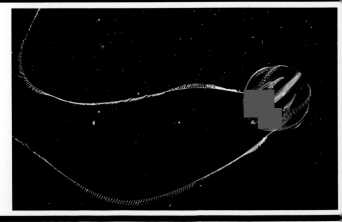

| 226 Clapper Hydromedusa | *Sarsia tubulosa* p. 449 | Width: 4" |

Rocky and Sandy shores

Phylum Cnidaria, Class Hydrozoa

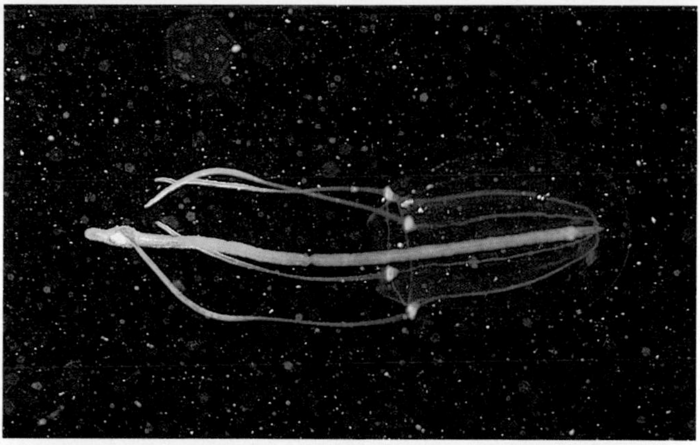

| 227 Common Northern Comb Jelly | *Bolinopsis infundibulum* p. 450 | Height: 6" |

Rocky Shores

Phylum Ctenophora, Class Tentaculata

| 228 Leidy's Comb Jelly | *Mnemiopsis leidyi* p. 450 | Height: 4" |

Sandy Shores; Bays and Estuaries

Phylum Ctenophora, Class Tentaculata

| 229 Common Salp | *Salpa fusiformis* | Length: 3¼" |
| | *p. 450* | |

Offshore waters along
Atlantic Coast

Phylum Chordata, Class
Thaliacea

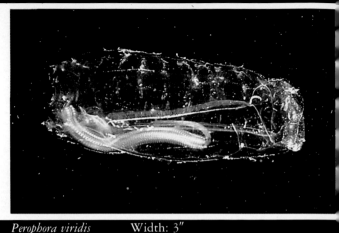

| 230 Creeping Tunicate | *Perophora viridis* | Width: 3" |
| | *p. 451* | |

Sandy Shores; Bays and
Estuaries

Phylum Chordata, Class
Ascidiacea

| 231 Painted Tunicate | *Clavelina picta* | Width: 12" |
| | *p. 451* | |

Mangrove Shores and Coral
Reefs

Phylum Chordata, Class
Ascidiacea

232 Sea Peach

Halocynthia pyriformis Height: 5"
p. 451

Rocky Shores

Phylum Chordata, Class
Ascidiacea

233 Sea Vase

Ciona intestinalis Height: 6"
p. 452

Rocky Shores

Phylum Chordata, Class
Ascidiacea

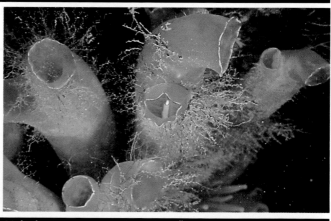

234 Orange Sea Grape

Molgula citrina Length: ⅝"
p. 452

Rocky and Sandy shores;
Bays and Estuaries

Phylum Chordata, Class
Ascidiacea

235 Mangrove Tunicate *Ecteinascidia turbinata* Length: 1"
p. 453

Mangrove and Gulf shores

Phylum Chordata, Class
Ascidiacea

236 Northern Sea Pork *Aplidium constellatum* Width: 3"
p. 453

Rocky, Sandy, and Gulf
shores; Bays and Estuaries;
Coral Reefs

Phylum Chordata, Class
Ascidiacea

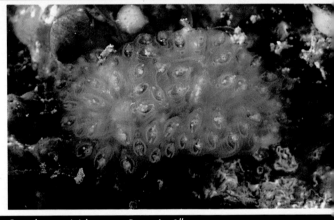

**237 Green Encrusting
Tunicate** *Symplegma viride* Length: 3"
p. 453

Sandy Shores and Coral
Reefs

Phylum Chordata, Class
Ascidiacea

238 Little Gray Barnacle
Chthamalus fragilis
Width: ⅜″
p. 454

Rocky Shores

Phylum Arthropoda, Class
Crustacea

239 Bay Barnacle
Balanus improvisus
Width: ½″
p. 454

Rocky Shores; Bays and
Estuaries

Phylum Arthropoda, Class
Crustacea

240 Northern Rock
Barnacle
Balanus balanoides
Height: 1″
p. 454

Rocky Shores; Bays and
Estuaries

Phylum Arthropoda, Class
Crustacea

241 Common Goose Barnacle

Lepas anatifera
p. 455

Length: 6″

Offshore waters

Phylum Arthropoda, Class Crustacea

242 Ivory Barnacle

Balanus eburneus
p. 455

Width: 1″

Rocky and Sandy shores; Bays and Estuaries

Phylum Arthropoda, Class Crustacea

243 Lined Anemone

Fagesia lineata
p. 455

Height: 1⅜″

Off Sandy Shores

Phylum Cnidaria, Class Anthozoa

244 Striped Anemone

Haliplanella luciae
p. 456

Height: ¾"

Rocky, Sandy, and Gulf shores

Phylum Cnidaria, Class Anthozoa

245 Ghost Anemone

Diadumene leucolena
p. 456

Height: 1½"

Rocky and Sandy shores

Phylum Cnidaria, Class Anthozoa

246 Frilled Anemone

Metridium senile
p. 456

Height: 18"

Rocky and Sandy shores

Phylum Cnidaria, Class Anthozoa

247 Trumpet Stalked Jellyfish
Haliclystus salpinx
p. 457
Height: 1″

Rocky Shores

Phylum Cnidaria, Class Scyphozoa

248 Stalked Tunicate
Boltenia ovifera
p. 457
Length: 3″

Rocky Shores

Phylum Chordata, Class Ascidiacea

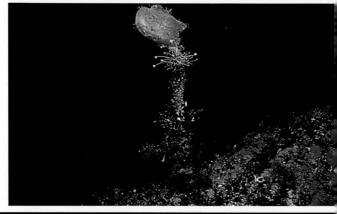

249 Club Hydroid
Clava leptostyla
p. 458
Width: 1″

Rocky Shores; Bays and Estuaries

Phylum Cnidaria, Class Hydrozoa

| 250 **Large-eyed Feather Duster** | *Potamilla reniformis* p. 458 | Length: 4″ |

Rocky and Sandy shores; Bays and Estuaries

Phylum Annelida, Class Polychaeta

| 251 **Spiral-gilled Tube Worm** | *Spirobranchus giganteus* p. 458 | Length: 4″ |

Coral Reefs and Gulf Shores

Phylum Annelida, Class Polychaeta

| 252 **Spiral-tufted Bryozoan** | *Bugula turrita* p. 459 | Length: 12″ |

Rocky and Sandy shores

Phylum Bryozoa, Class Gymnolaemata

253 Banded Feather Duster

Sabella crassicornis
p. 459

Length: 2"

Rocky Shores; Bays and Estuaries

Phylum Annelida, Class Polychaeta

254 Snail Fur

Hydractinia echinata
p. 459

Height: ⅛"

Rocky, Sandy, and Gulf shores; Bays and Estuaries

Phylum Cnidaria, Class Hydrozoa

255 Red Soft Coral

Gersemia rubiformis
p. 460

Height: 6"

Rocky Shores

Phylum Cnidaria, Class Anthozoa

256 Tubularian Hydroid *Tubularia crocea* Width: 12"
p. 460

Rocky, Sandy, and Gulf
shores

Phylum Cnidaria, Class
Hydrozoa

**257 Thick-based
Entoprocts** *Barentsia* spp. Width: 1¼"
p. 461

Rocky Shores

Phylum Entoprocta

258 Porcupine Bryozoan *Flustrellidra hispida* Length: 4"
p. 461

Rocky Shores

Phylum Bryozoa, Class
Gymnolaemata

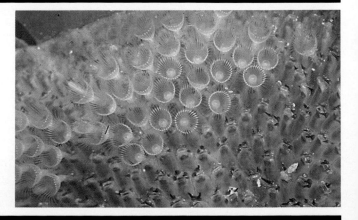

259 Feathered Hydroid

Pennaria tiarella
p. 461

Height: 6″

Rocky, Sandy, and Gulf shores; Coral Reefs

Phylum Cnidaria, Class Hydrozoa

260 Bushy Wine-glass Hydroids

Obelia spp.
p. 462

Height: 8″

Rocky, Sandy, and Gulf shores; Bays and Estuaries

Phylum Cnidaria, Class Hydrozoa

261 Zig-zag Wine-glass Hydroid

Obelia geniculata
p. 462

Width: 12″

Rocky, Sandy, and Gulf shores

Phylum Cnidaria, Class Hydrozoa

262 Wine-glass Hydroids
Campanularia spp.
p. 463
Height: 10″

Rocky, Sandy, and Gulf shores

Phylum Cnidaria, Class Hydrozoa

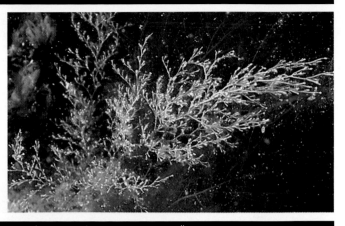

263 Garland Hydroid
Sertularia pumila
p. 463
Height: 2″

Rocky and Sandy shores; Bays and Estuaries

Phylum Cnidaria, Class Hydrozoa

264 Sea Plumes
Pseudopterogorgia spp.
p. 464
Height: 36″

Coral Reefs

Phylum Cnidaria, Class Anthozoa

265 Organ-pipe Sponge *Leucosolenia botryoides* Height: ½″
p. 464

Rocky Shores

Phylum Porifera, Class
Calcispongiae

**266 Elegant Burrowing
Anemone** *Edwardsia elegans* Height: 2″
p. 464

Rocky and Sandy shores

Phylum Cnidaria, Class
Anthozoa

267 Sea Whip *Leptogorgia virgulata* Height: 36″
p. 465

Sandy Shores and Coral
Reefs

Phylum Cnidaria, Class
Anthozoa

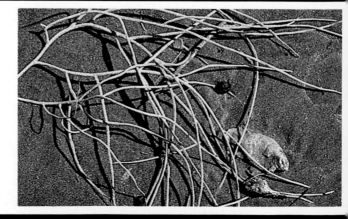

268 Pink-tipped Anemone

Condylactis gigantea
p. 465

Width: 12"

Coral Reefs and Gulf Shores

Phylum Cnidaria, Class Anthozoa

269 Ringed Anemone

Bartholomea annulata
p. 465

Height: 2"

Coral Reefs and Gulf Shores

Phylum Cnidaria, Class Anthozoa

270 Finger Sponge

Haliclona oculata
p. 466

Height: 18"

Rocky and Sandy shores; Bays and Estuaries

Phylum Porifera, Class Demospongiae

271 Sea Fans

Gorgonia spp.
p. 466

Height: 36"

Coral Reefs

Phylum Cnidaria, Class
Anthozoa

272 Elkhorn Coral

Acropora palmata
p. 466

Height: 120"

Coral Reefs and Gulf
Shores

Phylum Cnidaria, Class
Anthozoa

273 Staghorn Coral

Acropora cervicornis
p. 467

Height: 10'

Coral Reefs

Phylum Cnidaria, Class
Anthozoa

274 Fire Coral

Millepora alcicornis
p. 467

Height: 24"

Coral Reefs

Phylum Cnidaria, Class
Hydrozoa

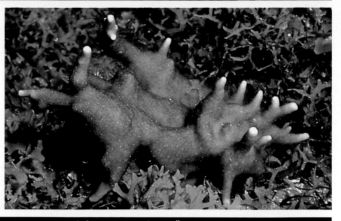

275 Red Beard Sponge

Microciona prolifera
p. 467

Width: 8"

Rocky and Sandy shores;
Bays and Estuaries

Phylum Porifera, Class
Demospongiae

276 Rubbery Bryozoan

Alcyonidium hirsutum
p. 468

Width: 3"

Rocky Shores; Bays and
Estuaries

Phylum Bryozoa, Class
Gymnolaemata

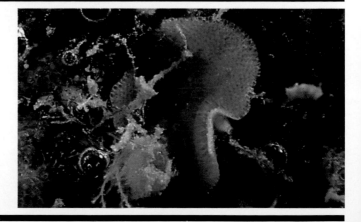

277 Encrusted Tunicate *Polycarpa obtecta* Length: 2"
p. 468

Coral Reefs and Gulf
Shores

Phylum Chordata, Class
Ascidiacea

278 Vase Sponge *Ircinia campana* Height: 36"
p. 468

Sandy and Gulf shores;
Coral Reefs

Phylum Porifera, Class
Demospongiae

**279 Labyrinthine Brain
Coral** *Diploria* Height: 96"
labyrinthiformis
p. 469

Coral Reefs and
Gulf Shores

Phylum Cnidaria, Class
Anthozoa

280 Reef Starlet Coral   *Siderastrea siderea*   Width: 36"
p. 469

Coral Reefs and Gulf
Shores

Phylum Cnidaria, Class
Anthozoa

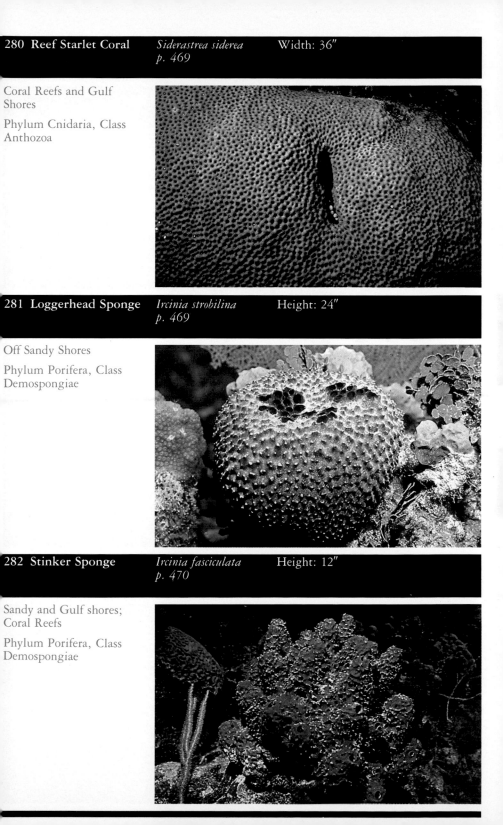

281 Loggerhead Sponge   *Ircinia strobilina*   Height: 24"
p. 469

Off Sandy Shores

Phylum Porifera, Class
Demospongiae

282 Stinker Sponge   *Ircinia fasciculata*   Height: 12"
p. 470

Sandy and Gulf shores;
Coral Reefs

Phylum Porifera, Class
Demospongiae

283 Clubbed Finger Coral   *Porites porites*   Length: 12″
p. 470

Coral Reefs and Gulf
Shores

Phylum Cnidaria, Class
Anthozoa

284 Porous Coral   *Porites astreoides*   Height: 24″
p. 470

Coral Reefs and Gulf
Shores

Phylum Cnidaria, Class
Anthozoa

285 Large Star Coral   *Montastrea cavernosa*   Width: 60″
p. 471

Coral Reefs and Gulf
Shores

Phylum Cnidaria, Class
Anthozoa

Coral Reefs and Gulf
Shores

Phylum Cnidaria, Class
Anthozoa

Rocky and Sandy shores;
Bays and Estuaries

Phylum Bryozoa, Class
Gymnolaemata

Rocky and Sandy shores;
Bays and Estuaries

Phylum Bryozoa, Class
Gymnolaemata

| 289 Starlet Coral | *Siderastrea radians*
p. 472 | Width: 12″ |

Coral Reefs

Phylum Cnidaria, Class
Anthozoa

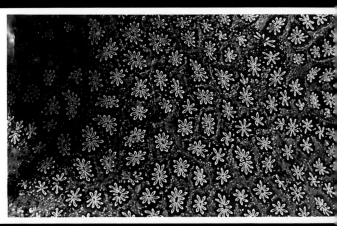

| 290 Golden Star
Tunicate | *Botryllus schlosseri*
p. 472 | Width: 4″ |

Rocky and Sandy shores;
Bays and Estuaries

Phylum Chordata, Class
Ascidiacea

| 29 Single-horn
Bryozoan | *Schizoporella unicornis*
p. 473 | Width: 4″ |

Rocky, Sandy, and Gulf
shores; Bays and Estuaries

Phylum Bryozoa, Class
Gymnolaemata

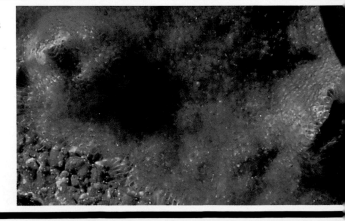

292 Boring Sponge *Cliona celata* Width: ⅛″
p. 473

Rocky, Sandy, and Gulf
shores; Bays and Estuaries

Phylum Porifera, Class
Demospongiae

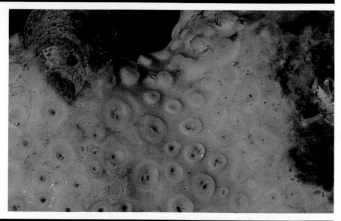

293 Ornate Worm *Amphitrite ornata* Length: 15″
p. 474

Rocky and Sandy shores;
Bays and Estuaries

Phylum Annelida, Class
Polychaeta

294 Sinistral Spiral Tube *Spirorbis borealis* Length: ⅛″
Worm *p. 474*

Rocky Shores

Phylum Annelida, Class
Polychaeta

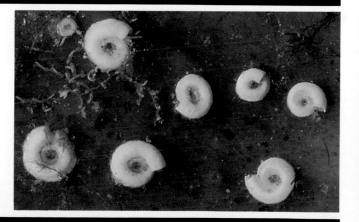

295 Red Terebellid Worm   *Polycirrus eximius*   Length: 2¾"
p. 474

Rocky and Sandy shores; Bays and Estuaries

Phylum Annelida, Class Polychaeta

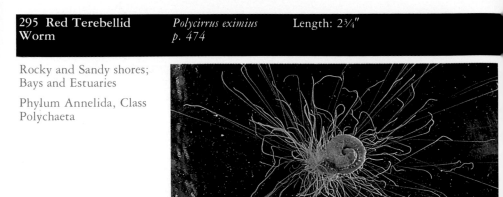

296 Plumed Worm   *Diopatra cuprea*   Length: 12"
p. 475

Rocky, Sandy, and Gulf shores; Bays and Estuaries

Phylum Annelida, Class Polychaeta

297 Orange-footed Sea Cucumber   *Cucumaria frondosa*   Length: 19"
p. 475

Rocky Shores

Phylum Echinodermata, Class Holothuroidea

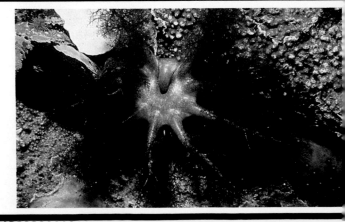

298 Hairy Sea Cucumber *Sclerodactyla briareus* Length: 4¾"
p. 475

Sandy and Gulf shores;
Bays and Estuaries

Phylum Echinodermata,
Class Holothuroidea

299 Scarlet Psolus *Psolus fabricii* Length: 4"
p. 476

Rocky Shores

Phylum Echinodermata,
Class Holothuroidea

300 Eyed Fringed Worm *Cirratulus cirratus* Length: 4¾"
p. 476

Rocky Shores

Phylum Annelida, Class
Polychaeta

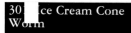

301 Ice Cream Cone Worm   *Pectinaria gouldii*   Length: 1⅝"
p. 477

Rocky and Sandy shores;
Bays and Estuaries

Phylum Annelida, Class
Polychaeta

302 Twelve-scaled Worm   *Lepidonotus squamatus*   Length: 2"
p. 477

Rocky and Sandy shores;
Bays and Estuaries

Phylum Annelida, Class
Polychaeta

303 Green Fire Worm   *Hermodice carunculata*   Length: 10"   ⊗
p. 478

Gulf shores and Coral Reefs

Phylum Annelida, Class
Polychaeta

304 Leafy Paddle Worms

Phyllodoce spp.
p. 478

Length: 18"

Rocky, Sandy, and Gulf shores; Bays and Estuaries

Phylum Annelida, Class Polychaeta

305 Clam Worm

Nereis virens
p. 478

Length: 36"

Rocky and Sandy shores; Bays and Estuaries

Phylum Annelida, Class Polychaeta

306 Green Paddle Worm

Eulalia viridis
p. 479

Length: 6"

Rocky and Sandy shores; Bays and Estuaries

Phylum Annelida, Class Polychaeta

307 Polydora Mud Worm   *Polydora ligni*   Length: 1"
                          p. 479

Rocky and Sandy shores;
Bays and Estuaries

Phylum Annelida, Class
Polychaeta

308 Two-gilled Blood Worm   *Glycera dibranchiata*   Length: 15⅜"
                              p. 480

Rocky, Sandy, and Gulf
shores; Bays and Estuaries

Phylum Annelida, Class
Polychaeta

309 Chevron Amphiporus   *Amphiporus angulatus*   Length: 6"
                           p. 480

Rocky Shores; Bays and
Estuaries

Phylum Rhynchocoela,
Class Enopla

310 Limulus Leech

Bdelloura candida
p. 481

Length: ⅝″

Rocky, Sandy, and Gulf
shores; Bays and Estuaries

Phylum Platyhelminthes,
Order Tricladida

311 Red Lineus

Lineus ruber
p. 481

Length: 8″

Rocky and Sandy shores;
Bays and Estuaries; Salt
Marshes

Phylum Rhynchocoela,
Class Anopla

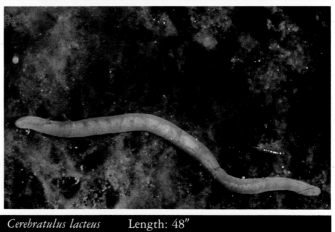

312 Milky Nemertean

Cerebratulus lacteus
p. 481

Length: 48″

Rocky, Sandy, and Gulf
shores; Bays and Estuaries

Phylum Rhynchocoela,
Class Anopla

313 Gould's Peanut Worm   *Phascolopsis gouldii*   Length: 12"
   p. 482

Rocky and Sandy shores;
Bays and Estuaries

Phylum Sipuncula

314 Bamboo Worm   *Clymenella torquata*   Length: 6"
   p. 482

Rocky and Sandy shores;
Bays and Estuaries

Phylum Annelida, Class
Polychaeta

**315 Common White
Synapta**   *Leptosynapta inhaerens*   Length: 6"
   p. 483

Rocky and Sandy shores;
Bay Mouths

Phylum Echinodermata,
Class Holothuroidea

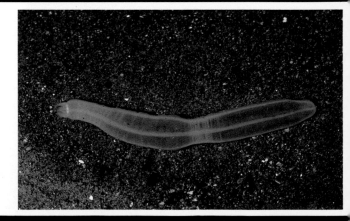

316 Keyhole Urchin Spoon Worm   *Thalassema mellita*   Length: 1½"
p. 483

Sandy Shores

Phylum Echiura

317 Lug Worm   *Arenicola cristata*   Length: 12"
p. 483

Sandy and Gulf shores;
Bays and Estuaries

Phylum Annelida, Class
Polychaeta

318 Florida Sea Cucumber   *Holothuria floridana*   Length: 10"
p. 484

Sandy Shores and Coral
Reefs

Phylum Echinodermata,
Class Holothuroidea

319 Risso's Dolphin
Grampus griseus
p. 488
Length: to 13'

Offshore Waters

Range
Eastern Newfoundland to
Lesser Antilles, including
northern and eastern Gulf
of Mexico

320 Harbor Porpoise
Phocoena phocoena
p. 488
Length: to 6'

Offshore Waters, Bays and
Estuaries

Range
Davis Straits and
southeastern Greenland to
North Carolina

321 Bottlenosed Dolphin
Tursiops truncatus
p. 488
Length: to 12'

Offshore Waters, Bays and
Estuaries

Range
Nova Scotia to Venezuela,
including Gulf of Mexico

| 322 Common Dolphin | *Delphinus delphis*
p. 489 | Length: to 8'6" | |

Offshore Waters

Range
Newfoundland and Nova
Scotia to northern South
America

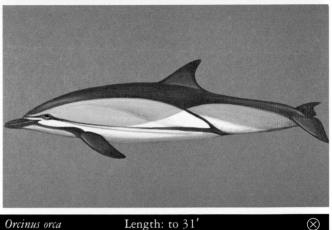

| 323 Killer Whale | *Orcinus orca*
p. 489 | Length: to 31' | ⊗ |

Offshore Waters, Bays

Range
Arctic to Lesser Antilles

| 324 Right Whale | *Eubalaena glacialis*
p. 490 | Length: to 53' | |

Offshore Waters

Range
Iceland to eastern Florida;
occasionally into southern
Gulf of Mexico; rarely to
West Indies

325 Long-finned Pilot Whale | *Globicephala melaena* p. 490 | Length: to 20′

Offshore Waters, Bays

Range
Iceland and Greenland to
North Carolina

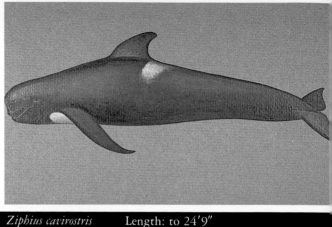

326 Cuvier's Beaked Whale | *Ziphius cavirostris* p. 491 | Length: to 24′9″

Offshore Waters

Range
Massachusetts to West
Indies, including Gulf of
Mexico

327 Blue Whale | *Balaenoptera musculus* p. 491 | Length: to 98′

Offshore Waters

Range
Arctic Circle to Panama,
including northwestern
Gulf of Mexico

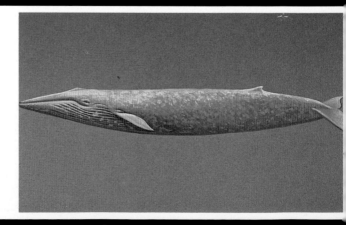

| 328 Minke Whale | *Balaenoptera acutorostrata* p. 492 | Length: to 33' |

Offshore Waters

Range
Arctic to Lesser Antilles, including eastern and northwestern Gulf of Mexico

| 329 Fin Whale | *Balaenoptera physalus* p. 492 | Length: to 79' |

Offshore Waters

Range
Arctic Circle to Greater Antilles, including Gulf of Mexico

| 330 Humpback Whale | *Megaptera novaeangliae* p. 492 | Length: to 53' |

Offshore Waters

Range
Northern Iceland and western Greenland south to West Indies, including northern and eastern Gulf of Mexico

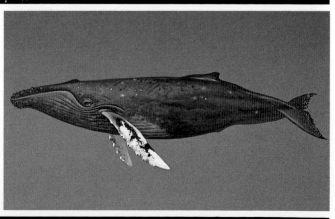

331 Manatee
Trichechus manatus
p. 493
Length: to about 15′

Bays and Estuaries; Gulf
Shores; Mangrove Shores

332 Hooded Seal
Cystophora cristata
p. 494
Length: 6′–8′2″

Offshore Waters

333 Harp Seal
Phoca groenlandica
p. 494
Length: 4′7″–6′7″

Offshore Waters

334 Hooded Seal	*Cystophora cristata* p. 494	Length: 6'–8'2" Pup

Offshore Waters

335 Harbor Seal	*Phoca vitulina* p. 495	Length: 4'–5'7"

Rocky and Sandy shores; Bays and Estuaries

336 Gray Seal	*Halichoerus grypus* p. 495	Length: to 9'10" (males); 7'6" (females)

Rocky Shores

337 Yellowtail Damselfish

Microspathodon chrysurus
p. 497

Length: to 7½"

Coral Reefs and Gulf Shores

Habitat
Reefs in shallow water or offshore

338 Tautog

Tautoga onitis
p. 497

Length: to 3'

Rocky and Sandy shores

Habitat
Coastal waters, near wrecks, piers, and steep, rocky shores

339 Bigeye

Priacanthus arenatus
p. 497

Length: to 16"

Rocky and Gulf shores; Coral Reefs

Habitat
Coral reefs and over rocks

340 Longspine Squirrelfish

Holocentrus rufus
p. 498

Length: to 12"

Coral Reefs

Habitat
Coral reefs

341 Cunner

Tautogolabrus adspersus
p. 498

Length: to 10"

Rocky and Northern Sandy shores; Bays and Estuaries

Habitat
Shallow coastal waters, in eelgrass, around piers and rock piles

342 Spanish Hogfish

Bodianus rufus
p. 498

Length: to 24"

Coral Reefs and Gulf Shores

Habitat
Coral and rocky reefs

343 Princess Parrotfish
Scarus taeniopterus
p. 499

Length: to 13"

Coral Reefs and Gulf
Shores

Habitat
Coral reefs

344 Queen Parrotfish
Scarus vetula
p. 499

Length: to 24"

Coral Reefs and Gulf
Shores

Habitat
Coral reefs

345 Blue Parrotfish
Scarus coeruleus
p. 500

Length: to 4'

Coral Reefs

Habitat
Coral reefs

346 Lumpfish

Cyclopterus lumpus
p. 500

Length: to 23"

Rocky and Northern Sandy
shores; Bays and Estuaries

Habitat
Over rocks in shallow
water

347 Florida Pompano

Trachinotus carolinus
p. 501

Length: to 17"

Sandy and Gulf shores

Habitat
Shallow water along sandy
beaches

348 Scrawled Filefish

Aluterus scriptus
p. 501

Length: to 3'

Sandy and Gulf shores

Habitat
Seagrass beds in tropical
and subtropical seas

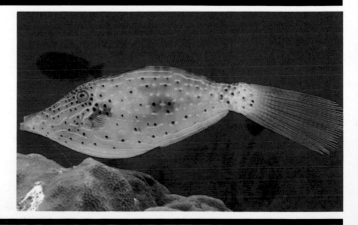

349 Sharpnose Puffer
Canthigaster rostrata
p. 501
Length: to 3¾"

Southern Sandy and Gulf shores; Coral Reefs

Habitat
Coral reefs and grass beds

350 Planehead Filefish
Monacanthus hispidus
p. 502
Length: to 9"

Rocky, Sandy, and Gulf shores; Offshore Waters

Habitat
Open seas or near shore around vegetation

351 Sargassumfish
Histrio histrio
p. 502
Length: to 6"

Rocky, Sandy, and Gulf shores; Bays and Estuaries; Offshore Waters

Habitat
Floating sargassum weed

352 Striped Burrfish

Chilomycterus schoepfi
p. 503

Length: to 10″

Southern Sandy and Gulf
shores

Habitat
Shallow grass beds in
summer, deeper waters in
winter

353 Sheepshead

*Archosargus
probatocephalus*
p. 503

Length: to 30″

Gulf Shores; Bays and
Estuaries

Habitat
Muddy, shallow water or
over oyster beds; around
piles and piers

354 Northern Puffer

Sphoeroides maculatus
p. 503

Length: to 10″

Sandy and Gulf shores;
Bays and Estuaries

Habitat
Bays and estuaries over
sand, silt, or mud

355 Goosefish *Lophius americanus* Length: to 4'
p. 504

Rocky and Sandy shores;
Bays and Estuaries

Habitat
On bottom and in shallows

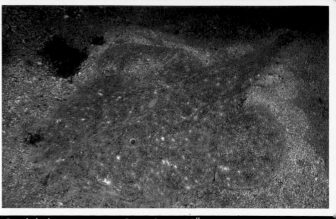

356 Windowpane *Scophthalmus aquosus* Length: to 18"
p. 504

Rocky and Sandy shores

Habitat
Over sand

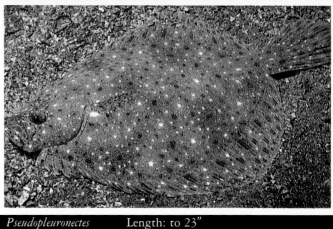

357 Winter Flounder *Pseudopleuronectes
americanus* Length: to 23"
p. 505

Rocky and Sandy shores;
Bays and Estuaries

Habitat
Over mud or sand, with or
without vegetation

358 Eyed Flounder

Bothus ocellatus
p. 505

Length: to 7″

Sandy and Gulf shores

Habitat
Shallow water in protected
areas over sand

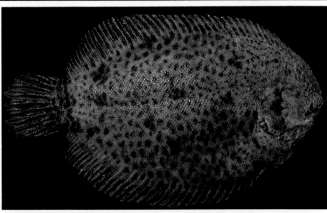

359 Hogchoker

Trinectes maculatus
p. 505

Length: to 6″

Sandy and Gulf shores;
Bays and Estuaries

Habitat
Shallow coastal waters over
mud, silt, or sand in bays
and estuaries

360 Naked Sole

Gymnachirus melas
p. 506

Length: to 6¼″

Sandy Shores

Habitat
Over sand on continental
shelf

361 Gray Angelfish

Pomacanthus arcuatus
p. 506

Length: to 24″

Rocky and Gulf shores;
Coral Reefs

Habitat
Shallow reefs

362 French Angelfish

Pomacanthus paru
p. 507

Length: to 14″

Coral Reefs

Habitat
Shallow reefs

363 Queen Angelfish

Holocanthus ciliaris
p. 507

Length: to 18″

Coral Reefs and Gulf
Shores

Habitat
Coral reefs in shallow water

364 Harvestfish
Peprilis alepidotus
p. 508
Length: to 12"

Sandy and Gulf shores

Habitat
Surface of inshore and
offshore waters over
continental shelf

365 Ocean Surgeon
Acanthurus bahianus
p. 508
Length: to 14"

Rocky, Sandy, and Gulf
shores

Habitat
Shallow reefs and rocky
areas, and nearby sand

366 Blue Tang
Acanthurus coeruleus
p. 508
Length: to 14"

Rocky and Gulf shores;
Coral Reefs

Habitat
Shallow coral and rock reefs

367 Foureye Butterflyfish   *Chaetodon capistratus*   Length: to 6"
   p. 509

Coral Reefs and Gulf
Shores

Habitat
Coral and rocky reefs

368 Reef Butterflyfish   *Chaetodon sedentarius*   Length: to 6"
   p. 509

Rocky and Gulf shores;
Coral reefs

Habitat
Coral and rocky reefs

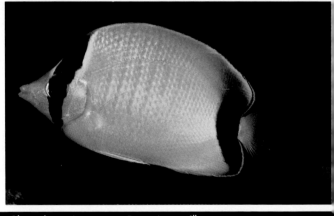

369 Banded Butterflyfish   *Chaetodon striatus*   Length: to 6"
   p. 510

Coral Reefs and Gulf
Shores

Habitat
Coral and rocky reefs

370 Sergeant Major
Abudefduf saxatilis
p. 510
Length: to 7"

Rocky and Gulf shores;
Coral Reefs

Habitat
Shallow reefs, rock jetties,
grass beds, and around
pilings

371 Porkfish
Anisotremus virginicus
p. 510
Length: to 14"

Southern Sandy and Gulf
shores; Coral Reefs

Habitat
Shallow water over reefs
and rocks

372 Pinfish
Lagodon rhomboides
p. 511
Length: to 15"

Sandy and Gulf shores

Habitat
Shallow water around
vegetation

373 Striped Bass
Morone saxatilis
p. 511
Length: to 6′

Rocky, Sandy, and Gulf
shores; Bays and Estuaries

Habitat
Inshore over various
bottoms; some
permanently in fresh water

374 Gray Snapper
Lutjanus griseus
p. 512
Length: to 3′

Rocky, Sandy, Mangrove,
and Gulf shores; Bays and
Estuaries; Coral Reefs

Habitat
Offshore, around estuaries,
mangrove swamps, and
coral reefs, and over rocks

375 Red Snapper
Lutjanus campechanus
p. 512
Length: to 31″
Juvenile

Sandy and Gulf shores

Habitat
Over rocks and natural and
artificial reefs

376 Tripletail

Lobotes surinamensis
p. 512

Length: to 3′4″

Bays and Estuaries; Gulf Shores

Habitat
Inshore in bays and estuaries near buoys and channel markers; offshore

377 Jewfish

Epinephelus itajara
p. 513

Length: to 7′10″

Southern Sandy and Gulf shores; Coral Reefs

Habitat
Inshore in shallow water; moderately deep water

378 Northern Searobin

Prionotus carolinus
p. 513

Length: to 17″

Rocky and Sandy shores; Bays and Estuaries

Habitat
On bottom in shallow to deep coastal waters

379 Sand Perch

Diplectrum formosum Length: to 12"
p. 514

Sandy and Gulf shores;
Coral Reefs

Habitat
Over sand or mud in
coastal waters, or near reefs

380 Black Drum

Pogonias cromis Length: to 3'3"
p. 514

Sandy and Gulf shores;
Bays and Estuaries

Habitat
Over sand or sandy mud in
bays and estuaries

381 Black Sea Bass

Centropristis striata Length: to 24"
p. 514

Rocky, Sandy, and Gulf
shores

Habitat
Continental shelf, over
rocks around jetties,
pilings, and wrecks

Southern Sandy and Gulf
shores; Coral Reefs

Habitat
Over coral reefs

Southern Sandy and Gulf
shores; Coral Reefs

Habitat
Over coral reefs and rocks
in shallow waters

Sandy and Gulf shores;
Bays and Estuaries

Habitat
Over mud or sand in
coastal waters and estuaries

385 Red Drum
Sciaenops ocellatus
p. 516
Length: to 5'

Sandy and Gulf shores;
Bays and Estuaries

Habitat
Surf zone to offshore waters

386 Southern Kingfish
*Menticirrhus
americanus*
p. 516
Length: to 20"

Sandy and Gulf shores

Habitat
Usually over sand but also
over mud or silt

387 Weakfish
Cynoscion regalis
p. 516
Length: to 35"

Sandy Shores; Bays and
Estuaries

Habitat
Shallow coastal waters over
sand or mud

388 Haddock

*Melanogrammus
aeglefinus
p. 517*

Length: to 3′8″

Rocky and Northern Sandy
shores

Habitat
Usually 25–75 fathoms,
rarely in shoal water

389 Atlantic Cod

*Gadus morhua
p. 518*

Length: to 6′

Rocky and Northern Sandy
shores

Habitat
Usually on or near bottom
of continental shelf

390 Pollock

*Pollachius virens
p. 518*

Length: to 3′6″

Rocky and Northern Sandy
shores; Bays and Estuaries

Habitat
Over rocks; sometimes at
midwater or on surface

391 Gizzard Shad
Dorosoma cepedianum
p. 519
Length: to 16"

Sandy and Gulf shores;
Bays and Estuaries

Habitat
Salt water; fresh water in
large rivers, reservoirs,
lakes, and estuaries

392 Mosquitofish
Gambusia affinis
p. 519
Length: to 2½"

Bays and Estuaries

Habitat
Near surface of fresh or
brackish water in ponds,
lakes, backwaters, and
sluggish streams

393 Gulf Killifish
Fundulus grandis
p. 519
Length: to 6"

Bays and Estuaries; Salt
Marshes; Gulf Shores

Habitat
Over sand or mud in bays,
tidal marshes, pools, and
ditches

394 Diamond Killifish   *Adinia xenica*   Length: to 2″

p. 520

Salt Marshes, Lagoons in
Coral Reefs, and Gulf
Shores

Habitat
Shallow lagoons, tide
pools, ditches, and salt
marshes

395 Sheepshead Minnow   *Cyprinodon variegatus*   Length: to 3″
p. 520

Bays and Estuaries, Salt
Marshes, and Gulf Shores

Habitat
Shallow waters of coastal
marshes and tide pools,
usually over sand; enters
fresh water

396 Sailfin Molly   *Poecilia latipinna*   Length: to 5″
p. 521

Salt Marshes

Habitat
Saltwater marshes, ponds,
and ditches; also in
fresh water

397 Atlantic Menhaden *Brevoortia tyrannus* Length: to 18″
p. 521

Rocky and Sandy shores;
Bays and Estuaries

Habitat
At or near surface over
continental shelf, near
large estuaries

398 American Shad *Alosa sapidissima* Length: to 30″
p. 521

Bays and Estuaries

Habitat
Bays, estuaries, and fresh
water

399 Atlantic Mackerel *Scomber scombrus* Length: to 22″
p. 522

Rocky and Northern Sandy
shores

Habitat
Open seas and over
continental shelf in
temperate water

400 Chub Mackerel
Scomber japonicus
p. 522
Length: to 25"

Rocky and Northern Sandy
shores

Habitat
Warm coastal waters over
continental shelf

401 Bluefish
Pomatomus saltatrix
p. 523
Length: to 3'7"
⊗

Rocky, Sandy, and Gulf
shores

Habitat
Surface waters, near shore
or offshore

402 Tarpon
Megalops atlanticus
p. 523
Length: to 8'

Sandy and Gulf shores;
Bays and Estuaries

Habitat
Primarily shallow coastal
waters and estuaries

403 Striped Anchovy

Anchoa hepsetus
p. 524

Length: to 6"

Sandy and Gulf shores;
Bays and Estuaries

Habitat
Shallow coastal·waters

404 Bonefish

Albula vulpes
p. 524

Length: to 3′

Rocky and Sandy shores;
Lagoons in Coral Reefs

Habitat
Shallow waters over soft
bottoms

405 Striped Mullet

Mugil cephalus
p. 524

Length: to 18"

Sandy and Gulf shores;
Bays and Estuaries

Habitat
Coasts, estuaries, and fresh
water

406 Snook

Centropomus undecimalis
p. 525

Length: to 4'7"

⊗

Bays and Estuaries, Lagoons in Coral Reefs, and Gulf Shores

Habitat
Shallow coastal waters, estuaries, lagoons, canals, and fresh water

407 Inland Silverside

Menidia beryllina
p. 525

Length: to 6"

Sandy and Gulf shores; Bays and Estuaries

Habitats
Along coast and in freshwater streams and rivers, usually over sand

408 Cobia

Rachycentron canadum
p. 526

Length: to 6'7"

Sandy and Gulf shores; Coral Reefs

Habitat
Open seas; some also found near shore around barrier islands and coral reefs

Rocky and Sandy shores;
Bays and Estuaries

Habitat
Marine, estuarine, and fresh
water, usually in
vegetation

Bays and Estuaries, Salt
Marshes, and Gulf Shores

Habitat
Shallow grass flats in salt
and fresh waters

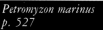

Rocky and Sandy shores;
Bays and Estuaries

Habitat
At sea; along coasts, in
estuaries and fresh water

412 Atlantic Needlefish
Strongylura marina
p. 527

Length: to 25"

Rocky and Sandy shores

Habitat
Coastal marine waters and
into freshwater coastal
streams

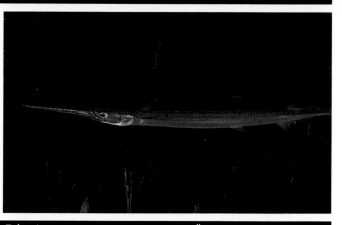

413 Sharksucker
Echeneis naucrates
p. 528

Length: to 32"

Offshore Waters

Habitat
Open seas

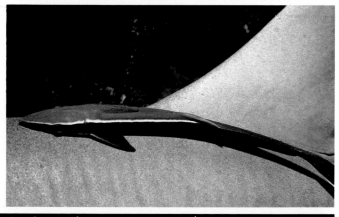

414 Spiny Dogfish
Squalus acanthias
p. 528

Length: to 5'

Rocky and Sandy shores;
Bays and Estuaries

Habitat
In temperate waters over
soft bottoms

415 Blue Shark

Prionace glauca
p. 528

Length: to 12'7"

Rocky and Northern Sandy shores

Habitat
In shallow coastal waters over sand or mud, and far out at sea

416 Bonnethead

Sphyrna tiburo
p. 529

Length: to 4'6"

Rocky, Sandy, and Gulf shores; Bays and Estuaries

Habitat
Shallow inshore waters, bays, estuaries, usually over sand

417 Blacktip Shark

Carcharhinus limbatus
p. 529

Length: to 8'

Rocky, Sandy, and Gulf shores; Bays and Estuaries

Habitat
Coastal waters and offshore

418 Sandbar Shark
Carcharhinus plumbeus　Length: to 8′
p. 529

Sandy and Gulf shores;
Bays and Estuaries

Habitat
Bottom-dwelling in
shallow bays, estuaries, and
inshore

419 Bull Shark
Carcharhinus leucas　Length: to 11′
p. 530
⊗

Sandy and Gulf shores;
Bays and Estuaries

Habitat
Inshore, never far from
land; ascends rivers

420 White Shark
Carcharodon carcharias　Length: to 21′
p. 530
⊗

Rocky, Sandy, and Gulf
shores; Bays and Estuaries

Habitat
Coastal surface waters

421 Sand Tiger

Odontaspis taurus
p. 531

Length: to 10'

⊗

Sandy Shores; Bays and Estuaries

Habitat
On or near bottom in shallow inshore waters

422 Smalltooth Sawfish

Pristis pectinata
p. 531

Length: to 18'

Sandy and Gulf shores; Bays and Estuaries

Habitat
Estuaries, lower parts of large rivers, and shallow coastal waters

423 Scalloped Hammerhead

Sphyrna lewini
p. 531

Length: to 13' 9"

⊗

Sandy and Gulf shores; Bays and Estuaries

Habitat
In oceans near surface, sometimes in estuaries

424 Spotted Eagle Ray   *Aetobatus narinari*   Length: to 9'
                             p. 532

Sandy and Gulf shores;
Bays and Estuaries

Habitat
Coastal surface waters

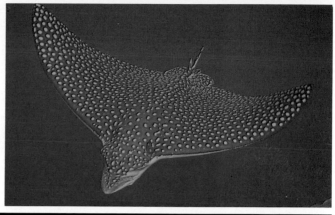

425 Southern Stingray   *Dasyatis americana*   Length: to 5'   ⊗
                             p. 532

Sandy and Gulf shores;
Bays and Estuaries

Habitat
Near shores and in bays

426 Clearnose Skate   *Raja eglanteria*   Length: to 3' 1"
                           p. 533

Sandy and Gulf shores

Habitat
Shallow shores

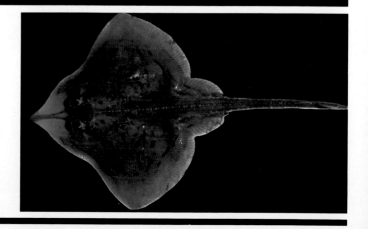

427 Oyster Toadfish   *Opsanus tau*   Length: to 15"
                             p. 533

Sandy Shores; Bays and
Estuaries; Lagoons in Coral
Reefs

Habitat
Shallow water over sand or
mud, in vegetation or
among debris

428 Striped Blenny   *Chasmodes bosquianus*   Length: to 3"
                            p. 533

Sandy and Gulf shores

Habitat
Shallow grass flats over
sand

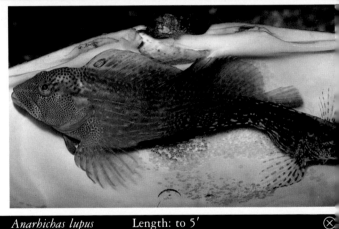

429 Atlantic Wolffish   *Anarhichas lupus*   Length: to 5'
                               p. 534

Rocky Shores

Habitat
Over hard bottoms

430 Ocean Pout

Macrozoarces americanus
p. 534

Length: to 3' 6"

Rocky and Northern Sandy shores; Bays and Estuaries

Habitat
On bottoms near sand, mud, rocks, or seaweed

431 Spotted Moray

Gymnothorax moringa
p. 535

Length: to 3' 3"

Sandy and Gulf shores; Coral Reefs

Habitat
Shallow coral reefs and rocky coasts

432 Lined Seahorse

Hippocampus erectus
p. 535

Length: to 5"

Rocky, Sandy, and Gulf shores

Habitat
Usually associated with vegetation such as eelgrasses and sargassum

433 Snapping Turtle   *Chelydra serpentina*   Length: 8–18½"
p. 538

Bays and Estuaries; Salt
Marshes; Lagoons in Coral
Reefs; Gulf Shores

434 Loggerhead   *Caretta caretta*   Length: 31–48"
p. 538

Sandy and Gulf shores;
Bays and Estuaries;
Lagoons in Coral Reefs

**435 Diamondback
Terrapin**   *Malaclemys terrapin*   Length: 4–5½"
p. 538

Bays and Estuaries; Salt
Marshes; Lagoons in Coral
Reefs; Gulf Shores

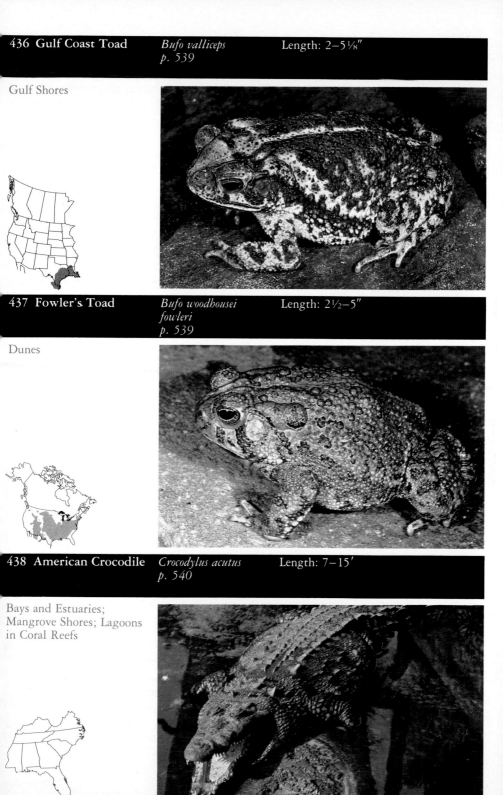

436 Gulf Coast Toad   *Bufo valliceps*   Length: 2–5⅛″
p. 539

Gulf Shores

437 Fowler's Toad   *Bufo woodhousei fowleri*   Length: 2½–5″
p. 539

Dunes

438 American Crocodile   *Crocodylus acutus*   Length: 7–15′
p. 540

Bays and Estuaries;
Mangrove Shores; Lagoons
in Coral Reefs

439 American Alligator

Alligator mississippiensis
p. 540

Length: 6'–19'2"

Bays and Estuaries; Salt Marshes; Lagoons in Coral Reefs; Gulf Shores

440 Green Anole

Anolis carolinensis
p. 540

Length: 5–8"

Mangrove and Gulf shores

441 Mole Skink

Eumeces egregius
p. 541

Length: 3½–6½"

Southern Sandy Shores

442 Cottonmouth   *Agkistrodon piscivorus*   Length: 20–74½"
p. 541

Bays and Estuaries; Salt
Marshes; Lagoons in Coral
Reefs; Gulf Shores

443 Southern Water Snake   *Nerodia fasciata*   Length: 16–62½"
p. 542

Bays and Estuaries; Salt
Marshes; Mangrove and
Gulf shores; Lagoons in
Coral Reefs

444 Eastern Hognose Snake   *Heterodon platyrhinos*   Length: 20–45½"
p. 542

Sandy and Gulf shores

445 White Mangrove
Laguncularia racemosa
p. 544
Plant height: 20–40'

Mangrove Shores

Range
Southern Florida

446 Black Mangrove
Avicennia germinans
p. 544
Plant height: 10–40'

Mangrove Shores

Range
North-central Florida to
the Keys, west to southern
Louisiana and southern
Texas

447 Red Mangrove
Rhizophora mangle
p. 544
Plant height: 15–20'

Mangrove Shores

Range
Primarily southwestern
Florida; also numerous
islets on Gulf side of
Florida Keys

448 Salt Marsh Aster *Aster tenuifolius*   Plant height: to 2½'
p. 545

Salt Marshes

Range
Massachusetts to Florida,
west along Gulf Coast to
Mississippi

449 Sea Rocket *Cakile edentula*   Plant height: 6–20"
p. 545

Sandy Shores

Range
Southern Labrador to
Florida

450 Beach Rose *Rosa rugosa*   Plant height: 3–6'
p. 546

Sandy Shores

Range
Quebec to New Jersey

451 Sea Lavender   *Limonium*   Plant height: 1–2'
                        carolinianum
                        p. 546

Salt Marshes

Range
Newfoundland and Quebec
to Florida, west along Gulf
Coast to Mississippi and
Texas

452 Beach Pea   *Lathyrus maritimus*   Creeper
                     p. 546   Length: 2–3'

Sandy Shores

Range
Along northwestern
Atlantic Coast, south to
New Jersey

453 Bayberry   *Myrica pensylvanica*   Plant height: 1½–6'
                    p. 547

Sandy Shores

Range
Maritime Provinces to
Louisiana

454 Beach Plum
Prunus maritima
p. 547

Plant height: to 6'

Sandy Shores

Range
New Brunswick to New
Jersey

455 Beach Heather
Hudsonia tomentosa
p. 548

Plant height: less than 1'

Sandy Shores

Range
New Brunswick to North
Carolina

456 Prickly Pear Cactus
Opuntia compressa
p. 548

Flower width: 2–3"

Sandy Shores

Range
Massachusetts to Georgia;
also Alabama on Gulf
Coast

457 Seaside Goldenrod

Solidago sempervirens
p. 548

Plant height: 2–8'

Sandy Shores

Range
The Gulf of St. Lawrence
to Florida, west along Gulf
Coast to Texas

458 Dusty Miller

Artemisia stelleriana
p. 549

Plant height: over 2'

Sandy Shores

Range
Quebec to Virginia

459 Sand Bur

Cenchrus tribuloides
p. 549

Plant height: 1–1½'

Sandy Shores

Range
Southern New York to
Florida, and west to
Louisiana

460 Saltmarsh Bulrush

Scirpus robustus
p. 549

Plant height: to 6'

Salt Marshes

Range
Nova Scotia to Florida, west along Gulf Coast to Texas

461 Spike Grass

Distichlis spicata
p. 550

Plant height: 1–2'

Salt Marshes

Range
Prince Edward Island to Texas

462 Sea Oats

Uniola paniculata
p. 550

Plant height: 3–6'

Sandy Shores

Range
Southern Virginia to Florida, west along Gulf Coast to Texas

463 Short Dune Grass   *Panicum amarum*   Plant height: up to 2'
p. 551

Sandy Shores

Range
Connecticut to Florida;
along Gulf Coast to
Louisiana

464 Saltmeadow Cordgrass   *Spartina patens*   Plant height: 12–40"
p. 551

Salt Marshes

Range
Quebec to central Florida;
also central Florida to
Texas on Gulf Coast

465 American Beach Grass   *Ammophila breviligulata*   Plant height: 2–4'
p. 552

Sandy Shores

Range
Newfoundland to North
Carolina

Salt Marshes

Range
Quebec to central Florida;
also central Florida to
Texas on Gulf Coast

Bays and Estuaries

Range
Greenland to Florida

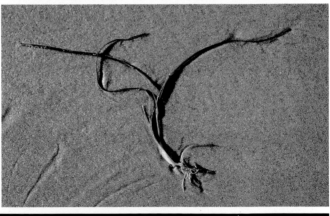

Coral Reefs; Gulf Shores

Range
Florida Keys and shallow
bays and lagoons along
Gulf Coast

469 Glassworts

Salicornia spp.
p. 553

Plant height: to 12"

Salt Marshes

Range
Massachusetts to Florida, west along Gulf Coast to Texas

470 Glassworts

Salicornia spp.
p. 553

Plant height: to 12"

Salt Marshes

Range
Massachusetts to Florida, west along Gulf Coast to Texas

471 Channeled Rockweed

Pelvetia spp.
p. 554

Length: 2–6"

Rocky Shores

Range
North Atlantic and Britain; unconfirmed, spotty records from northernmost portion of our Atlantic Coast

| 472 **Knotted Rockweed** | *Ascophyllum nodosum* p. 554 | Length: usually 3–4′, occasionally longer |

Rocky Shores

Range
Maritime Provinces to
northern New Jersey

| 473 **Bladder Rockweed** | *Fucus vesiculosus* p. 555 | Plant height: 1–4′ |

Rocky Shores

Range
Maritime Provinces to
North Carolina

| 474 **Sea Lettuce** | *Ulva lactuca* p. 555 | Length: 1′ or more |

Rocky Shores

Range
Most portions of Atlantic
and Gulf coasts

475 Green Thread Alga	*Enteromorpha* spp.	Length: up to 2'
	p. 555	Frond diameter: 1/4–3/4"

Rocky Shores

Range
All Atlantic and Gulf
shores of North America

476 Purple Laver	*Porphyra umbilicalis*	Diameter: about 6"
	p. 556	

Rocky Shores

Range
Northward from South
Carolina

477 Irish Moss	*Chondrus crispus*	Plant height: about 2"
	p. 556	

Rocky Shores

Range
Maritime Provinces to New
Jersey

478 Coralline Alga   *Corallina officinalis*   Plant height: to 5″
                          p. 556

Rocky Shores

Range
Maritime Provinces to
Long Island

479 Coralline Alga   *Corallina officinalis*   Plant height: to 5″
                          p. 556

Rocky Shores

Range
Maritime Provinces to
Long Island

480 Encrusting Stony   *Lithothamnium* spp.   Size: highly variable
Red Alga   *p. 557*   Thickness: to ½″

Rocky Shores; Coral Reefs

Range
Common on Atlantic and
Gulf coasts

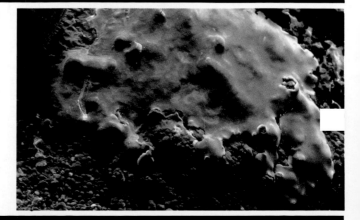

481 Bearded Robber Fly
Efferia pogonias
p. 559
Length: ½–¾"

Sandy Shores and Dunes

Food
Other flies, flying ants, small bees, true bugs, grasshoppers, butterflies, and moths

482 Eastern Sand Wasp
Bembix americana spinolae
p. 559
Length: ½–⅝"

Sandy Shores and Dunes

Food
Adult drinks nectar; larva eats flies of various kinds

483 Deer Flies
Chrysops spp.
p. 559
Length: ⅜–⅝"

Sandy Shores, Salt Marshes, and Dunes

Food
Male drinks plant juices; female sucks blood from mammals

484 American Horse Fly
Tabanus americanus
p. 560

Length: ¾–1⅛"

Sandy Shores and Salt
Marshes

Food
Male eats pollen and
nectar; female takes blood
of large mammals

485 Bee Fly
Anthrax analis
p. 560

Length: ¼–⅜"

Sandy Shores and Dunes

Food
Adult drinks nectar; larva
is parasite of tiger beetle
larvae

486 Cow Killer
*Dasymutilla
occidentalis*
p. 561

Length: ⅝–1"

Sandy Shores and Dunes

Food
Adult drinks nectar; larva
feeds on bee larvae

Golden Saltmarsh Mosquito   *Aedes solicitans*   Length: ⅛–¼"
                                    p. 561

Salt Marshes

Food
Male feeds on plant juices;
female sucks blood from
wild and domestic animals
and humans

Black-headed Soft-winged Flower Beetle   *Collops nigriceps*   Length: ¼"
                                          p. 562

Sandy Shores and Dunes

Food
Soft-bodied adult insects,
insect eggs and larvae

489 Beautiful Tiger Beetle   *Cicindela formosa*   Length: ⅝–¾"
                                 p. 562

Sandy Shores and Dunes

Food
A wide variety of surface-
dwelling insects

490 Seaside Grasshopper · *Trimerotropis maritima*   Length: ¾–1⅜"
p. 563

Dunes

Food
Herbaceous plants on range
and arid land

491 Field Cricket   *Gryllus pennsylvanicus*   Length: ⅝–1"
p. 563

Dunes

Food
Plant materials outdoors,
and when available, dying
and dead insects.

492 Dune Wolf Spider   *Geolycosa pikei*   Length: ½–⅞" (males); ¾–⅞"
p. 564   (females)

Sandy Shores and Dunes

Food
A wide variety of surface-
dwelling adult and larval
insects

493 Parasitic Jaeger   *Stercorarius parasiticus*   Length: 21″
p. 566

Offshore Waters

494 Magnificent Frigatebird   *Fregata magnificens*   Length: 38–40″
p. 566

Gulf Shores

495 Great Skua   *Catharacta skua*   Length: 21″
p. 566

Offshore Waters

496 Cory's Shearwater   *Calonectris diomedea*   Length: 20–22"
p. 567

Offshore Waters

497 Greater Shearwater   *Puffinus gravis*   Length: 18–20"
p. 567

Offshore Waters

498 Wilson's Storm-Petrel   *Oceanites oceanicus*   Length: 7"
p. 568

Offshore Waters

Sandy Shores

Rocky Shores

Offshore Waters

502 Ring-billed Gull   *Larus delawarensis*   Length: 18–20″
                              p. 569

Rocky, Sandy, and Gulf
shores; Bays and Estuaries

503 Herring Gull   *Larus argentatus*   Length: 23–26″
                              p. 570

Rocky, Sandy, and Gulf
shores; Bays and Estuaries

504 Great Black-backed *Larus marinus*   Length: 30″
Gull   *p. 570*

Rocky and Sandy shores;
Bays and Estuaries

505 Laughing Gull *Larus atricilla* Length: 15–17"
p. 570

Rocky, Sandy, and Gulf
shores; Bays and Estuaries

506 Bonaparte's Gull *Larus philadelphia* Length: 12–14"
p. 571

Sandy and Gulf shores

507 Roseate Tern *Sterna dougallii* Length: 14–17"
p. 571

Sandy and Gulf shores

508 Sandwich Tern
Sterna sandvicensis
p. 572
Length: 16"

Sandy Shores; Bays and
Estuaries

509 Caspian Tern
Sterna caspia
p. 572
Length: 19–23"

Sandy and Gulf shores;
Bays and Estuaries; Salt
Marshes

510 Royal Tern
Sterna maxima
p. 572
Length: 18–21"

Sandy and Gulf shores;
Bays and Estuaries

Rocky, Sandy, and Gulf
shores; Bays and Estuaries

Rocky, Sandy, and Gulf
shores; Bays and Estuaries;
Salt Marshes

Rocky and Sandy shores;
Bays and Estuaries

514 Least Tern
Sterna antillarum
p. 574
Length: 8–10"

Sandy and Gulf shores;
Bays and Estuaries; Salt
Marshes

515 Sooty Tern
Sterna fuscata
p. 574
Length: 16"

Sandy Shores

516 Black Skimmer
Rynchops niger
p. 575
Length: 18"

Rocky, Sandy, and Gulf
shores; Bays and Estuaries

517 Northern Gannet *Sula bassanus* Length: 35–40″
p. 575

Rocky and Sandy shores

518 American White Pelican *Pelecanus erythrorhynchos* Length: 55–70″
p. 576

Bays and Estuaries; Gulf Shores

519 Brown Pelican *Pelecanus occidentalis* Length: 45–54″
p. 576

Bays and Estuaries; Mangrove and Gulf shores

520 Common Murre *Uria aalge* Length: 17"
p. 577

Rocky Shores

521 Atlantic Puffin *Fratercula arctica* Length: 12"
p. 577

Rocky Shores

522 Razorbill *Alca torda* Length: 17"
p. 578

Rocky Shores

523 Dovekie	*Alle alle* *p. 578*	Length: 8″

Rocky Shores

524 Horned Grebe	*Podiceps auritus* *p. 578*	Length: 12–15″

Bays and Estuaries; Gulf
Shores

525 Common Loon	*Gavia immer* *p. 579*	Length: 28–36″

Bays and Estuaries; Gulf
Shores

526 Pied-billed Grebe
Podilymbus podiceps
p. 579
Length: 12–15″

Bays and Estuaries

527 Red-necked Grebe
Podiceps grisegena
p. 580
Length: 18–20″

Bays and Estuaries

528 Red-throated Loon
Gavia stellata
p. 580
Length: 24–27″

Bays and Estuaries

| 529 Northern Pintail | *Anas acuta*
p. 581 | Length: 25–30″ (males); 21–23″ (females) |

Bays and Estuaries; Salt Marshes

| 530 Canvasback | *Aythya valisineria*
p. 581 | Length: 19–24″ |

Bays and Estuaries; Gulf Shores

| 531 Redhead | *Aythya americana*
p. 581 | Length: 18–22″ |

Bays and Estuaries; Salt Marshes; Gulf Shores

532 Mottled Duck

Anas fulvigula
p. 582

Length: 21"

Bays and Estuaries; Salt
Marshes; Gulf Shores

533 Gadwall

Anas strepera
p. 582

Length: 18–21"

Bays and Estuaries; Salt
Marshes

534 American Black Duck

Anas rubripes
p. 583

Length: 19–22"

Bays and Estuaries; Salt
Marshes; Gulf Shores

| 535 American Wigeon | *Anas americana*
p. 583 | Length: 18–23" |

Salt Marshes

| 536 Fulvous Whistling-
Duck | *Dendrocygna bicolor*
p. 583 | Length: 18–21" |

Bays and Estuaries; Gulf
Shores

| 537 Blue-winged Teal | *Anas discors*
p. 584 | Length: 14–16" |

Bays and Estuaries; Gulf
Shores

| 538 Harlequin Duck | *Histrionicus histrionicus* p. 584 | Length: 14–20″ |

Rocky Shores

| 539 Ruddy Duck | *Oxyura jamaicensis* p. 585 | Length: 14–16″ |

Bays and Estuaries

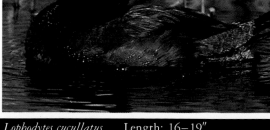

| 540 Hooded Merganser | *Lophodytes cucullatus* p. 585 | Length: 16–19″ |

Bays and Estuaries; Salt Marshes

541 Red-breasted Merganser *Mergus serrator* Length: 19–26"
p. 586

Bays and Estuaries; Gulf Shores

542 Bufflehead *Bucephala albeola* Length: 13–15"
p. 586

Bays and Estuaries; Gulf Shores

543 Greater Scaup *Aythya marila* Length: 15–20"
p. 586

Bays and Estuaries; Gulf Shores

544 Mallard   *Anas platyrhynchos*   Length: 18–27"
                  p. 587

Bays and Estuaries; Salt
Marshes

545 Northern Shoveler   *Anas clypeata*   Length: 17–20"
                            p. 587

Bays and Estuaries; Salt
Marshes; Gulf Shores

546 Ring-necked Duck   *Aythya collaris*   Length: 14–18"
                           p. 588

Bays and Estuaries; Salt
Marshes; Gulf Shores

547 Common Eider   *Somateria mollissima*   Length: 23–27"
p. 588

Rocky Shores; Bays and
Estuaries

548 King Eider   *Somateria spectabilis*   Length: 18–25"
p. 589

Rocky Shores; Bays and
Estuaries

549 Surf Scoter   *Melanitta perspicillata*   Length: 17–21"
p. 589

Rocky and Sandy shores;
Bays and Estuaries

550 Black Scoter

Melanitta nigra
p. 589

Length: 17–21″

Rocky and Sandy shores;
Bays and Estuaries

551 White-winged Scoter

Melanitta fusca
p. 590

Length: 19–24″

Rocky and Sandy shores;
Bays and Estuaries

552 Oldsquaw

Clangula hyemalis
p. 590

Length: 19–22″ (males); 15–17″ (females)

Rocky and Sandy shores;
Bays and Estuaries

553 Snow Goose
Chen caerulescens
p. 591
Length: 22–30"

Bays and Estuaries; Salt
Marshes; Gulf Shores

554 Canada Goose
Branta canadensis
p. 591
Length: 22–26" (small races); 35–45"
(large races)

Bays and Estuaries; Salt
Marshes; Gulf Shores

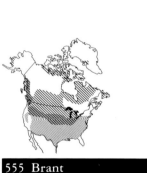

555 Brant
Branta bernicla
p. 592
Length: 22–30"

Bays and Estuaries; Salt
Marshes

556 Snow Goose   *Chen caerulescens*   Length: 22–30″
                   p. 591

Bays and Estuaries; Salt
Marshes; Gulf Shores

557 Tundra Swan   *Cygnus columbianus*   Length: 48–55″
                   p. 592

Bays and Estuaries

558 Mute Swan   *Cygnus olor*   Length: 58–60″
                   p. 592

Bays and Estuaries

559 Roseate Spoonbill   *Ajaia ajaja*   Length: 30–32"
                                p. 593

Bays and Estuaries;
Mangrove and Gulf shores

560 Wood Stork   *Mycteria americana*   Length: 40–44"
                               p. 593

Bays and Estuaries; Salt
Marshes; Mangrove and
Gulf shores

561 White Ibis   *Eudocimus albus*   Length: 23–27"
                               p. 594

Bays and Estuaries; Salt
Marshes; Mangrove Shores

Bays and Estuaries; Salt
Marshes; Mangrove and
Gulf shores

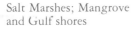

Salt Marshes; Mangrove
and Gulf shores

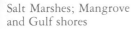

Salt Marshes; Mangrove
and Gulf shores

565 Great Blue Heron

Ardea herodias
p. 595

Length: 39–52"

Bays and Estuaries; Salt
Marshes; Gulf Shores

566 Reddish Egret

Egretta rufescens
p. 596

Length: 30"

Bays and Estuaries; Salt
Marshes; Gulf Shores

567 American Bittern

Botaurus lentiginosus
p. 596

Length: 23–34"

Salt Marshes and Gulf
Shores

568 Tricolored Heron

Egretta tricolor
p. 596

Length: 25–30"

Salt Marshes; Mangrove
and Gulf shores

569 Glossy Ibis

Plegadis falcinellus
p. 597

Length: 22–25"

Salt Marshes

570 Little Blue Heron

Egretta caerulea
p. 595

Length: 25–30"

Salt Marshes; Mangrove
and Gulf shores

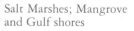

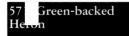

Bays and Estuaries; Salt
Marshes; Mangrove Shores

Salt Marshes and Gulf
Shores

573 Yellow-crowned Night-Heron   *Nycticorax violaceus*   Length: 22–27″
p. 598

Salt Marshes and Mangrove
Shores

574 Anhinga   *Anhinga anhinga*   Length: 34–36"
                                     p. 598

Bays and Estuaries; Gulf
Shores

**575 Double-crested
Cormorant**   *Phalacrocorax auritus*   Length: 30–35"
                                     p. 599

Rocky, Sandy, Mangrove,
and Gulf shores; Bays and
Estuaries

**576 American
Oystercatcher**   *Haematopus palliatus*   Length: 17–21"
                                     p. 599

Sandy, Mangrove, and
Gulf shores; Bays and
Estuaries

| 577 American Avocet | *Recurvirostra americana* p. 600 | Length: 16–20″ |

Bays and Estuaries; Salt Marshes; Gulf Shores

| 578 Black-necked Stilt | *Himantopus mexicanus* p. 600 | Length: 13–16″ |

Bays and Estuaries; Salt Marshes; Gulf Shores

| 579 Red Phalarope | *Phalaropus fulicaria* p. 601 | Length: 8″ |

Sandy Shores; Bays and Estuaries

| 580 Snowy Plover | *Charadrius*
alexandrinus
p. 601 | Length: 5–7″ |

Sandy and Gulf shores

| 581 Piping Plover | *Charadrius melodus*
p. 601 | Length: 6–7″ |

Sandy Shores

| 582 Semipalmated
Plover | *Charadrius*
semipalmatus
p. 602 | Length: 6–8″ |

Sandy and Gulf shores;
Bays and Estuaries

| 583 **Ruddy Turnstone** | *Arenaria interpres*
p. 602 | Length: 8–10″ |

Rocky and Gulf shores;
Bays and Estuaries

| 584 **Black-bellied Plover** | *Pluvialis squatarola*
p. 603 | Length: 10–13″ |

Rocky, Sandy, and Gulf
shores; Bays and Estuaries;
Salt Marshes

| 585 **Dunlin** | *Calidris alpina*
p. 603 | Length: 8½″ |

Sandy Shores

586 Sanderling
Calidris alba
p. 603
Length: 8″

Sandy and Gulf shores

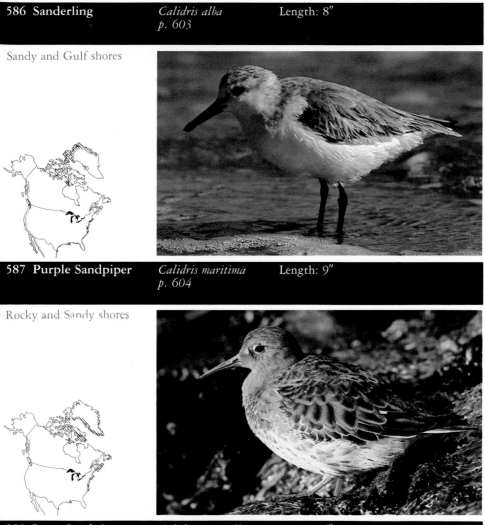

587 Purple Sandpiper
Calidris maritima
p. 604
Length: 9″

Rocky and Sandy shores

588 Least Sandpiper
Calidris minutilla
p. 604
Length: 6″

Bays and Estuaries; Salt
Marshes; Gulf Shores

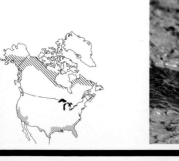

589 Stilt Sandpiper   *Calidris himantopus*   Length: 8½"
p. 605

Salt Marshes and Gulf
Shores

590 Willet   *Catoptrophorus*   Length: 15"
semipalmatus
p. 605

Sandy and Gulf shores;
Bays and Estuaries; Salt
Marshes

591 Spotted Sandpiper   *Actitis macularia*   Length: 7½"
p. 605

Bays and Estuaries; Salt
Marshes; Gulf Shores

592 Whimbrel

Numenius phaeopus Length: 17"
p. 606

Sandy Shores; Bays and
Estuaries

593 Lesser Yellowlegs

Tringa flavipes Length: 10½"
p. 606

Bays and Estuaries; Salt
Marshes; Gulf Shores

594 Short-billed Dowitcher

Limnodromus griseus Length: 12"
p. 607

Bays and Estuaries; Salt
Marshes; Gulf Shores

595 Long-billed Dowitcher

Limnodromus scolopaceus
p. 607

Length: 12¼"

Bays and Estuaries; Salt Marshes

596 Hudsonian Godwit

Limosa haemastica
p. 607

Length: 15"

Bays and Estuaries

597 Marbled Godwit

Limosa fedoa
p. 608

Length: 18"

Bays and Estuaries; Gulf Shores

598 Clapper Rail
Rallus longirostris
p. 608
Length: 14–16"

Salt Marshes and Gulf
Shores

599 Sora
Porzana carolina
p. 608
Length: 8–10"

Bays and Estuaries; Gulf
Shores

600 Purple Gallinule
Porphyrula martinica
p. 609
Length: 11–13"

Mangrove and Gulf shores

601 American Coot

Fulica americana
p. 609

Length: 15"

Bays and Estuaries; Gulf
Shores

602 Belted Kingfisher

Ceryle alcyon
p. 610

Length: 13"

Bays and Estuaries;
Mangrove Shores

603 Peregrine Falcon

Falco peregrinus
p. 610

Length: 15–21"

Rocky and Sandy shores

| 604 **Northern Harrier** | *Circus cyaneus* p. 611 | Length: 16–24″ |

Salt Marshes

| 605 **Osprey** | *Pandion haliaetus* p. 611 | Length: 21–24″ |

Sandy, Mangrove, and Gulf shores; Bays and Estuaries; Salt Marshes

| 606 **Bald Eagle** | *Haliaeetus leucocephalus* p. 611 | Length: 30–31″ |

Bays and Estuaries; Gulf Shores

| 607 Boat-tailed Grackle | *Quiscalus major* p. 612 | Length: 16–17″ (males); 12–13″ (females) |

Sandy, Mangrove, and Gulf shores; Bays and Estuaries; Salt Marshes

| 608 Fish Crow | *Corvus ossifragus* p. 612 | Length: 17″ |

Sandy Shores; Bays and Estuaries; Salt Marshes

| 609 Red-winged Blackbird | *Agelaius phoeniceus* p. 613 | Length: 7–9½″ |

Bays and Estuaries; Salt Marshes; Gulf Shores

Bays and Estuaries; Salt
Marshes

Mangrove and Gulf shores

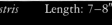

Sandy Shores

613 Marsh Wren
Cistothorus palustris Length: 4–5½"
p. 614

Salt Marshes and Gulf Shores

614 Swamp Sparrow
Melospiza georgiana Length: 5"
p. 614

Bays and Estuaries; Salt Marshes

615 Black-whiskered Vireo
Vireo altiloquus Length: 5½"
p. 615

Sandy, Mangrove, and Gulf shores

616 Sharp-tailed Sparrow

Ammodramus caudacutus
p. 615

Length: 5½"

Bays and Estuaries; Salt Marshes; Gulf Shores

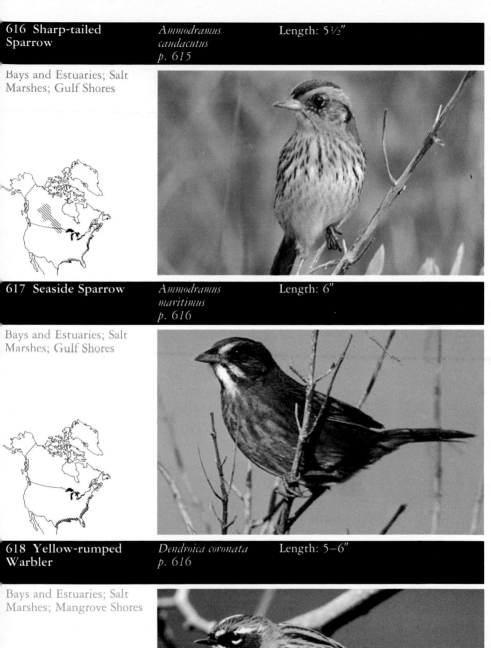

617 Seaside Sparrow

Ammodramus maritimus
p. 616

Length: 6"

Bays and Estuaries; Salt Marshes; Gulf Shores

618 Yellow-rumped Warbler

Dendroica coronata
p. 616

Length: 5–6"

Bays and Estuaries; Salt Marshes; Mangrove Shores

SEASHELLS

As every beachcomber knows, a visit to the seashore offers the pleasure of collecting the shells that have been washed ashore by the tides. On the Atlantic and Gulf coasts, the most spectacular shells include the Pink Conch and the Knobbed Whelk; smaller species, many of them amazingly intricate, are equally absorbing. This section describes some of the most typical and interesting shells that can be found along North America's eastern shores.

Queen Helmet
Cassis madagascariensis
31

4–14" (10.2–35.6 cm) high. Roughly triangular, large, heavy; pale yellowish white. Spire low. Body whorl large, with strong triangular knobs on shoulder, 2 rows of shorter blunt knobs below, whole surface with irregular spiral cords and crowded axial ridges that may become obscure. Large, thick parietal shield and broad outer lip pale brown or salmon; strong, elongated teeth and ridges pale against a deep chestnut-brown background. Inner side of outer lip with 10–12 teeth.

Habitat
On sand, in shallow depths to water 30' (9 m) deep.

Range
North Carolina to the larger islands of the West Indies.

Comments
Also known as the Emperor Helmet, this is among the largest species of helmet shells living today. Colonies have been seen plowing through the sand to find the heart urchin on which they feed; they may also feed on the long-spined urchin *Diadema*. The Latin species name was given more than 150 years ago under the erroneous impression that the shell was found in Madagascar. A more rounded form with smaller and more numerous spines is found off the shores of southeastern states. It was originally named as a distinct subspecies, Clench's Helmet (*C. m. spinella*).

Pink Conch
Strombus gigas
32, 121

7–12" (17.8–30.5 cm) high. Large, heavy; yellowish white with irregular brownish markings; fresh shells with thin, brown periostracum that flakes off when dry. Spire high, strongly angled, with pointed knobs where obscure axial ribs cross angles; knobs large and pointed on last 3 whorls. Interior of outer lip and aperture pinkish, suffused with white or yellow. Outer lip has broad upper expansion generally as high as or higher than spire; lower half somewhat wavy.

Habitat
In sand and rubble, usually among or near eelgrass, in water 5–15' (1.5–5 m) deep.

Range
SE. Florida to the West Indies and Venezuela.

Comments
Immature shells have a quite different appearance, with a high spire of strongly angled whorls, a narrow, pointed base, and an unexpanded lip. This is among the largest shells in the Florida-Caribbean area and long a favorite of collectors and souvenir hunters. Early travelers brought this shell back to Europe, and later, in Victorian England and America, it was used as a decoration and displayed prominently. Conch meat is delicious and an important source of food in the West Indian islands; numerous dishes featuring conchs are served at restaurants in Florida and the islands. Overfishing for food and souvenirs has severely depleted this species in some places.

Knobbed Whelk
Busycon carica
33

4–9″ (10.2–22.9 cm) high. Somewhat spindle-shaped, large, with a low, conical spire and a large body whorl that is narrowed below, ending in a long, wide, open canal; grayish white to pale grayish brown; younger shells with narrow, dark axial streaks, and commonly a whitish band below middle of body whorl. Spire whorls with low spiral cords and small, rounded knobs. Body whorl with strong, triangular knobs. Aperture elongate, whitish or deep orange, merging gradually at base into canal, which is weakly twisted below curved columellar wall. Outer lip thin, slightly wavy.

Habitat
On sand, in shallow depths to water 6–12′ (1.8–3.7 m) deep; also dredged in water to 15′ (4.6 m) or more deep.

Range
Cape Cod, Massachusetts, to Cape Canaveral, Florida.

Comments
These common shells are often cast up on beaches during storms. They may also be found buried in sand flats exposed by low tides, or caught in crab or lobster pots. Females lay their egg capsules, which resemble flattened pillboxes, near the low-tide line; these, too, are often tossed up on beaches. A subspecies, Kiener's Whelk (*B. c. eliceans*), found from North Carolina to Florida, is heavier, with stronger spines on the body whorl, which has a strong, broad spiral swelling near the base.

Channeled Whelk
Busycon canaliculatum
34

3½–7½″ (8.9–19 cm) high. Pear-shaped, large, with a moderately elevated, conical spire and a broad body whorl that narrows abruptly into a long, slender, open, slightly curved canal; grayish to yellowish white; covered with a gray periostracum bearing minute hairs. Spire whorls strongly angled, with a deep, narrow channel at suture, margined by a low ridge, and with a strong, knobby, or beaded ridge at shoulder; each whorl with low spiral cords; spiral sculpture and knobs on sharp ridge becoming weak and obscure on body whorl. Aperture broad, oval, yellowish to orange-brown inside.

Habitat
On sand or mud, intertidally to just below low-tide level.

Range
On both coasts: Cape Cod, Massachusetts, to N. Florida; introduced into San Francisco Bay, California.

Comments
This shell is abundant in the shallow bays of southern New England and Long Island Sound, and has at times been used for food. As late as the first quarter of this century, bushel baskets of these snails were sold at market in Boston's North End. They are known to feed on mollusks, but are also probably scavengers. The egg capsules are attached to a string and resemble small, oval change purses.

Lightning Whelk
Busycon contrarium
35

2½–16" (6.4–40.6 cm) high. Somewhat spindle-shaped, large, sinistral, with a low, conical spire and a large body whorl that is narrowed below, ending in a long, slightly twisted, open canal; yellowish to grayish white, with fine, narrow axial lines of reddish brown, often with obscure, dark axial streaks and an obscure, broad, whitish band below middle of body whorl. Spire whorls with strong, low spiral cords and a rounded angle just above suture, angle without knobs in early whorls and with low knobs in later whorls. Body whorl with broad, triangular knobs on shoulder, and numerous low spiral threads above and below. Aperture whitish within. Outer lip occasionally faintly grooved within.

Habitat
In sand, from near low-tide line to water 10′ (3 m) deep.

Range
North Carolina to Florida and Texas.

Comments
This whelk can be distinguished easily because it is sinistral, with its aperture on the left. The related Perverse Whelk (*B. perversum*) is also sinistral but stouter and heavier. The body whorl has strong triangular spines and a strong spiral swelling on the bottom.

Florida Crown Conch
Melongena corona
36, 124

1–8" (2.5–20.3 cm) high. Variable. Broadly to elongately ovate, with spire high to broadly conical; whitish, with dark brown spiral bands that sometimes cover most of shell. Whorls strongly convex, with indented suture, a shelflike shoulder below suture, strong axial ribs, and many fine spiral threads; tops of ribs project above shoulder, becoming strong, hollow, triangular spines; additional spines sometimes present on body whorl and base. Aperture ovate, rounded at top. Outer lip arched, thin, smooth inside, with external brown color bands showing through. Inner lip smooth, slightly twisted. Canal broad, open.

Habitat
On mud or muddy sand in quiet bays and lagoons, often among mangroves, intertidally to water about 6′ (1.8 m) deep.

Range
Both coasts of Florida; E. Alabama.

Comments
This common species is also known as the Common Crown Conch or the Crown Conch. Some shells lack spines and have fine spiral sculpture. The animal is a scavenger, feeding on dead fish, crabs, and other mollusks, but it also attacks and feeds on living bivalves. The female lays egg capsules that are attached to long strings anchored to a solid object. The young usually hatch as crawling larvae.

Apple Murex
Phyllonotus pomum
37

2–4¾" (5.1–12.1 cm) high. Ovate, with an elevated, conical spire; grayish white or yellowish brown, usually with dark brown spiral bands or blotches on outer lip. About 7 convex whorls; each whorl has 3 ridges, with 2–3 axial ribs between ridges; ribs and growth lines crossed by numerous spiral cords and fine threads; hollow spines or knobs present where larger cords cross ridges. Parietal callus has a thin, upturned margin and a brownish blotch. Aperture oval. Outer lip slightly flaring, toothed. Canal broad, moderately long, narrowly open, with an upturned end that has strong, hollow spines on outer edge.

Habitat
Among rocks or on sand intertidally.

Range
North Carolina to Brazil.

Comments
This is one of the abundant murex snails in Florida and the West Indies. In Florida it feeds principally on the common Eastern Oyster, boring almost round holes in the shells. The female lays compressed, tongue-shaped egg capsules formed into towerlike masses, each containing 80–200 capsules. After about 3 weeks, the young emerge as crawling individuals, immediately seeking out young snails and clams as prey.

Florida Lace Murex
Chicoreus florifer dilectus
38, 123

1–3¼" (2.5–8.3 cm) high. Elongately ovate, with an elevated, conical spire; whitish to pale brown, nuclear whorls often pinkish. Whorls each have 3 ridges bearing long, scaly, hollowed spines, with a low knob between ridges, and occasionally 1–2 smaller axial ribs and fine, irregular spiral cords. Aperture almost circular. Canal long, narrowly open, with 4 open, leafy spines on 1 side and a broad, flattened flange on other side. Operculum stout, almost circular.

Habitat
Among coral rubble or in sandy or muddy areas, intertidally to shallow water.

Range
North Carolina to S. Florida, and the Gulf Coast to Panama.

Comments
This is the most common Florida murex. It preys on various kinds of bivalves, boring a hole in the shell to feed on the soft parts. The Florida Lace Murex has been listed as a distinct species, *C. arenarius* or *C. rufus*, but it is so closely related to the West Indian Lace Murex (*C. florifer*) that it is now considered a subspecies of it.

Florida Horse Conch
Pleuroploca gigantea
39, 122

4–19" (10.2–48.3 cm) high. Spindle-shaped, large, with an elongate, conical spire; whitish yellow, orange, or brown; covered with a thin, brown periostracum. Spire whorls angled by 8–10 strong axial ribs that form triangular knobs, and with fine spiral cords and threads; on later whorls, knobs may become very large or disappear, leaving only strong spiral cords. Columella has 2 strong spiral ridges near base. Aperture oval. Canal long, open, slightly twisted. Operculum thick, horny, oval, pointed at 1 end.

Habitat
On sand and muddy sand, from low-tide level to water 20′ (6.1 m) deep.

Range
North Carolina to Florida and Texas.

Comments
This is the largest gastropod in our range, and one of the largest in the world. It feeds mainly on larger gastropods, such as the Tulip Shell, Lightning Whelk, and Lace Murex, and on the bivalve pen shells. It attacks gastropods by firmly holding on to the victim's operculum, preventing it from closing the aperture; the conch then inserts its proboscis and eats the soft parts of the prey. The egg masses are found on sand and consist of clusters of flattened, vase-shaped capsules that have horizontal ridges on the outside.

Thick-lipped Drill
Eupleura caudata
40

½–1⅝″ (1.3–4.1 cm) high. Ovate, with an elevated, conical spire; grayish white. Whorls strongly angled, with axial ribs, about 4–6 between growth lines on body whorl; 2–3 large, often obscure spiral cords on spire whorls, more than 8 on body whorl, with slender cords between. Body whorl has a thin ridge on each side, giving shell a flattened appearance. Columella smooth. Aperture ovate, yellowish to pale reddish brown within. Outer lip thick, white, toothed, with 6 small, short teeth inside. Canal moderately long, straight, narrowly open.

Habitat
On and near oyster beds in shallow water.

Range
S. Massachusetts to S. Florida.

Comments
The sculpture may be obscure because of erosion. The Thick-lipped Drill feeds mainly on oysters, but also on other species. The female lays her eggs from about February to May singly in slender, flattened, vase-shaped capsules on a slender stalk. A related species, the Sharp-ribbed Drill (*E. sulcidentata*), similar size, is found on the western coast of Florida. It is slightly more compressed, with more strongly angled whorls, which are frequently spiny, and with obscure spiral cords.

Atlantic Oyster Drill
Urosalpinx cinerea
41

½–1¾″ (1.3–4.4 cm) high. Oval, with elevated spire about half shell length; grayish or yellowish white, often with brown spiral bands. Whorls convex, with about 12 low, rounded axial ribs crossed by numerous spiral cords; finer scaly spiral threads between ribs. Aperture elongately ovate, white, yellowish or brownish within. Outer lip sometimes thickened within, with 2–6 small teeth inside. Canal open, fairly broad.

Habitat
On and among rubble near oyster beds, intertidally to water 25′ (76 m) deep.

Range
On both coasts: Nova Scotia to NE. Florida, and Washington to central California.

Comments
This species was introduced at the same time as oysters into both California and England about 100 years ago. It is probably the greatest predator of the common Eastern Oyster, although it also feeds on other bivalves, some gastropods, and even crabs. Using its radula, it drills a hole in the prey's shell, then inserts its proboscis to feed. The eggs are laid in rounded, vaselike capsules attached by a narrow stem to a solid object. Spawning takes place all summer, and the larvae emerge as crawling young in 6–8 weeks. The closely related Gulf Oyster Drill (*U. perrugatus*), same size, is found on both coasts of Florida; it has fewer and larger axial ribs, which are angled at the shoulder.

Florida Rock Shell
Thais haemastoma floridana
42

1½–4″ (3.8–10.2 cm) high. Ovate, with a broadly conical spire; grayish to yellowish, with fine, reddish-brown spots and short lines. Spire whorls have numerous spiral cords crossed by axial ribs, sharp on early whorls but broad and obscure on later whorls; spiral cord on periphery strongest, knobby at ribs. Body whorl large, convex, with or without 2 rows of strong, pointed knobs. Aperture ovate, yellowish or orange within. Margin of outer lip with fine, white spiral ridges. Canal broad, short.

Habitat
On rocks and oyster reefs, intertidally to below low-tide line.

Range
North Carolina to Florida and the Caribbean islands.

Comments
A common and variable species both in size and in the prominence of the series of knobs. The eggs are laid in vaselike capsules from which the young emerge as free-swimming larvae after 2–4 weeks. A subspecies, Hays' Rock Shell (*T. h. canaliculata*), has been proposed for the large, knobby specimens from the Gulf of Mexico. They are found near and on oyster beds, where they feed mainly on young oysters, but also on adult oysters and mussels; they also prey on other clams and barnacles.

Banded Tulip
Fasciolaria lilium
43

2¼–4⅛" (5.7–10.5 cm) high. Spindle-shaped; whitish to grayish yellow, with gray, bluish gray, or orange axial splotches or streaks, and with fine, dark reddish-brown spiral lines, 2 on spire whorls and 7–10 on body whorl. Whorls convex, smooth, except for third whorl, which has axial riblets and several shallow grooves. Body whorl has a narrow, elongated base, long canal, and strong descending ridges on lower part. Columella twisted, with a strong ascending spiral ridge at base. Aperture narrowly ovate, pointed above, where there is a long, narrow spiral ridge on parietal wall.

Habitat
On sand or muddy sand, in water 2–150' (0.6–46 m) deep.

Range
Dry Tortugas, Florida, and Louisiana to Texas and Yucatán, Mexico.

Comments
This species is closely related to the more common Florida Banded Tulip (*F. l. hunteria*), which is sometimes listed as a distinct species (*F. hunteria*). The Florida Banded Tulip is found from North Carolina to Florida and Alabama, and is generally smaller, with a broader body whorl and a somewhat shorter canal; the color splotches usually have a bluish-gray cast.

True Tulip
Fasciolaria tulipa
124, 125

2½–9½" (6.4–24.1 cm) high. Spindle-shaped; grayish white, yellowish, orange, or grayish green, usually with many fine reddish-brown lines and brown to orange axial splotches. Whorls convex; early whorls smooth except for a low, broad, raised, slightly knobby spiral ridge below suture, and a shallow groove immediately below ridge; later whorls smooth or with low, crowded spiral ridges. Body whorl has spiral ridges on base and canal. Columella curved, with 2 spiral ridges at base. Aperture ovate, notched and pointed above. Outer lip margin finely and sharply toothed, with teeth dark; densely spirally ridged within. Canal moderately long, slightly twisted, broad, open.

Habitat
On sand and mud, intertidally to water 30' (9 m) deep.

Range
North Carolina to Florida, Texas, and the West Indies.

Comments
This abundant species preys on a variety of gastropods and bivalves, but prefers large gastropods, such as the Florida Banded Tulip, the Pear Whelk, and young Queen Conchs. The female's egg capsules resemble flattened, V-shaped, stemmed vases with a frilly edge, clumped together in masses. The larvae emerge as crawling young.

Junonia
Scaphella junonia
45, 126

2½–4" (6.4–11.4 cm) high. Elongately ovate, large, with spire about a third shell length; white or yellowish white, with numerous spiral rows of large, squarish or oblong red-brown spots; fresh shells covered with a thin, pale brownish or yellowish periostracum. Nuclear whorls dome-shaped, smoothish, brown; later spire whorls gently convex; first 1½–2 whorls axially ribbed and usually with fine, distant spiral threads, later whorls smooth, often with very obscure spiral threads. Body whorl spirally ridged near base. Aperture elongate, pointed at both ends. Outer lip sharp, whitish or yellowish within. Columella has 4 strongly ascending spiral ridges. Columellar callus yellowish white, bordered by pale brownish siphonal ridge. No operculum.

Habitat
In sand, in water 40–250' (12–76 m) deep.

Range
North Carolina to both coasts of Florida.

Comments
Little is known about this handsome, distinctive species because it lives in moderately deep water. The many spots on this shell resemble those on the tail of the peacock, which was known to the ancients as the bird of Juno—hence the species name.

Alphabet Cone
Conus spurius atlanticus
46

1¾–3" (4.4–7.6 cm) high. Spire short, conical, concave, stepped; white, with spiral rows of irregular reddish-brown or yellowish-orange spots; fresh specimens have a thin, pale brown periostracum. Early whorls smooth except for very fine curved growth lines; later whorls flattened or with a shallow, wide furrow. Body whorl smooth except for narrow spiral ridges near base. Aperture narrow, white within.

Habitat
In sand, in water 1–50' (0.3–15 m) deep.

Range
Both coasts of Florida to Mexico.

Comments
This moderately abundant species is found in fairly shallow water, where it feeds on worms. The female's lens-shaped egg capsules are attached to a hard bottom and often laid in as many as 3–4 layers. The young escape as free-swimming larvae.

Scotch Bonnet
Phalium granulatum
47

1–3⅝" (2.5–9.2 cm) high. Broadly ovate; pale yellowish white to white, with 3 or more spiral rows of squarish, reddish-brown to reddish-yellow spots. Axial grooves usually present, which may result in a beaded or checkered appearance, especially on spire whorls and upper part of body whorl. Body whorl large, convex, often with spiral grooves, sometimes smooth. Parietal wall usually covered by a callus, which extends over lower columellar area as a freestanding, roughened shield. Outer lip usually thickened and with teeth.

Habitat
On sand in shallow water.

Range
North Carolina to Texas and Brazil.

Comments
Large numbers of these shells may be tossed up on our beaches after storms or long periods of strong winds blowing toward shore. Because this species is quite variable, numerous names have been given to the varieties that at some time or another have been considered distinct species or subspecies. The female deposits egg capsules that resemble elevated, round towers; she sits on them as she lays the eggs. The Scotch Bonnet is the official state shell of North Carolina.

Common Northern Whelk
Buccinum undatum
48

1⅜–5½" (3.5–14 cm) high. Broadly ovate, large, thick-shelled, with elevated, conical spire about half shell length; yellowish white to pale yellowish brown; fresh shells covered with a thin, light brown periostracum. Whorls convex, with strong, broad, curved ribs; on body whorl ribs reach to middle; ribs crossed by low, strong spiral cords with one to several finer threads between. Columella somewhat twisted. Aperture broadly ovate; interior, parietal callus, and columella white. Outer lip flared, faintly grooved within. Canal broad.

Habitat
On rocks, sand, or gravel, near low-tide line to water 200' (61 m) deep or deeper.

Range
Arctic to New Jersey.

Comments
This common and well-known species also occurs in Europe. It is also called the Common Northern Buccinum, the Waved Whelk, and, in England, the Common Whelk or Buckie. The height of the spire is somewhat variable, as is the strength of the spiral cords; the shells on our coasts do not reach the size of those in Europe. The animal is a scavenger, feeding on dead and dying marine animals. In England it was once an important food source and is still sold in some markets in the southeast. Egg capsule clusters were once used by sailors for washing their hands and were called "sea wash balls."

Common Nutmeg
Cancellaria reticulata
49

1–2¼" (2.5–5.7 cm) high. Broadly ovate, heavy, with spire less than half shell length; yellowish white, with reddish-brown axial or spiral splotches. Spire whorls shouldered below suture, almost straight-sided below shoulder, with 4–5 flattened spiral cords. Body whorl convex, with about 12 spiral cords. Spiral cords crossed by equidistant, narrow axial riblets that form beads on cords and result in latticed sculpture. Columella has 2 strong ridges, upper one larger, spirally grooved. Aperture elongate, pointed. Outer lip sharp, with strong, even ridges within. Canal short, twisted. Siphonal ridge strong.

Habitat
In sand among turtle grasses, from low-tide line to water 50' (15 m) deep.

Range
North Carolina to Texas and Brazil.

Comments
The radular teeth of this species are shaped like slender blades of grass; the tips bear many minute open tubes. The animal probably uses these to feed on soft sand-dwelling animals.

Common Dove Shell
Columbella mercatoria
50

⅜–⅞" (10–22 mm) high. Broad, with a conical spire and a bluntly triangular body whorl; shades of brown or yellow and white in varying patterns of splotches and spots. 5–6 slightly angled whorls, bluntly angled at periphery, with broad, low, rounded spiral cords; early whorls with low ribs, later whorls with cords sometimes obscurely beaded. Columella strong toothed. Aperture narrow, slightly curved. Outer lip thickened, finely toothed, curved. Canal short, open.

Habitat
On sand and stones among turtle grasses, from low-tide level to water 20' (6 m) deep.

Range
E. Florida to Brazil.

Comments
This abundant and common shell is highly variable in color and color patterns. The animal probably feeds on algae. The female lays single, oval, dome-shaped capsules on stones or turtle grass leaves. About a month after the capsules are deposited, the young larvae crawl out to begin life.

Atlantic Dogwinkle
Nucella lapillus
51

⅞–2" (2.2–5.1 cm) high. Ovate, thick-shelled, with a short, broad, moderately elevated, conical spire; whitish or yellowish to pale brownish or reddish brown, sometimes banded. Whorls convex, with numerous low, rounded spiral cords, often faintly knobby and occasionally scaly. Columella broad. Aperture ovate, yellowish or pale brown within. Outer lip thick, flaring; inner margin white to reddish brown.

Habitat
On rocks, often among seaweeds, intertidally.

Range
Newfoundland to New York.

Comments
This species is sometimes called *Thais lapillus*. It also occurs in

Europe. Diet can influence its color: those that feed on the Blue Mussel tend to be darker than those that prey on other mollusks or barnacles. Specimens with scaly sculpture are usually found below the low-tide mark, where there is diminished wave action. The female lays clusters of eggs in vase-shaped capsules, which are attached by a small stalk to rocks, mainly in crevices and on the undersides of stones. After about 4 months the young emerge and crawl about to begin feeding.

New England Basket Whelk
Nassarius trivittatus
52

½–⅞" (13–22 mm) high. Elongately ovate, with a high, conical spire more than half shell length; yellowish gray, southern specimens sometimes with 3 reddish-brown spiral bands on body whorl. Whorls strongly shouldered, giving shell a stepped appearance; strong axial ribs present, beaded by spiral cords. Body whorl convex, constricted above short, open canal. Aperture ovate. Parietal callus white, small, thin, glossy; rounded projection present at upper end of parietal wall and at toothed inner margin of outer lip.

Habitat
On sand and muddy sand, intertidally to water 300' (91 m) deep.

Range
Canada to NE. Florida.

Comments
This shell is also called the New England Dog Whelk, the Three-lined Basket Shell, and the New England Nassa. It is abundant on intertidal sand flats and just below the low-tide line, but is also commonly dredged in moderately deep waters. The animal is whitish with pale violet spots. Large numbers have been observed feeding on the egg cases of the Northern Moon Shell. It is probably also a scavenger.

Greedy Dove Shell
Anachis avara
53

⅜–¾" (10–19 mm) high. Broadly elongate, with spire about half shell length; light to dark brown, usually with white spots, sometimes yellowish with brown splotches; tops of ribs usually white below suture. Spire whorls slightly convex; first 3 whorls axially ribbed, next 2 usually smooth, sometimes ribbed. Body whorl has about 12 strong axial ribs crossed by fine spiral grooves. Aperture elongate, pointed at upper end. Outer lip has elongate teeth within. Canal broad, open. Operculum horny, elliptical.

Habitat
In eelgrass near or below low-tide line; on stones in water 30–150' (9–46 m) deep.

Range
Massachusetts to Florida.

Comments
This species is often found living together with the

Well-ribbed Dove Shell (*A. lafnesnayi*), with which it has been confused in the past. Its feeding habits are not known, but probably it is carnivorous and may be a scavenger. The egg capsules are volcano-shaped, with fine radial lines on the sides and without concentric ridges; the young hatch as free-swimming larvae.

Brown Sargassum Snail
Litiopa melanostoma
54

⅛" (3 mm) high. Elongately ovate, thin, with a pointed spire and a large body whorl; pale yellow to light brown. Whorls smoothish, moderately convex, marked by microscopic spiral grooves. Columella has a ridgelike projection at base. Aperture narrowly ovate. Outer lip thin, occasionally thickened in adults, and dark brown just inside.

Habitat
On floating sargassum weeds; dead shells in beach drift.

Range
The Gulf Stream along the Atlantic and Gulf coasts of North America; also Bermuda to Brazil.

Comments
This pelagic snail spends its entire life on sargassum weed. Because of its distinctive smooth, thin shell, large body whorl, and unusual habitat, it is placed in a separate subfamily (Litiopinae). It is often washed ashore on coasts bordering warm parts of the Atlantic.

Common Eastern Dog Whelk
Nassarius vibex
55

⅜–¾" (10–19 mm) high. Broadly ovate, with an elevated, conical spire half shell length; gray, often with reddish-brown bands or spirally arranged spots. Spire whorls separated by a well-marked suture, with strong, rounded axial ribs crossed by 3 strong, low spiral cords. Body whorl has 8–10 narrow, flattened spiral cords, top cord strongest, and a strong, broad basal ridge that marks former ends of canal. Aperture oval. Outer lip thickened above, toothed within, flaring below, marked externally by a strong axial thickening. Parietal wall and lower part of body whorl covered by a broad, shiny callus, with a vertical ridge at upper edge of aperture, and several small beads at base with a strong fold within. Operculum ovate, with strong spines at one end.

Habitat
On sand near low-tide line.

Range
Cape Cod, Massachusetts, to Florida, and Gulf Coast to Mexico.

Comments
This species is also called the Common Eastern Nassa, Mottled Dog Whelk, and Bruised Basket Shell. It has been observed feeding on the egg masses of polychaete worms. The female deposits oval, flattened, erect egg capsules, with a stalk at the narrower end that is attached to a hard surface. The young

emerge first as free-swimming larvae; after they develop a foot they may swim or creep for a while before losing the lobes used for swimming and settling down on the bottom.

Eastern Mud Whelk
Ilynassa obsoleta
56

⅝–1¼" (1.6–3.2 cm) high. Ovate, thick-shelled, with spire about half shell length; light brown, reddish brown, or dark brown. Whorls convex, with moderately deep suture, usually eroded apex, and crowded, low, slanting axial ribs crossed by low, flat spiral cords. Body whorl with obscure axial ribs. Columella curved, with a projecting spiral edge at base. Aperture oval. Outer lip with spiral ridges within. Canal broad, short. Parietal wall callused, often reddish brown.

Habitat
On mud flats, especially near low-tide line.

Range
On both coasts: Gulf of St. Lawrence, Canada, to NE. Florida; introduced on the Pacific Coast from Vancouver Island, British Columbia, to central California.

Comments
This abundant species is also called the Eastern Mud Nassa, the Mud Dog Whelk, the Mud Basket Shell, and the Common Mud Snail, and is often listed in the genus *Nassarius.* The shell is usually eroded. The animal prefers to feed on microscopic plant life, but will also eat dead animal matter and has been seen feeding on living marine worms. The egg capsules are erect, vase-shaped, and somewhat flattened. The young emerge as free-swimming larvae.

Common Periwinkle
Littorina littorea
57

⅝–1½" (1.6–3.8 cm) high. Broadly ovate, thick, sharply pointed except when eroded; grayish to gray-brown, often with dark spiral bands. Whorls smooth, slightly convex; young or unworn shells may show fine, low spiral lines. Columellar area and inside of outer lip whitish, the latter with a dark margin and dark brown deep within.

Habitat
On rocks intertidally.

Range
Labrador to Maryland.

Comments
Eggs are laid by the female in floating, disklike, horny capsules that eventually disintegrate, allowing the young larvae to escape and swim about for a while before settling down to a crawling life. This species is very common and abundant in Europe, and is still gathered and eaten by many people. In a more leisurely time, before World War II, pubs along the coast of England often had bowls of boiled periwinkles on the bar; small villages still carry on this tradition today. Their patrons pick the snails from their shells with "winkle pins" and dunk them in a sauce.

Marsh Periwinkle
Littorina irrorata
58

¾–1¼″ (1.9–3.2 cm) high. Broad, heavy, with aperture equal in length to spire; grayish white; spiral ridges marked with elongate reddish-brown spots; callus of inner lip chestnut-brown, and inside of sharp outer lip marked with red-brown streaks. Whorls almost flat, sculptured with many regular spiral ridges. Body whorl well-rounded at periphery.

Habitat
On and among vegetation in brackish-water marshes.

Range
New York to central Florida and along the Gulf Coast to Texas.

Comments
This common and abundant salt marsh species, usually living just at or above the water line, is not found in southern Florida or the West Indies. A fine algal growth may occasionally give this shell a greenish tinge. The female produces floating egg capsules.

Alternate Bittium
Bittium alternatum
59

⅛–⅜″ (3–10 mm) high. Elongately ovate, small; various shades of brown or very pale, occasionally spotted on spiral cords; immature specimens often very dark brown. Whorls slightly convex, with spiral cords crossing low axial ribs, rendering them knobby. In adults, sculpture on body whorl sometimes reduced. Base has numerous spiral cords. Columella slightly twisted at base. Aperture has a distinct inner margin and a thin, flaring outer lip; interior of lip and columella usually yellowish or pale reddish brown.

Habitat
On tidal flats to water 120′ (37 m) deep.

Range
Gulf of St. Lawrence to Virginia.

Comments
This species may be abundant locally along the shores and bays and estuaries, and is often found living on eelgrass. A related species is the Variable Bittium (*B. varium*), found from Maryland to Texas; it is smaller, with reduced spiral sculpture, especially on the body whorl, and with a white axial ridge on the body whorl.

Angulate Wentletrap
Epitonium angulatum
60

½–⅞″ (13–22 mm) high. Elongate, slender to moderately broad, with pointed spire; white. Whorls smooth, rounded, separated, attached at suture by 9–10 thin, bladelike ribs, bent slightly backward; ribs on early whorls strongly angled, and usually angled on later whorls. Aperture oval, with lip thickened and somewhat bent backward.

Habitat
In sand or rubble, probably near sea anemones, in shallow water.

Range
New York to Florida and Texas.

Comments
This is one of the most common wentletraps on the Atlantic Coast. It is commonly found among beach drift.

Costate Horn Shell
Cerithidea costata
61

⅜–⅝" (10–16 mm) high. Slender, elongate, with a pointed spire; light to dark brown or grayish. Whorls strongly rounded, with smooth, rounded, slightly curved, whitish axial ribs. On body whorl, ribs end at a spiral cord at upper limit of smooth base; ribs on last 2 whorls may become obscure; occasionally 1 or more whitish, swollen axial ridges on body whorl. Aperture round, with flaring, thickened outer and basal lips. Operculum horny, with a central nucleus and few turns.

Habitat
On mud in shallow water.

Range
W. and S. Florida to the West Indies.

Comments
Large numbers of these mollusks often live in quiet places, such as estuaries or mangrove swamps. They are also called Ribbed Horn Shells. A related species, the Plicate Horn Shell (*C. pliculosa*), ranging from Louisiana to Venezuela and in the larger West Indies, is higher and broader, with obscure spiral cords that make the axial ribs knobby; it has several broad, yellowish ribs that represent former outer lips.

Common American Auger
Terebra dislocata
62

1¼–2⅜" (3.2–6 cm) high. Sharply elongate, with about 14 whorls in a 1½" (3.8 cm) shell; bluish gray to yellowish brown, upper third sometimes paler, with a whitish band on periphery of body whorl. 1½ smooth, tan nuclear whorls; later whorls have distant, narrow axial ribs crossed by a strong spiral groove a third distance down from suture, and about 3–4 fine spiral cords; axial ribs on upper third of whorls become larger and broader on later whorls. Columella has prominent, twisted ridge at base. Aperture oblong. Canal twisted to left.

Habitat
In sand, from low-tide level to water 100′ (30 m) deep.

Range
Virginia to the West Indies.

Comments
This species, which is also called the Atlantic Auger, has neither a radula nor poison glands. It is commonly found near burrows of the acorn worm *Balanoglossus,* and probably preys on it.

West Indian Worm Shell
Vermicularia spirata
63

1–5" (2.5–12.7 cm) long. Irregular, wormlike; early whorls whitish or brown, subsequent whorls pale yellow to reddish brown. Young shells elongate, pointed, whorls with 1–2 spiral cords, becoming obscure; subsequent whorls gradually uncoil, forming an irregular, wormlike tube, with spiral cords either retained or becoming somewhat obscure or irregularly roughened.

Habitat
Often growing in or with sponges or other colonial marine animals in shallow water.

Range
SE. Florida and the West Indies.

Comments
This unusual shell is frequently found tossed up on beaches; clumps containing numerous living individuals are common. The apex resembles a turret shell, but after ¼–1" (6–25mm) the shell becomes uncoiled.

North Atlantic Top Shell
Calliostoma occidentale
64

⅜–½" (10–13 mm) high and equally wide. Conical; white. Whorls moderately convex, with 3–4 strong spiral cords and occasionally finer intermediate cords, cords smooth on later whorls but beaded on early ones; generally iridescent between cords. Base convex, with flattened spiral cords. Umbilicus closed.

Habitat
On sand and rubble, in shallow water to water 35–6000' (10.7–1829 m) deep.

Range
Nova Scotia to New Jersey.

Comments
This fairly common species, which also occurs in Europe, is the only member of the genus *Calliostoma* found in the colder waters of the northern Atlantic. The North Atlantic Top Shell is distinctive because of its relatively small size, white color, and iridescent sheen.

Common American Sundial
Architectonica nobilis
65

1–2½" (2.5–6.4 cm) wide. Broadly conical, low; whitish yellow, with a row of red-brown spots below suture, paler spots on cords and interspaces both above and on base. Numerous flattened whorls with several strong spiral cords and grooves of various widths; cords beaded in early whorls, beads gradually flattening out and becoming absent on body whorl. Body whorl strongly angled. Base flattened, with spiral cords and smoothish intervals. Inner cords strongly beaded around deep, narrow umbilicus, which is bordered by a heavy, white, strongly knobbed margin. Operculum horny, brown.

Habitat
In sand in shallow water.

Range
On both coasts; North Carolina to Brazil, and Baja California to Peru.

Comments
This sundial is often tossed up on beaches. One of the old German names for this species was the Architecture Shell, and the generic name was adopted from this popular name.

Bleeding Tooth
Nerita peloronta
66

¾–1½" (1.9–3.8 cm) high. Broadly ovate, thick, low-spired; grayish or yellowish, with irregular black and red zigzag markings. Whorls with spiral cords, strongest on early whorls. Columella has a flattened orange to scarlet area, with a large and small tooth at edge. Inner side of outer lip with numerous fine, obscure, elongate teeth; 1–2 larger teeth at each end. Operculum has an orange-brown semicircular ridge surrounding a gray-brown area, with some fine beads.

Habitat
On rocks at or near low-tide line.

Range
SE. Florida and the West Indies.

Comments
This abundant shell is very popular and is commonly sold in souvenir shops or used to make costume jewelry and trinkets. The ancient Romans called a certain sea snail *nerita*, in reference to their sea god, Nereus; hence the generic name.

Virgin Nerite
Neritina virginea
67

¼–¾" (6–19 mm) high. Round to slightly elevated, smooth, shiny; variably colored: black, white, greenish, red, purple, in a variety of patterns, with spots, mottlings, irregular axial streaks or lines, sometimes with a spiral band. Columellar area white to yellowish, convex, smooth, with small, irregular teeth. Operculum shelly, smooth, black.

Habitat
On stones or mangrove roots, intertidally and in brackish-water mud flats.

Range
Florida and the West Indies to Texas, Panama and Brazil.

Comments
This species is strictly a brackish-water inhabitant, particularly in mangrove swamps, and lives at the low-tide level, where it is exposed to the air for only short periods. It is especially common around the mouths of creeks and rivers, but it cannot tolerate fresh water and does not occur far up rivers. It is an extremely variable shell. The related Clench's Nerite (*N. clenchi*), also variable in color and pattern, is larger, less rounded, and more elevated; the outer edge of the columellar area opposite the teeth is dark orange-yellow. It is found in brackish and fresh water from Florida to Texas.

Northern Yellow Periwinkle
Littorina obtusata
68

⅜–¾" (10–19 mm) high and wide. Low-spired, smooth; yellow or orange to dark brown, occasionally with a brown or white spiral band; early whorls may be paler. Columella white. Operculum horny, yellow or dark orange.

Habitat
On rocks among seaweeds near or at low-tide level.

Range
Labrador to New Jersey.

Comments
This species is sometimes known as the Round Periwinkle. It also occurs along the Atlantic coast of Europe. It deposits its jellylike egg masses on seaweeds; the newly hatched larvae are free swimming. It is often found with the less common Northern Rough Periwinkle (*L. saxatilis*), which ranges from the Arctic seas to Cape May, New Jersey. This species is more elevated and gray to dark brown, with convex whorls bearing smooth spiral cords. The females produce live, shelled young.

Common Purple Snail
Janthina janthina
69

1–1½" (2.5–3.8 cm) wide. Round, smooth, thin, with a low spire; whitish purple with a deep purple base. Body whorl large, slightly angled at periphery.

Habitat
Suspended upside down from a frothy bubble raft on ocean surface.

Range
On both coasts: south of Nantucket, Massachusetts, and San Diego, California; also found worldwide in all tropical and subtropical waters.

Comments
The purple base of the Common Purple Snail may serve as camouflage from both fish and birds; from below, it appears to blend in with the sky, and from above, with the blue of the sea. The warm Gulf Stream carries these snails as far north as Massachusetts and England; however they cannot survive cold water and die when they encounter it. Like other species of *Janthina,* large numbers of these mollusks live on the open sea; but after steady, constant easterly winds, they are often found cast up in great numbers on our southern beaches. A vivid account of such an occurrence in Key West, Florida, was given by the malacologist Charles T. Simpson writing in 1897: ". . . as far as the eye could see, it [the beach] was a mass of the most intense, glowing violet color . . . from below low water to highest tide mark they were piled up . . . over shoe-top deep."

Common Northern Moon Shell
Lunatia heros
70

1½–5" (3.8–12.7 cm) high, equally wide or almost as wide. Almost round, smooth; grayish white to brownish gray, early whorls darker. Spire low, broadly conical, with gently convex whorls. Body whorl evenly rounded, or in large specimens slightly flattened below suture. Umbilicus deep, only slightly covered by thickened, white columella. Aperture semicircular. Operculum thin, horny, light brown.

Habitat
In sand, intertidally to water 1200' (366 m) deep; only in deeper water in the southern part of its range.

Range
New Brunswick and Gulf of St. Lawrence to North Carolina.

Comments
This shell is very common in New England. In the moist sands exposed at low tide, low mounds may betray the presence of live snails as they plow below the surface with their powerful foot, looking for clams. Using their radulae, they attack the clams by boring neat, round holes in the valves. A related species, same range, is the Spotted Northern Moon Shell (*L. triseriata*), which is much smaller, has 3 rows of brownish spots, and is found in water 6–350' (1.8–107 m) deep.

Shark Eye
Neverita duplicata
71, 129

⅞–3" (2.2–7.6 cm) high, somewhat wider. Dome-shaped, smooth; bluish to brownish gray, early whorls darkest, sometimes with a large brown spot on back. Spire low, with slightly convex whorls. Body whorl strongly rounded. Base convex. Umbilicus fairly broad and partially covered by a whitish to chestnut-brown, buttonlike pad. Aperture semicircular. Operculum thin, horny.

Habitat
On sandy shores, intertidally to just below low-tide line.

Range
Massachusetts to Florida and the Gulf states.

Comments
The Shark Eye is very common on the sandy coasts of the Atlantic. It preys on clams and other bivalves that it finds in the sand, boring neat, round holes in their valves and then feeding on the soft tissues within. Some specimens from the southern part of the range have a lower spire. The dark early whorls are surrounded by paler succeeding whorls, giving the appearance of an eye—hence the common name.

Common Atlantic Margin Shell
Marginella apicina
72

⅜–½" (10–13 mm) high. Ovately triangular, with a short, low spire and a large body whorl. Whorls smooth, shiny; whitish to yellow or orange-tan; tip of spire orange or deep yellow; body whorl often with 1 dark band below suture, 1 below periphery, and 1 near base. Aperture narrow, pointed above. Outer lip thickened within, smooth; margin round, raised, extending over preceding whorl, generally with 4 small reddish-brown spots: 1 at top, 2 in middle, and 1 at base. Columella has 4 slanting ridges, the lowest bordering short, open canal.

Habitat
In sand and among grasses, in water 1–30' (0.3–9 m) deep.

Range
North Carolina to the West Indies.

Comments
This shell is abundant on both sides of Florida, but especially common on the southwestern coast; occasionally sinistral specimens are found. The female lays dome-shaped, pimpled egg capsules singly, and the young emerge crawling.

Coffee Melampus
Melampus coffeus
73

½–¾" (13–19 mm) high. Top-shaped, smooth, with a low, broadly conical spire, and a broad, strongly angled body whorl; grayish, with a narrow, white spiral band at angle of body whorl and usually 1 or more below that. Spire whorls almost flat-sided. Body whorl very slightly convex below shoulder angle. Columella with spiral ridge at base. Aperture narrow, rounded below. Outer lip thin, with a brownish inner margin and a series of white teeth and spiral ridges within, rounded below. Inner lip pale brown, turned backward, thickened. Parietal wall has several teeth.

Habitat
On mud in mangrove areas intertidally.

Range
S. Florida to the West Indies.

Comments
The jellylike egg masses of this species are laid on stones, sticks, and dead leaves at high-tide level. About 10 days after the tide reaches the egg mass, free-swimming young emerge.

Eastern Melampus
Melampus bidentatus
74

⅜–¾" (10–19 mm) high. Ovate, with a broadly conical to elevated conical spire a quarter to a third shell length; yellowish brown to pale brown, sometimes with brown spiral bands and axial streaks. Apex usually eroded. Spire whorls flat-sided, usually worn, with microscopic, slightly wavy spiral grooves. Body whorl with rounded angles and fine spiral grooves toward top, narrowed toward rounded base. Columella with strong spiral ridge at base, another ridge above it. Aperture elongate, narrowed above, rounded below. Outer lip thin, with numerous strong, thin, white spiral ridges within.

Habitat
On edges of marshes or mangrove swamps or on seacoasts, near high-tide mark.

Range
Southern Canada to the West Indies.

Comments
This abundant species will occasionally climb on grasses to escape high water. In the marshes of New England, eggs are deposited when the area is flooded by spring high tides every

2 weeks. The eggs are laid in long, gelatinous strings that become covered by debris, which keeps the eggs moist when the water is low. The eggs hatch as free-swimming young, and after about 2 weeks settle down as crawling individuals.

Bubble Melampus
Detracia bullaoides
75

⅜–½″ (10–13 mm) high. Ovate to elongately ovate, with spire a third to a half shell length; brown, often with white to bluish-gray axial streaks and bands on spire. Spire elevated, convex; apex small, glassy, dome-shaped. Smoothish, sutures often irregular. Columella thickened, pale brown, with a strong spiral ridge. Aperture narrow, sharply pointed above. Outer lip thin, brown within, with a short, white spiral ridge near bottom.

Habitat
In mud in mangrove areas intertidally, and under debris at the high-tide line.

Range
S. Florida to the Virgin Islands.

Comments
The related Florida Melampus (*D. floridana*) is a smaller, broadly ovate shell found from Chesapeake Bay to Louisiana.

Lettered Olive
Oliva sayana
76, 127

1¾–2¾″ (4.4–7 cm) high. Elongate, almost cylindrical, smooth, glossy, with a small, pointed, conical spire; grayish or yellowish, with fine, irregular, reddish-brown zigzag markings, which are darker below suture and in 2 broad spiral bands on body whorl; sometimes all orange or white. Spire whorls smooth, flat-sided, flaring out at bottom to a sharp spiral ridge bordering narrow, deep, channeled suture. Body whorl long, slightly convex. Base has a sharp, raised edge bordering low, broad, flat siphonal band. Aperture narrow, wider at base. Parietal wall has a callus with spiral ridges, and a broader, raised callus at base, with about 4 strong, slanting ridges. Siphonal notch broad.

Habitat
In sand, from near low-tide line to water 150′ (46 m) deep.

Range
North Carolina to Florida, Texas, and Brazil.

Comments
This abundant species usually lives just below the surface with only its siphon extended above the sand. It preys on bivalves, especially egg cockles and coquina shells, seizing them and folding them in the hind part of the foot, then carrying them under the sand to digest. Apparently it also feeds on small crustaceans, such as sand crabs (*Emerita*), since it is often caught on hooks fishermen bait with them. Females release round egg capsules that float about in the water currents for about a week before the young escape.

Flamingo Tongue
Cyphoma gibbosum
77, 128

⅞–1¾" (2.2–4.4 cm) long. Broadly oblong, slightly flattened, smooth, shiny; back orange, except for an elongate white central area and a thickened white margin around edge. Upper end broadly rounded, lower end more narrowly rounded; back has a conspicuous transverse ridge in middle. Aperture broad. Outer lip thickened, untoothed.

Habitat
On sea fans and sea whips in shallow water.

Range
North Carolina to Brazil.

Comments
The animal's mantle, which covers most of its back, is yellowish orange with many large, irregular rings. The eggs are laid singly in clear, domed capsules, and the young emerge as free-swimming larvae. McGinty's Cyphoma (*C. macgintyi*), ranging from North Carolina and Bermuda to the Bahamas, is similar in size but more elongate. It is white and has a thicker and more conspicuous margin on the right edge of the back. The animal's mantle is yellow with solid dark spots.

Common Atlantic Bubble
Bulla umbilicata
78

½–1⅛" (1.3–2.8 cm) high. Oval to almost oblong; moderately thick-shelled; whitish, densely spotted or streaked with pink, red, or brown. Spire has a deep depression, narrowed below, with straight-sided walls and strong spiral grooves. Body whorl smooth, glossy, with fine, shallow, irregular grooves on base. Aperture narrow above, rounded and sacklike below, longer than body whorl. Outer lip thin, strongly arched at top, rounded below, merging into strongly curved columella, which is thickened and turned backward over base of shell.

Habitat
In mud and sand near low-tide line.

Range
Florida to Brazil.

Comments
This species has been erroneously listed as *B. striata,* a species that occurs in the Mediterranean, West Africa, and Central America.

Florida Slender Chiton
Stenoplax floridana
79

½–1⅞" (1.3–4.7 cm) long. Elongate, slender; yellowish to greenish white, irregularly spotted with white, grayish green, or brown. Valves strongly arched; sides of central valves and tail valve well differentiated, raised, with strong, radial, branching ridges, made beaded by irregular concentric grooves; central areas with narrow, crowded, longitudinal ridges becoming more slanting, stronger, and beaded toward edges; head valve with strong radial ridges beaded by concentric grooves. Girdle whitish, yellow, or gray, with small, crowded, thin, finely ribbed scales.

Habitat
Under stones between tide levels.

Range
Florida Keys to the West Indies and Panama.

Comments
Young specimens show a more sharply defined sculpture. The genus name is derived from 2 Greek words, *stenos* ("narrow") and *plax* ("plate"), referring to the narrow shape.

Common Eastern Chiton
Chaetopleura apiculata
80

⅜–¾" (10–19 mm) long. Oblong to broadly oval; pale brown to yellowish white, sometimes with a dark streak in central area. Valves distinctly angled in center; side areas slightly raised. End valves with tiny scattered beads; central areas with tiny beads in linear rows. Girdle leathery, microscopically beaded, and with scattered, fine, curved, hairlike spines.

Habitat
On shells or stones, near low-tide level to water 90' (27 m) deep.

Range
Cape Cod, Massachusetts, to Florida.

Comments
In the north this species is usually found on slipper shells (*Crepidula*), and on the west coast of Florida on pen shells (*Pinna*). Southern specimens may have a light or dark streak in the center. The female lays eggs, each of which is surrounded by a bristly capsule and set singly on a solid substance. In about a day the larva escapes as a free-swimming form, and in 6–10 days it settles on the bottom as a creeping animal.

Red Northern Chiton
Tonicella rubra
81

½–1" (13–25 mm) long. Elongately oval; pale yellowish, mottled with red or orange-red, often appearing orange-red with whitish zigzag markings. Valves bluntly angled; smooth except for growth ridges. Girdle reddish or grayish-brown, occasionally mottled with white, with microscopic, crowded, elongate scales.

Habitat
On and among rocks, near or just below low-tide level to water 450' (137 m) deep.

Range
On both coasts: Arctic to Connecticut, and to Monterey, California.

Comments
A related species is the Mottled Red Chiton (*T. marmorea*), which has a similar northern range. It is slightly larger, and the girdle is naked, lacking scales or spines.

Atlantic Slipper Shell
Crepidula fornicata
82

¾–2½" (1.9–6.4 cm) long. Strongly arched, or sometimes low, limpetlike, with coiled apex bent downward to 1 side of rear; base ovate. Exterior whitish, with irregular brownish blotches or radiating lines; usually smooth, but sometimes faintly wrinkled. Interior shiny, white, sometimes marked with brown; flat shelf covering a third to a half of rear has a sinuous edge with a slight central indentation.

Habitat
On rocks, other shells, and horseshoe crabs, intertidally to water 50′ (15 m) deep.

Range
On both coasts: Canada to Florida and Texas; introduced into Washington State.

Comments
This common shell is sometimes known as the Boat Shell or Quarterdeck. The species also occurs in parts of Europe. Its form may be influenced by the object to which it is attached; those living on scallops or mussels may take on the sculpture of those shells. Individuals are often found stacked on top of each other. In oyster beds, communities of slipper shells may be harmful, smothering the oysters. The related Spotted Slipper Shell (*C. maculosa*), 1–1⅜" (2.5–3.5 cm) long, is found from Florida to Mexico; it has small reddish-brown spots on its surface, and a straight or only slightly convex edge on the internal shelf.

Atlantic Plate Limpet
Notoacmaea testudinalis
83

⅞–1¾" (2.2–4.4 cm) long. Moderately high, with a nearly central apex; base broadly oval. Exterior grayish white, usually irregularly mottled with reddish brown in either rays or a netlike pattern; appearing smooth but with many microscopic radial threads and very fine growth lines. Interior shiny, whitish or pale bluish with a large, central, chestnut-brown spot; external mottling often showing through; sometimes a dark, mottled border at edge.

Habitat
Abundant on rocks intertidally.

Range
On both coasts: Arctic to New York, and to Alaska.

Comments
This is the common large limpet found on the rocky shores of New England and eastern Canada. Like many other limpets, it varies considerably in the height of the shell and in the extent and shape of the internal brown scar. The Latin species name means "like a tortoise shell," probably referring to the shell's mottled appearance.

Cayenne Keyhole Limpet
Diodora cayenensis
84

⅝–1¾" (1.6–4.4 cm) long. Moderately high, with a long dumbbell-shaped hole slightly in front of the centrally located apex; base broadly oval. Exterior whitish to gray, with many rough, radial ribs; every fourth rib larger. Interior white, with a truncate callus and deep pit behind it.

Habitat
On and among rocks, intertidally to water 90' (27 m) deep.

Range
Maryland to S. Florida and Brazil.

Comments
The Cayenne Keyhole Limpet is our most common representative of genus *Diodora*. It was formerly known as *D. alternata*. The elongate 2-lobed or dumbbell-shaped hole found in many species of *Diodora* is the source of the name "keyhole limpet." The related Lister's Keyhole Limpet (*D. listeri*), same size, has coarser sculpture of alternating large and small radial ribs, crossed by strong concentric ridges, forming squarish pits. Its color is sharper, whitish or gray, often with black markings, and it is found from southern Florida to Brazil.

Atlantic Bay Scallop
Argopecten irradians
85

1½–4" (3.8–10.2 cm) long. Almost circular, valves moderately convex; ears equal, byssal notch small, triangular, with few or no teeth on lower edge. Exterior white to dark gray or brown, often with concentric color bands or radial rays, ribs often darker than interspaces; 17–18 radial ribs, rounded except for fine, threadlike growth lines. Interior whitish, gray, or pinkish with dark margin, ears often spotted with brown; radial grooves present between broad, flattened ridges, which are strongly angled at margin.

Habitat
On muddy sand in eelgrass; in water 1–60' (0.3–18 m) deep.

Range
North shore of Cape Cod, Massachusetts, to New Jersey.

Comments
This and the Atlantic Deep-sea Scallop are the most important scallop species fished commercially on our East Coast. Once extensively gathered, especially in New England, the Atlantic Bay Scallop has become scarce because of overfishing and because eelgrass, which is an important element in its habitat, is largely disappearing. The southern forms have been placed in 2 subspecies. *A. i. concentricus,* found from Maryland to western Florida and Louisiana, is more circular and has a greater number of squarish ribs; its generally white right valve is much more convex than the darker left valve. *A. i. amplicostatus,* from Louisiana to Mexico, is similar to *A. i. concentricus,* but is more inflated and has fewer ribs.

Turkey Wing
Arca zebra
86

1¾–3½" (4.4–8.9 cm) long. Oblong, large, inflated; umbones a fourth shell length from front end, separated by broad, flattened, straight ligament area; an angled ridge runs from umbones toward lower part of hind end. Exterior yellowish white or yellowish brown, with oblique zigzag bands of reddish brown; covered with a brown, matted periostracum; numerous radial ridges present, crossed by fine concentric ridges. Interior whitish, with exterior color patterns showing through; darker along lower margin.

Habitat
Attached to coral rocks and in crevices, from low-tide line to water 20′ (6.1 m) deep.

Range
North Carolina to Bermuda and Brazil.

Comments
In the West Indies this abundant species is used by fishermen for bait; in Bermuda and Venezuela it is often eaten. The related Mossy Ark (A. imbricata), same range, is slightly smaller, with beaded ribs and a larger hind end; there is no oblique striping.

Blood Ark
Anadara ovalis
87

1⅛–3″ (2.8–7.6 cm) long. Broadly oval, sometimes almost round, inflated; front end convex, shorter than angled hind end; umbones close together; ligament area forms a V-shaped depression. Exterior whitish or yellowish white, usually covered with a thick, fibrous, dark brown periostracum; numerous flattened, often centrally grooved ribs present; concentric sculpture limited to irregular growth ridges. Interior white, with strong radial grooves in lower half; ligament area narrow, vertical; hinge line gently curved, with about 7 small, irregular, partly fused teeth in front of umbo; about 30 teeth behind umbo, first 18 or so narrow and flattened, later ones larger and angled; margin scalloped.

Habitat
In sand and mud, from low-tide line to water 10′ (3 m) deep.

Range
Cape Cod, Massachusetts, to the West Indies and Brazil.

Comments
This species is called the Blood Ark or Bloody Clam because, unlike most mollusks, it has hemoglobin and consequently red blood.

Ponderous Ark
Noetia ponderosa
88

1½–2¾″ (3.8–7 cm) long. Broadly ovate, trapezoidal, inflated, thick-shelled; strongly angled from umbones to lower part of hind end; umbones large, in middle of upper margin, turned toward hind end; ligament area moderately broad, spearhead-shaped, vertically grooved. Exterior whitish, covered with a thick, feltlike, dark brown periostracum; strong, flattened radial ribs present, with a central groove toward lower margin; interspaces have fine, crowded, flattened concentric threads, which become finer toward margins. Interior yellowish white; hind muscle scar elongately ovate, raised, with a sharp margin; hinge line narrow in middle, with many variously shaped teeth, those toward front end angled, vertical; margin toothed, scalloped.

Habitat
In sand, from just below low-tide line to water 60′ (18 m) deep.

Range
Virginia to Florida and Texas.

Comments
Fossil shells of this species are sometimes found on beaches as far north as southern Massachusetts; washed out from fossil beds, they show that the waters in that area were once warmer.

Atlantic Strawberry Cockle
Americardia media
89

⅞–2″ (2.2–5.1 cm) high. Obliquely squarish, inflated; umbones high, prominent; a pronounced angle runs from umbones to lower, straight-sided hind end. Exterior yellowish white, with transversely oblique series of reddish-brown spots; many flat ribs present, with densely crowded, curved scales. Interior white, sometimes with faint yellowish tinge under hinge, often with brown or purplish stain near lower hind angle of margin; margin strongly scalloped and grooved.

Habitat
In sand, in water 1–18′ (0.3–5.5 m) deep.

Range
North Carolina to Brazil.

Comments
This shell is also called the American Cockle or the Antillean Strawberry Cockle and is sometimes listed as *Trigoniocardia media*.

Giant Atlantic Cockle
Dinocardium robustum
90, 130

2¼–5¼″ (5.7–13.3 cm) high. Large, broadly ovate, somewhat oblique, inflated; rounded angle runs from umbones to lower end of hind margin; hind end flattened. Exterior whitish yellow, with scattered reddish-brown spots on ribs, often in concentric series, hind end brownish; numerous radial ribs present; on hind two thirds of shell ribs flattened, on front third ribs rounded, with strong, scalelike ridges. Interior pale reddish or purplish brown, white toward front, hind margin brown; radially grooved; front and lower margins strongly scalloped; in front of central teeth a white calcareous projection extends onto umbones.

Habitat
In mud and sand, from near low-tide line to water 100′ (30 m) deep.

Range
Virginia to N. Florida, Texas, and Mexico.

Comments
The largest cockle on our Atlantic Coast, it is common on the

beaches from North Carolina to northern Florida. Its flesh
makes an excellent chowder. Van Hyning's Cockle (*D. r.
vanhyningi*), a subspecies found in southwestern Florida, is
more elongate and oblique and more vividly colored.

Yellow Cockle
Trachycardium muricatum
91

1¼–2½" (3.2–6.4 cm) high. Broadly oval to almost circular,
moderately thick-shelled and inflated; umbones almost central.
Exterior whitish yellow, often with irregular reddish or orange
splotches; with 30–40 radial ribs bearing small scales; ribs on
front fourth of shell have small scales on front side; ribs
elsewhere have small scales on hind side. Interior whitish or
yellowish, with a yellowish splotch under hinge area, which
often has reddish-brown streaks on each side; margin strongly
toothed, especially hind margin, which often has a reddish or
purplish tinge.

Habitat
In sand or mud, in water 1–30' (0.3–9 m) deep.

Range
North Carolina to Argentina.

Comments
Like most of our cockles, this species has short siphons and
therefore can bury itself only a little below the surface.

Dwarf Tiger Lucine
Codakia orbiculata
92

½–1" (13–25 mm) long. Small, almost circular, moderately
thick-shelled and flattened; umbones somewhat behind
middle. Exterior white or yellowish; with crowded, rounded
riblets crossing many concentric ridges, forming elongate
beads or scales on riblets. Interior yellowish white; 2 teeth
under umbones and 2 parallel side teeth on each side in left
valve, 1 each in right valve; ligament on deeply placed shelf;
margin faintly grooved.

Habitat
In sand and mud, from low-tide to water 500' (152 m) deep.

Range
North Carolina to Brazil.

Comments
Also called Little White Lucine, this species varies
considerably in sculpture; some smaller and more ornate
specimens have reduced concentric ridges. The similar Costate
Lucine (*Parvilucina costata*), same range, is ⅜–½" (10–13 mm)
long, and has stronger concentric ridges. It is more inflated,
with a pointed hind muscle scar and a finely toothed margin.
It is often placed in the genus *Codakia*.

Coquina Shell
Donax variabilis
93, 131

½–1" (13–25 mm) long. Elongately triangular, wedge-
shaped; hind margin slightly angled behind ligament,
strongly toothed; front end rounded. Exterior whitish, usually
suffused, rayed, or banded with pink, orange, purple, yellow,

brown, or blue; shiny, with crowded, low radial riblets, obscure on front end, strong on hind end. Interior whitish, suffused with yellow, reddish, or purplish; margin strongly grooved and toothed, especially hind part.

Habitat
In sand on beaches, above and at low-tide line.

Range
New York to Florida and northern Mexico.

Comments
The species is also known as the Butterfly Shell, Wedge Shell, and Pompano; it is the basis for a famous chowder. Beds of compacted dead shells form a rock called coquina, which has been mined since colonial times. Living shells can be collected readily by quickly digging in the wet sand as a wave retreats.

Sunray Venus
Macrocallista nimbosa
94

3–6″ (7.6–15.2 cm) long. Large, elongately ovate, somewhat compressed, moderately thick-shelled; umbones slightly more than a fourth shell length from front end. Exterior pale brown, with darker brownish, interrupted radial rays of varying widths and irregular, dark concentric bands; periostracum thin, glossy, varnishlike; smooth except for fine growth lines and wrinkles. Interior white; pallial sinus small, pointed; front side tooth in left valve erect, triangular, fitting into pit in right valve.

Habitat
In sandy mud or sand, from just below low-tide line to water 25′ (7.6 m) deep.

Range
North Carolina to Brazil.

Comments
This large, striking shell is often cast up on Florida beaches. The animals bury themselves just below the surface; their presence is revealed by grooves in the sand. Gulls and terns dig great numbers of them up to feed on. These shells are plentiful in parts of northwestern Florida.

False Angel Wing
Petricola pholadiformis
95

1½–2¼″ (3.8–5.7 cm) long. Elongate, cylindrical, thin-shelled; front end inflated, becoming gradually flatter toward hind end; umbones a fifth shell length from front end; ligament short, external. Exterior white; front end with low, scaly riblets; riblets finer and without scales on rest of shell. Interior white; ribs in front end visible as grooves; pallial sinus deep, narrow.

Habitat
In heavy mud, clay, and peat, in lower part of intertidal zone.

Range
On both coasts: Gulf of St. Lawrence to Texas; introduced into California and Washington.

Comments
This species, which has also been introduced into Europe, is sometimes found boring into waterlogged wood. As its common name suggests, the shell closely resembles members of the Angel Wing Family.

Angel Wing
Cyrtopleura costata
96

4–8″ (10.2–20.3 cm) long. Large, elongately ovate; hind end slightly narrowed; umbones a fourth shell length from front end; front part of upper margin expanded, curving over umbones, hind part touching umbones; 1 horny accessory plate covers umbones; behind it a thick, winged, transverse, shelly plate present. Exterior white, sometimes tinged with pink; with scaly radial riblets, sharp and angular at front end, strongly scalloping lower margin, broader at hind end; surface smooth at upper margin. Interior white; external riblets show through as grooves; shield-shaped extension of upper margin over umbones ridged with an irregular thickening at hind end; projection under umbones broad, triangular, spoon-shaped.

Habitat
In deep, soft, sandy mud, at or just below low-tide level to water 60′ (18 m) deep.

Range
S. Massachusetts to the northern West Indies, Texas, and Brazil.

Comments
This well-known collector's item is common on the west coast of Florida, where it can be found burrowing as deep as 2′ (0.6 m) into mud. It is good eating and was once sold in markets throughout Cuba.

File Yoldia
Yoldia limatula
97

1–2½″ (2.5–6.4 cm) long. Large, elongately ovate, flattened; hind end pointed, front end evenly rounded; umbones small, in middle of upper margin, projecting only slightly above upper margin. Exterior white, covered with a shiny, greenish or pale brown periostracum, marked by a few dark concentric lines; smooth except for fine, irregular growth ridges, and a fine, sharply angled ridge running from umbones to hind end. Interior shiny, white to bluish white; lower margin sharp, smooth; shelf large, triangular; about 30 small, erect teeth in front of umbones, about 26 behind.

Habitat
In mud and muddy sand, in water 4–100′ (1.2–30 m) deep.

Range
Nova Scotia to North Carolina.

Comments
This shell is especially common in bays and estuaries. The genus name refers to a member of the Danish court who collected shells.

Great Piddock
Zirfaea crispata
98

1¼–3½" (3.2–8.9 cm) long. Broadly ovate; hind end broad, rounded, front end pointed; umbones slightly in front of center, covered by reflected part of front upper margin; a small, thin, triangular accessory plate present just behind umbones. Exterior grayish white; an oblique groove runs from umbones to center of lower margin, with irregular concentric growth wrinkles behind groove, and crowded, wavy, scaly concentric ridges in front; lower margin sharply saw-toothed. Interior whitish; an oblique ridge marks presence of external furrow; a narrow, flattened projection present under umbones.

Habitat
In salt marsh peat, or mud or clay, from low intertidal zone to water 240' (73 m) deep.

Range
From Labrador to S. New Jersey.

Comments
This species, also known as the Common Piddock, is occasionally found in waterlogged wood cast up on beaches. It also occurs in Europe. The size and shape of the shells vary according to the substance in which they burrow. A related species, the Rough Piddock (*Z. pilsbryi*), found from Alaska to southern Baja California, grows to a larger size, and has a longer hind end with a straighter lower margin.

Soft-shell Clam
Mya arenaria
99

1–5½" (2.5–14 cm) long. Ovate, moderately thin-shelled; front end rounded; hind end narrowed, rounded; umbones near center. Exterior grayish white, chalky, with a thin, light brown periostracum; irregular concentric growth lines and ridges present. Interior white; pallial sinus deep, squared off; internal ligament in left valve on large, horizontally projecting shelf with sharp, raised edges; right valve with ligament in oval pit deep under umbo.

Habitat
In sand and mud, intertidally to water 240' (73 m) deep.

Range
On both coasts: Labrador to North Carolina, and British Columbia to central California.

Comments
This species also occurs in Europe. In England it is known as the Sand-gaper, and northeastern American Indians called it the Manninose. It has long been important as a food source. In about 1865 or 1870, it was introduced into California, and has gradually spread north to British Columbia.

Atlantic Surf Clam
Spisula solidissima
100

1¾–7" (4.4–17.8 cm) long. Large, oval or elongately triangular, thick-shelled; umbones prominent, in front of middle, turned forward; ligament small; an obscure low angle runs from umbones to lower end of hind margin. Exterior yellowish white or grayish, with grayish-yellow periostracum, fibrous near hind end, less so on front end; smooth except for concentric growth lines. Interior dull white to cream-colored; ligament depression large, triangular.

Habitat
Just beneath surface in sand, mud, or gravel, from below low-tide line to water 140′ (42 m) deep.

Range
Nova Scotia to South Carolina.

Comments
In the Middle Atlantic states this shell is called the Beach Clam or Skimmer Clam, in Maine the Hen Clam, and in Canada the Bar Clam. It is the basis of important commercial fisheries, especially off New Jersey, Delaware, and northern Virginia.

Northern Quahog
Merceneria mercenaria
101

2¾–4¼″ (7–10.8 cm) long. Broadly ovate, moderately inflated, thick-shelled; hind end slightly sinuous, pointed below; umbones near front end; lunule margined by sharply incised line; broad, narrow escutcheon bounded by low umbonal ridge. Exterior grayish yellow, often with pale brownish tinge; with erect concentric ridges that are strong near umbones, more crowded near front and hind ends, with finer threads between; ridges broader and lower near lower margin; surface smooth near center. Interior white, usually with purple spot near hind end; pallial sinus small, sharply pointed; margin finely toothed.

Habitat
In sand or mud in bays or inlets, from intertidal flats to water 50′ (15 m) deep.

Range
Gulf of St. Lawrence to Florida and Texas.

Comments
Also known as the Hard-shelled Clam or the Littleneck Clam. The name "Quahog," or "Quahaug," is of Algonquin Indian origin. The Indians used the animal as food and the shell for tools and ornaments. Beads made from the thick shell were strung together and used as wampum, or shell-money; those with purple spots were twice as valuable as the white ones. Today this clam is the basis of an important commercial fishery. The related larger and heavier Southern Quahog (*M. campechiensis*), found from southern New Jersey to Florida and Texas, grows to 6″ (15.2 cm) in length; it is more inflated and lacks the smoothish area in the center of the valves; the interior is white and rarely marked with purple.

Carolina Marsh Clam
Polymesoda caroliniana
102

1–2″ (2.5–5.1 cm) long. Broadly ovate to almost circular, inflated, moderately thick-shelled; umbones large, central. Exterior pale olive-green or olive-brown; with a thin, brown periostracum forming distant, fibrous, scaly ridges that may be dense and wavy; with fine, concentric, elongately beaded growth ridges. Interior white; each valve with 3 central teeth; right valve with 2 minutely grooved side teeth on each side, left valve with 1; pallial sinus small, narrow, pointed.

Habitat
In mud in tidally influenced rivers, intertidally or just below low-tide line.

Range
Virginia to N. Florida, and Gulf of Mexico to Texas.

Comments
This species is abundant at the mouths of rivers and creeks, where the water is brackish to almost fresh. The related Florida Marsh Clam (*Pseudocyrena maritima*), found from Florida to Texas, is smaller, thinner, triangularly elongate, with the umbones nearer the front end; the periostracum is thinner and paler, and the interior is flushed with purple.

Ocean Quahog
Arctica islandica
103

2–5″ (5.1–12.7 cm) long. Large, broadly ovate, thick-shelled; both ends rounded; umbones large, curved forward, in front of middle; ligament large. Exterior whitish, with thick, olive-brown, dark brown, or almost black periostracum with fine concentric ridges, strongly wrinkled in older shells; smooth except for growth lines. Interior white; right valve with 3 central teeth, a small front side tooth close to central teeth, and an elongate hind side tooth; left valve with 2 strong central teeth, 1 small, rough front side tooth; no pallial sinus.

Habitat
In sand, in water 30–840′ (9–256 m) deep.

Range
Newfoundland to North Carolina.

Comments
Also known as the Black Clam and the Mahogany Clam, this is a highly esteemed food source and the basis of an extensive commercial fishery from Rhode Island south to Virginia. Its range also includes Iceland and western Europe. The Ocean Quahog somewhat resembles the common Northern Quahog, but differs in being more circular, thinner, with smaller umbones and a heavier periostracum, and in lacking a pallial sinus.

Disk Dosinia
Dosinia discus
104

1¾–3″ (4.4–7.6 cm) long. Nearly circular, flattened, thick-shelled; umbones small, curved forward; lunule impressed; ligament long, immersed in narrow cleft. Exterior white; periostracum thin, grayish, translucent, varnishlike; with crowded, flattened concentric ridges separated by fine grooves. Interior white; pallial sinus long, narrow, pointed; hinge area broad; left valve with small, low front side tooth and very thin front central tooth that fits into narrow cleft between 2 front central teeth in right valve.

Habitat
In sand and sandy mud in protected beaches, in lower
intertidal zone, rarely to water 10' (3 m) deep.

Range
Virginia to Florida, Texas, and the Bahamas.

Comments
This species is not found on open beaches, but only within
bays or estuaries where it burrows in loose sand. The related
Elegant Dosinia (*D. elegans*), found from North Carolina to
Texas and the Caribbean, is approximately the same size; its
concentric ridges are broader and less numerous.

Common Egg Cockle
Laevicardium laevigatum
105

1¼–3" (3.2–7.6 cm) high. Obliquely ovate, inflated;
umbones prominent; 2 fine, curving incised lines run from
umbones to each end of lower margin. Exterior white, often
tinged or spotted with pale orange, rose, purple, or brown;
covered with a thin, grayish-brown periostracum that is
usually worn off; smooth, often with obscure radial ribs and
fine concentric lines. Interior white, tinged with yellow,
reddish orange, or purplish; margin finely grooved; hinge
angled.

Habitat
In sand or mud, in water 2–65' (0.6–20 m) deep.

Range
North Carolina to Brazil.

Comments
Young shells are transversely ovate, gradually becoming more
obliquely ovate. Using its muscular foot, the animal can leap
considerable distances. The related Morton's Egg Cockle
(*L. mortoni*), 1" (25 mm) high, ranges from Cape Cod,
Massachusetts, to Florida and Texas. It is more oval or almost
circular, with fine concentric ridges set with fine beads.
Another species, Ravenel's Egg Cockle (*L. pictum*), is obliquely
ovate, flatter, and more brightly colored; it is found from
North Carolina to Brazil.

Northern Dwarf Tellin
Tellina agilis
106

½–⅝" (13–16 mm) long. Small, ovate, translucent,
compressed, thin-shelled; front end rounded; umbones behind
middle. Exterior whitish, sometimes pinkish; front part shiny,
often iridescent, smooth except for very fine, delicate growth
lines; hind part duller because of microscopic concentric
threads. Interior whitish; right valve with 2 central teeth and
1 large front side tooth, hind side tooth small; left valve with
1 large and 1 small central tooth.

Habitat
In sandy mud, in water 2–150' (0.6–46 m) deep.

Range
Gulf of St. Lawrence to Georgia.

Comments

Formerly known as *T. tenera,* this species is rather commonly found washed ashore along the northeastern coast. Related is Say's Tellin (*T. texana*), found from North Carolina to Florida, Texas, and the Bahamas. It is the same size, but thicker, more inflated, with stronger concentric sculpture. DeKay's Dwarf Tellin (*T. versicolor*), from Rhode Island to the West Indies, is also the same size; it is more elongately ovate and usually pink and iridescent.

Atlantic Nut Clam
Nucula proxima
107

¼–⅜″ (6–10 mm) long. Obliquely ovate, almost triangular; front end convex; umbones near hind end, pointed backward. Exterior white, with distant, microscopic radial threads, which appear as dark lines through shiny, olive-green periostracum. Interior pearly, smooth, with external radial sculpture showing through as fine lines; lower margin finely toothed; 24–30 crowded, pointed, flattened, triangular teeth on both sides of shelf.

Habitat
In mud and sand, in water 10–2500′ (3–762 m) deep.

Range
Nova Scotia to Florida and Texas.

Comments
These mollusks serve as food for bottom-feeding fish and are often found in the stomachs of haddock. The genus name is Latin for "little nut," referring to the shape.

Common Jingle Shell
Anomia simplex
108

¾–2¼″ (1.9–5.7 cm) long. Irregularly circular to broadly ovate, thin-shelled, translucent; right valve flat, thin. Exterior yellowish, orange, or silvery-white; smooth except for fine growth lines, or irregularly wrinkled, or radially ridged. Interior shiny, pearly; left valve with an oval, dull white central area and 3 roundish muscle scars; right valve with 1 round muscle scar.

Habitat
On rocks, shells, logs, boats, and piers, from near low-tide line to water 30′ (9 m) deep.

Range
S. Massachusetts to Brazil.

Comments
This jingle shell has a large byssus. Usually only the left valves are found on beaches, because the right valves are thinner and fragile and more likely to break. If this species attaches itself to another shell, the sculpture and shape of the left valve may resemble that of the shell to which it is attached.

Atlantic Thorny Oyster
Spondylus americanus
109

1½–5½" (3.8–14 cm) long. Large, broadly ovate to almost circular, thick-shelled, usually attached by right valve. Exterior whitish, yellow, or orange to reddish brown; early part of left valve often lighter or reddish and spotted; ribs and riblets on left valve with erect spines; right valves may have dense, leafy concentric ridges. Interior smooth, whitish, light brown or reddish on ears, with finely grooved margin often purple, brownish, orange, or yellowish.

Habitat
On rocks, coral reefs, submerged wrecks, and sea walls, in water 1–150' (0.3–46 m) deep.

Range
North Carolina to Brazil.

Comments
In deep, quiet waters the spines grow very long and delicate. The closely interlocking hinge teeth work so effectively that it is difficult to separate the valves without damaging the teeth.

Frons Oyster
Dendrostrea frons
110

1–2¾" (2.5–7 cm) high. Irregular, broadly ovate to elongately ovate, thick-shelled, narrowed at upper end, with hinge area curved backward. Exterior yellowish white, usually strongly tinged with purplish red; strong, irregular radial ridges present, giving margin a sharply angled, scalloped edge; ridges often wrinkled and developing clasping spines in shells attached to sea whips. Interior whitish or greenish; muscle scar near middle of hind margin or near hinge; series of small beads usually present along margin.

Habitat
On gorgonians, corals, cables, or wire nets, in water 2–15' (0.6–4.6 cm) deep.

Range
S. Florida to Brazil.

Comments
This variable species is also called the Leafy Oyster. Those shells without claspers may belong in a separate species.

Eastern Oyster
Crassostrea virginica
111

2–8" (5.1–20.3 cm) long. Large, irregularly and broadly ovate to elongate, usually thick-shelled, narrowed at upper end; right valve flatter than left valve. Exterior grayish or yellowish white, sometimes rayed with reddish purple; smoothish except for irregular wrinkles and growth lines, or with several radial ridges, especially on lower half; often with strong, platelike growth ridges. Interior white, with oval muscle scar near hind margin, scar usually purple; ligament large; margin smooth, gray.

Habitat
On hard or soft bottom, in water 10–40' (3–12 m) deep, especially in areas of low salinity.

Range
Gulf of St. Lawrence to Gulf of Mexico and the West Indies.

Comments
This is the common edible oyster of the Atlantic Coast. The principal fisheries are in the Middle Atlantic area; from these more than half the oysters in the United States are harvested. The eggs of this and the Giant Pacific Oyster are fertilized and develop in the water outside the parents. An unsuccessful attempt was made to introduce this species to the Pacific Coast.

Flat Tree Oyster
Isognomon alatus
112

1–4¼" (2.5–10.8 cm) long. Ovate to almost circular, often irregularly shaped, flattened, thin to moderately thick-shelled; hinge line straight, umbones pointed; byssal gap forms V-shaped depression between valves. Exterior grayish white, usually mottled with reddish purple, or reddish purple sometimes rayed with white; smooth except for irregular growth lines, which are often scaly, especially near margins. Interior has whitish to bluish-black pearly area, with a nonpearly, glossy margin that is usually paler, often yellowish mottled with reddish purple; hinge line thick, often wide above, with perpendicular grooves that contain horny ligament at lower end; margin thickened below umbones.

Habitat
On mangroves, rocks, or concrete structures, at low-tide line.

Range
S. Florida to Brazil.

Comments
The specimens found on mangrove roots are usually larger, flatter, and lighter than those found on rocks or concrete structures.

Stiff Pen Shell
Atrina rigida
113

5–11" (12.7–28 cm) long. Large, fan-shaped, moderately thick-shelled; upper margin straight, lower margin concave behind beaks and convex toward thin, sharp-edged hind margin. Exterior dark grayish brown, with 15–20 radiating ribs, upper ribs large, usually bearing many erect, hollow, sometimes tubular spines. Interior grayish brown, often mottled with dark orange or brownish orange near hind end; pearly layer covers front end, with large muscle scar protruding above edge of pearly layer.

Habitat
In sandy mud, from low-tide line to water 90' (27 m) deep.

Range
North Carolina to S. Florida and the West Indies.

Comments
The hind end of this pen shell is often covered with marine growth. Blackish pearls, which are used in making jewelry,

are sometimes found inside them. The Half-naked Pen Shell (*A. seminuda*), found from North Carolina to Texas and Brazil (absent in southern Florida and the Bahamas), is very similar and was formerly confused with *A. rigida*. It is slightly smaller, thinner, more narrow, and lighter in color; the internal muscle scar is slightly smaller and lies wholly within the pearly area.

Saw-toothed Pen Shell
Atrina serrata
114

6–12″ (15.2–30.5 cm) long. Large, elongate, fan- or wedge-shaped, thin-shelled; upper margin long, straight; front half of lower margin gently concave, hind part convex; hind margin straight, at right angle with upper margin. Exterior yellowish gray to grayish brown with more than 30 narrow radial riblets bearing many broad, hollow spines. Interior pale brownish, with a large, purplish or pearl-gray pearly layer covering three quarters of interior.

Habitat
In sandy mud, in water 2–20′ (0.6–6.1 m) deep.

Range
North Carolina to Texas and northern South America; rare in the West Indies.

Comments
Small shrimp and crab species spend their adult lives in the mantle cavity of this and other pen shells. Here they are sheltered and protected, and feed on particles brought into the mantle cavity.

Atlantic Ribbed Mussel
Geukensia demissa
115

2–5″ (5.1–12.7 cm) long. Elongately ovate or fan-shaped, moderately thin-shelled; upper margin straight or slightly and gently convex; broad umbones a short distance behind narrowed, rounded front end. Exterior grayish white, with a shiny, olive-brown to dark brown periostracum; and with strong radiating riblets, largest on upper part of hind end above broad umbonal ridge, fine to obscure along lower margin. Interior bluish gray or whitish, tinged with purplish blue or purplish red at hind end; hind margin scalloped by external ribs; no teeth at hinge.

Habitat
Buried in mud or peat or fastened to pilings at surface of mud in salt marshes and bays.

Range
On both coasts: Gulf of St. Lawrence to NE. Florida; also introduced into San Francisco Bay, California.

Comments
This mussel was formerly placed in the genus *Modiolus*. It is abundant in the salt marshes of the Middle Atlantic states, especially from Delaware to North Carolina, where it occurs in clumps buried in mud among the roots of the marsh cordgrass *Spartina*. A subspecies, the Beaded Ribbed Mussel

(*G. d. granosissima*), is found from Florida to Texas and Yucatán, Mexico; it is usually more slender and larger, with more numerous and beaded riblets.

Northern Horse Mussel
Modiolus modiolus
116, 132

2–9″ (5.1–22.9 cm) long. Large, oval, inflated, moderately heavy; middle of upper margin bluntly angled, lower margin straight or very slightly concave; rounded umbones just behind narrowed front end. Exterior pale purplish gray, covered with a pale to dark brown, hairy periostracum; smooth except for irregular, concentric growth ridges. Interior grayish white; margin smooth.

Habitat
Among gravel and rocks, from just below low-tide line to water 600′ (183 m) deep.

Range
On both coasts: Arctic to New Jersey, and to Monterey, California.

Comments
The periostracum easily flakes off dry adult shells, and in young shells it is drawn out into triangular, pointed projections. This large mussel is frequently used as fish bait, and in some parts of Europe, where it also occurs, as food.

Blue Mussel
Mytilus edulis
117

1¼–4″ (3.2–10.2 cm) long. Elongately fan-shaped, thin-shelled, with hind end rounded; middle of top margin bluntly angled, lower margin straight; umbones at pointed front end. Exterior purplish gray, covered with a tough, thin, smooth, dark brownish to bluish black periostracum. Interior bluish white, with margin and oval muscle scar near hind end bluish gray to bluish black; ligament long, narrow, under front half of upper margin on a narrow, chalky shelf that is pitted below; 4–7 small teeth at front end.

Habitat
Attached to rocks and wooden structures near low-tide line.

Range
On both coasts: Arctic to South Carolina, and Alaska to S. Baja California; also South America.

Comments
This is among the most common and widespread marine bivalves. It also occurs in Europe. It has been widely used as food for centuries, especially in Europe, where it is raised commercially in marine "farms." According to Rachel Carson, it is a "virtually untapped shellfish resource."

Atlantic Razor Clam
Siliqua costata
118

1½–2⅝″ (3.8–6.7 cm) long. Elongately oblong, compressed, thin-shelled; ends rounded; upper and lower margins almost parallel; umbones small, about a fourth shell length from front end; ligament stout, in a narrow cleft. Exterior whitish or pale purplish; periostracum thin, smooth, shiny, olive-green to brownish yellow; smooth except for faint growth lines. Interior purplish white; with low, white ridge running from hinge area toward lower margin, straight or slightly slanted toward front; hinge area on elongate shelf; 2 diverging central teeth in right valve; 2 separated central teeth in left valve.

Habitat
In sand or mud, just below low-tide line.

Range
Gulf of St. Lawrence south to North Carolina.

Comments
This species is commonly found burrowing vertically in sand or mud flats.

Green Jackknife Clam
Solen viridis
119

2–2⅝" (5.1–6.7 cm) long. Elongately oblong, gaping at both ends; hind end narrowed, rounded; upper margin straight; lower margin slightly curved; umbones at front end; ligament narrow, long. Exterior grayish white; periostracum thin, shiny, pale yellowish or yellowish green, with a widening gray band from umbones to hind end. Interior grayish white; 1 central tooth in each valve.

Habitat
In sand in bays and inlets intertidally.

Range
Rhode Island to Florida and Louisiana.

Comments
The genus name is a Latin word for "pipe" and refers to the elongate, narrow shell, open at both ends.

Atlantic Jackknife Clam
Ensis directus
120

3–8" (7.6–20.3 cm) long. Elongately oblong, slightly curved; both ends strongly squared off, front lower corner rounded; umbones at front end; a low, flat, broadening ridge runs from umbones to hind end; ligament moderately long, narrow. Exterior whitish; periostracum olive-green, grayish on ridge; smooth except for fine growth lines that become vertical on ridge, and above it turn back toward umbones. Interior bluish white; 2 small, vertical central teeth in left valve, 1 narrow central tooth in right valve; a long side tooth in each valve behind central teeth.

Habitat
In sand intertidally.

Range
Labrador to South Carolina.

Comments
These clams are common on tidal flats in New England, where they burrow vertically into the sand with their strong foot. They make good eating and are frequently sold in markets.

SEASHORE CREATURES

The intertidal areas and the nearshore waters of the Atlantic and Gulf coasts harbor a world of fascinating animal life. Hundreds of creatures—long or round, large or minute—find shelter among sand grains, burrow deep into the muddy bottoms of bays, or live attached to wave-lashed rocks. Crabs scuttle along the bottom of the sea, searching for a meal; jellyfishes drift by, a floating mass of tentacles. Some of these seashore creatures are so bushy that early biologists classified them as plants. To a visitor who is wading, swimming, or snorkeling along these shores, the intertidal and underwater worlds hold tremendous promise of discovery. This section describes some of the most interesting and beautiful of these seashore creatures.

Flat Mud Crab
Eurypanopeus depressus
133

¾" (19 mm) wide, ⅝" (16 mm) long. Small, fan-shaped. Grayish olive to olive-brown, lighter underneath; fingers of pincers dark brown. Carapace rounded in front, sides slanting in toward rear border; area between eye sockets almost straight, notched in middle; 4 teeth on side margin, last 2 sharp-pointed. Pincers stout, unequal, larger pincer with fingers almost straight, tips hollowed out, or spoon-shaped.

Habitat
On mud bottoms, among oysters; in bays and brackish estuaries.

Range
Massachusetts Bay to Florida and Texas; Bermuda; West Indies.

Comments
Phylum Arthropoda, Class Crustacea. This mud crab shows a preference for oyster shells. It preys on newly settled oysters, but is not considered a serious pest by oystermen.

Stone Crab
Menippe mercenaria
134

4⅝" (117 mm) wide, 3⅛" (79 mm) long. Oval. Mottled brownish red with gray spots, tannish beneath, fingers of pincers black. Carapace oval, convex, smooth. Between eye socket and side, margin divided into 4 lobes, first 2 wide, last 2 toothlike. Pincers heavy, unequal, largest about one-fourth longer than carapace width; inner surface of hand rasplike. Walking legs stout, hairy.

Habitat
Adults in burrows in sandy mud shoals just below low-tide line; young in turtle-grass beds and shell and rock bottoms of channels.

Range
North Carolina to Florida and Texas; Bahamas; West Indies to the Yucatán.

Comments
Phylum Arthropoda, Class Crustacea. This is the largest of the mud crabs, and the source of the delectable seafood dish, crab claws. Its catch is carefully regulated in most states, and in Florida it is illegal to take females. When a male is taken, one may break off and keep the larger pincer—which must be at least 4" from tip to first joint—but must return the crab to the water so that it can regenerate a new pincer. Most crustaceans are able to regenerate an appendage in 2 molts.

Lady Crab
Ovalipes ocellatus
135

3⅛" (79 mm) wide, 2½" (64 mm) long. Fan-shaped. Carapace yellowish gray, with closely set rings of reddish-purple spots, metallic iridescence; pincers light brown, with bluish tips and purple spots on top. Carapace slightly wider than long; convex, granular; with 3 sharp teeth between eye sockets, 5 strong teeth directed forward from eye socket to widest part. Pincers large, sharp; finger one-half length of hand; joint next to hand with spine on inner and outer side; fifth pair of walking legs paddlelike.

Habitat
On sand, rock, or mud bottoms; from low-tide line to water 130′ (40 m) deep.

Range
Cape Cod to South Carolina. Isolated population on Prince Edward Island.

Comments
Phylum Arthropoda, Class Crustacea. This handsome crab is known for its aggressive disposition and sharp pincers. It must be handled with great caution.

Sargassum Crab
Portunus sayi
136

2⅛″ (54 mm) wide, 1⅛″ (28 mm) long. Wide, spindle-shaped. Chocolate-brown, light brown, or olive, with irregular whitish spots, orange spines on pincers. Width of carapace twice length, with sharp spine at side; front margin nearly semicircular; 8 teeth between eye and spine on each side. Pincers large, long, equal; spine on outer margin of hand; 2 spines on next joint, 4 spines on long joint beyond; fifth pair of walking legs broad, paddle-shaped.

Habitat
Among floating sargasso weed.

Range
Nova Scotia to Florida and Texas; Bermuda; West Indies to Brazil.

Comments
Phylum Arthropoda, Class Crustacea. Although this crab is normally a creature of the high seas and a member of the sargasso weed community, it is frequently seen among weeds blown ashore by storms. Gibbes' Crab (*P. gibbesii*) is 2⅜″ (60 mm) wide and 1⅛″ (28 mm) long, and brownish red with carmine-red pincers and spines. The front margin of the carapace has 7 teeth between the eye and the large spine at each side. Its pincers are twice body length, strong and sharp; the last pair of walking legs are paddle-shaped. It ranges from Massachusetts to Florida, Texas, and Venezuela. The Spiny-handed Crab (*P. spinimanus*) has a carapace width less than twice its length, and a spine at each side the same size as the 8 teeth on the margin. It is 3½″ (89 mm) wide and 2⅛″ (54 mm) long. The length of the pincers is more than twice the body width, the hand slender and ridged, the fingers straight and curved in at the tips. The joint next to the hand has 2 strong spines and the long joint next to that has 5. It ranges from New Jersey to Florida and Texas, to Bermuda, through the Gulf of Mexico, and the West Indies to Brazil.

Toad Crab
Hyas araneus
137

2½" (64 mm) wide, 3¾" (95 mm) long. Violin-shaped. Reddish to olive, legs banded red and orange. Older specimens less colorful. Carapace widest at rear half, narrow at middle and slightly wider from middle forward. Sharp corners behind eye sockets, continuing to rear as row of low, round projections; long, triangular beak deeply cleft along midline. Legs moderately long, pincers small, hands narrow, fingertips white.

Habitat
On rock and pebble bottoms, among kelps; from low-tide line to water 170' (52 m) deep.

Range
Arctic to Rhode Island.

Comments
Phylum Arthropoda. Class Crustacea. Older Toad Crabs bear coralline or green algae or bryozoans on their carapaces, making them difficult to see and hard to identify. The Lesser Toad Crab (*H. coarctatus*) ranges from the Arctic to Cape Hatteras. It is smaller, 1¼" (32 mm) wide and 2" (51 mm) long, and has a prominent toothed ridge behind the eye socket.

Common Spider Crab
Libinia emarginata
138

3¾" (95 mm) wide, 4" (102 mm) long. Round, spiny. Grayish yellow or brown, tips of fingers white. Carapace globular; beak extended, with shallow, V-shaped notch; midline with 9 spines in a row, border with 7 spines behind eye socket, numerous smaller spines of different sizes, and hairs, on upper surface. Pincers equal; hand long, narrow; movable finger slightly curved, both fingers toothed; walking legs long, hairy. Legs and pincers of male almost twice as long as female's.

Habitat
Various kinds of bottoms; from low-tide line to water 410' (125 m) deep.

Range
Nova Scotia to Florida and Texas.

Comments
Phylum Arthropoda, Class Crustacea. Common Spider Crab males frequently have walking legs and pincers more than 6" (15 cm) long, and are impressive in their slow, careful locomotion. They are often overgrown with fine algae, which accumulates dirt and debris. The Doubtful Spider Crab (*L. dubia*) lives a similar life in comparable habitat, and ranges from Cape Cod to Florida, Texas, the Bahamas, and Cuba. It differs in having a longer beak with a deeper central notch, 6 spines down the midline, and 6 spines along the margin, the last nearly 3 times as long as the others.

Jonah Crab
Cancer borealis
139

6¼" (16 cm) wide, 4" (102 mm) long. Fan-shaped. Upper side dull rosy to brick-red, yellowish beneath, legs yellow mottled with reddish purple. Carapace oval, granular, length two-thirds of width, front border rounded. 3 teeth between eye sockets, middle one largest; 9 teeth to side of eye socket, each with several smaller points. Pincers stout, short, fingers bent downward, black at tips; joint next to hand with sharp spine on inside upper border. Walking legs short, hairy, black-tipped.

Habitat
On rocky shores and bottoms; from low-tide line to water 2620' (799 m) deep.

Range
Nova Scotia to Florida; Bermuda.

Comments
Phylum Arthropoda, Class Crustacea. This crab is a common species among seaweeds along the open rocky coast of northern New England, but it seldom moves into brackish estuaries. Though it has strong pincers, it is not at all aggressive and can be handled safely with moderate precautions.

Atlantic Rock Crab
Cancer irroratus
140

5¼" (133 mm) wide, 3½" (89 mm) long. Fan-shaped. Upper side yellow, closely dotted with reddish or purplish spots, whitish to creamy yellow underneath. Carapace oval, fairly smooth, front border rounded. 3 teeth between eye sockets, middle one longest; 9 simple teeth to side of eye socket. Pincers stout, short, fingers bent downward, black at tips. Walking legs short, hairy at edges.

Habitat
On rock, sand, or gravel bottoms, in estuaries and on open shores; from low-tide line to water 2600' (780 m) deep.

Range
Labrador to South Carolina.

Comments
Phylum Arthropoda, Class Crustacea. This crab enters lobster pots, and until a short time ago was regarded by lobstermen as a pest and a bait-stealer. But the rise in seafood prices has made it profitable to market the crabs as well as the lobsters.

Coral Crab
Carpilius corallinus
141

6" (15 cm) wide, 3½" (89 mm) long. Oval. Brick-red, with large, scarlet to dark red spots and small, white or yellowish dots and irregular lines; pale yellow beneath; tips of pincers black. Carapace convex, smooth, oval, with 1 blunt spine at rear corners. Pincers heavy, smooth.

Habitat
On reefs and coral rubble; in shallow water.

Range
Florida; West Indies.

Comments
Phylum Arthropoda, Class Crustacea. This handsome crab—
an unlikely relative of the generally unprepossessing mud
crabs—is the largest in the West Indies and is highly prized
as food.

Sand Fiddler
Uca pugilator
142

1½" (38 mm) wide, 1" (25 mm) long. Square-bodied, with 1
large pincer. Males: upper surface purplish or grayish blue,
with purple patch on front half and irregular markings of
black, brown, or gray; brownish at side; hand of large pincer
bluish, lavender, or reddish brown; fingertips white. Females:
similar but with more subdued colors, darker. Carapace nearly
rectangular; convex, smooth, H-shaped depression near center;
sides curved outward behind eye sockets; eyestalks long,
slender; antennae small. Pincers of male greatly unequal, one
very large, one small; those of female small, equal. Outer
surface of hand with low, round projections on upper part,
diminishing downward. Inner surface without oblique ridge.
Fingers strong, movable one curved.

Habitat
On protected sand and sandy mud beaches, marshes, and tidal
creeks.

Range
Boston Harbor to Florida and Texas; West Indies.

Comments
Phylum Arthropoda, Class Crustacea. The forbidding-looking
large pincer of the male Sand Fiddler is not at all dangerous.
It is used in a courtship display prior to mating, when the
crab rises on tiptoes, extending the pincer, then flexing it and
bowing down. The Mud Fiddler (*U. pugnax*) is a little smaller,
⅞" (22 mm) wide and ⅝" (16 mm) long. It ranges from Cape
Cod to northeastern Florida, and from northwestern Florida to
Texas. The male has an oblique ridge on the inner surface of
the hand of the large pincer. It is dark olive or almost black
above, sometimes speckled white near the front, has a royal
blue spot near the middle, and is grayish below. The large
pincer is brownish yellow at the base, becoming yellow on the
hand; the fingertips are almost white. Females are similar in
color, but lack the blue spot. This crab prefers a muddy
habitat and frequently digs into mud banks along tidal
marshes, sharing burrows with the Marsh Crab. Where sand
and mud intergrade, populations of Sand Fiddlers and Mud
Fiddlers may be intermixed, though they do not interbreed.

Brackish-water Fiddler
Uca minax
143

1½" (38 mm) wide, 1" (25 mm) long. Square, with 1 large
pincer. Chestnut-brown above, gray at front; large pincer red
at movable joints, hand white; walking legs olive or grayish
brown. Carapace nearly rectangular, somewhat narrowed at
rear, convex, smooth, H-shaped depression near center.
Eyestalks long, slender, antennae small. Male's large pincer

with an oblique ridge of low, round projections on inner surface of hand; pincers of female equal, small.

Habitat
In muddy marshes of low salinity, sometimes at great distance from ocean; in burrows above high-tide line.

Range
Cape Cod to Florida and Texas; West Indies to Colombia.

Comments
Phylum Arthropoda, Class Crustacea. This fiddler strongly prefers brackish-water mud habitats, and can survive at least 3 weeks in fresh water. It is omnivorous.

Ghost Crab
Ocypode quadrata
144

2" (51 mm) wide, 1¾" (44 mm) long. Square-bodied. Upper surface gray, grayish white, yellowish white, or straw-colored; white underneath; pincers white or pale lavender; young mottled gray and brown. Carapace rectangular, sides nearly parallel and vertical, front corner acutely angled, H-shaped depression on front half, surface granulated. Eyestalks large, club-shaped. Pincers unequal, strong, rough, margins saw-toothed, both fingers toothed. Walking legs long, strong, hairy.

Habitat
On sandy beaches.

Range
Rhode Island to Florida and Texas; West Indies to Brazil.

Comments
Phylum Arthropoda, Class Crustacea. If careful not to disturb them, one can watch these crabs walking along the beach, facing the moon when it is full. They are called Ghost Crabs with good reason: they blend closely with the sand on which they live, and are very swift. They seem to appear from nowhere, run, and suddenly disappear again.

Green Crab
Carcinus maenas
145

3⅛" (79 mm) wide, 2⅝" (67 mm) long. Fan-shaped. Greenish, with blackish mottlings above, yellowish below, adult females orange-red underneath, young variable in color and pattern. Carapace slightly wider than long, with 3 teeth between eye sockets and 5 strong teeth, forward, curved toward the side of each eye socket. Pincers moderately large, equal. Fifth pair of walking legs normal, not paddle-shaped.

Habitat
On rocks, jetties, and mud banks in wetlands; in tide pools; from open shore to brackish water.

Range
Nova Scotia to New Jersey. Introduced into Brazil, Panama.

Comments
Phylum Arthropoda, Class Crustacea. Introduced from

Europe, the Green Crab was unknown north of Cape Cod in the last century, but is now the most common crab along the shores of the Gulf of Maine.

Wharf Crab
Sesarma cinereum
146

⅞" (22 mm) wide, ¾" (19 mm) long. Squarish. Upper surface brown to olive, gray beneath. Carapace almost square, nearly smooth, with few low, round projections toward front, sides hairy; eyes at front corners. Pincers stout, short, joints between hand and body with granular cross-bands; immovable finger with large tooth. Third pair of walking legs over twice length of carapace.

Habitat
Among rocks and drift logs, on wharf piles and boat hulls; in shallow burrows above high-tide line.

Range
Chesapeake Bay to Florida and Texas; Honduras; West Indies to Venezuela.

Comments
Phylum Arthropoda, Class Crustacea. This crab leads a semiterrestrial life, and is often called the "Friendly Crab" because of its habit of climbing into boats. The Marsh Crab (*S. reticulatum*) lives in salt marshes from Cape Cod to Florida and Texas. It is larger, 1⅛" (28 mm) wide and ⅞" (22 mm) long, is olive, blackish, or purplish, and has purplish pincers. It lives in burrows in salt marshes, frequently sharing the burrow with the Mud Fiddler Crab.

Blue Crab
Callinectes sapidus
147

9¼" (23 cm) wide, 4" (102 mm) long. Spindle-shaped. Grayish or bluish green, spines red; male with blue fingers on hand, female with red; underside white, with yellow and pink tints. Carapace 2½ times as wide as long, moderately convex, smooth; 4 triangular teeth between eye sockets, 8 sharp, strong teeth between eye socket and large spine at side. Pincers powerful; hand ribbed, with spine at base; fingers nearly straight, toothed; long joint between wrist and body with 3 large teeth on front margin; fifth pair of walking legs broad, paddle-shaped.

Habitat
In shallows and brackish estuaries; from low-tide line to water 120' (37 m) deep.

Range
Nova Scotia to Florida and Texas; Bermuda; West Indies to Uruguay.

Comments
Phylum Arthropoda, Class Crustacea. Because of its commercial importance, this species has been studied more extensively than any other crab. It supports a large seafood industry in Chesapeake Bay and along the entire southeastern and Gulf coasts.

Flat-browed Crab
Portunus depressifrons
148

1⅝" (41 mm) wide, 1" (25 mm) long. Spindle-shaped. Upper surface mottled light and dark gray, lower surface bluish white; pincers and walking legs bright blue or purple on undersurface, darker above. Carapace with blunt spine at widest part, width less than twice length, 8 triangular teeth between spine and eye socket; 6 short teeth between eye sockets. Pincers long, fingers toothed, outer surface of thumb hairy; long joint, with 6 spines on front border, between wrist and body; walking legs long, last pair broad, paddle-shaped.

Habitat
On sand bottoms of coves and inlets; in shallow water.

Range
North Carolina to Florida; Texas to Yucatán Peninsula; Bermuda; Bahamas; West Indies.

Comments
Phylum Arthropoda, Class Crustacea. In the Carolinas it is found in the stomach contents of bottom-feeding fish.

Commensal Crabs
Pinnotheres spp.
149

⅝" (16 mm) wide, ½" (13 mm) long. Oval. White, salmon, brown, or blue, with or without white spots. Carapace round, smooth, soft, flexible. Pincers small; hand flat on inside, swollen on outside; fingers curve to meet; walking legs slender, last 2 joints of walking legs with fringe of hair. Female's abdomen wider than carapace.

Habitat
In mantle cavity of various bivalve mollusks, tubes of Parchment Worms, or pharynx of tunicates, or in sea stars.

Range
Massachusetts to Florida and Texas; West Indies to Argentina; British Columbia to Peru.

Comments
Phylum Arthropoda, Class Crustacea. These crabs live as commensals or parasites on the body or in the cavity of a host animal that feeds by capturing organic particles that the crab shares.

Say's Mud Crab
Neopanope texana
150

⅞" (22 mm) wide, ⅝" (16 mm) long. Small, fan-shaped. Dark blue-green, slate-gray, buff, or brown, with reddish or purplish speckles. Black color on fingers extends onto hand of pincer. Carapace rounded across front, sides slanting toward straight rear border; 4 teeth between eye sockets and side margin, last 2 teeth sharp-pointed. Pincers nearly equal, major one with large tooth at base of finger.

Habitat
On mud bottoms in bays and brackish estuaries, among oysters; from low-tide line to water 90' (27 m) deep.

Range
Prince Edward Island to Florida.

Comments
Phylum Arthropoda, Class Crustacea. This species shows
variation in different parts of its range. From Virginia
southward, these crabs lack the black color on the fingers of
their pincers, and are slightly larger, 1⅛" (28 mm) wide and
⅞" (22 mm) long.

Sponge Crab
Dromia erythropus
151

5" (127 mm) wide, 3¼" (83 mm) long. Fan-shaped, hairy.
Carapace whitish, densely covered with stiff, brown to
blackish hairs. Tips of legs light red. Front margin of carapace
with 5 teeth between eye socket and side. Back convex, with
several wide, low bumps. Pincers and walking legs hairy
except at tips; last pair folded upward at rear of carapace.

Habitat
On rocks and reefs, among sponges and other growth; below
low-tide line to fairly deep water.

Range
Florida; West Indies.

Comments
Phylum Arthropoda, Class Crustacea. This crab camouflages
itself with a piece of living sponge that it cuts to fit the top of
its carapace, and holds there by the sharp tips of the upturned
fifth pair of walking legs. The sponge continues to grow.

Lesser Sponge Crab
Dromidia antillensis
152

1¼" (32 mm) wide, 1⅜" (35 mm) long. Fan-shaped, hairy.
Yellowish green, buff, gray, orange-buff, or reddish, hairs
paler. Tips of pincers red. Carapace densely hairy, convex,
with 4–5 teeth between eye socket and side. Pincers and
walking legs hairy except at tips; last pair of walking legs
folded upward at rear of carapace.

Habitat
On rocks and coral reefs, among sponges and other growth;
from low-tide line to water 1020' (310 m) deep.

Range
Cape Hatteras to Florida and Texas; Mexico; Bermuda;
Bahamas; West Indies to Brazil.

Comments
Phylum Arthropoda, Class Crustacea. The Lesser Sponge Crab
usually camouflages itself with a piece of living sponge, but
sometimes decorates itself with compound tunicates or a
colony of mat anemones instead of a sponge. When the crab is
quiet it almost completely escapes notice.

Flame-streaked Box Crab
Calappa flammea
153

5½" (140 mm) wide, 4" (102 mm) long. Semicircular,
convex. Grayish, with flame-shaped, purplish-brown markings
on carapace; pincers reddish blue on outer surface, white on
inside and at fingertips. Carapace straight across at rear,
arched, round in front; sides at rear with 5 strong teeth.

Pincers heavy, unequal, fitting snugly against body; hands triangular, with finger at top; large hand with 7 teeth on upper margin, smaller hand with 6.

Habitat
On sand bottoms; from below low-tide line to water 240' (73 m) deep.

Range
Cape Hatteras to Florida, Texas, and Mexico; Bermuda; Bahamas.

Comments
Phylum Arthropoda, Class Crustacea. The powerful pincers of this crab are used to chip open snail shells occupied by hermit crabs. The action is like that of a hand-operated can opener.

Atlantic Mole Crab
Emerita talpoida
154

1" (25 mm) long, ¾" (19 mm) wide. Egg-shaped. Pale grayish tan. Carapace convex, crosswise-creased line immediately behind beak, another curved one farther back; rear end of carapace smooth. First pair of antennae hairy. Second pair of antennae long, feathery, usually concealed under edge of carapace. Eyestalks long, slender. First pair of walking legs broad, sturdy, without pincers; second, third, and fourth pairs less sturdy, leaflike; fifth pair very slender. Abdomen broad at front, tapering rapidly, with pair of forked, leaflike appendages, and long, spearhead-shaped tailpiece on last segment, bent forward underneath body.

Habitat
On open sandy beaches; between high- and low-tide lines.

Range
Cape Cod to Florida and Texas; Mexico.

Comments
Phylum Arthropoda, Class Crustacea. This species is frequently used for bait, and can be collected in large numbers by attaching a wire mesh net to a common garden rake, and then raking the wave-swept beach.

Flat-clawed Hermit Crab
Pagurus pollicaris
155

1¼" (32 mm) long, 1" (25 mm) wide. Living in snail shell. Oblong. Whitish or pale tannish gray, eyestalks brown. Carapace widest at rear. Right pincer larger than left, covered with low, rounded projections, especially at borders; hand broad and rounded, width two-thirds of length, finger with blunt angle midway along its border. Fifth pair of walking legs turned up. Abdomen long, soft, cylindrical, with reduced appendages.

Habitat
On sand bottoms along open shores, and in brackish estuaries; from low-tide line to water 150' (46 m) deep.

Range
Cape Cod to Florida and Texas.

Comments
Phylum Arthropoda, Class Crustacea. This large hermit crab is
frequently found living in shells of moon snails and the larger
whelks. The Zebra Flatworm often shares the shell as a
commensal.

Land Hermit Crab
Coenobita clypeatus
156

1½" (38 mm) long, ½" (13 mm) wide. Living in snail shell.
Nearly cylindrical. Reddish or purplish brown, pincers purple
or bluish with orange tips, beak and mouthparts yellowish.
Carapace widest at rear. Eyestalks long, not set in sockets.
Antennae retractable. First pair of walking legs with rounded
pincers, left one much larger. Second and third pairs of
walking legs reduced, turned upward. Abdomen long, soft,
with only left appendages developed; reduced tail fan.

Habitat
Among plants; above high-tide line.

Range
S. Florida; West Indies.

Comments
Phylum Arthropoda, Class Crustacea. This is one of the few
species of terrestrial hermit crabs in the world.

Acadian Hermit Crab
Pagurus acadianus
157

1¼" (32 mm) long, 1" (25 mm) wide. Living in snail shell.
Oblong. Carapace brownish; legs orange or reddish brown,
white near bases; hand of pincers with orange or reddish-
orange stripe down middle, almost white at borders; eyestalks
and first pair of antennae blue; eyes yellow. Carapace widest at
rear. Eyestalks moderately long, not set in sockets. First pair
of walking legs pincers, right walking leg much larger, both
covered with low, round projections. Second and third pairs of
walking legs longer than pincers. Fourth and fifth pair
reduced, fifth pair turned upward. Abdomen long, soft,
cylindrical, with reduced appendages.

Habitat
In rocky tide pools and just below low-tide line in northern
part of its range; to water 1600' (488 m) in southern part.

Range
Labrador to Chesapeake Bay.

Comments
Phylum Arthropoda, Class Crustacea. Hermit crabs, which
must change shells as they grow, will readily do so when they
find one that suits them better.

**Long-clawed Hermit
Crab**
Pagurus longicarpus
158

½" (13 mm) long, ⅜" (10 mm) wide. Living in snail shell.
Oblong. Grayish or greenish white, pincers with tannish-gray
or tannish stripe down middle, edged with white. Carapace
widest at rear. Right pincer larger than left, hand nearly
cylindrical, 3 times longer than wide, smooth except for row

of weak spines at edge and down middle. Fifth pair of walking legs turned up. Abdomen long, soft, cylindrical, with reduced appendages.

Habitat
On sand, mud, rock, and weed bottoms, along open shores and in brackish estuaries; from low-tide line to water 150' (45 m) deep.

Range
Nova Scotia to Florida and Texas.

Comments
Phylum Arthropoda, Class Crustacea. This is the most common hermit crab in Atlantic waters. It usually uses periwinkle, mud snail, or oyster drill shells as a home.

Giant Hermit Crab
Petrochirus diogenes
159

4¾" (121 mm) long, 2¼" (57 mm) wide. Living in snail shell. Oblong. Reddish, with white spots on pincers, red-and-white-banded antennae, blue eyes. Rear end of carapace twice as wide as front. Antennae retractable. Eyestalks long, not in sockets. First pair of walking legs with pincers, right one somewhat larger, both covered with heavy irregular scales. Second and third pairs of walking legs long, sturdy, scaly. Fourth and fifth pairs of walking legs reduced, turned upward. Abdomen long, cylindrical, soft, with only left appendages developed; reduced tail fan.

Habitat
On sand bottoms and seagrass flats; from shallows to water 300' (91 m) deep.

Range
North Carolina to Florida and Texas; West Indies.

Comments
Phylum Arthropoda, Class Crustacea. This is the largest hermit crab in American waters.

Horseshoe Crab
Limulus polyphemus
160

24" (61 cm) long, 12" (30 cm) wide. Horseshoe-shaped carapace convex, with triangular abdomen and spikelike tail; older individuals usually covered with algae. Greenish tan. Pair of compound eyes on each side of carapace, 2 simple eyes on forepart of midline. Sides of abdomen scalloped, with 6 spines. 1 pair of pinchers in front of mouth. Mouth surrounded by 5 pairs of walking legs, each walking leg with a burrlike base; last pair of walking legs with circle of leaflets; first pair on male heavy and rounded; others with pincher tips. Underside of abdomen has 6 pairs of overlapping flaps, the first covering openings of 6 ducts, the others covering 5 pairs of book gills comprised of many flat sheets.

Habitat
On mud or sand bottoms; from near low-tide line to water 75' (23 m) deep.

Range
Gulf of Maine to Gulf of Mexico.

Comments
Phylum Arthropoda, Class Merostomata. This animal is the
only one of its kind in American waters, and cannot be
confused with anything else. It feeds on clams, worms, and
other invertebrates, which it grinds with the burrlike bases of
the walking legs that surround its mouth. In spring,
Horseshoe Crabs congregate near the shore, males holding
onto the abdomens of females with their heavy walking legs.
When the tide is high, each female digs a hole above the low-
tide line and lays 200–300 pale greenish eggs. As she does so,
the male spawns sperm to fertilize them. The eggs are then
buried in sand, where they remain for several weeks,
eventually hatching as miniature Horseshoe Crabs.

**West Indies Spiny
Lobster**
Panulirus argas
161

24" (61 cm) long, 6" (15 cm) high. Long, cylindrical, spiny.
Pale gray, tan, greenish, brownish, or mahogany, with large
yellowish spots on carapace and tail, paler underneath; legs
longitudinally striped with blue. Carapace has rows of strong
spines, largest pair of spines above eyestalks, bent forward.
First pair of antennae slender, branched, two-thirds of body
length; second pair of antennae longer than body, large,
heavy, spiny, base with strong spines. No pincers on walking
legs. Abdomen smooth, each segment with furrow across
middle.

Habitat
Among rocks, sponges and other growth, and reefs; from low-
tide line to water 300' (91 m) deep.

Range
North Carolina to Florida; Gulf of Mexico; Bermuda; West
Indies to Brazil.

Comments
Phylum Arthropoda, Class Crustacea. Although called
"crawfish" in many places, this lobster should not be confused
with the freshwater crawfish or crayfish. It is heavily fished
throughout its range, and in Florida is now abundant only in
the Keys.

Northern Lobster
Homarus americanus
162

34" (86 cm) long, 9" (23 cm) high. Long, cylindrical, with
large pincers. Greenish black above, paler underneath;
appendages and beak tipped with red. Rarely yellow or blue.
Carapace cylindrical. Beak pointed, with 3 teeth on upper
side, 1 behind level of eyestalk. First pair of antennae short,
branch of second pair of antennae longer than body. First 3
pairs of walking legs with pincers, first pair of walking legs
greatly enlarged, not alike. One, usually left, heavier, blunt,
with rounded teeth; other, usually right, less heavy, sharp,
pointed; abdomen somewhat flattened. First 2 pairs of
swimmerets of male modified for copulation.

Habitat
On rock bottoms, both in bays and open ocean; from near shoreline to continental shelf.

Range
Labrador to Virginia.

Comments
Phylum Arthropoda, Class Crustacea. The lobster's two dissimilar pincers serve different purposes. The heavier one, or "crusher," is designed to crack hard objects like snails and bivalves. The sharper one, the "cutter," is used for tearing apart the prey, carrion, or plant material on which the animal feeds.

Red Opossum Shrimp
Heteromysis formosa
163

⅜" (10 mm) long, ¹⁄₁₆" (2 mm) wide. Slender, shrimplike. Red, pink, or brownish. First pair of antennae with 1 short and 1 long slender branch; second pair of antennae with 1 long, slender branch and 1 flattened, broad, oval, leaflike branch, the scale. Eyes large, stalked, black. Carapace covers most of thorax. Thoracic appendages 2-branched, many-jointed, bristly. Female usually red, with pouch for young under thorax. Abdomen long, slender, with 5 pairs of forked appendages and notched tailpiece with bristles along half of the margin, making up tail fan.

Habitat
In tide pools, under rocks and shells; from above low-tide line to water more than 800' (243 m) deep.

Range
Bay of Fundy to New Jersey.

Comments
Phylum Arthropoda, Class Crustacea. This species is more of a bottom-dweller than part of the plankton, and is usually found among rocks and shells, especially shells of the Surf Clam.

Banded Coral Shrimp
Stenopus hispidus
164

2" (51 mm) long, ⅜" (10 mm) high. Slender, elongate. White, with red-edged purple bands on body and pincers. Antennae twice body length. First pair of walking legs nearly body length, hand of pincer long. Pincers and body surface spiny.

Habitat
On coral reefs.

Range
Florida; West Indies.

Comments
Phylum Arthropoda, Class Crustacea. This beautiful cleaning shrimp advertises its availability by standing in one place and waving its antennae to attract a fish in need of having its external and mouth parasites removed.

Spotted Cleaning Shrimp
Periclimenes yucatanicus
165

1" (25 mm) long, ¼" (6 mm) high. Slender, elongate. Transparent, with brown speckles at front end; 3 large, round, white-bordered, tannish spots on the back; 3 white-bordered blue-black spots on the side of the carapace, and similar spots on the flat paired appendages in the tail fan. Legs and antennae banded with black and white. Third segment of abdomen enlarged and bent downward almost at a right angle.

Habitat
Among the tentacles of the Pink-tipped Sea Anemone, Ringed Anemone, and others; around coral reefs in shallow water.

Range
Florida; West Indies; Yucatán.

Comments
Phylum Arthropoda, Class Crustacea. Like other cleaning shrimps, this species cleans parasites from the skin and mouth of fishes.

Pink Shrimp
Penaeus duorarum
166

Males 6½" (17 cm) long, 1" (25 mm) high. Females 8⅜" (21 cm) long, 1⅛" (28 mm) high. Sides somewhat flattened. Gray, bluish gray, or reddish brown; dark spot between third and fourth abdominal segments. Beak continuous with ridge extending almost to rear end of carapace, with broad, rounded groove on each side. 10 pointed teeth along ridge, extending onto beak; 2 teeth on underside of beak. First 3 pairs of legs with pincers. Surface of carapace and abdomen smooth.

Habitat
On various bottoms; from low-tide line to water 300' (91 m) deep.

Range
Chesapeake Bay to Florida and Texas; Bermuda; Bahamas; West Indies to Brazil.

Comments
Phylum Arthropoda, Class Crustacea. The Pink Shrimp is sought by fisheries from North Carolina through the Gulf Coast. The Brown Shrimp (*P. aztecus*) ranges from New Jersey to Florida and Texas, and from the West Indies to Uruguay; it is found from the shoreline to a depth of 300' (91 m). It is similar to the Pink Shrimp, but has a groove down the middle of the rear half of the ridge, and it lacks a brown abdominal spot. It is brown or grayish brown. The White Shrimp (*P. setiferus*) is bluish white with dusky bands and scattered black dots, with the beak and sides tinged with pink, and with red swimmerets. Its beak is continuous with a ridge that extends only about two-thirds of the distance to the rear of the carapace, does not have a groove in its midline, and is flanked by a pair of shallow grooves that extend only half the length of the carapace. Males measure 7¼" (18 cm) long and 1" (25 mm) high, and females 7⅞" (20 cm) long and 1⅛" (28 mm) high. These 3 species are the backbone of our Atlantic shrimping industry.

Common Mantis Shrimp
Squilla empusa
167

10" (25 cm) long, 2½" (64 mm) wide. Shrimplike, somewhat flattened. Greenish or bluish green, with darker green or blue margins to segments. Large, jacknifelike appendage near front with 6 sharp spines on claw. 3 pairs of walking legs. Tailpiece with blunt ridge down middle, and 6 strong marginal spines.

Habitat
Burrows in sand or mud; from low-tide line to water 500′ (152 m) deep.

Range
Cape Cod to Florida and Texas; south to Brazil.

Comments
Phylum Arthropoda, Class Crustacea. This is the "shrimp snapper" well known and respected by shrimp trawlers. A quick slash of one of its large appendages can cut a shrimp or fish in two—or lacerate a finger. It is edible, and said to be delicious.

Red-eyed Amphipod
Ampithoe rubricata
168

¾" (19 mm) long, ⅛" (3 mm) high. Arched, width equal to height. Grayish green, pale below. Antennae almost equal to body in length, first pair slender, second pair heavier. Eyes oval, small, bright red. 7 pairs of walking legs, first 2 pairs heavy, with large claw, last 2 pairs bent back along abdomen. Tailpiece a rounded trapezoid. Body smooth.

Habitat
Among seaweeds and in mussel beds on rocky coasts and in estuaries; above and just below low-tide line.

Range
Labrador to Long Island Sound.

Comments
Phylum Arthropoda, Class Crustacea. These amphipods are early summer breeders, the female holding developing young in a pouch on her underside.

Red-lined Cleaning Shrimp
Lysmata wurdemanni
169

2¾" (70 mm) long, ½" (13 mm) high. Long, tapered toward rear. Translucent white, with longitudinal red stripes down back, transverse ones on side. Beak prominent, half as long as antennal scale, ridged, with 4–5 teeth above and 3–5 below. 2 longest joints of second walking leg beaded.

Habitat
On rocks, jetties, and coral reefs, among hydroids on pilings and buoys; from low-tide line to water 100′ (30 m) deep.

Range
Chesapeake Bay to Florida and Texas; Bahamas; West Indies to Brazil.

Comments
Phylum Arthropoda, Class Crustacea. Specimens of this shrimp from South America differ from the North American

ones in minor details, such as the number of teeth on the beak and the number of beads on the second walking leg.

Brown Pistol Shrimp
Alpheus armatus
170

1½" (38 mm) long, ⅜" (10 mm) high. Brown, with light tan markings on side of body. Antennae banded red and white. Beak short, eyes small. Part of socket over eye with small tooth at front margin. First pair of walking legs with pincers, one almost length of carapace.

Habitat
Among rocks and coral rubble, and on reefs; near low-tide line and below in shallow water.

Range
Florida; West Indies.

Comments
Phylum Arthropoda, Class Crustacea. The red-and-white-banded antennae make this species easy to distinguish from other species of pistol or snapping shrimps.

Long-horn Skeleton Shrimp
Aeginella longicornis
171

2⅛" (54 mm) long, ¹⁄₁₆" (2 mm) wide. Long, slender, arched, jointed. Tannish, reddish, or almost colorless. Head short, with spiny bumps. First pair of antennae two-thirds body length, second pair of antennae shorter, less than one-third body length. Eyes small, round. Large second thoracic appendage with 2–3 sharp teeth on underside of palm, long claw. Pair of saclike gills on next 2 segments. Last 3 segments with nonbristly grasping appendages directed backward.

Habitat
On seaweeds, hydroids, and sponges; from low-tide line to water 7450' (2271 m) deep.

Range
Labrador to North Carolina.

Comments
Phylum Arthropoda, Class Crustacea. This is the largest skeleton shrimp in American Atlantic waters.

Linear Skeleton Shrimp
Caprella linearis
172

¾" (19 mm) long, ¹⁄₃₂" (1 mm) wide. Long, slender, arched, jointed. Pale buff. Head rounded at front, long. First pair of antennae one-third body length, twice as long as second pair. Second pair of antennae with row of long bristles on underside. Eyes small, round, red. First and second thoracic appendages enlarged, with grasping claw, second thoracic appendage much larger. Pair of saclike gills on next 2 segments. Last 3 segments with bristly grasping appendages directed backward.

Habitat
Among seaweeds, bushy hydroids and other growth; from low-tide line to water 660' (201 m) deep.

Range
Arctic to Long Island Sound.

Comments
Phylum Arthropoda, Class Crustacea. Males of this species are larger than females, each of which has a brood-pouch of leaflike plates on the underside.

Opossum Shrimps
Mysis spp.
173

1¼" (32 mm) long, ⅛" (3 mm) wide. Slender, shrimplike. Translucent, greenish, each segment with dark brownish spot. First pair of antennae with 1 short and 1 long slender branch; second pair of antennae with 1 flattened, long, narrow, bladelike branch, the scale, and 1 long, slender branch. Eyes large, stalked, black. Carapace covers most of thorax. Fourth pair of abdominal appendages in male long and pointed. Thoracic legs 2-branched, many-jointed, bristly. Female with pouch for young under thorax. Abdomen long, slender, with 5 pairs of forked, bristly appendages; last segment with pair of flattened, forked appendages and notched tailpiece with bristles along entire margin, making up tail fan.

Habitat
Among seaweed and eelgrass ranging into brackish estuaries; from low-tide line to water 600' (183 m) deep.

Range
Gulf of St. Lawrence to New Jersey.

Comments
Phylum Arthropoda, Class Crustacea. Opossum Shrimps are so named because, like opossums, the females have a pouch. It is made up of flat, folding plates that close toward the midline, and hold the developing eggs.

Common Shore Shrimp
Palaemonetes vulgaris
174

Males 1½" (38 mm) long, ¼" (6 mm) high, females 1¾" (44 mm) long, ¼" (6 mm) high. Slender, elongate. Transparent, with a few red, yellow, white, and blue spots on back. Beak reaches beyond antennal scale, beak tip directed upward; 8–11 teeth along top of beak, 2 teeth behind eye socket. First 2 pairs of walking legs with pincers, second pair larger. Carapace and back of abdomen smooth.

Habitat
In bays and estuaries, usually among submerged seaweeds; from low-tide line to water 45' (14 m) deep.

Range
Gaspé Peninsula to Yucatán Peninsula.

Comments
Phylum Arthropoda, Class Crustacea. This shrimp has been used to study the hormonal control of color in crustaceans. It has cells—containing red, yellow, blue, or white pigment—whose independent expansion or contraction changes the animal's hue.

**Flat-browed Mud
Shrimp**
Upogebia affinis
175

2½" (64 mm) long, ⅜" (10 mm) high. Long, slender. Bluish
or yellowish gray. First pair of antennae small, second pair of
antennae half of body length, bristly. Beak squarish, flattened,
extending beyond tiny eyes. First pair of walking legs coated
with long bristles. Abdomen large, twice length of carapace,
separated from it by deep constriction. Tail fan large.

Habitat
Burrows in sand and mud flats; in lower and midtidal zones.

Range
Cape Cod to Florida and Texas; West Indies to Brazil.

Comments
Phylum Arthropoda, Class Crustacea. This crustacean is not a
true shrimp, but is more closely related to the hermit crabs. It
lives with a mate in a permanent burrow.

Mottled Tube-maker
Jassa falcata
176

⅜" (10 mm) long, 1/16" (2 mm) high. Arched, slender, nearly
as wide as high. Reddish, mottled with paler spots. Antennae
bristly, second pair nearly twice as long as first. Oval eyes
beside base of first antennae. Second walking leg with huge
hand nearly one-third body length, with large thumb and
long, sharp claw opposite it; last 2 pairs bent along abdomen.

Habitat
In tubes on pilings, wharves, buoys, eelgrass, and hydroid
stems; near low-tide line and below to water 33′ (10 m) deep.

Range
Newfoundland to Florida and Texas; British Columbia to
S. California.

Comments
Phylum Arthropoda, Class Crustacea. This amphipod builds a
tube out of mud, debris, and mucus, attaching it to almost
any solid surface where there is good water flow. It feeds both
by straining out suspended organic particles with its bristly
antennae, and by preying on small invertebrates, grasping
them with its huge second walking leg.

Sand Shrimp
Crangon septemspinosa
177

2¾" (70 mm) long, ½" (13 mm) high. Somewhat flattened,
top to bottom. Transparent, colorless, pale gray, buff, with
many irregular, tiny, star-shaped, black spots; tail fan often
blackish. Beak short, without teeth, reaching forward to level
of eyestalks; spine in middle of back behind beak. First
walking leg heavy, with backward-bending claw at tip; second
and third walking legs very slender.

Habitat
On sandy bottoms and in eelgrass beds, on open shores and in
bays and estuaries; from low-tide line to water more than 300′
(91 m) deep.

Range
Arctic to Florida.

Comments
Phylum Arthropoda, Class Crustacea. Sand shrimps have a great tolerance for variations in salinity.

Baltic Isopod
Idotea baltica
178

1" (25 mm) long, ¼" (6 mm) wide. Elongate, straight, somewhat widened in middle, flattened. Tannish green, dark green, or mottled red, brown, or black, with white. Second pair of antennae directed forward and bent to the side. Eyes at side of head. 7 thoracic segments, each with pair of walking legs out to side, all similar. Tailpiece one-fourth body length, squarish at end with point in middle. Last pair of appendages forms doors enclosing gill-like abdominal appendages under tailpiece.

Habitat
On seaweeds and rocks near shore, or swimming nearby in shallow water.

Range
Gulf of St. Lawrence to North Carolina.

Comments
Phylum Arthropoda, Class Crustacea. This is the largest isopod along the northeastern coast. In early summer copulating pairs swim about, the larger female holding the smaller male beneath her. A closely related species, ranging from the Gulf of St. Lawrence to Cape Cod, is the Sharp-tailed Isopod (*I. phosphorea*), which grows to ½" (13 mm) long and ⅛" (3 mm) wide, has an arrowhead-shaped tailpiece, and occurs in a great variety of colors and patterns: solid, banded, or mottled brown, white, red, yellow, gray, or greenish.

Big-eyed Beach Flea
Talorchestia megalophthalma
179

1" (25 mm) long, ⅜" (10 mm) high. Arched, broad, heavy. Gray to reddish brown. First pair of antennae very short, second pair of antennae less than one-half body length. Eyes large, bulging, covering most of side of head. 7 bristly walking legs, second enlarged at tip with claw; last 3 bent back along abdomen, last 2 long. Tailpiece triangular, with blunted end.

Habitat
On clean, sandy surf of exposed beaches, in burrows, or under logs and debris; near high-tide line and above.

Range
Newfoundland to Florida.

Comments
Phylum Arthropoda, Class Crustacea. These lively creatures can leap a foot or more, much like fleas. Some bathers are unnecessarily apprehensive about being bitten by beach fleas, which feed only on organic debris. The Long-horned Beach Flea (*T. longicornis*) is the same size as *T. megalophthalma* and occurs in the same range. Its second pair of antennae are almost body length and its eyes do not bulge.

Northern Sea Roach
Ligia oceanica
180

1″ (25 mm) long, ½″ (13 mm) wide. Oval, flattened, roachlike. Tannish gray, mottled. Second pair of antennae one-half body length, slender. Eyes at side of head. 7 clearly defined thoracic segments, each with pair of walking legs, all similar. Tailpiece short. Last pair of appendages slender, one-fourth body length, forked, extending backward from sides of tailpiece.

Habitat
On rocks and pilings; near high-tide line and above.

Range
Cape Cod north, at least to Maine.

Comments
Phylum Arthropoda, Class Crustacea. This animal's shape, speed, and habit of rushing into hiding when disturbed are reminiscent of a cockroach. The Exotic Sea Roach (*L. exotica*) ranges from Chesapeake Bay to Florida and the West Indies, and is extremely abundant along the Florida inland waterway. It is 1¼″ (32 mm) long and ⅝″ (16 mm) wide, and its last pair of appendages is about half of its body length.

Atlantic Long-fin Squid
Loligo pealei
181

17″ (43 cm) long, 3⅝″ (92 mm) wide. Cylindrical, tapered toward rear. White, with variable red, purplish, yellow, and brown speckles. Head with pair of large eyes, 4 pairs of arms one-half mantle length and 1 pair of tentacles two-thirds mantle length; siphon under neck; triangular fin one-half mantle length on each side of rear end.

Habitat
Ocean surface to water 300′ (91 m) deep over continental shelf.

Range
Bay of Fundy to the West Indies.

Comments
Phylum Mollusca, Class Cephalopoda. These fast-swimming squid are abundantly used as fish bait and, to a lesser degree, as human food. They occur in large schools and are eaten by many commercially important fish, including sea bass, bluefish, and mackerel.

Long-armed Octopus
Octopus macropus
182

Body plus longest arm 36″ (1 m) long. Globe-shaped, with 4 pairs of arms. Tan to reddish brown, with whitish spots; color changeable. Arms long, more than 7 times body length, with 2 alternating rows of suckers; tubular siphon under neck. Head almost as broad as body; eyes high on sides of head, with bump above each. Skin with small warts.

Habitat
Among coral reefs and coral rock.

Range
Florida Keys; West Indies.

Comments
Phylum Mollusca, Class Cephalopoda. This octopus discharges a dark brownish ink when disturbed, thus confusing possible predators. *O. macropus* feeds principally on various kinds of crabs, which it captures with one or more of its arms.

Common Atlantic Octopus
Octopus vulgaris
183

Body plus longest arm 120″ (3 m) long. Globe-shaped, with 4 pairs of arms. Usually reddish brown; color highly variable. Thick arms 4 times length of mantle, with 2 alternating rows of suckers; tubular siphon under neck; head almost as broad as body, eyes high on sides of head. Skin mostly smooth, but can temporarily raise variously shaped bumps.

Habitat
Among rocks and coral reefs near shore; near low-tide line and below in shallow water.

Range
Connecticut to Florida and Texas; Mexico; West Indies.

Comments
Phylum Mollusca, Class Cephalopoda. This octopus is secretive, hiding during the day in crevices and caves and under rocks. Small specimens may be found above the low-tide line. The Briar Octopus (*O. briareus*) ranges from southern Florida throughout the West Indies, among coral rocks and reefs, and in turtle-grass beds. Its length is 18″ (46 cm), its arms are thick at the base and over 5 times the mantle length. It is usually pinkish brown, but changeable, and its skin is smooth or finely granular.

Dwarf Brittle Star
Axiognathus squamatus
184

Disk diameter ¼″ (6 mm), arm length 1″ (25 mm). Tiny, long-armed. Tan, gray, or orange; white spot at margin near base of each arm. Disk round, plump, surface covered with fine scales, 2 large scales at base of each arm; jaws with 2 rounded teeth on each side. Arms with oval plate on top of each joint, vertical row of 3 short spines on each side.

Habitat
Among rocks and gravel in tide pools, in crevices and algal holdfasts, on rocky shores; from between high- and low-tide lines to water 2716′ (828 m) deep.

Range
Arctic to Florida.

Comments
Phylum Echinodermata, Class Stelleroidea, Subclass Ophiuroidea. This little brittle star is bioluminescent, capable of emitting light.

Daisy Brittle Star
Ophiopholis aculeata
185

Disk diameter ¾″ (19 mm), arm length 3⅝″ (92 mm). Long-armed. Red, orange, pink, yellow, white, blue, green, tan, brown, gray, and black, in infinite variety of spots, lines, bands, and mottlings. Central disk scalloped, a lobe protruding between adjacent arms, covered with fine, blunt spines and roundish plates. Plates on top of arms surrounded by row of small scales; joints with 5–6 bluntly-tapered spines in vertical rows on side of arm.

Habitat
Under rocks in tide pools, among kelp holdfasts; from low-tide line to water 5435' (1657 m) deep.

Range
Arctic to Cape Cod; Bering Sea to S. California.

Comments
Phylum Echinodermata, Class Stelleroidea, Subclass Ophiuroidea. These elegant brittle stars are an exotic sight in a tide pool, scrambling into hiding when one exposes them by lifting away their rock.

Slender Sea Star
Leptasterias tenera
186

Radius 1½" (38 mm). Long-rayed. Red, rose, pink, lavender, or purplish above, whitish underneath. Usually 5, sometimes 6 slender arms tapering to blunt tips; moderately large central disk, upper surface rough with irregular rows of conspicuous slender spines, ring of pinchers around each; red eyespot at tip of arm; sieve plate white. 2 rows of long, sucker-tipped tube feet in each groove.

Habitat
On rock or gravel bottoms; from low-tide line to water 495' (151 m) deep.

Range
Nova Scotia to Cape Hatteras.

Comments
Phylum Echinodermata, Class Stelleroidea, Subclass Asteroidea. Like other species in this genus, *L. tenera* is a brooder, the female laying a small number of large, yolky eggs, which she holds in the area around the mouth, assuming the humped-up position taken while feeding. The developing eggs, however, obstruct such feeding during their incubation, and she endures an enforced fast.

Blood Star
Henricia sanguinolenta
187

Radius 4" (102 mm). Slender-armed. Upper side usually blood-red, sometimes rose, purplish, orange, yellow, cream-colored, or white; underside whitish. Central disk small, arms nearly cylindrical, long; surface smooth, covered with closely set, equal-sized, blunt spines; red eyespot at tip of arm. Sieve plate whitish; 2 rows of sucker-tipped tube feet in grooves.

Habitat
On rock bottoms; from low-tide line to water 7920' (2414 m) deep.

Range
Arctic to Cape Hatteras.

Comments

Phylum Echinodermata, Class Stelleroidea, Subclass Asteroidea. Besides trapping organic particles on its mucus and then moving them into its mouth by ciliary action, the Blood Star can also absorb dissolved nutrients through its skin.

Northern Sea Star
Asterias vulgaris
188

Radius 8″ (20 cm). Long-armed. Pink, rose, orange, tan, cream-colored, gray, greenish, bluish, lavender, or light purple. Body soft, flabby. Central disk moderately large; 5 arms tapered to narrow tip, somewhat flattened, widest just beyond juncture with disk; upper surface with abundant short, pointed spines, usually a row of spines down middle of arm. Red eyespot at each arm tip. Sieve plate cream-colored to whitish, prominent. Small, delicately tapered pinchers around spines at sides of arms. 4 rows of tube feet in each groove.

Habitat

On rock or gravel bottoms; from between high- and low-tide lines to water 1145′ (349 m) deep.

Range

Labrador to Cape Hatteras.

Comments

Phylum Echinodermata, Class Stelleroidea, Subclass Asteroidea. In some coves in Maine this sea star is so abundant around mussel beds that one can see several hundred in a few minutes.

Forbes' Common Sea Star
Asterias forbesi
189

Radius 5⅛″ (130 mm). Long-armed. Tan, brown, olive, with tones of orange, red, or pink; sieve plate orange. Similar to the Northern Sea Star, but with firmer skeleton, arms blunter and thicker, and spines scattered, not usually in rows.

Habitat
On rock, gravel, or sand bottoms; from low-tide line to water 160′ (49 m) deep.

Range
Gulf of Maine to Texas.

Comments

Phylum Echinodermata, Class Stelleroidea, Subclass Asteroidea. Like the Northern Sea Star, this species feeds chiefly on bivalve mollusks. Experiments have shown that a star 3″ in radius can exert a 12-pound pull. A 2″ cherrystone clam exerts a 10-pound pull to keep its valves closed. This star needs only a tiny gape, ¹⁄₂₅₀″ (.1 mm) to gain its meal. It everts its stomach through its mouth, slips it between the mollusk's valves, and secretes digestive juices that begin to consume the clam's soft tissues. The clam soon dies, its valves gape, and the sea star finishes its meal.

Thorny Sea Star
Echinaster sentus
190

Radius 2¼″ (57 mm). Small, with heavy spines. Red, reddish brown, reddish orange, or dark purple. Central disk small; 5 blunt, moderately long arms, upper surface of each having 5 irregular rows of large spines, middle row largest, each spine mounted on a rounded base; spines scattered over disk. Sieve plate raised, rough. 2 rows of long tube feet in each groove.

Habitat
On rocky shores, grass beds, reefs; in shallow water.

Range
North Carolina to Florida; West Indies.

Comments
Phylum Echinodermata, Class Stelleroidea, Subclass Asteroidea. This is one of the commonest shallow-water sea stars in southern Florida. Certain species of *Echinaster* have been shown to be attracted to light, and *E. sentus* probably responds similarly, as it is found in the open on sunny days.

Cushion Star
Oreaster reticulatus
191

Radius 10″ (25 cm). 5-pointed, thick-bodied, highly arched. Larger specimens reddish brown, orange-red, or yellowish, with spiny meshwork of contrasting lighter or darker color; young specimens olive-green or mottled purplish brown; all ages cream-colored, yellow, or tan underneath. Arms not clearly demarked from oval disk; upper surface with knobby spines joined by raised ridges to form network of squares and triangles; margin with row of equally spaced knobby spines, under surface covered with knobby spines in neat rows, sharper spines bordering grooves. 2 rows of whitish tube feet. Firm, hard skeleton.

Habitat
On sand, coral, rubble, and growth-covered bottoms; below low-tide line in shallow water.

Range
North Carolina to Florida; West Indies to Brazil.

Comments
Phylum Echinodermata, Class Stelleroidea, Subclass Asteroidea. This is the largest sea star on our Atlantic Coast. Its remarkably hard skeleton maintains the animal's shape even when it is dried. One frequently sees garishly painted specimens of dried Cushion Stars in the windows of beachwear stores.

Smooth Sun Star
Solaster endeca
192

Radius 8″ (20 cm). Many-armed. Purplish, red, pink, or orange. 7–14 arms.

Habitat
On rock and gravel bottoms; from low-tide line to water 900′ (274 m) deep.

Range
Arctic to Cape Cod; Alaska to Puget Sound.

Comments
Phylum Echinodermata, Class Stelleroidea, Subclass
Asteroidea. This sun star preys chiefly on small sea cucumbers
and on other small sea stars. Its development is direct from
egg to adult form; it does not pass through a free-swimming
stage.

Spiny Sun Star
Crossaster papposus
193

Radius 7" (18 cm). Many-armed. Scarlet above, with
concentric bands of white, pink, yellowish or dark red; white
underneath. Central disk large, with netlike pattern of raised
ridges; 8–14 arms, length one-half radius. Entire upper
surface sparsely covered with brushlike spines; marginal spines
larger. Mouth area bare. 2 rows of sucker-tipped tube feet in
grooves.

Habitat
On rock bottoms; from low-tide line to water 1080' (329 m)
deep.

Range
Arctic to Gulf of Maine; Alaska to Puget Sound.

Comments
Phylum Echinodermata, Class Stelleroidea, Subclass
Asteroidea. Among the most beautiful of echinoderms, these
sea stars seem to be sunbursts of color. They are predatory on
smaller sea stars, swallowing them whole.

Slate-pencil Urchin
Eucidaris tribuloides
194

2½" (64 mm) wide, 1¼" (32 mm) high. Heavy-spined, oval.
Tan with brown spots or stripes, sometimes mottled white, or
tinged with green or red. Test red-orange to brown. Primary
spines thick, blunt, length of test width, one per plate; other
spines tiny, flattened, abundant. Area around anus with small
spines. No gills.

Habitat
On coral reefs, rocks, and coral rubble; near low-tide line and
below in shallow water.

Range
South Carolina to Florida; Bermuda; Bahamas; West Indies;
Mexico to Brazil.

Comments
Phylum Echinodermata, Class Echinoidea. The large spines on
this urchin are frequently coated with white or pink coralline
algae, bryozoans, or sponges.

Rock-boring Urchin
Echinometra lucunter
195

2" (51 mm) wide, ¾" (19 mm) high. Spiny, oval. Reddish
brown or brownish black, tinged with purple or green, spines
light green, violet, light or dark reddish brown. Somewhat
oval, spine size variable, longest ¾" (19 mm), pointed. Area
around anus with many small spines and many plates of
different sizes. 10 clusters of gills.

Habitat
In rocks with holes in areas of heavy wave action; near low-tide line and slightly below.

Range
Florida to Texas and Mexico; Bermuda; Jamaica; West Indies to Brazil.

Comments
Phylum Echinodermata, Class Echinoidea. This urchin bores its burrow during years of scraping with the teeth of its Aristotle's lantern. When the urchin braces its spines against the burrow, it is very difficult to remove.

Atlantic Purple Sea Urchin
Arbacia punctulata
196

2″ (51 mm) wide, ¾″ (19 mm) high. Spiny, oval. Spines purplish brown, reddish gray, or sometimes nearly black; skin blackish. Spines longitudinally grooved, cylindrical, pointed, variable in size; longest spines near top 1″ (25 mm) long; top nearly free of spines. Area around anus with 4 plates, each one-fourth of a circle. 10 clusters of blue-black gills.

Habitat
On rock and shell bottoms, among seaweeds, in tide pools; from low-tide line to water 750′ (229 m) deep.

Range
Cape Cod to Florida; Texas; Yucatán; Cuba; Jamaica; West Indies; Trinidad.

Comments
Phylum Echinodermata, Class Echinoidea. This species is the most intensively studied of all sea urchins. It is omnivorous, and will eat various algae, sponges, coral polyps, mussels, sand dollars, and dead or dying urchins and other animals.

Green Sea Urchin
Strongylocentrotus droebachiensis
197

3¼″ (83 mm) wide, 1½″ (38 mm) high. Spiny, oval. Test brownish green, spines light green, gray-green, or, more rarely, brownish green or reddish green; tube feet brownish. Spines not greatly variable in length, never over one-third diameter of test. Area around anus with many scalelike plates of different sizes. 10 clusters of gills.

Habitat
On rocky shores and in kelp beds; from low-tide line to water 3795′ (1157 m) deep.

Range
Arctic to New Jersey; Alaska to Puget Sound.

Comments
Phylum Echinodermata, Class Echinoidea. These urchins are so abundant in certain protected bays that it is impossible to walk through a bed of them without stepping on some.

Long-spined Urchin
Diadema antillarum
198

4" (102 mm) wide, 1¾" (44 mm) high. Long-spined, oval.
Adults dark, purple or black; young urchins frequently with
white bands or speckles on spines. Spines greatly variable in
size, longest spines on upper surface 16" (41 cm) long. Scaly
plates on area around anus. 10 sets of gills.

Habitat
On coral reefs, rocks, coral rubble, reef flats, and tide pools;
near low-tide line and below in shallow water.

Range
Florida; Bermuda; Bahamas; West Indies; Mexico to
Suriname.

Comments
Phylum Echinodermata, Class Echinoidea. Bathers and divers
in the American tropics know and respect the long, sharp
spines of this urchin, which can puncture a wetsuit or tennis
shoe and cause intense irritation if lodged in the skin.

Lentil Sea Spider
Anoplodactylus lentus
199

¼" (6 mm) long, 1⁄16" (2 mm) wide. Slender, flattened, long-
legged, with long neck and tiny abdomen. Reddish brown to
reddish purple. Proboscis rising under long neck, cylindrical,
rounded at tip, one-fourth as long as body, with pinchers
longer than proboscis on each side, but no feelerlike
appendages. 4 eyes on projection behind proboscis. Length of
abdomen twice width. 4 pairs of slender legs ¾" (19 mm)
long. Only male has pair of accessory legs.

Habitat
On hydroids and tunicates on rock or shell bottoms; near low-
tide line and below to water 900' (274 m) deep.

Range
Bay of Fundy to Florida; West Indies.

Comments
Phylum Arthropoda, Class Pycnogonida. The Lentil Sea Spider
owes its color to a dark reddish pigment in its blood. It has
longer legs than any other sea spider in the American Atlantic
and looks like a tangled knot. This species feeds on hydroids.

Arrow Crab
Stenorhynchus seticornis
200

½" (13 mm) wide, 2¼" (57 mm) long. Arrowhead-shaped.
Pale gray, cream-colored, buff, or orange with inverted, V-
shaped, light-and-dark-brown or black stripes; legs reddish,
bright red at joints; fingers of pincers blue, eyes maroon.
Carapace triangular, smooth, widest at rear, narrowing toward
eyes, extending forward as long, slender, spiny beak. Pincers
twice body length, slender; legs slender, over 3 times body
length, with 2–3 rows of fine spines on longest joints.

Habitat
On rock, shell, sand, and coral-rubble bottoms, coral reefs,
jetties, and wharf pilings; from low-tide line to water 4884'
(1489 m) deep.

Range
North Carolina to Florida and Texas; Bermuda; Bahamas; West Indies to Brazil.

Comments
Phylum Arthropoda, Class Crustacea. This dainty and elegant little crab is a delight to watch as it walks delicately among the rocks or on a reef. In recent years it has appeared in pet stores.

Northern Basket Star
Gorgonocephalus arcticus
201

Disk diameter 4" (102 mm), arm length 14" (36 cm). Highly branching. Upper surface of disk yellowish brown or darker brown; arms yellowish tan, white at tips; white underneath. Disk pentagonal, naked, leathery, with 5 pairs of spiny ridges radiating from near center to sides of arms. 5 stout arms dividing into 2 equal branches near disk, then arms dividing equally again 5 or more times to many coiling, tendril-like branches; arm joints with short, hooked spines, small tube feet. Mouth with 5 sawlike jaws.

Habitat
On rock bottoms; in water 18–4831' (6–1472 m) deep.

Range
Arctic to Cape Cod.

Comments
Phylum Echinodermata, Class Stelleroidea, Subclass Ophiuroidea. This creature is a slowly coiling, squirming mass of branched arms, usually completely entangled in anything it can grasp. It is frequently seen when hauled up to the surface in lobster pots.

Keyhole Urchin
Mellita quinquiesperforata
202

5½" (140 mm) long, 6" (15 cm) wide. 5-slotted disk. Tan, light brown, or grayish. Test covered with fine spines, almost circular, flat, with 2 pairs of slots and a single larger one between the rear 2. Mouth central, anus at rear margin. 5 branched furrows leading toward mouth.

Habitat
On sand bottoms; below low-tide line in shallow water.

Range
Cape Cod to Florida; Bermuda; Jamaica; Puerto Rico; Mexico to Brazil.

Comments
Phylum Echinodermata, Class Echinoidea. This species is more closely related to other sand dollars than to sea urchins. Its 5 slots are notches when the animal is small, and are closed off by growth.

Six-hole Urchin
Mellita sexiesperforata
203

4" (102 mm) long, 4¼" (108 mm) wide. 6-slotted disk. Silvery gray to tan or yellowish brown. Test with 6 slots: 2 pairs, 2 single slots in midline—1 toward front, 1 toward rear. Otherwise similar to the Keyhole Urchin.

Habitat
On sand bottoms; below low-tide line in shallow water.

Range
South Carolina to Florida; Bermuda; Bahamas; West Indies to Uruguay.

Comments
Phylum Echinodermata, Class Echinoidea. This urchin is similar in life habits to *M. quinquiesperforata*. Its species name, *sexiesperforata*, means "six holes" in Latin and is descriptive of its most distinctive characteristic.

Common Sand Dollar
Echinarachnius parma
204

3⅛" (79 mm) wide, ¼" (6 mm) high. Flat, disklike. Reddish brown or purplish brown, darker above, paler below. Outline nearly circular, test flattened, covered with many close-set, short spines; 5 petal-shaped loops of tube feet on upper surface. Mouth central on lower surface, anus at rear margin. 5 branched furrows leading to mouth.

Habitat
On sand bottoms; from low-tide line to water 5280' (1613 m) deep.

Range
Labrador to Maryland.

Comments
Phylum Echinodermata, Class Echinoidea. Sand dollars feed on fine particles of organic matter and are, in turn, eaten by flounder, cod, haddock, and other bottom-feeding fishes.

Variegated Urchin
Lytechinus variegatus
205

3" (76 mm) wide, 1¼" (32 mm) high. Spiny, oval. Green, white, pinkish red, brownish red, or reddish purple; color variable. Spines short, stout, abundant. Area around anus with many scalelike plates.

Habitat
On turtle-grass flats and sand-and-gravel bottoms with abundant plant growth, and among mangroves; from low-tide line to water 180' (55 m) deep.

Range
North Carolina to Florida; Bahamas; West Indies.

Comments
Phylum Echinodermata, Class Echinoidea. This urchin is usually camouflaged with bits of shell, plant material, and other debris held over its body by tube feet.

Long-spined Sea Biscuit
Plagiobrissus grandis
206

10″ (25 cm) long, 8¼″ (21 cm) wide. Spiny, oval. Yellow, tan, or reddish. Test irregularly oval, convex, indented at front, sides nearly parallel; covered with sharp, medium-sized spines; some long spines at top 4″ (102 mm) long. 5 rows of tube feet in deep furrows. Flat underneath, mouth near front end, anus at rear margin.

Habitat
In coral sand around reefs; to water more than 50′ (15 m) deep.

Range
Florida; West Indies.

Comments
Phylum Echinodermata, Class Echinoidea. *P. grandis* is the largest and one of the handsomest of the irregular echinoids. Its chief predators are large helmet snails, which grab it out of the sand and eat it.

Spotted Sea Hare
Aplysia dactylomela
207

5″ (127 mm) long, 2½″ (64 mm) wide. Plump, with long foot. Yellow or yellowish green, with irregular violet-black circles. Head with 1 pair of antennae below, near mouth, 1 larger pair above, farther back, with eyes in front of base. Pair of long, winglike flaps along upper side of body. Shell small, internal. Foot extends from head to beyond body mass.

Habitat
In turtle-grass beds and protected sand flats, and on reef flats; below low-tide line in shallow water.

Range
Florida and Texas; West Indies.

Comments
Phylum Mollusca, Class Gastropoda, Subclass Opisthobranchia. Like other sea hares this species is hermaphroditic and lays long, sticky strings of a million or more eggs, which are entangled in seaweeds.

Bushy-backed Sea Slug
Dendronotus frondosus
208

4⅝″ (117 mm) long, 1″ (25 mm) wide. Widest in middle, tapered to point at rear end. Grayish brown to rusty red mottled with white spots, or pure white. Head blunt, with 6 branched projections extending forward. Comblike antennae set in sheaths with whorl of branched projections; 2 rows of 5–8 bushy projections along back.

Habitat
On rocks and among seaweeds; from low-tide line to water 360′ (110 m) deep.

Range
Arctic to New Jersey.

Comments
Phylum Mollusca, Class Gastropoda, Subclass

Opisthobranchia. The Bushy-backed Sea Slug is commonly found wherever there is an abundance of the hydroids on which it feeds. It is also known to browse on bryozoans and colonial tunicates.

Red-gilled Nudibranch
Coryphella rufibranchialis
209

1¼" (32 mm) long, ⅜" (10 mm) wide. Long, narrow; rear end tapered to sharp point. Translucent white, with opaque white line down middle of back. 100 long, fingerlike projections with bright red, occasionally brown, core; projections rise in clumps from each side of back, opaque white ring near tip. Head with 2 pairs of long antennae. Front end of foot with sharp, hooklike extension on each side.

Habitat
Among seaweeds and hydroids; near low-tide line and below to deep water.

Range
Arctic to New York; British Columbia.

Comments
Phylum Mollusca, Class Gastropoda, Subclass Opisthobranchia. Although this animal is called the Red-gilled Nudibranch, the projections on its back are not gills. Each contains a slender extension of the gut. When the nudibranch feeds on certain kinds of hydroids, it can incorporate the stinging cells from the digested prey into the tissues of these projections so that they can explode on contact just as they would in the hydroid's tentacles.

Rough-mantled Doris
Onchidoris bilamellata
210

1" (25 mm) long, ¾" (19 mm) wide. Mixed pattern of chocolate- to rusty-brown and cream-color. Broadly oval. Back covered with many short, thick, knobby projections. Comblike antennae; 16–32 simple featherlike gills arranged in 2 half-rings on back near rear end.

Habitat
On rocks and pilings near mud bottoms; from well above low-tide line to water 25′ (8 m) deep.

Range
Bay of Fundy to Rhode Island.

Comments
Phylum Mollusca, Class Gastropoda, Subclass Opisthobranchia. This nudibranch feeds on acorn barnacles. In New England it can frequently be found in large numbers, 20 or more per rock, under barnacle-covered boulders in quiet estuaries. Formerly known as *O. fusca.*

White Atlantic Cadlina
Cadlina laevis
211

1" (25 mm) long, ⅜" (10 mm) wide. Oval. Slightly convex. White, semitransparent, with opaque white specks and larger, lemon-yellow spots near the margin of the back. Comblike antennae and ring of feathery gills, usually yellow at tips.

Habitat
On rock bottoms; near low-tide line and below.

Range
Arctic to Massachusetts.

Comments
Phylum Mollusca, Class Gastropoda, Subclass
Opisthobranchia. Although the populations of slime sponges
on which it feeds are abundant on rocky New England shores,
the White Atlantic Cadlina is found only locally, in widely
separated populations.

Hairy Doris
Acanthodoris pilosa
212

1¼″ (32 mm) long, ⅝″ (16 mm) wide. Oval, convex. Pale
lemon-yellow or purplish brown. Covered with soft, slender,
conical projections. Antennae comblike, nearly equal in size,
bent backward. Ring of 7–9 plumelike gills on back at rear
end.

Habitat
On seaweeds, with a heavy growth of bryozoans; in shallow
water, near low-tide line and below.

Range
Arctic to Connecticut.

Comments
Phylum Mollusca, Class Gastropoda, Subclass
Opisthobranchia. The Hairy Doris feeds on the rubbery
Porcupine Bryozoan, which is usually found growing on the
base of rockweed and knotted wrack. It lays eggs in the form
of white ribbons that attach onto the seaweed or the rock to
which the animal is fastened.

Atlantic Ancula
Ancula gibbosa
213

½″ (13 mm) long, ⅛″ (3 mm) wide. Plump, elongated
and tapered toward rear. Transparent, whitish. Tentacles
with 2 extra projections; ring of gills on middle of back
surrounded by ring of clublike projections; antennae and all
projections lemon-yellow at tips.

Habitat
On various large seaweeds; near low-tide line and below.

Range
Arctic to Massachusetts.

Comments
Phylum Mollusca, Class Gastropoda, Subclass
Opisthobranchia. The Atlantic Ancula's yellowish internal
organs can be seen through the transparent whitish body wall.
When out of the water, the soft body collapses, and some say
it resembles a lightly fried egg.

Common Lettuce Slug
Tridachia crispata
214

1½" (38 mm) long, ¼" (6 mm) wide. Long. Greenish or bluish green, with white speckles. Head wide, rounded at sides, with 1 pair of knobby antennae. 2 curly folds of mantle run length of back.

Habitat
In quiet places such as grass beds; near low-tide line and below in shallow water.

Range
S. Florida and the West Indies.

Comments
Phylum Mollusca, Class Gastropoda, Subclass Opisthobranchia. The Common Lettuce Slug is herbivorous, and is equipped with a specialized radula that permits it to puncture cells of algae and suck out the juice.

Warty Sea Cat
Dolabrifera dolabrifera
215

6" (15 cm) long, 2" (51 mm) wide. Oval, soft, rough. Gray to gray-green; sole of foot light green with pale dots. Head with 2 pairs of tentacles, pair of black eyes between tentacle pairs. Rear half of body wide, rounded, plump; surface rough, warty.

Habitat
On algal growth; near low-tide line in shallow water.

Range
Florida; Bahamas; West Indies to Brazil.

Comments
Phylum Mollusca, Class Gastropoda, Subclass Opisthobranchia. Also called the Green Sea Hare, this species is well-camouflaged among the algae on which it feeds.

Zebra Flatworm
Stylochus zebra
216

1½" (38 mm) long, ½" (13 mm) wide. Oblong, with rounded head end and bluntly pointed rear end. Yellowish to white, with many thin, dark brown crossbands, some branching near the margin. Row of eyespots around margin, and short, stubby tentacles and brain area difficult to see because of worm's striking coloration. Mouth near middle of underside.

Habitat
In snail shells occupied by large hermit crabs.

Range
Cape Cod to Florida and Texas.

Comments
Phylum Platyhelminthes, Order Polycladida. This worm is especially common in whelk shells occupied by the Flat-clawed Hermit Crab.

By-the-wind Sailor
Velella velella
217

Float 4″ (102 mm) long, 3″ (76 mm) wide, 2″ (51 mm) high. Float consisting of flat, oval, cartilagelike skeleton full of gas-filled pockets, with vertical triangular crest set diagonally across the top, serving as a snail. Blue, transparent. Single large-mouthed feeding tube, surrounded by rows of reproductive bodies. Numerous blue tentacles around the rim.

Habitat
Surface of the sea.

Range
Warm waters. Driven ashore from the Gulf Stream by storms, as far north as Cape Hatteras, occasionally farther.

Comments
Phylum Cnidaria, Class Hydrozoa. Although they contain stinging cells, the tentacles of the Sailor are harmless to man. The By-the-wind Sailor can "tack" in the manner of a sailboat.

Portuguese man-of-war ⊗
Physalia physalis
218

Float 12″ (30 cm) long, 6″ (15 cm) high, 5″ (127 mm) wide. Float gas-filled. Iridescent pale blue and pink, with large, deflatable, pink-ridged crest above. Dense cluster of 3 kinds of polyps suspended underneath. Tentacles of different lengths, some more than 60′ (18 m) long, containing blue, beadlike stinging cells; blue tubular feeding parts with terminal mouths and no tentacles; treelike, branching gonads, salmon-pink when mature.

Habitat
Surface of the sea.

Range
Florida to Texas and Mexico; Bahamas; West Indies. Driven ashore by storms from Gulf Stream to Cape Cod.

Comments
Phylum Cnidaria, Class Hydrozoa. Highly toxic. This siphonophore floats on the surface by means of a gas-filled, balloonlike float that changes shape to catch the prevailing wind. Its tentacles contain one of the most powerful poisons known in marine animals and can inflict severe burns and blisters even when the animal is dead on the beach. The Man-of-War Mackerel (*Nomeus gronovii*) lives among the tentacles with impunity, acting as a lure to other fish while receiving protection and fragments of food from the man-of-war.

Lion's Mane ⊗
Cyanea capillata
219

24″ (61 cm) high, 96″ (244 cm) wide. Bell saucer-shaped, upper surface smooth. Color varies with age and, thus, size: pink and yellowish to 5″ (127 mm), reddish to yellow-brown to 18″ (46 cm), darker red-brown when larger. 16 marginal lobes. Shaggy clusters of more than 150 tentacles attached beneath 8 deep clefts between lobes, marginal sense organs in 8 shallower clefts. Feeding tube stout, extending as 4 much-folded, membranous lips around mouth. 4 highly folded, ribbonlike gonads suspended under bell alternate with lips.

Habitat
Floats near surface.

Range
Arctic to Florida and Mexico.

Comments
Phylum Cnidaria, Class Scyphozoa. Highly toxic. This is the largest jellyfish in the world. Specimens 8 feet wide have been found. Contact with *Cyanea*'s tentacles produces severe burning and blistering. Prolonged exposure may cause muscle cramps and breathing difficulties. In Sir Arthur Conan Doyle's story, "The Adventure of the Lion's Mane," Sherlock Holmes solves a homicide caused by contact between the victim and this medusa in a tide pool.

Sea Nettle ⊗
Chrysaora quinquecirrha
220

5″ (127 mm) high, 10″ (25 cm) wide. Pink with radiating red stripes. 40 tentacles. Bay form 2″ (51 mm) high, 4″ (102 mm) wide. White. 24 tentacles. Bell covered with fine warts. Margin divided into scalloped, shallow lobes. Long, yellow tentacles alternate with marginal sense organs between lobes. Feeding tube extends well below bell margin as 4 long, ruffled, lacy lips. 4 gonads, each a convoluted loop.

Habitat
Floats near surface.

Range
Cape Cod to Florida and Texas. Abundant in Chesapeake Bay.

Comments
Phylum Cnidaria, Class Scyphozoa. Mildly toxic. Contact with a Sea Nettle usually results in a mild itchy irritation, but a person stung severely may require hospitalization.

Upside-down Jellyfish ⊗
Cassiopeia xamachana
221

2″ (51 mm) high, 12″ (30 cm) wide. Bell gray-green to brownish yellow. Rather flat, with rounded edges. 80 marginal lobes, with 16 marginal sense organs, no marginal tentacles. Feeding tube stout, with 8 long, green or brown, fleshy oral arms with grapelike clusters on 15 primary branches and several large, ribbon-shaped filaments suspended beneath. Mouth subdivided into many tiny pores on oral arms.

Habitat
In shallow waters, back-reef lagoons, and mangrove bays.

Range
Florida to Texas and Mexico; Bahamas; West Indies.

Comments
Phylum Cnidaria, Class Scyphozoa. Mildly toxic. Contact with the Upside-down Jellyfish causes itching followed by a rash. Thousands of these creatures lie side by side on their backs in shallow water, basking in the sun and exposing their oral arms to the currents.

Cannonball Jellyfish
Stomolophus meleagris
222

5″ (127 mm) high, 7″ (18 cm) wide. Hemispherical, thick, tough. Milky bluish or yellowish, with pale-spotted brown band around margin. Margin has 128 small lobes with 8 deep notches containing prominent sense organs; no marginal tentacles. Feeding tube stout, with 16 short, forked oral arms. Primary mouth present.

Habitat
Floats near shore.

Range
Chesapeake Bay to Florida and Texas; Bahamas; West Indies.

Comments
Phylum Cnidaria, Class Scyphozoa. This jellyfish occurs in huge swarms along shores of the Gulf of Mexico. One swarm observed at Port Aransas, Texas, was estimated drifting through the channel at a rate of 2 million per hour.

Moon Jellyfish ⊗
Aurelia aurita
223

3″ (76 mm) high, 16″ (41 cm) wide. Saucer-shaped. Whitish, translucent. 8 shallow marginal lobes, sense organs in 8 clefts between lobes. Numerous short, fringelike tentacles. Feeding tube short, stout, expanding as 4 long oral arms with frilly margins. Numerous branching radial canals. Reproductive organs horseshoe-shaped or round. Ripe female organs: yellowish, pink, or violet; males': yellow, yellow-brown, or rose; immatures': whitish.

Habitat
Floats near surface; just offshore.

Range
Arctic to Florida and Mexico; Alaska to S. California.

Comments
Phylum Cnidaria, Class Scyphozoa. Mildly toxic. This is the jellyfish most commonly washed up on beaches during high tide or after a storm. Its sting causes a slight rash that may itch for several hours.

Angled Hydromedusa
Gonionemus vertens
224

Medusa ½″ (13 mm) high, ¾″ (19 mm) wide. Dome-shaped. Transparent. Feeding tube not quite reaching bell margin, thickest where attached. Mouth has 4 slightly frilled lips. Ruffled sex organs extend along most of length of 4 radial canals, creating cross-shaped marking. 60 long marginal tentacles, each with spiral or ringlike clusters of stinging cells and an adhesive sucker near end. Feeding tube, gonads, and tentacle bases yellowish tan to reddish brown. Polyp stage unknown.

Habitat
Floating in shallow water; sometimes found clinging to eelgrass.

Range
Arctic to Cape Cod; Alaska.

Comments
Phylum Cnidaria, Class Hydrozoa. When the medusa attaches itself to a rock or seaweed, the tentacles form an angle at the sucker, hence the species' name.

Sea Gooseberry
Pleurobrachia pileus
225

1⅛" (28 mm) high, 1" (25 mm) wide. Round to egg-shaped. Transparent, iridescent. 2 tentacles, each fringed on 1 side, can extend over 20 times body length or retract completely. 8 rows of comb plates, equally spaced, extend nearly full length of body. Pharynx, stomach and its branches, and tentacles and sheaths white, pink, yellow, or orange-brown.

Habitat
Near shore; usually in large swarms.

Range
Maine to Florida and Texas.

Comments
Phylum Ctenophora. Unlike many jellyfish, Sea Gooseberries do not sting. The sticky filaments of the trailing tentacles capture small crustaceans, fish eggs and larvae, and other planktonic animals. The tentacles then contract and wipe the prey off on the mouth, which immediately swallows it. The Arctic Sea Gooseberry (*Mertensia ovum*) is more egg-shaped, flatter, and larger, 2" (51 mm) high and 1" (25 mm) wide. It occurs from the Arctic to the Gulf of Maine, and sometimes in winter to Cape Cod; it is also found along the coast of central California.

Clapper Hydromedusa
Sarsia tubulosa
226

Polyp colony ¾" (19 mm) high, 4" (102 mm) wide. Polyp small. Colorless to pink. On sparsely branching stem. Head bulbous, with 12 or more knobbed tentacles scattered over surface. Reproductive buds attached near base of head. Medusa ¾" (19 mm) high, ⅝" (16 mm) wide. Thimble-shaped. Feeding tube, canals, and tentacle bases yellowish, red, brown, or blue. Feeding tube extends below rim of bell. Mouth simple. 4 radial canals, 4 long, trailing tentacles, each with black eyespot at base.

Habitat
Polyps attached to rocks; below low-tide line. Medusa floats near surface.

Range
Arctic to Chesapeake Bay.

Comments
Phylum Cnidaria, Class Hydrozoa. In this species' medusa stage, the mouth tube hangs below the body like the clapper of a bell.

**Common Northern
Comb Jelly**
Bolinopsis infundibulum
227

6″ (15 cm) high, 2″ (51 mm) wide. Elongate, oval, somewhat flattened, narrow at top. Transparent, iridescent. 2 large lobes less than half the total body length. 4 fingerlike structures around mouth; 8 comb plate rows, 2 extending down each lobe nearly to end, 1 down each structure. Comb plate rows, pharynx, stomach and its branches faintly white.

Habitat
In shallow water.

Range
Arctic to Gulf of Maine; sometimes in Massachusetts Bay.

Comments
Phylum Ctenophora. This species is the most common comb jelly north of Cape Cod in the summer.

Leidy's Comb Jelly
Mnemiopsis leidyi
228

4″ (102 mm) high, 2″ (51 mm) wide. Oval, somewhat flattened, broad at top end. Milky-transparent; iridescent. 2 large lobes longer than half the total body length. 1 pair of short tentacles in sheaths between lobes, 4 ribbonlike structures around mouth, between lobes. 8 rows of comb plates, 2 extending down each lobe nearly to end, 1 down each structure.

Habitat
In shallow water; penetrates into brackish waters.

Range
South of Cape Cod to the Carolinas; common in Chesapeake Bay as far north as Baltimore.

Comments
Phylum Ctenophora. Leidy's Comb Jelly has been used in marine laboratories to study bioluminescence and problems of regeneration. Its relative, McCrady's Comb Jelly (*M. mccradyi*), ranges from Florida through the West Indies. It is about the same size and shape as *M. leidyi*, but is greenish tan and less transparent, and sometimes has 2 brown spots on each side.

Common Salp
Salpa fusiformis
229

3¼″ (83 mm) long, 1⅝″ (41 mm) wide. Transparent cylinder. Colorless; muscle bands whitish; contents of digestive system visible, yellowish. Body an open-ended cylinder, slightly wider in rear half; tunic variable, sometimes thick, sometimes thin. 9 prominent, incomplete muscle bands, not reaching midline underneath, first 3 and last 2 muscle bands touching each other at top midline; smaller muscles to close openings at ends. Front opening leads into large pharynx with a pair of single slanting gills bounded by slits on each side. Food groove long, joining rest of digestive system between last 2 muscle bands.

Habitat
Floating in plankton; near ocean surface.

Range
Entire Atlantic Coast; Alaska to California.

Comments
Phylum Chordata, Class Thaliacea. The asexually reproducing form of the Common Salp, described above, develops a long chain of buds that trails from the lower rear end. The sexual form is smaller, 1" (25 mm) long and ⅜" (10 mm) wide, and its tunic tapers to a point at both ends.

Creeping Tunicate
Perophora viridis
230

⅛" (3 mm) long and nearly as wide. Colony 3" (76 mm) or more long, 3" (76 mm) wide. Creeping, vinelike. Translucent greenish yellow. Oval individuals rising on short stalks from creeping stems. 2 siphons clearly visible with aid of hand lens.

Habitat
On rocks, pilings, bases of algae, and other solid substrates, in bays and estuaries; low-tide line to water 90' (27 m) deep.

Range
Cape Cod to Florida and Texas.

Comments
Phylum Chordata, Class Ascidiacea. Both the vinelike character and green color of this tunicate might readily lead one to confuse it with a plant. But a pair of sharp eyes, especially if aided by a hand lens, can make out tiny individual sea squirts with their siphons.

Painted Tunicate
Clavelina picta
231

Individuals ¾" (19 mm) long, ¼" (6 mm) wide. Colony a cluster 8" (20 cm) high, 12" (30 cm) wide. Tunic translucent white to yellowish, with red, purple, or cream-colored band around upper part, and red purple internal organs. This species buds asexually to form colonies of separate individuals.

Habitat
On mangrove roots, soft corals, stony corals, and other hard objects; near low-tide line and below in shallow water.

Range
S. Florida; West Indies.

Comments
Phylum Chordata, Class Ascidiacea. A colony 12" wide includes over 1000 individuals formed by budding from the rootlike base of older individuals. Small swimming tadpole larvae are released and settle, developing into miniature adults within a day.

Sea Peach
Halocynthia pyriformis
232

5" (127 mm) high, 3" (76 mm) wide. Barrel-shaped. Yellow to orange, strongly tinged with red at top and on one side. Tunic tough, fuzzy; siphons 4-lobed, both on top, incurrent siphon larger and higher, excurrent siphon smaller, lower. Attached to substrate by rootlike fibers.

Habitat
On rock and gravel bottoms; from low-tide line to water 637'
(194 m) deep.

Range
Arctic to Massachusetts Bay.

Comments
Phylum Chordata, Class Ascidiacea. The shape, color, and
fuzzy surface of this handsome solitary tunicate are reminiscent
of a peach. The largest specimens are found near the Arctic.

Sea Vase
Ciona intestinalis
233

6" (15 cm) high, 1" (25 mm) wide. Slender, vaselike. Pale
yellow or greenish, translucent, openings ringed with yellow.
Pharynx long; longitudinal muscles and digestive system
visible through translucent body wall. Openings close together
near tip.

Habitat
On rocks, pilings, floats, and boat hulls in harbors and
protected bays; from low-tide line to water 1650' (500 m)
deep.

Range
Arctic to Rhode Island.

Comments
Phylum Chordata, Class Ascidiacea. The ubiquity, abundance,
size, and easy availability of this species have made it the best-
studied tunicate in the world. A large *Ciona* pumps 4 or 5
gallons of seawater each day to filter its food, obtain oxygen,
and excrete waste products.

Orange Sea Grape
Molgula citrina
234

⅝" (16 mm) long, ½" (13 mm) wide. Rounded, with slightly
flattened sides. Translucent; orange sex organs visible. Siphons
widely separated, prominent. Tunic usually clean.

Habitat
Attached under rocks; near low-tide line and below in shallow
water.

Range
Arctic to Rhode Island.

Comments
Phylum Chordata, Class Ascidiacea. This species is a brooder,
its tadpole larvae developing in its atrium. A close relative,
the Common Sea Grape (*M. manhattensis*), is a spawner,
shedding eggs and sperm into the water. It is 2" (51 mm)
long and 1⅝" (41 mm) wide, and gray to greenish, its siphons
prominent but less far apart, and its tunic usually muddy. It
lives on rocks, pilings, boat hulls, and various seaweeds in
bays and estuaries, and is tolerant of a range of salinity,
temperature, and pollution. It ranges from Maine to Texas,
but does not occur in Florida, and has been introduced into
several bays in central California, where it thrives.

Mangrove Tunicate
Ecteinascidia turbinata
235

1" (25 mm) long, ⅜" (10 mm) wide. Colony 10" (25 cm) high, 8" (20 cm) wide. Cluster of globules. Transparent, colorless tunic, clearly visible internal organs yellow, orange, or pink. Long, globe-shaped individuals, spiralling in dense clusters of several hundred growing from creeping stem.

Habitat
On roots of mangroves and stems of turtle grass; near low-tide line and below in shallow water.

Range
S. Florida to Texas; West Indies.

Comments
Phylum Chordata, Class Ascidiacea. This attractive compound tunicate looks like a cluster of long, fluid-filled glass bulbs growing around a plant root or stem.

Northern Sea Pork
Aplidium constellatum
236

⅜" (10 mm) high, ⅟₃₂" (1 mm) wide. Colony 1" (25 mm) high, 3" (76 mm) wide. Colony of stalked lobes. Cream-colored, with red or orange individuals. Colony fleshy, soft, with long, slender individuals embedded in the soft substance.

Habitat
On rocks, pilings, and other hard objects; from low-tide line to water 20' (6 m) deep.

Range
Maine to Gulf of Mexico.

Comments
Phylum Chordata, Class Ascidiacea. A large colony of this compound tunicate resembles a piece of salt pork. A related species, the Common Sea Pork (*A. stellatum*), is similar in color and in range, but forms colonies 12" (30 cm) wide and 1" (25 mm) high, and is firmer and more rubbery.

Green Encrusting Tunicate
Symplegma viride
237

Colony more than 3" (76 mm) long and equally wide. Thin, gelatinous encrustation. Translucent, greenish; individuals purple, greenish, or black; area around siphons white, pale green, yellow, or orange. Tunic soft, thin layer, individuals uniformly scattered throughout, each with 2 siphons to surface.

Habitat
On rocky areas and in sea grass beds; near low-tide and below in shallow water.

Range
Florida; West Indies.

Comments
Phylum Chordata, Class Ascidiacea. This species encrusts rocks, shells, sea grass, and bryozoan stems, assuming the shape and contours of the substrate. Its individuals are uniformly scattered rather than arranged in flowerets.

Little Gray Barnacle
Chthamalus fragilis
238

¼" (6 mm) high, ⅜" (10 mm) wide at base. Conical, low, top flattened. Grayish-white. Sides composed of 2 pairs of limy plates overlapping 2 unpaired end plates. Top 2 pairs of plates with gape between pairs. 6 pairs of fine, feathery appendages extend through gape when open. Surface of plates smooth. Base membranous, without limy deposit.

Habitat
On rocks, singly or in small, uncrowded groups; near high-tide line.

Range
Cape Cod to Florida and Texas; West Indies.

Comments
Phylum Arthropoda, Class Crustacea. This little barnacle lives high between the tide lines and above in the splash zone when it is wet; consequently, it can feed only at high tide, a short time in each tidal cycle.

Bay Barnacle
Balanus improvisus
239

¼" (6 mm) high, ½" (13 mm) wide. Conical, flat at top. White. Sides composed of 2 pairs of limy plates overlapping only 1 of 2 unpaired plates. 2 pairs of plates at top with gape between. Side plates smooth. Base limy.

Habitat
On rocks, pilings, oysters and other hard-shelled animals, in brackish estuaries; from low-tide line to water 120' (37 m) deep.

Range
Nova Scotia to Florida and Texas; Mexico; West Indies to Brazil.

Comments
Phylum Arthropoda, Class Crustacea. This estuarine form was introduced from the East Coast to the West Coast before the middle of the 19th century along with the Eastern Oyster.

Northern Rock Barnacle
Balanus balanoides
240

1" (25 mm) high, ½" (13 mm) wide at base. Conical if not crowded, flat at top. White. Sides composed of 2 pairs of limy plates overlapping only 1 of 2 unpaired plates. 2 pairs of plates at top with gape between pairs. 6 pairs of feathery appendages extend through gape when feeding. Plates smooth, with few vertical grooves, scalloped at base. Base membranous, without limy deposit.

Habitat
On hard objects; from between high- and low-tide lines to below low-tide line in shallow water.

Range
Arctic to Delaware.

Comments
Phylum Arthropoda, Class Crustacea. This barnacle occurs in

such dense populations in some places that it can grow only in length, and its shape becomes greatly distorted. The sharp edges of its plates pose a hazard to any bare skin that touches them.

Common Goose Barnacle
Lepas anatifera
241

6" (15 cm) long, 2¾" (70 mm) wide. Flattened, lance-shaped, stalked. Enclosed in 5 strong, limy, white, orange- or yellow-edged plates; stalk purplish brown. 6 pairs of feathery feeding appendages extendible through gape between plates. Stalk one-half total length, thick, rubbery. Surface of plates almost smooth, with fine lines; stalk smooth.

Habitat
Floating; attached to drifting objects, buoys, bottles, tar masses, and the Common Purple Sea Snail.

Range
Washed ashore on both coasts of the United States.

Comments
Phylum Arthropoda, Class Crustacea. The Common Goose Barnacle is a creature of the high seas. Its swimming larvae are attracted by the shaded undersides of floating objects, where they settle gregariously. Anything long afloat, such as a navigational buoy, may be completely covered below with thousands of these barnacles.

Ivory Barnacle
Balanus eburneus
242

1" (25 mm) high, 1" (25 mm) wide. Conical, flat at top. Ivory-white. Sides composed of 2 pairs of limy plates overlapping only 1 of 2 unpaired plates. 2 pairs of grooved plates at top with gape between. Side plates smooth. Base limy and full of hollow tubes.

Habitat
On rocks and pilings in bays and estuaries; near low-tide line and below in shallow water.

Range
Maine to South America.

Comments
Phylum Arthropoda, Class Crustacea. This is the common estuarine barnacle. It occurs in brackish habitats almost into fresh water.

Lined Anemone
Fagesia lineata
243

1⅜" (35 mm) high, ¼" (6 mm) wide. Cylindrical, slender. Cream-colored to tan or brownish, with pale longitudinal lines. Oral disk surrounded by 40 slender tentacles in 3 rings; inner ones longest. Base in thin mucus tube, flattened or rounded. Column smooth.

Habitat
Among worm tubes and other growth on and under rocks; from below low-tide line to water more than 76' (23 m) deep.

Range
Cape Cod to Cape Hatteras.

Comments
Phylum Cnidaria, Class Anthozoa, Order Actiniaria. This little anemone occurs locally in numbers great enough to carpet the bottom.

Striped Anemone
Haliplanella luciae
244

¾" (19 mm) high, ¼" (6 mm) wide. Brown to olive-green. Column usually with longitudinal stripes of orange, yellow, or cream; some specimens lack stripes. Tentacles surrounding oral disk long, slender, numbering up to 50 in larger specimens. White threads of stinging cells discharged through mouth when animal is disturbed.

Habitat
On solid objects in shallow water; also found in brackish water and in salt marshes.

Range
Maine to Chesapeake Bay; reported from Texas.

Comments
Phylum Cnidaria, Class Anthozoa, Order Actiniaria. The Striped Anemone was apparently introduced from Japan in the late 19th century. Its species name, *luciae*, was given by the American naturalist A. E. Verrill in honor of his daughter Lucy.

Ghost Anemone
Diadumene leucolena
245

1½" (38 mm) high, ½" (13 mm) wide. Translucent, whitish, pink, or olive. Columnar. Mostly smooth, but with low, scattered projections. 60 slender, pale, ½" (13 mm) long tentacles surrounding mouth. White threads of stinging cells discharged when animal is disturbed.

Habitat
On or under rocks, among marine growth on pilings and jetties; in shallow water of bays and other protected areas.

Range
Maine to North Carolina.

Comments
Phylum Cnidaria, Class Anthozoa, Order Actiniaria. This little anemone is easily confused with immature forms of the Frilled Anemone, but it lacks the thread of stinging cells found in that species.

Frilled Anemone
Metridium senile
246

18" (46 cm) high, 9" (23 cm) wide. Smooth. Reddish brown to olive-brown or lighter, to cream-colored and white; paler forms may be mottled. Oral disk lobed; tentacles slender and very abundant, 1000 in large specimens, producing a frilled appearance. Long, white threads of stinging cells discharged when animal is disturbed.

Habitat
Attached to rocks, wharf piles, and other solid objects; near low-tide line and below in shallow water.

Range
Arctic to Delaware.

Comments
Phylum Cnidaria, Class Anthozoa, Order Actiniaria. These anemones reproduce either sexually or asexually, the latter by dividing lengthwise or by leaving behind, as they creep over a surface, bits of tissue from the pedal disk that regenerate into complete anemones.

Trumpet Stalked Jellyfish
Haliclystus salpinx
247

1″ (25 mm) high, ½″ (13 mm) wide. Translucent, with red, orange, yellow, or tan. Widely flared when expanded, with each of 8 short arms ending in a pompom of 100 knobbed tentacles. Notches between arms spaced equally, each notch with trumpet-shaped anchor that has small tentacle in middle and ridged ring around base. Mouth has 4 lips. Reproductive organs situated along length of arms.

Habitat
Attached to eelgrass, kelp, rockweed, other seaweeds, and to rocks; near low-tide line and below in shallow water.

Range
New Brunswick to Cape Cod.

Comments
Phylum Cnidaria, Class Scyphozoa. The Trumpet Stalked Jellyfish is a trap for small crustaceans, and when one of these comes into contact with a tentacle, it is immediately put into the mouth and swallowed. The Eared Stalked Jellyfish (*H. auricula*) is similar in appearance, but with a somewhat shorter stalk and holdfasts that are plump, oval, and shaped like an earlobe with a short tentacle in the center. It ranges farther south, to the south side of Cape Cod.

Stalked Tunicate
Boltenia ovifera
248

Body 3″ (76 mm) long, 2″ (51 mm) wide; stalk ¼″ (6 mm) wide, 12″ (30 cm) or more high. Oval body on long stalk. Tannish yellow to orange or red; reddish around siphons. Body on long, sturdy, upright stalk; surface lightly hairy, sometimes wrinkled. Siphons on one side, prominent, incurrent siphon aimed upward, excurrent siphon aimed downward.

Habitat
On rock and gravel bottoms; from low-tide line to water 1640′ (500 m) deep.

Range
Arctic to Cape Cod.

Comments
Phylum Chordata, Class Ascidiacea. The long stalk of older

specimens of this tunicate is usually encrusted with bryozoans, hydroids, and algae. Arctic specimens blown ashore by storms are eaten by Eskimos.

Club Hydroid
Clava leptostyla
249

Polyp colony ⅜" (10 mm) high, 1" (25 mm) wide. Unbranched, rising from a network of creeping horizontal stems. Pink to reddish orange. 30 threadlike tentacles scattered over top ¼ of club-shaped heads. Clusters of reproductive organs just below tentacles. No medusa stage.

Habitat
Usually attached to rockweeds and knotted wrack, occasionally on rocks; just above low-tide line and in bays and shallow water.

Range
Labrador to Long Island Sound; central California.

Comments
Phylum Cnidaria, Class Hydrozoa. These hydroids can be found growing in velvety clusters in tide pools.

Large-eyed Feather Duster
Potamilla reniformis
250

4" (102 mm) long, ⅛" (3 mm) wide. In thin, leathery tubes encrusted with sand, more than 6" (15 cm) long. Slender, tapered toward rear. 60 segments. Yellowish green. Plume of about 20 gills, united at base, orange-red to reddish brown, ringed with white, yellowish at tips, each with 1–8 large, red eyes, irregularly spaced.

Habitat
On rocks and shells; from near low-tide line to water 340' (104 m) deep.

Range
Maine to North Carolina.

Comments
Phylum Annelida, Class Polychaeta, Subclass Sedentaria. This delicate and graceful worm is abundant on shelly bottoms on the south side of Cape Cod.

Spiral-gilled Tube Worm
Spirobranchus giganteus
251

4" (102 mm) long, ⅜" (10 mm) wide. In long, limy tube with a single spine on one side of opening. Bluish to tan. 200 segments. Prominent flared collar, 2 sets of yellow, orange, red, pink, blue, white, or tan spirally-wound gills, each 1" (25 mm) long, conical. Rounded lid on a long stalk with a pair of antlerlike projections with few short spikes at margins.

Habitat
On dead coral, or burrowed into living coral heads; below low-tide line in shallow seas.

Range
Florida, Bahamas, West Indies, and Gulf of Mexico wherever coral reefs occur.

Comments
Phylum Annelida, Class Polychaeta, Subclass Sedentaria.
These beautiful worms look like flowers on the surface of coral
heads.

Spiral-tufted Bryozoan
Bugula turrita
252

Colony 12″ (30 cm) long, 4″ (102 mm) wide. Erect, flexible,
branching. Orange-brown to tan. Individuals arranged in 2
parallel rows, main branches having secondary branches
arranged in a spiral pattern about the long axis. Individuals
1/32″ (1 mm) long and half as wide, tapering downward, with
several spines at their upper ends and with stalked bird's-beak
pinchers located halfway down the front margins. Mature
colonies with globular brood chambers.

Habitat
On seagrasses, algae, pilings, and rocks; from low-tide line to
water 90′ (27 m) deep.

Range
Massachusetts to Florida.

Comments
Phylum Bryozoa, Class Gymnolaemata. Species of the genus
Bugula may easily be confused with seaweeds.

Banded Feather Duster
Sabella crassicornis
253

2″ (51 mm) long, 1/8″ (3 mm) wide. In stiff, leathery tube 4″
(102 mm) long. Tapered. Creamy pink to orange-tan. 4-lobed
collar at head end, head with plume of 24 straight, feathery
gills, united at base, banded with various shades of red, each
with 2–6 paired, dark red eyespots, evenly spaced in rows
across plume.

Habitat
Attached to rocks and shells; from near to low-tide line to
water 170′ (52 m) deep.

Range
Maine to Cape Cod.

Comments
Phylum Annelida, Class Polychaeta, Subclass Sedentaria.
Living in a dead-end tube presents a problem in voiding fecal
pellets. Members of this genus have a ciliated groove that runs
the length of the body and carries the pellets to the top of the
tube so the worm can dump them outside. The Black-eyed
Feather Duster Worm (*S. melanostigma*), which also has evenly
spaced rows of eyes on the plume and, in addition, a few wide
bands of red, is about the same size as *S. crassicornis*. It is
common in Florida and the Caribbean Sea.

Snail Fur
Hydractinia echinata
254

Polyp colony 1/8″ (3 mm) high. Dense, furry. Whitish, pale
pink, or reddish orange. Tough, jagged-spined crust that coats
entire snail shell occupied by hermit crab. 3 kinds of polyps,
connected by creeping stem: slender feeding polyps, with up

to 30 threadlike tentacles in irregular whorl below mouth; long, flexible protective polyps with no mouth or tentacles, ending in large knob of stinging cells; reproductive polyps with stalked, saclike organs, either male or female. No medusa stage.

Habitat
On snail shells occupied by hermit crabs; occasionally on stones.

Range
Labrador to Florida and Texas.

Comments
Phylum Cnidaria, Class Hydrozoa. As the hermit crab moves, the Snail Fur polyps reach new water in which to capture food. The stinging cells of the hydroid may in turn protect the crab from being eaten.

Red Soft Coral
Gersemia rubiformis
255

6″ (15 cm) high, 3″ (76 mm) wide. Soft, fleshy, with stout, club-shaped branches or cluster of pear-shaped lobes rising from main stem. Red to orange. Branches terminate in clusters of polyps set close together, each with 8 short, featherlike tentacles.

Habitat
Attached to rocks, pilings, and other solid objects; below low-tide line.

Range
Arctic to Gulf of Maine.

Comments
Phylum Cnidaria, Class Anthozoa, Subclass Octocorallia. The needlelike limestone spicules imbedded in the Red Soft Coral's stem lend support to its structure.

Tubularian Hydroid
Tubularia crocea
256

Polyp colony more than 12″ (30 cm) wide. Single pink polyps 5″ (127 mm) high on sparsely branched stems rising from a creeping horizontal stem. Head pear-shaped, with whorl of short, threadlike tentacles around mouth, longer ones around base; 24 tentacles in each whorl. Grapelike clusters of reproductive organs, attached above basal whorl, hang down below it. No medusa stage.

Habitat
Attached to almost any solid object continuously submerged in shallow water.

Range
Nova Scotia to Cape Hatteras, possibly to Florida.

Comments
Phylum Cnidaria, Class Hydrozoa. These hydroids commonly encrust boat hulls. Related species are the Ringed Tubularian (*T. larynx*), 2″ (51 mm) high, which has highly branched

stems with circular constrictions; the Tall Tubularian
(*T. indivisa*), with about 40 tentacles per whorl and polyps up
to 12″ (30 cm) high; and the Sparsely-branched Tubularian
(*T. spectabilis*), distinguished from *T. crocea* only by details of
its reproductive organs.

Thick-based Entoprocts
Barentsia spp.
257

⅜″ (10 mm) high, 1¼″ (32 mm) wide. Dense. Whitish or
yellowish; visible digestive contents yellow to brown. Slender
stalks rising from creeping stem, each stalk with thickened,
muscular base and globular individual at tip. Some species
branched. Individual with ring of 10–20 ciliated tentacles
that curl toward center when disturbed.

Habitat
On rocks, shells, pilings, seaweeds, and other solid objects;
near low-tide line and below in shallow water.

Range
Atlantic Coast.

Comments
Phylum Entoprocta. Colonies of these small animals may at
first be mistaken for hydroids. However, their habits of
curling rather than contracting their tentacles, and of bowing
at the stem when disturbed, quickly mark them as entoprocts.

Porcupine Bryozoan
Flustrellidra hispida
258

Colony 4″ (102 mm) long, 2″ (51 mm) wide. Rubbery.
Reddish brown. Encrusting, bristling with small spines.
Individuals ¹⁄₁₆″ (2 mm) long, ¹⁄₃₂″ (1 mm) wide, 6-sided,
structures visible only at edge of colony where spines have not
yet developed.

Habitat
On stems of rockweeds, on rocks and shells; from low-tide line
to water 62′ (19 m) deep.

Range
Arctic to Long Island Sound.

Comments
Phylum Bryozoa, Class Gymnolaemata. This colony's
expanded tentacles, when seen through the shallow water of a
tide pool, look like a pale blue mist hovering over its surface.

Feathered Hydroid ⊗
Pennaria tiarella
259

Polyp colony 6″ (15 cm) high, 6″ (15 cm) wide. Bushy,
branched alternately in one plane like a feather. Stems covered
with tough, horny, yellow to black sheath, and ringed above
attachment of each branch. White to pink flask-shaped head
has 5 irregular whorls of knobbed tentacles below mouth,
basal whorl of 12 threadlike tentacles, and a few white to rosy
pink reproductive organs above basal tentacles. Medusa ¹⁄₁₆″
(2 mm) high, ¹⁄₂₅″ (1 mm) wide. Cup-shaped. Deep pink. 4
pink-spotted radial canals and 4 short, white tentacle bulbs
along rim.

Habitat
Attached to solid objects; in shallow water below low-tide line. Medusa floats near surface.

Range
Maine to Florida and Texas; West Indies.

Comments
Phylum Cnidaria, Class Hydrozoa. Mildly toxic. This hydroid is capable of delivering a mild sting when handled.

Bushy Wine-glass Hydroids
Obelia spp.
260

Colony 8″ (20 cm) high, 4″ (102 mm) wide. Bushy. Whitish. Colony highly branched, each branch with rings just above attachment to stem. Feeding heads, head sheath, and sheath around reproductive buds like those of the Zig-zag Wine-glass Hydroid.

Habitat
Attached to rocks, shells, pilings, floats, and other solid objects; from low-tide line to water 165′ (50 m) deep.

Range
Entire Atlantic Coast.

Comments
Phylum Cnidaria, Class Hydrozoa. Recent work on the classification of *Obelia* suggests that there are only 2 species of Bushy Wine-glass Hydroids, *O. bidentata* and *O. dichotoma*. They cannot be distinguished in the field. The Double-toothed Bushy Wine-glass Hydroid (*O. bidentata*) ranges from Cape Cod to Florida and the West Indies.

Zig-zag Wine-glass Hydroid
Obelia geniculata
261

Polyp colony 1″ (25 mm) high, more than 12″ (30 cm) wide. Stems simple, unbranched, zigzagged, rising in a row from creeping horizontal base. Whitish. Ringed stalks of polyps rising from each "knee" of zigzag stem. Head sheath conical, margin smooth, feeding head with flared mouth. Single whorl of up to 20 basal tentacles. Sheath around reproductive buds urn-shaped, with collar, attached by short, ringed stalk in angle between stem and stalk of head sheath. Medusa ⅟₁₆″ (2 mm) high, ¼″ (6 mm) wide. Almost flat. 100 short tentacles at rim; 8 marginal sense organs; 4 radial canals with yellow gonad under each. Feeding tube yellow, short. Mouth has 4 simple lips.

Habitat
Polyps attached to large kelp, sargasso weed, rocks; in shallow water. Medusa floats near surface.

Range
Arctic to Florida and Texas; West Indies.

Comments
Phylum Cnidaria, Class Hydrozoa. The medusae of *O. geniculata* often swim with the bell turned inside out like windblown umbrellas.

Wine-glass Hydroids
Campanularia spp.
262

Polyp colony 10″ (25 cm) high, 6″ (15 cm) wide. Sheathed stems regularly or irregularly branched, or unbranched; single, or several fused together. Whitish. Upright stems arise from creeping base; stems and branches with or without circular constrictions. Feeding head sheath flaring, wine-glass-shaped, stalked; margin smooth or toothed. Polyp has flaring mouth, single whorl of 20 threadlike tentacles. Sheath surrounding reproductive buds more than twice as long as feeding head sheath; cylindrical; slightly flared, stalkless, without neck. No medusa stage.

Habitat
On rocks, pilings, and other hard objects, and on seaweeds; from low-tide line to water 1380′ (420 m) deep.

Range
Labrador to Florida; Bermuda; Bahamas; West Indies to Venezuela; Alaska to S. California.

Comments
Phylum Cnidaria, Class Hydrozoa. These hydroids belong to a large family characterized by the stalked, wine-glass-shaped sheath that surrounds and protects the feeding head. Unlike its close relative *Obelia, Campanularia* does not release free-swimming medusae. Instead, the medusae remain within the sheath without developing mouth or tentacles, mature sexually, and produce ciliated larvae that escape into the water and disperse. Laboratory examination is necessary to determine species.

Garland Hydroid
Sertularia pumila
263

Polyp colony 2″ (51 mm) high, 1″ (25 mm) wide. Clusters of stiff stems with opposite branching. Creamy to pale tan. Head sheaths in opposite pairs, tubular, lower half attached to stem, upper half curved outward. Margins have 2 teeth. Aperture closed by lid with 2 flaps. Feeding heads small, slender, with a single whorl of 12 threadlike tentacles. Gonad sheath large, egg-shaped, smooth, with short collar and large opening. No medusa stage.

Habitat
Attached in tufts to rockweed, knotted wrack, rocks, and other solid objects; near low-tide line and below.

Range
Arctic to Cape Hatteras.

Comments
Phylum Cnidaria, Class Hydrozoa. This species is representative of a large family of widely distributed hydroids of similar structure. *Sertularella* differs in having the head sheaths alternate instead of opposite on the stem. *Abietinaria* also has alternate head sheaths, and is highly branched in 1 plane.

Sea Plumes
Pseudopterogorgia spp.
264

36″ (91 cm) or more high, 12″ (30 cm) wide. Plumy, branching. Bluish gray, violet, purple, yellow, or whitish. Branches alternate or opposite on stem, long or short, with round or slitlike openings along edges of branches into which polyps retract.

Habitat
Attached to rocks around reefs; below low-tide line in shallow water.

Range
Florida; Bahamas; West Indies.

Comments
Phylum Cnidaria, Class Anthozoa, Subclass Octocorallia. Sea plumes, along with their relatives the sea fans and sea whips, are sensitive to bright light and expand their polyps only at night or on overcast days.

Organ-pipe Sponge
Leucosolenia botryoides
265

¹⁄₁₆″ (2 mm) wide, ½″ (13 mm) high. Branching, cylindrical tube rising from a creeping base. White. Spicules limy, 3- or 4-pronged, visible with a hand lens. Grows in clusters of 2 or 3 to several hundred tubes.

Habitat
On the underside of overhanging rocks; on seaweeds and wharf piles, in protected areas; near low-tide line and below.

Range
Gulf of St. Lawrence to Cape Cod.

Comments
Phylum Porifera, Class Calcispongiae. This small sponge spreads in patches whose surface resembles a web of starched lace.

Elegant Burrowing Anemone
Edwardsia elegans
266

2″ (51 mm) high, ¼″ (6 mm) wide. Slender, wormlike. Usually enclosed in thin, parchmentlike tube to which sand grains adhere. Pale red or purplish brown, with pale lemon-yellow spots. Collar bearing mouth smooth, surrounded by ring of 16 slender tentacles; middle section grooved and warty; basal section inflatable, whitish or pinkish. Tentacles yellowish, with orange to red stripe.

Habitat
Under stones, in sandy mud; near low-tide line and below.

Range
New Brunswick to Chesapeake Bay.

Comments
Phylum Cnidaria, Class Anthozoa, Order Actiniaria. Unlike most sea anemones, which have flat basal disks, the Elegant Burrowing Anemone has an inflatable basal section with which it can probe and dig in the sandy mud.

Sea Whip
Leptogorgia virgulata
267

36" (91 cm) high, ½" (13 mm) wide. Stems and branches long, whiplike, tough, pitted with small, evenly distributed pores. Purple, red, yellow-orange, or tan.

Habitat
Attached to rocks and other hard objects in shallow water; near low-tide line and below.

Range
New Jersey to N. Florida.

Comments
Phylum Cnidaria, Class Anthozoa, Subclass Octocorallia. This horny coral is so named because its branches have a horny central core. The closely related Straight Sea Whip (*L. setacea*), 72" (183 cm) high and ½" (13 mm) wide, is unbranched. It ranges up into Chesapeake Bay as far north as the Patuxent River in Maryland.

Pink-tipped Anemone
Condylactis gigantea
268

6" (15 cm) high, 12" (30 cm) wide. Large, showy, columnar. White, light blue, pink, orange, pale red, or light brown. Mouth surrounded by 100 or more long, tapering tentacles tipped with pink, scarlet, blue, or green in several rings, usually paler than body. Basal disk firmly attached.

Habitat
Attached to hard objects in shallow water; common around reefs in both forereef and lagoonal areas and in turtle-grass beds.

Range
From S. Florida through the Florida Keys; West Indies.

Comments
Phylum Cnidaria, Class Anthozoa, Order Actiniaria. This impressive anemone is the largest in American Atlantic tropical waters. It is sometimes called the "passion flower" of the Caribbean.

Ringed Anemone
Bartholomea annulata
269

More than 2" (51 mm) high, 1½" (38 mm) wide. Columnar, smooth. Brownish; whitish at base. 200 tentacles with pale rings varying in size, light brown.

Habitat
On or beneath rocks and other solid objects; in shallow water.

Range
Florida to Texas; Bahamas; West Indies.

Comments
Phylum Cnidaria, Class Anthozoa, Order Actiniaria. The rings on this anemone's tentacles are actually batteries of stinging cells.

Finger Sponge
Haliclona oculata
270

More than 12" (30 cm) wide, 18" (46 cm) high. Erect, branched. Attached at base by short, narrow stalk; variable in number and shape of branches. Tan to gray-brown, sometimes rosy or red-orange. Pores conspicuous, scattered over surface.

Habitat
Attached to rocks; from low-tide line to water 400' (124 m) deep.

Range
Labrador to North Carolina.

Comments
Phylum Porifera, Class Demospongiae. This species is sometimes called the "Eyed Sponge" because its pores are reminiscent of so many eyes. It is frequently broken free by storms and tossed up on the beach, where its skeleton bleaches to white.

Sea Fans
Gorgonia spp.
271

36" (91 cm) high, 36" (91 cm) wide. Flattened; outline egg-shaped with small branches fusing to make a continuous latticework. Pinkish purple, yellow, or, rarely, white. Smaller branches wider than thick, compressed in same plane as stem. Numerous fine pores on branches.

Habitat
Attached to rocks around reefs and on reef flats; below low-tide line.

Range
S. Florida; Bermuda; Bahamas; West Indies.

Comments
Phylum Cnidaria, Class Anthozoa, Subclass Octocorallia. Sea fans evoke idyllic tropical seas, and are often collected, dried, and sometimes spray-painted for souvenirs.

Elkhorn Coral
Acropora palmata
272

10' (3 m) high, more than 60" (152 cm) wide. Treelike, with flattened, fanlike branches of extremely variable length and width extending outward from a short, thick stalk. Brownish yellow to cream-colored, tips of branches white. Surface of branches covered with small, protruding, round cups oriented toward growing edge.

Habitat
On windward side of reefs; below low-tide line.

Range
Florida Keys; Bahamas; West Indies to Brazil.

Comments
Phylum Cnidaria, Class Anthozoa, Order Scleractinia. In more protected areas of the reef, this coral forms fingerlike margins on its branches that resemble the flat, branching antlers of a moose or European elk. Cuts and scratches resulting from contact with this coral can be slow to heal.

Staghorn Coral
Acropora cervicornis
273

10′ (3 m) high, more than 60″ (152 cm) wide. Loosely branched, with 1″ (25 mm) wide, cylindrical branches of variable length that do not fuse together. Yellowish or purplish brown, paler at the tips. Surface covered with small, protruding, round cups oriented toward branch tip.

Habitat
In protected areas of reefs; on windward side of reefs in water more than 10′ (3 m) deep.

Range
Florida Keys; Bahamas; West Indies.

Comments
Phylum Cnidaria, Class Anthozoa, Order Scleractinia. This coral is heavily collected for tourists, to the great detriment of many reefs.

Fire Coral ⊗
Millepora alcicornis
274

More than 24″ (61 cm) high, more than 18″ (46 cm) wide. Upright, branching or platelike, on coral rock or encrusting mollusk shells or skeletons of horny corals. Brown to creamy yellow. Covered with tiny pores occupied by whitish polyps.

Habitat
Coral reefs, cement pilings, and other submerged structures.

Range
Florida to Mexico; Bahamas; West Indies.

Comments
Phylum Cnidaria, Class Hydrozoa. Highly toxic. People touching the Fire Coral suffer a severe burning sensation and blistery rash.

Red Beard Sponge
Microciona prolifera
275

Varies from a thin encrusting layer less than ⅛″ (3 mm) high and covering a few square inches to 8″ (20 cm) wide and 8″ (20 cm) high with many fanlike branches. Red to orange. Pores inconspicuous.

Habitat
On rocks, pilings, oysters and other shells, and hard objects in protected bays and estuaries; below low-tide line.

Range
Nova Scotia to Florida and Texas.

Comments
Phylum Porifera, Class Demospongiae. The Red Beard Sponge was the first animal shown to reorganize its form from experimentally separated cells. Cells divided by squeezing the sponge through a fine mesh cloth into a bowl of sea water creep about on the bottom, stick to each other, and finally form a mass that reorganizes into a sponge. This sponge tolerates both the pollution and the reduced salinities of bays and estuaries.

Rubbery Bryozoan
Alcyonidium hirsutum
276

Colony more then 3" (76 mm) wide, ⅛" (3 mm) high. Fleshy, encrusting. Yellowish brown or reddish. Colony gelatinous, usually encrusting stems of rockweed and other plants; sometimes erect, branched. Surface covered with many conical projections. Closely packed individuals retract into puckered openings.

Habitat
On stems of seaweeds and on rocks; near low-tide line and below in shallow water.

Range
Arctic to Long Island Sound.

Comments
Phylum Bryozoa, Class Gymnolaemata. *A. hirsutum* is extremely variable in form, but is unlike all other species of *Alcyonidium* in having conical bumps on its surface. The Pussley Bryozoan (*A. verrilli*), which ranges from Cape Cod to Chesapeake Bay, grows in branching colonies 15" (38 cm) high and 4" (102 mm) wide, and is yellowish brown.

Encrusted Tunicate
Polycarpa obtecta
277

2" (51 mm) long, 1¾" (44 mm) wide. Tough-coated, sand-encrusted globe. Body yellowish, brownish gray, or mud-colored; siphons red, purplish brown, or brown. Tunic wrinkled, usually encrusted with sand and bits of shell; thick, rough attached to substrate by mossy fibers; siphons prominent, 4-lobed.

Habitat
On rocks, grass stems, and other solid objects; near low-tide line and below in shallow water.

Range
Florida to Texas; West Indies to Brazil.

Comments
Phylum Chordata, Class Ascidiacea. These solitary tunicates may be easily overlooked because of their encrusting habit. Those that settle on rocks well above the bottom, as on a seawall, may be relatively free of sand coating.

Vase Sponge
Ircinia campana
278

24" (61 cm) wide, 36" (91 cm) high. Vase-shaped or bell-shaped, with a deep central cavity. Reddish to reddish brown. Surface irregular, with small pores and coarse longitudinal ribs.

Habitat
Attached to rocks projecting a short distance above the bottom; from below low-tide line to water 50' (15 m) deep.

Range
Florida to Mexico; Bahamas; West Indies.

Comments
Phylum Porifera, Class Demospongiae. An accumulation of

coral sediment is usually present in this sponge's central cavity, apparently with no ill effects. This species, often washed ashore during storms, becomes tough and shrunken when dried.

Labyrinthine Brain Coral
Diploria labyrinthiformis
279

96″ (244 cm) high, 96″ (244 cm) wide. Convex, heavy boulders with winding, interconnected valleys ¼″ (6 mm) deep, and ⅜″ (10 mm) wide. Bright orange-yellow to brownish yellow. Walls between valleys thick, with longitudinal groove.

Habitat
Abundant on reefs; in shallow water.

Range
Florida to Texas and Mexico; Bermuda; Bahamas; West Indies.

Comments
Phylum Cnidaria, Class Anthozoa, Order Scleractinia. The young brain coral newly settled on a solid substrate has one polyp in a round cup. The cup begins to elongate as it grows, folding and twisting into "valleys." The polyp is thus stretched into a long and contorted mass that appears brainlike.

Reef Starlet Coral
Siderastrea siderea
280

36″ (91 cm) wide, 36″ (91 cm) high. Boulderlike. Brown or grayish. Surface covered with round cups ¼″ (6 mm) wide and equally high, shallow, with 60 septa.

Habitat
Associated with reefs, usually in protected areas and shallow water; sometimes on reef front in water more than 15′ (5 m) deep.

Range
Florida; Bermuda; Bahamas; West Indies to Brazil.

Comments
Phylum Cnidaria, Class Anthozoa, Order Scleractinia. A common inhabitant of the reef and surrounding area.

Loggerhead Sponge
Ircinia strobilina
281

18″ (46 cm) wide, 24″ (61 cm) high. Cylindrical, cake-shaped. Dark gray to dull black. Surface with irregular "peaks"; pores large. Soft and resilient.

Habitat
Attached to rocky outcrops rising short distances from the bottom; from shallow water to water 50′ (15 m) deep.

Range
Florida to Mexico; Bahamas; West Indies.

Comments
Phylum Porifera, Class Demospongiae. The sponge

Spheciospongia vesparia, a species totally different from *I. strobilina* but found in the same range, is known by the same common name. Consequently *I. strobilina* is also sometimes called the Cake Sponge.

Stinker Sponge
Ircinia fasciculata
282

8″ (20 cm) wide, 12″ (30 cm) high. Nodes, lobes, or thick branches. Yellow to brown or purplish. Surface with many short, rounded lobes. Pores large, conspicuous.

Habitat
Attached to rocks rising a little above the substrate; in shallow water, on reefs, to water 50′ (15 m) deep.

Range
Florida to Mexico; Bahamas; West Indies.

Comments
Phylum Porifera, Class Demospongiae. While most sponges have an unpleasant smell, the Stinker Sponge, as its name implies, emits an especially repulsive odor. Though the sponge is resilient while alive, it becomes hard and brittle when dried. Stinker Sponges often wash ashore after storms.

Clubbed Finger Coral
Porites porites
283

Colony 12″ (30 cm) or more long, 12″ (30 cm) wide, forming thick clumps of irregular branches swollen at their ends, 1″ (25 mm) wide. Pale beige, yellowish brown to purplish. Branches covered with closely set cups about 1/16″ (2 mm) wide and equally high.

Habitat
Throughout the reef; in shallow water.

Range
Florida to Mexico; Bermuda; Bahamas; West Indies.

Comments
Phylum Cnidaria, Class Anthozoa, Order Scleractinia. This species is a common inhabitant of the back reef, although in that habitat it does not achieve the large size of specimens growing on the fore reef.

Porous Coral
Porites astreoides
284

Encrusting colony 24″ (61 cm) high, 24″ (61 cm) wide. Flattened or rounded, lump-covered masses. Yellow or greenish brown to neon-green. Surface covered with closely set, small cups 1/16″ (2 mm) high, each with 12 septa.

Habitat
Back-reef areas, sand bottoms, and turtle-grass beds; in shallow water.

Range
Florida to Mexico; Bermuda; Bahamas; West Indies to Brazil.

Comments
Phylum Cnidaria, Class Anthozoa, Order Scleractinia. The

massive coral boulders of this species are among the most common features of American reefs. The Spiral-gilled Tube Worm is a frequent inhabitant of the Porous Coral.

Large Star Coral
Montastrea cavernosa
285

36″ (91 cm) high, 60″ (152 cm) wide. Massive, boulderlike. Greenish or yellowish brown. Cups crowded, large, elevated above the surface, ½″ (13 mm) wide, ⅛″ (3 mm) deep. 48 septa extending into the space around cups.

Habitat
On coral rock bottom; in shallow water.

Range
Florida to Texas; Mexico; Bahamas; West Indies; Bermuda.

Comments
Phylum Cnidaria, Class Anthozoa, Order Scleractinia. An important reef species, but also occurs by itself on flats behind the reef. It feeds actively on plankton.

Stokes' Star Coral
Dichocoenia stokesii
286

12″ (30 cm) high, 12″ (30 cm) wide. Heavy, convex boulders. Yellowish tan; tentacles of polyps white. Cups of various shapes—round, oval, elongate, or Y-shaped. Cups form short valleys ¼″ (6 mm) wide, ¼″ (6 mm) deep. 10 thick septa per cm, alternately thick and thin.

Habitat
Back-reef and fore-reef areas; in water 5′ (2 m) or more deep, with good circulation.

Range
Florida; Bahamas; West Indies.

Comments
Phylum Cnidaria, Class Anthozoa, Order Scleractinia. The retracted polyps of this coral show the starlike pattern of its septa against a darker yellow or brown background.

Common Red Crust Bryozoan
Cryptosula pallasiana
287

Colony ¹⁄₃₂″ (1 mm) high, more than 3″ (76 mm) wide. Hard, encrusting, thin, roundish. Red to orange, or pink. Individuals in elongate, limy, boxlike cases arranged radially and spirally, with keyhole-shaped opening, rounded at head end, widest at rear end, with 2 toothlike points, separating fore from rear parts, through which feeding tentacles extend; 16–20 smaller pores irregularly scattered over case surface.

Habitat
On rocks, shells, and other hard objects; near low-tide line and below in shallow water.

Range
Nova Scotia to Florida.

Comments
Phylum Bryozoa, Class Gymnolaemata. The crown of tentacles

used in filtering microscopic organisms from the water as food can be seen only if a rock or shell encrusted with this bryozoan is placed in a bowl of sea water and kept at ocean temperature. The extended tentacles will appear as white fuzz on the surface of the colony.

Hairy Bryozoan
Electra pilosa
288

Colony 2″ (51 mm) wide, paper-thin lacy network, circular, lobed, or irregularly star-shaped. White, with long, gold spines. Colony shape variable; patches on stones or broad-bladed seaweeds; may take a cylindrical shape around narrow stems or blades of seaweeds. Individuals elongated, oval, 1/32″ (1 mm) long, with oval, membranous frontal area bordered by 4–12 spines, the middle bottom spine usually longer than the rest. No brood chambers.

Habitat
On almost any substrate, but particularly common on seaweeds, especially the Irish Moss (*Chondrus crispus*); from low-tide line to water 100′ (30 m) deep.

Range
Arctic to Long Island Sound.

Comments
Phylum Bryozoa, Class Gymnolaemata. This is one of the most common bryozoans in the New England region. Its long golden spines give it a delicately hairy appearance. Both the colony and the individual zooids are extremely variable in form.

Starlet Coral
Siderastrea radians
289

12″ (30 cm) wide, 12″ (30 cm) high. Rounded mass. Brown, salmon, yellow, or gray. Young forms encrust and eventually cover small stones. Surface covered with deep, starlike cups 1/8″ (3 mm) wide, with 40 septa.

Habitat
On coral reefs and reef flats in shallows.

Range
Florida to Texas and Mexico; Bermuda; Bahamas; West Indies to South America.

Comments
Phylum Cnidaria, Class Anthozoa, Order Scleractinia. This very common species tolerates the great temperature fluctuations of a shallow reef flat as well as considerable variations in salinity.

Golden Star Tunicate
Botryllus schlosseri
290

Colony 1/8″ (3 mm) high, 4″ (102 mm) wide. Thin, rubbery crust. Yellow, olive, greenish, tan, brown, purple, or black; individuals outlined in yellow or white.

Habitat
On rocks, shells, pilings, bases of seaweeds, eelgrass, and

other solid surfaces, on open shores and in brackish estuaries; near low-tide line and below in shallow water.

Range
Bay of Fundy to North Carolina.

Comments
Phylum Chordata, Class Ascidiacea. This species can be cultured easily by tying a bit of a colony to a glass slide placed in a pint of sea water. It has been used in studies of reproduction, development, and the genetics of color patterns.

Single-horn Bryozoan
Schizoporella unicornis
291

Colony $\frac{1}{32}$″ (1 mm) high, more than 4″ (102 mm) wide. Limy, encrusting, variable in form. White, pale reddish orange to dull red. Usually several layers thick, new layers growing over old dead ones. Individuals squarish, less than $\frac{1}{32}$″ (1 mm) wide and high, aperture round, with indentation at rear, single spine below aperture, surface perforated with many pores. Brood chambers rounded, perforated; stalkless bird's-beak pinchers on some individuals, sometimes scarce.

Habitat
On rocks, shells, pilings, worm tubes, and various seaweed stalks, on open shores and in estuaries; near low-tide line and below in shallow water.

Range
Arctic to Florida.

Comments
Phylum Bryozoa, Class Gymnolaemata. This bryozoan's habit of growing new layers over older ones sometimes results in the formation of thick, round nodules around a pebble or shell. The Staghorn Bryozoan (*S. floridana*), which ranges from North Carolina through Florida, the Gulf of Mexico, and the West Indies, forms branching colonies several layers thick, 4″ (102 mm) high, 2″ (51 mm) wide.

Boring Sponge
Cliona celata
292

One or more $\frac{1}{8}$″ (3 mm) wide, $\frac{1}{16}$″ (2 mm) high yellowish pores protruding from holes in mollusk shells or coral. Sponge may overgrow the host entirely.

Habitat
In living and dead mollusk shells and corals.

Range
Gulf of St. Lawrence to Gulf of Mexico; Washington to California.

Comments
Phylum Porifera, Class Demospongiae. The larvae of these sponges settle on shells and coral, develop into tiny sponges and, secreting sulfuric acid, excavate pits and galleries, loosening chips of the shell or coral, which are then ejected. The host is weakened to the point of disintegration, and the sea bottom is thus kept free of accumulating shells.

Ornate Worm
Amphitrite ornata
293

15" (38 cm) long, ¾" (19 mm) wide. In a firm tube of sand, mud, or mucus. Thick thorax and more slender, tapered abdomen. Orange-pink to reddish or orange-brown. Head with numerous long, yellowish-orange tentacles and 3 pairs of branched, red gills; appendages with bristles on 50 body segments.

Habitat
In quiet, shallow bays, often brackish, in bottoms ranging from soft mud to firm muddy sand; near low-tide line and just below.

Range
Maine to North Carolina.

Comments
Phylum Annelida, Class Polychaeta, Subclass Sedentaria. The tubes of this worm extend downward a foot or more. The opening is usually found in the center of a low hillock made of mud and sand excavated by the worm. South of Cape Cod, one can commonly find the Many-scaled Worm (*Lepidametria commensalis*) living commensally in the tube with the Ornate Worm.

Sinistral Spiral Tube Worm
Spirorbis borealis
294

⅛" (3 mm) long, ⅛" (3 mm) wide. In limy tube coiled like a snail shell, counterclockwise to left from opening toward center. Tiny worm inside. Whitish, translucent. 9 feathery gills; stalked lid; collar of 3 segments.

Habitat
Attached to kelps, Irish moss, and other algae, and to rocks and shells; from above low-tide line to shallow depths.

Range
Maine to Cape Cod.

Comments
Phylum Annelida, Class Polychaeta, Subclass Sedentaria. These worms are unusual among polychaetes in being hermaphroditic, the forward segments of the abdomen being female and the rear ones male. The tube of the Dextral Spiral Tube Worm (*S. spirillum*) coils to the right. The worm itself is similar to *S. borealis* in measurements, habitat, and distribution.

Red Terebellid Worm
Polycirrus eximius
295

2¾" (70 mm) long, ¼" (6 mm) wide. Cylindrical, tapered toward rear. Wide thorax and narrower abdomen. Blood-red. Head with numerous tentacles, but no gills or eyes. 25 segments with appendages bearing bristles.

Habitat
Without well-defined tubes; in burrows in soft mud bottoms, among eelgrass roots, or under rocks in muddy places, ranging into brackish water; from low-tide line to water 55' (17 m) deep.

Range
Maine to North Carolina.

Comments
Phylum Annelida, Class Polychaeta, Subclass Sedentaria. This worm has no circulatory system, but its body fluid is full of red blood cells.

Plumed Worm
Diopatra cuprea
296

12″ (30 cm) long, ⅜″ (10 mm) wide. In a leathery tube. Front cylindrical, rear flattened and tapered. Reddish to brown, speckled with gray; appendages yellowish brown; ripe males yellowish, females gray-green. Cuticle thick, wrinkled, iridescent. Lobe above mouth oval, short, with 1 pair of short, conical antennae in front, and 5 long antennae with ringed bases on top. Proboscis with large jaws, segments 4 or 5 through 35 with bushy gills on upper surfaces.

Habitat
On protected mud flats and sand flats, mixed with shell debris and gravel; from low-tide line to water 270′ (82 m) deep.

Range
Massachusetts to Florida and Louisiana.

Comments
Phylum Annelida, Class Polychaeta, Subclass Errantia. Although the Plumed Worm dwells in a tube, it is an active predator, an unusual combination among polychaete worms. This worm can bite, so care in handling it is advised.

Orange-footed Sea Cucumber
Cucumaria frondosa
297

19″ (48 cm) long, 5″ (127 mm) wide. Cucumber-shaped. Dark reddish brown above, paler beneath, paler in young specimens, tube feet orange-tinted. Round, long, tapered to rounded point at rear, somewhat tapered at head end; soft, smooth. Neck with mouth and tentacles retractable; 10 highly branched tentacles that can extend half of body length or more. 5 crowded rows of tube feet, 2 on upper side, 3 below.

Habitat
On rocky shores, under overhanging rocks, in crevices; from low-tide line to water 1208′ (368 m) deep.

Range
Arctic to Cape Cod.

Comments
Phylum Echinodermata, Class Holothuroidea. This is the largest and most conspicuous sea cucumber in New England.

Hairy Sea Cucumber
Sclerodactyla briareus
298

4¾″ (121 mm) long, 2″ (51 mm) wide. Hairy, sweet-potato-shaped. Blackish, brownish, greenish, or purplish. Wide in middle, strongly tapered, mouth and tail ends bent upward; nearly covered with slender tube feet, not in rows; soft. 10 large, bushy tentacles, 2 lowest ones smaller.

Habitat
On mud or sand bottoms; from low-tide line to water 20′ (6 m) deep.

Range
Cape Cod to Florida and Texas; West Indies.

Comments
Phylum Echinodermata, Class Holothuroidea. The Hairy Sea Cucumber lies buried in mud or sand with only its tentacles, mouth, and anal end above the surface. It can regenerate lost tentacles in 3 weeks.

Scarlet Psolus
Psolus fabricii
299

4″ (102 mm) long (contracted), 2″ (51 mm) wide. Scaly, flat-bottomed, oval. Scarlet above, sole tannish orange. Covered with granular scales; front end extends as neck, with mouth surrounded by 10 long, red, highly branched tentacles, front ones longer, rear ones shorter. Anus on cone, pointing upward, with 5 anal teeth, surrounded by 1–2 rows of 5–6 scales. Lower side a flattened sole, with crowded rows of tube feet around margin, and partial row in center at front and rear, not meeting each other in middle.

Habitat
On boulders and rock walls; below low-tide line to water 1320′ (402 m) deep.

Range
Arctic to Cape Cod.

Comments
Phylum Echinodermata, Class Holothuroidea. The Scarlet Psolus is a striking creature when fully extended, but appears as a mere red lump when contracted. It can be found on seashores at low tide, only in places of extreme tidal fluctuation, such as Passamaquoddy Bay.

Eyed Fringed Worm
Cirratulus cirratus
300

4¾″ (121 mm) long, ⅛″ (3 mm) wide. In mud tubes. Cylindrical. Orange to yellowish. Head bluntly pointed, with 2–9 pairs of eyes on top, arranged in an arc. Cluster of long filaments on first bristle-bearing segment, 1 or more pairs on most of the rest.

Habitat
Under rocks, mussel beds, and sponges; from near low-tide line to shallow depths.

Range
Maine to Cape Cod.

Comments
Phylum Annelida, Class Polychaeta, Subclass Sedentaria. The Eyed Fringed Worm feeds by extending its filaments out of the tube and sweeping them over the bottom, picking up small organic particles for food. The filaments are fragile, and are easily broken off when the worm is handled.

Ice Cream Cone Worm
Pectinaria gouldii
301

1⅝" (41 mm) long, ¼" (6 mm) wide. In cone-shaped, slightly curved tube of sand grains, 2½" (64 mm) long and ¾" (19 mm) wide at front end. Conical; terminal segment flared. Creamy pink mottled with red and blue. Head obliquely flattened, with 2 pairs of long, tapered antennae, 2 comblike sets of 15 large, golden bristles; clusters of pale, flattened feeding tentacles extending forward from beneath mouth. 2 pairs of bright red gills on sides of head.

Habitat
In a vertical tube in sandy mud. Invading brackish estuaries with low salinities; from near low-tide line to water 90' (27 m) deep.

Range
Maine to Florida.

Comments
Phylum Annelida, Class Polychaeta, Subclass Sedentaria. Its tube proves this worm nature's stonemason *par excellence*. A wall made of a single layer of sand grains selected for size and fit, then firmly cemented together by dense mucus, forms the delicate, graceful tube, open at both ends.

Twelve-scaled Worm
Lepidonotus squamatus
302

2" (51 mm) long, ⅝" (16 mm) wide. Stout. Grayish, tan, or mottled brown. Covered above by 12 pairs of oval scales, with tan, reddish, or greenish projections of several sizes; tentacles and antennae with dark bands, pointed tips.

Habitat
Under rocks, among marine growth, on pilings, and on gravel and shell bottoms; from above low-tide line to water more than 8000' (2438 m) deep.

Range
Labrador to New Jersey.

Comments
Phylum Annelida, Class Polychaeta, Subclass Errantia. The name *Lepidonotus* means "scaly back," and when this worm is disturbed it rolls up like an armadillo into a scale-covered ball. It is tough and, unlike some of its relatives, does not easily lose its scales. The Commensal Twelve-scaled Worm (*L. sublevis*) is 1⅜" (35 mm) long and ⅜" (10 mm) wide. It is grayish, greenish, or reddish brown, and has scales with low, conical projections of uniform size. It lives commensally in a shell with the Flat-clawed Hermit Crab, and among oysters and under rocks, from Cape Cod to Florida and Texas. The Variable Twelve-scaled Worm (*L. variabilis*) measures 1" (25 mm) long and ¼" (6 mm) wide, and has mottled gray or brown scales, each with its rear border edged in short hairs. It ranges from Florida to Texas and the West Indies, and is found among oyster shells, rocky rubble, and clumps of algae.

Green Fire Worm ⊗
Hermodice carunculata
303

10" (25 cm) long, ¼" (6 mm) wide. Squarish in cross section. Greenish or reddish, with tufts of orange gills on upper surface of each appendage, and abundant white bristles on the side. Head with 5 short tentacles; 2 pairs of eyes; large, folded or wrinkled, lance-shaped pad from back of head to 5th segment.

Habitat
Under rocks, in turtle grass beds, on coral reefs and flats; from low-tide line to water 50' (15 m) deep.

Range
Florida; Bahamas; West Indies.

Comments
Phylum Annelida, Class Polychaeta, Subclass Errantia. This fire worm is very toxic. Like the related Orange Fire Worm (*Eurythoe complanata*) it inflicts a painful sting when handled.

Leafy Paddle Worms
Phyllodoce spp.
304

18" (46 cm) long, ⅜" (10 mm) wide. Long, slender. Whitish, tan, brownish, greenish, or gray, some with dark band down middle of back, or with cross-stripes. Head with 4 pairs of long tentacles; lobe above mouth heart-shaped, with 4 short antennae and 2 prominent eyes. Body segments with large, leaflike, oval paddles on upper side of appendages, smaller ones on lower side.

Habitat
Under rocks, among shells and gravel, and in algal holdfasts; from low-tide line to water 5000' (1524 m) deep.

Range
Arctic to Florida and Texas.

Comments
Phylum Annelida, Class Polychaeta, Subclass Errantia. These worms prey on other polychaetes, and on nemertean worms and other small creatures, and are themselves eaten by several species of fish, including cod, haddock, and plaice. Laboratory examination is usually necessary to determine the species of these worms.

Clam Worm
Nereis virens
305

36" (91 cm) long, 1¾" (44 mm) wide. Thicker in head region, tapered toward rear. 200 segments. Iridescent greenish, bluish, or greenish brown above, usually with fine red, gold, or white spots; paler beneath; appendages red, showing blood vessels. Head with 4 pairs of tentacles of equal length; a fleshy lip on each side of mouth, lobe above mouth broad, rectangular, with pair of short tentacles; proboscis with pair of strong, black jaws. 2 pairs of eyes; body appendages 2-lobed, upper part of appendages broad and leaflike.

Habitat
In sand, sandy mud, mud, clay, and various peat bottoms, among roots of eelgrass, in protected waters and in brackish

estuaries; from near high-tide line to water more than 500'
(152 m) deep.

Range
Maine to Virginia.

Comments
Phylum Annelida, Class Polychaeta, Subclass Errantia. The
Clam Worm is a swift and voracious predator, feeding on
other worms and invertebrates, carrion, and certain algae. It
has a keen sense of smell and in captivity can readily locate
bits of fresh clam meat.

Green Paddle Worm
Eulalia viridis
306

6" (15 cm) long, ⅛" (3 mm) wide. Slender. Pale to dark
green. 200 segments, first 3 with 4 pairs of tentacles equal in
length; lobe above mouth oval, with 5 antennae. 1 pair of
large eyes. Appendages with spearhead-shaped paddles above.

Habitat
Under rocks in tide pools, in gravelly sand, on pilings and
rocks among marine growth; from above low-tide line to water
500' (152 m) deep.

Range
Arctic to New Jersey.

Comments
Phylum Annelida, Class Polychaeta, Subclass Errantia. This
worm was one of the most abundant animals found in an
oceanographic study of organisms growing on ship hulls,
floats, and harbor installations in New England.

Polydora Mud Worm
Polydora ligni
307

1" (25 mm) long, 1/16" (2 mm) wide. In a mud-covered tube.
Slender, cylindrical. Translucent, reddish. Head with 2 long
antennae (which are easily lost), lobe above mouth forked in
front, with 4 eyes arranged in a rectangle; fifth bristle-bearing
segment with large group of long bristles pointing upward;
tail somewhat flared. 14 pairs of gills, usually beginning with
segment 12.

Habitat
In soft, fragile tubes covered with mud and attached to hard
objects in protected places on mud and clay bottoms; near
low-tide line and in shallow water.

Range
Entire East Coast.

Comments
Phylum Annelida, Class Polychaeta, Subclass Sedentaria.
These worms are sometimes so abundant in oyster beds that
they bury the oysters in several inches of mud tubes. There are
many species in the genus *Polydora*, some of them boring into
oyster shells or snail shells occupied by hermit crabs.

Two-gilled Blood Worm
Glycera dibranchiata
308

15⅜" (38 cm) long, ½" (13 mm) wide. Long, round. Pink. Lobe above mouth conical, with 4 tiny antennae at tip. Pharynx everts as long, bulbous proboscis with 4 black jaws at tip. Each appendage with red, fingerlike, nonretractable gill on upper and lower side.

Habitat
In mud, sandy mud, and sandy gravel bottoms in bays and open waters; from near low-tide line to water 1322' (403 m) deep.

Range
Gulf of St. Lawrence to Florida and Texas.

Comments
Phylum Annelida, Class Polychaeta, Subclass Errantia. This worm is sometimes called a Beak Thrower because it can suddenly and forcefully shoot out its proboscis. It uses this mechanism for burrowing, for ingesting prey, and for nipping the unwary person handling them. This species is used as fish bait, and is shipped all over the United States by bait diggers in Maine. The Tufted-gilled Blood Worm (*G. americana*) ranges from Cape Cod to Florida and Texas and along the entire Pacific Coast. It measures 14" (36 cm) long and ½" (13 mm) wide and differs from *G. dibranchiata* chiefly in having a retractable tuft of gills on only the upper side of each appendage.

Chevron Amphiporus
Amphiporus angulatus
309

6" (15 cm) long, ⅜" (10 mm) wide. Thick, slimy. Reddish brown to purplish above, whitish or pinkish below, rounded head demarked by whitish sensory grooves, forming a rear-pointing chevron. Pale area with 12 small eyespots on each side in front of chevron; 20 larger eyespots along each side of front margin, separated from other eyespots by a thin, pale line; proboscis thick, pinkish.

Habitat
Beneath rocks in sandy or gravelly places; from above low-tide line to water more than 450' (137 m) deep.

Range
Maine to Cape Cod.

Comments
Phylum Rhynchocoela, Class Enopla. This species may be mistaken for a leech. The Blood Nemertean (*A. cruentatus*), similar in shape to *A. angulatus*, is 1⅜" (35 mm) long and ⅛" (3 mm) wide, and is translucent yellow, pink, or orange, with 3 longitudinal vessels containing red blood. It ranges from Massachusetts to both coasts of Florida, and the entire Pacific Coast, and is found among hydroids, bryozoans, and algae, on rock and shell bottoms, from low-tide line to water 240' (73 m) deep.

Limulus Leech
Bdelloura candida
310

⅝" (16 mm) long, ¼" (6 mm) wide. Elongate, with narrow head end and squarish rear with "sucker." White to pale yellowish. Brown intestine has 1 front and 2 rear branches that do not join at rear. 2 black eyes near front end. Mouth in center of underside, from which long, white feeding tube can be extended.

Habitat
Gills and legs of the Horseshoe Crab.

Range
Gulf of Maine to Florida and Texas.

Comments
Phylum Platyhelminthes, Order Tricladida. This active worm can attach its sucker firmly to a Horseshoe Crab, where it feeds on food particles brought in by the host. When removed from a crab and kept in sea water, the worm will not feed and begins to shrink in size. The Limulus Leech lays eggs enclosed in a capsule fastened to the tissues of the Horseshoe Crab's gills by an anchorlike stalk.

Red Lineus
Lineus ruber
311

8" (20 cm) long, ⅛" (3 mm) wide. Slender, slightly flattened, head wider than adjacent part of body. Dark red, brownish, or greenish, pale at borders, sometimes ringed with faint, white lines, with 4–8 black eyespots and longitudinal sensory groove on each side.

Habitat
Under rocks and shells, and among mussels and algal growth on both sand and mud bottoms; above low-tide line and below to shallow depths.

Range
Maine to Long Island Sound.

Comments
Phylum Rhynchocoela, Class Anopla. Some biologists regard the greenish form of this animal as a separate species. The Social Lineus (*L. socialis*), a gregarious worm frequently found in clumps, is about the same size, shape, and color as *L. ruber*, but is distinguished by its habit of coiling into a tight spiral when disturbed. It ranges from Maine to Florida and Texas. The Striped Lineus (*L. bicolor*), which ranges from Cape Cod to Cape Hatteras, is smaller, 2" (51 mm) long and 1/16" (2 mm) wide, and is greenish or brownish, with a white or pale yellow stripe down the back, and a pale undersurface.

Milky Nemertean
Cerebratulus lacteus
312

48" (122 cm) long, ⅝" (16 mm) wide. Cylindrical and firm at front end; flat, wide, and soft, very thin at the edges over most of the length; tail present, head shaped like a spearhead, wider than adjacent body. Milky white, yellowish, or pinkish in young forms, mature males red, females brownish. Deep longitudinal sensory grooves on head. No eyespots; mouth an elongate slit.

Habitat
Burrowing in sand or sandy mud, under rocks, in sheltered bays and estuaries; near low-tide line and below.

Range
Maine to Florida and Texas.

Comments
Phylum Rhynchocoela, Class Anopla. This nemertean is by far the largest ribbon worm on the Atlantic Coast of the United States.

Gould's Peanut Worm
Phascolopsis gouldii
313

12″ (30 cm) long, ½″ (13 mm) wide. Long and slender; no appendages. Whitish, creamy, pink, tan, or gray. Cylindrical, tapering to blunt point at rear, front end more slender, extending to a length equal to one-half contracted body length; mouth surrounded by ring of short, unbranched tentacles.

Habitat
Mud, and muddy or gravelly sand; near low-tide line and below in shallow water.

Range
Bay of Fundy to Cape Hatteras.

Comments
Phylum Sipuncula. This worm is one of the more common animals found on sandy mud flats on the south side of Cape Cod.

Bamboo Worm
Clymenella torquata
314

6″ (15 cm) long, ¼″ (6 mm) wide. In a sandy 10″ (25 mm) long tube. Cylindrical, slender. Brick-red with bright red joints, or green with green joints. 22 segments: head segment obliquely slanted, with bulbous, eversible proboscis; flared collar at front end of fourth segment; 17 segments elongate and bearing short appendages with bristles; the last of 4 tail segments funnel-shaped, with fingerlike projections around the edge.

Habitat
In vertical tube in sand or sandy-mud bottoms in protected places, ranging into brackish water; from near low-tide line to water more than 330′ (100 m) deep.

Range
Maine to North Carolina.

Comments
Phylum Annelida, Class Polychaeta, Subclass Sedentaria. The long segments of these worms vividly recall sticks of bamboo. The green color of some populations of Bamboo Worms results from their eating 1-celled algae present in the mud. A green worm with several segments removed, placed in mud lacking those algae, will regenerate red segments.

Common White Synapta
Leptosynapta inhaerens
315

6" (15 cm) long, ⅜" (10 mm) wide. Wormlike. Translucent white. Long, slender, smooth, fragile; 5 white longitudinal muscle bands visible through body wall. No tube feet. 12 retractable featherlike tentacles, each with 5–7 branches on opposite sides of stalk.

Habitat
On sand and sandy mud; from low-tide line to water 637' (194 m) deep.

Range
Maine to South Carolina and Bermuda; British Columbia to S. California.

Comments
Phylum Echinodermata, Class Holothuroidea. Its weight, when its digestive system is full of sand, and its delicate construction make this animal difficult to handle without breaking it. The Pink Synapta (*L. roseola*) ranges from the Bay of Fundy to Long Island Sound, in shallow water, sand, and under rocks; it is translucent rosy red and has tentacles with 2–3 branches on each side of the stalk.

Keyhole Urchin Spoon Worm
Thalassema mellita
316

1½" (38 mm) long, ¼" (6 mm) wide. Sausage-shaped, with proboscis. Brick-red; proboscis pale yellow. Trunk cylindrical, smooth, with pair of large, hooklike bristles near head end on underside; no bristles around anus; scooplike proboscis about one-third total length.

Habitat
In skeletons of dead keyhole urchins; below low-tide line in shallow water.

Range
Virginia to Florida.

Comments
Phylum Echiura. These worms enter the skeletons of dead keyhole urchins when quite young, and become too large to escape. They feed by extending the scooplike proboscis, whose mucus-covered surface traps tiny organic particles.

Lug Worm
Arenicola cristata
317

12" (30 cm) long, 1" (25 mm) wide. Firm and sturdy, thick in front, with tapering head and tail end; skin coarse and checkered. Greenish black. Head without appendages or eyes; mouth with bulbous proboscis covered with short, fingerlike projections. Each segment with 5 rings, the thickest with tufts of long bristles above and ridged furrows with shorter hooks below.

Habitat
Burrowing in sandy mud flats in protected places; near low-tide line and just below.

Range
Cape Cod to Florida and Louisiana; entire Pacific Coast.

Comments
Phylum Annelida, Class Polychaeta, Subclass Sedentaria. To feed, the Lug Worm pumps water into its burrow, thus irrigating its gills and collapsing the muddy sand at the end of the burrow. It then eats that sand, from which it digests the organic matter. Periodically, the worm backs up to the surface to void the undigested sand and mud. Another species, the Northern Lug Worm (*A. marina*), 8" (20 cm) long and ¾" (19 mm) wide, found north of Cape Cod, extrudes its feces as a "casting," a rope of sandy mud lightly held together by mucus.

Florida Sea Cucumber
Holothuria floridana
318

10" (25 cm) long, 2" (51 mm) wide. Cucumber-shaped. Dark brown, reddish brown, brick-red, rarely paler, sometimes spotted, tentacles yellowish. Upper surface with many conical projections. 2 rows of slender tube feet; lower surface with many larger tube feet not arranged in rows. 20 larger tentacles with knobby tips, mouth pointing downward.

Habitat
In grass beds and on reef flats; in shallow water just below low-tide line.

Range
Florida; West Indies; Yucatán; Panama.

Comments
Phylum Echinodermata, Class Holothuroidea. This sea cucumber sometimes occurs in great numbers just below the low-tide line on sandy shores. It produces sticky threads that are extruded from the anus when the animal is disturbed, doubtless a valuable deterrent to predators. This characteristic is locally known as "cotton spinning."

Sea Mouse
Aphrodita hastata

6" (15 cm) long, 3" (76 mm) wide. Plump. Yellow, bronze, blackish, occasionally iridescent. 40 segments. Upper surface covered with numerous long bristles of various sizes and mucus and mud.

Habitat
In soft mud bottoms; below low-tide line, from water 6' (2 m) to more than 6000' (1829 m) deep.

Range
Gulf of St. Lawrence to Chesapeake Bay.

Comments
Phylum Annelida, Class Polychaeta, Subclass Errantia. The Sea Mouse, which is sometimes tossed ashore in large numbers during storms, has abundant bristles that give it a furry appearance, especially when the mud and mucus have been washed out.

Northern Stony Coral
Astrangia danae

5″ (127 mm) long, 5″ (127 mm) wide. Forms thin crust over rocks or shells, sometimes with short, thick branches. Pinkish to white. Cups to ¼″ (6 mm) wide, closely set, 30 in a colony 4″ (102 mm) wide, with 30 septa.

Habitat
Attached to rocks and shells; from shallow water to water 135′ (40 m) deep.

Range
Cape Cod to Florida.

Comments
Phylum Cnidaria, Class Anthozoa, Order Scleractinia. This is the only shallow-water species of stony coral found north of Cape Hatteras. Dwarf Cup Coral (*A. solitaria*), a related tropical species, ranges from Bermuda to Brazil.

Caribbean Lancelet
Branchiostoma caribaeum

2″ (51 mm) long; ¼″ (6 mm) high. Elongate. Translucent, whitish; colored digestive contents visible. Fishlike body without distinct head; flattened, vertical; rounded beak at front end, with chamber below leading into mouth; row of tentacles on either side curved toward midline. Ridgelike fin above from beak to tail; tail fin spearhead-shaped. Paired fins, from mouth chamber to excurrent opening of gill chamber, unite to form single fin in lower midline to tail. V-shaped muscle segments pointing forward on both sides of body. Large pharynx with many slits slanting downward and toward the rear; food groove in floor continuous with rest of digestive system. Row of rounded sex organs below pharynx.

Habitat
Fine sand and sandy-mud bottoms; near low-tide line and below in shallow water.

Range
Chesapeake Bay to Florida and Texas; Mexico; also occurs in the West Indies.

Comments
Phylum Chordata, Subphylum Cephalochordata. The lancelet is a good swimmer but spends most of its time buried in the sand with only its head end out. Cilia on the gills bring water, strained of coarse particles by the tentacles, into the pharynx through the mouth.

Parchment Worm
Chaetopterus variopedatus

10″ (25 cm) long, 1″ (25 mm) wide. Soft. Divided into 3 distinct regions. In U-shaped, parchmentlike tubes more than 24″ (61 cm) long. Whitish, translucent. Front end has shovel-shaped head with pair of short tentacles, pair of winglike appendages on segment 12, cup on segment 13 from which a food groove extends to the mouth; middle section with 3 prominent "fans" on back of segments 14–16; rear section of 30 segments, each with pair of appendages loaded with sperm or eggs in the ripe adult.

Habitat
Buried in mud, sandy mud flats, and eelgrass beds in protected bays and estuaries; from near low-tide line to water 25′ (8 m) deep.

Range
Cape Cod to Florida and Louisiana.

Comments
Phylum Annelida, Class Polychaeta, Subclass Sedentaria. The tube of this worm is distinctive enough to identify it. It is wide enough to accommodate the worm along most of its length, but each end tapers and rises about 1″ (25 mm) above the surface of the bottom. The worm cannot get out.

Atlantic Tube Worm
Hydroides uncinata

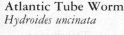

3″ (76 mm) long, ⅛″ (3 mm) wide. In white, limy, twisted tube. Cylindrical, tapered toward rear. Translucent, yellowish or greenish, with green blood vessels visible. Head with solid or mottled purple, red, orange, yellow, tan, greenish, or white plume of 18 pairs of gills, each pointed and without side branches at tip, abundant branches near base. Lid stalked, funnel-shaped, edged with about 30 teeth. Collar of 7 segments. Abdomen tapering.

Habitat
On hard objects; from low-tide line to water 50′ (15 m) deep.

Range
Cape Cod to Florida and Texas.

Comments
Phylum Annelida, Class Polychaeta, Subclass Sedentaria. These worms are common wherever there are rocks or shells. The tubes may be solitary or in masses.

Florida Honeycomb Worm
Sabellaria floridensis

3″ (76 mm) long, ¼″ (6 mm) wide. In sandy tube. Conical. Yelowish; 2 adjacent semicircular parts on top of head form dark, disk-shaped lid edged by golden bristles and surrounded by row of reddish, retractable tentacles. Tail slender, unsegmented, bent under body at sharp angle.

Habitat
Along open coast, attached to rocks, forming reefs of tubes of cemented sand grains; near low-tide line and below in shallow water.

Range
West coast of Florida.

Comments
Phylum Annelida, Class Polychaeta, Subclass Sedentaria. Sand tubes of the Florida Honeycomb Worm form reefs more than 10′ (3 m) across. The worm extends its tentacles to trap fine plankton, organic particles, and sand. The food is moved to the mouth by cilia, and the sand is moved to the edge of the tube, where it is cemented on by mucus.

MAMMALS

Few animals have inspired as much legend and inquiry as the mammals of the seas—the whales, dolphins, seals, and related creatures. Their ease and agility in a world of water is a source of fascination, and their intelligence and ability to communicate have long intrigued observers. This section describes some of the most frequently seen marine mammals of the Atlantic and Gulf shores, from the ungainly Manatee to the sleek Killer Whales and Harbor Seals.

Risso's Dolphin
Grampus griseus
319

To 13' (4 m). Robust toward front, tapers rapidly to narrow tail; dark gray at birth; darkening to almost black when young, with distinctive grayish-white regions on belly; numerous scars; color lightens overall, particularly on head, with increasing age; dorsal fin, flippers, and flukes usually remain dark. Head bulbous, V-shaped crease on front pointing downwards, dividing melon, or bump, into 2 parts; no distinct beak. Dorsal fin tall, crescent-shaped, at mid-back.

Habitat
Near surface of open temperate and tropical seas, most often seaward from outer edge of continental shelf; possibly coastal waters where shelf edge is close to shore.

Range
In Atlantic from E. Newfoundland to Lesser Antilles, including northern and eastern Gulf of Mexico. In Pacific from off N. Washington to tropics.

Comments
Occurs in herds of several hundred, but is more common in groups of a dozen or less. They sometimes ride bow waves and stern wakes, and may leap clear of the surface.

Harbor Porpoise
Phocoena phocoena
320

To 6' (1.8m). Chunky; back dark brown or gray fading to lighter grayish brown on sides, often speckled in transition zone; white on belly extends up sides, especially in front of dorsal fin. Head small, rounded; beak very short, indistinct. Dorsal fin small, dark, triangular, tip blunt.

Habitat
Subarctic and cold temperate waters, usually inshore within 10-fathom curve, rarely to 100 fathoms offshore. Often in bays, harbors, estuaries, and river mouths.

Range
In Atlantic from Davis Straits and southeastern Greenland to North Carolina. In Pacific from Gulf of Alaska and eastern Aleutian chain to S. California.

Comments
This species tends to be wary of vessels and does not ride bow waves. It often swims quietly at the surface. Harbor Porpoises are known to feed on octopuses, squids, and fishes, including herrings. In turn they may be preyed upon by large sharks and by Killer Whales. Because they live mostly inshore, they are often adversely affected by human activities.

Bottlenosed Dolphin
Tursiops truncatus
321

To 12' (3.7 m). Robust; back usually dark gray, sides lighter gray, shading to pink or white on belly; individuals vary from albino to nearly black; distinct dark cape often on head and back; old females may have spots on belly. Beak well defined but relatively short; transverse groove between forehead and snout. Dorsal fin near center of back, prominent, broad-based, crescent-shaped, tip pointed.

Habitat
Inshore waters including estuaries, shallow bays, waterways, and freshwater rivers; sometimes to edge of continental shelf.

Range
In Atlantic from Nova Scotia to Venezuela, including Gulf of Mexico. In Pacific from S. California to tropics.

Comments
This species is particularly adept at locating prey using echolocation, that is, projecting a sound beam and listening to the echo. It rides the bow waves of boats and even surf waves. There are many records of wild Bottlenosed Dolphins voluntarily approaching humans closely enough to be touched. While these dolphins do communicate among themselves (as probably all cetaceans do), there is no good evidence that they talk to people.

Common Dolphin
Delphinus delphis
322

To 8'6" (2.6 m). Spindle-shaped, slender, not robust; back black or brownish black, coloration and markings variable; chest and belly cream to white. Sides distinctly marked with hourglass or crisscross pattern of tan or yellowish tan. Beak defined, moderately long, often dark with white tip. One or more dark stripes from center of lower jaw to flipper. Dorsal fin nearly triangular to distinctly crescent-shaped, usually black with lighter grayish region of varying size near middle, tip pointed.

Habitat
Offshore over outer continental shelf, often near ridges. Rarely inshore.

Range
In Atlantic from Newfoundland and Nova Scotia to northern South America. In Pacific from Victoria, British Columbia, to equator.

Comments
These animals often travel in huge herds of more than a thousand. They frequently leap clear of the water and ride bow waves of vessels for a long time.

Killer Whale ⊗
Orcinus orca
323

To 31' (9.4 m). Males more robust than females; black with white, tan or yellow region on undersides from lower jaw to anus extending onto sides behind dorsal fin; oval, white patch just above and behind eye; usually light gray saddle behind dorsal fin; undersides of flukes usually white. Head broad, rounded; mouth large; teeth large, pointed; no pronounced beak. Flippers large, paddle-shaped, rounded. Dorsal fin tall, distinctly crescent-shaped in females and juveniles, taller and erect in adult males, sometimes appears to bend forward.

Habitat
Upper layers of cooler coastal seas; occasionally large rivers and tropical seas.

Range
In Atlantic from pack ice to Lesser Antilles, including
northern, eastern, and western Gulf of Mexico. In Pacific from
Chukchi Sea to equator.

Comments
Fierce in their feeding habits. On occasion groups of these
animals attack baleen whales, pinnipeds such as seals, and
small Odontocetes. They are also known to feed on fishes,
squids, sea turtles, and sea birds. They have been known to
attack and mortally wound baleen whales, and then leave
without eating them. While there are no reliable records of
unprovoked attacks on humans, people should be extremely
cautious of these animals.

Right Whale
Eubalaena glacialis
324

To 53' (16.2 m). Large, rotund; brown to almost black,
mottled overall, with some white on chin and belly, baleen
plates dark brownish to dark gray or black, may appear pale
yellowish gray further offshore. Jaw highly arched, curves
upward along side of head; bumps on head light yellowish,
largest bump, or "bonnet," in front of large, paired
blowholes. No dorsal fin or ridge. Flukes broad, tips pointed,
concave toward deep notch, dark below. Blow V-shaped.

Habitat
Often near shore in shallow water; sometimes in large bays.

Range
In Atlantic from Iceland to E. Florida, occasionally into
southeastern and southwestern Gulf of Mexico, rarely to West
Indies. In Pacific from Gulf of Alaska and southeastern Bering
Sea to central Baja California.

Comments
Also called the Black Right Whale, this species was named
the Right Whale by early whalers who believed it to be the
"right" or "correct" whale to take, since it swims slowly, is
easy to approach and kill, and does not sink when dead. One
animal measuring 51' (15.4 m) weighed 46.2 tons (42,000
kg). Once killed, the Right Whale yielded an abundance of
valuable oil and baleen to be used for corset stays and other
decorative or utilitarian objects. As an endangered species,
these whales are fully protected and more are being seen.
There is growing evidence that calves are born when the
whales are in the South—in the Atlantic off northeastern
Florida, Georgia, and possibly the Carolinas.

Long-finned Pilot Whale
Globicephala melaena
325

To 20' (6.1 m). Robust; black with anchor-shaped patch of
grayish white on chin, gray area on belly, both variable in
intensity and shape; gray saddle behind dorsal fin in some
large individuals. Head thick, bulbous, sometimes flattened,
squarish in front, especially in adult males. Flippers long, to
one-fifth body length; dorsal fin crescent-shaped, low, with
long base, set far forward on back.

Habitat
Generally offshore waters; inshore waters and bays in summer.

Range
From Iceland and Greenland to North Carolina; possibly to Georgia.

Comments
Long-finned Pilot Whales sometimes "spy-hop" or "pitchpole," that is, hang vertically in the water with the head and part of the back out of water. They also slap their flukes on the surface, or "lobtail," but do not ride bow waves.

Cuvier's Beaked Whale
Ziphius cavirostris
326

To 24'9" (7.5 m). Robust; dark rust-brown, slate-gray, or fawn-colored, belly lighter, frequently covered with light blotches; juveniles and some females lighter; head frequently pale, distinctly white on old males. Head small, upper profile slightly concave; mouth opening small; beak indistinct in larger individuals; paired teeth at tip of lower jaw, erupt only in adult males. Pronounced indentation on back behind head. Dorsal fin tall, distinct, nearer tail than head.

Habitat
Upper layers of open seas; often near shore.

Range
In Atlantic from Massachusetts to West Indies, including Gulf of Mexico. In Pacific from southern Bering Sea to equator. Widely distributed in nonpolar seas.

Comments
These deepwater whales, reputedly very vigorous swimmers, may appear and disappear suddenly as they rise from deep water and dive again after a short rest at the surface.

Blue Whale
Balaenoptera musculus
327

To 98' (29.9 m). Spindle-shaped, tapering toward rear; light bluish above mottled with gray or grayish white, belly sometimes yellowish, baleen plates black. Rostrum broad, flat, nearly U-shaped, with single median ridge along top; paired blowholes on top of head. Dorsal fin extremely small, nearly triangular to crescent-shaped, far back on tail stock. Grooves on underside extend to or slightly past navel. Blow high, oval.

Habitat
Usually open seas, but sometimes in shallow inshore waters.

Range
In Atlantic from Arctic Circle to Panama, including northwestern Gulf of Mexico. In Pacific from southern Chukchi Sea to Panama.

Comments
The yellowish coloring on the belly of this species is due to diatoms accumulated in colder water. The Blue Whale is probably the largest animal known, even larger than the dinosaurs. It weighs about 196 tons (178,000 kg).

Minke Whale
Balaenoptera acutorostrata
328

To 33' (10.1 m). Spindle-shaped, tapering toward rear; dark gray to black above, belly and underside of flippers white, crescent-shaped marks sometimes present on upper side in front of flippers, diagonal white band on flippers. Baleen plates yellowish white toward front, sometimes dark toward rear. Rostrum flat, narrow, pointed, triangular, with single median ridge along top; paired blowholes on top of head. Dorsal fin tall, crescent-shaped. Grooves along throat and chest end slightly before navel.

Habitat
Open seas, but mainly over continental shelf; sometimes in bays, inlets, and estuaries.

Range
In Atlantic from pack ice to Lesser Antilles, including eastern and northwestern Gulf of Mexico. In Pacific from Bering and Chukchi seas to equator. Seasonal variations in both oceans.

Comments
The Minke Whale is the smallest baleen whale in North American waters. Its seasonal distribution is contingent upon food availability. Individuals often approach vessels.

Fin Whale
Balaenoptera physalus
329

To 79' (24.1 m). Spindle-shaped, tapering toward rear; blue-black above, undersides white. Grayish-white chevron behind head, apex on midline of back, arms extending backward. Right lower lip, including mouth cavity, yellowish white, right upper lip occasionally also white, left lips dark. Right front baleen plates white, remainder striped with alternate yellowish white and bluish gray to grayish white. Snout V-shaped with single median ridge along top; top of head flat, with paired blowholes. Dorsal fin steeply angled, placed far back. Back distinctly ridged behind dorsal fin. Grooves on throat and chest extend at least to navel.

Habitat
Inshore and offshore.

Range
In Atlantic from Arctic Circle to Greater Antilles, including Gulf of Mexico. In Pacific from Bering Sea to Cabo San Lucas, Baja California.

Comments
Because of its crescent-shaped dorsal fin, an obvious characteristic, the Fin Whale is easily seen at sea. It feeds on fishes, pelagic crustaceans, and squids. It sometimes leaps clear of the surface, yet is also a deeper diver than some of the other baleen whales.

Humpback Whale
Megaptera novaeangliae
330

To 53' (16.2 m). Robust, narrowing rapidly to tail; mostly black, belly sometimes white, flippers and underside of flukes nearly all white, baleen plates black with black or olive-black bristles. Top of head and lower jaw with string of fleshy knobs or protuberances randomly distributed; paired blowholes on top of head; distinctive, rounded projection on tip of lower jaw. Flippers very long, front edges scalloped. Dorsal fin small, variably shaped, placed on small hump slightly more than two-thirds of way back from head. Flukes deeply notched, concave, rear scalloped. Blow balloon-shaped.

Habitat
Along coast; usually on continental shelf or island banks; sometimes in open seas.

Range
Migratory. In Atlantic from northern Iceland and western Greenland south to West Indies, including northern and eastern Gulf of Mexico. In Pacific from Bering Sea to southern Mexico.

Comments
These whales "sing" a series of repeated phrases; the vocal patterns are apparently specific to separate populations of whales but may vary from year to year. It is possible that individual animals can be recognized by some of their sounds. Humpbacks sometimes leap clear of the water and may be seen slapping their flukes or a flipper on the surface.

Manatee
Trichechus manatus
331

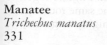

To about 15′ (460 cm) long. Massive, torpedo-shaped, nearly hairless aquatic mammal. Grayish to blackish when wet. Tail broad, flattened, paddle-shaped. Broad head with upper lip deeply cleft and bearing stiff bristles. Front legs like large flippers with 3 nails; hind legs absent. No external ears.

Habitat
Shallow coastal waters, bays, rivers, and lakes; mangrove shores.

Range
Gulf and Atlantic coastal waters off southeastern United States north to Beaufort, North Carolina. Florida's waters have the largest remaining populations.

Comments
The Manatee is primarily nocturnal and moderately social; while not part of a herd, Manatees congregate in warm water in winter. They cavort together when they meet, embracing each other with flippers and even pressing their thick lips together in a "kiss." They spend their days browsing on aquatic vegetation, which they grasp in lips and bristles, with flippers helping to hold loose grass blades; they consume 60–100 pounds per day. Propelling themselves with undulations of the hind end of their streamlined bodies, they use flippers and tails mainly for steering and stabilization. Flippers are also used to clean their teeth and rub their sides, which they do often and with apparent pleasure, also rubbing against underwater objects like rocks. Manatees are now an endangered species.

Hooded Seal
Cystophora cristata
332, 334

6'–8'2" (180–250 cm) long. Steel gray above, often with irregular whitish or brownish blotches; paler below. Females paler, with less distinct markings. Both sexes have hood on head, larger in males; when inflated, this elastic nasal sac stretches from nostrils to forehead; when deflated, appears wrinkled. Juveniles bluish-gray above. Claws light colored and strong. Males larger than females.

Habitat
Edge of Arctic pack ice; in deep water.

Range
Gulf of St. Lawrence to Greenland waters; not in Hudson Bay.

Comments
When a bull is angry or threatened, it inflates its hood, which greatly increases the apparent size of its head and may make the seal more formidable to an enemy. Usually in small groups, this seal is more social when breeding or migrating. After mating, in groups segregated by sex, seals follow the retreating ice through Davis Strait to waters east of Greenland, where they haul out onto the ice to molt. At this time, late June–early July, they fast, and their weight drops significantly. Then they slowly migrate south, feeding far out to sea, and finally winter off the Grand Banks of Newfoundland. Hooded and Harp seals often migrate together but do not intermingle. Pups migrate by the same route as adults but a month later. Members of this highly migratory species may stray as far south as Florida.

Harp Seal
Phoca groenlandica
333

4'7"–6'7" (140–200 cm) long. Males yellowish white to grayish above, with harp-shaped black saddle on back; silvery with scattered small spots below. Females less distinctly marked or markings broken up into irregular spots. Black or dark brown face. Juveniles blue-gray with darker gray markings. Males slightly larger than females.

Habitat
Drifting pack ice; occasionally up streams.

Range
Arctic seas from northern Hudson Bay and western coast of Greenland south along Labrador into Gulf of St. Lawrence, west to mouth of Mackenzie River.

Comments
Annual oceanic migrations of this seal cover 6000 miles. Harp Seals can dive to 900' and remain submerged up to 15 minutes. Small fish, especially such schooling kinds as capelin and herring, are chief foods along with some crustaceans. In February, migrating adults move to the edge of the ice pack, where cows give birth to a single pup, weighing about 12 lb and covered with white fur (lanugo). After being nursed only 2 weeks, the baby seal has grown to 90–100 lb and is then abandoned. For the next couple of weeks it does not feed; its weight drops to about 50 lb, and the lanugo is molted. Many

pups perish, but the rest learn to gather food for themselves and will migrate north with the herd. Meanwhile, the bulls, which have a musky odor during breeding season, have congregated in the water between ice floes, where they court cows by swimming about furiously and perhaps even battling among themselves. Mating occurs in the water.

Harbor Seal
Phoca vitulina
335

4'–5'7" (120–170 cm) long. Usually yellowish-gray or brownish with dark spots above, but highly variable from cream to dark brown; spotted creamy white below. Males and females about same size.

Habitat
Coastal waters, mouths of rivers; some northern populations permanently inland in freshwater lakes.

Range
In East, southern Greenland and Hudson Bay coasts south to Carolinas; in West, southern Arctic from Yukon and N. Alaska south along California coast.

Comments
Harbor Seals spend much time basking on beaches and rocky shores in groups of several individuals to 500. At the first sign of danger, they give an alarm bark and dive into the water. They can dive to 300' and remain submerged up to 28 minutes. They feed when the tide comes in, sometimes ascending rivers with the tide, and haul out at low tide, sleeping high and dry until the next rising tide unless disturbed. In the spring they may follow fish runs upriver for hundreds of miles, returning to coastal waters in the fall. Feeding mostly on fish, including rockfish, herring, cod, mackerel, flounder and salmon, they eat some mollusks (about 5 percent of their diet), including squid, clams, and octopus; and sometimes crayfish, crab, and shrimp. Some learn to steal fish from nets, which are often damaged, incurring the wrath of commercial fishermen. Populations vary in their breeding season, and pupping may occur from March to August.

Gray Seal
Halichoerus grypus
336

Males: to 9'10" (300 cm) long. Females: 7'6" (230 cm) long. Large. Grayish to almost black above, usually with lighter splotches; somewhat paler below. Head squarish, snout long. Males larger than females and have wrinkled necks.

Habitat
Waters along rocky coasts and islands.

Range
Labrador to New England; includes Gulf of St. Lawrence.

Comments
This relatively rare seal has a world population of 50,000–70,000, with more than 5000 in North American waters. Quite gregarious, it gathers in groups to feed on such bottom fish as pollock, cod, flounder, whiting, and cuttlefish.

FISHES

The fishes that dominate the underwater world of the Atlantic and Gulf coasts range from the bizarre, oddly-shaped eels and rays to the more familiar flatfishes, snappers, and perches. Many fishes spend their lives in deep ocean waters, while others ascend rivers inland to spawn or feed. Some are chiefly solitary; others travel in enormous schools. Many of these fishes—such as anchovies, cods, and bass—are important commercially; others, such as the Tarpon, Blue Marlin, and some sharks, provide challenging recreation for the sport fisherman. This section describes many of the most frequently seen fishes in the waters of the Atlantic and the Gulf.

Yellowtail Damselfish
Microspathodon chrysurus
337

To 7½" (19 cm). Depth about one-half length; entire body and all fins except caudal dark blue to almost black, bronzy on cheeks and breast, light blue spots on back and dorsal fin, caudal fin either yellowish or white. Young have more blue spots on back and dorsal fin, caudal fin dark. Upper profile of head steep; mouth small, at tip of snout; eye small, relatively high on head; deep notch in front of eyes; bone in front of gill cover smooth; 1 nostril on each side of snout. Rear edges of soft dorsal and anal fin squared off. Lateral line ends under soft dorsal fin.

Habitat
Reefs in shallow water or offshore.

Range
From N. Florida to Venezuela; Gulf of Mexico, West Indies, and Caribbean.

Comments
This species feeds on algae, organic detritus, and certain corals. The young pick parasites from larger fishes.

Tautog
Tautoga onitis
338

To 3' (91 cm). Depth one-third length; color varies with background; dull-colored: mousy, chocolate-gray, deep dusky green, brownish, or dull black, sides irregularly mottled with paler shades; chin white in large specimens. Head profile steep; snout blunt; mouth at tip of snout; lips thick; jaws stout. Long-based dorsal fin notched; caudal fin squared off, slightly rounded at corners. Cheeks scaleless, velvety to touch.

Habitat
Coastal waters, usually at depths of less than 60' (18 m); near wrecks, piers, docks, mussel beds, and steep, rocky shores.

Range
From Nova Scotia to South Carolina; most abundant from Cape Cod to Delaware.

Comments
Despite reported lengths of 3' (91 cm), most catches are less than half that size. Tautogs feed by crushing shelled invertebrates with their strong teeth. Although considered good food and sport fishes, they are not plentiful.

Bigeye
Priacanthus arenatus
339

To 16" (41 cm). Compressed, depth one-third length; bright red, pelvic fins black. Profile of head less curved above than below, nearly straight from snout to dorsal fin origin. Mouth large, oblique, lower jaw projects well beyond upper; spine in front of gill cover very small; eyes large, diameter greater than length of snout. Pelvic fins connected to body by membrane; dorsal fin continuous, without notch; anal fin evenly rounded; caudal fin notched.

Habitat
Coral reefs and over rocks, to about 72' (22 m).

Range
From Massachusetts south to Argentina, including Bermuda, Gulf of Mexico, and West Indies.

Comments
The Bigeye Snapper is a carnivore and feeds on small fishes, crustaceans, and polychaete worms.

Longspine Squirrelfish ⊗
Holocentrus rufus
340

To 12″ (30 cm). Oblong and relatively slender; caudal peduncle very narrow; bright silvery red with diffuse red lines above becoming indistinct and pink on sides and belly; dorsal fin membranes with white spots near upper margin. Top of head and area below eye brick-red; spines in front of gill cover long, slender. 4 anal spines; front rays of soft dorsal fin and upper lobe of caudal fin elongate.

Habitat
Coral reefs, from near surface to about 15 fathoms.

Range
Bermuda; SE. Florida, West Indies, western Caribbean, and western Gulf of Mexico.

Comments
These squirrelfishes are active at night, feeding away from the coral reefs where they hide during the day. They eat a variety of crustaceans, gastropods, and brittle stars. The sharp spines can inflict painful wounds.

Cunner
Tautogolabrus adspersus
341

To 10″ (25 cm). Moderately slender; reddish brown above with bluish or brownish tinge, mottled with blue, brown, and red; some specimens uniformly brown, others deep sepia; color varies with background. Snout pointed; lips moderately thick. Dorsal fin notched, base long. Cheek scaled.

Habitat
Shallow coastal waters, in eelgrass, around pilings, piers, and rock piles.

Range
From Newfoundland to New Jersey, occasionally to Chesapeake Bay.

Comments
Cunners are so variably colored that it is difficult to describe them. Those that live among red seaweeds or in deep water are reddish or rust-colored, whereas over sand they are pale and speckled with blackish dots. Cunners are omnivorous. Popular with anglers, they are good pan fishes.

Spanish Hogfish
Bodianus rufus
342

To 24″ (61 cm). Moderately deep, depth about one-third length; front two-thirds, including dorsal fin and upper part of head, bluish purple; rear third and entire belly yellow; pectoral fins unpigmented. Head pointed, forehead not steep in profile; upper jaw has large canine tooth, curved backwards, on each side. Dorsal fin continuous; upper and lower caudal fin rays form short filaments. Lateral line not interrupted.

Habitat
Coral and rocky reefs to depths of about 16 fathoms.

Range
Bermuda; from S. Florida to northern Brazil, including offshore reefs in Gulf of Mexico; Caribbean.

Comments
The young of the Spanish Hogfish pick parasitic crustaceans off other fishes. As a defense mechanism, the bluish-purple color becomes reddish in deep water, protecting the fishes from predators, because red is not visible at great depths.

Princess Parrotfish
Scarus taeniopterus
343

To 13″ (33 cm). Moderately deep, depth about one-third length. Adult-phase males blue-green and orange with broad, pale yellow stripe above pectoral fin, 2 narrow blue-green stripes on head; dorsal and anal fins blue with orange band through middle, caudal fin blue, edges orange. Juvenile-phase female has 3 dark brown stripes alternating with white, fins pale blue. Teeth form beaklike plates, lower plates hidden by upper when mouth closed. Single dorsal fin long; caudal fin squared off or slightly rounded. 3 scale rows on cheek; 7 scales in series under eye; 7–8 scales on back between snout and dorsal fin insertion.

Habitat
Coral reefs.

Range
Bermuda, S. Florida, Florida Keys, northwestern Gulf of Mexico, Bahamas, and throughout Caribbean to northwestern Brazil.

Comments
It is difficult to determine the exact geographical limits of this and other parrotfishes, due to the similarity of the species and the many color phases.

Queen Parrotfish
Scarus vetula
344

To 24″ (61 cm). Moderately deep, depth one-third length. Adult-phase males blue-green, scale edges red-orange; head green with alternating orange and blue-green stripes on lower snout and chin, caudal fin green, orange band on upper and lower rays. Juvenile-phase females dark reddish to purplish brown with broad, whitish band on lower sides. Teeth form beaklike plates, lower plate hidden by upper when mouth closed. Single dorsal fin long, caudal fin squared off, crescent-shaped in adult males. 4 scale rows on cheek, 7 scales on back between snout and dorsal fin insertion.

Habitat
Coral reefs.

Range
Bermuda; from S. Florida to Colombia, including
northwestern Gulf of Mexico and Caribbean.

Comments
This fish is one of the most noticeable members of the coral
reef community. This and other parrotfishes are believed to be
the major factor in reef attrition and sand production in calm
areas.

Blue Parrotfish
Scarus coeruleus
345

To 4' (1.2 m). Moderately deep, depth more than one-third
length; large adults deep blue; smaller specimens light blue,
head yellow, bases of scales yellowish pink. Teeth white,
forming beaklike plates, lower plate hidden by upper when
mouth closed. Single dorsal fin long; caudal fin squared off,
upper and lower lobes become longer as size increases. 3 scale
rows on cheek; 6 scales on back between snout and dorsal fin
insertion.

Habitat
Coral reefs.

Range
From Maryland to Rio de Janeiro, Brazil, including Bermuda,
Caribbean, and West Indies.

Comments
The Blue Parrotfish, like other parrotfishes, uses the molarlike
teeth on its upper and lower pharyngeal bones to grind algae
along with soft coral.

Lumpfish
Cyclopterus lumpus
346

To 23" (58 cm). Very robust, more or less triangular-shaped in
cross section; variably bluish, olive, brownish, reddish,
greenish; paler below, often with darker blotches and black
dots. Mouth small, at tip of snout, oblique. Pectoral fins
broad-based, almost meet at throat; pelvic fins inserted just
behind throat, modified to sucking disk on underside; dorsal
and anal fins similar, toward rear placed opposite each other,
not attached to squared-off caudal fin. Skin rough with 7
lengthwise ridges formed by large tubercles, tips of largest
sometimes black.

Habitat
Primarily over rocks in shallow water.

Range
From Newfoundland to Hudson Bay, and along coast to
Chesapeake Bay.

Comments
This ungainly fish clings to rocks or debris. Males make good
eating, and this species is noted for its tasty roe, but females
are inedible while breeding.

Florida Pompano
Trachinotus carolinus
347

To 17" (43 cm). Short, deep, moderately compressed; dorsal and ventral profiles similar; back bluish gray or bluish green; sides silvery; belly silvery and yellowish. Snout blunt, mouth slightly underneath head. Fins dusky or yellowish; pectoral fin shorter than head; pelvic fins shorter than pectorals; first dorsal fin has 6 short spines; base of second dorsal only slightly longer than base of anal fin. Caudal peduncle relatively deep, without plates or grooves at base of caudal fin; no finlets.

Habitat
Shallow water along sandy beaches.

Range
From Massachusetts to Brazil, including shores of Gulf of Mexico; occurs irregularly in West Indies. Migrates north in summer, south in winter.

Comments
The Florida Pompano is a favorite food fish and commands high prices. It is caught using light tackle over shallow sand flats. Pompanos often make long "flights" out of the water.

Scrawled Filefish
Aluterus scriptus
348

To 3' (91 cm). Elongate, very compressed; light bluish gray to olive or brown, body and head have blue or blue-green spots, irregular lines, and scattered small, black spots. Snout very long; lower jaw projects well beyond upper; 6 outer teeth in each jaw. Gill slits oblique. Pelvic bone lacks external spine; first dorsal fin spine long, slender, often broken; caudal peduncle deeper than long; caudal fin long, rear profile rounded. Scales numerous, minute.

Habitat
Seagrass beds in tropical and subtropical seas.

Range
From New England south to Brazil, including Bermuda, Gulf of Mexico, and Caribbean.

Comments
This fish will often assume a vertical head-down position, to mimic blades of grass or to survey the bottom for food.

Sharpnose Puffer
Canthigaster rostrata
349

To 3¾" (9.5 cm). Elongate, round in cross section; orange-brown to purple-brown on upper third, lower two-thirds abruptly white to orange; blue lines radiate from eye onto caudal peduncle, lower part of caudal peduncle slightly darker, with narrow, blue, parallel bars; upper and lower caudal rays dark, middle rays and all other fins pale orange. Each jaw with 2 teeth. No pelvic fins; dorsal fin opposite anal fin; caudal fin notched. Ridge or keel on back in front of dorsal fin. Prickles absent or greatly reduced; no fleshy flaps.

Habitat
Coral reefs and grass beds to depths of 85' (26 m); always in clear water.

Range
From North Carolina, Bermuda, Bahamas, and Florida south
to northern coast of South America, including Gulf of Mexico
and West Indies.

Comments
In the United States the Sharpnose Puffer is most abundant in
southern Florida. It is frequently found around sea fans and
stinging coral. This species, like other puffers, feeds primarily
on shellfishes.

Planehead Filefish
Monacanthus hispidus
350

To 9″ (23 cm). Very deep, greatly compressed; gray, tan, and
brown, sometimes greenish, with irregular, darker blotches or
spots; color varies with background; caudal fin dusky yellow,
other fins yellow. 6 outer teeth in each jaw. Gill slits
almost vertical. Pelvic bone has prominent external spine,
disappearing in large specimens; first dorsal fin spine strong,
second dorsal soft ray forms 1 long filament in adult males;
caudal fin roughly rounded. Scales on side of caudal peduncle
prolonged to form bristles; skin velvetlike.

Habitat
Open seas or near shore around vegetation.

Range
From Nova Scotia to Brazil, including Bermuda and Gulf of
Mexico.

Comments
These fishes, especially the young, are found in the open ocean
among floating sargassum or inshore around seagrass beds.
Adults move seaward in winter.

Sargassumfish
Histrio histrio
351

To 6″ (15 cm). Short, deep, irregular in profile, moderately
compressed; creamy white to yellowish, mottled light and
dark spots and blotches; blends with sargassum plant in which
it lives; coloring changeable depending on amount of light
and on mood of fish. Mouth relatively small, gape very wide.
Pectoral fins limblike, with long base; small gill opening
behind base. First dorsal spine forms lure; second and third
spines large, depressible, and covered with skin bearing fleshy
fingerlike projections (cirri). Skin smooth with numerous
fleshy flaps.

Habitat
Floating sargassum weed.

Range
From New England to Brazil, including Bermuda, Gulf of
Mexico, Caribbean, and West Indies.

Comments
The only commercial value of the Sargassumfish is in the
aquarium trade. It is fun to watch it lurking in the vegetation
and luring prey to its cavernous mouth.

Striped Burrfish
Chilomycterus schoepfi
352

To 10″ (25 cm). Oval, broad, slightly depressed; covered with stout, 3-rooted, immovable spines; green to olive-green or brownish above, upper sides with irregular, oblique, black or brown lines, lower sides whitish, belly whitish or golden yellow; dark blotch at dorsal and anal fin bases, and above and behind pectoral fin base. Single tooth in each jaw, fused to form parrotlike beak. No pelvic fins; dorsal and anal fins short-based; pectoral and caudal fins well developed.

Habitat
Shallow grass beds in summer, deeper waters in winter.

Range
From Cape Hatteras, North Carolina, south to Brazil, including Bahamas and Gulf of Mexico; to Nova Scotia and Maine as stragglers.

Comments
Striped Burrfishes are quite common, especially south of the Carolinas during the summer months. Those under 3″ (7.5 cm) make good aquarium pets and will readily inflate when gently rubbed on the belly.

Sheepshead
Archosargus probatocephalus
353

To 30″ (76 cm). Deep, compressed; gray, 5–6 dark bars on body, 1 on nape, with slightly wider pale interspaces; bars darker in young than adults. Head profile very steep; snout pointed; mouth at tip of snout; jaws have broad incisor teeth in front, molars on sides. Pectoral fin long; single dorsal fin preceded by small, forward-directed spine embedded in skin.

Habitat
In muddy, shallow water or over oyster beds; frequently around piles and piers of bridges; occasionally enters fresh water in Florida.

Range
From Cape Cod to Brazil, including Gulf of Mexico, but absent from the Caribbean.

Comments
The Sheepshead gets its name from its large incisor teeth, which protrude a little beyond the lips. Its stout dorsal and anal spines can cause punctures. This food fish is a bottom-dweller; it does not school, but forms feeding groups.

Northern Puffer
Sphoeroides maculatus
354

To 10″ (25 cm). Elongate, round in cross section, globular when inflated; gray to brown above with vague black spots or saddlelike blotches, belly yellow to white; back, sides, and cheeks with tiny black spots; lower sides with series of barlike markings. 2 teeth in each jaw. No pelvic fins; caudal fin slightly rounded. Covered with prickles; no fleshy flaps.

Habitat
Bays and estuaries over sand, silt, or mud to about 30 fathoms. Inshore in summer, offshore in winter.

Range
From Newfoundland to NE. Florida.

Comments
The Northern Puffer is used as food and marketed as "sea squab." Care should be taken not to confuse it with the Bandtail Puffer, which is definitely toxic, and the Southern Puffer, which is reported to be mildly toxic.

Goosefish
Lophius americanus
355

To 4' (1.2 m). Tapering; tan to chocolate-brown and finely mottled above, whitish below; fin membranes behind head black, other fins darker than body. Head flattened, rounded; mouth wide, opens upward; teeth numerous, thin, sharp. Gill openings in form of round hole behind axis of pectoral fins. Lower jaw, head, and side of body have fringe of fleshy flaps. Pectoral and dorsal fins squarish; pelvic fins broad, stubby. Anterior dorsal spines present, foremost modified as "fishing lure"; third spine on top of head shorter than width of ridge between eyes.

Habitat
On bottom to about 200 fathoms, but frequents shallows in north of range.

Range
From Bay of Fundy to N. Florida.

Comments
Goosefishes have an enormous capacity for food and eat almost any kind of fish, various species of birds (they have been reported to eat geese), turtles, and invertebrates. They apparently can swallow fishes that are equal to their own weight.

Windowpane
Scophthalmus aquosus
356

To 18" (46 cm). Highly compressed; depth about two-thirds length, eyes on left side. Eyed side translucent, olive, brownish, reddish, or grayish, mottled with numerous small, irregular, lighter or darker blotches on head, sides, and fins; blind side white, sometimes with dusky blotches. Lower jaw projects slightly beyond upper. Pelvic fin bases very long, extend toward head; dorsal fin origin over snout, first few rays free without membrane between them. Lateral line highly arched toward front.

Habitat
Over sand, from near shore to depths of about 25 fathoms.

Range
From Gulf of St. Lawrence and Nova Scotia to Florida.

Comments
The Windowpane is most common in the New England states, where it is a year-round resident. It is of little importance as a food or game fish.

Winter Flounder
Pseudopleuronectes americanus
357

To 23" (58 cm). Highly compressed, elliptical, eyes on right side, top and bottom profiles evenly curved. Color varies with substrate from reddish brown to olive-green to almost black, sometimes mottled; fins plain; blind side white. Head small. Dorsal fin origin over front edge of upper eye. Lateral line almost straight, slightly arched above pectoral fins; scales strongly spiny on eyed side, smoother on blind side.

Habitat
Over mud or sand, with or without vegetation, to 20 fathoms or more.

Range
From Labrador to Georgia; rarely south of Chesapeake Bay; most abundant in Gulf of Maine.

Comments
The Winter Flounder has a thicker body and broader caudal peduncle than any other small flounder species in its range. South of New York, it goes into deep water in the summer and reappears in shoal waters during the winter; hence the common name Winter Flounder. This species is an important food fish.

Eyed Flounder
Bothus ocellatus
358

To 7" (18 cm). Highly compressed, depth two-thirds length, eyes on left side; light tan or gray, usually with rings or blotches; 3 diffuse, dark blotches along lateral line; caudal fin has 2 small, vertically placed, black dots; blind side white. Eyes well separated, more so in males; foremost bone of gill cover free, visible. Pectoral fin base on eyed side twice as long as on blind side; dorsal fin origin in front of eyes, front rays not branched. Lateral line distinctly arched over pectoral fin.

Habitat
Shallow water in protected areas over sand; less frequently over mud.

Range
From Long Island to Rio de Janeiro, Brazil, including Bermuda, parts of Gulf of Mexico, Caribbean, and West Indies.

Comments
This species and its relatives the Peacock Flounder (*B. lunatus*) and Twospot Flounder (*B. robinsi*) are good food fishes, but they are of little commercial value due to their small size and the fact that they are infrequently caught by anglers. They burrow into sand or mud, behavior shared with other lefteye flounders.

Hogchoker
Trinectes maculatus
359

To 6" (15 cm). Depth more than half length, eyes on right side; dusky usually with 7–8 narrow, black bars; fins have dark streaks or spots, particularly in juveniles; blind side white, often partly pigmented. Head blunt; mouth and eyes very small. No pectoral fins; right pelvic fin connected to anal fin; dorsal fin origin over snout, first ray shortest. Lateral line visible as nearly straight, narrow, dark stripe; no fleshy flaps; scales small, strongly spiny.

Habitat
Shallow coastal waters over mud, silt, or sand in bays and estuaries; occasionally in fresh water.

Range
Along coast from Maine to Yucatán, including Gulf of Mexico.

Comments
Young Hogchokers ascend streams for distances of 150 miles (240 km) or more. However, spawning takes place in the estuaries.

Naked Sole
Gymnachirus melas
360

To 6¼" (16 cm). Oval, depth half to three-fifths length, eyes on right side; eyed side, including caudal fin, dark brown or black with beige or brown zebralike stripes extending onto dorsal, anal, and caudal fins; blind side whitish, with dusky edges on dorsal, anal, and caudal fins. Head very small; mouth small, twisted. Pectoral fin small on eyed side only, sometimes hidden under skin; pelvic fins small, concealed by skin, continuous with anal fin; dorsal and anal fins enclosed in loose skin. Skin unscaled, soft and fleshy. Lateral line has branches at right angles.

Habitat
Over sand on continental shelf to 100 fathoms.

Range
From Massachusetts south along coast to Pensacola, Florida.

Comments
This fish and a similar species, the Fringed Sole (*G. texae*), overlap in a very narrow zone east and west of Mobile Bay, Alabama. This is probably because of the difference in the bottom, which is sandier east of the zone of overlap and muddier west of it.

Gray Angelfish
Pomacanthus arcuatus
361

To 24" (61 cm). Compressed, depth about three-fourths length; gray or brown, most large scales dark with pale edges, dorsal, anal, and caudal fin edges light blue or white, chin and mouth area white; juveniles black with 5 yellow bars across head and body. Head profile very steep; mouth small, lower jaw projects beyond upper; spine in front of gill cover well developed. Soft dorsal and anal fins filamentous; caudal fin squared off.

Habitat
Shallow reefs.

Range
From New England to southeastern Brazil, including West Indies; rare on offshore reefs in Gulf of Mexico.

Comments

The Gray Angelfish, perhaps the largest of the angelfishes, is reported to be among the least wary of the reef fishes. Apparently it is also hardy, as it is known to straggle north as far as New England. The species has been introduced in Bermuda.

French Angelfish
Pomacanthus paru
362

To 14″ (36 cm). Deep, compressed; blackish, most scales with crescent-shaped yellow marks, yellow ring around eye, yellow bar at pectoral fin base, dorsal fin filament yellow; juveniles black with 5 yellow bars on head, body, and caudal fin base. Head profile very steep; mouth small, lower jaw projects beyond upper; spine in front of gill cover well developed. Dorsal and anal fins filamentous; caudal fin rounded.

Habitat
Shallow reefs.

Range
Bermuda; from N. Florida and West Indies to northern South America. Reported in Gulf of Mexico around West Flower Gardens Reef.

Comments
Juvenile specimens of the French Angelfish and the Gray Angelfish are very similar, and this has undoubtedly led to some confusion regarding the geographical distribution and relative abundance of the 2 species.

Queen Angelfish
Holacanthus ciliaris
363

To 18″ (46 cm). Deep, compressed; bluish, scale edges yellow-orange; head yellowish with blue markings on snout, gill cover, and chest; large, black spot encircled by blue ring on nape; pectoral, pelvic, and caudal fins yellow, black blotch at base of pectorals; dorsal and anal fins with narrow, light blue edges. Juveniles yellowish green with narrow light blue bars; bluish-black band through eye. Upper profile of head nearly straight to slightly concave above eye; spine in front of gill cover present. Dorsal and anal fins long, filamentous, extending beyond end of caudal fin; caudal fin rounded, without upper filament.

Habitat
Coral reefs in shallow water.

Range
From Florida to Brazil, including Gulf of Mexico and Caribbean.

Comments
Queen Angelfishes blend well with their natural habitat, despite their bright colors. Juveniles may exhibit cleaning behavior typical of some wrasses. The Queen and Blue angelfishes commonly hybridize, producing offspring that are intermediate in appearance.

Harvestfish
Peprilus alepidotus
364

To 12" (30 cm). Very deep, compressed, upper and lower profiles similar; pale blue or greenish above, silvery with yellowish tinge below. Snout short, length less than diameter of eye. Pectoral fin longer than head; no pelvic fins; front edges of dorsal and anal fins crescent-shaped; caudal fin deeply forked. No pores below dorsal fin; scales small, loosely attached, easily shed, extend to cheeks and bases of dorsal, anal, and caudal fins.

Habitat
Surface of inshore and offshore waters over continental shelf to depths of about 15 fathoms.

Range
From Maine to Uruguay, including Gulf of Mexico and West Indies, but not western Caribbean; infrequent north of Chesapeake Bay.

Comments
Adult Harvestfishes swim in large schools and feed on jellyfishes, crustaceans, worms, and small fishes. The juveniles are plankton feeders and often live among floating weeds or large jellyfishes. Although most individuals are less than 6" (15 cm) long, the Harvestfish is an excellent food fish.

Ocean Surgeon
Acanthurus bahianus
365

To 14" (36 cm). Deep, compressed, depth half length; grayish brown to yellow with pale bluish- to greenish-gray lengthwise lines; gill-cover membrane purple or black; pelvic fin rays pale blue; dorsal fin has alternating narrow bands of dull orange and light bluish green; anal fin has dark gray to grayish-blue bands; area around blade violet; caudal fin olive to yellow-brown to dark blue with edge bluish white. Mouth small, slightly underneath head. Dorsal fin continuous, without notch; bladelike spine on caudal peduncle; caudal fin notched or crescent-shaped.

Habitat
Shallow reefs and rocky areas, and nearby sand.

Range
From Massachusetts to Rio de Janeiro, Brazil, including Caribbean and West Indies; absent from Gulf of Mexico.

Comments
The Ocean Surgeon is a bottom dweller. The algae that it scrapes off hard substrates is ground in its gizzardlike stomach.

Blue Tang
Acanthurus coeruleus
366

To 14" (36 cm). Deep, almost disk-shaped, compressed, depth more than half length; adults blue to purplish gray, frequently with narrow, gray bands; sheath of blade white; narrow, purplish-gray bands on dorsal and anal fins. Juveniles lemon-yellow; preadults sometimes part yellow, part blue, or blue with yellow fins. Eyes high on head; mouth small. Dorsal fin continuous, uninterrupted; bladelike spines on caudal peduncle; caudal fin distinctly concave in adults, notched in juveniles.

Habitat
Shallow coral and rock reefs.

Range
From New York to Brazil; center of abundance West Indies; stragglers in northern and southern parts of range; known off Louisiana in Gulf of Mexico.

Comments
This species belongs to the family of surgeonfishes, which have 3 color phases: juvenile, preadult, and adult. They are active during the day and often occur in rather large groups. Their teeth are adapted for feeding on algae that grow on or among coral rocks.

Foureye Butterflyfish
Chaetodon capistratus
367

To 6″ (15 cm). Deep, compressed, disk-shaped; silvery gray to pale yellow or whitish with dark, oblique lines above and horizontal lines below, meeting to form chevrons; black bar on head through eye; pelvic fins mostly yellow; large black eyespot below back of end of dorsal fin. Snout pointed; mouth small; jaws protractile. Dorsal fin continuous, long. Lateral line extends onto caudal peduncle.

Habitat
Coral and rocky reefs.

Range
From New England to Panama, including Gulf of Mexico and West Indies.

Comments
The Foureye Butterflyfish, one of the most common butterflyfishes, rarely exceeds 4″ (10 cm). It feeds primarily on coral polyps, sea anemones, tubeworms, and algae.

Reef Butterflyfish
Chaetodon sedentarius
368

To 6″ (15 cm). Deep, compressed, disk-shaped; yellow above shading to white below, dark bar on head through eye; broad, black bar extending from dorsal and anal fins to caudal peduncle. Snout pointed; mouth small, jaws protractile. Soft dorsal and anal fins more rounded toward rear. Lateral line extends onto caudal peduncle.

Habitat
Coral and rocky reefs.

Range
From North Carolina to S. Florida, eastern Gulf of Mexico, and Caribbean.

Comments
The adult Reef Butterflyfish is probably seen less often than some other butterflyfishes because it frequents deeper water. In the Tortugas it has been reported at 40 fathoms.

Banded Butterflyfish
Chaetodon striatus
369

To 6″ (15 cm). Deep, compressed, disk-shaped; whitish with lines forming chevrons, black band on head through eye, 2 broad, black bars on sides; black or dusky bar from soft dorsal fin base to caudal peduncle; dorsal, anal, and caudal fins with black bands near margin, white edges; pelvic fin spine white, rays black. Soft dorsal and anal fins do not appear noticeably rounded.

Habitat
Coral and rocky reefs.

Range
From New Jersey to Brazil, including Gulf of Mexico and Caribbean.

Comments
In the Gulf of Mexico the Banded Butterflyfish is known only around offshore reefs.

Sergeant Major
Abudefduf saxatilis
370

To 7″ (18 cm). Oblong, deep, compressed; bluish white, back under spiny dorsal fin yellow or greenish yellow, 5 prominent dark bars on sides with wider, light interspaces, dark spot at pectoral fin base. Mouth small, at tip of snout, slightly oblique; 1 nostril on each side of snout. Dorsal fin spines continuous with soft rays; soft dorsal and anal fins pointed, similar in size and shape; caudal fin forked. Lateral line ends under soft dorsal fin.

Habitat
Shallow reefs, rock jetties, grass beds, and around pilings. Juveniles part of sargassum fauna.

Range
From Rhode Island to Uruguay, including Bermuda, Gulf of Mexico, and Caribbean.

Comments
The Sergeant Major is apparently most abundant on shallow reefs in the Caribbean; far fewer occur north of Florida. It feeds on plankton, deep-sea invertebrates, and even sometimes on plants.

Porkfish
Anisotremus virginicus
371

To 14″ (36 cm). Deep, compressed; alternating silvery blue and yellow stripes on sides, diagonal black band from chin through eye to nape, another from below first dorsal spine to base of pectoral fin; spiny dorsal and pelvic fins dusky to black, other fins yellow. Head short; snout blunt; mouth small, lips thick. Scales only on bases of soft dorsal and anal fins.

Habitat
Shallow water over reefs and rocks.

Range
From Florida to Brazil, including Bermuda, eastern and western Gulf of Mexico, Caribbean, and West Indies.

Comments

Adult Porkfishes feed on a variety of invertebrates; the young, however, are known to pick parasites from the skin of larger fishes.

Pinfish
Lagodon rhomboides
372

To 15″ (38 cm). Oval, compressed; back olive; sides bluish with yellow stripes and 5–6 faint dusky bars, silvery sheen overall, dark spot on shoulder, fins yellow, no dark blotch on caudal peduncle. Head profile slightly concave at eye; snout relatively short, rather pointed; rear nostril oval; mouth at tip of snout; front teeth strongly flattened, incisorlike, deeply notched; side teeth molarlike. Pectoral fins long; dorsal fin single, forward-directed spine at origin.

Habitat

Primarily shallow water around vegetation.

Range

From Cape Cod south along coast to Yucatán, Mexico; possibly including northern Cuba.

Comments

This is a very common porgy, but because of its small size it is seldom used as food. Its greatest value is as forage for larger fishes.

Striped Bass
Morone saxatilis
373

To 6′ (1.8 m). Elongate, moderately compressed; back olive-green to dark blue, sides silvery, belly white; upper sides with 6–9 dark uninterrupted stripes; dorsal, anal, and caudal fins dusky. Mouth large, lower jaw slightly projecting. Teeth small. Gill cover has 2 flat spines near rear edge. First dorsal fin separated from second dorsal by deep notch. Scales extend onto all fin bases except spiny dorsal.

Habitat

Inshore over various bottoms; some permanently in fresh water.

Range

Atlantic Ocean and associated rivers from St. Lawrence River to St. Johns River, Florida; Apalachicola River, W. Florida, to Lake Ponchartrain, Louisiana. Most abundant from Hudson River to Chesapeake Bay. Widely introduced into rivers and lakes in much of Mississippi River system, Colorado River, and coastal streams in Washington, Oregon, and California.

Comments

The Striped Bass is a very important sport and commercial fish throughout its range, and large individuals are caught by surf fishing, especially on the Atlantic Coast. It is a delicious food fish. It is anadromous, and spawns prolifically in fresh water.

Gray Snapper
Lutjanus griseus
374

To 3′ (91 cm). Relatively slender; gray or olive above with reddish tinge or blotches, grayish or yellowish pink below; scale centers sometimes orange, edges white; no black spot on sides; spiny dorsal fin edge red. Snout long, pointed; lower jaw projects slightly beyond upper; dorsal profile of head slightly concave; large pair of canine teeth in upper jaw. Pectoral fin relatively short, not reaching anus; soft dorsal fin and anal fin rounded; caudal fin notched.

Habitat
Juveniles and young inshore, even in fresh water; adults offshore to about 90 fathoms, around estuaries, mangrove swamps and coral reefs, and over rocks.

Range
From Massachusetts to Rio de Janeiro, Brazil, including Bermuda, Gulf of Mexico, Antilles, and Caribbean.

Comments
This species can change color instantly to match its background. Although the Gray Snapper is reported to reach 3′ (91 cm) in length, most are less than half that long.

Red Snapper
Lutjanus campechanus
375

To 31″ (79 cm). Rather deep, depth one-fourth length; scarlet above fading to rosy red below, sometimes with silvery sheen; fins red or reddish orange, some with dusky borders; small specimens, to 12″ (30 cm), have dark spot on upper sides below front dorsal fin soft rays. Head large, front profile steep, rounded behind eye; snout long; eye small. Single dorsal fin long; caudal fin notched.

Habitat
Over rocks and natural and artificial reefs at 5–100 fathoms.

Range
From Massachusetts south to Florida, but rare north of Carolinas; Gulf of Mexico to Yucatán, Mexico. Absent in Antilles and Caribbean.

Comments
Red Snappers account for a substantial part of the food fishery on the Gulf Coast of the United States and Mexico. In the northeastern Gulf, artificial reefs have been constructed to attract these and other fishes for sport fishing.

Tripletail
Lobotes surinamensis
376

To 3′4″ (1 m). Deep, compressed, soft dorsal and anal fins long, with rounded caudal fin giving appearance of 3 tails; dark brown to bronzy to yellow-brown, often blotched or mottled, especially in young. Pectoral fins pale, other fins dark; single dorsal fin without pronounced notch; 3 anal fin spines. Scales adherent, strongly spiny.

Habitat
Inshore in bays and estuaries near buoys and channel markers; offshore.

Range
From Cape Cod to Argentina, including Gulf of Mexico, Caribbean, and tropics; most south of Cape Hatteras.

Comments
This excellent food fish can be caught around piers, pilings, wrecks, or flotsam using live shrimps for bait. It feeds primarily on crustaceans. Adult Tripletails float on their sides in the shade of flotsam; the young do the same, mimicking drifting leaves. There is a single species found worldwide.

Jewfish
Epinephelus itajara
377

To 7'10" (2.4 m). Very robust, broad; greenish or gray with small, black spots. Head large, somewhat flattened; eye small; mouth oblique. Pelvic fins smaller than pectorals; dorsal fin continuous, 11 spines much shorter than foremost soft rays; soft dorsal, anal, and caudal fins rounded; 3 anal fin spines. Lateral line continuous to base of caudal fin. Scales small but strongly spiny; bases of soft dorsal and anal fins covered with scales and thick skin.

Habitat
Inshore in shallow water; also in moderately deep water.

Range
Both coasts of Florida, Gulf of Mexico, Greater Antilles, and southwestern Caribbean.

Comments
Although the world's angling record for Jewfishes is 680 lbs, specimens in the 90 lb (40 kg) class or under are more likely to be caught. They are sought by spearfishers around oil rigs in Louisiana and Texas. Jewfishes feed mostly on crustaceans, but are known to feed on fishes and even on turtles.

Northern Searobin
Prionotus carolinus
378

To 17" (43 cm). Elongate, robust toward front, tapering toward rear; grayish or reddish above, pale below. Head large with many ridges and spines, some disappearing with growth. Pectoral fins winglike, reddish brown to black above, grayish or whitish below, extend to middle of soft dorsal fin; pelvic fins white. Black spot between fourth and sixth dorsal spines, surrounded by light halo extending through membrane between third and fourth, sixth and seventh spines.

Habitat
On bottom in shallow to deep coastal waters.

Range
From Bay of Fundy to Palm Beach, Florida; most common north of Bermuda. Migrates offshore and south in winter.

Comments
This is thought to be the most common searobin in Chesapeake Bay. It feeds on various crustaceans, including shrimps and crabs, and on bivalves, squids, and fishes. Searobins are a good food fish.

Fishes

Sand Perch
Diplectrum formosum
379

To 12" (30 cm). Small, slender, elongate; indistinct, dark bars and alternating blue and orange stripes, narrow, blue lines on cheek. Head and mouth large; 2 bony lobes in front of gill cover, 1 at angle, 1 above, each with radiating spines; 3 flat spines on gill cover. Dorsal fin continuous; 3 anal fin spines; caudal fin slightly forked, upper rays sometimes threadlike. Lateral line continuous to caudal fin base.

Habitat
Over sand or mud in coastal waters, or near reefs or upper edges of depressions in ocean floor to about 40 fathoms.

Range
From Virginia to Florida, throughout Gulf of Mexico and West Indies to Brazil.

Comments
Rather common in certain areas, this little sea bass is often caught by anglers who are pursuing something larger.

Black Drum
Pogonias cromis
380

To 3'3" (99 cm). Deep, moderately compressed, back elevated, bottom profile nearly straight; silvery to dark gray; 4–5 broad, black bars on sides, bars less intense in large fish; all fins dusky or black. Mouth nearly horizontal, underneath head; chin has numerous small barbels, longer toward rear on chin; gill cover smooth. 2 anal fin spines, second much larger than first; caudal fin squared off to slightly notched. Lateral line extends to tip of caudal fin; scales large, spiny.

Habitat
Over sand or sandy mud in bays and estuaries.

Range
From Gulf of Maine to S. Florida; Gulf of Mexico west from S. Florida to Laguna Madre, Mexico; Brazil.

Comments
Black Drums feed on fishes, crustaceans, and oysters, which they crush with their huge pharyngeal teeth. Although they may weigh more than 100 pounds (45.4 kg), and are often caught, they are not popular as game or food fishes.

Black Sea Bass
Centropristis striata
381

To 24" (61 cm). Elongate, moderately compressed, depth one-third length; dark brown or bluish black, light centers of scales form stripes above, dorsal fin striped. Head large; lower jaw projects beyond upper; no large spines in front of gill cover. Dorsal fin high, continuous, with notch between spiny and soft parts, interspinal membrane has deep notches, spines have fleshy flaps. 3 anal fin spines; caudal fin round or ending in 3 lobes, upper lobe often has elongate ray in adults. Lateral line extends to caudal fin base. Bases of dorsal and anal fins lack thick skin and scales.

Habitat
Continental shelf, over rocks around pilings and wrecks.

Range
From Maine south to Florida Keys and eastern Gulf of Mexico.

Comments
Black Sea Bass from the eastern Gulf of Mexico represent a subspecies (*C. s. melana*) that attains a length of only about half that of the Atlantic populations. The Black Sea Bass is an important food fish, especially in the mid-Atlantic states. It is often caught by anglers fishing with rods from boats for other kinds of fishes.

Nassau Grouper
Epinephelus striatus
382

To 4′ (1.2 m). Robust, not strongly compressed; brownish or brownish orange above, but often pinkish or red in deep water, 5 dusky bars on sides; dark blotch on top of caudal peduncle, intense dark dots around eye, dark stripes between eye and dorsal fin origin. Head long. Single dorsal fin with shallow notch between spines and rays, interspinal membranes notched; 3 anal fin spines; caudal fin rounded in young, becoming squared off in adults. Small, dense scales on bases of dorsal and anal fins.

Habitat
Over coral reefs and to depths of 15 fathoms.

Range
From North Carolina to Brazil, including Bermuda, southern Gulf of Mexico, and Antilles.

Comments
The Nassau Grouper changes color phases rapidly. It is not very wary, and readily takes food from the hands of divers. It is an important sport fish, a good fighter, and will take various kinds of bait. The Nassau Grouper averages a weight of about 8 to 10 lbs (3.6 to 4.5 kg) and is considered excellent eating.

Rock Hind
Epinephelus adscensionis
383

To 24″ (61 cm). Robust, not strongly compressed; light olive, body and fins covered with reddish-brown spots larger on undersides than sides; 2–3 dark saddles on back under dorsal fin, 1 on caudal peduncle; soft dorsal, caudal, and anal fins greenish, without black margins. Head long; mouth oblique, some dorsal fin spines longer than front soft rays, interspinal membrane notched; 3 anal fin spines; caudal fin rounded. Lateral line continuous to base of caudal fin. Bases of soft dorsal and anal fins covered with scales and thick skin.

Habitat
Over coral reefs and rocks in shallow water.

Range
Bermuda, S. Florida, Gulf Coast, West Indies, and shores of Caribbean, south to Brazil. Occasionally strays north to Massachusetts.

Comments
The Rock Hind is reported to be a better food fish than the

Red Hind, but is more wary of taking bait. It is common in shallow depths, and tolerates rough inshore waters, although it has been found as deep as 16 fathoms.

Atlantic Croaker
Micropogonias undulatus
384

To 24″ (61 cm). Moderately elongate and compressed; dusky bluish or grayish above, silvery-bronze below, small brownish dots form irregular lines on sides and 1–2 horizontal rows on soft dorsal, other fins clear or pale yellowish. Snout conical; mouth small, slightly oblique, underneath head; chin with 3–5 pairs of minute barbels and 5 pores; strong spines in front of gill cover. 2 anal fin spines; caudal fin doubly notched in adults. Lateral line extends to tip of caudal fin.

Habitat
Over mud or sand in coastal waters and estuaries.

Range
Along coast from Cape Cod to Texas, south to Yucatán, Mexico; not common north of New Jersey or in S. Florida.

Comments
In the southern part of its range, the Atlantic Croaker matures in 1 year and lives another 1 or 2 years; in the north it matures later and survives longer. Important commercially, it is caught by the thousands of tons.

Red Drum
Sciaenops ocellatus
385

To 5′ (1.5 m). Elongate, moderately compressed; iridescent silvery gray, copper, bronze, or reddish; 1 or more large, black eyelike spots on caudal peduncle; dorsal and caudal fins dusky; anal and pelvic fins pale. Snout conical; mouth horizontal, underneath head; no chin barbels. Third and fourth dorsal spines longest; caudal fin squared off in adults. Lateral line extends to tip of caudal fin; scales large, spiny.

Habitat
Surf zone to offshore waters, depending on season and age of individuals; also occasionally enters fresh water.

Range
Along coast from New York to Florida, west to Laguna Madre, Mexico. Most abundant from Florida to Texas.

Comments
Red Drums run in schools during their spring and fall migrations. They migrate in response to temperature, salinity, and food availability.

Southern Kingfish
Menticirrhus americanus
386

To 20″ (51 cm). Elongate, spindle-shaped, moderately compressed; dusky, darker above, lighter below, almost white on belly, sides with 7 or 8 dark, dusky oblique bands. Pelvic, anal, and caudal fins dusky, sometimes tinged with yellow; pectoral fins dusky, outer edges black; spiny dorsal fin dusky, apex black; soft dorsal fin plain. Snout conical; mouth small, horizontal, underneath head; chin with single, short, stout barbel. When flattened, longest dorsal spine falls short of first soft ray; 1 anal fin spine. Scales small, spiny, adherent. Lateral line extends to caudal fin edge.

Habitat
Usually over sand but also over mud or silt at depths of at least 60′ (18 m).

Range
From Cape Cod to Florida, Gulf of Mexico, and western Caribbean.

Comments
One of several kingfishes called "ground mullets," the tasty Southern Kingfish is caught in the northeastern Gulf of Mexico by baitcasting in the surf.

Weakfish
Cynoscion regalis
387

To 35″ (89 cm). Elongate, spindle-shaped, moderately compressed; greenish-olive above, sides iridescent, silvery below, small, irregular dark dots on back form oblique streaks on scale rows, pelvic and anal fins usually yellow, other fins dusky, tinged with yellow. Mouth oblique; lower jaw projecting; no barbels or pores. Soft dorsal fin covered with scales up to basal half; caudal fin crescent-shaped or notched. Lateral line extends to caudal fin tip; scales spiny, large, smooth on head.

Habitat
Shallow coastal waters over sand or mud; summer feeding and nursery grounds in estuaries.

Range
From Nova Scotia to Florida, and W. Florida to Tampa Bay. Most abundant from New Jersey to Chesapeake Bay.

Comments
Although this important game and commercial fish is reported to reach about 35″ (89 cm), the majority caught by anglers are 18″ (46 cm) or smaller.

Haddock
Melanogrammus aeglefinus
388

To 3′8″ (1.1 m). Moderately elongate, slightly compressed, tapering to slender caudal peduncle; dark gray above, whitish below; large, dark blotch on shoulder; lateral line black. Chin barbel very small. Pelvic fins not filamentous; 3 dorsal fins, front rays of first long, ending in sharp point; dorsal and caudal fins dusky; 2 anal fins.

Habitat
Usually at 25–75 fathoms, rarely in shoal water.

Range
Grand Banks; from Nova Scotia Banks to Cape Cod, and in deep water off Cape Hatteras.

Comments
Haddock live in deeper waters than cod and prefer smooth

bottoms of sand, gravel, or clay. They feed indiscriminately on
available fauna. Most specimens weigh up to 4 lbs (1.8 kg).
They are somewhat more important commercially than cod.

Atlantic Cod
Gadus morhua
389

To 6' (1.8 m). Moderately elongate, slightly compressed,
tapering to slender caudal peduncle; variably greenish,
brownish, yellowish, whitish, or reddish; back and sides with
numerous brownish spots; lateral line pale; no black blotch on
shoulder. Eye large; chin barbel large; upper jaw projects
beyond lower. Fins dark; pelvic fins not filamentous; 3 dorsal
fins; 2 anal fins; caudal fin notched.

Habitat
Usually on or near bottom of continental shelf at depths of 6–
20 fathoms, sometimes deeper, over hard, irregular substrates.

Range
From western Greenland south to Cape Hatteras; most
abundant from Labrador to New York.

Comments
Reported at over 200 lbs (90 kg) but considered large at one-
third of that weight, Atlantic Cod average 6 to 12 lbs (2.7 to
5.4 kg). They feed on a variety of animals, mostly mollusks,
sea squirts, and other fishes. The annual catch of this
commercially important fish amounts to tens of thousands of
tons. It is often caught on a handline by anglers in New
England.

Pollock
Pollachius virens
390

To 3'6" (1.1 m). Rather elongate, somewhat compressed;
olive-green, brownish green, or grayish above, sides paler,
belly silvery; lateral line white; dorsal, anal, and caudal fins
olive-gray or greenish; paired fins have pinkish tinge. Lower
jaw projects beyond upper; chin barbel minute or absent. First
dorsal fin roughly triangular; pelvic fin short; caudal fin deeply
notched or crescent-shaped.

Habitat
Over rocks to depths of 100 fathoms; sometimes at midwater
or on surface.

Range
From Gulf of St. Lawrence to New Jersey, occasionally to
Chesapeake Bay and North Carolina. Most abundant in Gulf
of Maine.

Comments
Pollock usually run in schools and are an important part of the
New England and North Atlantic fishery, but less so than
Atlantic Cod and Haddock. Adults average from 4 to 15 lbs
(1.8 to 6.8 kg).

Gizzard Shad
Dorosoma cepedianum
391

To 16″ (41 cm). Deep, moderately compressed; back dark blue or gray, sides silvery, belly white; 6 or 8 horizontal dusky stripes on upper sides; dusky spot behind gill cover. Head small, mouth small and underneath head; transparent membranous eyelid present. Pelvic fin almost directly under origin of dorsal fin. Last ray of dorsal fin elongate, filamentous. Belly scales platelike, forming distinct keel.

Habitat
Salt water; fresh water in large rivers, reservoirs, lakes, and estuaries.

Range
Atlantic Coast and associated rivers from New York to mid-Florida, Gulf of Mexico from mid-Florida to central Mexico; St. Lawrence River, Great Lakes, and Mississippi River system.

Comments
The Gizzard Shad is a very common herbivorous fish associated primarily with freshwater habitats. It has no commercial value, but is forage for larger, carnivorous fishes.

Mosquitofish
Gambusia affinis
392

To 2½″ (6.5 cm). Rather robust, particularly females; compressed. Tan to olive above, pale yellowish below; scales have small, dusky spots near edges; dark bar below eye; many spots present on dorsal and caudal fins; females have conspicuous black spot on belly during reproductive period. Head flattened; mouth small, oblique, lower jaw projects beyond upper; teeth small. Anal fin of male modified to form reproductive organ.

Habitat
Near surface of fresh or brackish water in ponds, lakes, ditches, backwaters, and sluggish streams.

Range
From New Jersey to central Mexico along coast and in associated freshwater streams; Mississippi River basin south from Illinois.

Comments
Because it eats aquatic mosquito larvae, the Mosquitofish has been introduced into many areas to control mosquitoes.

Gulf Killifish
Fundulus grandis
393

To 6″ (15 cm). Elongate, moderately robust. Males dark greenish blue or olive above; sides lighter with small, pearly spots; belly yellowish; dorsal, anal, and caudal fins with small, light spots; pelvic and anal fins yellowish. Females olive above, silvery below; sides have 12–15 narrow bars; anal fin yellow. Head rather large; snout bluntly rounded; 10 pores on lower jaw. Dorsal fin origin over or in front of anal fin.

Habitat
Over sand or mud in bays, tidal marshes, pools, and ditches.

Range
Along coast from NE. Florida to Veracruz, Mexico.

Comments
The Gulf Killifish can tolerate adverse conditions such as low
oxygen and great variation in salinity ranging from fresh water
to salt concentration several times that of sea water. It feeds
primarily on crustaceans and small fishes, and has increased in
value as bait in the past few years.

Diamond Killifish
Adinia xenica
394

To 2" (5 cm). Very deep and compressed, depth about half
length. Dark green with 10–14 narrow, pearly bands with
wider interspaces; belly yellow; lower jaw orange; pelvic fins
dusky, tips yellow; dorsal and anal fins dusky with pale blue
or orange spots; caudal fin barred with some pale spots. Snout
pointed; head flat above, front profile concave; mouth at tip of
snout, teeth conical. Dorsal fin origin in front of anal fin
origin. Caudal peduncle deep.

Habitat
Shallow lagoons, tide pools, ditches, and salt marshes.

Range
Gulf of Mexico from S. Florida to S. Texas.

Comments
This beautiful killifish is often locally abundant in shallow
tidal areas of marshes and barrier islands.

Sheepshead Minnow
Cyprinodon variegatus
395

To 3" (7.5 cm). Robust, moderately compressed. Males olive,
iridescent blue, or greenish blue above, sides with poorly
defined bars, belly yellowish, caudal fin edge and base with
black bar. Females olive or brassy, sometimes light orange
above, black bars on sides, 1–2 spots on rear rays of dorsal fin.
Snout blunt, mouth small, at tip of snout. Teeth incisor-like,
tricuspid. Dorsal fin origin midway between snout and caudal
fin, in front of anal fin base. Caudal peduncle deep; caudal fin
squared off. Scale behind gill cover present.

Habitat
Shallow water of coastal marshes and tide pools, usually over
sand; enters fresh water.

Range
Along coast from Massachusetts to northern Mexico.

Comments
The Sheepshead Minnow rarely frequents water more than a
few feet deep and is tolerant of extreme temperatures and
salinities. It is usually found in brackish water, but can
survive in water up to 4 times saltier than sea water.

Sailfin Molly
Poecilia latipinna
396

To 5" (12.5 cm). Oblong, compressed; depth of male about same from dorsal fin toward rear; belly rounded in female and caudal peduncle narrower. Olive with blackish or reddish-orange to yellowish dots on side scales forming stripes. Head small, flattened; mouth small; teeth in several series, outer ones largest. In males, dorsal fin very tall, with blackish spots on membranes between rays forming interrupted narrow bands; caudal fin has dark spots forming bars. Anal fin of males located forward and modified to form reproductive organ.

Habitat
Saltwater marshes, ponds, and ditches; also freshwater pools, ponds, and ditches.

Range
Along coast from North Carolina to Yucatán. Inland streams in Florida, Louisiana, and Texas. Introduced in lower Colorado River system.

Comments
These strikingly beautiful fishes feed primarily on plants and organic detritus. A variety with black coloring is bred as a popular aquarium fish. Like many killifishes, they are extremely tolerant of wide ranges in salinity.

Atlantic Menhaden
Brevoortia tyrannus
397

To 18" (46 cm). Oval, deep and compressed; blue or green, sometimes bluish brown above; sides and belly silvery, fins yellowish; distinct spot behind gill cover often followed by several rows of smaller spots. Head very large; mouth oblique. Pectoral fins slightly crescent-shaped, near bottom profile; dorsal fin origin slightly behind pelvic fin insertion. Exposed scales on belly almost vertical, fringed.

Habitat
At or near surface over continental shelf, near large estuaries.

Range
From New Brunswick to S. Florida.

Comments
This fish and a related species, the Gulf Menhaden (*B. patronus*), both also called "pogy," occur in huge schools, often weighing hundreds of tons. They support a large industry on the Atlantic and Gulf coasts. Although all parts of the fish have value, its oil is the principal product.

American Shad
Alosa sapidissima
398

To 30" (76 cm). Elongate, strongly compressed; top and bottom profiles evenly rounded; depth about one-fourth length. Back dark bluish or greenish, sides much paler, belly silvery; dusky spot behind gill cover usually followed by several small, less distinct dusky spots. Head one-fifth or less of length; mouth oblique; eye diameter much less than length of snout. Dorsal fin origin slightly in front of pelvic fin insertion.

Habitat
Bays, estuaries, and fresh water.

Range
From S. Labrador to St. Johns River, Florida; introduced in Pacific from Alaska to Mexico.

Comments
All *Alosa* are schooling species that enter freshwater streams to spawn. None remain long in fresh water, nor do they go far out at sea.

Atlantic Mackerel
Scomber scombrus
399

To 22″ (56 cm). Elongate, spindle-shaped, slightly compressed; dark bluish green to blue-black above, top of head darker; usually 27–30 transverse, wavy, dark bands to just below lateral line; silvery below. Head large, pointed; transparent, membranous eyelid present. First dorsal fin triangular, second slightly concave, with spines depressible into dorsal groove; 5 dorsal and 5 anal finlets. 2 small keels on each side of caudal peduncle, no large median keel. Scales minute, barely visible except around pectoral fin base, lacks girdle of scales.

Habitat
Open seas and over continental shelf in temperate water below 68° F (20° C).

Range
Migratory. From Newfoundland to Cape Hatteras.

Comments
The Atlantic Mackerel, an extremely abundant fish that travels in large schools, is important commercially for food. The fishing industry makes no distinction between the Atlantic and Chub mackerels.

Chub Mackerel
Scomber japonicus
400

To 25″ (64 cm). Elongate, spindle-shaped, slightly compressed; dark green to blue-black above with many wavy, dark streaks extending to just below lateral line, silvery below with numerous dusky blotches. Head pointed, flattened between eyes; snout conical, shorter than rest of head; transparent, membranous eyelid present. 2 dorsal fins widely separated, first triangular, with 8–10 spines; second slightly concave; 5 dorsal and 5 anal finlets. 2 small keels on each side of caudal peduncle, no large median keel. Lacks girdle of scales, largest scales around pectoral fins.

Habitat
Warm coastal waters over continental shelf.

Range
In Atlantic from Nova Scotia to Florida, Gulf of Mexico, and Venezuela.

Comments
Chub Mackerels, usually schooling fishes themselves, feed on

other schooling fishes like anchovies and herrings, and on invertebrates. This species is an excellent food fish. Members of the mackerel family (Scombridae) are fast swimmers. There are 23 species that are found in North America.

Bluefish ⊗
Pomatomus saltatrix
401

To 3'7" (1.1 m). Elongate, compressed; greenish or grayish blue above, silvery below, median fins yellowish. Head large; mouth large, at tip of snout; teeth prominent, sharp, arranged in single series. First dorsal fin has 7–8 spines, separated from soft dorsal fin by deep notch; anal fin with 2 spines, similar to soft dorsal; caudal fin forked. Scales small, present on head, body, and bases of fins; lateral lines complete, straight, follows top profile.

Habitat
Surface waters, near shore or offshore.

Range
From Nova Scotia to Argentina, including Florida and Gulf of Mexico.

Comments
Bluefishes are voracious creatures, often foraging on squids or schools of small fishes. They are reported to feed until their bellies are full, regurgitate, and feed again as long as food is present. They have been known to attack people. Bluefishes are exciting sport fishes and good food if consumed when fresh.

Tarpon
Megalops atlanticus
402

To 8' (2.4 m). Large, elongate, moderately deep and compressed; back blue-gray, sides and belly silvery, fins dusky or pale. Mouth huge, oblique, lower jaw projects well beyond upper; upper jawbone reaches well beyond eye; bony plate present in lower jaw. Pectoral and pelvic fins with large axillary scale; pelvic fins abdominal and in front of dorsal fin origin. Single dorsal fin short, last ray elongate and threadlike; anal fin origin behind dorsal fin base; caudal fin deeply forked. Scales extremely large, smooth.

Habitat
Primarily shallow coastal waters and estuaries. Spawn offshore, larvae develop inshore; juveniles and sometimes adults enter fresh water.

Range
From Nova Scotia south to Brazil, including Bermuda, Gulf of Mexico, and Caribbean. Infrequently north of North Carolina.

Comments
The Tarpon is also known as the Silverking and is indeed the king of sport fishes. It takes an experienced angler to land a large Tarpon, for this extremely strong fish is a fast swimmer and can make spectacular leaps out of the water in an effort to throw the hook. It is not regarded as good food.

Striped Anchovy
Anchoa hepsetus
403

To 6″ (15 cm). Elongate, compressed; dusky green or greenish blue above; broad, bright silver band on sides; whitish below. Snout conical, overhangs mouth; eye large, width greater than length of snout. Pelvic fins abdominal; pectoral fins inserted well below axis of body; anal fin origin under or behind midpoint of dorsal fin base; caudal fin deeply forked. Scales large, loosely attached, easily shed; no keel on belly.

Habitat
Shallow coastal waters to about 35 fathoms.

Range
From Massachusetts to northern Brazil, including Gulf of Mexico, Caribbean, West Indies.

Comments
There are 10 species of anchovies on the Atlantic Coast, and 4 on the Pacific Coast. Anchovies occur in large schools, filter feed on plankton, and are eaten extensively by predators such as mackerels and Bluefishes. They play an invaluable role in the marine energy web. Anchovies are also important commercially, as they are widely used for bait and food.

Bonefish
Albula vulpes
404

To 3′ (91 cm). Elongate, spindle-shaped; bluish or greenish, silvery overall, occasionally with dusky side stripes and bars that fade upon death; base of fins often yellow. Upper jaw overhangs lower. Pelvic fins abdominal. Caudal fin large, deeply forked. Scales smooth.

Habitat
Shallow waters over soft bottoms.

Range
In Atlantic from Bay of Fundy to Rio de Janeiro, Brazil, most common in S. Florida, Bermuda, and Bahamas; in Pacific from San Francisco, California, to Peru.

Comments
Bonefishes eat clams, snails, shrimps, and small fishes. Although they have been virtually ignored on the West Coast, they are prized game fishes on the East Coast, since they are easier to catch on shallow sand flats.

Striped Mullet
Mugil cephalus
405

To 18″ (46 cm). Elongate, cylindrical toward front, compressed toward rear; silvery, back olive-green or bluish green, 6–7 darker stripes on sides. Head flat between eyes; transparent, membranous eyelid well developed; mouth small, wide, at tip of snout, lower jaw has fleshy knob at tip. Pectoral fins inserted high on shoulders; pelvic fins abdominal; dorsal fin has 4 weak spines well separated from soft dorsal; 3 anal fin spines; caudal fin forked. Scales spiny, cover body, top of head, and bases of soft dorsal and anal fins. No lateral line.

Habitat
Coasts, estuaries, and fresh water.

Range
In Atlantic from Cape Cod to Brazil, including Gulf of
Mexico, Caribbean, and West Indies. In Pacific from San
Francisco Bay, California, to Chile.

Comments
These important food fishes occur in schools. Striped Mullets
are known to travel several hundred miles up rivers, but
spawning always takes place in the sea. They feed on small
algae and detritus that they glean from the mud.

Snook ⊗
Centropomus undecimalis
406

To 4'7" (1.4 m). Slender, elongate; yellowish brown or
greenish brown above, silvery below with dark lateral line on
sides extending through caudal fin. Snout pointed, lower jaw
projecting; mouth large with teeth in jaw and on roof. Fins
dusky; dorsal fins well separated, second dorsal spine very
strong; anal fin with 3 spines. Scales spiny.

Habitat
Shallow coastal waters, estuaries, lagoons, canals, and fresh
water.

Range
From Cape Fear River, North Carolina, south to S. Florida;
along Gulf Coast of Florida to Destin, disjunctly to Texas;
West Indies and Caribbean south to Brazil. Probably only
summer migrants north of S. Florida.

Comments
The Snook, a highly esteemed food and sport fish, feeds on
other fishes and various crustaceans. Sensitive to low
temperatures, it avoids water cooler than about 61° F (16° C).
The Snook should be handled carefully, as the sharp gill covers
can cause deep cuts.

Inland Silverside
Menidia beryllina
407

To 6" (15 cm). Elongate, slender, moderately compressed; pale
greenish above, pale below, lateral band silvery, with dark
line above; rear scale edges dusky, fins pale. Mouth at tip of
snout, oblique; snout shorter than eye. 2 dorsal fins well
separated; anal fin long; caudal fin forked. Scales with smooth
edges, not rough to touch.

Habitat
Along coast and in freshwater streams and rivers, usually over
sand.

Range
From Massachusetts to Veracruz, Mexico, along coast, and in
associated freshwater streams. Inland in lower Mississippi
River drainage and Rio Grande.

Comments
This fish is tolerant of wide fluctuations in salinity but is never
found offshore. Until recently the freshwater form was known
as the species *Menidia audens*.

Cobia
Rachycentron canadum
408

To 6'7" (2 m). Elongate, almost cylindrical; dark brown above with 2 narrow, silvery bands, belly gray or yellowish. Head large, broad, flattened; mouth at tip of snout, lower jaw projects. First dorsal fin has short, disconnected spines; second dorsal fin long, elevated toward front; anal fin smaller, similar to second dorsal; caudal fin rounded to slightly crescent-shaped. Scales small, embedded.

Habitat
Open seas; some also found near shore around barrier islands and coral reefs.

Range
From mid-Atlantic states to Argentina, including Gulf of Mexico, Antilles, and Caribbean; rarely found off Massachusetts.

Comments
Cobias are often seen basking on the surface around boats or flotsam, where they will take a hook baited with almost any fish, squid, or crustacean. They may be confused with members of the Remora Family when they are viewed from the side.

Threespine Stickleback
Gasterosteus aculeatus
409

To 4" (10 cm). Spindle-shaped; gray to olive-brown, sides paler, belly silvery; breeding adults reddish on head and belly. Head one-fourth length; lower jaw projects beyond upper. Usually 3 stout, widely separated dorsal spines preceding soft dorsal fin. Caudal peduncle narrow; caudal fin triangular. Sides covered with series of bony plates.

Habitat
Marine, estuarine, and fresh water, usually in vegetation.

Range
In Atlantic, from Hudson Bay to Chesapeake Bay; in Pacific, from Bering Sea to N. Baja California and in associated freshwater streams.

Comments
These shore fishes enter brackish water or ascend freshwater streams to spawn from April to July. The female deposits 75 to 100 eggs on a nest built by the male, which guards the eggs and remains with the fry until they can fend for themselves.

Gulf Pipefish
Syngnathus scovelli
410

To 6" (15 cm). Slender, very elongate; females have deeper body and V-shaped belly. Females usually olive-brown with white or silvery bars, pectoral fins plain, dorsal and caudal fins dusky; males similar but usually lighter. Snout moderately short; no pelvic fins; dorsal fin usually located over 3 bony rings on body and 5 on tail; caudal fin present.

Habitat
Shallow grass flats in salt and fresh waters.

Range
From Florida to Mexico in Gulf of Mexico; fresh water in
Louisiana and Florida.

Comments
There are 24 species of pipefishes on the coasts of North
America. Most are similar in shape, and the species are
distinguished by the number of bony rings on the body and
tail and the position of the dorsal fin relative to the body
rings. They are found primarily near shore and prefer areas of
dense vegetation. Only the Gulf Pipefish enters fresh water.

Sea Lamprey
Petromyzon marinus
411

To 33″ (84 cm). Eel-like; olive-brown above, usually mottled
yellowish brown on sides, pale below; some have shades of red,
blue, and green on sides, others blackish. Mouth without
jaws, with numerous rasplike teeth; eyes small; 7 pairs of gill
openings. Dorsal fins separated, distinct from caudal fin; no
paired or anal fins. 67–74 muscle segments between last gill
opening and anus.

Habitat
At sea to 500 fathoms or more; along coasts, in estuaries and
fresh water.

Range
From Gulf of St. Lawrence south to N. Florida and associated
streams; Great Lakes.

Comments
The adult Sea Lamprey is parasitic. The larvae live on the
bottom in silt and mud for up to 5 years.

Atlantic Needlefish
Strongylura marina
412

To 25″ (64 cm). Very elongate, round in cross section;
greenish to bluish green above, silvery below; dark stripe often
on sides from above pectoral fin to caudal fin base. Upper and
lower jaws very elongate, armed with numerous sharp teeth.
No spines in fins; pelvic fins small, abdominal; pectoral fins
inserted high on sides; dorsal and anal fins far back; caudal fin
not deeply forked, lower lobe slightly longer than upper.
Caudal peduncle without keels, not strongly flattened. Lateral
line follows belly profile. Scales small.

Habitat
Coastal marine waters and into freshwater coastal streams.

Range
From Maine to Rio de Janeiro, Brazil; absent from Bahamas
and Antilles.

Comments
This and other needlefishes often occur in small schools, and
are most active at night. They feed primarily on small fishes.
Spawning is believed to occur in both fresh and salt water.

Sharksucker
Echeneis naucrates
413

To 32″ (81 cm). Very elongate, depth about one-tenth length, head about one-fifth length; dark gray, brown, or blackish; belly whitish; dark band from snout through eye to caudal fin, with whitish zone on each side. Lower jaw projects beyond upper; oval sucking disk present. Dorsal and anal fins same shape, with long base and whitish edges.

Habitat
Open seas.

Range
From Nova Scotia to Brazil, including Gulf of Mexico.

Comments
This remora, unlike some others, is indiscriminate in choosing a host. It has been observed to remain with the Bull Shark (*Carcharhinus leucas*) even in fresh water.

Spiny Dogfish
Squalus acanthias
414

To 5′ (1.5 m). Elongate, slender; gray or brown above; dirty white below; young have light spots on back. Snout long, pointed. Spine in front of each dorsal fin; origin of first dorsal fin slightly behind rear of pectorals; origin of second dorsal fin behind rear of pelvics. Lacks anal fin; upper lobe of caudal fin larger than lower, tip rounded.

Habitat
In temperate waters over soft bottoms, off coast to 200 fathoms.

Range
On Atlantic Coast from Newfoundland to North Carolina; a few stray to Cuba; on Pacific Coast from Bering Sea to central Baja California.

Comments
The fully developed young are born in broods of 2 to 20 and average 8″ to 12″ (20 to 30 cm) long at birth. Tagging studies off California suggest that Spiny Dogfishes are migratory. These sharks are considered pests in North America.

Blue Shark
Prionace glauca
415

To 12′7″ (3.8 m). Very slender, spindle-shaped; dark blue above, bright blue on sides, white below; tips of pectoral, dorsal, and anal fins dusky. Snout long, narrowly rounded, longer than width of mouth. Teeth serrate, triangular and curved in upper jaw, narrower in lower jaw. Pectoral fins very long, narrow, and somewhat crescent-shaped. Dorsal fins relatively small, no ridge of skin. Keel on caudal peduncle weak; caudal fin crescent-shaped.

Habitat
In shallow coastal waters over sand or mud, and far out at sea.

Range
In Atlantic from Nova Scotia to Gulf of Maine, rarely to Chesapeake Bay, disjunctly to Brazil. In Pacific from S. Alaska to Chile.

Comments

Blue Sharks are common and well known to commercial fishers and whalers. Ordinarily they feed on small schooling fishes; however, they are known to follow vessels for days feeding on offal. They are not considered dangerous to people.

Bonnethead
Sphyrna tiburo
416

To 4'6" (1.4 m). Elongate; gray or grayish brown above, paler below. Head flattened, expanded laterally, with eyes at end of lateral expansions; front margin rounded or bonnetlike, without indentations; slightly concave opposite nostrils. Teeth smooth, cusps slanted in upper jaw, erect in lower jaw, becoming flattened in corners of both jaws.

Habitat
Shallow inshore waters, bays, and estuaries, usually over sand.

Range
In Atlantic from New England to northern Argentina, including Gulf of Mexico and Caribbean; in Pacific from S. California to Peru.

Comments
The Bonnethead, harmless to people, feeds on a variety of crustaceans, mollusks, and fishes. It is often caught on hook and line, and sometimes eaten.

Blacktip Shark
Carcharhinus limbatus
417

To 8' (2.4 m). Moderately slender, spindle-shaped; back gray, belly white; tips of pelvic fins black, other fin tips black, but color fades with age. Snout relatively long, pointed; no spiracle; front teeth erect, sharp-pointed, serrate. Gill openings moderately long. Pectoral fins crescent-shaped; dorsal fins lack spines, first larger than second; anal fin present.

Habitat
Coastal waters and offshore.

Range
In Atlantic from New England to southern Brazil, including Caribbean and Gulf of Mexico; in Pacific from Baja California and Gulf of California to Peru, including offshore islands.

Comments
These sharks are noted for their leaping and spinning antics. In pursuit of food or when hooked, they leap high and rotate on their long axis. They often swim in packs of 6 to 12.

Sandbar Shark
Carcharhinus plumbeus
418

To 8' (2.4 m). More robust than most sharks in the Requiem Shark Family; brown to grayish brown above, lighter on sides, whitish below; no conspicuous markings on body or fins. Snout relatively short, broadly rounded; teeth weakly serrate, upper teeth broadly triangular; lower teeth erect, slender, symmetrical. First dorsal fin large, origin over axil of pectoral fins; origins of second dorsal and anal fins opposite each other. Ridge of skin on midline of back between dorsal fins.

Habitat
Bottom-dwelling in shallow bays, estuaries, and inshore.

Range
From Massachusetts to Brazil; more common north of Cape
Hatteras; less frequent in Gulf of Mexico.

Comments
The Sandbar Shark feeds on a variety of mollusks, crustaceans,
and fishes and, due to its relatively small size, is not known to
be a threat to people.

Bull Shark ⊗
Carcharhinus leucas
419

To 11' (3.5 m). Spindle-shaped, relatively robust; back
grayish, belly white, tips of fins dusky in young. Snout short,
rounded, length less than width of mouth; teeth strongly
serrate, those in upper jaw broadly triangular, in lower jaw
slender. No spiracle; no ridge between dorsal fins or keel on
caudal peduncle. Pectoral fins large, broad, with pointed tips;
first dorsal fin much larger than second, first dorsal fin origin
in front of axil of pectoral fins.

Habitat
Inshore, never far from land. Ascends rivers for considerable
distances.

Range
In Atlantic from New York to Rio de Janeiro, Brazil,
including Bermuda, Gulf of Mexico, and Antilles; in Pacific
from S. Baja California to Peru.

Comments
Bull Sharks are often caught on hook and line but do not rise
to the surface and leap as do some of the other members of the
family. Several attacks on humans have been reported.

White Shark ⊗
Carcharodon carcharias
420

To 21' (6.4 m). Elongate, spindle-shaped; gray or brown
above, dirty white below. Snout bluntly pointed; teeth
triangular and serrate. Origin of first dorsal fin above rear of
pectorals; anal fin beneath or behind second dorsal fin. Caudal
peduncle has keel; caudal fin crescent-shaped, upper and lower
lobes almost equal.

Habitat
Coastal surface waters.

Range
On Atlantic Coast south from S. Newfoundland to Brazil,
including Gulf of Mexico; on Pacific Coast from Alaska south
to Gulf of California.

Comments
White Sharks bear live young hatched from eggs held inside
the mother's body; the young are about 5' (1.5 m) long at
birth. These savage predators feed on fishes, sea otters, seals,
sea lions, and even crabs. This species is the most dangerous
shark that occurs in North America and has attacked and

killed humans on both the Atlantic and Pacific coasts. It is
occasionally caught by commerical fishermen.

Sand Tiger ⊗
Odontaspis taurus
421

To 10′ (3 m). Elongate; light gray-brown above, becoming
paler on belly; darker spots behind pectoral fins on trunk and
fins. Teeth tricuspid, middle cusp very long and pointed.
Pectoral fins entirely behind fifth gill opening; 2 dorsal fins
without spines, about equal in size, first in front of pelvic fins;
anal fin present; caudal fin low in profile.

Habitat
On or near the bottom in shallow inshore waters.

Range
From Gulf of Maine to S. Brazil and from W. Florida to
Texas. Common north of Cape Hatteras, but relatively rare in
Gulf of Mexico.

Comments
The Sand Tiger has been known to attack people. It is
especially interesting as an example of prebirth cannibalism. A
single embryo develops in each uterus using nutrients it
obtains by consuming yolks and fellow embryos.

Smalltooth Sawfish
Pristis pectinata
422

To 18′ (5.5 m). Moderately flattened and shark-shaped, tail
sector large and not distinct from body; color nearly uniform
mousy gray to blackish above, paler on sides, whitish below.
Snout large, bladelike, with 24 or more teeth on each side.
Pectoral fins not greatly expanded; origin of first dorsal fin
over pelvic fin insertion. 2 dorsal fins about same size and
shape. Caudal fin large and sharklike.

Habitat
Estuaries, lower parts of large rivers, and shallow coastal
waters.

Range
From Chesapeake Bay to Brazil; Gulf of Mexico; rarely north
to New York.

Comments
Used to obtain food, the saw is slashed from side to side
among schooling fishes, stunning or killing them.

**Scalloped
Hammerhead** ⊗
Sphyrna lewini
423

To 13′9″ (4.2 m). Elongate, compressed; head greatly
expanded laterally, with eyes at each end of lateral expansion;
gray above, white below. Front margin of head with median
indentation; corners of mouth in front of line drawn between
rear corners of head. Eye large, separated from nostril by
distance equal to diameter of eye; front of mouth on or near
line drawn between eyes.

Habitat
In oceans near surface, sometimes in estuaries.

Range
From New Jersey south to southern Brazil including Gulf of
Mexico and Caribbean.

Comments
Hammerhead sharks are usually found near the surface where
they feed on fishes and squids. They are known to attack their
own kind as well as people.

Spotted Eagle Ray
Aetobatus narinari
424

To 9' (2.8 m) wide. Disk broader than long; head distinct
from body; tail very long and whiplike; dorsal fin and,
usually, 2 spines at tail base. Upper surface gray, olive-gray,
or chestnut-brown with whitish, yellowish, or bluish spots,
variable in size and shape; lower parts white. Eyes and spiracle
at juncture of back and sides; teeth in both jaws like large, flat
plates, arranged in single series. Pectoral fins taper to acute
point, more or less crescent-shaped. Skin smooth.

Habitat
Coastal surface waters.

Range
From Chesapeake Bay to Brazil; Gulf of Mexico and
Caribbean; abundant in E. Florida and Antilles.

Comments
Spotted Eagle Rays are solitary, and are found in large schools
only when spawning and migrating. They are capable of
sustaining long-distance travel. They are graceful swimmers
and look as if they are flying through the water. When
pursued, they make spectacular leaps into the air.

Southern Stingray ⊗
Dasyatis americana
425

To 5' (1.5 m) wide. Disk roughly rhombic in shape; outer
corners sharply rounded; front edges of disk nearly straight.
Upper surface light brown, gray, or olive, varies depending on
surroundings; lower surface whitish with gray or brownish
margins; ridge and skin fold of tail dark brown. Lacks dorsal
fin; long, whiplike tail with spine near base; skin fold on
underside of tail about as deep as tail diameter; no conspicuous
tubercles on tail.

Habitat
Near shores and in bays.

Range
From New Jersey to Brazil; rare north of Cape Hatteras; Gulf
of Mexico and Caribbean.

Comments
These stingrays lie partly buried in the sand with only the
eyes, spiracle, and tail exposed. Stingrays can inflict serious
wounds with the tail spine.

Clearnose Skate
Raja eglanteria
426

To 3'1" (94 cm). Disk rhombic, flattened, wider than long, angle of snout about 100°, broadly rounded toward rear; light to dark brown above with darker brown or black roundish spots and irregular bars, white below; sides of snout translucent; no eyespots. Thorns on shoulder region near eye and spiracle; single row of thorns along midline of back. Dorsal fins separate, same size and shape. Entire tail thorny; half of total length.

Habitat
Shallow shores.

Range
From Massachusetts to Florida and northern Gulf of Mexico.

Comments
More common inshore during warm months, this skate moves into deeper water in winter.

Oyster Toadfish ⊗
Opsanus tau
427

To 15" (38 cm). Robust, compressed; olive-brown above, belly paler with pale bars or irregular blotches. Head large and flattened; mouth very large, wide, fleshy flaps on upper and lower lips; teeth strong, blunt. Dorsal, anal, and caudal fins dusky, paired fins pale. Pectoral fins broad at base, fanlike, with bars or blotches, insertion behind pelvic fins. Anal fin lacks spines, similar to soft dorsal but shorter; caudal fin rounded. Scaleless.

Habitat
Shallow water over sand or mud, in vegetation or among debris.

Range
From Cape Cod to S. Florida.

Comments
All 3 North American species in this genus have powerful jaws and should be handled with caution. They remain in hiding, awaiting their prey, which includes a variety of crustaceans, annelids, mollusks, and fishes.

Striped Blenny
Chasmodes bosquianus
428

To 3" (7.5 cm). Elongate, compressed; brownish; sides with dark blotches forming wide irregular bands, dark spots sometimes forming horizontal lines; breeding males have blue spot or band on front part of dorsal fin, and orange streak extending toward rear. Snout pointed; maxilla reaches beyond eye; teeth in single row, slender, curved backward. Dorsal fin long, continuous, spines slightly shorter than soft rays, last ray attached to caudal fin by membrane; usually 2 anal fin spines, with fleshy knobs at ends in males.

Habitat
Shallow grass flats over sand.

Range
From New York to NE. Florida, disjunctly to Pensacola,

Florida, and south to Veracruz, Mexico; rarely north of
Maryland.

Comments
The Striped Blenny has an interesting distribution because it
is found on the Atlantic and Gulf coasts but not off peninsular
Florida.

Atlantic Wolffish ⊗
Anarhichas lupus
429

To 5′ (1.5 m). Elongate, greatest depth at nape, tapering to
slender caudal peduncle; color varies with substrate: purplish,
brownish, bluish gray, olive, or combinations of these; 10 or
more irregular bars on sides. Pectoral fin broad at base,
fanlike; no pelvic fins; dorsal fin spines numerous, flexible;
dorsal fin long, continuous, begins at nape and of uniform
height throughout; dorsal and anal fins separate from caudal
fin.

Habitat
Over hard bottoms from near shore to depths of 85 fathoms.

Range
From Greenland and Davis Strait to Cape Cod, occasionally to
New Jersey.

Comments
This solitary species is not abundant anywhere. Its large jaws,
formidable teeth, and habit of attacking objects and people—
in the water or when caught—make it a potentially dangerous
fish. It feeds on a variety of shelled mollusks, echinoderms,
and crustaceans.

Ocean Pout
Macrozoarces americanus
430

To 3′6″ (1.1 m). Elongate, eel-like, depth about one-eighth
length; color variable: pinkish yellow, brownish, reddish
brown, mottled with darker hues above; belly dirty white or
yellowish. Head conical; teeth large, conical; eye small. Pelvic
fins small, not filamentous, insertion in front of pectoral fins,
pectoral fins broad-based, fanlike. Dorsal fin origin at nape,
continuous, about same height throughout, not connected to
caudal fin; anal fin long, low, continuous, connected to caudal
fin. Flesh soft, scales small, slimy.

Habitat
On bottom over sand, mud, rocks, or seaweed from shore to
105 fathoms.

Range
From Gulf of St. Lawrence and SE. Newfoundland to
Delaware.

Comments
Though there is little demand for them as food, the flesh of
Ocean Pouts is reputedly lean and wholesome.

Spotted Moray
Gymnothorax moringa
431

To 3′3″ (99 cm). Robust; moderately compressed; yellow
above, white or yellow elsewhere, with dense, irregular,
brownish to purplish-black spots and small blotches. Area
where head joins nape elevated; rear nostril simple, without
tube. Lacks pectoral fins; front edge of dorsal fin black; rear
edges of dorsal, anal, and caudal fins white.

Habitat
Shallow coral reefs and rocky coasts.

Range
From North Carolina south to Rio de Janeiro, Brazil,
including Gulf of Mexico, Caribbean, West Indies.

Comments
The Spotted Moray is reported to be very common in the
Bahamas but is not often seen due to its secretive nature.

Lined Seahorse
Hippocampus erectus
432

To 5″ (13 cm). Head perpendicular to vertical body; body
portion deep, compressed. Color changes with background;
light brown, dusky, gray, blackish, or brick-red; unmarked
or variously mottled; sometimes speckled with fine white or
golden dots. Dorsal fin fan-shaped; tail prehensile, without
caudal fin.

Habitat
Usually associated with vegetation such as eelgrasses and
sargassum.

Range
From Nova Scotia to Argentina; Bermuda and Gulf of Mexico.

Comments
Seahorses are poor swimmers and depend on their camouflage
both to hide from enemies and conceal themselves from prey.
They blend so well into their background that the casual
observer rarely sees them. They feed by rapid intake of water.
The incubation period in the abdominal pouch is thought to
be about 2 weeks.

Swordfish
Xiphias gladius

To 15′ (4.6 m). Elongate, spindle-shaped, compressed,
greatest depth near first dorsal fin; dark gray or black above;
gray, sometimes yellowish, below. Snout very elongate,
forming flattened beak or sword; no teeth in jaws. Pectoral fin
length about equal to first dorsal fin height. No pelvic fins;
first dorsal fin large, widely separated from second. Single keel
on caudal peduncle. Caudal fin crescent-shaped, lobes very
long. Adults lack scales.

Habitat
Surface near shore and in open seas to depths of at least 33
fathoms.

Range
In Atlantic from Newfoundland south to Argentina. In Pacific
from Oregon south to Chile.

Comments
Swordfishes feed on crustaceans, squids, anchovies, hakes, mackerels, rockfishes, and other fishes. Although the Swordfish is highly prized as a game fish, few are taken by anglers because of the great expense involved in their pursuit. The annual commercial catch off southern California has grown to over 500 tons (453,590 kg). Most of the catch is now taken with gill nets, and a smaller portion with harpoons.

Blue Marlin
Makaira nigricans

To 14'8" (4.5 m). Deep, moderately compressed; deep blue to rich brown above, silvery below, 15 bars formed by pale blue spots on sides; first dorsal fin blue-black, usually without spots, other fins brownish black. Head profile steep; snout elongate, forms spear. Tips of pectoral, first dorsal, and anal fins pointed; pectorals can be folded against body; pelvic fins long, slender, shorter than pectorals; first dorsal fin long, tall toward front, abruptly becoming lower, height less than body depth. Lateral line in netlike pattern; scales dense, embedded, ending in 1–2 long spines.

Habitat
Usually near surface of open seas.

Range
Migratory. In Atlantic from New England to Gulf of Mexico, Caribbean, and Uruguay; uncommon in Gulf of Maine. In Pacific rarely from S. California to Chile.

Comments
The Blue Marlin is highly prized as a large game fish; it is also caught in significant numbers on commercial longlines. Although the record size is reported to be about a ton, most Blue Marlins weigh between 200 and 400 lbs (91 to 181 kg). The females attain much larger sizes than males.

REPTILES AND AMPHIBIANS

The shorelines of the Atlantic Ocean and the Gulf of Mexico provide shelter and food for a wide array of handsome and colorful reptiles, and even a very few amphibians in areas removed from direct exposure to salt water. Several kinds of turtles, both brackish-water and marine, live along these shores, together with lizards, snakes, and toads, and the impressive American Alligator, which roams the margins of brackish marshes. This section describes these and other typical amphibians and reptiles of the coasts.

Snapping Turtle
Chelydra serpentina
433

8–18½" (20–47 cm). The familiar "snapper," with massive head and powerful jaws. Carapace tan to dark brown, often masked with algae or mud, bearing 3 rows of weak to prominent keels, and serrated toward the back. Plastron yellow to tan, unpatterned, relatively small, and cross-shaped in outline. Tail as long as carapace; with saw-toothed keels. Tubercles on neck.

Habitat
Fresh water. Likes soft mud bottoms and abundant vegetation. Also enters brackish waters.

Range
S. Alberta to Nova Scotia, south to the Gulf of Mexico.

Comments
Highly aquatic, the Snapping Turtle likes to rest in warm shallows, often buried in mud, with only its eyes and nostrils exposed. It emerges in April from a winter retreat beneath an overhanging mudbank or vegetative debris. Snappers strike viciously when lifted from water or teased and can inflict a serious bite.

Loggerhead
Caretta caretta
434

31–48" (79–122 cm). Ocean-dwelling, with paddlelike limbs. Carapace elongated and heart-shaped, keeled (3 keels in young), reddish brown; 5 or more scales on sides, first touching plate at nape; 3 plates on part of shell connecting carapace and plastron. Plastron cream-yellow, with 2 ridges (lost with age). 2 pairs of scales between eyes and nostrils. Male's tail extends well beyond shell.

Habitat
Coastal bays, lagoons, estuaries, open seas.

Range
Warm waters of Atlantic and Pacific. In summer, ranges from Gulf waters north to New England (also Newfoundland).

Comments
There are reports of Loggerheads taken in the past weighing 1000 pounds (455 kg), but such giants are gone now. Omnivorous, their diet includes sponges, mollusks, crustaceans, sea urchins, and marine plants.

Diamondback Terrapin
Malaclemys terrapin
435

Males, 4–5½" (10.2–13.8 cm); females, 6–9⅜" (15.2–23.8 cm). Carapace keeled; light brown or gray to black; bear deep growth rings, giving sculpted appearance. Plastron oblong; yellowish or greenish, with dark flecks or blotches; not hinged. Head and neck gray, peppered with black. Eyes black and prominent; jaws light-colored.

Habitat
Salt-marsh estuaries, tidal flats, and lagoons.

Range
Cape Cod to Texas along Atlantic and Gulf coasts.

Comments
Diamondback meat was highly esteemed as a delicacy at the turn of the century and the numbers of these turtles were greatly reduced. Despite destruction of coastal marshes, recent protective legislation has restored some populations.

Gulf Coast Toad
Bufo valliceps
436

2–5⅛" (5–13.0 cm). Medium-sized, with light-bordered dark band along side. Brown to black, with orange highlights and white spots. Usually a light stripe down middle of back. Bony ridges on head prominent, creating a depression between them on top of the skull. Ridges connected to triangular parotoid glands. Male has yellow-green throat.

Voice
A short trill, repeated often.

Habitat
Various humid locations, from roadside ditches to the barrier beaches of the Gulf of Mexico.

Range
Gulf Coast from S. Mississippi, west through E. Texas and south into Mexico. Also, a small section of south-central Arkansas.

Comments
Active at twilight, this toad is common in gardens. It is frequently seen catching insects under streetlights. It even turns up in city storm sewers.

Fowler's Toad
Bufo woodhousei fowleri
437

2½–5" (6–12.7 cm). Large toad with back blotched, chest unspotted. Prominent bony ridges on head contact elongate parotoid glands. Yellow to green to brown.

Voice
Like the bleat of a sheep with a cold.

Habitat
Sandy areas near marshes, irrigation ditches, backyards, and temporary rain pools.

Range
Lake Michigan east through most of Pennsylvania to SE. New York and southern New England, south to the Gulf Coast (excluding coastal South Carolina, Georgia, and most of Florida), west to E. Texas and north to Missouri and S. Illinois.

Comments
Fowler's is a subspecies of Woodhouse's Toad, which is widespread throughout most of the United States. Primarily nocturnal, this is the toad commonly seen at night catching insects beneath lights. Occasionally it is active during the day, but more frequently remains in its burrow or hides in vegetation.

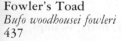

American Crocodile
Crocodylus acutus
438

7–15′ (2.1–4.6 m). Long slender snout distinguishes it from American Alligator. Gray-green, dark olive-green, or gray-brown with dark crossbands on back and tail; crossbands obscure in old adults. Large fourth tooth on bottom jaw. No curved bony ridge in front of eyes.

Habitat
Florida Bay in Everglades National Park, Biscayne Bay, and Florida Keys; bogs and mangrove swamps.

Range
Extreme coastal S. Florida and the Keys.

Comments
The American Crocodile may have reached 23′ (7 m) in South America. The Florida population, fewer than 500 in number, was declared endangered in 1975. Poaching and construction of highways, beachfront homes, and mobile home parks have reduced their numbers.

American Alligator
Alligator mississippiensis
439

6′–19′2″ (1.8–5.84 m). Largest reptile in North America. Distinguished from American Crocodile by broad and rounded snout. Generally black with yellowish or cream crossbands that become less apparent with age. Large fourth tooth on bottom jaw fits into a socket in upper jaw, is not visible when mouth is closed. No curved bony ridge in front of eyes.

Voice
During the breeding season adults produce a throaty, bellowing roar heard over considerable distance. Young give a high-pitched call: *y-eonk, y-eonk, y-eonk.*

Habitat
Fresh and brackish marshes, ponds, lakes, rivers, swamps, bayous, and big spring runs.

Range
Coastal SE. North Carolina to the Florida Keys and west along the coastal plain to S. Texas; north to extreme SE. Oklahoma and S. Arkansas.

Comments
Alligators are important to the ecology of their habitat. During droughts they dig deep holes, or "dens," which provide water for wildlife. They hibernate in the winter. Much reduced in numbers, under state and federal protection they are beginning to make a comeback in some areas.

Green Anole
Anolis carolinensis
440

5–8″ (12.7–20.3 cm). A slender lizard with extensible pink throatfan, large toe pads. Snout long, wedge-shaped. No back crest. Usually green, but in seconds can change to brown or intermediate colors. Tail round.

Habitat
Arboreal. Encountered on vertical surfaces like fence posts and walls; but favors tree trunks, shrubs, grasses, palm fronds.

Range
S. Virginia to the Florida Keys, west to central Texas and
Oklahoma.

Comments
Diurnal. Basking anoles are typically brown; fighting males
turn green with a black patch behind the eyes. They slowly
stalk their prey: flies, beetles, moths, spiders, crabs.

Mole Skink
Eumeces egregius
441

3½–6½" (8.9–16.5 cm). Relatively long-bodied brownish
skink with 4 light stripes on head and body. Upper 2 stripes
confined to second scale rows counting from middle of back.
Legs tiny; 5 toes. Ear opening partly closed. 3 scales above
eyes. Tail orange, red, pink, or blue. Breeding male has
reddish chin and belly.

Habitat
Sandy soils of coastal dunes; inland sandhill scrub and turkey-
oak. Also, under rocks and tidal wrack on beaches.

Range
Coastal plain of Georgia, Alabama, Florida, and Keys.

Comments
Diurnal. Adapted for tunneling and digging, as its name
implies, this species successfully preys on burrowing or
secretive insects, spiders, and small crustaceans. A number of
subspecies occur in its range.

Cottonmouth ⊗
Agkistrodon pisicivorus
442

20–74½" (50.8–189.2 cm). A dark, heavy-bodied water
snake; broad-based head is noticeably wider than neck. Olive,
brown, or black above; patternless or with serrated-edged dark
crossbands. Wide, light-bordered, dark brown cheek stripe
distinct, obscure, or absent. Head flat-topped; eyes with
vertical pupils (not visible from directly above as are eyes of
harmless water snakes); heat-sensitive facial pit (for locating
prey) between eye and nostril. Young strongly patterned and
bear bright, yellow-tipped tails. Scales keeled.

Habitat
Lowland swamps, lakes, rivers, bayheads, sloughs, irrigation
ditches, canals, rice fields, to small clear rocky mountain
streams; sea level to about 1500' (450 m).

Range
SE. Virginia south to upper Florida Keys, west to S. Illinois,
S. Missouri, south-central Oklahoma, and central Texas.
Isolated population in north-central Missouri.

Comments
Do not disturb or attempt to handle! Its bite is far more
serious than that of the Copperhead and can be fatal. When
annoyed, the Cottonmouth tends to stand its ground, opening
its mouth to expose the light "cotton" lining. Unlike other
water snakes, it swims with its head out of water.

Southern Water Snake
Nerodia fasciata
443

16–62½" (40.6–158.8 cm). Stout-bodied aquatic snake with dark crossbands over most of body, light stripes on back and at juncture of back and sides, or essentially patternless. Color and pattern highly variable; dark stripe from eye to angle of mouth and large squarish blotches or wormlike markings on belly scales. Some darken with age, obscuring pattern. Scales keeled. Scale in front of anus divided.

Habitat
Freshwater and saltwater situations; permanent lakes, ponds, cypress and mangrove swamps, marshes, and sluggish streams; sea level to about 1000' (300 m).

Range
Coastal plain, North Carolina to Florida Keys, west to E. Texas; north in Mississippi River Valley to extreme S. Illinois.

Comments
This snake is fond of sunning, but is active mostly at night after heavy rains when frogs are moving about. In cool weather it is often found under vegetative debris. Commonly mistaken for the venomous Cottonmouth, it defends itself vigorously when disturbed. It feeds on frogs, tadpoles, and fish. A number of subspecies occur.

Eastern Hognose Snake
Heterodon platyrhinos
444

20–45½" (50.8–115.6 cm). A stout-bodied snake with pointed, slightly upturned snout and wide neck. Color extremely variable; yellow, tan, brown, gray, or reddish with squarish dark blotches on back interspaced with round dark blotches at juncture of back and sides. All-black individuals common in some areas. Belly mottled; underside of tail conspicuously lighter than belly color. Scales keeled. Scale in front of anus divided.

Habitat
Prefers open sandy-soiled areas; thinly wooded upland hillsides, cultivated fields, woodland meadows. Sea level to 2500' (750 m).

Range
East-central Minnesota to extreme S. New Hampshire south to S. Florida, west to E. Texas and W. Kansas.

Comments
The Eastern Hognose Snake is commonly called puff, or spreading adder or blow viper. It is active in the daytime, and burrows deep into loose earth during cold winter months. When disturbed, it "hoods" its neck, inflates its body, hisses loudly, and strikes. If this fails to discourage a would-be predator, it rolls over and plays dead with mouth agape and tongue hanging out. It becomes limp and will remain "dead" when picked up; however, it will roll over again if placed right-side up. In captivity it loses willingness to display such behavior. Enlarged teeth on the rear upper jaw are believed to inject mild venom into toads and frogs, upon which it feeds. It rarely bites people.

PLANTS

Although many plants cannot tolerate the salty air and soils of North America's coastlines, several hardy species of trees, wildflowers, and grasses manage to thrive along the ocean's edge. American Beach Grass is a familiar sight along sand dunes, while salt marshes and bays support populations of various salt-tolerant grasses and rushes. Along portions of the Gulf of Mexico and the shores of southern Florida, the land is being extended seaward by the incursions of three different kinds of mangrove. And on the hard bottoms and intertidal regions of rocky coasts are found a wide variety of marine algae —more commonly known as seaweeds. This section describes many of the most common species of plants found along the Atlantic and Gulf coasts.

White Mangrove
Laguncularia racemosa
445

Tree with shiny, leathery leaves and reddish-brown stems.
Height: 20–40' (6–12 m).
Leaves: 1½–2½" (3.8–6 cm) long; oval, dark green, leathery.
Bark: brown, flaky.
Flowers: near-white; produced most of the year.

Habitat
Landward fringe of mangrove swamps.

Range
S. Florida.

Comments
White Mangroves are able to grow only after pioneering Red
Mangroves and Black Mangroves have established themselves.
Thus they are found well back in a mangrove swamp, forming
a third zone behind the other 2 species. These trees have no
prop roots and no, or only a few small, aerial roots because
they live on elevated ground above the high-tide mark.

Black Mangrove
Avicennia germinans
446

A massive coastal tree with leathery, yellow-green leaves and
fragrant white flowers. Numerous upright breathing roots
surround the plant, projecting into the air from the mud.
Height: 10–40' (3–12 cm).
Leaves: 2–4" (5–10 cm) long; evergreen; coated with fine
grayish hairs.
Bark: dark brown, scaly.
Flowers: rounded or notched, white; crowded in upright
clusters branched on 4-angled stalks at ends of twigs; nearly
year-round.

Habitat
Silt seashores; in salt and brackish water; mangrove swamp
forest along coast and islands.

Range
North-central Florida to the Keys, west to S. Louisiana and S.
Texas.

Comments
There are several different groups of plants known as
mangroves. Black Mangrove is the hardiest of the 3 species
forming the mangrove swamps of southern Florida; it
penetrates farthest north along the Gulf Coast, where it
becomes smaller and shrubby and is killed in cold winters.
Though not closely related to the pioneering Red Mangrove,
Black Mangrove grows in the same localities, but in a zone
closer to the original shoreline, appearing after the Red
Mangrove has established itself. As the Red Mangrove
advances seaward, the Black Mangrove replaces it.

Red Mangrove
Rhizophora mangle
447

A small tree with spreading branches and high, branching,
arched and stiltlike prop roots that enter the water.
Height: 15–20' (4.5–6 m).
Leaves: evergreen; elliptical, leathery; black dots below.

Flowers: light yellow in clusters of 2–3.
Fruit: long, spearlike seedlings that hang down, then fall into mud or water.

Habitat
Shallow bays and coastal waters.

Range
Primarily SW. Florida; also numerous islets along Gulf side of Keys, from Key West north to Ten Thousand Islands.

Comments
The Red Mangrove is the pioneer species of this diversified and often unrelated group of treelike plants collectively known as mangroves. The first to establish itself in a mangrove swamp, this tree is always the one farthest out in the water, followed by the Black Mangrove and then the White Mangrove. It is the only one of the three to have prop roots. Its dangling seedlings germinate while on the parent tree and are ready to root once they drop into the soft swamp bottom.

Salt Marsh Aster
Aster tenuifolius
448

A perennial with curved, slightly zigzag, widely spreading branches that create a weak, straggly appearance.
Height: to 2½' (70 cm).
Leaves: long, narrow, alternate; upper leaves reduced in size.
Flowers: white or pale lavender; late August–October.

Habitat
Brackish-water and salt marshes, especially depressions.

Range
Massachusetts to Florida, west along Gulf Coast to Mississippi.

Comments
The Salt Marsh Aster has a wide range, but is never a major member of the salt marsh plant community. It occurs within regions dominated by Saltmarsh Cordgrass (*Spartina alterniflora*) and becomes conspicuous only when it blooms in late summer and early fall.

Sea Rocket
Cakile edentula
449

A low, prostrate, branched annual plant with succulent stems and leaves.
Height: 6–20" (15–50 cm).
Flowers: pale blue or lavender; July–September.
Fruit: fleshy green seed pods developing into rocket-shaped capsules.

Habitat
On sandy beaches between wrack line and primary dune.

Range
S. Labrador to Florida.

Comments
Sea Rocket is one of the few plants sufficiently salt-tolerant to

live on open beaches unprotected by barrier dunes. Its fleshy stems and leaves enable it to retain water under saline conditions lethal to most dune plants and other vegetation.

Beach Rose
Rosa rugosa
450

A dense, shrublike plant with very spiny, hairy stems.
Height: 3–6' (1–2 m).
Leaves: leaflets, 5–9 per leafstalk; curving backward, appearing wrinkled; margins toothed. Dark green.
Flowers: purplish-rose to white; June–September.
Fruit: smooth, bright red hip.

Habitat
Coastal thickets; depressions among secondary dunes.

Range
Quebec to New Jersey.

Comments
A native of eastern Asia, the Beach Rose is an important stabilizer of dunes.

Sea Lavender
Limonium carolinianum
451

A slender stem arises from the center of a basal rosette of spoon-shaped leaves.
Height: 1–2' (30–60 cm).
Flowers: small, lavender-pink, appearing along one side of each lateral branching stem; July–October.

Habitat
Coastal salt marshes.

Range
Newfoundland and Quebec to Florida, west along Gulf Coast to Mississippi and Texas.

Comments
Dense colonies of these small, shrubby perennial herbs delicately color coastal salt marshes in late summer and early fall. Like other marsh plants, Sea Lavender is tolerant of highly saline conditions and is able to retain water in its fleshy basal leaves and taproot.

Beach Pea
Lathyrus maritimus
452

A vinelike perennial with curling tendrils at the leaf tips.
Height: creeper; stems 2–3' (60–90 cm) long.
Leaves: composed of 3–6 pairs of leaflets.
Flowers: violet to purple; June–August.
Fruit: brown seed pods.

Habitat
Sea beaches and sand dunes.

Range
Along northeastern Atlantic Coast, south to New Jersey.

Comments
This legume provides food for insects, birds, and small

mammals of coastal dune areas. The plant tends to sprawl on the sand, with some of its stems and leaves rising erect, often supported as the tendrils wind around adjacent dune grasses.

Bayberry
Myrica pensylvanica
453

Woody shrub with fragrant, dark green leaves and waxy berries.
Height: 1½–6′ (0.5–2 m).
Leaves: to 4″ (10 cm) long; slightly toothed near tip.
Fruit: round, grayish-white, wax-covered berry, ⅛–¼″ (3–4 mm) in diameter, growing in clusters from stem below the leaves.

Habitat
Secondary coastal sand dunes.

Range
Maritime Provinces to Louisiana on the Gulf Coast.

Comments
The closely related Wax Myrtle (*Myrica cerifera*) occurs from New Jersey to Florida and along the Gulf Coast to Texas. It is a much larger plant, reaching a tree-size height of up to 30 feet (10 m). Distinguishing between *M. cerifera* and *M. pensylvanica* in regions where they both are found may be difficult, since they hybridize readily. The thick wax that coats the fruits of these plants is used to make candles, but large quantities of berries are needed to produce even one candle.

Beach Plum
Prunus maritima
454

A straggling, sometimes treelike, fruiting shrub; branches are brown with tan dots.
Height: to 6′ (2 m); occasionally to 13′ (4 m).
Leaves: alternate; elliptical, finely toothed; to 2¾″ (7 cm) long.
Flowers: snowy white, becoming pinkish before dropping; early June.
Fruit: ½″ (15 mm) in diameter; ranges in color from dark red to bluish purple; maturing September–October.

Habitat
Secondary coastal sand dunes.

Range
New Brunswick to New Jersey.

Comments
Dense stands of this shrub may be found between sand hills in secondary dunes behind a beach. In early summer, the dunes are bright with multitudes of Beach Plum blossoms, their flowers forming clusters toward the tips of the stems. In late summer and early fall, the fruit is eaten by birds and small mammals; the plums may be eaten fresh or cooked, and are often used to make preserves.

Beach Heather
Hudsonia tomentosa
455

A shrubby plant, bushy and much branched, often forming dense mats that trap sand.
Height: usually less than 1' (30 cm).
Leaves: scalelike; small, downy, pressed close to the stem.
Flowers: abundant, very small, yellow, in ovoid clusters; opening wide in the sun and lasting only 1 day; May–July.

Habitat
Beaches and coastal sand dunes.

Range
New Brunswick to North Carolina.

Comments
Where Beach Heather grows in profusion, its ability to trap sand is evident: small hillocks develop around and within each cluster of plants, elevating their stems. In flowering season, this plant's yellow blossoms brighten the entire dune area.

Prickly Pear Cactus
Opuntia compressa
456

Prickly Pears sprawl upon the sand in thick mats consisting of flattened, oval, fleshy pads that are modified stems. Essentially spineless, but may have 1 or 2 spines, and minute, detachable brownish bristles.
Flowers: 2–3″ (5–8 cm) wide; bright yellow.
Fruit: 1¼–2″ (3–5 cm) long, reddish or purple.

Habitat
Secondary coastal sand dunes.

Range
Massachusetts to Georgia; also Alabama on the Gulf Coast.

Comments
The Prickly Pear Cactus, like other water-conserving cacti, has lost normal leaf structure through evolutionary adaptation to a hot, desiccating environment. Most types of leaves have stomates, or pores, through which water is evaporated. The leaves of cacti remain in the form of protective spines, although this coastal species has almost completely lost them as well. Its brownish bristles may cause skin irritation if the pads are handled.

Seaside Goldenrod
Solidago sempervirens
457

A towering perennial with lance-shaped, fleshy leaves.
Height: 2–8' (0.6–2.4 m).
Leaves: 4–15″ (10–40 cm) long.
Flowers: bright yellow, in sprays along much of the stem, most profusely on the upper half; June–December, depending on latitude.

Habitat
Leeside of primary and secondary coastal dunes, and on fringes of salt marshes.

Range
The Gulf of St. Lawrence to Florida, west along Gulf Coast to Texas.

Comments
This plant is tolerant of saline conditions and, because of its
fibrous roots, is an effective dune stabilizer. When in flower,
the blossoms of Seaside Goldenrod are visited by a wide variety
of insects.

Dusty Miller
Artemisia stelleriana
458

A pale green, introduced perennial plant with tall clusters of
yellow flowers.
Height: over 2' (60 cm).
Leaves: densely covered on both sides with fine, white woolly
hairs.
Flowers: in tall clusters, yellow; July–September.

Habitat
Sandy beaches and coastal dunes.

Range
Quebec to Virginia.

Comments
Dusty Miller, originally an inhabitant of the Japanese
archipelago and Kamchatka, is now well established along the
Atlantic Coast, where it is a common, solitary plant on
secondary dunes. This plant survives the heat and effects of
salt spray partly through its woolly leaves: the dense coating of
white hairs not only reflects sunlight, but also provides good
insulation.

Sand Bur
Cenchrus tribuloides
459

A sprawling, branching annual grass with long narrow leaves
and spiny burs.
Height: 1–1½' (30–45 cm).
Leaves: long, narrow.
Flowers: on spikes; one or several single purple or yellow spiny
burs borne at the tips of shoots; June–October.

Habitat
Coastal sands; land side of barrier dunes and across secondary
dunes.

Range
S. New York to Florida, and westward to Louisiana.

Comments
The burs on this plant have tiny, backward-pointing spines
that resist removal from clothing and skin. Not only do the
painfully sharp spines on Sand Bur protect the plant against
disturbance, but also they provide an effective mechanism for
seed dispersal to other areas. Seeds are produced by
midsummer and at first are green, turning to tan or purple.
Sand Bur is a useful stabilizer of dunes.

Saltmarsh Bulrush
Scirpus robustus
460

A sturdy, tall perennial grass that grows from a stout rhizome.
In cross section the stem is triangular and prominently bears a
number of long, sharp leaves.

Height: to 6' (2 m).
Flowers: spikelets of many small flower clusters growing
either close to the stem or held out on very short
peduncles.
Leaves: prominent, long, slender but robust, remaining
attached throughout the growing season.
Fruit: shiny, brown-black seeds developing in dense clusters of
seed heads; each seed protected by thin, brown scales. Seeds
develop in late summer, growing from the juncture between
leaves and stem.

Habitat
Primarily intertidal regions of brackish-water and salt
marshes.

Range
From Nova Scotia to Florida, west along the Gulf Coast
to Texas.

Comments
Because of its 3-sided stem, Saltmarsh Bulrush is sometimes
called Threesquare; however, other grass species with this
name have fewer leaves that usually disappear as the plants
grow. The small, lustrous dark seeds are a favorite food of
waterfowl.

Spike Grass
Distichlis spicata
461

A short, wiry grass found in the higher elevations of a salt
marsh, often in dense stands.
Height: 1–2' (30–60 cm).
Leaves: 1–5" (1½–11 cm) long; opposite, on a slender
stem.
Flowers: thick, compact cluster; pale green; August–early
autumn.

Habitat
Salt marshes.

Range
From Prince Edward Island south to Florida, west along the
Gulf Coast to Texas.

Comments
Spike Grass tolerates wet, saline regions of a salt marsh better
than Saltmeadow Cordgrass (*Spartina patens*). It often grows
along the margins of evaporation basins, where salt content is
especially high.

Sea Oats
Uniola paniculata
462

A tall, erect grass that has a crowded, robust flower and
seed head.
Height: 3–6' (1–2 m).
Leaves: 8–16" (20–40 cm) long, about ¼" (0.6 cm) wide;
slender, narrowing into pointed tips.
Flowers: crowded; seed heads becoming straw-colored in late
summer.

Habitat
Mostly primary dunes.

Range
S. Virginia to Florida, west along Gulf Coast to Texas.

Comments
Tolerant of strong winds, sand abrasion, and salt spray from the ocean, Sea Oats is one of the most important stabilizers of primary dunes along the Gulf Coast. Its large seed heads are more prominent than those of American Beach Grass, or Marram Grass (*Ammophila breviligulata*), but like that species, Sea Oats colonizes dunes more by subsurface rhizomes than by germinating seeds.

Short Dune Grass
Panicum amarum
463

A grass with very elongated, light blue-green leaves. Seed head is slender, bearing many small ellipsoid seeds supported on short branches.
Height: up to 2'.

Habitat
Back side of primary dune and on secondary dunes and sand flats, where it may grow in abundance.

Range
Connecticut to Florida, then west along the Gulf Coast to Louisiana.

Comments
Short Dune Grass is not as effective as other dune grasses in binding sand. As a result, it becomes buried or uprooted when sand movement is extensive.

Saltmeadow Cordgrass
Spartina patens
464

A tousled-looking, wiry grass, growing amid flattened mats of previous years' growth. Wind causes stems to twist around one another, creating swirling depressions and crests in broad expanses.
Height: 12–40" (0.3–1 m).
Leaves: slender, with edges rolled together, appearing cylindrical.
Flowers: minute, brownish; attached along one side of stem.
Fruit: tiny, brownish.

Habitat
Salt marshes and wet beaches.

Range
Quebec along East Coast to central Florida; on Gulf Coast west from central Florida to Texas.

Comments
The smallest and most delicate of the cordgrasses, Saltmeadow Cordgrass is an important soil-binder. A wide variety of native and visiting animals eat its fruits, leaves, stems, and rhizomes. Big Cordgrass (*Spartina cynosuroides*), the largest and coarsest species, develops massive flower clusters that may reach more

than 6 feet (2m) above the marsh bed, but seldom grows in dense stands like the other 2 species.

American Beach Grass
Ammophila breviligulata
465

A tall, erect, stiff perennial grass arising from long subsurface rhizomes. A leaf cluster surrounds an elongated flowering spike, unlike other beach grasses.
Height: 2–4′ (60–120 cm).
Leaves: long, narrow.
Flowers: on cylindrical spikes; July–September.

Habitat
Back beaches and sand dunes.

Range
Newfoundland to North Carolina.

Comments
American Beach Grass, the most common dune plant along much of the Atlantic Coast, is important as a dune stabilizer, for it can withstand burial within a shifting dune by sending up vertical rhizomes that produce new emerging stems. This plant's rhizome mat is both horizontal and vertical, and its roots over 20′ deep beneath the sand, thus serving to knit a dune together.

Saltmarsh Cordgrass
Spartina alterniflora
466

The dominant salt marsh plant.
Height: to 8′ (2.5 m) along marsh creeks; 1–2′ (0.3–0.6 m) to rear of marshes along upper tidal limits.
Leaves: flat, smooth, tough; to 2′ (0.6 m) long, with alternating spikelets.
Flowers: minute greenish-white blossoms in clusters on flowering head; August. Cluster turns tannish as fruit develops.

Habitat
Salt marshes, especially along borders of creeks.

Range
Quebec along East Coast to central Florida; on Gulf Coast west from central Florida to Texas.

Comments
The wettest of the cordgrasses, Saltmarsh Cordgrass varies greatly in height according to the zone of the salt marsh in which it lives. The short form growing at upper tidal levels seldom flowers. Propagation for both forms occurs primarily through spreading rhizomes, which penetrate marsh mud and bind it together. This species is always larger and coarser than the closely related Saltmeadow Cordgrass (*Spartina patens*).

Eelgrass
Zostera marina
467

This grasslike marine herb is a seed plant, its leaves streaming with the current.
Height: to 4′ (1.2 m).
Leaves: tapelike.

Flowers: at leaf bases; small, green, sheathed. Inconspicuous male flowers are reduced to a single slender stamen; female flowers consist of 1 ovary containing a single ovule; June–September.
Fruit: oval, oblong.

Habitat
Shallow bays and coves, tidal creeks, estuaries.

Range
Greenland to Florida.

Comments
Neither a seaweed nor an alga, Eelgrass is a true seed plant that has evolved an ability to live in saline waters. Currents distribute both pollen and the small fruit; propagation also occurs by means of rhizomes underneath the mud or sand. Unlike marine algae, it offers no resistance to attaching organisms, so the outer half of each blade usually is coated with a wide variety of very small marine plants and animals. Eelgrass beds are havens for scallops, crabs, and many fishes.

Turtle Grass
Thalassia testudinum
468

Broad, straplike leaves grow in dense clusters from a horizontal rhizome lying under the bottom, often forming great underwater "meadows."
Blades: about 1' tall or less.

Habitat
Shallow water, from low-tide level to about 30', on sandy and sand-mud bottoms. Grows best in sea water that is only slightly brackish.

Range
Florida Keys, and shallow bays and lagoons along the Gulf Coast.

Comments
Turtle Grass grows outside the range of Eelgrass, so it cannot be confused with this similar, more slender marine species. Like Eelgrass it supports a dense population of epibiota attached to its broad leaves. Vast underwater fields of Turtle Grass provide nourishment for a wide variety of marine animals.

Glassworts
Salicornia spp.
469, 470

Mats consisting of perennial, prostrate woody main stems, from which single, erect, translucent jade-green stems grow. Plants turn yellow, brown, or bright red in autumn.
Height: to 12" (30 cm).
Leaves: flat leaves lacking; stems terminate in a spike.
Flowers: minute, inconspicuous; each recessed into a separate pit; August–October.

Habitat
Salt marshes.

Range
Massachusetts to Florida, west along Gulf Coast to Texas.

Comments
The thick, succulent stems of Woody Glasswort (*Salicornia virginica*) and its close relatives, Jointed Glasswort (*S. europaea*) and Dwarf Glasswort (*S. bigelovii*), retain large quantities of water within their tissues, which is necessary for metabolism in a saline habitat. Glassworts are capable of growing under conditions where other salt marsh plants fail to survive.

Channeled Rockweed
Pelvetia spp.
471

An olive-green to brown fucoid rockweed growing in dense tufts.
Length: 2–6".
Fronds: channeled.

Habitat
Rocky shores.

Range
North Atlantic and Britain; unconfirmed reports of spotty growth on northernmost portion of our Atlantic Coast.

Comments
This rockweed is easily confused with *Fucus* species growing on the North American Atlantic Coast, where isolated populations have occasionally been reported but not confirmed. Like other rockweeds, *Pelvetia* lies flat on rocks when the tide is low and becomes dark with exposure to air. Unlike Knotted Rockweed it has no swollen bladders, and unlike *Fucus* it has no midrib. *Pelvetia* can grow up into the splash zone, above the high-tide mark, but plants that do so are dwarfed. In northern Scotland this rockweed is eaten by sheep and cattle.

Knotted Rockweed
Ascophyllum nodosum
472

An olive-green rockweed with smooth, flattened fronds.
Length: usually 3–4', occasionally longer.
Fronds: branch dichotomously several times along length of stem; every few inches 1 frond enlarges to form an air bladder.
Reproduction: small notches, 1–2" (2.5–5 cm) apart along edges of fronds, give rise to stalked, club-shaped receptacles, fertile branches bearing reproductive organs.

Habitat
Mid-tidal zone of rocky shores.

Range
Maritime Provinces to N. New Jersey.

Comments
At low tide, Knotted Rockweed drapes downward over exposed rocks in protected waters in smooth array, usually crowding out the smaller, slower-growing *Fucus* rockweeds. Underwater, buoyed by its air-filled vesicles (cavities), this plant stands erect in dense colonies, swaying in the wave surge.

Bladder Rockweed
Fucus vesiculosus
473

A highly variable, extremely common intertidal seaweed species with small, pea-sized air bladders—often paired—on the flattened, leafy parts of fronds.
Height: 1–4′.
Fronds: branch dichotomously; clearly defined midrib; olive-green.
Reproduction: receptacles containing reproductive organs at tips of fronds; generally ovoid or pointed; swelling when ripe and changing color from olive-green to yellowish (female) or orange (male).

Habitat
Mid-tidal zone of rocky shores.

Range
Maritime Provinces to North Carolina.

Comments
Bladder Rockweed is extremely common and prevails over Knotted Rockweed where wave action is too powerful for the larger plant. Its form varies according to habitat conditions: its growth in sheltered waters differs from that in heavy wave surge, and estuarine forms differ from those of normal ocean salinity.

Sea Lettuce
Ulva lactuca
474

A bright green, wrinkled frond that is broad and flat and attached to a solid substrate.
Length: 1′ (30 cm) or more.
Fronds: walls are 2 cells thick.

Habitat
In clear water of lower intertidal zone and just below where there are jetties, buoys, pilings, and other solid objects to which plants can adhere.

Range
Most shores covered in this book.

Comments
Sea Lettuce lives lower in the intertidal zone and is more conspicuous than its relative Green Thread Alga (*Enteromorpha*). It may even be found growing in sandy beach areas anchored to a pebble, shell, or living mole crab.

Green Thread Alga
Enteromorpha spp.
475

A bright green, filamentous alga that often grows in dense, tangled masses and is extremely variable in form.
Length: up to 2′.
Fronds: tubular, 1 cell thick, ¼–¾″ (6–20 mm) in diameter; sometimes buoyed to surface by gas bubbles trapped within and not attached to substrate.

Habitat
Cosmopolitan; extensive in upper intertidal rock pools and in salt marshes; beaches, attached to shells; on jetties and buoys; on mangrove prop roots and intertidal coral masses.

Range
All shores covered in this book.

Comments
An upper intertidal rock pool may become brilliant green with this tolerant, very common alga. *Enteromorpha* withstands increasing salt content, resulting from evaporation, as well as lessened salinity from collected rainfall. When it dies, it quickly turns white; dried, its delicate structure crumbles and disintegrates.

Purple Laver
Porphyra umbilicalis
476

A silky, purplish-red plant that is broad and thin, growing singly or in dense clusters, anchored to a hard surface. Diameter: 6".

Habitat
Lower intertidal zone and below on rocks, jetties, pilings, and hard surfaces.

Range
Northward from South Carolina.

Comments
In some parts of the world this seaweed is valued as an edible and is cultivated for that purpose. It often flourishes best during the cold months in southerly regions.

Irish Moss
Chondrus crispus
477

A leathery, tough, purplish-red alga of variable form and color (may be purplish green or yellowish), generally growing in clusters of 10–20 fronds from a disklike holdfast on a rock surface.
Height: about 2".
Fronds: usually widening into a flat, repeatedly branching fanlike structure, sometimes becoming greenish in strong sunlight. Male plant has pinkish or whitish patches.

Habitat
Lower intertidal zone of rocky shores, continuing into subtidal levels.

Range
Maritime Provinces to New Jersey.

Comments
Irish Moss, also known as Carragheen, has long been an ingredient used in medicines, flavored drinks, and jellies, and a stabilizer in salad dressings and numerous other products.

Coralline Alga
Corallina officinalis
478, 479

A branched, tufted plant, varying in color from yellowish to rose-red to purple. Calcareous segments along stem nearly cylindrical, becoming flattened and wedge-shaped toward the tips. Branching most abundant toward end of each tuft, creating a fanlike effect.
Height: to 5".

Habitat
Lower intertidal zone along rocky shores on sloping rock faces; also in tide pools.

Range
Maritime Provinces to Long Island.

Comments
Although this plant can withstand strong wave action, it does not tolerate the drying effects of air and so is restricted to the lower intertidal zone. Plants at the uppermost levels of this zone are dwarfed. Clusters of Coralline Alga feel stiff and gritty when they are pinched. Their tufted branches provide an excellent habitat for a variety of small invertebrate animals.

Encrusting Stony Red Alga
Lithothamnium spp.
480

An attractive, red-violet calcareous growth that follows the contours of rocks or shells it grows upon. Its margin may be light-colored and slightly lobed. Depending upon species, the surface of the alga may be smooth or warty. Size is highly variable; thickness, to several millimeters.

Habitat
Grows best in shaded crevices or on seaweed-covered rocks; also on shells of hermit crabs and large snails living in protected regions of a rocky shore.

Range
Common on Atlantic and Gulf coasts.

Comments
These plants are easily overlooked because they appear to be a rock coloration or a mineral coating rather than living organisms.

INSECTS AND SPIDERS

Among the most numerous animals on earth, insects and spiders are also fascinating. Some have carved out a niche for themselves as tiny predators in an immense landscape; others have developed complex social systems of communal life. The coastal areas serve as breeding grounds for many species, such as the American Horse Fly, whose larvae live in or near the water; other insects, such as the Eastern Sand Wasp, spend most of their adult lives in sand. Included here are descriptions of the most common and typical insects found on North America's eastern shores.

Bearded Robber Fly
Efferia pogonias
481

½–¾" (13–19 mm). Humpbacked. Head and thorax sandy to dark brown, with white or yellow beardlike bristles. Male's abdomen steel-gray with last segments silvery; female's lighter gray with 2 black spots in middle. Legs spiny, silvery gray with orange and black tibiae. Wings clear to smoky.

Habitat
Pastures, open fields, and dunes.

Range
Southern United States east of the Rocky Mountains.

Life Cycle
Eggs are laid on soil, into which larvae burrow in search of prey. They overwinter underground and pupate in spring. Adults fly August–September.

Comments
The Bearded Robber Fly often overtakes horse flies or deer flies in flight, whirring at high speed. It captures them and sucks them dry while standing on a leaf or twig.

Eastern Sand Wasp
Bembix americana spinolae
482

½–⅝" (13–16 mm). Short "waist" between thorax and abdomen. Head, thorax, and most of abdomen black. Abdomen has greenish-yellow bands interrupted by black along midline. Short white hair on sides of thorax and over back. Femora black, most of tibiae and all outermost leg segments are pale greenish or yellow. Wings are clear with pale brownish veins.

Habitat
Sandy meadows, lakeshores, beaches, and dunes.

Range
Throughout North America, except the Pacific Coast.

Life Cycle
Female digs sloping burrows with terminal cells below the ground surface. Female then catches fly, paralyzes it with stinger, and transports it to cell. Female lays 1 egg, then closes burrow with a sand door. Wasp later brings further flies to larva, provisioning it for about 5 days, opening and reclosing door each time. When full grown, larva spins cocoon in cell, while female constructs another nest nearby. Adults are active in summer.

Comments
Females often dig multiple burrows but raise young in only 1 or 2, perhaps using partly closed extra burrows to distract would-be predators and parasites.

Deer Flies
Chrysops spp.
483

⅜–⅝" (9–15 mm). Body somewhat flattened, head smaller than that of horse fly. Black with yellow-green markings on thorax and most of abdomen. Antennae cylindrical. Eyes bright green or gold with zigzag or other patterns. Hind tibiae have 2 spurs at tip. Wings have distinctive brownish-black pattern. Larva is yellowish white or greenish with brown rings.

Habitat
Deciduous and mixed forests, meadows, roadsides, and suburbs near water.

Range
Throughout North America.

Life Cycle
Shiny black eggs are laid in clusters on leaves of emergent plants just above water. Fully grown larvae pupate in mud at edge of water. Adults emerge May–August.

Comments
A deer fly circles over its intended victim before settling, then immediately bites. Some transmit bacteria that cause tularemia in rabbits, hares, and occasionally people. The most common species, the Callidus Deer Fly (*C. callidus*), has black on its thorax and V-shaped black marks on abdominal segments 2, 3, and 4. It pesters animals and people during June and July and ranges from Maine to Florida, west to Texas, north to British Columbia.

American Horse Fly
Tabanus americanus
484

¾–1⅛″ (20–28 mm). Large, broad. Head tan to ash-gray between large green eyes and on rear surface. Antennae reddish brown. Thorax brownish to blackish with gray hair. Abdomen is blackish red-brown with short gray hair across rear margin. Hind tibiae do not have spurs. Wings smoky; brown to black near base.

Habitat
Near swamps, salt marshes, and ponds.

Range
Newfoundland to Florida, west to Texas and northern Mexico, north to Canadian Northwest Territories.

Life Cycle
Egg masses are attached to plants overhanging fresh water, into which larvae drop. Larvae overwinter in muddy bottom 2 winters, then pupate in spring. Males are short-lived, but females may survive until fall.

Comments
When the female bites, the wound inflicted often continues to bleed for several minutes because the fly's saliva contains an anticoagulant that prevents clotting. A single animal may suffer a debilitating loss of blood if many of these insects attack it.

Bee Fly
Anthrax analis
485

¼–⅜″ (7–8 mm). Velvety black. Head large with eyes above and forward rather than on sides. Wings clear in outer third; remainder opaque black or brownish black, conspicuous when wings outstretched at rest.

Habitat
Meadows, open fields, gardens with sandy soil, and sand dunes.

Range
Quebec and New England to Florida, west to Arizona, north to Montana.

Life Cycle
Eggs are deposited singly on ground close to burrow of tiger beetle larva. Each fly larva enters beetle burrow, attaches itself to larva and overwinters there. When host pupates in spring, fly larva sheds its skin, cuts into beetle pupa, and completes growth as internal parasite. Fully grown fly larva pupates, working its way to soil surface. Then adult emerges in early spring.

Comments
The related Tiger Bee Fly (*A. tigrinus*), ½–⅝″ (12–15 mm), is purplish black with mottled black patterns on its wings. It is found from the Canadian Maritime Provinces south to Florida and the Gulf states, and from California to southern Alberta.

Cow Killer
Dasymutilla occidentalis
486

⅝–1″ (15–25 mm). Antlike, with only slight constriction (pedicel) between thorax and abdomen. Antennae beadlike. Thorax and abdomen red above, covered with short erect red hair. Body below and head black. Males winged, females wingless.

Habitat
Meadows, forest edges, clover fields, and sand dunes.

Range
New York south to Florida and the Gulf states, west to Texas.

Life Cycle
Female searches for bumble bee nests and drops 1 egg beside each brood chamber. Cow Killer larvae invade brood chambers, feed on the bee larvae, kill them, and scavenge on their remains. Cow Killer larvae pupate in victim's brood chambers.

Comments
Adult Cow Killers can run quickly and fight ferociously. They get their name from their painful sting—so severe that many people claim it could kill a cow.

Golden Saltmarsh Mosquito
Aedes solicitans
487

⅛–¼″ (4–6 mm). Golden brown; male unmarked, female's abdomen with silvery-white stripe along middle of back and silvery-white or golden-yellow bands. Female's proboscis and outermost leg segments have white and black bands. Thorax feathery. Male's antennae feathery, female's threadlike. Wings smoky, female's spotted.

Habitat
Near brackish and salt water; in salt marshes; larvae also in
swimming pools.

Range
New Brunswick to Florida, west to Texas, north to Nebraska.

Life Cycle
Eggs are laid singly on vegetation or other surface at
waterline. Larvae hatch and pupate in stagnant water.

Comments
The Black Saltmarsh Mosquito (*A. taeniorhynchus*), ⅛"
(4 mm), is black with broad white bands, no stripe along
middle of back, and a different pattern of white on the
proboscis and outermost leg segments. It is found in
Massachusetts, south along the Atlantic Coast, and west along
the Gulf of Mexico into southern California.

**Black-headed Soft-
winged Flower Beetle**
Collops nigriceps
488

¼" (5–6 mm) long, black head, yellowish thorax with central
spot, wing covers (elytra) iridescent bluish-black, abdomen
rusty-red; third joint of antennae (in males) greatly enlarged.

Habitat
Common in beach wrack and on grasses on primary and
secondary dunes; also found along inland margins of salt
marshes.

Range
From Massachusetts to Florida; also along Gulf Coast to
Mobile, Alabama.

Comments
This small, colorful beetle is predaceous upon smaller
arthropods in dune vegetation, beach debris, and along inland
marsh vegetation. Its food consists of insect eggs and larvae,
and adult soft-bodied insects. Larvae of the beetle also are
carnivorous with the same general feeding habits as adults,
but usually in damp regions. Mating pairs are often found
clinging to dune grass stems. While they are capable fliers,
these beetles spend much of their time crawling upon a surface
in search of food and avoiding vigorous sea breezes.

Beautiful Tiger Beetle
Cicindela formosa
489

⅝–¾" (15–18 mm). Head, thorax, and underside are
metallic blackish bronze with a few short white hairs. Elytra
have reddish-brown pattern with iridescent green on midline
and edge, white along sides.

Habitat
Sand dunes and other sandy places with scattered vegetation.

Range
Throughout North America.

Life Cycle
Eggs are left singly in the shade of a plant. Larvae make

vertical burrows under plants, later use these hideaways as pupal shelters. 1 generation a year.

Comments
This tiger beetle is usually found alone, feeding on small insects.

Seaside Grasshopper
Trimerotropis maritima
490

¾–1⅜″ (19–34 mm). Pale brown to pale gray body, finely speckled with black; buff to pink hind tibiae; and pale yellow hind wings edged with dark gray.

Habitat
Coastal sand dunes.

Range
Massachusetts to Florida.

Life Cycle
Up to 12 egg masses, with 100 eggs each, are deposited in soft soil. Eggs overwinter, hatch in late spring. Nymphs become adults by June in the South or October in the North. 1 generation a year.

Comments
The Seaside Grasshopper often snuggles into beach sand along the Atlantic Coast and the Great Lakes. The related Pallid-winged Grasshopper (*T. pallidipennis*) is slightly larger with 2 black crossbands on fore wings and whitish to yellow hind wings except for dark edge. Hind tibiae yellow or brownish.

Field Cricket
Gryllus pennsylvanicus
491

⅝–1″ (15–25 mm). Black to dark reddish brown. Black antennae longer than body; projections from tail hairy, longer than head and front portion of thorax combined. Wings do not project beyond tail projections.

Habitat
Undergrowth where there is moderate humidity and protection from night winds and cold.

Range
Throughout North America to Alaska.

Sound
Common song is a series of triple chirps. Courtship song is a continuous trill at a pitch near the upper limits of audibility for the human ear.

Life Cycle
Female inserts eggs singly deep into the soil. Eggs overwinter in the North, where all unmatured nymphs and adults die of the frost. In the South nymphs and adults may overwinter and produce 3 generations a year.

Comments
This cricket enters houses in autumn, attracted by the warmth. In courtship the male dances about and "sings" to excite the female.

Dune Wolf Spider
Geolycosa pikei
492

Male ½–⅞″ (14–22 mm), female ¾–⅞″ (18–22 mm). Body and legs gray to sand-colored, speckled with black. Legs have many black spines.

Habitat
Sand dunes and other sandy areas.

Range
Throughout North America, individual species more restricted.

Life Cycle
Vertical burrows up to a few feet deep are dug in sand. Spider cements sand particles for walls with silk, throwing loose sand out doorway. Female brings up egg sac and exposes it to warmth of sun in doorway.

Comments
This spider seldom emerges from its burrow, but lies in wait for insects to pass within reach. If it senses vibrations in the ground, it disappears down the burrow and waits minutes before climbing up to the doorway again.

BIRDS

No visit to the seashore is complete without the pleasure of watching birds in action. As tight little flocks of Sanderlings race up and down at the water's edge, terns and gulls cry out and dive for food. Farther out, over the water, cormorants glide evenly along, while the large shearwaters and the songbird-sized Wilsons' Storm-Petrel may be seen well out to sea over the open ocean. In fall and spring, the air over bays and estuaries is rich with the calls of migrating ducks and geese; from time to time, a Bald Eagle may be seen swooping down from the sky for fishes. This section describes some of the most common birds that occur along our Atlantic and Gulf shores.

Parasitic Jaeger
Stercorarius parasiticus
493

21″ (53 cm). A fast-flying, gull-like seabird. Typical adults are brown above, white or light dusky below, with a gray-brown band across the breast and a dark, almost black crown. Dark-phase birds are uniform dusky brown with pale cheeks. Intermediates between the 2 color phases occur. Distinguished from other jaegers by pointed central tail feathers extending up to 3 inches beyond rest of tail and moderate white flash in outer wing. Often seen disturbing gulls and terns.

Voice
Usually silent; a variety of mewing and wailing notes on the breeding grounds.

Habitat
Grassy tundra and stony ground near inland lakes in summer; at other times on the ocean.

Range
Aleutians, N. Alaska, Canada, and Greenland south to central Canada; winters in warm waters south to Argentina.

Comments
This is the most familiar of our jaegers, since it comes more readily into bays and estuaries and feeds more often close to shore. Like the other jaegers, it usually obtains food by pursuing gulls and terns and forcing them to drop food.

Magnificent Frigatebird
Fregata magnificens
494

38–40″ (96–102 cm). Wingspan: 90″ (2.5 m). Black with very long, pointed wings, deeply forked tail, and long hooked bill. Male has a brilliant red throat pouch in breeding season and inflates it to huge size during courtship; female has a white breast. Young have white head and underparts.

Voice
Usually silent; harsh, guttural notes during courtship.

Habitat
Mangrove islets in shallow waters.

Range
Local on islets in Florida Bay. In the nonbreeding season, ranges to the coasts of Florida, Louisiana, and Texas.

Comments
Frigatebirds, also known as Man-o'-War-birds, are masters of flight—whether soaring on outstretched wings, circling in the sky, swooping down on flying fish, or giving chase to boobies and other seabirds. They have the largest wingspread in proportion to weight of any bird. A frigatebird will harass a booby until the latter drops its catch, which the frigatebird deftly snatches in midair.

Great Skua
Catharacta skua
495

21″ (53 cm). A large, dark, heavy-bodied, gull-like bird, grayish brown with conspicuous white patches in the outer wing. Tail short and blunt. Immatures of the larger gulls lack the white wing patches.

Voice
A harsh *hah-hah-hah-hah;* quacking and croaking notes.

Habitat
Breeds on bare ground near the sea; ranges over the open sea.

Range
Nests on Iceland and islands north of Britain, ranging widely over the North Atlantic. Also breeds on islands in the Southern Hemisphere.

Comments
Skuas occur off the shores of the Northern Hemisphere most often in late summer and early fall, where they are abundant on the fishing banks off Newfoundland. They feed on a variety of shrimp, fish, rodents, and the eggs and young of colonial seabirds.

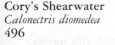

Cory's Shearwater
Calonectris diomedea
496

20–22″ (51–56 cm). Dull gray above, white below; pale bill (usually yellow). Dull gray crown of Cory's Shearwater blends evenly with the white sides of the face, without the abrupt contrast seen in the Greater Shearwater.

Voice
Howling, gurgling calls heard only on breeding grounds.

Habitat
Open oceans.

Range
Breeds in eastern Atlantic and Mediterranean, and occurs in summer and fall off the East Coast of North America.

Comments
This is the only one of our large shearwaters that breeds in the Northern Hemisphere. After the breeding season the birds move westward into American waters, usually becoming common in July and remaining until late in the fall. A powerful bird, it does not resort to burrows for protection from predators during the breeding season. Like the Greater Shearwater, it often follows ships in search of food.

Greater Shearwater
Puffinus gravis
497

18–20″ (46–51 cm). Narrow-winged, gull-sized seabird usually seen skimming over the waves in the wake of ships. Dull brown above, white below; dark cap contrasting sharply with white on face; may show white at base of tail; black bill.

Voice
Usually silent in our area; a snarling *eeyah,* given by birds resting in flocks on the water.

Habitat
Open ocean.

Range
Islands of the Tristan da Cunha group in the South Atlantic. Nonbreeding summer visitor to the North Atlantic.

Comments
These birds follow a "Great Circle" route around the Atlantic, appearing in North American waters in May, then moving on to the eastern Atlantic in late summer. Expert divers, they feed mainly on small fish and squid.

Wilson's Storm-Petrel
Oceanites oceanicus
498

7" (18 cm). A small seabird that skims over the surface like a swallow. Black with a white rump; tail not forked.

Voice
A soft peeping, heard when the birds are feeding.

Habitat
Open ocean; breeds on rocky cliffs and offshore islands.

Range
Breeds in Antarctic and subantarctic seas; in nonbreeding season ranges over Atlantic, Pacific, and Indian oceans, in the western Atlantic north to Labrador.

Comments
One of the most abundant birds in the world, this species, formerly called Wilson's Petrel, nests in countless millions on islands in the Southern Hemisphere, and visits the Northern Hemisphere during our summer months. It often hovers at the surface of the water, its wings held over its back and its feet gently touching the water.

Brown Noddy
Anous stolidus
499

15" (38 cm). Robin-sized. Dark sooty-brown with pale grayish-white crown; wedge-shaped tail; slender, black bill.

Voice
Low *cah*, similar to call of a young crow.

Habitat
Open ocean; breeds on coastal and oceanic islands.

Range
Breeds on the Dry Tortugas, Florida. Found nearly throughout the warmer regions of the world.

Comments
These dark brown terns with light caps associate commonly with Sooty Terns, at least at breeding colonies. Unlike them, however, the Noddy does not wander northward after the nesting season and, as a result, few are reported in our area north of southern Florida. Noddies get their name from their habit of nodding and bowing to each other during courtship.

Black-legged Kittiwake
Rissa tridactyla
500

16–18" (40–46 cm). Small, seagoing gull. Adult white with pale gray back and wings; sharply defined black wing tip, as if dipped in black ink; black feet; yellow bill; slightly forked tail. Winter adult has dusky gray patch on nape. Young bird has dusky band on nape, dark diagonal wing band, and black-tipped tail.

Voice
Variety of loud, harsh notes. Very noisy on the breeding ground. With a little imagination, its common call can be said to resemble its name, *kittiwake*.

Habitat
Cliffs and seacoasts in the Arctic; winters at sea.

Range
North Pacific and Arctic Ocean to the Gulf of St. Lawrence. Winters from the edge of the sea ice south to the Sargasso Sea.

Comments
If the nest is disturbed, the young of this cliff-nesting species stay put no matter how close a human observer gets; to leave a nest on a high, narrow ledge could result in a fatal plunge to the rocks below. This is the only gull that dives and swims underwater to capture food.

Northern Fulmar
Fulmarus glacialis
501

18″ (46 cm). A stocky, gull-like seabird; typical birds are pale gray on back and wings, white elsewhere, but uniformly dark gray individuals occur, as well as intermediates between pale and dark gray. Yellow bill. Easily distinguished from gulls by its flight: several fast wingbeats, then a stiff-winged glide.

Voice
Chuckling and grunting notes when feeding; various guttural calls during the breeding season.

Habitat
Rocky cliffs; open seas.

Range
Arctic Ocean south to Newfoundland, wintering at sea south to New Jersey.

Comments
The Fulmar feeds on fish, squid, shrimp, and the refuse of the whaling industry. The expansion of the fishing industry in this century has caused an increase in the North Atlantic.

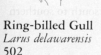

Ring-billed Gull
Larus delawarensis
502

18–20″ (45–50 cm). Adult silvery gray on back, white on head, tail, and underparts. Similar to Herring Gull but smaller, with yellow feet and with narrow black ring around bill. Young birds are mottled brown, and have a blackish tail band and flesh-colored legs.

Voice
Loud, raucous mewing cry, like the Herring Gull but higher-pitched.

Habitat
Lakes and rivers; many move to salt water in the winter.

Range
Alaska and Labrador south to the Great Lakes and California. Winters from southern New England south to Cuba.

Comments
In most of the northern part of the United States, the Ring-billed Gull is known as a winter visitor, less common than the Herring Gull. But in some inland areas and in the Deep South, it is the more numerous of the two species. It often nests in very large colonies.

Herring Gull
Larus argentatus
503

23–26" (58–66 cm). Adult white with light gray back and wings; black wing tip with white spots. Feet pink or flesh-colored. First-year birds brownish.

Voice
Loud, rollicking call, *kuk-kuk-kuk, yucca-yucca-yucca,* and other raucous cries.

Habitat
Lakes, rivers, estuaries, and beaches; all aquatic habitats.

Range
Breeds from Alaska and Greenland south to the Carolinas.

Comments
This is the common "sea gull" inland and along the coast. In recent years it has become abundant, probably due to the amount of food available at garbage dumps, and has extended its range southward along the Atlantic Coast, often to the detriment of colonial birds such as terns and Laughing Gulls.

Great Black-backed Gull
Larus marinus
504

30" (76 cm). Very large gull. Adult has black back and wings, rest of plumage white. Bill yellow and legs pinkish. Immature mottled with brown, has a black tip to its tail, and dark bill.

Voice
Deep and guttural. A deep *keeow.*

Habitat
Coastal beaches, estuaries, and lagoons; also at refuse dumps. Less commonly on inland lakes and rivers.

Range
Coasts on both sides of the North Atlantic, south to southern United States and the Mediterranean.

Comments
Our largest gull, this conspicuous bird accompanies the ever-present Herring Gull at all times of the year, even during the summer, when they nest together in mixed colonies. However, the Black-backed always asserts dominance.

Laughing Gull
Larus atricilla
505

15–17" (38–43 cm). In summer the adult has a black hood and dark gray back and wings; hind edge of wing is white; wing tip is black, without white spots. Lacks a hood in winter. Young bird is dark brown with contrasting white rump. The similar Franklin's Gull has a black wing tip separated from the gray wing by a white band.

Voice
Loud, high-pitched *ha-ha-ha-ha-haah-haah-haah-haah*.

Habitat
Salt marshes, bays, and estuaries. Very rare inland.

Range
Maine to the Caribbean. Winters regularly north to Virginia, in smaller numbers farther north.

Comments
The common summer gull along the Atlantic and Gulf coasts, it has declined in numbers in recent years perhaps due to the destruction of coastal marshes and the increase in Herring Gulls, which prey on its eggs and young.

Bonaparte's Gull
Larus philadelphia
506

12–14" (30–35 cm). A small, delicate gull, silvery gray above with conspicuous white patches on leading edge of outer wing. Black on head of breeding adults is lacking in winter. Young have dark on upper wings and a black band on tail.

Voice
Rasping *tea-ar;* a soft, nasal, snarling note.

Habitat
Forested lakes and rivers; winters along the coast, in estuaries, and at the mouths of large rivers.

Range
Breeds in interior of northwestern Canada and in Alaska. Winters along both coasts, on the Atlantic from southern New England southward.

Comments
Breeding in the Far North, these beautiful gulls are most often seen on lakes and rivers during migration or along the coast in winter. They keep to themselves, seldom joining the gulls at dumps. They feed in inlets and at sewage outlets.

Roseate Tern
Sterna dougallii
507

14–17" (35–43 cm). Robin-sized. White with a black cap and very pale gray back and wings. Bill usually solid black, upperparts pale, long tail deeply forked.

Voice
Loud, harsh *zaap,* likened to the sound of tearing cloth. Also a softer *cue-lick.*

Habitat
Coastal beaches, islands, and inshore waters.

Range
Along the coast from Gulf of St. Lawrence south to Venezuela; winters from Gulf Coast to Brazil. Also breeds in Atlantic.

Comments
The Roseate Tern is much less numerous than other terns of similar size, and its patchy distribution around the world

suggests that it is an old species, perhaps more abundant and widespread ages ago. It probably suffers from competition with the Common Tern for nesting sites, at least in America.

Sandwich Tern
Sterna sandvicensis
508

16″ (40 cm). Robin-sized. White with gray back and upper surface of wing, black cap, short crest, and long, black, yellow-tipped bill.

Voice
Loud, harsh *curr-it*.

Habitat
Coastal beaches and islands.

Range
Locally on the Atlantic and Gulf coasts from Virginia to Florida and Texas. Winters south to Panama, Brazil, Africa, and India.

Comments
The Sandwich Tern is one of three crested terns occurring along our coasts. Its range is most unusual. It breeds much farther north in Europe than it does in America because of the warming influence of the Gulf Stream.

Caspian Tern
Sterna caspia
509

19–23″ (48–58 cm). Gull-sized. Largely white, with black cap and pale gray back and wings; heavy bright red bill and dusky underwing.

Voice
Low, hoarse *kraa*. Also a shorter *kow*.

Habitat
Sandy or pebbly shores of lakes and large rivers; seacoasts.

Range
Mackenzie, the Great Lakes, and Newfoundland south to the Gulf Coast and Baja California. Winters north to California and North Carolina.

Comments
Much less gregarious than other terns, Caspians usually feed singly. Pairs breed by themselves, in small colonies, or may attach themselves to colonies of other birds.

Royal Tern
Sterna maxima
510

18–21″ (46–53 cm). Crow-sized. A large tern with a heavy yellow-orange to orange-red bill. Black cap, pale gray back and wings, white forehead, black crest. Tail moderately forked. Similar Caspian Tern has blood-red bill, darker underwing, and shorter tail.

Voice
Harsh, high-pitched *Kak*.

Habitat
Sandy beaches.

Range
Breeds along the coast from Virginia to Texas and Mexico, wandering regularly farther north in summer. Winters from the Gulf Coast southward.

Comments
It nests in large, dense colonies. Nests are sometimes washed away by storm tides, but the birds usually make a second attempt, often at a new location. It feeds mostly on small fish, rather than on crustaceans and insects taken by other terns.

Common Tern
Sterna hirundo
511

13–16″ (33–40 cm). Pigeon-sized. White with black cap and pale gray back and wings. Red bill with black tip. Deeply forked tail.

Voice
Kip-kip-kip. Also *TEEaar.*

Habitat
Lakes, ponds, rivers, coastal beaches, and islands.

Range
Labrador south to the Caribbean and west to Wisconsin and Alberta. Winters from Florida to southern South America.

Comments
During breeding season, whole colonies often fail to breed successfully because of disruption by humans, and as a result, their numbers are slowly declining. They will attack human intruders in the nesting colonies, often striking them on the head with their bills.

Forster's Tern
Sterna forsteri
512

14–15″ (35–38 cm). White with pale gray back and wings, black cap, and deeply forked tail. Orange bill with black tip. Similar to the Common Tern, but wing tips are frosty white and, at very close range, outer web of outermost tail feathers white instead of dusky. Lacks black cap in winter but has distinctive black mark behind eye.

Voice
Harsh nasal *beep.*

Habitat
Salt marshes in the East; freshwater marshes in the West.

Range
Breeds along the Atlantic Coast from Maryland to Texas and in the interior from Alberta and California east to Illinois. Winters from Virginia to Guatemala.

Comments
One of the few exclusively North American terns, it is so similar to the Common Tern that, until 1831, it was not recognized as a distinct species. Its preference for marshes enables it to avoid competition with the Common Tern, whi favors sandy or pebbly beaches and rocky islands.

Arctic Tern
Sterna paradisaea
513

14–17″ (35–43 cm). Whitish, with white streak below the black cap and pale gray upperparts. Deeply forked tail. Similar to Common Tern but underparts grayer, bill blood-red, legs shorter, tail longer.

Voice
Harsh *TEE-ar* or *kip-kip-kip-TEE-ar,* high in pitch.

Habitat
Coastal islands and beaches; also on tundra in summer.

Range
Aleutians, N. Alaska, Ellesmere Island east to Newfoundland, Massachusetts, Quebec, N. Manitoba, and British Columbia. Winters at sea in the Southern Hemisphere.

Comments
Seldom seen south of its breeding grounds in the East, these terns annually perform spectacular migrations, every fall heading eastward across the Atlantic and down the west coasts of Europe and Africa to winter in the Antarctic Ocean. In spring they retrace the same route, a round trip totaling as much as 22,000 miles.

Least Tern
Sterna antillarum
514

8–10″ (20–25 cm). Size of a large sparrow. Very small tern with a yellow bill and a fast, shallow wingbeat. White with black cap, pale gray back and wings, and forked tail; forehead white.

Voice
Sharp *killick* or *kip-kip-kip-killick.*

Habitat
Sandy and pebbly beaches along the coast; sandbars in large rivers. Often on landfills.

Range
Maine south to Venezuela; occasionally along rivers in the Mississippi Valley; coastal California. Winters from Gulf Coast southward. Also breeds in Eurasia, Africa, and Australia.

Comments
Because of its habit of nesting on low sandbars, whole colonies are sometimes destroyed by extra-high tides. It is most often seen hovering over the water, peering downward in search of small minnows and other marine or freshwater organisms.

Sooty Tern
Sterna fuscata
515

16″ (40 cm). Robin-sized. Adult black above with white forehead; white below. Deeply forked tail; thin, black bill. Immature birds are dark brown.

Voice
Harsh, squeaky notes and croaks.

Habitat
Open ocean; breeds on coastal and oceanic islands.

Range
Tropical seas; in North America breeds only on the Dry
Tortugas, Florida.

Comments
Sooty Terns are notorious wanderers, and when not nesting
they range far and wide over the seas. These birds have a
remarkable homing ability: when individuals marked with a
dye were taken from their breeding grounds on the Dry
Tortugas, and released along the coasts of North Carolina and
Texas, all returned to their breeding grounds in one to seven
days. Sooty Terns feed largely at dusk and at night. Unlike
most other terns they do not dive, but pluck small fish and
squid from the surface of the water. They spend most of their
time in the air, rarely perching or alighting on the water.

Black Skimmer
Rynchops niger
516

18″ (46 cm). Crow-sized. Black above, white below; red legs.
Bill red with black tip; flattened laterally, bladelike; unique
among birds in having lower mandible much longer (about
one-third) than the upper.

Voice
Barking call; cooing notes at the nesting site.

Habitat
Breeds chiefly on sandbars and beaches; feeds in shallow bays,
inlets, and estuaries.

Range
Atlantic and Gulf coasts from Massachusetts and Long Island
to Florida and Texas, and from Mexico to southern South
America. Winters regularly north to the Carolinas.

Comments
This extraordinary bird can hardly fail to attract attention
from even the most blasé observer, especially when in flight.
Usually only one or two individuals are seen as they skim the
surface (hence their name) for fish, with the tip of the lower
mandible cutting through the water. They also wade in
shallow water, jabbing at the fish scattering before them. At
other times compact flocks may be seen flying in unison,
wheeling in one direction and then another—showing first the
jet-black of the wings, then the white of the underparts.

Northern Gannet
Sula bassanus
517

35–40″ (89–102 cm). Goose-sized. Adult white with black
wing tips; head tinged with rich orange-buff in breeding
season. Long, pointed tail and wings. Immature bird is dark
gray speckled with white. Alternately flaps and glides in
flight—shaped like a flying cross.

Voice
Guttural croak or grunt, heard only on the breeding islands.

Habitat
Large colonies on rocky cliffs of coastal islands.

Range
Breeds on a few islands off Newfoundland, in the Gulf of St.
Lawrence, and off Nova Scotia. Winters in coastal waters
south to Florida.

Comments
This strictly maritime species, the only northern member of
the Booby family, is one of the most spectacular birds. During
migrations they may be observed offshore, either gliding above
the water or diving into the sea after fish, sometimes plunging
headlong from heights as great as 50 feet or more. A
remarkable system of interconnected air sacs under the skin of
the breast serves as a cushion to protect the bird from the
shock of striking the water. A trip to the breeding colony on
Bonaventure Island, off the Gaspé Peninsula, Quebec, yields
one of the great sights in the bird world; over 15,000 pairs of
gannets brooding their young. Gannets take part in quite an
elaborate series of displays. When one bird returns to the nest
site, it is greeted by its mate. Both birds raise their heads and
cross bills, which they clash together like fencers, then bow to
each other with wings and tails raised. This is followed by
mutual preening of the head and neck. Usually the bird who
has been relieved at the nest will pick up sticks or seaweed to
present to its mate. Finally, the departing bird stands with
head and neck extended straight up and wings raised over the
back, then leaps into the air.

American White Pelican
Pelecanus erythrorhynchos
518

55–70″ (140–179 cm). Wingspan: 96″ (2.8 m). Huge white
bird with a massive yellow bill and black wing tips. Usually
rests bill on breast.

Voice
Low grunts or croaks at the nesting site; usually silent.

Habitat
Marshy lakes and along the Pacific and Texas coasts. Winters
chiefly in coastal lagoons.

Range
Breeds from British Columbia and Mackenzie south to W.
Ontario and California; also on the Texas coast. Winters from
Florida and S. California south to Panama.

Comments
A flock of migrating American White Pelicans is a majestic
sight—a long line of ponderous birds, flapping and sailing
in unison. These birds ride rising air currents to great
heights, where they soar gracefully in circles. They fish
cooperatively.

ヘn Pelican
occidentalis

45–54″ (114–137 cm). Wingspan: 90″ (2.5 m). Very large,
stocky bird with a dark brown body and a massive bill and
throat pouch. Head whitish in adults, dark brown in young.
Usually rests its bill on its breast.

Voice
Adults are silent, but young birds in nesting colonies are very noisy, emitting loud grunts and screams.

Habitat
Sandy coastal beaches and lagoons.

Range
Atlantic Coast from North Carolina south to Venezuela; on the Pacific Coast from British Columbia to Chile.

Comments
Unlike its larger relative, the White Pelican, it is an expert diver, often plunging spectacularly in pursuit of fish just beyond the breakers. Its pouch is not used to store or carry fish as is generally believed, but rather serves to separate the fish from the water.

Common Murre
Uria aalge
520

17″ (43 cm). Crow-sized. Long, slender, pointed bill. In breeding plumage, head, back, and wings brownish black; underparts and wing lining white. Winter plumage similar, but throat and cheeks white. Small populations with "bridling"—a narrow white eye-ring and line behind the eye.

Voice
Low-pitched, growls, *arr* or *arrriarrr*.

Habitat
Rocky coasts.

Range
Arctic and subarctic shores; breeds in America south to California on the Pacific side, but only to islands in the Gulf of St. Lawrence on the Atlantic. Winters south to California and Massachusetts.

Comments
Very gregarious, resting in large colonies on open, rocky cliff ledges. Occasionally observed in rafts on water. Winters at sea. The murres, like all alcids, use their wings for swimming and diving, and seem to fly through the water.

Atlantic Puffin
Fratercula arctica
521

12″ (30 cm). Short, stocky bird. Black above and white below, with a white face and red legs; its remarkable triangular bill is brilliant red and yellow. In fall the horny outer covering of the bill peels off, leaving the bill smaller and duller in appearance.

Voice
Deep, throaty purrs and croaks. One call sounds like *Hey, Al*.

Habitat
Chiefly rocky coasts.

Range
Greenland south to Maine. It is essentially nonmigratory and winters chiefly offshore in the breeding range.

Comments
This clown of the sea is a comical-looking bird with a short
dumpy figure, red-rimmed gleaming yellow eyes, gaudy
triangular bill, and a habit of waddling around, jumping from
rock to rock. It nests in much smaller colonies than do most of
the other alcids. Their food consists of fish, shellfish, and
shrimp.

Razorbill
Alca torda
522

17″ (43 cm). A crow-sized diving bird. Black above, white
below. Very deep bill, laterally compressed.

Voice
Low croaks and growls.

Habitat
Coastal waters.

Range
Greenland south to Maine. Winters to New Jersey.

Comments
These birds can often be recognized at a distance on the water
by their large heads, stout bills, and upward-pointed tails. As
with many alcids, Razorbills migrate southward after severe
cold spells and visit our shores in the midst of winter. They
are hardy birds, spending most of their time at sea and
approaching land only after strong easterly gales.

Dovekie
Alle alle
523

8″ (20 cm). Robin-sized. Very small, chunky, black-and-white
seabird. Black above, white below. Bill very short.

Voice
Lively chattering.

Habitat
Breeds on rocky cliffs, and winters chiefly at sea.

Range
High Arctic south to Greenland. Winters to New Jersey.

Comments
The little Dovekie, smallest of Atlantic Alcidae, exists in
countless thousands in the cold Arctic regions and is
considered by some to be the most abundant bird in the
world. Greenland Eskimos catch large numbers of them,
eating the birds raw and making shirts from their skins.

Horned Grebe
Podiceps auritus
524

12–15″ (30–38 cm). Small, slender-necked, with a short,
sharply pointed bill. In breeding plumage, dark body, rufous
neck, blackish head, and conspicuous buff ear plumes. In
winter, dark upperparts and white chin and neck.

Voice
Usually silent, but on the breeding grounds it gives a loud
series of croaks, shrieks, and chatters.

Habitat
Marshes and lakes in summer; in winter, mainly on salt water but also on the Great Lakes.

Range
Alaska and northern Canada southeast to Wisconsin. In winter, Aleutians and along Atlantic Coast to Texas.

Comments
Thought of as saltwater birds, these grebes are rarely seen in flight; once on the wintering grounds they seldom fly, and they migrate almost entirely at night. Like other grebes, the young can swim and dive immediately after hatching, but are often seen riding on the parents' backs. Grebes have a remarkable ability to control their specific gravity so that they can swim high in the water or almost submerged.

Common Loon
Gavia immer
525

28–36" (71–91 cm). Goose-sized. Heavy, long-bodied water bird with thick, pointed bill held horizontally. In summer, head and neck black with white collar; back black with white spots. In winter, crown, hind neck, and upperparts grayish; throat and underparts white. When swimming it rides low in the water.

Voice
Wild maniacal laugh, also a mournful yodeled *oo-AH-ho* with middle note higher, and a loud ringing *kee-a-ree, kee-a-ree* with the middle note lower. Often calls at night.

Habitat
Forested lakes and rivers; oceans and bays in winter.

Range
Breeds from Aleutian Islands, Alaska, and northern Canada south to New Hampshire, Montana, and California. Winters south to the Gulf Coast.

Comments
It is known for its call, a far-carrying wail heard on its northern breeding grounds and occasionally during migration. Loons are expert divers and have been caught in nets as much as 200 feet below the surface. Their principal food is fish.

Pied-billed Grebe
Podilymbus podiceps
526

12–15" (30–38 cm). Pigeon-sized. A stocky, uniformly brownish water bird, with stubby bill; whitish with a prominent black band that is lacking in winter.

Voices
Series of hollow *cow-cow-cow* notes.

Habitat
Marshes, ponds; salt water in winter if fresh water frozen.

Range
British Columbia to S. Mackenzie, and Nova Scotia to southern Argentina. Winters as far north as New England.

Comments
Although easily overlooked, it announces itself in the breeding season with its loud, barking call notes. When alarmed, it slowly sinks below the water, surfacing again out of sight among the reeds.

Red-necked Grebe
Podiceps grisegena
527

18–20" (46–51 cm). Largest grebe in eastern North America. A slender water bird with long rufous neck; whitish cheeks; dark cap; long, pointed yellow bill. Grayish body. Similar in winter, but neck gray. The long yellow bill separates this species from all other North American grebes. In flight it can be distinguished from loons by its smaller size and white wing patches.

Voice
Nasal honk. Also a loonlike wail.

Habitat
Ponds and lakes in summer; bays and estuaries in winter.

Range
Northern Canada and Alaska southeast to S. Minnesota; more rarely to Quebec and New Hampshire. Winters south to Long Island, rarely to Florida.

Comments
Highly aquatic, grebes can swim with only their head above water, concealing themselves in low pond vegetation. The young, striped in black and white, are often seen riding on the parents' backs. Like loons, grebes are expert divers.

Red-throated Loon
Gavia stellata
528

24–27" (61–68 cm). Goose-sized. Large, long-bodied bird seldom seen away from salt water. In breeding plumage, gray head and neck, rusty throat, black back spotted with white. In winter, similar to the Common Loon but smaller, paler, with bill thinner and seemingly upturned.

Voice
Its call, more rarely heard than that of the Common Loon, is a high-pitched wail. Often heard is a low, gooselike growl.

Habitat
Salt bays and tundra ponds during the summer; bays, estuaries, and ocean in winter.

Range
Aleutian Islands and coastal tundra south to Newfoundland and N. Manitoba. In winter, south to Florida and the Gulf.

Comments
The attractive breeding plumage of this loon is seldom seen in southern latitudes, for it is acquired just before the birds depart for their nesting grounds. Loons have difficulty walking on land because their legs are located at the extreme rear of their bodies, so they are seldom seen away from the water.

Northern Pintail
Anas acuta
529

Males 25–30″ (63–76 cm); females 21–23″ (53–58 cm). Slim, graceful duck with a slender neck. Male has brown head and white neck with white line extending up the side of the head. Central tail feathers long, black, and pointed. Female streaked brown, similar to female Mallard but paler, grayer, and slenderer, with brown patch on inner flight feathers that is bordered with white at the rear edge only; tail is more pointed than in female Mallard.

Voice
Distinctive 2-toned whistle. Females quack.

Habitat
Marshes, prairie ponds, and tundra; salt marshes in winter.

Range
Breeds from Alaska and Greenland south to W. Pennsylvania, Nebraska, and California. Locally and occasionally farther east. Winters south to Central America and the West Indies.

Comments
The Pintail, a widely distributed and common duck, is a strong flier and long-distance migrant like the Mallard. Seeds of aquatic plants are its main food, but in winter small aquatic animals are also taken.

Canvasback
Aythya valisineria
530

19–24″ (48–61 cm). Male has a whitish body, black chest, and reddish head with low forehead. The long bill gives the head a distinctive sloping profile. Female gray-brown, with similar profile. At a distance males can be distinguished from Redheads by their white bodies, the male Redhead's body being largely gray.

Voice
Males grunt or croak. Females quack.

Habitat
Nests on marshes; winters on lakes, bays, and estuaries.

Range
Alaska, Mackenzie, and Manitoba south to Minnesota, Nebraska, and California. Winters from British Columbia and Massachusetts south to the Gulf Coast and to Central America.

Comments
Although they breed mainly in the West, each fall large numbers migrate eastward to winter on the Great Lakes and along the Atlantic Coast. They are considered among the best-tasting ducks, and many thousands are shot annually.

Redhead
Aythya americana
531

18–22″ (46–56 cm). Male gray, with brick-red head and black breast. Female duller and browner, with a light area around base of bill, more round-headed than female Ring-necked Duck. Both sexes have a pale gray wing stripe and a pale blue-gray bill. Similar Canvasback has a whitish body and sloping forehead and bill.

Voice
Like the meow of a cat; also quacks.

Habitat
Nests in marshes, but at other times is found on lakes and bays; often on salt water in winter.

Range
Breeds from British Columbia, Mackenzie, and Manitoba south to New Mexico, and rarely in eastern states. Winters from California, the Great Lakes, and southern New England south to Guatemala and the West Indies.

Comments
Redheads do most of their feeding at night, spending the daylight hours resting on water. This beautiful duck has suffered from hunting and the destruction of its habitat.

Mottled Duck
Anas fulvigula
532

21″ (53 cm). Mottled dark brown and sandy. Similar to a female Mallard, but bill clear yellow or orange-yellow, and tail dark, rather than sandy brown.

Voice
A loud *quack,* like that of a Mallard.

Habitat
Coastal marshes and lagoons.

Range
Resident in S. Florida and along the Gulf Coast of Louisiana and Texas.

Comments
This southern duck is a very close relative of the more widespread Mallard. Until recently, no other duck of the genus *Anas* nested in these coastal marshes, and so the distinctive male plumage, which among these birds serves in species recognition, was gradually lost. After thousands of years of evolutionary change, the two sexes are colored alike.

Gadwall
Anas strepera
533

18–21″ (46–53 cm). A medium-sized duck with a white patch on hind edge of wing. Male mottled gray with a black rump and sandy brown head. Female similar but brown.

Voice
Ducklike quack. Also utters *kack-kacks* and whistles.

Habitat
Freshwater marshes, ponds, and rivers; locally in salt marshes.

Range
Alaska and New England south to North Carolina and California. Winters north to southern New England.

Comments
This relative of the Mallard has the widest range of any duck, breeding almost throughout the North Temperate Zone.

Known to hunters as the "Gray Duck." It feeds mainly on seeds, leaves, and stems of aquatic plants.

American Black Duck
Anas rubripes
534

19–22" (48–56 cm). Sooty brown with conspicuous white wing linings, olive or greenish bill. Sexes alike. The female Mallard is paler and sandier; its bill is mottled with orange.

Voice
Typical duck quack.

Habitat
Marshes, lakes, streams, coastal mud flats, and estuaries.

Range
Eastern and central North America, from Manitoba and Labrador to Texas and Florida.

Comments
It is believed that widespread interbreeding between Black Ducks and Mallards has resulted in recent years in a decrease of "pure" Blacks. Actually the name is a misnomer, for the bird appears black only at a distance. In areas of heavy shooting, these and other dabbling ducks ingest enough lead shot to cause extensive mortality from lead poisoning.

American Wigeon
Anas americana
535

18–23" (46–58 cm). Male is brownish with white crown, green ear patch, and bold white shoulder patches easily visible in flight. Female is mottled brown with grayish head and whitish shoulder patch. Pale blue bill and feet in both sexes.

Voice
Distinctive whistled *whew-whew-whew*. Also quacks.

Habitat
Marshes, ponds, and shallow lakes.

Range
Alaska, Mackenzie, and Minnesota south to Nebraska and N. California, rarely farther east. Winters south to Central America and the West Indies.

Comments
The American Wigeon, or "Baldpate," is a wary species, often seen on marshy ponds in the company of diving birds such as coots, Redheads, and Canvasbacks. They wait at the surface while the other birds dive, then snatch the food away.

Fulvous Whistling-Duck
Dendrocygna bicolor
536

18–21" (46–53 cm). A long-legged, long-necked, gooselike duck. Body mainly tawny, with a white stripe on the side; rump and underside of the base of the tail are white.

Voice
Clear double whistle. Called Squealer by hunters.

Habitat
Coastal marshes.

Range
Resident in S. California, Texas, and S. Florida, and locally southward to Brazil.

Comments
Although Fulvous Whistling-Ducks in North America breed only in southern Texas and southern California, they occasionally wander; small flocks have turned up as far away as Utah and Nova Scotia.

Blue-winged Teal
Anas discors
537

14–16″ (35–40 cm). A small brownish duck with pale blue shoulder patches. Male has a gray head and white crescent in front of eye. Female mottled brown, with pale blue shoulder patches like the male.

Voice
Soft lisping or peeping note. Female utters a soft quack.

Habitat
Marshes, shallow ponds, and lakes.

Range
British Columbia, Quebec, and Newfoundland to North Carolina, the Gulf Coast, and S. California. Winters south to northern South America.

Comments
On low marshy prairies in the central part of the continent, where this duck is most numerous, virtually every pond and pothole has a breeding pair. The male commonly "stands guard" on the pond while the female is incubating. Unlike other dabbling ducks that form pairs in the fall, this teal begins courting in the spring and often does not acquire the familiar breeding plumage until December or January. Like most ducks they go through an eclipse plumage and molt most of their feathers, including the primaries, and so are flightless until new feathers grow in.

Harlequin Duck
Histrionicus histrionicus
538

14–20″ (35–51 cm). A small, dark duck. Male is blue-gray, appearing black at a distance, with chestnut flanks and distinctive white patches on the head and body. Female is dusky brown with 3 whitish patches on sides of face. In flight, this species lacks white patches on the wings.

Voice
Call has been described as a mouselike squeak; hence the local name Sea Mouse.

Habitat
Swift-moving streams in summer; rocky, wave-lashed coasts and jetties in winter.

Range
Alaska, Baffin Island, and N. Quebec south to Labrador and California. Winters along the coast south to Long Island and central California.

Comments

In the Northeast these ducks are known locally as Lords and Ladies. They spend most of their lives on salt water, visiting inland streams only during the breeding season. As soon as the female begins incubating, her mate returns to the ocean and undergoes the annual molt.

Ruddy Duck
Oxyura jamaicensis
539

14–16" (35–40 cm). A small, chunky duck with a long tail that is often held straight up. Male in breeding plumage has a chestnut body, black crown, and white cheeks. Female and winter male are dusky brown with whitish cheeks—crossed by a brown stripe in the female. Bill of male is blue in breeding season, black at other times.

Voice

Mostly silent. Courting male makes a series of clucking notes.

Habitat

Freshwater marshes, marshy lakes and ponds; sometimes shallow salt bays and rivers in winter.

Range

Breeds from British Columbia, Mackenzie, and Quebec south to the Gulf Coast and through Central America to northern South America. Winters north to British Columbia and Massachusetts.

Comments

This duck is one of the most aquatic members of the family, and like a grebe can sink slowly out of sight. They seldom fly, escaping from danger by diving or concealing themselves in marsh vegetation. Once airborne, however, they are fast fliers.

Hooded Merganser
Lophodytes cucullatus
540

16–19" (40–48 cm). A small duck with a slender, pointed bill. Male has white, fan-shaped, black-bordered crest; dark blackish body; dull rusty flanks; white breast with 2 black stripes down side. Female is dull gray-brown with head and crest warm brown. Both show white wing patch in flight.

Voice

Hoarse grunts and chatters.

Habitat

Wooded ponds, lakes, and rivers; tidal channels in winter.

Range

Alaska, Manitoba, and Nova Scotia south to Tennessee, Nebraska, and Oregon; occasionally in southeastern states. Winters from British Columbia, Nebraska, and New England south to Mexico and the Gulf Coast.

Comments

The smallest of our mergansers, they are most often seen along rivers and in estuaries during the fall and winter. They are usually found in flocks of up to a dozen, and when startled are among the fastest-flying of our ducks.

Red-breasted Merganser
Mergus serrator
541

19–26" (48–66 cm). Male has a green head, gray sides, white neck-ring, and rusty breast. Female grayish, with brown head shading gradually into white of breast. Both sexes are crested and have red bills.

Voice
Usually silent; croaking and rasping notes during courtship.

Habitat
Northern lakes and tundra ponds; in winter, principally on the ocean and in salt bays.

Range
Alaska, Baffin Island, and Labrador south to Maine, Michigan, and British Columbia. Winters chiefly along the coast south to the Gulf Coast and northern Mexico.

Comments
This is the only one of our three mergansers commonly found on salt water. Like the others it lives mainly on fish, which it captures in swift underwater pursuit, aided by its long, pointed bill lined with sharp, toothlike projections.

Bufflehead
Bucephala albeola
542

13–15" (33–38 cm). Small, chubby duck. Male largely white, with black back, black head with greenish and purplish gloss, and a large white patch from eye to top and back of head. Female all dark with a single whitish patch on cheek. It is a fast flier and has a rapid wingbeat.

Voice
A squeaky whistle (male); a soft, hoarse quack (female).

Habitat
Northern lakes and ponds; in winter, mainly on salt bays and estuaries.

Range
Alaska, Mackenzie, and Ontario south to Manitoba and the mountains of California. Winters on both coasts south to Mexico, the Gulf Coast, and Florida.

Comments
The Bufflehead, or "Butterball" as it is known to hunters, is a smaller relative of the goldeneyes and like them breeds in tree cavities. Usually in small parties, it does not form great rafts as do scaups, Redheads, and Canvasbacks.

Greater Scaup
Aythya marila
543

15–20" (38–51 cm). Male has very light gray body; blackish chest; and black-appearing, green-glossed head. Female is a uniform dark brown with white patch at base of bill. Often seen in large flocks on open water.

Voice
Usually silent; discordant croaking calls when breeding.

Habitat
Lakes, bays, and ponds; in winter, often on salt water.

Range
Alaska and northern Canada east to Hudson Bay and in
Maritime Provinces. Winters mainly along Pacific, Gulf, and
Atlantic coasts.

Comments
It is most commonly seen in large rafts, often composed of
thousands of birds, on big inland lakes. When these lakes
freeze over, the birds move to salt water. Although the two
scaups can be difficult to tell apart, any very large flock of
scaups on the northeast coast in winter may be assumed to be
the Greater. Because it dives for many small animals and is
not as much of a vegetarian as the Redhead or the Canvasback,
the Greater Scaup is not considered as choice a game bird but
is still shot in large numbers annually.

Mallard
Anas platyrhynchos
544

18–27″ (46–68 cm). Male has a green head, white neck-ring,
chestnut breast, and grayish body. Inner feathers of wing
(speculum) are metallic purplish blue, bordered on front and
back with white. Female mottled brown with white tail and
purplish-blue speculum, bill mottled orange and brown.

Voice
Males utter soft, reedy notes; females, a loud quack.

Habitat
Ponds, lakes, and marshes. Semidomesticated birds may be
found on almost any body of water.

Range
Breeds from Alaska and Greenland south to Virginia, Texas,
and northern Mexico. Winters south to Central America and
the West Indies.

Comments
Ancestor of the common white domestic duck, wild Mallards
frequently interbreed with domestic stock, producing a
bewildering variety of patterns and colors. They also hybridize
with wild species such as the closely related American Black
Duck and even occasionally with Northern Pintails.

Northern Shoveler
Anas clypeata
545

17–20″ (43–51 cm). Large "shovel" bill. Male has green
head, white body, and chestnut flanks. Female streaked brown
with pale blue wing patches; similar to female Blue-winged
Teal but larger, with the distinctive bill. Both sexes have pale
blue shoulder patches.

Voice
Low croak, cluck, or quack.

Habitat
Marshes and prairie potholes. Sometimes on salt or brackish
marshes.

Range
Alaska, Manitoba, south to Nebraska, Colorado, and S.

California; occasionally farther east and south. Winters north to British Columbia and Georgia, and to New England.

Comments
Like the closely related Blue-winged Teal, the Northern Shoveler, formerly called Shoveler, is among the first ducks to arrive in the fall and the last to leave in the spring. It feeds on minute aquatic animals by straining water through comblike teeth along the sides of its long, expanded bill.

Ring-necked Duck
Aythya collaris
546

14–18″ (35–46 cm). Male has black back and breast; purple-glossed, black-appearing head; pale gray flanks; vertical white mark on side of breast. Female brownish, paler around the base of the bill, and has a narrow white eye-ring. Bill pale gray with a white ring. The shape of the head—high and angular—distinguishes this bird from the scaups.

Voice
Soft purring notes, but usually silent.

Habitat
Wooded lakes, ponds, and rivers; seldom on salt water except in the southern states.

Range
Alaska, Manitoba, and Newfoundland south to Maine, Colorado, and California. Winters south to Mexico and the West Indies.

Comments
This species might better be called the Ring-billed Duck, for its chestnut neck-ring is usually seen only at close range, while the white ring on the bill is a prominent field mark.

Common Eider
Somateria mollissima
547

23–27″ (58–68 cm). Our largest duck. Male has black underparts; white back, breast, and head; dark crown; back of head has greenish tinge. Female is mottled brown. Long, sloping bill gives the bird a distinctive profile.

Voice
During courtship the male gives a humanlike moan. Female quacks.

Habitat
Rocky coasts and coastal tundra.

Range
Alaska across the Arctic to Greenland and south to Maine. Winters along the coast south to Alaska and Long Island.

Comments
Eiders are best known for their down—very soft feathers plucked from the breast of the female. For hundreds of years down has been gathered from nests in northern Europe and used to make pillows and quilts. Only eiders in the Arctic are strongly migratory.

King Eider
Somateria spectabilis
548

18–25" (46–63 cm). A large duck. Male has a black back and a conspicuous orange-yellow bill and "shield" on forehead. Female similar to female Common Eider but bill is shorter, not extending as far toward the eye, and lacks the sloping profile.

Voice
A guttural croaking.

Habitat
Rocky coasts and islands.

Range
Usually in freshwater ponds and lakes in Alaska and Arctic islands east to Greenland, south locally to Hudson Bay. Winters along coasts south to S. Alaska and New Jersey; rarely farther south and on the Great Lakes.

Comments
Although the world population of the King Eider is large, the birds are seldom seen in the United States; most winter farther north and favor deeper water than the Common Eider. They often dive for food, and have been caught in nets as much as 150 feet below the surface.

Surf Scoter
Melanitta perspicillata
549

17–21" (43–53 cm). Male black with white patches on the crown and nape; hence the local name "Skunk-head." Bill swollen at the base and bearing a large black spot. Female brownish black with 2 whitish patches on cheek. Both sexes lack white wing patch.

Voice
A low, guttural croaking.

Habitat
Northern lakes; winters almost entirely on the ocean and in large coastal bays.

Range
Aleutians, Alaska, and northern Canada south to N. Quebec, Saskatchewan, and British Columbia. Winters on Atlantic, Pacific, and Gulf coasts.

Comments
When alighting on the water, these birds have a habit of holding their wings up over their backs while coasting to a stop. Because they consume little plant food, hunters do not consider their flesh good to eat; nevertheless, many thousands are shot annually for sport.

Black Scoter
Melanitta nigra
550

17–21" (43–53 cm). Male black; black bill with large yellow knob at base, hence the local name "Butterbill." Female duller, with pale cheeks and all-dark bill.

Voice
In spring a musical, whistled *cour-oo*.

Habitat
Ponds in northern or high-elevation coniferous forests; winters on the ocean and in large salt bays.

Range
W. Alaska, Labrador, and Newfoundland. Winters along the coast south to California and South Carolina, more rarely in the interior.

Comments
Like other scoters it preys on mollusks, but also spends time tearing barnacles and limpets from submerged rocks and reefs. Newly hatched young remain on fresh water for several days, but then move to salt water.

White-winged Scoter
Melanitta fusca
551

19–24″ (48–61 cm). Male black with bold white wing patches and yellow bill with a large black knob at the base. Females are dull brown with 2 whitish facial spots and white wing patches.

Voice
A hoarse croak.

Habitat
Large lakes; in winter most birds move to the ocean or coastal bays, but a few remain on big lakes in the interior.

Range
Aleutians, Alaska, and Manitoba south to North Dakota and Washington. Winters regularly south to British Columbia, Colorado, Louisiana, and South Carolina.

Comments
During the height of migration, in October and November, the long, irregular lines of thousands of scoters migrating southward just offshore provide a most impressive sight. This scoter is the most widespread of the three species.

Oldsquaw
Clangula hyemalis
552

Males 19–22″ (48–56 cm); females 15–17″ (38–43 cm). Male boldly patterned in black and white (chiefly white in winter, chiefly black in summer), with very long, slender central tail feathers. Females are duller and lack the long tail feathers. In all plumages has all-dark, unpatterned wings.

Voice
Various clucking and growling notes; a musical *ow-owdle-oo*, frequently repeated, during courtship.

Habitat
Tundra; in winter on open bays and inshore waters.

Range
Aleutian Islands, N. Alaska, eastward along the Arctic coast of Canada and the islands to Greenland, south to southern Hudson Bay and N. British Columbia. Winters along the coast south to Oregon and the Carolinas.

Comments

The Oldsquaw is one of the very few of our diving ducks that travels under water by using its wings; other species propel themselves with their feet. This fact may explain the birds' ability to dive to such great depths—as deep as 80 fathoms.

Snow Goose
Chen caerulescens
553, 556

22–30" (56–76 cm). The white color phase with black wing tips is most common in the East, while in the West and along the Gulf Coast the "Blue Goose"—dark gray with white head and neck—is numerous. Pinkish bill and feet.

Voice
High-pitched nasal barking.

Habitat
Breeds on the tundra and winters in salt marshes and marshy coastal bays; also in freshwater marshes and grain fields.

Range
Arctic regions of North America. Winters on the Pacific Coast south to Baja California and along the Atlantic Coast from New Jersey to Texas. In smaller numbers in the interior.

Comments
Until recently the two color phases were considered separate species, but it is now known that they interbreed where their ranges overlap. They breed on Baffin Island and nearby Southampton Island. Each fall virtually the entire population gathers at the southern end of Hudson Bay and makes a single nonstop flight to the Gulf Coast.

Canada Goose
Branta canadensis
554

Small races 22–26" (56–66 cm); large races 35–45" (89–114 cm). Brownish body with black head and long black neck; conspicuous white cheek patch. The smaller Brant lacks the white cheek patch.

Voice
Rich, musical honking.

Habitat
Lakes, bays, rivers, and marshes. Often feeds in open grassland and stubble fields.

Range
Alaska and Baffin Island south to Massachusetts, North Carolina, and California. Winters south to northern Mexico and the Gulf Coast. Widespread as a semidomesticated bird in city parks and reservoirs.

Comments
When people speak of "wild geese" it is generally this species they have in mind. Familiar in every state and province; a common sight is their V-shaped flocks in migration. There is much geographical variation in size; some birds are scarcely larger than Mallards, others are at least twice that size. Tolerant of man, some even nest in city parks and suburbs.

Brant
Branta bernicla
555

22–30" (56–76 cm). Similar to the Canada Goose but smaller, shorter-necked, and lacking the conspicuous white cheek patch. Dark brown above with black head and neck, and an inconspicuous white mark on the side of the neck.

Voice
Low, guttural croaking, unlike the clear, rich honking of Canada Goose.

Habitat
Tundra and coastal islands in the Arctic; salt marshes and estuaries in winter.

Range
Breeds in the Arctic; winters along the coasts south to California and the Carolinas.

Comments
Flocks can be identified at a great distance as they travel in erratic, constantly shifting bunches unlike the V-shaped flocks of Canada Geese or the long, irregular lines of Snow Geese. Birds from far western North America have black underparts and until recently were considered a separate species, the "Black Brant."

Tundra Swan
Cygnus columbianus
557

48–55" (122–140 cm). The only swan likely to be seen in most of the East. Large, all white; black bill usually with small yellow spots at base of upper mandible. Holds neck straight up, unlike the Mute Swan's gracefully curved neck.

Voice
Mellow, rich bugling call, from migrating birds.

Habitat
Arctic tundra; winters on marshy lakes and bays.

Range
Breeds in Alaska and northern Canada east to Baffin Island. Winters in Aleutians and from Washington to Baja California and from Maryland to Texas; occasionally on the Great Lakes.

Comments
Each fall large numbers of Tundra Swans pause briefly on the Great Lakes before moving to their winter headquarters along the Atlantic Coast from Chesapeake Bay to North Carolina. They often travel in flocks of several hundred.

Mute Swan
Cygnus olor
558

58–60" (147–152 cm). Wingspan: 95" (2.3m). All white; bill of adults is orange with black knob at the base. Young birds are similar, but dingy.

Voice
Unlike other swans, it is usually silent except for some hissing and grunting notes. Loud trumpeting call is rarely heard.

Habitat
Ponds, rivers, coastal lagoons, and bays.

Range
Introduced from Europe into the northeastern United States; most frequent in southern New England, SE. New York, New Jersey, and Maryland; also established in Michigan.

Comments
With its wings arched over its back and its neck in a graceful S-curve, the male is extremely handsome on the water. A breeding pair will defend the nest and young against all comers, including humans, using their wings and bills.

Roseate Spoonbill
Ajaia ajaja
559

30–32" (76–81 cm). Wingspan: 53" (1.3 m). Brilliant pink with white neck and back, orange tail. Straight bill with broad flattened tip, hence its name. Immatures are white.

Voice
Low croak or cluck.

Habitat
Mangroves.

Range
Locally on the coasts of S. Florida, Louisiana (rare), and Texas. Also West Indies, Mexico, and Central and South America.

Comments
These birds spend much time feeding on shrimps and fish in the shallow waters of Florida Bay and the Gulf of Mexico. They obtain food by sweeping their bills from side to side and scooping up whatever they encounter. Early in the century their numbers were severely depleted by plume hunters but, with protective laws, they have increased once again.

Wood Stork
Mycteria americana
560

40–44" (102–112 cm). Wingspan: 66" (1.5 m). White with black flight feathers and tail. Head and neck bare, dark gray. Bill long, stout, and slightly curved, black in adults and yellow in immatures. Flies with its neck extended.

Voice
Dull croak. Usually silent except around nest. Young clatter endlessly.

Habitat
On or near the coast, breeding chiefly in cypress swamps; also in mangroves.

Range
Breeds in Florida; wanders to South Carolina and Texas, occasionally farther. Also in South America.

Comments
Often wrongly called Wood Ibis, this is a true stork. These birds perch motionless on a bare branch or slowly stalk through marshes in search of food. They are sometimes seen circling high in the air on rising thermal air currents. They nest in enormous colonies numbering up to 10,000 pairs.

White Ibis
Eudocimus albus
561

23–27" (58–68 cm). Wingspan: 38" (1 m). Adult white with
black wing tips (usually hidden at rest); bare face and
downcurved, red bill; red legs in breeding seasons, otherwise
slate-colored. Immature birds are brown above and white
below with brown bill and legs.

Voice
Grunts and growls.

Habitat
Marshy sloughs, mud flats, lagoons, and swamp forests.

Range
Coastal from South Carolina to Florida and Texas. South to
northern South America.

Comments
Around their colonies, ibises eat crayfish, which in turn
devour quantities of fish eggs. By keeping down the numbers
of crayfish, the birds help increase fish populations. In
addition, their droppings fertilize the water, greatly increasing
the growth of plankton, the basic food of all marsh life.

Great Egret
Casmerodius albus
562

35–41" (89–104 cm). Wingspan: 55" (1.4 m). A large, all-
white heron with a yellow bill and black legs.

Voice
Deep guttural croak. Also loud squawks when nesting.

Habitat
Freshwater and salt marshes, marshy ponds, and tidal flats.

Range
Oregon, Wisconsin, and Massachusetts to southern South
America. Winters north to South Carolina and Gulf Coast.

Comments
The Great Egret is one of the most magnificent herons; it has
fortunately recovered from long persecution by plume hunters.
Like the Great Blue Heron, it feeds alone, stalking fish, frogs,
snakes, and crayfish in shallow water.

Snowy Egret
Egretta thula
563

20–27" (51–68 cm). Wingspan: 38" (1 m). A small white
heron with a slender black bill, black legs, and yellow feet. In
the breeding season it has long lacy plumes on its back.
Similar to young of the Little Blue Heron, but that species has
a stouter, bluish-gray bill and greenish-yellow legs and feet.

Voice
Harsh squawk.

Habitat
Salt marshes, ponds, rice fields, and shallow coastal bays.

Range
N. California, Oklahoma, and Maine to southern South
America. Winters north to California and South Carolina.

Comments
During the 19th and early 20th centuries, Snowy Egrets were slaughtered almost to extinction for their fine plumes, used to decorate hats. Fortunately, complete protection has enabled them to increase their numbers again. Snowies are agile, often seen sprinting about in shallow water. Although they breed on freshwater marshes in the West, in the eastern states they are best known as salt marsh birds.

Little Blue Heron
Egretta caerulea
564, 570

25–30″ (63–76 cm). Wingspan: 41″ (1 m). Adult slate-blue with maroon neck; immature is white, usually with dark tips to primaries. Grayish bill with black tip; greenish legs. Young birds have a spotted or patched appearance.

Voice
Usually silent. Squawks when alarmed. Croaks, grunts, and screams at the nest site.

Habitat
Freshwater swamps and lagoons in the South; coastal thickets on islands in the North.

Range
East Coast from New York to Texas and inland to Oklahoma. Winters north to South Carolina. Also in South America.

Comments
This is one of the most numerous herons in the South and may be observed in large mixed concentrations of herons and egrets. It eats more insects than the larger herons and is sometimes seen following a plow to pick up insect larvae.

Great Blue Heron
Ardea herodias
565

39–52″ (99–132 cm). Wingspan: 70″ (1.8 m). A common, large, grayish heron with a yellowish bill. Flies with neck folded, whereas the Sandhill Crane flies with the neck extended. In Florida an all-white form, the "Great White" Heron, differs from the Great Egret in having greenish-yellow rather than black legs.

Voice
Hoarse, guttural squawk.

Habitat
Lakes, ponds, rivers, and marshes.

Range
Alaska, Quebec, and Nova Scotia south to Mexico and West Indies. Winters north to New England and S. Alaska.

Comments
This large heron is frequently found standing at the edge of a pond or marshy pool, watching for fish or frogs, which are its principal food. It also feeds on small mammals, reptiles, and occasionally birds. Most Great Blue Herons migrate south in the fall, but a few remain in the North during the winter; such lingering birds often fall victim to severe weather.

Reddish Egret
Egretta rufescens
566

30" (76 cm). Wingspan: 46" (1 m). Medium-sized heron.
Slaty with shaggy rufous head and neck; black legs; pink bill
with black tip. Also a white phase.

Voice
Squawks and croaks.

Habitat
Salt and brackish waters, breeding in shallow bays and
lagoons; in mangroves (Florida); among cacti, willows, and
other shrubs (Texas).

Range
Local in extreme S. Florida and along the Texas coasts, south
to the West Indies and Mexico.

Comments
Both color phases may be seen on the Gulf Coast, the dark one
predominating in Florida waters, the white in Texas, but this
varies according to locality; sometimes both occur together.
During the nuptial display the plumes on its head, neck, and
back stand out in a bristly ruff.

American Bittern
Botaurus lentiginosus
567

23–34" (58–86 cm). A medium-sized, brown heron. Outer
wing appears blackish in flight, contrasting with mustard-
brown of inner wing and body. At close range the bird shows
a black streak on each side of the throat.

Voice
Peculiar pumping sound, *oong-KA-chunk!*, repeated a few
times and often audible for half a mile.

Habitat
Freshwater and brackish marshes and marshy lake shores.

Range
British Columbia, Manitoba, and Newfoundland to Maryland,
Kansas, and S. California; also in Texas, Louisiana, and
Florida. Winters north to British Columbia, Ohio, and
Delaware, occasionally farther north.

Comments
Its call has given such names to the bird as "Thunder-pumper"
and "Stake-driver." It is secretive, preferring to freeze and
trust its concealing coloration when approached rather than
flush like other herons. When an observer is nearby it will
often raise its head, point its bill skyward, and sway slowly
from side to side, as if imitating waving reeds. If the observer
gets too close the bittern will fly off, uttering a low barking
call.

Tricolored Heron
Egretta tricolor
568

25–30" (63–76 cm). Wingspan: 38" (1 m). A gray-blue heron
with rufous neck and white belly.

Voice
Guttural croaks and squawks.

Habitat
Swamps, bayous, coastal ponds, salt marshes, mangrove islands, mud flats, and lagoons.

Range
Atlantic and Gulf coasts from Massachusetts southward. Winters north to Virginia. Also in South America.

Comments
A numerous heron in the Deep South, it is very slender and with graceful movements searches about for frogs or fish. Like bitterns, it has a habit of standing motionless among the grasses with bill pointing straight up to avoid detection.

Glossy Ibis
Plegadis falcinellus
569

22–25" (56–63 cm). Wingspan: 37" (0.9 m). A large, all-dark marsh bird with a downcurved bill. Plumage rich chestnut, wings glossy greenish.

Voice
Low grunt and higher-pitched bleats.

Habitat
Marshes, swamps, flooded fields, coastal bays, and estuaries.

Range
On or near the coast, chiefly from Maine to Florida and Texas. In recent years, inland to the Great Lakes.

Comments
It is now a common breeder where it was once rare or absent. Inland it frequently eats crayfish, but along the coast it feeds mostly on fiddler crabs. It also eats insects and snakes, including the poisonous water moccasin.

Green-backed Heron
Butorides striatus
571

15–22" (38–56 cm). Crow-sized. A small dark heron with bright orange or yellowish legs. Head and neck chestnut, crown black, small crest, back and wings dark green-gray.

Voice
Explosive, rasping *skyow!* Also croaks, cackles, and clucks.

Habitat
Lake margins, streams, ponds, and marshes.

Range
British Columbia, Minnesota, and New Brunswick south to southern South America. Winters north to South Carolina, the Gulf Coast, and California.

Comments
The most common heron in much of its range, all it requires is a pond or stream with thick bushes or trees nearby for nesting and soft, muddy borders in which to search for its prey. It stretches its neck and bill forward as if taking aim, nervously flicking its short tail, and, after a few elaborately cautious steps, seizes the fish with a jab of its bill. A retiring bird, it often flushes unexpectedly from the edge of water.

Black-crowned Night-Heron
Nycticorax nycticorax
572

23–28″ (58–71 cm). Wingspan: 44″ (1.1 m). A medium-sized, stocky, rather short-necked heron with black crown and back, gray wings, and white underparts; short, black bill; pinkish or yellowish legs. In breeding season it has 2 or more long white plumes on back of head. Young birds are dull gray-brown lightly spotted with white. May be confused with young Yellow-crowned Night-Herons and American Bitterns.

Voice
Harsh, barking *quawk!*, most often heard at night or at dusk. A bewildering variety of croaking, barking, and screaming calls are uttered in the nesting colony.

Habitat
Marshes, swamps, and wooded streams.

Range
Washington, Saskatchewan, Minnesota, and New Brunswick, to southern South America. Winters in South.

Comments
As its name implies it is largely nocturnal, spending daylight hours roosting in trees or reedbeds. It is therefore best known for its call. These birds keep to themselves.

Yellow-crowned Night-Heron
Nycticorax violaceus
573

22–27″ (56–68 cm). Wingspan: 44″ (1.1 m). Medium-sized heron. Adult is slate-gray with black head, white cheeks, yellowish crown and plumes, black bill, and orange legs. In flight the feet extend beyond the tail. Immature birds are grayish, finely speckled with white above, like young Black-crowned Night-Herons but with a thicker bill and longer legs.

Voice
High-pitched *quawk*.

Habitat
Wooded swamps and coastal thickets.

Range
Massachusetts to Florida and west to Texas; mainly near the coast, but north along the Mississippi River and its larger tributaries, rarely to the central states. Also warmer portions of Middle and South America and West Indies.

Comments
Contrary to popular opinion, herons do not stab a fish (it would then be difficult to release) but grasp it in their bill, toss it in the air, and swallow it head first.

Anhinga
Anhinga anhinga
574

34–36″ (86–91 cm). A blackish bird of southern swamps with a very long, slender neck and long tail. Male's plumage has greenish iridescence; upper surface of wings silvery gray. Female has tawny brown neck and breast, and black belly.

Voice
Generally silent. Low grunts reported.

Habitat
Freshwater ponds and swamps with thick vegetation, especially cypress.

Range
Atlantic and Gulf coasts from North Carolina to Texas and in the Mississippi Valley north to Arkansas and Tennessee. South to southern South America.

Comments
It is also known as the Snakebird because its body is submerged when swimming so that only its head and long, slender neck are visible above the water. Its long, dagger-shaped, serrated bill is ideally suited for catching fish, which it flips into the air and gulps down head first. Cormorants and Anhingas lack oil glands with which to preen and so must perch with their wings half-open to dry them in the sun. Unlike cormorants, Anhingas often soar in circles high overhead.

Double-crested Cormorant
Phalacrocorax auritus
575

30–35″ (76–89 cm). Goose-sized. Slender-bodied, dark bird with a long neck and a slender, hooked bill that is usually tilted upward when swimming. Orange throat pouch. Stands upright when perched. Tufts on the crown rarely visible.

Voice
Deep guttural grunt.

Habitat
Lakes, rivers, swamps, and coasts.

Range
Breeds from Alaska and Newfoundland south to Mexico and the Bahamas. Winters north to Long Island and S. Alaska.

Comments
The Double-crested is the most familiar cormorant in the East. Except in the Northeast during the winter, and along the Gulf Coast, it is the only cormorant seen. Cormorants migrate in large, V-shaped flocks like migrating geese but are silent when flying.

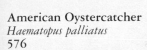

American Oystercatcher
Haematopus palliatus
576

17–21″ (43–53 cm). Chicken-sized. Boldly patterned in blackish brown and white. Long red bill, pink feet. Shows a bold white wing patch in flight.

Voice
Piercing *kleep!* Also a ploverlike *cle-ar*.

Habitat
Sandy and pebbly beaches, mud flats, borders of salt marshes.

Range
Along the coast from Baja California and Massachusetts south to Argentina and Chile. Winters from North Carolina southward.

Comments

Oystercatchers are large, conspicuous birds that were quickly shot out along the Atlantic Coast. Given total protection, they have once again become numerous and now nest in numbers as far north as Massachusetts, where just a few years ago they were very rare. Oystercatchers insert their long, bladelike bills into mussels and other bivalves, severing the powerful adductor muscles before the shells can close. They also feed on barnacles and snails. Although they do not breed in colonies, these birds gather in large flocks on migration and in winter.

American Avocet
Recurvirostra americana
577

16–20″ (40–51 cm). Pigeon-sized. Slender and long-legged. Upperparts and wings patterned in black and white; underparts in white. Head and neck rust-colored in summer, white in winter. Bill very thin and strongly upturned.

Voice
Loud repeated *wheep*.

Habitat
Freshwater marshes and shallow marshy lakes; breeds locally in salt or brackish marshes. Many move to the coast in winter.

Range

Washington and Manitoba south to Texas and California. Winters from S. Texas and California to Guatemala. Uncommon but regular on Atlantic Coast in fall.

Comments
During their southward migration every fall, a few Avocets stray eastward to the Atlantic Coast, where they may be seen singly or in small flocks on shallow lagoons and coastal ponds. Avocets feed much like Spoonbills, sweeping their bills from side to side along the surface of the water to pick up crustaceans, aquatic insects, and floating seeds.

Black-necked Stilt
Himantopus mexicanus
578

13–16″ (33–40 cm). Black above, white below; head patterned in black and white; long neck; very long red legs; straight, very thin bill.

Voice
Sharp *kip-kip-kip-kip*.

Habitat
Salt marshes and shallow coastal bays.

Range

Oregon and Saskatchewan to the Gulf Coast, and along the Atlantic Coast from Delaware and the Carolinas to northern South America. Winters mainly south of the United States.

Comments
At nesting season they are particularly aggressive and will often fly low over an approaching human being, uttering a loud alarm call with their long red legs trailing behind them.

Red Phalarope
Phalaropus fulicaria
579

8" (20 cm). In summer, rich chestnut, dark crown, white face; short, stout, yellow bill with a black tip. In winter, gray above and white below, bill darker. Unstreaked back, wing stripe. Like other phalaropes, the female is more brightly colored than the male.

Voice
Sharp metallic *beek*.

Habitat
The most oceanic of all shorebirds, mostly in the nonbreeding season; otherwise it is found in bays, inlets, inland lakes, shores, coasts, and on the tundra in the breeding season.

Range
Islands and coasts along the Arctic Ocean of both hemispheres; in America south to northern Canada. Winters at sea, chiefly in the Southern Hemisphere.

Comments
Far at sea, these birds look like bobbing corks or miniature gulls riding the waves. The greater part of their diet while they are at sea is made up of tiny marine animals known as plankton. On land they forage for aquatic larvae.

Snowy Plover
Charadrius alexandrinus
580

5–7" (13–17 cm). Whitish with pale brown upperparts, black legs, slender black bill, and a small black mark on each side of the breast. The similar Piping Plover has a stubbier, yellow bill and yellow legs.

Voice
Plaintive *chu-we* or *o-wee-ah*.

Habitat
Flat, sandy beaches; alkali beds; and sandy areas with little vegetation.

Range
Locally from Washington, Colorado, and Oklahoma to South America, and along the Gulf Coast as far east as NW. Florida. Winters from California and the Gulf Coast south.

Comments
The Snowy Plover's patchy distribution is due to its habitat requirements. Keeping to large, flat expanses of sand, it avoids competition for food in a habitat in which few other species can exist.

Piping Plover
Charadrius melodus
581

6–7" (15–17 cm). Sparrow-sized. Pale whitish with complete or incomplete black breast band; yellow legs; bill yellowish in spring, dark in fall.

Voice
Clear, whistled *peep-lo*.

Habitat
Bare, dry, sandy areas, both inland and on the coast.

Range
Lakes in interior Canada and Newfoundland south along the Atlantic Coast to Virginia, rarely to the Carolinas. Winters on the Atlantic and Gulf coasts, north as far as the Carolinas.

Comments
The color of dry sand, the Piping Plover is difficult to see on the beach. The eggs and downy chicks also blend with the sand. Many of its former nesting sites have been destroyed.

Semipalmated Plover
Charadrius semipalmatus
582

6–8″ (15–20 cm). A dark-backed shorebird with white underparts and a conspicuous black breast band from which it gets its common name of "Ring-necked Plover." Bill stubby, yellow-orange, with dark tip. The Piping Plover is similar but is much paler above.

Voice
Plaintive 2-note whistle: *tsuwee*. Also a soft chuckle.

Habitat
Beaches and tidal flats, shallow pools in salt marshes; lakeshores in the interior during migration.

Range:
Breeds from the Aleutians, Alaska and the islands of the Canadian Arctic south to Nova Scotia, Quebec, N. Manitoba, and N. British Columbia. Winters regularly from California and the Gulf Coast south; in smaller numbers farther north.

Comments
This is one of the most familiar American shorebirds. The birds usually migrate in flocks, but otherwise tend to scatter when feeding. They have the typical plover habit of running along the beach for several paces, then stopping abruptly and raising their heads.

Ruddy Turnstone
Arenaria interpres
583

8–10″ (20–25 cm). A stocky shorebird with orange legs. Upperparts rusty red in summer, duller in winter; white below. Face and breast have conspicuous black markings, duller but still visible in winter. Because of their striking flight pattern they are sometimes called Calico-backs.

Voice
A metallic but musical *netticut* or *kek-kek*.

Habitat
Coastal tundra; in winter on rocky, pebbly, and sandy coasts and beaches.

Range
Islands and coasts in the Arctic. Winters regularly from California and the Carolinas south to South America, in smaller numbers farther north.

Comments
Turnstones are named from their method of feeding, in which

they walk along the beach, deftly rolling small stones and pebbles and seizing the animals hiding underneath. They also dig holes in the sand, often larger than themselves, in pursuit of burrowing crustaceans.

Black-bellied Plover
Pluvialis squatarola
584

10–13" (25–33 cm). Quail-sized. Gray with a bold white stripe on the wing visible when the bird flies. In flight it always shows a black patch under the wing. At any season it has a white rump.

Voice
Clear, whistled *pee-a-weee*.

Habitat
Tundra; in migration and in winter it occurs on beaches and coastal marshes, less commonly on inland marshes, lakeshores, and plowed fields.

Range
N. Alaska and Arctic islands to S. Alaska, Southampton Island, and southern Baffin Island. Winters to South America.

Comments
The Black-bellied Plover is usually found singly or in small groups. Our largest plover, it is conspicuous among its usual companions, the smaller plovers, turnstones, and sandpipers. It is wary and is usually the first to fly off.

Dunlin
Calidris alpina
585

8½" (21 cm). Robin-sized. Fairly long bill with a distinct droop at the tip. In summer, reddish black; white below with a conspicuous black belly. In winter, dull gray; paler below.

Voice
Cheerp or *chit-lit*.

Habitat
Beaches, extensive mud and sand flats, tidal inlets and lagoons; also inland lake and river shores.

Range
Arctic coasts on both hemispheres. In America, south to Alaska and Hudson Bay. Winters on the Pacific Coast from British Columbia and on the Atlantic Coast from New England south to Mexico and Florida.

Comments
These handsome birds, also known as Red-backed Sandpipers, are very tame and thus easy to approach and study. Among the hardiest of the shorebirds, thousands sometimes spend the winter months on sandbars or inlets along the coast as far north as Long Island.

Sanderling
Calidris alba
586

8" (20 cm). Robin-sized. In summer, rufous head and breast and white belly; in winter the rufous areas are replaced by pale gray; black bill and legs; conspicuous white wing stripe.

Voice
Sharp *kip*. Conversational chatter while feeding.

Habitat
Ocean beaches, sandbars, occasionally mud flats; inland lake and river shores.

Range

Worldwide. In the Americas it breeds along the coasts of the Arctic Ocean south to Hudson Bay. Winters from the United States (both coasts) to southern South America.

Comments
Practically every day of the year these birds may be found on any ocean beach. As a wave comes roaring in, the birds run up on the beach just ahead of the breaker, then rush after the retreating surf to feed on the tiny crustaceans and mollusks stranded by the outgoing water.

Purple Sandpiper
Calidris maritima
587

9″ (23 cm). Dark slate with orange-yellow legs; bill dull orange with black tip. Paler and more streaked in winter.

Voice
Single or double *twit*.

Habitat
Rocky coasts and promontories.

Range

Arctic and subarctic Canada. Winters on the Atlantic Coast south to South Carolina.

Comments
These hardy birds remain through the coldest winters on wave-washed rocks along the ocean front. Sometimes flocks of as many as fifty or more may be found on stone jetties. Purple Sandpipers can be approached closely.

Least Sandpiper
Calidris minutilla
588

6″ (15 cm). Sparrow-sized; smallest of American shorebirds. Brownish with yellowish or greenish legs, a short thin bill, and a streaked breast. Grayer in winter plumage.

Voice
A loud clear *treep;* when feeding, a soft chuckle.

Habitat
Grassy pools, bogs, and marshes with open areas; also flooded fields and mud flats.

Range

Breeds in Aleutians, Alaska, and Canada. Winters from southern United States to central South America.

Comments
These are probably the tamest of shorebirds and at times fly off only when almost underfoot. They prefer grassy areas to the more open flats frequented by most shorebirds.

Stilt Sandpiper
Calidris himantopus
589

8½" (21 cm). Robin-sized. Chestnut head stripes and barring below identify this bird in breeding plumage. Nonbreeding birds have much paler plumage with a white line over the eye. Long bill, slightly downcurved at the tip. Has long, greenish legs. Wings unpatterned.

Voice
Simple *tu-tu* similar to that of Lesser Yellowlegs.

Habitat
Grassy pools and shores of ponds and lakes.

Range
Breeds in N. Alaska and Canada. Winters in Florida and South America. Uncommon along the Atlantic Coast.

Comments
Often associated with dowitchers and yellowlegs, Stilt Sandpipers resemble both species and appear to be intermediate between the two. While yellowlegs move about continually in nervous, jerky motions and dowitchers feed slowly, probing deep into the mud, Stilt Sandpipers move like yellowlegs but cover more ground, at the same time feeding deliberately like dowitchers.

Willet
Catoptrophorus semipalmatus
590

15" (38 cm). Pigeon-sized. Grayish brown with gray legs. Best told in flight by its flashy black-and-white wing pattern.

Voice
Extremely vocal; their *will-will-willet* calls identify them immediately. They also utter a rapid *kuk-kuk-kuk-kuk-kuk*.

Habitat
Coastal beaches, freshwater and salt marshes, lakeshores, and wet prairies.

Range
Breeds locally in southern Canada, United States, and the West Indies. Winters from southern United States to central South America.

Comments
Willets look quite nondescript on the ground, but once in flight or even with wings spread out, they are distinguished by their striking black-and-white color pattern. They frequently accompany godwits on migration.

Spotted Sandpiper
Actitis macularia
591

7½" (19 cm). Robin-sized. In breeding plumage olive-brown above, many black spots below; lacks spotting in fall and winter.

Voice
Clear *peet-weet;* also a soft trill.

Habitat
Almost anyplace with water nearby, both in open country and in wooded areas.

Range
N. Alaska and Canada to southern United States. Winters from southern United States to South America.

Comments
This is one of the best known of American shorebirds. Its habit of endlessly bobbing the rear part of its body up and down has earned it the vernacular name "teeter-tail." When flushed from the margin of a pond or stream it is easily identified by its short bursts of rapid wingbeats alternating with brief glides.

Whimbrel
Numenius phaeopus
592

17″ (43 cm). Crow-sized, with long legs. Gray-brown with striped crown and medium-length curved bill.

Voice
5–7 loud, clear, whistled notes.

Habitat
Arctic tundra, preferring freshwater pools near the coast. On migration, chiefly coastal salt meadows, mud flats, and grassy slopes along the coast.

Range
North America. In America winters from Virginia, Texas, and California to southern South America.

Comments
The Whimbrel, or Hudsonian Curlew, is found not only along both coasts but in the center of the continent. It is numerous because of its wary behavior, its remote nesting grounds on the Arctic tundra, and its successful competition with other big shorebirds for food and breeding territory. Like many other tundra breeders, those in the east fly offshore during their autumn migration to South America, returning in spring mainly through the interior.

Lesser Yellowlegs
Tringa flavipes
593

10½″ (26 cm). Legs yellowish orange. Black bill relatively thin and short for body size. Breeding plumage shows white belly, streaked breast, and fine barring on sides and flanks.

Voice
A flat, unmelodious *tu-tu,* normally given in doublets.

Habitat
Marshy ponds, lake and river shores, mud flats; in the breeding season, northern bogs.

Range
Alaska and Canada. Winters from southern United States to southern South America.

Comments
This species usually occurs in large flocks. The Lesser Yellowlegs is tame, allowing an observer a close approach.

Short-billed Dowitcher
Limnodromus griseus
594

12″ (30 cm). Rich rust-brown in spring, gray in fall; very long bill, greenish legs, barred tail, white rump and back.

Voice
Loud, rapid, whistled *tu-tu-tu.*

Habitat
Mud flats, creeks, salt marshes, and tidal estuaries.

Range
S. Alaska to eastern Canada. Winters from southern United States to central South America.

Comments
Dowitchers often occur in large flocks—sometimes in the thousands—on coastal flats during migrations, remaining well bunched whether in flight or feeding in the mud. They probe deeply with their long bills with rapid up-and-down motion.

Long-billed Dowitcher
Limnodromus scolopaceus
595

12¼″ (31 cm). A stocky shorebird with a very long, straight bill. Breeding birds have rusty underparts and dark, streaked upperparts; winter birds are gray. In all plumages shows a conspicuous white rump and lower back, most easily seen in flight. Very similar to Short-billed Dowitcher, but darker and more coarsely streaked above, and with a longer bill.

Voice
A sharp, thin *keek,* very different from soft *tu-tu-tu* of Short-billed Dowitcher.

Habitat
Breeds in swampy bogs; in migration and winter occurs on mud flats, marshy pools, and margins of freshwater ponds.

Range
N. Alaska, and northwestern Canada. Winters from southern United States south to Guatemala.

Comments
Dowitchers are often seen during migration. The main fall migration of Long-bills takes place in September and October, when a majority of Short-bills have already departed.

Hudsonian Godwit
Limosa haemastica
596

15″ (38 cm). Underparts rufous in the breeding season, otherwise gray above, whitish below. Conspicuous black-and-white tail, broad white wing stripe, and black wing lining. Long, slightly upturned bill.

Voice
High-pitched *chip-ta-it* and *quit-quit.* Usually silent.

Habitat
Tundra; chiefly mud flats on migration.

Range
Breeds on the Canadian tundra and migrates through the United States; winters in the southern parts of South America.

Comments
Never common, the Hudsonian Godwit was for many years
hunted for food and became scarce. Now completely
protected, its numbers have increased considerably. This large
shorebird can be seen in flocks of up to several dozen or more
during fall passage on the coastal mud flats of the northeastern
states.

Marbled Godwit
Limosa fedoa
597

18″ (46 cm). Crow-sized. A large, pale, buff-brown shorebird
with cinnamon wing linings and buffy underparts, and a long,
pinkish upturned bill.

Voice
Prolonged, far-reaching, whistled *god-wit, god-wit,* or *go-wit,
go-wit*—hence its name.

Habitat
Extensive grasslands; on migration, salt marshes, tidal creeks,
mud flats, and sea beaches.

Range
South-central Canada and north-central United States.
Winters from southernmost United States to Central America
and on the Pacific Coast of South America to Chile.

Comments
One of our largest shorebirds, it breeds on the vast grassy
plains of the West but less abundantly than in former days. It
is a rich buff color, blending perfectly with the brown grass of
the plains.

Clapper Rail
Rallus longirostris
598

14–16″ (25–40 cm). Chicken-sized. Long-billed, grayish
brown above, buff-cinnamon below; cheeks gray.

Voice
Harsh clattering *kek-kek-kek-kek-kek.*

Habitat
Salt marshes.

Range
Breeds along the coasts from California and Massachusetts to
South America. Winters north to New Jersey, rarely farther
north.

Comments
Its call is one of the most familiar sounds in the salt marshes
in summer. Although generally secretive, the birds are
sometimes forced into view by high tides, when they may be
seen along roads in the marsh or standing on floating boards.

Sora
Porzana carolina
599

8–10″ (20–25 cm). Quail-sized. Gray-breasted with a black
face and stubby yellow bill. Upperparts mottled brown; lower
abdomen banded with black and white. Young birds in fall
lack the black face and have buff breasts.

Voice
Most familiar call is a musical series of piping notes rapidly descending the scale. When an intruder approaches a nest the adults come boldly into view, uttering an explosive *keek!*

Habitat
Chiefly freshwater marshes and marshy ponds; rice fields and salt marshes in winter.

Range
British Columbia, Mackenzie, and Newfoundland south to Pennsylvania, Oklahoma, and Baja California; winters north to California and to the Carolinas.

Comments
These birds are especially numerous in fall and winter in southern marshes and rice fields, where they are primarily seed-eaters. Although shot in large numbers every year, their high reproductive rate ensures a stable population.

Purple Gallinule
Porphyrula martinica
600

11–13″ (28–33 cm). Chicken-sized. Rich purplish blue with green upperparts, white underside of base of tail, yellowish-green legs, red-and-yellow bill, and light blue frontal shield.

Voice
Squawking and cackling. Also guttural grunts.

Habitat
Freshwater marshes with lily pads, pickerelweed, and other aquatic vegetation.

Range
The Carolinas and Tennessee to Florida and Texas; wanders to the northern states. South to southern South America.

Comments
This beautiful bird is often observed walking on lily pads, using its very long toes, and may even sometimes be seen climbing up into low bushes. When walking or swimming it constantly jerks its head and tail.

American Coot
Fulica americana
601

15″ (38 cm). Slate-gray with a conspicuous white bill; greenish legs and lobed feet.

Voice
Variety of calls, some fowl-like clucking, and cackles, grunts, and other harsh notes.

Habitat
Open ponds and marshes; in winter, also in saltwater bays and inlets.

Range
Southern Canada to northern South America.

Comments
Coots are the most aquatic members of their family, moving

on open water like ducks and often feeding with them. They are excellent swimmers and divers, and they eat various aquatic plants. They also come out on land to feed on seeds, grass, and waste grain. They often become tame when fed scraps and bits of bread.

Belted Kingfisher
Ceryle alcyon
602

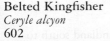

13″ (33 cm). Pigeon-sized. Bushy crest; daggerlike bill; blue-gray above, white below. Male has a blue-gray breast band; female similar but with a chestnut belly band.

Voice
Loud, penetrating rattle, given on the wing and when perched.

Habitat
Rivers, lakes, and saltwater estuaries.

Range
Breeds from Alaska and Canada and throughout United States. Winters south to Panama and the West Indies.

Comments
Kingfishers often hover like a tern over water where a fish is visible and dive vertically for the prey. They may also take crabs, crayfish, salmanders, lizards, mice, and insects.

Peregrine Falcon
Falco peregrinus
603

15–21″ (38–53 cm). Wingspan: 40″ (1 m). Crow-sized. Adults slate-gray above and pale below, with fine bars and spots of black; narrow tail; long pointed wings; conspicuous black "mustaches." Young birds darker below and browner.

Voice
Rasping *kack-kack-kack*. Also a long ascending wail, *WEEchew-WEEchew.*

Habitat
Open country, especially along rivers, also near lakes, and the coast. Migrates chiefly along the coast. Also eastern urban centers with large pigeon populations.

Range
Formerly bred from Alaska and Greenland south to Georgia and Baja California, but now restricted to the northern parts of its range in the East. Winters north to British Columbia and Massachusetts. Also breeds in southern South America.

Comments
Spectacular on the wing, in former times they were a favorite choice for the sport of falconry, plunging from tremendous heights at speeds estimated at 180 miles per hour to capture flying birds. The Peregrine has been drastically reduced in numbers by pesticides. These falcons are quite tolerant of man and formerly nested on windowsills and ledges of buildings in our largest cities, where they preyed on pigeons, prompting the successful reintroduction of captive-raised birds in eastern, pigeon-plagued urban centers.

Northern Harrier
Circus cyaneus
604

16–24" (40–61 cm). Wingspan: 42" (1.1 m). Long-winged, long-tailed hawk with a white rump, usually seen soaring unsteadily over marshes with its wings held in a shallow V. Female and young are brown above, streaked below, young birds with a rusty tone. Male, seen less than young birds and females, has pale gray back, head, and breast.

Voice
Usually silent. At the nest a *kee-kee-kee-kee* or a sharp whistle.

Habitat
Marshes.

Range
Eastern Aleutians, Alaska, Mackenzie, and Newfoundland to Virginia and northern Mexico. Winters north to British Columbia, Wisconsin, and New Brunswick.

Comments
This is the only North American member of a group of hawks known as harriers. All hunt by flying close to the ground, taking small animals by surprise. They seldom pursue their prey in the air or watch quietly from an exposed perch.

Osprey
Pandion haliaetus
605

21–24" (53–61 cm). Wingspan: 54–72" (1.4–1.8 m). A large, long-winged "fish hawk." Brown above and white below; white head with dark brown line through eye and on side of face. Wing shows distinct bend at the "wrist."

Voice
Loud, musical chirping.

Habitat
Lakes, rivers, and seacoasts.

Range
Breeds from Alaska and Newfoundland south to Florida and the Gulf Coast and California south to Argentina.

Comments
This hawk is well adapted for capturing fish, which comprise its entire diet. The soles of Ospreys' feet are equipped with sharp, spiny projections that give the bird a firm grip.

Bald Eagle
Haliaeetus leucocephalus
606

30–31" (76–79 cm). Wingspan: 72–90" (1.8–2.3 m). A large blackish eagle with white head, white tail, and a long, heavy yellow bill. Young birds colored with variable shades of brown, mottled with white.

Voice
Squeaky cackling.

Habitat
Lakes, rivers, marshes, and seacoasts.

Range
Formerly bred throughout most of North America, but now

restricted as a breeding bird to Aleutians, Alaska, parts of northern and eastern Canada, northern United States, and Florida. In winter, along almost any body of water, especially the larger rivers in the interior of the continent.

Comments
Eating dead fish stranded on beaches and riverbanks has caused many Bald Eagles to absorb large amounts of pesticides, which interfere with the birds' calcium metabolism and result in thin-shelled and often infertile eggs. Once a familiar sight along rivers and coasts, our national bird is today known mainly as an occasional migrant; adults now usually outnumber young birds. Unless these pesticides can be removed from the birds' environment, we may face the loss of one of North America's most magnificent birds.

Boat-tailed Grackle
Quiscalus major
607

Males 16–17" (40–43 cm); females 12–13" (30–33 cm). Tail very long and keel-shaped. Male black, iridescent blue on back and breast; yellow or brown eyes. Female smaller, brown with a paler breast.

Voice
Harsh *jeeb-jeeb-jeeb-jeeb*.

Habitat
Marshes along the coast; in Florida also in farmlands.

Range
Resident along the coast from New Jersey south to Louisiana; also inland in peninsular Florida.

Comments
This species and its close relative the Great-tailed Grackle were thought to be a single species until it was recently found that both nest in Louisiana without interbreeding.

Fish Crow
Corvus ossifragus
608

17" (43 cm). All black, thin bill. May be best told by its voice.

Voice
Two calls: a nasal *kwok* and a 2-noted nasal *ah-ah*.

Habitat
Low coastal country, near tidewater in the North; in the South also lakes, rivers, and swamps far inland.

Range
Atlantic and Gulf coasts from Massachusetts and extreme southern New England south to Florida and west to Texas. Also inland along the larger rivers north to Arkansas, SW. Tennessee, central Virginia, and south-central Pennsylvania.

Comments
Nearly all the heronries on the coast have attendant Fish Crows ever ready to plunder the heron nests for eggs. An omnivorous feeder like all crows, consuming everything.

Red-winged Blackbird
Agelaius phoeniceus
609

7–9½" (17–24 cm). Smaller than a Robin. Male is black with bright red shoulder patches. Female and young are heavily streaked with dusky brown.

Voice
Rich, musical *O-ka-LEEEE!*

Habitat
Marshes, swamps, and wet and dry meadows; pastures.

Range
Breeds from Alaska and Newfoundland south to Florida, the Gulf Coast, and central Mexico. Winters regularly north to Pennsylvania and British Columbia.

Comments
Although primarily a marsh bird, the Red-wing will nest near virtually any body of water and occasionally breeds in upland pastures. Each pair raises two or three broods a season. Flocks number in the hundreds of thousands or millions.

Tree Swallow
Tachycineta bicolor
610

5–6¼" (13–16 cm). Sparrow-sized. The only swallow in the East with metallic blue or blue-green upperparts and clear white underparts. Young are dull brown, whitish below.

Voice
Cheerful series of liquid twitters.

Habitat
Lake shores, flooded meadows, marshes, and streams.

Range
Alaska, N. Manitoba, and Newfoundland south to Maryland, Nebraska, Colorado, and California. Winters north to the Carolinas, the Gulf Coast, and S. California; occasionally to New York and Massachusetts.

Comments
This bird's habit of feeding on bayberries enables it to winter farther north than other swallows. They enjoy playing with a feather, which they drop and then retrieve as it floats in the air. They gather in enormous flocks along the coast in fall.

Mangrove Cuckoo
Coccyzus minor
611

12" (30 cm). Blue Jay-sized. Brown above, rich buff or tawny below; black facial mask; curved bill. Long, graduated tail with black-and-white spots at tip.

Voice
Low, guttural *gaw-gaw-gaw-gaw-gaw,* almost like a soft bark or the scolding of a squirrel.

Habitat
Only in Florida mangrove swamps.

Range
S. Florida through the West Indies and from Mexico to northern South America.

Comments
In North America, this species is found only in the Florida
Keys and on the adjacent Gulf Coast as far as Tampa Bay. It is
difficult to observe, remaining hidden in dense thickets.

Horned Lark
Eremophila alpestris
612

7–8″ (17–20 cm). Larger than a sparrow. Brown, with black
stripe below eye, black crescent on breast, and black "horns"
(not always seen). Walks rather than hops. In flight, tail seen
as black with white edges.

Voice
Ti-ti. Song delivered in flight is a high-pitched series of
tinkling notes.

Habitat
Plains, fields, airports, and beaches.

Range
Arctic south to North Carolina, Missouri, coastal Texas, and
northern South America.

Comments
The only true lark in the New World, this is one of our
earliest nesting birds. Even in the northern states, nests may
be found in February, when the first set of eggs is often
destroyed by severe snowstorms. As many as three broods.

Marsh Wren
Cistothorus palustris
613

4–5½″ (10–14 cm). Smaller than a sparrow. Brown above,
pale buff below; a white eyebrow and white back streaks.

Voice
Liquid gurgling song ending in a mechanical chatter.

Habitat
Fresh and brackish marshes with cattails, reeds, bulrushes, or
sedges.

Range
British Columbia, Manitoba, and New Brunswick south to
Florida, the Gulf Coast, and northern Mexico. Winters north
to New Jersey, along the Gulf Coast, and on the Pacific Coast
north to Washington.

Comments
The male has a number of mates, each of which builds a nest
of her own. In addition, the male may also build up to half a
dozen "dummy" nests, often incomplete, one of which may be
used as a roost.

Swamp Sparrow
Melospiza georgiana
614

5″ (13 cm). A chunky, dark sparrow with unstreaked
underparts, bright rufous cap, and rusty wings; back and tail
dark brown; face and breast gray; throat white.

Voice
Sweet, musical trill, all on 1 note.

Habitat
Freshwater marshes and open wooded swamps; in migration with other sparrows in weedy fields, parks, and brush piles.

Range
From east-central Canada south to east-central United States; winters south to the Gulf of Mexico.

Comments
A bird of the wetlands during the breeding season, the Swamp Sparrow appears in a variety of other habitats during migration and winter. It is rather shy, but responds readily to any squeaking noise, and can usually be lured into view.

Black-whiskered Vireo
Vireo altiloquus
615

5½" (14 cm). Olive-green above, white below with a dusky streak below the eye, giving the bird its name.

Voice
Song a continuous series of short, paired, Robin-like phrases, separated by brief pauses.

Habitat
Mangroves, thick scrub, and shade trees.

Range
Breeds in S. Florida and the West Indies. Winters in northern South America, less commonly in the Lesser Antilles.

Comments
They are not shy and come regularly into gardens and shade trees in Key West. They may also be seen in the dense scrub and tropical hammocks in the Upper Keys and occasionally in coconut palms and mangroves around Miami. They eat insects and, rarely, berries and other soft fruits.

Sharp-tailed Sparrow
Ammodramus caudacutus
616

5½" (14 cm). The combination of a dark cap, gray ear patch, and a bright orange-buff triangular area on the face distinguishes this species from the only other salt-marsh sparrow, the Seaside Sparrow.

Voice
A dry, insect-like *kip-kip-zeeeee*.

Habitat
Along the coast, in the drier, grassy portions of salt marsh and inland to grassy, freshwater marshes.

Range
Locally from central Canada to the Middle Atlantic states; winters chiefly on the south Atlantic and Gulf coasts.

Comments
These birds spend most of their lives in dense, coarse marsh grass, and by the end of the breeding season their plumage is so badly worn that little of the distinctive pattern remains visible. A month later, however, they have acquired a fresh coat of feathers.

Seaside Sparrow
Ammodramus maritimus
617

6″ (15 cm). A dark, gray-streaked salt-marsh sparrow with a dull yellow mustache and dull yellow spot in front of the eye.

Voice
2 short, sharp notes followed by a buzzy *zeeee*.

Habitat
Exclusively grassy salt marsh, favoring the wetter portions.

Range
Salt marshes of the Atlantic and Gulf coasts from southern New England to Florida and Texas, wintering in the southern portions of this range.

Comments
Literally a seaside bird; few other sparrows have so restricted a habitat. Favoring the wetter sections of salt marsh, it feeds much less on seeds than do other sparrows, but eats tiny young crabs, snails, and other small marine animals along the tidal creeks of salt meadows. Like all birds living near the ground in grass, it is difficult to detect until almost underfoot, whereupon it flushes, flies for a short distance, drops down into the thick grass, and runs along like a mouse. The best opportunity to view one is when it is in song atop a grass stem or small shrub.

Yellow-rumped Warbler
Dendroica coronata
618

5–6″ (13–15 cm). Breeding male dull bluish above, streaked with black; breast and flanks blackish. Rump yellow. 2 white wing bars. Crown and small area at sides of breast yellow. Eastern birds ("Myrtle Warbler") have white throats; western birds ("Audubon's Warbler") have yellow throats. Females, fall males, and young are streaked gray-brown, but always have yellow rump and white spots in tail.

Voice
A thin, buzzy warble; a sharp *chek!*

Habitat
Coniferous and mixed forests; winters in large numbers along the Atlantic Coast.

Range
N. Alaska, N. Manitoba, and central Quebec south in the West to northern Mexico and in the East to Maine, Massachusetts, N. New York, and Michigan. Winters from southern part of breeding range south to Costa Rica and the West Indies.

Comments
Until recently, the eastern and western populations of the Yellow-rumped Warbler were thought to be two distinct species, respectively the "Myrtle Warbler" and "Audubon's Warbler." However, it has been found that in the narrow zone where the ranges of the two come together, the birds hybridize freely. In the East, the "Myrtle Warbler" is an abundant migrant, and the only warbler that regularly spends the winter in the northern states.

PART IV APPENDICES

AN INTRODUCTION TO MARINE INVERTEBRATES

The term invertebrate is vaguely familiar to most people but somewhat mysterious to many. The word actually describes what certain animals lack—a backbone or spinal column. Fishes, amphibians, reptiles, birds, and mammals are vertebrates. All other animals lack a backbone and are, by definition, invertebrates.

Marine invertebrates are among the most fascinating animals on earth. They include creatures as diverse as sponges, jellyfishes, worms, snails, clams, squids, shrimps, lobsters, crabs, sea stars, and sea urchins. Many of the less familiar kinds of invertebrates, such as sponges, sea anemones, or hydroids, may be mistaken for plants. Closer investigation, however, reveals that they are animals.

The following essays and illustrations explain the principal anatomical features of the major phyla of marine invertebrates. A familiarity with the basics of invertebrate anatomy will help you identify the animals you encounter.

Sponges: Phylum Porifera

The simplest many-celled animals are sponges. Their shapes vary from tiny cups, broad branches, and tall vases to encrustations and large, rounded masses. Sponges come in a variety of colors. Grays and browns predominate in deeper waters, brighter hues in the shallows. With differing growing conditions a species may vary in size, shape, and color.

A sponge consists of a cooperating community of individual cells, each performing a specific function. The cells surround a system of canals through which water is carried, providing the basis for all the sponge's life functions. Water enters the canals through minute pores (ostia) that dot the surface of the sponge. It then passes into chambers lined with collar cells, each with a fine-meshed funnel-shaped collar. Out of each collar extends a flagellum, a hairlike structure whose beating creates a current. The combined action of all the collar cells drives water through the canals and out of the sponge through a larger pore, the osculum. The collar cells trap food particles brought in with the water, and either digest them or pass them to other cells to be digested. This flow of water through the animal also brings in oxygen and removes carbon dioxide and other waste products. A simple sponge has just one chamber and one osculum; more complex sponges have many of each.

Most sponges have a skeleton that is a meshwork of tough protein (spongin), or of clusters of microscopic hard geometric objects (spicules), or a combination of both. Spicules are either limy (calcareous) or glasslike (siliceous) and appear in many different forms.

The Phylum Porifera is divided into three classes: the Calcispongiae, or Calcarea, which have limy spicules; the Hyalospongiae, or Hexactinellida (glass sponges), which are found only in deep waters; and the Class Demospongiae, which comprises all the remaining sponges and may have skeletons of glasslike spicules or of spongin or both, or may lack a skeleton entirely.

Cnidarians: Phylum Cnidaria

The Phylum Cnidaria includes hydras, hydroids, jellyfishes, sea anemones, and corals. Members of this phylum are nearly all found in marine and brackish water.

The cnidarian body is radially symmetrical, and consists of a tube or sac with a single opening, the mouth, surrounded by tentacles. The body wall consists of an outer layer, the epidermis, which is separated from the gastrodermis, the layer lining the digestive cavity (coelenteron), by a middle layer, the mesoglea, which varies from a thin, noncellular film to a thick layer that, in some forms, has so many cells that it resembles connective tissue or muscle. The epidermis includes cells specialized for production of nematocysts, a distinctive characteristic of cnidarians. Nematocysts provide an effective means of snaring prey animals and also offer protection against predators. The nematocyst is a capsule containing a long thread that is forcefully everted when triggered by contact with prey or other animals. Some nematocysts are sticky, some wrap around prey, but most inject venom into other creatures. People coming into contact with certain cnidarians may sustain reactions ranging from a mild rash to severe blistering and, in extreme cases, will suffer fatal congestive respiratory failure.

Generally, the cnidarian body is an asexual polyp—a tube with a mouth surrounded by tentacles, specialized for a sedentary (sessile) life attached to some solid object—or a saucer- or bowl-shaped sexual medusa that floats free in the water and swims by pulsating contractions. The life cycle of a cnidarian may include one or both of these forms. Polyps may be solitary or colonial, increasing colony size by budding, the process of forming outgrowths that develop into new individuals. In a colony, polyps may be specialized for various functions, such as trapping food, defense, digestion, or reproduction. The body or bell of a medusa is umbrella-shaped. An extension (manubrium) bearing the mouth is suspended from the underside. Tentacles are generally located on the margin of the bell and trail behind as the medusa swims.

Class Hydrozoa

This class includes hydroids, hydromedusae, chondrophorans, siphonophorans, and hydrocorallines. These animals are characterized by a noncellular mesoglea, a gastrodermis lacking nematocysts, and, with a few exceptions, gonads, or reproductive organs, in the epidermis. They may have either the polyp or the medusa body form, and a number of species pass through both stages in the life cycle. The medusa-stage animal is usually small and simple in form. The polyp stage of marine forms is often marked by a variety of specialized individuals in a colony, including feeding, defensive, and reproductive polyps. Usually the polyp stage is dominant in size and longevity, and in some species is the only stage.

Class Scyphozoa

Forms commonly known as jellyfish are included in Class

Scyphozoa. The medusa is the dominant and in some cases the only stage. The small polyp stage (scyphistoma), when present, buds off small, lobed medusae (ephyrae) by a series of transverse constrictions. Scyphozoan medusae have a thick, firm mesoglea. The coelenteron is subdivided into a number of chambers and canals. Its lining is equipped with nematocysts. The manubrium—the extension bearing the mouth—may be long or short, with some species possessing oral arms surrounding the mouth. Gonads are located in pouches of the coelenteron.

Class Anthozoa

This class includes the soft corals, the sea anemones, and the stony corals, animals that also have a thick, firm mesoglea. All anthozoans are sexual polyps with no known medusa stage. The coelenteron is subdivided into chambers by radial partitions, the septa or mesenteries, which extend from the body wall toward the center. The mouth is situated on an oral disk, surrounded by tentacles. It is generally slitlike and may have one or two siphonoglyphs, ciliated grooves in the wall of the pharynx, at one or both ends; the pharynx opens into the coelenteron. The gastrodermis contains nematocysts and gonads. Sexes are usually separate. Some species are oviparous, shedding their eggs into the water. Others are viviparous, with fertilization taking place in the body of the female. After fertilization, the egg develops into a minute planula larva. Some sea anemones brood their young beyond the planula stage and release them as polyps, while others bud off new individuals asexually. Nearly all other anthozoans are colonial and undergo extensive budding.

Subclass Octocorallia. These colonial animals are sometimes called soft corals because of the tough, elastic matrix they secrete, into which the polyps can retract. The sea whips and sea fans have a horny core over which the softer tissues lie. Colonies may be bushy, whiplike, or fanlike. Their polyps have eight pinnately branched tentacles.

Subclass Zoantharia, order Actiniaria. Sea anemones are solitary, sessile cnidarians, generally cylindrical in form when fully extended. The anemone body consists of a column, at the bottom of which is a pedal disk that attaches the animal to the substrate. At the top of the column is an oral disk with a slitlike mouth. It is surrounded by one or more rows of tentacles that vary in size and number from one species to another. The fully retracted animal is hemispherical, with only an indentation at the site of the retracted oral disk. While some anemones live with the entire body exposed, others bury themselves in a sandy or muddy bottom, exposing the oral disk only when fully extended, and retracting into the bottom when disturbed at low tide. Many anemones are capable of creeping slowly about on the pedal disk.

Order Scleractinia. The stony corals are mostly warm-water creatures and are structurally similar to sea anemones. They deposit a skeleton of calcium carbonate at their base. The skeleton conforms to the configuration of the base of the polyp, including its pattern of internal septa. The deposited skeleton extends partially up the column of the polyp and forms a cup in which the polyp sits. Most species of coral are colonial, reproducing by budding and branching. The entire skeletal structure of the colony is called the corallum. The corallum of different species varies in form from highly branched or bushy outgrowths to solid, massive boulders. Many reef corals are nourished by symbiotic algae that live within their tissues.

Order Corallimorpharia. Cnidarians in this order resemble true corals, but lack skeletons. They are colonial, have a basal disk and radially arranged tentacles.

Comb Jellies: Phylum Ctenophora

Comb jellies share with cnidarians the presence of differentiated tissues without true organ systems, but possess a modified radial symmetry. Unlike cnidarians, comb jellies do not sting. Body form varies, but is commonly globular or somewhat compressed. Water makes up more than ninety-five percent of the comb jelly's body weight. Some species have a pair of tentacles equipped with adhesive cells, some have oral lobes (two large flaps around the mouth), and some have neither. The comb jelly's mouth leads into a gullet, or pharynx, which in turn opens into a digestive cavity, the stomach. From the stomach, numerous canals extend throughout the animal, and digested food thus reaches all parts of the body. Ctenophores are carnivorous, feeding on a large variety of planktonic prey.

The comb jelly's comb plates (ctenae) consist of transverse rows of cilia fused together by a thin membrane and arranged in eight lines down the long axis of the animal. The beat of the comb plates by progressive waves, or metachronal rhythm, moves the animal through the water, mouth-end forward, coordinated by a sensory structure, the apical organ—a dome-shaped cyst containing a heavy granule, the statolith. All species found in American waters swim feebly, and thus are at the mercy of ocean currents. Refraction of light upon the comb plates imparts a jewel-like quality to ctenophores seen in the sunlight. In the dark, many comb jellies are bioluminescent, and their whole form, including the rows of comb plates, can be seen outlined in flashes of light.

Flatworms: Phylum Platyhelminthes

Of all animals that have a head, flatworms have the simplest body plan. As their name suggests, flatworms' bodies are compressed, their thickness small compared with their length and breadth. As with cnidarians, the mouth is the only opening into the digestive cavity; through it food is taken in and wastes discharged. Unlike cnidarians, flatworms have well-defined nervous, muscular, excretory, and reproductive systems, which lie within a solid matrix of tissue (parenchyma). Distribution of digested food is achieved by a digestive cavity that in some of them branches into all parts of the body. Because of the worms' flatness, all cells are close enough to the surface for exchange of oxygen and carbon dioxide with the environment. The flat body—capable of great contortion—also enables these creatures to hide in narrow crevices or enter the body openings of other animals. The phylum includes three classes: the Turbellaria, Trematoda, and Cestoidea. The latter two parasitize various vertebrate animals and will not be considered here. The Class Turbellaria includes mostly free-living forms, of which only the order Tricladida and Polycladida have members large and obvious enough to catch the eye of the shore visitor. Triclads have a digestive cavity with three major branches, one toward the head and two toward the rear. Polyclads have numerous branches radiating from the central digestive cavity. Members of both orders have an epidermis covered with cilia, simple eyespots (ocelli), and sensory structures for taste and smell on the head end, as well as a mouth situated toward the rear on the underside, and a muscular, sucking pharynx. Locomotion is achieved by rippling contractions of body muscles aided by the action of cilia, allowing the worm to glide smoothly over a surface. Both groups include predators and scavengers that feed on dead animals. Some species are commensals, living in close relation with another kind of animal.

Nemertean Worms: Phylum Rhynchocoela

Most nemerteans are long, slender, and somewhat flattened. Color varies greatly; many are highly colored—red, orange, yellow, brown, or green—some patterned above with stripes or spots, and paler underneath. Nemerteans range in size from less than an inch (a millimeter) to several feet (30 meters) long. They are remarkably elastic and can stretch many times longer than their relaxed body length. They may be equipped with eyespots and sensory grooves, are covered with cilia, and consist internally of a solid mass of tissue, without a body cavity. Their nervous systems and excretory systems are like those of flatworms, and the digestive tract includes mouth and anus. Soft-bodied and seemingly vulnerable, nemerteans are in fact poisonous predators. They have a long sharp-tipped proboscis, which can be thrust out accurately to a distance almost as great as the animal's body length to capture prey—usually small annelid worms and crustaceans—with abundant mucus or paralyzing venom. The proboscis lies in a fluid-filled sac above the mouth; in all species it is coated with glandular secretions and in some species may be equipped with a dartlike barb through which toxic substances are injected.

Segmented Worms: Phylum Annelida

The Phylum Annelida includes about 9000 known species belonging to three classes: the Hirudinea, Oligochaeta, and Polychaeta. The Hirudinea are leeches, of which only a few species are parasitic on the gills, fins, and bodies of marine fishes. The Oligochaeta include the earthworms and most freshwater annelids, but only about 200 marine species. The Polychaeta are nearly all marine, and include over 5000 species, two-thirds of all annelids. Our discussion will deal only with the polychaetes.

An annelid's body is usually elongate, more or less cylindrical, and consists of a series of segments. The body wall is covered with a thin, elastic cuticle, beneath which lie layers of circular and longitudinal muscles. These surround a fluid-filled body cavity (coelom), which is usually divided between segments by cross-walls (septa). A series of elongations and contractions of the segments propels the worm forward.

The body plan is more advanced than that of phyla previously discussed. Annelids have a complete digestive system extending from the mouth on the first segment to the anus at the hind end of the body. Above the mouth is a lobe, the prostomium, a probing organ that often bears sensory structures and is useful in feeding and burrowing. Most annelids have well-developed circulatory, nervous, and excretory systems. Respiration is carried on through the cuticle, and some forms have specialized gills. All annelids are equipped with glands under the cuticle that produce abundant mucus that helps keep the cuticle moist and is used in some of these species to catch food, build tubes, or form their egg-masses.

The Polychaeta are divided into two subclasses, the Errantia and the Sedentaria. The Errantia are worms that move about, while the Sedentaria remain in a tube or burrow. Errant polychaetes generally have well-developed, paired appendages (parapodia), standard trunk segments, good locomotory ability, and a head with eyespots and sensory appendages. They are predators, browsers, or bottom-dwelling deposit feeders. Sedentary polychaetes usually have a head without eyes or sensory appendages, but sometimes with many gills and feeding tentacles; a trunk divided into a thick thorax followed by a slender abdomen—the segments of each quite different; and appendages reduced and modified for adhering to the inside of the tube or burrow. They are generally bottom-dwelling deposit or filter feeders.

Peanut Worms: Phylum Sipuncula

The small Phylum Sipuncula includes the peanut worms, a group with certain features in common with annelid worms, but several other characteristics that are unique. Both have similar developmental and reproductive patterns, a similar nervous system, and similar layers in the body and the walls of the digestive tract. In sipunculids, however, there is no sign of segmentation, and the digestive tract is U-shaped, doubling over and terminating in an anus in the upper midline, well toward the front end. These worms can extend and retract a large part of the front end into and out of the trunk and, when disturbed, contract into a plump, taut, elongate oval, in some species resembling a peanut kernel. The mouth and surrounding parts are the last to be seen when the worm extends fully, and the first to roll in and disappear as it retracts. The mouth is surrounded by tentacles. Animals with short tentacles feed on organic matter taken in with mud or sand; those with longer, branched tentacles filter organic particles from the water.

Spoon Worms: Phylum Echiura

The Phylum Echiura is a small group of worms, similar in many ways to the Annelids, but lacking any suggestion of segmentation. Their digestive and nervous systems, body wall structures, reproductive patterns, and even bristles (setae) are similar. Echiurids are plump-bodied, sausage-shaped, fluid-filled creatures with a nonretractable proboscis that has a deep groove or trough on the underside, leading into the mouth. One or more rings of bristles encircle the end of the worm.

Mollusks: Phylum Mollusca

In addition to the approximately 50,000 known living mollusk species, some 35,000 fossil mollusks have been described. The fossil record for this phylum extends over 600 million years and is extremely rich because the mineralized molluscan shell, or valve, fossilizes readily.

The body consists of three regions: a head, bearing the mouth and sense organs and containing the brain; a visceral mass surrounded by the body wall, containing most of the internal organs; and a foot, the muscular lower part of the body on which the animal creeps. A membranous extension of the body wall, the mantle, secretes the shell and encloses a mantle cavity containing the gills, anus, and excretory pores. The mouth in most groups is equipped with a long, tough, toothed, ribbonlike structure, the radula, by means of which the animal rasps food. Mollusks have well-developed organ systems—nervous, muscular, digestive, circulatory, respiratory, excretory, and reproductive—but, unlike annelids and arthropods, they lack body segmentation.

Class Polyplacophora

Chitons are flattened, oval creatures with a row of eight broad but short valves along the back. Surrounding the eight valves, and in some cases covering them, is a margin of the mantle called the girdle. On the underside is a large foot with which the animal clings tenaciously to a solid surface; when pried loose, it usually curls into a ball like a pill bug or a hedgehog. On each side of the foot in the mantle cavity lie paired gills. At the front of the foot is the head, bearing the mouth with its radula, but without tentacles; eyes are rare or absent. Most chitons feed by rasping fine algal growth from the surface of rocks and, in some cases, also prey on sedentary animals such as bryozoans, sponges, and protozoans.

Class Gastropoda

The Class Gastropoda contains about eighty percent of all living molluscan species, and includes the snails, limpets, abalones, sea slugs, and sea hares. Garden slugs and pond and land snails also belong to this group.

The general body plan of a gastropod includes a spiral shell into which the animal can retract, a head equipped with tentacles, eyes, and mouth, and a large foot. Forms such as sea hares have only a vestigial, internal shell. Nudibranchs, or sea slugs, have shells in the larval stage, but lose them on maturing. Terrestrial slugs lack a shell.

The snail shell is basically an elongate cone wound around an axis. Each turn around the axis is a whorl. The body whorl is the most recently formed and largest, and contains most of the snail's soft parts. The remaining whorls constitute the spire, which terminates in the apex. The inner side of the shell adjacent to the axis about which it spirals is the columella. The columella may be hollow, opening in an umbilicus at the end opposite the apex, or may be closed over by a shell growth, the umbilical callus. The groove between adjacent whorls is called a suture. The outer surface of the whorls may be smooth or sculptured. A prominent spiral ridge on a whorl is termed a shoulder. The surface may be coated with a tough, horny layer, the periostracum.

The opening of the body whorl through which the head and foot are extended is the aperture. The aperture has an outer lip and an inner lip. In some snails the aperture may have a slender forward extension, the siphonal canal, in which lies a tubular fold of the edge of the mantle, the siphon, through which the animal takes water into the mantle to aerate the gills and carry off waste products. Many species have a horny, leathery, or limy lid, or operculum, attached to the side of the foot. When the head and foot are completely retracted, the operculum neatly seals off the aperture.

By far the majority of snails are dextral, coiling to the right. A few species are sinistral, coiling to the left, and occasionally an individual of a normally dextral species will be sinistral. To make sure which "handedness" a snail exhibits, hold the shell with the apex up and aperture toward you. If the aperture is on your right, the snail is dextral; if it is on your left, the snail is sinistral.

In cited measurements, the term "length" represents that of the axis, even though anatomically it would be more correct to call this the height. In a few low, flattened forms, such as limpets, slipper snails, and abalones, the term "length" will designate true length, the distance from front to rear, and the term "height," the distance from top of shell to surface of substrate. The width is always the broadest dimension at right angles either to the axis or to the true length.

In an active marine snail the opening of the mantle cavity is above the head, not at the rear as the generalized molluscan body plan would indicate. Having the mantle open forward improves water flow over the gills. It also makes the snail asymmetrical internally. The paired nerve cords are twisted about each other, and organs from the original right side, such as the gill, auricle of the heart, and excretory opening, are diminished or eliminated.

The Class Gastropoda contains three subclasses: the Prosobranchia (meaning "gill forward"), the Opisthobranchia ("gill behind"), and the Pulmonata ("with a lung"), which are predominantly terrestrial and freshwater species. Only the Opisthobranchia and Prosobranchia will be considered here.

Class Bivalvia

The bivalves known to most people are those commonly used

as food: clams, oysters, mussels, cockles, and scallops. The Class Bivalvia (also known as Pelecypoda) includes mollusks whose shells consist of two parts, or valves, hinged together along the upper midline. There are about 15,000 species of bivalves, more than eighty percent of them in the sea, and the others in fresh water.

The basic body plan of a bivalve is well adapted to a life of burrowing through the bottom. The two valves that enclose the rest of the body are convex, giving the animal a wedgelike or hatchetlike shape. (Pelecypoda means "hatchet foot" in Greek.) The foot usually is bladelike and can be protruded forward from between the valves. The mantle, which completely lines the shell, forms two openings at the rear end: a lower one, the incurrent siphon, to admit water into the mantle cavity, and an upper one, the excurrent siphon, for its escape. The siphons may be merely two slitlike openings between the two parts of the mantle, or two separate extensible tubes, or the two tubes may be united into a single neck which contains the two passages. The gills, meshworks of strands united into large sheets, are suspended on either side of the visceral mass within the mantle cavity. They are used both for respiration and for food collecting. The gills secrete mucus which traps food from the water—mostly one-celled plants and fine particles of organic matter. The thin layer of food-laden mucus is moved down the gills, then forward along their edges, where long, flaplike palps transfer it to the mouth. The head of a bivalve is little more than a bump with a mouth and a pair of palps. It is probable that bivalves evolved from gastropods.

For purposes of identification, bivalve shells exhibit the most obvious and stable species characteristics. To determine the left valve from the right, hold the animal hinge-side upward and front end away from you. (The front end is the one from which the foot protrudes.) The right valve is then on your right and the left valve on your left. In some species you will find a gap between the valves for foot protrusion. Alternatively, the protrusion of the siphons between the valves at the rear end lets you know indirectly which end is the front. For bivalves that typically lie with one valve down and one up, such as oysters, jewel boxes, and scallops, we refer to the upper and lower valves.

Concentric growth lines can be seen on the shell surface in most bivalves. The center area surrounded by the lines is the oldest part of the shell, and is known as the umbo (plural umbones), or beak. It is usually located nearer the front end than the back, or bent forward. Many characteristics used by conchologists in identification of bivalves—such as teeth, muscle scars, and the pallial line, cannot be observed on living animals, so little reference will be made to them. In determining dimensions, the length of the shell is measured as a straight line between its front and rear edges. The height is the distance between uppermost (hinge line) and lowermost edges. However, in oysters the length is commonly considered as the distance from the umbo to the opposite end.

Class Cephalopoda

Members of the Class Cephalopoda, the squids, octopods, and nautiluses (the latter not included in this book), are specialized variations on the molluscan theme. The visceral mass is surrounded by a mantle enclosing gills and body openings. Cephalopods have a head—with a brain, sense organs, and a mouth with a radula—and a foot specialized into a numer of arms surrounding the mouth and equipped with suckers. Some people refer to the arms as tentacles, but biologists reserve that term for a special pair of long appendages found in squids, and used for capturing prey. The mouth is equipped with a sharp beak, like a parrot's, with which the animal kills and tears apart its prey.

Squids have thin flexible internal shells made of a horny substance, and octopods have none at all. Both use their mantle cavities and siphons for locomotion. Water is admitted into the mantle cavity through slits behind the head, and jetted with great force out the siphon beneath the neck. An ink gland opening into the mantle cavity enables cephalopods, when threatened, to squirt out a cloud of ink and, in the confusion, make their escape. Squids living in ocean depths where the only light is bioluminescence confuse their enemies with a cloud of luminescent particles.

Class Scaphopoda

A relatively small group of mollusks found worldwide, consisting of approximately 350 living species in four genera and two families; in our range all four genera and about ninety species occur. They live in water 10,000 to 10,500 feet (3000 to 3200 meters) deep, although most species are found in water more than 100 feet (30 meters) deep and are rarely found along Atlantic shorelines or on beaches. These mollusks first appeared in the Devonian period, about 300 million years ago. Their tubular shells are $1/8-5''$ (0.3–12.7 cm) long and open at both ends, with the front end, or aperture, larger than the hind end, or apex; the middle is either evenly tapered or swollen. The apex may have one or more slits or notches in the margin, or a projecting tube. The exterior is smooth, longitudinally ridged, or has circular rings.

Tusk shells live partially buried in sand or mud; water is drawn in and waste products are eliminated through the apex, which protrudes above the surface of the ocean floor. The foot is reduced in size and adapted for digging. The head bears no tentacles or eyes, and the mouth, furnished with a radula, is surrounded by lobes and threadlike appendages with which it captures the foraminifera and bivalves on which it feeds. Tusks lack gills and absorb oxygen through the mantle skin.

Arthropods: Phylum Arthropoda

Of all the major groups of invertebrate animals, by far the largest and most familiar are the arthropods. More than 1,000,000 species are known, of which all but about 85,000 are insects—invertebrates familiar to us all. Only a very few species are associated with the sea, but many occur along shorelines. These animals include the preponderantly marine

Crustacea, a class of more than 31,000 species, and the entirely marine Pycnogonida, or sea spiders (500 species). The Merostomata, or horseshoe crabs, also live on the Atlantic. An arthropod's most obvious characteristic is the tough encasement of armor, or exoskeleton, which gives the animal rigidity and protects its soft insides. This armor is made principally of a substance called chitin. The exoskeleton has joints, regions where the chitin is thin and flexible, permitting movement. Such joints are particularly obvious on the legs, and give the phylum its name, Arthropoda, which means "jointed foot" in Greek.

The presence of an exoskeleton prevents increase in body size. Growth can be achieved only by a series of molts, the periodic shedding of the exoskeleton. Before an arthropod molts, a new, soft exoskeleton is deposited beneath the old one. The old exoskeleton splits, the soft animal slowly climbs out and increases in size by taking in water or air. The new exoskeleton soon hardens, and the animal's size is again fixed until the next molt. During this process, the animal is soft and vulnerable to predators so it usually hides.

The arthropods share a number of characteristics with the annelids. Both are segmented and have a similarly organized nervous system, and a heart that lies above the gut. Unlike the annelids, however, the segments of arthropods are not all alike, but are usually grouped together in functional regions: head, thorax, and abdomen. In some groups the head and thorax are fused and covered with a single plate, the carapace. Arthropods are bristly, with nearly all their bristles sense organs—some sensitive to touch, currents, taste, odor, or sound. They have eyes that may be simple, with one lens and retina, or compound, composed of many lenses and nerve cells. Their circulatory system is said to be "open," that is, with blood coursing from large blood vessels into open spaces or sinuses to bathe the tissues, rather than through fine capillaries among the tissues. All marine forms have gills.

Class Pycnogonida

The sea spiders, or pycnogonids, are a strange group of small-bodied, long-legged marine arthropods. Though they walk on eight legs, they are not spiders. The pycnogonid body consist of a thorax of four segments, each with a pair of side projections bearing the legs. The first segment has a necklike projection with a single four-part eye on the top, and a sucking proboscis with a mouth at the tip. Beside the proboscis there may be paired accessory mouthparts in the form of pinchers and feelers. A given species may have one, both, or neither of these appendages. The rear end of the animal has a very small projection, the abdomen, the sole function of which is to bear the anus. In fact, there is so little room for organs in the body cavity of a pycnogonid that the sex organs are located in the long joints of the legs. In some pycnogonids, usually on the male, there is an extra pair of slender legs curled under the first body segment. It is on these that the female attaches her eggs.

Class Merostomata

Horseshoe crabs, members of the Subclass Xiphosura, consist of three genera and five similar species, only one of which lives along the Atlantic Coast and in the Gulf. The horseshoe crab is an ancient animal dating back nearly 400 million years, having changed little over that time. Its body consists mostly of a large rounded, domed shield, or carapace, a broad shielded abdomen with heavy lateral spines, and a long pointed tail, or telson. Turned over, the carapace is found to cover seven pairs of appendages: one pair of chelicerae used in feeding, four pairs of legs ending in weak pincers, and one pair of pushing legs, and a small pair of degenerate appendages. The abdomen bears six pairs of appendages, the first being a covering to the reproductive opening, the genital operculum. It is followed by five pairs of flaplike gills which constantly fan back and forth maintaining an exchange of water over their respiratory surfaces; in addition, they are able to serve as swimming paddles in young horseshoe crabs. The spikelike telson is not a weapon, but is jointed at its base and serves as a lever when the animal is turned upside down. Unlike that of true crabs, the exoskeleton of a horseshoe crab is not fortified with calcium salts but consists of a horny, chitinous substance. Sensory organs include a small pair of anterior simple eyes, or ocelli, located on either side of a median spine, and a large pair of widely separated compound eyes facing the sides. These compound eyes are capable of detecting movement and light filtering through the water.

Class Crustacea

The crustaceans include a number of animals familiar because they are edible: shrimps, lobsters, and crabs. They also include a variety of other forms seen along the shore—amphipods including beach fleas, isopods including sea roaches, and barnacles—as well as many tiny marine and freshwater creatures too small to be seen with the naked eye. A crustacean is an arthropod that usually possesses five pairs of appendages on five head segments: two pairs of antennae, one pair of jaws, or mandibles, one on each side of the mouth, and two pairs of manipulatory mouthparts, or maxillae. The number of segments in the body varies, depending on the group. In some forms the body may simply be a trunk. In more advanced types it may be divided into a thorax and an abdomen. The thorax has a maximum of eight segments, and the abdomen six, or, rarely seven. Each segment may bear a pair of basically Y-shaped appendages that have different forms and functions. The first three pairs on the thorax may be auxiliary mouthparts, or maxillipeds. The remaining five thoracic appendages may be walking legs, the first two or three ending in pincers. The first five segments on the abdomen bear forked, flattened appendages called swimmerets, and the last segment ends in a flattened tailpiece, or telson, flanked by a pair of broad, flat appendages (uropods) that together make up the tailfin. In crabs, the abdomen is folded forward and is recessed under the thorax.

Echinoderms: Phylum Echinodermata

The Phylum Echinodermata is an entirely marine group of animals including sea stars, brittle stars, sea urchins, sand dollars, sea cucumbers, and sea lilies, whose most obvious feature is their radial symmetry. The echinoderm body is nearly always arranged in five parts, or multiples thereof. There is a body axis with the mouth at one end and anus at the other. In some forms the mouth faces up, in others, down or to the side. Echinoderms have an internal limy skeleton, covered by skin, and may also have spines, some movable, some fixed, variable in size and shape. The unique characteristic of the phylum is an internal hydraulic system, termed the water vascular system, that operates numerous tube feet (podia). These are slender, fingerlike appendages, arranged in rows, which the animal extends by pumping full of fluid, and retracts with muscles within the tube foot itself. Tube feet are used in locomotion and feeding. Many echinoderms have tube feet equipped with suction disks at their tips, enabling them to cling tenaciously to a surface. Inside the body is a complex system of canals, filled with sea water (in sea cucumbers it is filled with body fluid) that operates the tube feet. Water passes back and forth between the canals and the sea through a sieve plate.

The phylum is divided into four classes: the Class Stelleroidea, the starlike echinoderms, which is divided into the Subclass Asteroidea, the sea stars, and the Subclass Ophiuroidea, the brittle stars; the Class Echinoidea, the sea urchins, sand dollars, and sea hearts; the Class Holothuroidea, the sea cucumbers; and the Class Crinoidea, the sea lilies.

Class Stelleroidea, Subclass Asteroidea. The asteroids include the sea stars, also called starfish, a term considered inappropriate by biologists, who reserve the word "fish" for finny vertebrates. The asteroid body has the form of a somewhat flattened star, with arms (rays) usually numbering five or a multiple of five, rarely six or some other number, each in contact with adjacent arms where it joins the central disk. The surface of the central disk has the anus in the center, the sieve plate near the junction of two arms, and openings of sex ducts at each juncture of adjacent arms. The upper surface of each arm has the spines and other features of the species, and an eyespot, usually red, at the tip. The underside of a sea star has the mouth in the middle of the central disk, and an open groove from the mouth to the tip of each arm. Two or four crowded rows of tube feet lie in each groove. In some sea stars there is a special skeletal structure for pinching small objects, a modification of two or three spines. These pinchers (pedicellariae) may be shaped like small tweezers or pliers, or flattened like the jaws of a vise.

Subclass Ophiuroidea. The brittle stars and basket stars make up the Subclass Ophiuroidea. In ophiuroids the base of an arm does not meet that of its neighbor as it does in a sea star; instead, a portion of the free border of the oral disk lies between them. The central disk may be round, pentagonal, or scalloped, its upper surface leathery or scaly. The mouth on

the underside is shaped like a five-pointed star, an arm joining
the disk at each star point alternating with a triangular
pointed jaw with toothed margins. At the base of each jaw is a
plate that may be perforated to form the sieve plate of the
water vascular system, the number of sieve plates ranging from
one to five. Beside the base of each arm are one or two slits
that open into a large respiratory pouch. The arms are long,
jointed, and flexible, unbranched in brittle stars, extensively
branched in basket stars. The segments commonly bear spines,
a feature used in identifying species. While there is no groove
on the underside of the arm, as there is in a sea star, there is a
double row of active, suckerless tube feet that serve as sense
organs, are used in feeding, and may be of some use in
locomotion. Arms are used for locomotion and grasping food.

Class Echinoidea
The Class Echinoidea includes the sea urchins, cake urchins,
sand dollars, and heart urchins. Unlike sea stars and brittle
stars, these creatures do not have arms, or rays. The skeleton,
called a test, consists of rows of radially arranged plates
immovably joined to one another. Movable spines, each with a
concave base, fit on correspondingly convex bumps on each
plate. Muscle fibers attached to each spine enable it to swing
about in any direction.
Regular species, such as the sea urchins, are almost perfectly
radially symmetrical, while irregular species, the cake urchins,
heart urchins, and sand dollars, have a bilateral symmetry
superimposed upon a radial pattern. In sea urchins, the
middle of the upper surface has a circular area, usually with
scaly plates, bearing the anus. It is surrounded by five petal-
shaped plates, each with a large pore, the opening of a sex
duct. One of these plates is also full of small pores, and is the
sieve plate. Alternating with these plates are five other plates
which may or may not touch the area bearing the anus.
Beyond these ten plates are twenty longitudinal rows of firmly
united plates extending toward the mouth, five pairs of rows
perforated for tube feet alternating with five unperforated
pairs. All plates bear spines. The long needlelike spines of one
reef species bear a toxin that causes a painful sting.
Tube feet on an urchin are arranged in five pairs of rows that
extend longitudinally around the test. They are tipped with
suckers, and are long enough to reach beyond the spines.
Urchins also have numerous stalked pinchers about the size of
the tube feet; all of the pinchers have three jaws, and some
have poison glands. These structures are defensive, protecting
against predators and discouraging larval animals from settling
on the urchins.
The body wall on the lower side extends beyond the border of
the rows of plates as a flexible tip surrounding the mouth.
Around the mouth are large tube feet, which can attach to the
substrate and pull the mouth against it for feeding. In all
cases, feeding involves gnawing with a toothed organ called
Aristotle's lantern. This remarkable structure consists of a set
of skeletal rods and muscles arranged to open and close five

teeth, like the jaws of a drill chuck. The area around the mouth is usually adorned with ten frilly gills.

Cake urchins, heart urchins, and sand dollars are modified for burrowing in sand. They have shorter and more numerous spines than do sea urchins; tube feet are confined to the upper and lower surfaces, absent from the sides; and they have assumed a bilateral symmetry while retaining most of the general pattern of an echinoid. In heart urchins the mouth is well forward, and the anus at the rear end. In cake urchins and sand dollars the mouth remains central, but the anus is to the rear. The upper surface of the test shows the pattern of five sets of tube feet, one directed forward, two to the left, and two to the right. Though the anus is to the rear, the plates with reproductive pores and sieve plates remain at the upper center. Aristotle's lantern is not well developed.

Class Holothuroidea

Members of the Class Holothuroidea are generally called sea cucumbers, though some of them bear no particular resemblance to the vegetable. They are elongated, with the axis running horizontally from mouth to anal end. More primitive forms have five well-developed longitudinal rows of tube feet equally spaced around the circumference, but since such long animals must lie with one side down, many of them have well-developed tube feet on the three rows in contact with the substrate, and the other two rows reduced or missing. This imposes an almost bilaterally symmetrical pattern on these radially symmetrical animals.

The mouth is surrounded by a row of tentacles, which may be fingerlike, stalked with a buttonlike tip, or branched. Tentacles are actually modified tube feet, part of the water vascular system. They are used in feeding. The holothuroids differ from the echinoderms previously discussed in having a water vascular system full of body fluid rather than sea water; no sieve plate communicates with the sea.

Bryozoans: Phylum Bryozoa

The Phylum Bryozoa, or Ectoprocta, includes more than 4000 species of colonial sedentary animals. Individuals (or zooids) in the colony are seldom as large as ¹⁄₃₂″ (1 mm), though the colony itself may be several feet across.

The individual lies within a body-covering that is continuous with or fused to the body-covering of adjacent colony members. The covering may be gelatinous, membranous, rubbery, chitinous (made of the same tough material found in the exoskeleton of an insect or shrimp), or limy. The form of the colony may be branching, creeping, bushy, leafy, tubular, fleshy, or encrusting.

The case around the individual has an opening through which a crown of tentacles can be extended. The tentacles are ciliated and surround the mouth. The anus lies outside the crown of tentacles. The extended tentacles are funnel-shaped. Cilia drive water and food particles, mostly one-celled plants and bacteria, into the funnel. Some species draw food into the mouth with their tentacles.

A colony increases in size asexually by budding, and new colonies are established by sexual reproduction. Most bryozoans are hermaphroditic, but in some species the sexes are distinct.

There are three classes of bryozoans: the Stenolaemata, which are all marine, and are tubular and limy, with circular openings for the crown of tentacles; the Gymnolaemata, which are mostly marine, and are either tubular, encrusting, gelatinous, membranous, chitinous, or limy; and the Phylactolaemata, which are all freshwater species.

Entoprocts: Phylum Entoprocta

The Phylum Entoprocta includes about sixty species of small sedentary animals, known as nodding heads, most of which are marine and colonial. An entoproct has an oval body mounted on a stalk. Its upper surface is surrounded by a crown of six to thirty-six ciliated tentacles. Within the crown lies the mouth at one end and the anus at the other; in this, entoprocts differ from bryozoans, whose anus is outside the crown of tentacles. The ciliated tentacles create a current of water, and organic particles are trapped on a coating of mucus on the tentacles and moved by cilia into the mouth and the U-shaped digestive tract consisting of esophagus, stomach, and intestine. When the feeding animal is disturbed, its tentacles retract by shortening and curling to the center.

Colonial entoprocts have an attached creeping stem from which arise a number of stalks, sometimes branched, with individuals at the tips. Within the stems are muscle fibers which cause the stalk to bend or "bow" at times, and then, as quickly, to straighten up again.

Brachiopods: Phylum Brachiopoda

The Phylum Brachiopoda includes about 260 living species of shelled animals, but over 30,000 fossil species have been described from as far back as 600 million years ago. The genus *Lingula* is the oldest genus of animal life of which there are still living species, and dates back over 425 years.

The brachiopod shell consists of two valves and superficially resembles that of the bivalve mollusks. Unlike those of mollusks, however, the valves are upper and lower instead of left and right. Brachiopods are sizable animals, with shells usually 1–3″ (25–76 mm) long. They have a stalk that anchors them to the substrate. The phylum contains two classes: Inarticulata and Articulata. These names refer to the nature of articulation, or joining, of the two valves.

Classes Inarticulata and Articulata

The valves of inarticulates are the same size and are joined to each other only by muscles, with the stalk emerging from between them at that juncture. The articulates have a larger lower valve to which the upper is hinged. The stalk emerges through a hole in the lower valve to the rear of the hinge line. The bowl-like lower shell with its hole looks like an ancient Roman oil lamp, inspiring the name of "lampshells." The interior of the valves is lined with a mantle that secretes

shell material. As the valves gape, they expose a large
crescentic structure with a coiled arm at either side bearing a
double row of long tentacles directed toward the gape. Cilia
on the tentacles drive water over them, trapping fine organic
particles and moving them to the mouth in the middle of the
crescent. Inarticulates have a digestive system that ends at an
anus; articulates have an intestine that ends as a blind pouch,
and undigested matter, bound by mucus into small pellets
that do not foul the tentacles, is expelled through the mouth.
Articulate brachiopods have a short, muscular stalk that is
attached to rocks or other solid objects.

Inarticulate brachiopods have a long stalk with a tuft of fibers
at the tip by which the animal is anchored in a mud or sand
bottom. The stalk can contract or extend, permitting the
animal to gape its valves at the surface of the bottom, or
retreat under the surface at low tide or when disturbed. In
some Asiatic countries these stalks are cooked and eaten.
Nearly all brachiopods have separate sexes, with ovaries or
testes in the rear part of the body cavity. Eggs or sperm are
discharged through the kidney ducts. Most species are
spawners, with development to swimming larvae taking place
in the sea, but a few brood the developing eggs. None is
capable of asexual reproduction.

Acorn Worms: Phylum Hemichordata

The acorn worms are burrowing forms with a three-part body
consisting of a muscular proboscis, usually short and cone-
shaped, attached by a stalk to a short collar which bears the
mouth just below the proboscis stalk, and a long trunk, the
first part of which has many paired gill slits on the upper
surface. These slits permit the escape of water taken in
through the mouth and passed over gills in the walls of the
foregut, or pharynx. The pharynx continues into the midgut,
where digestion takes place, and subsequently into the
hindgut, which terminates in the anus at the rear tip.

Chordates: Phylum Chordata

If it were not for the existence of sea squirts and lancelets, the
Phylum Chordata would consist only of vertebrate animals—
those with a vertebral skeleton or backbone; but sea squirts
and lancelets necessitate a broader view of the Phylum
Chordata. This phylum takes its name from the notochord, a
stiffened rod consisting of a fibrous sheath around translucent
cells whose turgid condition provides both firmness and
flexibility. No member of any other phylum has a notochord.
Possession of a notochord prevents a chordate's body from
telescoping when its longitudinal muscles contract. Instead, it
bends from side to side. Lancelets retain the notochord
throughout life, whereas sea squirts and vertebrates possess one
only during larval or embryonic stages of development.

Subphylum Urochordata

The Subphylum Urochordata includes tunicates, salps, and
larvaceans. Many are sedentary animals whose body is enclosed
in a jacket or tunic. Urochordates have a large pharynx with

slits in its walls and a food groove in its floor. The pharynx functions both in respiration and in filtering food. The adult shows no evidence of notochord or tubular nerve chord, which are found only in the tadpole-shaped larva and which the larva loses, along with its muscular tail, as it matures.

Class Ascidiacea. The tunicates or sea squirts (Class Ascidiacea) are attached forms, either solitary or colonial, the latter with many individuals produced by budding. They have a continuous tunic covering the body. There is one opening through which water enters the animal and another nearby through which water escapes. These are called the incurrent and excurrent siphons, respectively. The incurrent siphon opens into a large pharynx with slitted walls, surrounded by a cavity, the atrium, opening to the outside through the excurrent siphon. Water is thus moved by cilia into the pharynx through the incurrent siphon and the slits, into the atrium, and out of the atrium through the excurrent siphon. The pharynx is continuous with the rest of the digestive tract, which loops about the terminates in an anus situated just inside the excurrent siphon.

Class Thaliacea. Salps are small barrel-shaped, almost transparent members of the plankton that swim by taking water in the front end and forcing it out the rear by contractions of visible bands of body muscles. One Atlantic species occurs in enormous concentrations in inshore waters, while another may bud off a long sequence of individuals that stay linked together to form a transparent chain with orange- or rose-tinged internal organs.

Subphylum Cephalochordata
Of all the invertebrates, those most similar to the vertebrate animals are the cephalochordates, or lancelets. Adult lancelets clearly show the three chordate characteristics: pharyngeal slits, a tubular nerve cord above the digestive system, and notochord, the latter extending from the tip of the head to the tip of the tail. Lancelets, like urochordates, differ in having a chamber around the pharynx to receive and remove water coming through the slits, and they lack the brain, eyes, and internal ears common to vertebrates.

Phylum Porifera
Sponge

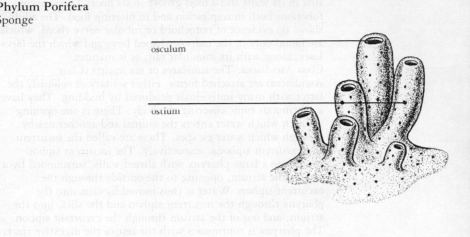

osculum

ostium

Phylum Cnidaria
Hydrozoan Polyp

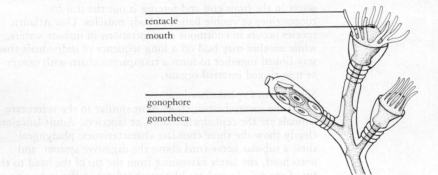

tentacle
mouth

gonophore
gonotheca

Phylum Cnidaria
Scyphozoan Medusa

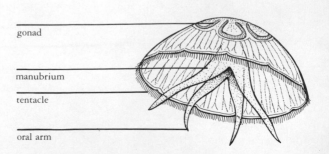

gonad

manubrium

tentacle

oral arm

Phylum Cnidaria
Sea Anemone

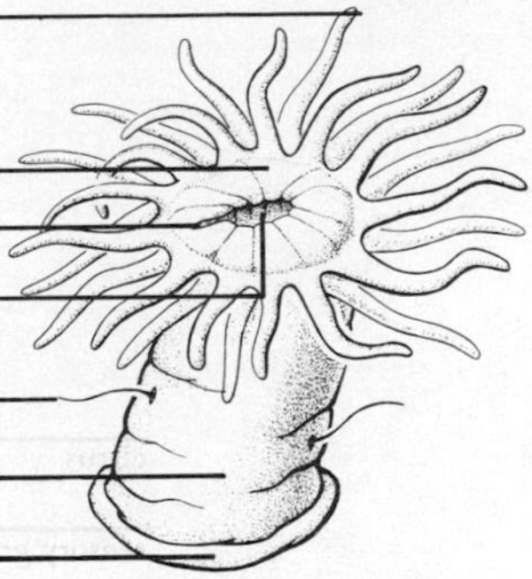

tentacle

oral disk

siphonoglyph

mouth

acontium

column

pedal disk

Phylum Ctenophora
Comb Jelly

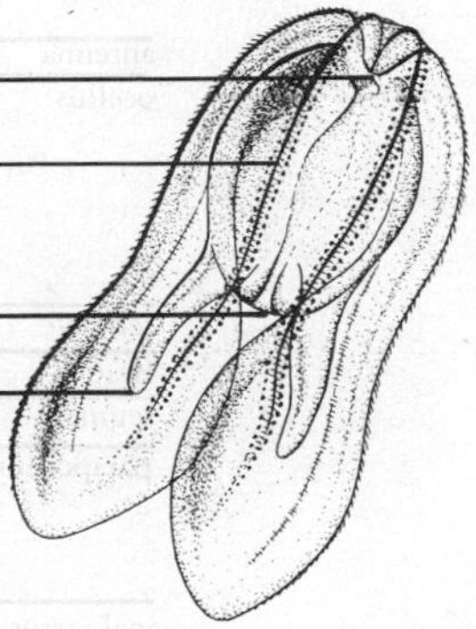

apical organ

comb plate

mouth

oral lobe

Phylum Platyhelminthes
Flatworm

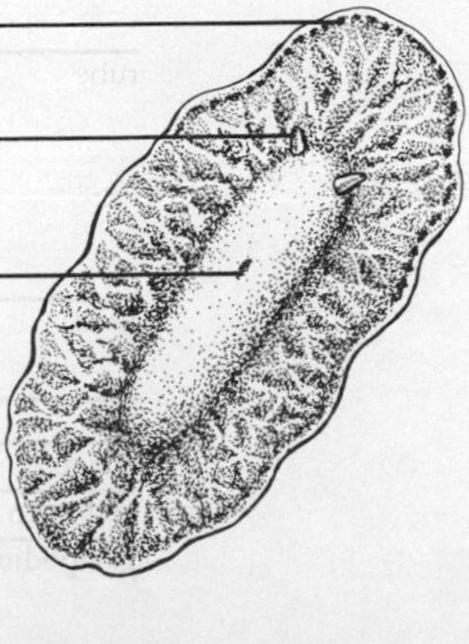

ocellus

tentacle

mouth

Phylum Rhynchocoela
Ribbon Worm

cirrus

sensory groove

Phylum Annelida
Clam Worm

antenna
ocellus

tentacle
head
segment
parapodium

anal cirrus

Phylum Annelida
Parchment Worm

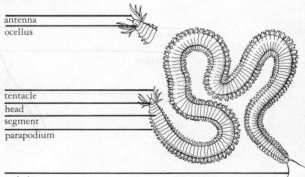

tube

head

cup
thorax
abdomen
parapodium

Phylum Sipuncula
Peanut Worm

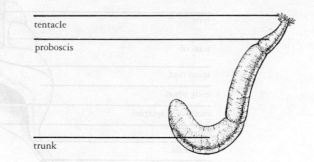

tentacle

proboscis

trunk

Phylum Echiura
Echiurid Worm

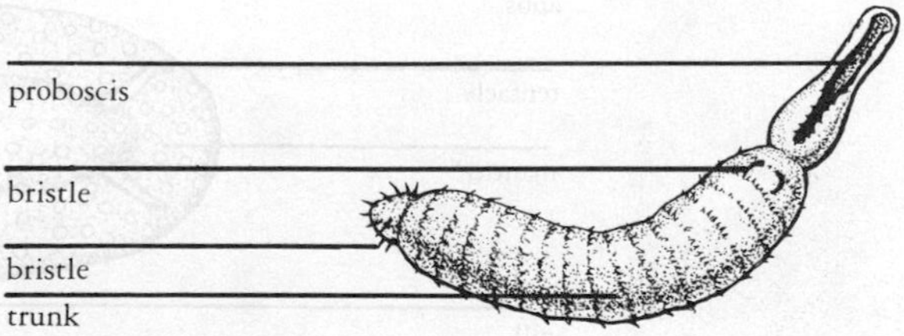

proboscis

bristle

bristle
trunk

Phylum Mollusca
Chiton

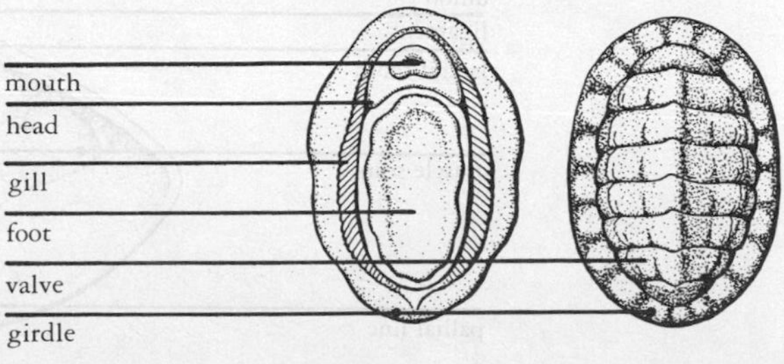

mouth
head

gill

foot

valve

girdle

Phylum Mollusca
Snail

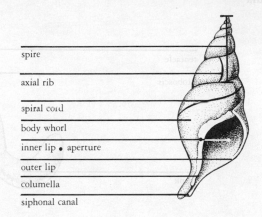

spire

axial rib

spiral cord

body whorl

inner lip • aperture

outer lip

columella

siphonal canal

Phylum Mollusca
Nudibranch

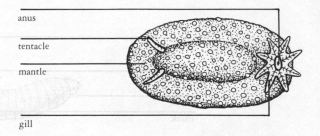

anus

tentacle

mantle

gill

Phylum Mollusca
Clam

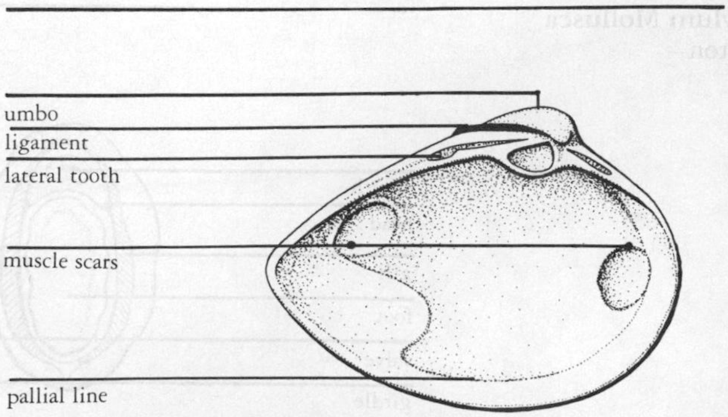

umbo
ligament
lateral tooth

muscle scars

pallial line

Phylum Mollusca
Squid

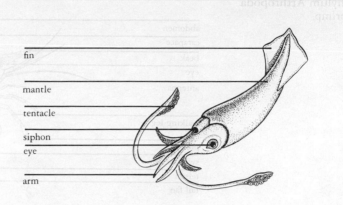

fin

mantle

tentacle

siphon

eye

arm

Phylum Arthropoda
Horseshoe Crab

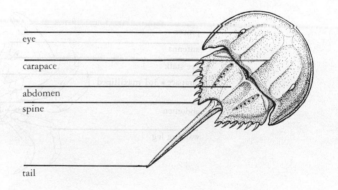

eye

carapace

abdomen

spine

tail

Phylum Arthropoda
Sea Spider

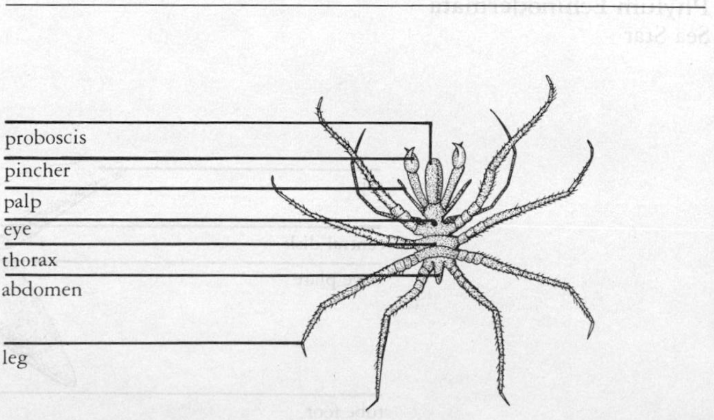

proboscis

pincher

palp

eye

thorax

abdomen

leg

Phylum Arthropoda
Shrimp

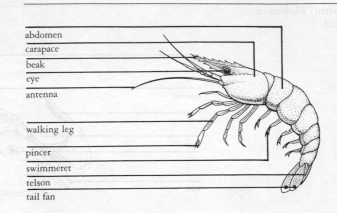

abdomen
carapace
beak
eye
antenna

walking leg

pincer
swimmeret
telson
tail fan

Phylum Arthropoda
Crab

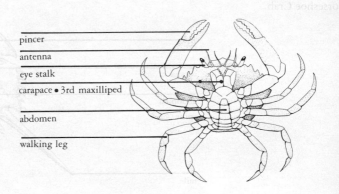

pincer
antenna
eye stalk
carapace • 3rd maxilliped
abdomen
walking leg

Phylum Echinodermata
Sea Star

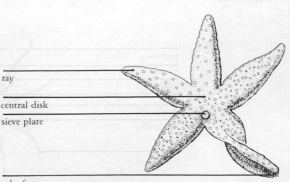

ray
central disk
sieve plate

tube foot

Phylum Echinodermata
Brittle Star

ray

central disk

spine

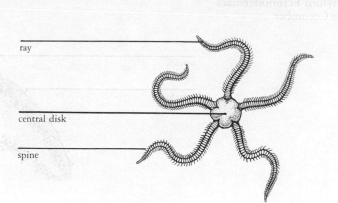

Phylum Echinodermata
Sea Urchin

spine

test

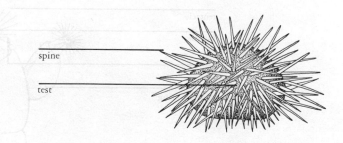

Phylum Echinodermata
Sand Dollar

spine

tube foot

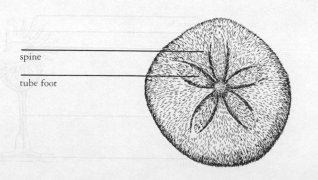

Phylum Echinodermata
Sea Cucumber

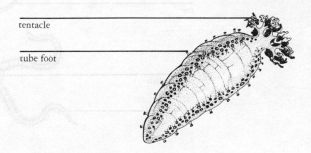

tentacle

tube foot

Phylum Bryozoa
Bryozoan

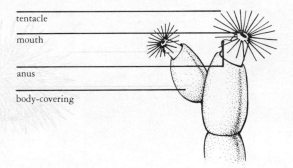

tentacle

mouth

anus

body-covering

Phylum Entoprocta
Entoproct

tentacle

anus

mouth

stalk

stem

Phylum Brachiopoda
Lampshell

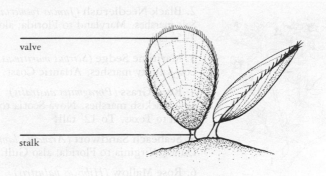

valve

stalk

Phylum Hemichordata
Acorn Worm

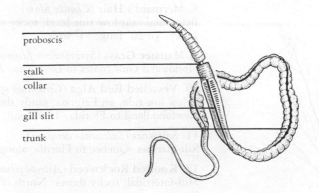

proboscis

stalk

collar

gill slit

trunk

Phylum Chordata
Tunicate

incurrent siphon

excurrent siphon

tunic

pharynx

stalk

PLANTS OF THE ATLANTIC AND GULF COASTS

1. Seaside Spurge *(Euphorbia polygonifolia)*
Sandy beaches and dunes. Quebec to Georgia. Runners about 1' long.

2. Black Needlerush *(Juncus roemerianus)*
Salt marshes. Maryland to Florida; along Gulf Coast to Texas. 2–5' tall.

3. Maritime Sedge *(Scirpus maritimus)*
Low-salinity marshes. Atlantic Coast. Up to 4½' tall.

4. Reed Grass *(Phragmites australis)*
Low brackish marshes. Nova Scotia to Florida; along Gulf Coast to Texas. To 12' tall.

5. Seabeach Sandwort *(Arenaria lanuginosa)*
Dunes. Virginia to Florida; also Gulf. 3–5" tall.

6. Rose Mallow *(Hibiscus palustris)*
Salt marshes. Massachusetts to Virginia. Up to 6' tall.

7. Tufted Green Alga *(Cladophora gracilis)*
Atlantic and Gulf coasts. Up to 3" tall.

8. Mermaid's Hair *(Chorda filum)*
Below and near low-tide level; rocky shores. North of New Jersey. To 20' long; ¼" wide.

9. Manatee Grass *(Syringodium filiforne)*
Florida and Gulf coasts to Louisiana. About 1' tall.

10. Vesselled Red Alga *(Ceramium* spp.*)*
Below low tide, on Eelgrass; sandy shores and bays. Newfoundland to Florida. 1–3" long.

11. Saltwort *(Salicornia europaea)*
Salt marshes. Quebec to Florida; along Gulf. To 1½' tall.

12. Knotted Rockweed *(Astrophyllum nodosum)*
Mid-intertidal; rocky shores. North of New Jersey. 15" or longer.

13. Spiral Rockweed *(Fucus spiralis)*
Mid-intertidal; rocky shores. New England. Up to 16" long.

14. Attached Sargassum Weed *(Sargassum filipendula)*
Lower intertidal; rocky shores. Cape Cod to Florida. 7" long.

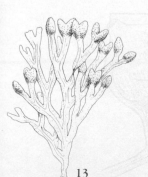

15. Toothed Rockweed *(Fucus serratus)*
Intertidal zone; rocky shores. New England. 2" long; fronds ¾" wide.

16. Dulse *(Rhodymenia palmata)*
Mid-intertidal; rocky shores. New England. About 12" long.

17. Sea Lettuce *(Ulva lactuca)*
Mid-intertidal; rocky and sandy shores. Atlantic and Gulf coasts. 1' or longer; width variable.

18. Sugar Kelp *(Laminaria saccharina)*
Below low-tide level; rocky shores. Maritime Provinces to New Jersey. About 5' long; up to 6" wide.

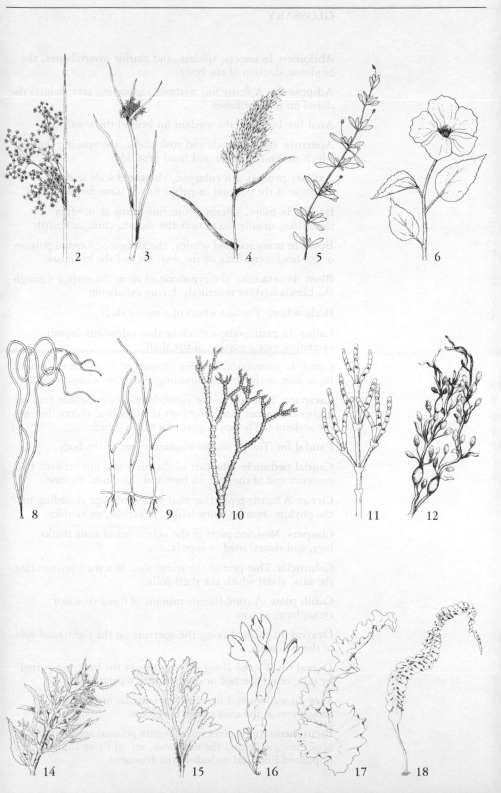

GLOSSARY

Abdomen In insects, spiders, and marine invertebrates, the hindmost division of the body.

Adipose fin A fleshy fin, without supporting rays; behind the dorsal fin in some fishes.

Anal fin In fishes, the median fin behind the anus.

Aperture In gastropods and tusk shells, the opening through which the animal's foot and head protrude.

Axillary process An enlarged, elongated scale at the insertion of the pectoral or pelvic fins of some fishes.

Barbel In fishes, a fleshy projection of the skin, often threadlike, usually found near the mouth, chin, or nostrils.

Beak In many toothed whales, the elongated forward portion of the head, consisting of the rostrum and the lower jaw.

Blow In cetaceans, the expulsion of air at the surface through the blowhole(s), or nostril(s), during exhalation.

Body whorl The last whorl of a snail's shell.

Callus In gastropods, a thick or thin calcareous deposit extending over a portion of the shell.

Canal In gastropods, an open channel or a tube on the outer lip or base of the shell, containing the living animal's siphons.

Carapace That part of the exoskeleton of a horseshoe crab or higher crustacean extending over the head and thorax, but not the abdomen. The upper part of a turtle's shell.

Caudal fin The fin on the hindmost part of the body.

Caudal peduncle The part of the body of a fish between the posterior end of the anal fin base and the caudal fin base.

Cirrus A tactile projection that varies in shape according to the phylum; may be tentaclelike, fingerlike, or hairlike.

Claspers Modified parts of the pelvic fins of male sharks, rays, and skates; used in copulation.

Columella That part of the spiral shell of a snail surrounding the axis, about which the shell coils.

Comb plate A comblike membrane of fused cilia in a ctenophore; a ctena.

Dextral In snails, having the aperture on the right-hand side of the columella.

Dorsal fin The fin along the midline of the back, supported by rays; often notched or divided into separate fins.

Ears In scallops and file shells, triangular or oblong projections at the ends of the hinge line.

Escutcheon In bivalves, an elongate pointed area on the upper margin behind the umbones, set off by an angle or impressed line, and including the ligament.

Flight feathers In birds, the long, well-developed feathers of the wings and tail, used during flight.

Flippers In cetaceans, the forelimbs.

Flukes In cetaceans, the horizontally positioned tail fin, resembling the tail of a fish, but not vertical.

Girdle In chitons, a band of muscular tissue that surrounds the valves and holds them together.

Heterocercal fin A caudal fin in which the upper lobe is larger than the lower; it contains the vertebral column.

Insertion In fishes the point at which each paired fin is joined to the body.

Keel A ridge on individual dorsal scales of some snakes; longitudinal ridge on the carapace or plastron of turtles; the raised edge along the upper edge of the tail in some salamanders.

Lateral line A series of tubes or pored scales associated with the sensory system; usually extending from just behind the opercle to the base of the caudal fin.

Ligament In bivalves, a horny structure on the hinge area, either external or internal, connecting the valves, which acts as a spring to keep the valves open.

Lip The outer edge of the aperture of a coiled gastropod.

Lunule In certain bivalves, a heart-shaped or elongate depression in front of the umbones.

Mantle A sheet of tissue that lines and secretes the shell of a mollusk, or covers the outside of a shell-less mollusk, and encloses the mantle cavity.

Mantle cavity The space enclosed by the mantle of mollusks containing the gills and the visceral mass.

Muscle scar The site on the inner surface of a bivalve shell where the muscle was attached.

Operculum A lid that closes an aperture; found in many gastropods and in certain tube-dwelling annelid worms.

Oral disk The flattened area around the mouth of an anthozoan polyp.

Origin The point at which the front of the dorsal or anal fin is attached to the body.

Paired fins The fins that occur in pairs—the pectorals and the pelvics.

Pallial line The line on the inner surface of a bivalve shell marking the site of attachment of the mantle.

Pallial sinus In bivalves, the shallow or deep embayment at the hind end of the pallial line.

Papilla A small, nipplelike projection.

Parietal callus In gastropods, a shelly thickening or deposit on the parietal wall.

Pectoral fins The paired fins attached to the shoulder girdle.

Pedal disk The flat base of a sea anemone, by which it adheres to a solid surface.

Pelvic fins The paired fins on the lower part of the body, usually just below or behind the pectoral fins.

Periostracum A smooth or fibrous horny layer covering part or all of a calcareous shell.

Pinnate Featherlike; with two rows of simple branches rising in one plane from opposite sides of an axis.

Plastron The lower part of a turtle's shell.

Pored scale One of a series of scales with a small opening into a sensory system; usually found along the lateral line.

Primaries The outermost and longest flight feathers on a bird's wing. Primaries vary in number from nine to eleven per wing, but always occur in a fixed number in any particular species.

Proboscis An extensible or permanently extended structure on the head, commonly associated with the mouth of an animal, used in feeding or sensing food or other substances.

Radial canal A canal branching from the central digestive cavity of a medusa, and extending to the margin of the bell.

Radula An organ located in the mouth cavity and consisting of minute teeth, either on a flexible muscular ribbon or unattached; used by snails, chitons, tusk shells, and cephalopods in feeding.

Ray One of the supporting structures in the fin membranes, either flexible (soft ray) or stiff (spine). The arm, or radiating appendage, of an echinoderm.

Rostrum In fishes, a forward projection of the snout; in cetaceans, a forward extension of the upper jaw.

Shield In gastropods, a thickened, distinctly margined callus on the body whorl near the inner lip.

Sinistral In snails, having the aperture on the left-hand side of the columella.

Siphonal canal In gastropods, a short or tubelike channel at the lower end of the aperture through which the siphon protrudes.

Spicule A small structure supporting the tissues of various sponges, soft corals, and compound tunicates.

Spine A usually rigid, unsegmented, unbranched structure that supports the thin membrane of a fin; a sharp, bony projection, usually on the head.

Spiracle In certain fishes, a respiratory opening, varying in size, on the back part of the head above and behind the eye; in whales, the blowhole.

Sucking disc An adhesive structure; a disc formed by a jawless mouth, the union of paired fins, or a modification of the dorsal spines.

Suture The seam between adjacent whorls of a snail's shell.

Tail fan A fanlike structure at the tip of the tail of some crustaceans, consisting of a telson, or tailpiece, and a pair of flattened abdominal appendages.

Tail stock In cetaceans, the tapered rear part of the body, just in front of the flukes.

Telson The unpaired terminal structure attached to the last abdominal segment of a Horseshoe Crab or crustacean.

Tentacle An elongated extension on the head of gastropods, on the mantle of bivalves, or around the mouth of an invertebrate, used for grasping or feeding, or as a sense organ.

Test The skeleton of an echinoid echinoderm, consisting of rows of fused plates

Thorax In insects and marine invertebrates, the division of the body between the head and the abdomen.

Tooth In gastropods, a small triangular or elongated protuberance on the columellar or parietal wall or inside the outer lip; in bivalves, a ridge along the hinge line.

Tube foot One of the numerous small appendages of an echinoderm, hydraulically operated and used in feeding or locomotion, or as a sense organ.

Tubercle A bump, node, or low, rounded projection on the surface of an animal.

Tunic The covering of a sea squirt's, or tunicate's, body; in compound tunicates, a thick mass in which many individuals are imbedded.

Umbilicus The hollow within the axis around which the whorls of a snail's shell coil.

Umbo In bivalves, the earliest part of the shell.

Umbonal ridge In bivalves, an angled or rounded ridge beginning at the umbo and usually extending to the hind end of a valve.

Valve In chitons, one of the eight plates comprising the shell; in bivalves, one of the two parts of the shell.

Wing In certain bivalves, a flattened projection located at one or both ends of the hinge line.

Wing bar A conspicuous crosswise wing mark.

Wing stripe A conspicuous mark along the opened wing.

BIBLIOGRAPHY

Abbott, Isabella A., and E. Yale Dawson.
How to Know the Seaweeds. 2nd edition.
Dubuque, Iowa: William C. Brown Company, 1978.

Amos, William H.
Assateague Island.
Washington, D.C.: National Park Service, 1980.
Life of the Seashore.
New York: McGraw-Hill Book Co., Inc., 1966.

Berrill, Michael and Deborah.
The North Atlantic Coast.
San Francisco: Sierra Club Books, 1981.

Daiber, Franklin C.
Animals of the Tidal Marsh.
New York: Van Nostrand Reinhold Co., 1982.

Fox, William T.
At the Sea's Edge.
Englewood Cliffs: Prentice-Hall, Inc., 1983.

Gosner, Kenneth L.
A Field Guide to the Atlantic Seashore.
Boston: Houghton Mifflin Company, 1979.

Kaplan, Eugene H.
A Field Guide to Coral Reefs of the Caribbean and Florida.
Boston: Houghton Mifflin Company, 1982.

MacGinitie, G. E. and Nettie.
Natural History of Marine Animals. 2nd edition.
New York: McGraw-Hill Book Co., Inc., 1968.

McConnaughey, Bayard H., and Robert Zottoli.
Introduction to Marine Biology. 4th edition.
St. Louis: C. V. Mosby Company, 1983.

McLusky, Donald S.
Ecology of Estuaries.
London: Heinemann Educational Books, Ltd., 1971.

Miner, Roy Waldo.
Field Book of Seashore Life.
New York: G. P. Putnam's Sons, 1950.

Roberts, Mervin F.
The Tidemarsh Guide.
New York: E. P. Dutton & Co., Inc., 1979.

Silberhorn, Gene M.
Common Plants of the Mid-Atlantic Coast: A Field Guide.
Baltimore: The Johns Hopkins University Press, 1982.

Stephenson, T. A. and Anne.
Life Between Tidemarks on Rocky Shores.
San Francisco: W. H. Freeman and Company, 1972.

Teal, John and Mildred.
Life and Death of the Salt Marsh.
New York: Ballantine Books, 1971.

CREDITS

Photo Credits
The numbers in parentheses are plate numbers. Some photographers have pictures under agency names as well as their own.

David H. Ahrenholz (489)
Ruth Allen (451)
William H. Amos (2nd frontispiece, 3rd frontispiece, 5th frontispiece, 7–12, 15, 17–22, 29, 30, 179, 216, 220, 240, 247, 257, 294, 478–480, 488, 492)

Animals Animals
E. R. Degginger (143) Zig Leszczynski (190, 435) Perry D. Slocum (440) Lynn M. Stone (438)

Ardea Photographics
P. Morris (218) J. S. Wightman (495)

Charles Arneson (141, 148, 152, 163, 165, 170, 182, 203, 206, 215, 239, 266, 285, 316, 343, 368, 370, 383, 417, 445)

Peter Arnold, Inc.
Fred Bavendam (299)

Ron Austing (613)
Stephen F. Bailey (592)
David L. Ballantine (136, 371)
Fred Bavendam (137, 139, 145, 157, 161, 162, 164, 173, 178, 183, 187, 188, 193, 195, 200, 201, 211, 219, 221, 225, 232, 233, 246, 250, 261, 268, 270, 279, 287, 297, 302, 305, 309)
John Behler (439)
D. W. Behrens (471)
Michael Berrill (234)
Gregory S. Boland (274)
Stephen A. Bortone (360)
Tom Brakefield (555)
Edward B. Brothers (398)
Richard T. Bryant (395, 396)
George H. Burgess (359, 426)
Karen Bussolini (14)
James H. Carmichael, Jr. (4th frontispiece, 31–120, 122, 124, 125, 127, 129, 131, 155, 159, 166, 169, 189)
Patrice Ceisel (338, 391)
Tony Chess (340, 365)
Roger Clapp (497)
Herbert Clarke (549, 556)

Bruce Coleman, Inc.
William H. Amos (259, 260) Jen and Des Bartlett (493) James H. Carmichael, Jr. (130, 142) Phil Degginger (277, 425) Harry Simmerman (147) Kim Taylor (176) Ron and Valerie Taylor (415, 420) Norman Owen Tomalin (347)

Stephen Collins (448, 449)

Cornell Laboratory of Ornithology

John S. Dunning (615) Caulion Singletary (599) K. Worden (520)

Allan Cruickshank (515)
Harry N. Darrow (508, 523, 573, 591, 604)
Thomas H. Davis (550, 587)
Edward R. Degginger (149, 156, 160, 167, 253, 392, 517)
Douglas Denninger (227)
David M. Dennis (437)
Jack Dermid (23, 24, 146, 202, 267, 293, 317, 434, 459 right, 464 right, 469, 470, 560, 562, 565, 576, 598)

Design Photographers International
Andrew Gifford (421) R. F. Head (318) Nancy Sefton (235, 264) Charles Steinmetz, Jr. (378)

John de Visser (1st frontispiece, 1–6)
Adrian J. Dignan (485, 487)
John DiMartini (255)
Larry Ditto (539)
Jim Dorau (222)
Georges Dremeaux (610)

DRK Photo
Stephen J. Krasemann (500, 505, 528) Wayne Lankinen (596)

Wilbur H. Duncan (447, 454 left, 455 left, 458 left, 459 left, 460, 461 right, 462, 463 left and right, 464 left, 465 left, 466)
Harry Ellis (486)
Harry Engels (605)
Douglas Faulkner (191, 198, 331, 351)
Davis Finch (589)
Kenneth W. Fink (501, 513, 533, 534, 537, 538, 564, 569, 577, 585, 597, 600)
David H. Firmage (192)
Jeff Foott (25, 584, 606)
Tom French (522)
Laurel Giannino (341, 355–357, 367, 369, 372, 390, 405, 414, 429, 430)
Brian Gibeson (401)
Susan Gibler (28)
Julius Gordon and Townsend Weeks (150)
William D. Griffin (559, 566, 567, 572)
Al Grotell (278, 282, 349, 382)
Pamela Harper (450)
James Hawkings (548)
Phil and Loretta Hermann (352)
Paul Humann (194, 205, 207, 231, 237, 269, 271, 273, 281, 283, 284, 289, 348, 363, 377, 413, 424, 431)

Jaçana
Claude Carré (229) Hervé Chaumeton (212, 258) R. Konig (180) Noailles (346) Fred Winner (306)

Warren Jacobi (516, 536)
Isidor Jeklin (540)

301, 304, 307, 310, 311, 314, 468, 472, 476)
John E. Randall (342, 358, 366)
Hans Reinhard (544)
Laura Riley (499)
Fred C. Rohde (403)
Edward S. Ross (481, 484)
Steve W. Ross (350)
William Roston (337)
Jeffrey L. Rotman (204, 242, 248, 256)
Leonard Lee Rue III (456 right)
Kjell B. Sandved (151)
Kenneth P. Sebens (138, 140)
John Shaw (483, 608)
Ervio Sian (506, 529, 542, 594)
Robert S. Simmons (441, 443)
Arnold Small (27, 524, 525, 530, 531, 563, 578, 586, 595)
Bruce A. Sorrie (496)

Tom Stack and Associates
Brian Parker (344) Kenneth Read (224) Tom Stack (411, 418)

Alvin E. Staffan (491, 614)
Douglas Stamm (412)
Lynn M. Stone (504)
Rick Sullivan and Diana Rogers (446)
Ian C. Tait (602)
Frank S. Todd (532, 546, 551, 552)
John L. Tveten (134)
U.S. Fish and Wildlife Service (354, 387, 400)
R. Van Nostrand (571)

VIREO (Academy of Natural Sciences of Philadelphia)
P. G. Connors (579)

Richard K. Wallace (407)
Richard E. Webster (588)
Wardene Weisser (509, 580)
Larry West (482)
Jack Wilburn (461 left, 510)
James D. Williams (393, 394, 410)
M. Woodbridge Williams (428)
Jon Witman (197)
Art Wolfe (541, 547)
Marilyn Wolff (16, 473–475)
Charles R. Wyttenbach (230, 249)
Gary R. Zahm (612)
C. Fred Zeillemaker (512)

Illustrations
Dolores R. Santoliquido contributed the drawings of fish and marine invertebrates. The drawings of plants were executed by Janice Rucker.

INDEX

ACKNOWLEDGMENTS

In writing this volume, we are indebted to many people. The senior author of this book taught life sciences for almost four decades, learning more from his experiences with students than a formal education had provided, while the junior author, reaching thousands of responsive visitors at the National Aquarium in Baltimore, reaps a rich harvest every day from their questions and observations.

Recognition must be given those who opened our eyes to worlds we could scarcely believe and those with whom we have shared much in marine biology: James H. Barrow, William Beebe, N. J. Berrill, Wendell Burger, Melbourne R. Carriker, Christopher Coates, William Cole, L. Eugene Cronin, Ulrich Dahlgren, Megumi Eri, Gairdner B. Moment, Thurlow C. Nelson, Carl N. Shuster, Jr., and John Tee Van. Several friends and authorities were of particular importance in supplying advice for this book: Ballard E. Ebbett and Sandra E. Ebbett, geologists, Lyndon State College; Robert Lake, entomologist, University of Delaware; Neil Robinson, former senior aquarist at the National Aquarium in Baltimore; and Franklin C. Daiber of the College of Marine Sciences, University of Delaware, who reviewed the manuscript and made many valuable suggestions.

We would also like to acknowledge the contributions of the authors of previously published National Audubon Society field guides whose work is incorporated into the present volume. Janice Rucker, an unusually perceptive and able nature artist, provided a major contribution to the book through drawings, each prepared after prolonged study of specimens and sources.

Finally, the secret to any book, especially if it is to be a useful one, is good editing. Both authors can state unequivocally that the staff at Chanticleer Press is the keenest and most supportive group of book editors they have ever worked with. Gudrun Buettner and Susan Costello, with whom the senior author has worked for many years, conceived the idea for the series; Ann Whitman was a brilliant and imaginative text editor; Marian Appellof skillfully coordinated the species accounts; Constance Mersel and David Allen checked every detail with meticulous and caring attention; and Jane Opper supervised the preparation of the maps that accompany the habitat essays. They and others who have assisted us along the way have become good friends as well as valued coworkers. But it is Mary Beth Brewer, Series Editor, for whom we reserve our deepest appreciation and affection, with the full knowledge that without her guidance and long hours of labor, this book would have been very much less.

William H. Amos
Stephen H. Amos

CHANTICLEER STAFF

Prepared and produced by Chanticleer Press, Inc.
Founding Publisher: Paul Steiner
Publisher: Andrew Stewart

Staff for this book:

Editor-in-Chief: Gudrun Buettner
Executive Editor: Susan Costello
Managing Editor: Jane Opper
Series Editor: Mary Beth Brewer
Text Editor: Ann Whitman
Associate Editor: Marian Appellof
Assistant Editor: David Allen
Editorial Assistant: Karel Birnbaum
Production: Helga Lose, Amy Roche
Art Director: Carol Nehring
Art Associate: Ayn Svoboda
Picture Library: Edward Douglas, Dana Pomfret
Maps and Symbols: Paul Singer
Natural History Consultant: John Farrand, Jr.

Design: Massimo Vignelli

All editorial inquiries should be addressed to:
Chanticleer Press
568 Broadway, Suite #1005A
New York, NY 10012

To purchase this book, or other National Audubon Society
illustrated nature books, please contact:
Alfred A. Knopf, Inc.
201 East 50th Street
New York, NY 10022
(800) 733-3000